www.wadsworth.com

wadsworth.com is the World Wide Web site fo
Wadsworth and is your direct source to dozer
online resources.

At *wadsworth.com* you can find out about
supplements, demonstration software, an
student resources. You can also send em
our authors and preview new publicati
new technologies.

wadsworth.com
Changing the way the world lear

The Structure
of Sociological Theory

Seventh Edition

JONATHAN H. TURNER
University of California, Riverside

Australia • Canada • Mexico • Singapore • Spain
United Kingdom • United States

THOMSON

WADSWORTH

Sociology Editors: *Robert Jucha, Lin Marshall*
Assistant Editor: *Stephanie Monzon*
Editorial Assistant: *Matthew Goldsmith*
Technology Project Manager: *Dee Dee Zobian*
Marketing Manager: *Matthew Wright*
Marketing Assistant: *Michael Silverstein*
Project Manager, Editorial Production:
    Erica Silverstein

Print/Media Buyer: *Tandra Jorgensen*
Permissions Editor: *Robert Kauser*
Production Service: *Scott Rohr, Buuji, Inc.*
Copy Editor: *Robin Gold*
Cover Designer: *Carole Lawson*
Text and Cover Printer: *R. R. Donnelley &*
    Sons/Crawfordsville
Compositor: *Buuji, Inc.*

For more information about our products,
contact us at:
Thomson Learning Academic Resource Center
1-800-423-0563

For permission to use material from this text,
contact us by:
Phone: 1-800-730-2214 **Fax:** 1-800-730-2215
Web: http://www.thomsonrights.com

ISBN 0-534-53599-2

Wadsworth/Thomson Learning
10 Davis Drive
Belmont, CA 94002-3098
USA

Asia
Thomson Learning
60 Albert Street, #15-01
Albert Complex
Singapore 189969

Australia
Nelson Thomson Learning
102 Dodds Street
South Melbourne, Victoria 3205
Australia

Canada
Nelson Thomson Learning
1120 Birchmount Road
Toronto, Ontario M1K 5G4
Canada

Europe/Middle East/Africa
Thomson Learning
Berkshire House
168-173 High Holborn
London WC1V 7AA
United Kingdom

Latin America
Thomson Learning
Seneca, 53
Colonia Polanco
11560 Mexico D.F.
Mexico

Spain
Paraninfo Thomson Learning
Calle/Magallanes, 25
28015 Madrid, Spain

Contents

Contents for Web Site for *The Structure of Sociological Theory*

PART VI: STRUCTURALIST THEORIZING

Preface

Over the last six editions of *The Structure of Sociological Theory,* the book has grown larger. Indeed, the last edition was so large that we had to go to double column format, but more fundamentally, the book had lost some of its focus in trying to be so comprehensive and detailed. In this edition, I have done something rarely performed in a long-running book: I have shortened the book by fourteen chapters, thus enabling me to go back to a single column format in a book that can actually be held in one's hand. I did this because I wanted the book to be more manageable and readable within a reasonable period of time. I sought to eliminate some of the "reference work" appearance of the book as it as has evolved and grown. Fortunately, in the computer age, materials put on the cutting room floor no longer disappear; rather, they reappear on a Web site where they can be downloaded and used. Indeed, I have gathered materials that I have cut over the last twenty years and placed them on the book's Web site (www.sociology/wadsworth.com). Thus, the reader can enjoy—if that is the right word—much of what I have eliminated over the years. Most of what has been taken out was not eliminated for intellectual reasons, but rather for considerations of space limitations between the covers of a hardback. I will return to the nature of the Web site, but first let me outline what is new in this version of the book.

First, I have restored the emphasis on the building of theory, making clear acknowledgment of the fact that many do not agree with this point of emphasis. But the book's strength (or weakness, depending on your viewpoint) is that it tries to present the theories in ways that make them testable, at least in principle.

Second, I have moved critical theory to a more prominent place in the text, juxtaposing it with conflict theory. There has always been a critical element in sociological theory, and this approach has gained more adherents in recent decades. Hence, this fact should be reflected in the organization of the book.

Third, I have retained the same basic schools of thought, with some modest revisions. The book organizes chapters in seven sections, roughly corresponding to distinctive theoretical orientations: functional, evolutionary, conflict, critical, exchange, interactionist, and structuralist theorizing. These are loose rubrics but I think that they capture the range of core theorizing in sociology today.

Fourth, I have shortened most of the chapters, although some, such as the introduction, and those on the rise of critical theory, the nature of postmodernism, and the rise of interactionist theorizing, are now longer than in previous editions.

Fifth, over the years, I have been eliminating my evaluations of theories, primarily for reasons of space. I continue this trend, making the book as neutral as is possible given my preference for scientific theorizing. Yet, the criticisms are not gone; they are back on the Web site and, as a result, can still be used to encourage discussion and debate.

Now, let me go back to the Web site. The wonderful thing about this option is that I can constantly update the site, and equally important, I can begin to put back much of what I have eliminated in past editions. The first edition of the book had a critical edge, evaluating and critiquing various approaches. I can now restore this feature for those who liked criticism and commentary, and theses can be used to encourage counter-commentaries and debates. Also, materials that have been cut from individual chapters as well as whole chapters from the last and previous editions are back on the Web site. These can be downloaded and used to supplement the materials between the hard covers of the book.

Other features of the book remain unchanged. This book has always been about the *structure* of theory, especially its assumptions and testable propositions, if any. It has also been more detailed and comprehensive than other textbooks. It goes into detail rather than skimming the surface of various approaches. This quality of the book does make it more difficult for some, but I have retained the emphasis on the emergence of a perspective, especially the key figures who inspired contemporary forms of the approach.

Thus, the book is very new this time around. I trust that it is more manageable for those reading between its covers, and more comprehensive and detailed for those consulting the Web site.

ACKNOWLEDGMENTS

I'd like to thank the following reviewers for their helpful suggestions for revising this seventh edition. I am grateful for the time and effort they put into making this a better book: Kooros Mahmoudi, Northern Arizona University; William Cross, Illinois College; Raghu Nath Singh, Texas A & M University; Guenther Lueschen, University of Alabama, Birmingham; Burton Wright, Troy State University, Dotham; Nita Bryant, Virginia Commonwealth University; James Crone, Hanover College; Norm Dolch, Louisiana State University, Shreveport; Robert Blain, Southern Illinois University; and Frank Taylor, Dana College.

1

Sociological Theory

Theories are explanations about how and why events in the universe occur. Sociological theories are thus explanations about how and why humans behave, interact, and organize themselves. There is, however, considerable controversy over this definition of theory. At the center of this controversy is the question of whether or not sociological theories can be scientific. Some argue that they can, others argue the opposite, and many offer some moderating position. To appreciate the dimensions of this controversy, let us begin by briefly outlining the nature of scientific theories. Then, we can return to what critics of scientific theory find objectionable.

THE NATURE OF SCIENTIFIC THEORY

Scientific theories begin with the assumption that the universe, including the social universe created by acting human beings, reveals certain basic and fundamental properties and processes that explain the ebb and flow of events in specific contexts. Because of this concern with discovering fundamental properties and processes, scientific theories are always stated abstractly, rising above specific empirical events and highlighting the underlying forces that drive these events. In the context of sociological inquiry, for example, theoretical explanations are not so much about the specifics of a particular economy as about the dynamics of production and distribution in general. Similarly, scientific theories are not so much about a particular form of government as about the nature of power as a basic social force. Or, to illustrate further, theories are not so much about particular behaviors and interactions among actual persons in a specific setting as about the nature of human interpersonal behavior in general. The goal, then, is always to see if the underlying forces that govern particulars of specific cases can be discovered. To realize this goal, theories must be about generic properties and processes transcending the unique character istics of any one situation or case. Thus, scientific theories always seek to tran scend the particular and the time bound, and in so doing, they focus on the generic, the fundamental, the timeless, and the universal.

Another characteristic of scientific theories is that they are stated more for mally than ordinary language. At the extreme, theories are couched in another language, such as mathematics, but more typically in the social sciences and particularly in sociology, theories are phrased in ordinary language. Still, even when using regular language, sociologists make an effort to speak in neutral, objective, and unambiguous terms so that the theory means the same thing to all who examine it. Terms denoting properties of the world and their dynam ics are defined clearly so that their referents are clear, and relationships among concepts denoting phenomena are stated in ways such that their interconnec tions are understood by all who examine the theory. At times, this attention to formalism can make theories seem stiff and dull, especially when these for malisms are couched at higher levels of abstraction. Yet, without attention to what terms and phrases denote and connote, a theory could mean very differ ent things to diverse audiences.

A final characteristic of scientific theories is that they are designed to be systematically tested with replicable methods against the facts of particular empirical settings. Despite being stated abstractly and formally, then, scientific theories do not stand aloof and alone from the empirical. Useful theories all suggest ways that they can be assessed against empirical events.

All scientific fields develop theories. For in the end, science seeks (1) to develop abstract and formally stated theories and (2) to test these theories against empirical cases to see if they are plausible. If the theory seems plausi ble in light of empirical assessment, then it represents *for the present time* the explanation of events. If a theory is contradicted by empirical tests, then it must be discarded or revised. If competing theories exist to explain the same phenomena, they too must be empirically assessed, with the better explanation winning out.

Science is thus a rather slow process of developing theories, testing them, and then rejecting, modifying, or retaining them, at least until a better theory is proposed. Without attention to stating theories formally and objectively assessing them against the empirical world, theory would become self- justifying and self-contained; it would be hard to refute such theories, and indeed, they would tend to reflect personal biases, ideological leanings, or reli gious convictions. The differences between scientific theory and other types of knowledge are presented in Figure 1.1.[1]

The typology asks two basic questions: (1) Is the search for knowledge to be evaluative or neutral? (2) Is the knowledge developed to pertain to actual

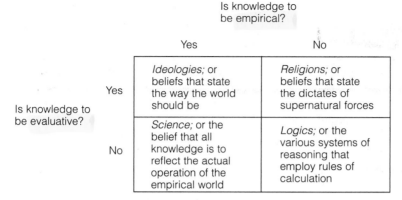

FIGURE 1.1 Types of Knowledge

empirical events and processes, or is it to be about nonempirical realities? In other words, should knowledge tell us *what should be* or *what is?* And should knowledge refer to the observable world or to unobservable realms? If knowledge is to tell us what should exist (and, by implication, what should not occur) in the empirical world, then it is ideological knowledge. If it informs us about what should be but does not pertain to observable events, then the knowledge is religious, or about forces and beings in another realm of existence. If knowledge is neither empirical nor evaluative, then it is a formal system of logic, such as mathematics. And if it is about empirical events and is nonevaluative, then it is science.

This typology is crude, but it makes the essential point: There are different ways to look at, interpret, and develop knowledge about the world. Science is only one way. Science is based on the presumption that knowledge can be value free, that it can explain the actual workings of the empirical world, and that it can be revised as a result of careful observations of empirical events. These characteristics distinguish science from other beliefs about how we should generate understanding and insight.[2]

The boundaries among these types of knowledge are often open, or at least permeable. Logics can be the language of science, as is the case when mathematics is used to state important relationships among forces driving the universe. The boundaries between these forms of knowledge can also be confrontational, as can be seen today in the controversy between religious and scientific explanations for the evolution of humans. Within sociology proper, the controversial relationship is between ideology and science. Many sociologists believe that theory must contain an ideological component; it must criticize undesirable conditions and advocate alternatives. Beliefs about "what should be" thus dominate the analysis of the social universe. This view of sociology contradicts the value-neutrality of science, where ideologies and other evaluative beliefs are not to contaminate analysis of social conditions. The debate between those who advocate scientific theory and those who argue for the infusion of ideology has been present for most of the history of sociology, and this debate still rages. In Part IV of this book, we devote a number of chapters to "critical theory," whose goal is to criticize existing conditions and to advocate potential alternatives.

These critical theories make a number of arguments. One is that no matter how hard scholars try to exclude ideology from their work, ideology will slip in. Every analyst is located at a particular position in society and will, therefore, have certain interests that guide both the problems selected for analysis and the mode of analysis itself. Inevitably what people think should occur will enter their work, and so, it is only an illusion that statements about the operation of the social world are free of ideology. Another line of criticism is that when "scientists" study what exists, they will implicitly see the social world as it is currently structured as the way things must inevitably be. As a result, theories about the world as it exists in the present can become ideologies legitimating the status quo and blinding thinkers to alternative social arrangements. And, a third line of attack on the value-neutrality of science is that humans can change the very nature of their universe; hence, there can be no immutable laws of human social organization because humans' capacity for agency allows them to alter the very reality described by these laws. Therefore, a natural science of society is not possible because the very nature of social reality can be changed by the actors in this reality.

Those who advocate a scientific approach reject these arguments by critical theorists.[3] Although they see ideological bias as always a potential problem, this problem can be obviated by careful attention to potential sources of bias. And even if one's position in the social world shapes the questions asked, it is still possible to answer these questions in an objective manner. Moreover, those committed to science reject the notion that the objective study of the social world ensures that inquiry will support the status quo. Real science seeks to examine the forces driving the current world, and theories are about these underlying forces that, in the very best theories, have operated in all times and places. Thus, science does not just describe the world as it is, but rather, scientists try to see how forces operating in the past and present (and future) generate the empirical world as it now appears and as it will appear in the future. These forces will thus change the present into the future, just as they transformed the past into a new present. There is no reason, therefore, for theories to legitimate a status quo; indeed, theories are about the dynamic potential of the forces that change social arrangements. And finally, scientists reject the notion that humans can change the very nature of the forces that drive the social world. Humans can, of course, change the social world as it exists, but this is very different from changing the generic and basic forces that shape the organization of the social universe. Agency is thus constrained by the underlying forces that drive the social universe. For example, humans can change the way they produce things, but they cannot eliminate production as a basic force necessary for the survival of the species; people can change political regimes, but they cannot eliminate power in social relations.

The debate about whether or not sociology can be a natural science will, no doubt, rage into the future. For our purposes, we simply must recognize that commitments to science vary among theorists in sociology. Yet, in the pages to follow, as well as on the Web site for this book (www. sociology.wadsworth.com), emphasis is on the contribution of theories to the science of sociology. Of course, those theories rejecting this orientation are also examined, but these alternatives will always be seen as deviating from scientific sociology.

THE ELEMENTS OF SCIENTIFIC THEORY

Theory is a mental activity revolving around the process of developing ideas that explain how and why events occur. Theory is constructed with several basic elements or building blocks: (1) concepts, (2) variables, and (3) statements/formats. Although there are many divergent claims about what theory is or should be, these four elements are common to all the claims. Let me examine each of these elements in more detail.

Concepts: The Basic Building Blocks of Theory

Theories are built from concepts. Most generally, concepts denote phenomena; in so doing, they isolate features of the world that are considered, for the moment at hand, important. For example, notions of atoms, protons, neutrons, and the like are concepts pointing to and isolating phenomena for certain analytical purposes. Familiar sociological concepts would include production, power, interaction, norm, role, status, and socialization. Each term is a concept that embraces aspects of the social world that are considered essential for a particular purpose.

Concepts are constructed from definitions.[4] A definition is a system of terms, such as the sentences of a language, the symbols of logic, or the notation of mathematics, that inform investigators about the phenomenon denoted by a concept. For example, the concept *conflict* has meaning only when it is defined. One possible definition might be this: *Conflict is interaction among social units in which one unit seeks to prevent another from realizing its goals.* Such a definition allows us to visualize the phenomenon that is denoted by the concept. A definition enables all investigators to "see the same thing" and to understand what it is that is being studied.

Thus, concepts that are useful in building theory have a special characteristic: They strive to communicate a uniform meaning to all those who use them. Because concepts are frequently expressed with the words of everyday language, however, it is difficult to avoid words that connote varied meanings—and hence point to different phenomena—for varying groups of scientists. This is why many concepts in science are expressed in technical or more "neutral" languages, such as the symbols of mathematics. In sociology, expressing concepts in such special languages is sometimes not only impossible but also undesirable. Hence, the verbal symbols used to develop a concept must be defined as precisely as possible so that they point to the same phenomenon for all investigators. Although perfect consensus might never be attained with conventional language, a body of theory rests on the premise that scholars will do their best to define concepts unambiguously.

The concepts of theory reveal another special characteristic: *abstractness.*[5] Some concepts pertain to concrete phenomena at specific times and locations. Other, more abstract concepts point to phenomena that are not related to concrete times or locations. For example, in the context of small-group research, *concrete concepts* would refer to the persistent interactions of particular individuals, whereas an *abstract* conceptualization of such phenomena would refer to those general properties of face-to-face groups that are not tied to particular individuals interacting at a specified time and location. Whereas abstract concepts are not tied to a specific context, concrete concepts are. In building theory, abstract concepts are crucial, although we will see shortly that theorists disagree considerably on this issue.

Abstractness poses a problem: How do we attach abstract concepts to the ongoing, everyday world of events? Although it is essential that some of the concepts of theory transcend specific times and places, it is equally critical that there be procedures for making these abstract concepts relevant to observable situations and occurrences. After all, the utility of an abstract concept can be demonstrated only when the concept is brought to bear on some specific empirical problem encountered by investigators; otherwise, concepts remain detached from the very processes they are supposed to help investigators understand. Just how to attach concepts to empirical processes, or the workings of the real world, is very controversial in sociology. Some argue for very formal procedures for attaching concepts to empirical events. Those of this persuasion contend that abstract concepts should be accompanied by a series of statements known as *operational definitions,* which are procedural instructions telling investigators how to go about discerning phenomena in the real world that are denoted by an abstract concept. Others argue that the nature of our concepts in sociology precludes such formalistic exercises. At best, concepts can be only sensitizing devices that must change with alterations of social reality, and so we can only intuitively and provisionally apply abstract concepts to the actual flow of events. To emulate the natural sciences in an effort to develop formal operations for attaching concepts to reality is to ignore the fact that social reality is changeable; it does not reveal invariant properties like the other domains of the universe.[6] Thus, to think that abstract concepts denote enduring and invariant properties of the social universe and to presume, therefore, that the concept itself will never need to be changed is, at best, naive.[7]

And so the debate rages, taking many different turns. We need not go into detail here because these issues will be brought out again and again as the substance of sociological theories is examined in subsequent chapters. For the present, it is only necessary to draw the approximate lines of battle.

Variables as an Important Type of Concept

When used to build theory, two general types of concepts can be distinguished: (1) those that simply label phenomena and (2) those that refer to phenomena that differ in degree.[8] Concepts that merely label phenomena would include such commonly employed abstractions as *dog, cat, group, social class,* and *star.* When stated in this way, none of these concepts reveals the ways in which the phenomena they denote vary in terms of such properties as size, weight, density, velocity, cohesiveness, or any of the many criteria used to inform investigators about *differences in degree* among phenomena.

Those who believe that sociology can be like other sciences prefer concepts that are translated into variables—that is, into states that vary. We want to know the variable properties—size, degree, intensity, amount, and so forth—of events denoted by a concept. For example, to note that an aggregate of people is a group does not indicate what type of group it is or how it compares with other groups by such properties as size, differentiation, and cohesiveness. And so, some of the concepts of scientific theory should denote the *variable* features of the world. To understand events requires that we visualize how variation in one phenomenon is related to variation in another. Others, who are less enamored by efforts to make sociology a natural science, are less compulsive about translating concepts into variables. These researchers are far more interested in whether or not concepts sensitize and alert investigators to important processes than they are in converting each concept into a metric that varies in some measurable way. They are not, of course, against the conversion of ideas into variables, but they are cautious about efforts to translate every concept into a metric.

Theoretical Statements and Formats

To be useful, the concepts of theory must be connected to one another. Such connections among concepts constitute theoretical statements. These statements specify how events denoted by concepts are interrelated, and at the same time they provide an interpretation of how and why events should be connected. When these theoretical statements are grouped together, they constitute a *theoretical format*. There are, however, different ways to organize theoretical statements into formats. Indeed, in sociological theory there is relatively little consensus about just how to organize theoretical statements; in fact, much of the theoretical controversy in sociology revolves around differences concerning the best way to develop theoretical statements and to group them together into a format. Depending on one's views about what kind of science, if any, sociology can be, the structure of theoretical statements and their organization into formats differ dramatically. Let us review the range of opinion on the matter.

There are four basic approaches in sociological theory for generating theoretical statements and formats: (1) meta-theoretical schemes, (2) analytical schemes, (3) propositional schemes, and (4) modeling schemes. Figure 1.2

FIGURE 1.2 The Elements of Theory in Sociology

summarizes the relations among these schemes and the basic elements of theory. Concepts are constructed from definitions; theoretical statements link concepts together; and statements are organized into four basic types of formats. These four formats can be executed in a variety of ways, however, and so in reality, there are more than just four strategies for developing theoretical statements and formats. Moreover, these various strategies are not always mutually exclusive, for, in executing one of them, we are often led to another as a kind of "next step" in building theory. Yet—and this point is crucial—these various approaches are often viewed as antagonistic, and the proponents of each strategy have spilled a great deal of ink sustaining the antagonism. Moreover, even within a particular type of format, there is constant battle over the best way to develop theory. This acrimony represents a great tragedy because, in a mature science, these approaches are viewed as highly compatible. Before pursuing this point further, we need to delineate each of these approaches.

Meta-theoretical Schemes This kind of theoretical activity is more comprehensive than ordinary theory. Meta-theoretical schemes are not, by themselves, theories that explain specific classes of events; rather, they explicate the basic issues that a theory must address. In many sociological circles, meta-theory is considered an essential prerequisite to adequate theory building,[9] even though the dictionary definition of *meta* emphasizes "occurring later" and "in succession" to previous activities.[10] Furthermore, in most other sciences, meta-theoretical reflection has occurred *after* a body of formal theoretical statements has been developed. Only after a science has used a number of theoretical statements and formats successfully do scholars begin to ask meta-theoretical questions[11]: What are the underlying assumptions about the universe contained in these statements? What strategies are demanded by, or precluded from, these statements and their organization into formats? What kind of knowledge is generated by these statements and formats, and, conversely, what is ignored? In sociological theory, however, advocates of meta-theory usually emphasize that we cannot develop theory until we have resolved these more fundamental epistemological and metaphysical questions.

For those who emphasize meta-theory, several preliminary issues must be resolved. These include the following: (1) What is the basic nature of human activity about which we must develop theory? For example, what is the basic nature of human beings? What is the fundamental nature of society? What is the fundamental nature of the bonds that connect people to one another and to society? (2) What is the appropriate way to develop theory, and what kind of theory is possible? For instance, can we build highly formal systems of abstract laws, as is the case in physics, or must we be content with general concepts that simply sensitize and orient us to important processes? Can we rigorously test theories with precise measurement procedures, or must we use theories as interpretative frameworks that cannot be tested by the same procedures as in the natural sciences? (3) What is the critical problem on which social theory should concentrate? For instance, should we examine the processes of social integration, or must we concentrate on social conflict? Should we focus on the nature of social action among individuals, or on structures of social organization? Should we stress the power of ideas, like values and beliefs, or must we focus on the material conditions of people's existence?

A great deal of what is defined as sociological theory involves trying to answer these questions. The old philosophical debates—idealism versus materialism, induction versus deduction, causation versus association, subjectivism versus objectivism, and so on—are re-evoked and analyzed with respect to social reality. At times, meta-theorizing has been true to the meaning of *meta* and has involved a reanalysis of previous scholars' ideas in light of these philosophical issues. The idea behind reanalysis is to summarize the metaphysical and epistemological assumptions of the scholars' work and to show where the schemes went wrong and where they still have utility. Furthermore, based on this assessment, there are some recommendations in reanalyses about how we should go about building theory and what this theory should be.

Meta-theorizing often gets bogged down in weighty philosophical matters and immobilizes theory building. The enduring philosophical questions persist because they are not resolvable. One must just take a stand on the issues and see what kinds of insights can be generated. But meta-theory often stymies as much as stimulates theoretical activity because it embroils theorists in inherently unresolvable and always debatable controversies. Of course, many sociologists reject this assertion, and for our present purposes, the more important conclusion is that a great deal of sociological theory is, in fact, meta-theoretical activity.

Analytical Schemes Much theoretical activity in sociology consists of concepts organized into a classification scheme that denotes the key properties, and interrelations among these properties, in the social universe. There are many different varieties of analytical schemes, but they share an emphasis on classifying basic properties of the social world. The concepts of the scheme chop up the universe; then, the ordering of the concepts gives the social world a sense of order. Explanation of an empirical event comes whenever a place in the classificatory scheme can be found for the empirical event.

There are, however, wide variations in the nature of the typologies in analytical schemes, although there are two basic types: (1) *naturalistic schemes,* which try to develop a tightly woven system of categories that is presumed to capture the way in which the invariant properties of the universe are ordered, and (2) *sensitizing schemes,* which are more loosely assembled congeries of concepts intended only to sensitize and orient researchers and theorists to certain critical processes. Figure 1.3 summarizes these two types of analytical approaches. Naturalistic/positivistic schemes assume that there are timeless and universal processes in the social universe, as much as there are in the physical and biological realms. The goal is to create an abstract conceptual typology that is isomorphic with these timeless processes. In contrast, sensitizing schemes are sometimes more skeptical about the timeless quality of social affairs. As a consequence of this skepticism, concepts and their linkages must always be provisional and sensitizing because the nature of human activity is to change those very arrangements denoted by the organization of concepts into theoretical statements. Hence, except for certain very general conceptual categories, the scheme must be flexible and capable of being revised as circumstances in the empirical world change. At best, then, explanation is simply an interpretation of events by seeing them as an instance or example of the provisional and sensitizing concepts in the scheme.

Some theorists argue that analytical schemes are a necessary prerequisite for developing other forms of theory. Until one has a scheme that organizes the properties of the universe, it is difficult to develop propositions and models about specific events. Without the general analytical framework, how can a theorist or researcher know what to examine? There is some merit to this position, but if the scheme becomes too complex and elaborate, it is not easily translated into other theoretical formats. Thus, analytical schemes can represent a useful way to begin theorizing, unless they are too rigid and elaborate to stimulate theorizing outside the parameters imposed by the scheme itself.

Propositional Schemes A proposition is a theoretical statement that specifies the connection between two or more variables. It tells us how variation in one concept is accounted for by variation in another. For example, the propositional statement "group solidarity is a positive function of external conflict with other groups" says that as group conflict escalates, the level of internal solidarity among members of the respective groups involved in the conflict increases. Thus, two properties of the social universe denoted by variable concepts, "group solidarity" and "conflict," are connected by the proposition that as one increases in value, so does the other.

Propositional schemes vary perhaps the most of all theoretical approaches. They vary primarily along two dimensions: (1) the level of abstraction and (2) the way propositions are organized into formats. Some are highly abstract and contain concepts that denote all cases of a type rather than any particular case (for example, group solidarity and conflict are abstract because no particular empirical instance of conflict and solidarity is addressed). In contrast, other propositional systems are tied to empirical facts and simply summarize relations

Naturalistic Scheme:

Explanation =
finding the place
in the typology of
an empirical event

◄──────► : Specify with concepts
processes that link
clearly defined
conceptual categories

Sensitizing Scheme:

Explanation =
interpreting events in
terms of categories

◄--------► : Loose and flexible linkages among sensitizing
conceptual categories

FIGURE 1.3 Types of Analytical Schemes

among events in a particular case (for example, as World War II progressed, nationalism in America increased). Propositional schemes vary not only in abstractness but also by how propositions are laced together into a format. Some are woven together by very explicit rules; others are merely loose bunches or congeries of propositions.

By using these two dimensions, several different types of propositional schemes can be isolated: (a) axiomatic formats, (b) formal formats, and (c) various empirical formats. (See Figure 1.4 on pages 14–15) The first two (axiomatic and formal formats) are clearly theoretical, whereas various empirical formats are simply research findings that test theories. But, these more empirical types of propositional schemes are often considered theory by practicing sociologists, and so they are included in our discussion here.

Axiomatic Format An axiomatic organization of theoretical statements involves the following elements. First, it contains a set of concepts. Some of the concepts are highly abstract; others are more concrete. Second, there is always a set of existence statements that describes those types and classes of situations in which the concepts and the propositions that incorporate them apply. These existence statements make up what are usually called the *scope conditions* of the theory. Third—and most nearly unique to the axiomatic format—propositional statements are stated in a hierarchical order. At the top of the hierarchy are *axioms,* or highly abstract statements, from which *all* other theoretical statements are logically derived. These latter statements are usually called *theorems* and are logically derived in accordance with varying rules from the more abstract axioms. The selection of axioms is, in reality, a somewhat arbitrary matter, but usually they are selected with several criteria in mind. The axioms should be consistent with one another, although they do not have to be logically interrelated. The axioms should be highly abstract; they should state relationships among abstract concepts. These relationships should be lawlike in that the more concrete theorems derived from them have not been disproved by empirical investigation. And the axioms should have an intuitive plausibility in that their truth appears to be self-evident.

The result of tight conformity to axiomatic principles is an inventory or set of interrelated propositions, each derivable from at least one axiom and usually more abstract theorems. This form of theory construction has several advantages. First, highly abstract concepts, encompassing a broad range of related phenomena, can be employed. These abstract concepts do not have to be directly measurable because they are logically tied to more specific and measurable propositions that, when empirically tested, can indirectly subject the more abstract propositions and the axioms to empirical tests. Thus, by virtue of this logical interrelatedness of the propositions and axioms, research can be more efficient because the failure to refute a particular proposition lends credence to other propositions and to the axioms. Second, the use of a logical system to derive propositions from abstract axioms can also generate additional propositions that point to previously unknown or unanticipated relationships among social phenomena.

There are, however, some fatal limitations on the use of axiomatic theory in sociology. Most interesting concepts and propositions in sociology cannot be legitimately employed because the concepts are not stated with sufficient precision and because they cannot be incorporated into propositions that state unambiguously the relationship between concepts. Axiomatic theory also requires controls on all potential extraneous variables so that the tight logical system of deduction from axiom to empirical reality is not contaminated by extraneous factors. Sociologists can create such controls, although in many situations, this kind of tight control is not possible.[12] Thus, axiomatic theory can be used only when precise definitions of concepts exist, when concepts are organized into propositions using a precise calculus that specifies relations unambiguously, and when the contaminating effects of extraneous variables are eliminated.

These limitations are often ignored in propositional theory building. The language of axiomatic theory is employed (axioms, theorems, corollaries, the like); but these efforts are, at best, pseudo-axiomatic schemes.[13] In fact, it is best to call them formal propositional schemes—the second type of proposition strategy listed earlier.

Formal Propositional Formats Formal theories are, in essence, watered-down or loose versions of axiomatic schemes. The idea is to develop highly abstract propositions that are used to explain some empirical event. Some highly abstract propositions are seen as higher-order laws, and the goal of explanation is to visualize empirical events as instances of this "covering law." Deductions from the laws are made, but they are much looser, rarely conforming to the strict rules of axiomatic theory. Moreover, extraneous variables cannot always be excluded, and so the propositions usually have the disclaimer "other things being equal." That is, if other forces do not impinge, then the relationship among concepts in the proposition should hold true. For example, our earlier example of the relationship between conflict and solidarity might be one abstract proposition in a formal system. Thus, a formal scheme might say, "Other things being equal, group solidarity is a positive function of conflict." Then we would use this law to explain some empirical event—say, for instance, the terrorist attacks on the World Trade Center (the conflict variable) and nationalism in America (the solidarity variable). And we might find an exception to our rule or law, such as America's involvement in the Vietnam War, that contradicts the principle, forcing its revision or the recognition that "all things were not equal." In this case, we might revise the principle by stating a condition under which it holds true: When parties to a conflict perceive the conflict as a threat to their welfare, then the level of solidarity of groups is a positive function of their degree of conflict. Thus, the Vietnam War did not produce internal solidarity in America because many did not see it as a direct threat to America's general welfare (whereas, for the North Vietnamese, it was a very real threat and produced solidarity).

The essential idea here is that, in formal theory, an effort is made to create abstract principles. These principles are often clustered together to form a group of laws from which we make rather loose deductions to explain empirical events. Much like axiomatic systems, formal systems are hierarchical, but the restrictions of axiomatic theory are relaxed considerably. Most propositional schemes in sociological theorizing are, therefore, of this formal type.

Empirical Propositional Formats Much of what is defined as theory in sociology is more empirical. These empirical formats consist of generalizations from specific events in particular empirical contexts. For example, Golden's Law states that "as industrialization increases, the level of literacy in the population increases." Such a proposition is not very abstract; it is filled with empirical content—industrialization and literacy. Moreover, it is not about a timeless process because industrialization is only a few hundred years old and literacy emerged, at best, only 6,000 years ago. Many such generalizations in sociology are considered theoretical. They represent statements of empirical regularities that scholars think are important to understand. Indeed, most

Axiomatic:

Formal:

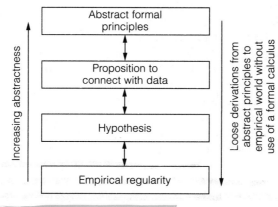

FIGURE 1.4 Types of Propositional Schemes

substantive areas and subfields of sociology are filled with these kinds of propositions.

Strictly speaking, however, these are not theoretical. They are too tied to empirical contexts, times, and places. In fact, they are generalizations that are in need of a theory to explain them. Yet, many scholars working in substantive areas see their empirical generalizations as theory; so, once again it is clear that there is no clear consensus in sociology about what constitutes theory.

Other kinds of empirical generalizations, however, raise fewer suspicions about their theoretical merits. These are often termed *middle-range theories* because they are more abstract than a research finding and because their empirical content pertains to variables that are also found in other domains of social reality. For example, a series of middle-range propositions from the complex

Middle-range:

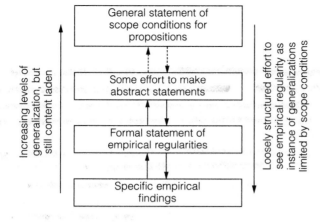

Explanation = ability to see specific empirical regularity as one of a general class of regularities or this type of phenomena

Empirical generalization:

Explanation = ability to generalize beyond one specific research finding

FIGURE 1.4 continued

organization's literature might be stated as follows: "Increasing size of a bureaucratic organization is positively related to (a) increases in the complexity (differentiation) of its structure, (b) increases in the reliance on formal rules and regulations, (c) increases in the decentralization of authority, and (d) increases in span of control for each center of authority."[14] These principles (the truth of which is not at issue here) are more abstract than Golden's Law because they denote a whole class of phenomena—organizations. They also deal with more generic variables—size, differentiation, centralization of power, spans of control, rules, and regulations—that have existed in all times and all places. Moreover, these variables could be stated more abstractly to apply to all organized social systems, not just bureaucratic organizations. For instance, a more abstract law might state this: "Increasing size of a social system is positively related to (a) increases in levels of system differentiation, (b) increases in the codification of norms, (c) increases in the decentralization of power, and (d) increases in the spans of control for each center of power." The truth or falsity of these propositions is not being asserted here; rather, these are illustrations of how empirical generalizations can be made more abstract and, hence, theoretical. The central point is that some empirical generalizations have more theoretical potential than others. If their variables are relatively abstract and if they pertain to basic and fundamental properties of the social universe that exist in other substantive areas of inquiry, then it is more reasonable to consider them theoretical.

In sum, then, there are three basic kinds of propositional schemes: axiomatic, formal, and various types of empirical generalizations. These propositional schemes are summarized in Figure 1.4. Although axiomatic formats are elegant and powerful, sociological variables and research typically cannot conform to their restrictions. Instead, we must rely on formal formats that generate propositions stating abstract relations among variables and then make loosely structured "deductions" to specific empirical cases. Finally, empirical formats consist of generalizations from particular substantive areas, and these are often considered theories of that area. Some of these theories are little more than summaries of research findings that require a theory to explain them. Others are more middle range and have more potential as theories because they are more abstract and pertain to more generic classes of variables.

Modeling Schemes At times it is useful to draw a picture of social events. Some models are drawn with neutral languages such as mathematics, in which the equation is presumed to map and represent empirical processes.[15] In reality, such equations are propositions (formal statements of relations among variables) *unless* they can be used to generate a picture or some form of graphic representation of processes. There is no clear consensus about what a model is, but in general, models array in visual space concepts denoting important social processes.

A model, then, is a diagrammatic representation of social events. The diagrammatic elements of any model include the following: (1) concepts that denote and highlight certain features of the universe, (2) the arrangement of these concepts in visual space so they reflect the ordering of events in the universe, and (3) symbols that mark the connections among concepts, such as lines, arrows, vectors, and so on. The elements of a model may be weighted in some way; they may be sequentially organized to express events over time; or, they may represent complex patterns of relations, such as lag effects, threshold effects, feedback loops, mutual interactions, cycles, and other potential ways in which properties of the universe affect one another.[16]

In sociology, most diagrammatic models are constructed to emphasize the causal connections among properties of the universe. That is, they are designed to show how changes in the values of one set of variables are related to changes in the values of other variables. Models are typically constructed when there are numerous variables whose causal interrelations an investigator wants to highlight. Figure 1.5 summarizes modeling strategies.

Analytical models:

= Lines can be weighted and signed

Explanation = ability to map crucial connections (perhaps weighted) among basic properties of a specific class of process or phenomenon

Causal models:

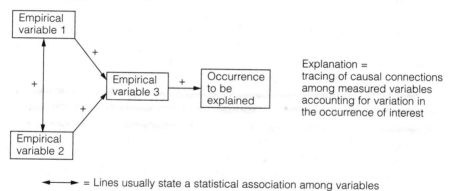

= Lines usually state a statistical association among variables

Explanation = tracing of causal connections among measured variables accounting for variation in the occurrence of interest

FIGURE 1.5 Types of Modeling Schemes

Sociologists generally construct two different types of models, which can be termed *analytical* models and *causal* models. This distinction is somewhat arbitrary, but it is a necessary one if we are to appreciate the kinds of models that are constructed in sociology. The basis for making this distinction is twofold: First, some models are more abstract than others in that the concepts in them are not tied to any particular case, whereas other models reveal concepts that simply summarize statistically relations among variables in a particular data set. Second, more abstract models almost always reveal more complexity in their representation of causal connections among variables. That is, one will find feedback loops, cycles, mutual effects, and other connective representations that complicate the causal connections among the variables in the model and make them difficult to summarize with simple statistics. In contrast, the less abstract models typically depict a clear causal sequence among empirical variables.[17] These models typically reveal independent variables that effect variation in some dependent variable; if the model is more complex, it might also highlight intervening variables and perhaps even some interaction effects among the variables.

Thus, analytical models are more abstract, they highlight more generic properties of the universe, and they portray a complex set of connections among variables. In contrast, causal models are more empirically grounded; they are more likely to devote particular properties of a specific empirical case; and they are likely to present a simple lineal view of causality.

Causal models are typically drawn to provide a more detailed interpretation of an empirical generalization. They are designed to sort out the respective influences of variables, usually in some temporal sequence, as they operate on some dependent variable of interest. At times, a causal model becomes a way of representing the elements of a middle-range theory so these elements can be connected to the particulars of a specific empirical context. For example, if we wanted to know why the size of a bureaucratic organization is related to its complexity of structure in a particular empirical case of a growing organization, we might translate the more abstract variables of size and complexity into specific empirical indicators and perhaps try to introduce other variables that also influence the relationship between size and complexity in this empirical case. The causal model thus becomes a way to represent with more clarity the empirical association between size and complexity in a specific context.

Analytical models are usually drawn to specify the relations among more abstract and generic processes. Often they are used to delineate the processes that connect the concepts of an axiomatic or, more likely, a formal theory. For example, we might construct a model that tells us more about the processes that generate the relationship between conflict and solidarity or between size and differentiation in social systems. Additional concepts would be introduced, and their weighted, direct, indirect, feedback, cyclical, lagged, and other patterns of effect on one another would be diagrammed. In this way, the analytical model tells us more about how and why properties of the universe are connected. In addition to specifying processes among formal propositions, analytical models can be used to describe processes that connect variables in the propositions of a middle-range theory. For example, we might use a model to map out how organization size and complexity are connected by virtue of other processes operating in an organization.

Of course, we can construct analytical models or causal models for their own sake, without reference to an empirical generalization, a middle-range theory, and a formal or axiomatic theory. We may simply prefer modeling to propositional formats. One of the great advantages of modeling is that it allows the presentation of complex relations among many variables in a reasonably parsimonious fashion. To say the same thing as a model, a propositional format might have to use complex equations or many words. Thus, by itself, modeling represents a tool that many theorists find preferable to alternative theoretical schemes.

CONCLUSION

It is important to recognize that there is far from complete consensus over which of these theoretical formats is the most desirable. The Web page for Chapter 1 provides an assessment of the relative merits of these formats from the perspective of science (www.sociology.wadsworth.com), but not all sociologists are committed to this epistemology, as we will come to appreciate as particular theoretical approaches are examined in the chapters to follow. Even among those committed to developing scientific theory, there is only a general sense that it is desirable to build formal propositions schemes. And so, as we approach the substance of sociological theory, we will see great diversity in the kinds of theories that various scholars seek to develop.

NOTES

1. I am borrowing the general ideal from Talcott Parsons, *The Social System* (New York: Free Press, 1951). For another version of this typology, see my *The Science of Human Organization* (Chicago: Nelson-Hall, 1985), Chapter 2.

2. Among several fine introductory works on the nature of scientific theory, the discussion in this chapter draws heavily on Paul Davidson Reynolds' excellent *A Primer in Theory Construction* (Indianapolis: Bobbs-Merrill, 1971). For excellent introductory works, see Arthur L. Stinchcombe, *Constructing Social Theories* (New York: Harcourt, Brace & World, 1968), pp. 3–56; Karl R. Popper, *The Logic of Scientific Discovery* (New York: Harper & Row, 1959); David Willer and Murray Webster, Jr., "Theoretical Concepts and Observables," *American Sociological Review* 35 (August 1970), pp. 748–757; Hans Zetterberg, *On Theory and Verification in Sociology*, 3rd ed. (Totowa, NJ: Bedminister, 1965); Jerald Hage, *Techniques and Problems of Theory Construction in Sociology* (New York: Wiley, 1972); Walter L. Wallace, *The Logic of Science in Sociology* (Chicago: Aldine, 1971); Robert Dubin, *Theory Building* (New York: Free Press, 1969); Jack Gibbs,

Sociological Theory Construction (Hinsdale, IL: Dryden, 1972); Herbert M. Blalock, Jr., *Theory Construction: From Verbal to Mathematical Formulations* (Englewood Cliffs, NJ: Prentice-Hall, 1969); Nicholas C. Mullins, *The Art of Theory: Construction and Use* (New York: Harper & Row, 1971); Bernard P. Cohen, *Developing Sociological Knowledge: Theory and Method* (Chicago: Nelson-Hall, 1989).

3. For my views on these controversial issues, see Jonathan H. Turner, "In Defense of Positivism," *Sociological Theory* 3 (Fall, 1985), pp. 24–30; and Stephan Fuchs and Jonathan H. Turner, "What Makes a Science Mature?," *Sociological Theory* 4 (Fall, 1986), pp. 143–150.

4. For more detailed work on concept formation, see Carl G. Hempel, *Fundamentals of Concept Formation in Empirical Science* (Chicago: University of Chicago Press, 1952).

5. For a useful and insightful critique of sociology's ability to generate abstract concepts and theory, see David and Judith Willer, *Systematic Empiricism: Critique of Pseudoscience* (Englewood Cliffs, NJ: Prentice-Hall, 1973).

6. For examples of this line of argument see Herbert Blumer, *Symbolic Interaction: Perspective and Method*

(Englewood Cliffs, NJ: Prentice-Hall, 1969); or Anthony Giddens, *New Rules of Sociological Method* (New York: Basic Books, 1977).

7. For the counterargument, see Jonathan H. Turner, "Toward a Social Physics: Reducing Sociology's Theoretical Inhibitions," *Humboldt Journal of Social Relations* 7 (Fall/Winter 1979–80), pp. 140–155; "Returning to Social Physics," *Perspectives in Social Theory,* vol 2 (1981); "Some Problematic Trends in Sociological Theorizing," *Wisconsin Sociologist* 15 (Spring/Summer 1978), pp. 80–88; and *Societal Stratification: A Theoretical Analysis* (New York: Columbia University Press, 1984).

8. Reynolds, *Primer in Theory Construction,* p. 57; see also Stinchcombe, *Constructing Social Theories,* pp. 38–47, for a discussion of how concepts not only point to variable properties of phenomena but also to the interaction effects of interrelated phenomena. For an interesting discussion of the importance of variable concepts and for guidelines on how to use them, see Hage, *Techniques and Problems of Theory Construction.*

9. For a forceful and scholarly advocacy of this point, see Jeffrey C. Alexander, *Theoretical Logic in Sociology,* 4 vols. (Berkeley: University of California Press, 1982–1984).

10. Webster's *New Collegiate Dictionary* (Springfield, MA: Merriman, 1976).

11. For the best review on the nature of metatheory, see George Ritzer, *Metatheorizing in Sociology* (Lexington, MA: Lexington, 1991).

12. For more details of this argument, see Lee Freese, "Formal Theorizing,"

Annual Review of Sociology 6 (1980), pp. 187–212; and Herbert L. Costner and Robert K. Leik, "Deductions from Axiomatic Theory," *American Sociological Review* 29 (December 1964), pp. 19–35.

13. See Freese.

14. I have borrowed this example from Peter M. Blau's "Applications of a Macrosociological Theory" in *Mathematizche Analyse von Organisationsstrukktaren und Prozessen* (Internationale Wissenschaftliche Fachkonferenz, vol. 5, March 1981).

15. Actually, these are typically "regression equations" and would not constitute modeling as I think it should be defined. A series of differential equations, especially as they are simulated or otherwise graphically represented, would constitute a model. Computer simulations represent, I think, an excellent approach to modeling. See, for example, Robert A. Hanneman, *Computer-Assisted Theory Building: Modeling Dynamic Social Systems* (Newbury Park, CA: Sage, 1988).

16. For examples of my efforts to develop such models, see my *Societal Stratification: A Theoretical Analysis* (New York: Columbia University Press, 1985), *A Theory of Social Interaction* (Stanford, CA: Stanford University Press, 1989), and *Macrodynamics: Towards a Theory on the Organization of Human Populations* (New Brunswick, NJ: Rutgers University Press, 1995).

17. The "path analysis" that was so popular in American sociology in the 1970s is a good example of such modeling techniques.

✳

PART I

Functional
Theorizing

2

Early Functional Theory

Auguste Comte (1798–1857) is usually credited as being the founder of sociology. Philosophizing about humans and society had, of course, long been a preoccupation of lay people and scholars alike, but Comte advocated a "science of society" and coined the term *sociology*. Although Comte's work soon fell into neglect and obscurity—leading him to live out his later years in frustration and bitterness—his work profoundly influenced social thought. It is regrettable that few recognize this influence even today, but despite Comte's current obscurity, the emergence of the functionalist perspective began with his work.[1] Comte created functionalism by comparing societies to biological organisms—a point of emphasis that remained for the entire nineteenth century.

THE ORGANISMIC ANALOGY

Auguste Comte's Early Statement

Comte felt that human evolution in the nineteenth century had reached the "positive stage" in which empirical knowledge could be used to understand the social world and to create a better society. Comte thus advocated applying the scientific method to the study of society—a strategy that, in deference to Comte, is still termed *positivism* in the social sciences. This application of the scientific method gave birth to a new science, sociology.

Comte's entire intellectual life represented an attempt to legitimate sociology. His efforts on this score went so far as to construct a "hierarchy of the sciences," with sociology as the "queen" of the sciences. Although this hierarchy allowed Comte to assert the importance of sociology and thereby separate it from social philosophy, his most important tactic for legitimating sociology was to borrow terms and concepts from the highly respected biological sciences. Sociology was thus initiated and justified by appeals to the biological sciences—which helps explain why functionalism was sociology's first and, until the 1970s, most dominant theoretical orientation.

Seeing the affinity between sociology and biology as residing in their common concern with organic bodies, Comte divided sociology into social "statics," or morphology, and "dynamics," or social growth and progress. But Comte was convinced that, although "Biology has hitherto been the guide and preparation for Sociology . . . Sociology will in the future . . . (provide) the ultimate systematization of Biology." Comte visualized that, with initial borrowing of concepts from biology and later with the development of positivism in the social sciences, the principles of sociology would inform biology. Thus, sociology must first recognize the correspondence between the individual organism in biology and the social organism in sociology:

> We have thus established a true correspondence between the Statistical Analysis of the Social Organism in Sociology, and that of the Individual Organism in Biology. . . . If we take the best ascertained points in Biology, we may decompose structure anatomically into *elements, tissues,* and *organs.* We have the same things in the Social Organism; and may even use the same names.[2]

Comte then began to make clear analogies between specific types of social structures and the biological concepts:

> I shall treat the Social Organism as definitely composed of the Families which are the true elements or cells, next the Classes or Castes which are its proper tissues, and lastly, of the cities and Communes which are its real organs.[3]

In Comte's hands, the organismic analogy was rough and crude, but it provided a model for legitimating sociology under the mantra of the more respected biological sciences as well as a strategy for conducting sociological inquiry. Yet, Comte never followed through on his advocacy; it was left to the British sociologist, Herbert Spencer, to develop more fully the implications of the organismic analogy.

Herbert Spencer's Analytical Functionalism

Herbert Spencer (1820–1903) was a broad-based philosopher who, before writing on sociology, had produced multivolume treatises on ethics,[4] biology,[5] and psychology.[6] All were a part of his Synthetic Philosophy, which was to unify the diverse realms of the universe under a common set of abstract principles.[7] In writing his major work on sociology, *The Principles of Sociology,*[8]

Spencer developed an organismic analogy that systematically compared society to organisms[9]:

1. As organic and superorganic (societal) bodies increase in size, they increase in structure. That is, they become more complex and differentiated.

2. Such differentiation of structures is accompanied by differentiation of functions. Each differentiated structure serves distinctive functions for sustaining the "life" of the systemic whole.

3. Differentiated structures and functions require in both organic and superorganic bodies integration through mutual dependence. Each structure can be sustained only through its dependence on others for vital substances.

4. Each differentiated structure in both organic and superorganic bodies is, to a degree, a systemic whole by itself (that is, organs are composed of cells, and societies are composed of groupings of individuals); thus, the larger whole is always influenced by the systemic processes of its constituent parts.

5. The structures of organic and superorganic bodies can "live on" for a while after the destruction of the systemic whole.

These points of similarity between organism and society, Spencer argued, must be qualified for their points of "extreme unlikeness"[10]:

1. There are great differences in the degree of connectedness of the parts, or structures, in organic and social wholes. In superorganic wholes, there is less direct and continuous physical contact and more dispersion of parts than in organic bodies.

2. There are differences in the modes of contact between organic and superorganic systems. In the superorganic, there is much more reliance on symbols than in the organic.[11]

3. There are differences in the levels of consciousness and voluntarism of parts in organic and superorganic bodies. All units in society are conscious, goal seeking, and reflective, whereas only one unit can potentially be so in organic bodies.

As Spencer continued to analogize the points of similarity between organicism and societies, he began to develop what can be termed *requisite functionalism*. That is, organic and superorganic bodies reveal certain universal requisites that must be fulfilled for these bodies to adapt to an environment. Moreover, these same requisites exist for all organic and superorganic systems. To quote Spencer on this point:

> Close study of the facts shows us another striking parallelism. Organs in animals and organs in societies have internal arrangements framed on the same principle. Differing from one another as the viscera of a living creature do in many respects, they have several traits in common. Each viscus

contains appliances for conveying nutriment to its parts, for bringing it materials on which to operate, for carrying away the product, for draining off waste matters; as also for regulating its activity.[12]

It is not hard to see the seeds of an argument for universal functional requisites in this passage. Indeed, on the next page from this quote, Spencer argued, "it is the same for society" and proceeded to list the basic functional requisites of societies. For example, each superorganic body

Has a set of agencies which bring the raw material . . . ; it has an apparatus of major and minor channels through which the necessities of life are drafted out of the general stocks circulating through the kingdom . . . ; it has appliances . . . for bringing those impulses by which the industry of the place is excited or checked; it has local controlling powers, political and ecclesiastical, by which order is maintained and healthful action furthered.[13]

Even though these universal requisites are not so clearly separated as they were to become in modern functional approaches, the logic of the analysis is clear. First, there are certain universal needs or requisites that structures function to meet. Spencer believed four classes of needs could be subsumed under three labels: (1) needs for *operation* by which he meant the necessity for (a) production and (b) reproduction; (2) needs for *regulation* or the necessity for coordinating and controlling members of a population through the use of power and symbols; and (3) needs for *distribution* or the movement of people, information, and resources among members of the population. As societies grow and differentiate, Spencer argued, they do so along these three axes; that is, first distinctive operative structures for production (gathering of resources and their conversion into usable commodities) and reproduction (generating new members for the society) become evident and distinct from each other. Then these become differentiated from regulating structures, such as centers of power (government) and centers of ideology like the church. Finally, distinctive, distributed structures (markets, ports, roads) and other systems for distributing people, information, and resources become separate from operative and regulatory structures. Thus, as societies grow, they differentiate between and within operative, regulatory, and distributive structures.

Thus, by recognizing that certain basic or universal needs must be met, analysis of organic and superorganic systems is simplified. One examines processes to determine needs for integrating differentiated parts, needs for sustaining the parts of the system, needs for producing and distributing information and substances, and needs for political regulation and control. In simple systems, these needs are met by each element of the system, but when structures begin to grow and to become more complex, they are met by distinctive types of structures that specialize in meeting one of these general classes of functions. As societies become highly complex, structures become even more specialized and meet only specific subclasses of these general functional needs.

The logic behind this form of requisite functionalism guided much of Spencer's substantive analysis and is the essence of functional analysis today. The list of basic needs to be met varies among theorists, but the mode of the analysis remains the same: Examine specific types of social processes and structures for the needs or requisites that they meet.

FUNCTIONALISM AND ÉMILE DURKHEIM

We should not be surprised that, as the inheritor of a long French tradition of social thought, especially Comte's organicism, Émile Durkheim's (1858–1917) early works were heavily infused with organismic terminology. Although his major work, *The Division of Labor in Society*, was sharply critical of Herbert Spencer, many of Durkheim's formulations were clearly influenced by the nineteenth-century intellectual preoccupation with biology.[14] Aside from the extensive use of biologically inspired terms, Durkheim's basic assumptions reflected those of the organicists: (1) Society was to be viewed as an entity in itself that can be distinguished from and is not reducible to its constituent parts. In conceiving society as a reality, *sui generis,* Durkheim in effect gave analytical priority to the social whole. (2) Although such an emphasis by itself did not necessarily reflect organismic inclinations, Durkheim, in giving causal priority to the whole, viewed system parts as fulfilling basic functions, needs, or requisites of that whole. (3) The frequent use of the notion "functional needs" is buttressed by Durkheim's conceptualization of social systems as "normal" and "pathological" states. Such formulations, at the very least, connote the view that social systems have needs that must be fulfilled if "abnormal" states are to be avoided. (4) When we view systems as normal and pathological, as well as by functions, the additional implication is that systems have equilibrium points around which normal functioning occurs.

Durkheim recognized the dangers in this kind of analysis and explicitly tried to deal with several of them. First, he was clearly aware of the dangers of teleological analysis—of implying that some future consequence of an event causes that very event to occur. Thus, he warned that the causes of a phenomenon must be distinguished from the ends it serves:

> When, then, the explanation of a social phenomenon is undertaken, we must seek separately the efficient cause which produces it and the function it fulfills. We use the word "function" in preference to "end" or "purpose," precisely because social phenomena do not generally exist for the useful results they produce.[15]

Thus, despite giving analytical priority to the whole and viewing parts as having consequences for certain normal states and, hence, meeting system requisites, Durkheim remained aware of the dangers of asserting that all systems have "purpose" and that the need to maintain the whole causes the existence of its constituent parts. Yet Durkheim's insistence that the function of a part for the social whole always be examined sometimes led him, and certainly many of his followers, into questionable teleological reasoning. For example, even when distinguishing *cause* and *function* in his major methodological statement, he leaves room for an illegitimate teleological interpretation: "Consequently, to explain a social fact, it is not enough to show the cause on which it depends; we must also, at least in most cases, show its function in the establishment of social order."[16] In this summary phrase, the words "in the establishment of" could connote that the existence of system parts can be explained only by the whole, or social order, that they function to maintain. From this view, it is only a short step to outright teleology: The social fact in question is caused by the needs of the social order that the fact fulfills. Such theoretical statements do not necessarily have to be illegitimate, for it is conceivable that a social system could be programmed to meet certain needs or designated ends and thereby have the capacity to cause variations in cultural items or "social facts" to meet these needs or ends. But if such a system is being described by an analyst, it is necessary to document how the system is programmed and how it causes variations in social facts to meet needs or ends. As the previous quotation illustrates, Durkheim did not have this kind of system in mind when he formulated his particular brand of functional analysis; thus, he did not want to state his arguments teleologically.

Despite his warnings to the contrary, Durkheim appears to have taken this short step into teleological reasoning in his substantive works. In his first major work on the division of labor, Durkheim went to great lengths to distinguish between cause (increased population and moral density) and function (integration of society). However, the causal statements often become fused with functional statements. The argument is, generally, like this: Population density increases moral density (rates of contact and interaction); moral density leads to competition, which threatens the social order; in turn, competition for resources results in the specialization of tasks as actors seek viable niches in which to secure resources; and specialization creates pressures for mutual interdependence and increased willingness to accept the morality of mutual obligation. This transition to a new social order is not made consciously, or by "unconscious wisdom"; yet, the division of labor is necessary to restore the order that "unbridled competition might otherwise destroy."[17] Hence, the impression is left that the threat or the need for social order causes the division of labor. Such reasoning can be construed as an illegitimate teleology because the consequence or result of the division of labor—social order—is the implied cause of it. At the very least, then, cause and function are not kept as analytically separate as Durkheim so often insisted.

In sum, then, despite Durkheim's warnings about illegitimate teleology, he often appears to waver on the brink of the very traps he wanted to avoid. The reason for this failing can probably be traced to the organismic assumptions built into this form of sociological analysis. In taking a strong sociologistic position on the question of emergent properties—that is, on the irreducibility of the whole to its individual parts—Durkheim separated sociology from the naive psychology and anthropology of his day.[18] However, in supplementing this emphasis on the social whole with organismic assumptions of function, requisite, need, and normality/pathology, Durkheim helped weld organismic principles to sociological theory for nearly three-quarters of a century. The brilliance of his analysis of substantive topics, as well as the suggestive features of his analytical work, made a functional mode of analysis highly appealing to subsequent generations of sociologists and anthropologists.

FUNCTIONALISM AND THE ANTHROPOLOGICAL TRADITION

Functionalism might have died with Durkheim except that anthropologists began to find it an appealing way to analyze simple societies. Indeed, functionalism as a well-articulated conceptual perspective was perpetuated in the first half of the twentieth century by the writings of two anthropologists, Bronislaw Malinowski and A. R. Radcliffe-Brown.[19] These thinkers were heavily influenced by the organicism of Durkheim, as well as by their own field studies among primitive societies. Despite the similarities in their intellectual backgrounds, however, the conceptual perspectives developed by Malinowski and Radcliffe-Brown reveal many dissimilarities.

A. R. Radcliffe-Brown's Functionalism

Recognizing that "the concept of function applied to human societies is based on an analogy between social life and organic life" and that "the first systematic formulation of the concept as applying to the strictly scientific study of society was performed by Durkheim," Radcliffe-Brown (1881–1955) tried to indicate how some problems of organismic analogizing might be overcome.[20] Radcliffe-Brown believed the most serious problem with functionalism was the tendency for analysis to appear teleological. Noting that Durkheim's definition of function pertained to the way in which a part fulfills system needs, Radcliffe-Brown emphasized that, to avoid the teleological implications of such analysis, it would be necessary to "substitute for the term 'needs' the term 'necessary condition of existence.'" In doing so, he felt that no universal human or societal needs would be postulated; rather, the question of which conditions were necessary for survival would be an empirical one, an issue that would have to be discovered for each given social system. Furthermore, in recognizing the diversity of conditions necessary for the survival of different systems, analysis would avoid asserting that every item of a culture must have a function and that items in different cultures must have the same function.

Once the dangers of illegitimate teleology were recognized, functional or (to use his term) structural analysis could legitimately proceed from several assumptions: (1) One necessary condition for survival of a society is minimal integration of its parts. (2) The term *function* refers to those processes that maintain this necessary integration or solidarity. (3) Thus, in each society, structural features can be shown to contribute to the maintenance of necessary solidarity. In such an analytical approach, social structure and the conditions necessary for its survival are irreducible. In a vein similar to that of Durkheim, Radcliffe-Brown saw society as a reality in and of itself. For this reason, he usually visualized cultural items, such as kinship rules and religious rituals, as explicable by needs for solidarity and integration. For example, in analyzing a lineage system, Radcliffe-Brown would first assume that some minimal degree of solidarity must exist in the system. Processes associated with lineage systems would then be assessed to determine their consequences for maintaining this solidarity. The conclusion was that lineage systems provided a systematic way of adjudicating conflict in societies where families owned land because such a system specified who had the right to land and through which side of the family it would always pass. The integration of the economic system—landed "estates" owned by families—is thus explained.[21]

This form of analysis poses a number of problems that continue to haunt functional theorists. Although Radcliffe-Brown admitted that "functional unity [integration] of a social system is, of course, a hypothesis," he failed to specify the analytical criteria for assessing just how much or how little functional unity is necessary for testing this hypothesis. As subsequent commentators discovered, without some analytical criteria for determining what is and what is not minimal functional integration and societal survival, the hypothesis cannot be tested, even in principle. Thus, what its typically done is to assume that the existing system is minimally integrated and surviving because it exists and persists. Without carefully documenting how various cultural items promote instances of both integration and malintegration of the social whole, such a strategy can reduce the hypothesis of functional unity to a tautology: If one can find a system to study, then it must be minimally integrated; therefore, lineages that are a part of this system must promote its integration. To discover the contrary would be difficult because the system, by virtue of being a surviving system, is already composed of integrated parts, such as a lineage system. There is a non sequitur in such reasoning because it is quite possible to view a cultural item like a lineage system as having both integrative and malintegrative (and other) consequences for the social whole. In his actual ethnographic descriptions, Radcliffe-Brown often slips inadvertently into a pattern of circular reasoning: The fact of a system's existence requires that its existing parts, such as a lineage system, be viewed as contributing to the system's existence. Assuming integration and then assessing the contribution of individual parts to the integrated whole led to an additional analytical problem: Such a mode of analysis implies that the causes of a particular structure— for example, lineages—reside in the system's needs for integration, which is most likely an illegitimate teleology.

Radcliffe-Brown would, of course, have denied this conclusion. His awareness of the dangers of illegitimate teleology would have seemingly eliminated the implication that the needs of a system cause the emergence of its parts. His repeated assertions that the notion of function "does not require the dogmatic assertion that everything in the life of every community has a function" should have led to a rejection of tautological reasoning.[22] Much like Durkheim, however, what Radcliffe-Brown asserted analytically was frequently not practiced in the concrete empirical analysis of societies. Such lapses were not intended but appeared to be difficult to avoid with functional needs, functional integration, and equilibrium as operating assumptions.[23]

Thus, although Radcliffe-Brown displayed an admirable awareness of the dangers of organicism—especially of the problem of illegitimate teleology and the hypothetical nature of notions of solidarity—he all too often slipped into a pattern of questionable teleological reasoning. Forgetting that integration was only a working hypothesis, he opened his analysis to problems of tautology. Such problems were persistent in Durkheim's analysis, and, despite his attempts to the contrary, their specter haunted even Radcliffe-Brown's insightful essays and ethnographies.

Bronislaw Malinowski's Functionalism

Functionalism might have ended with Radcliffe-Brown because it had very little to offer sociologists attempting to study complex societies. Both Durkheim and Radcliffe-Brown posited one basic societal need—integration—and then analyzed system parts to determine how they meet this need. For sociologists who are concerned with differentiated societies, this is likely to become a rather mechanical task. Moreover, it does not allow analysis of those aspects of a system part that are not involved in meeting the need for integration.

Bronislaw Malinowski's (1884–1942) functionalism removed these restrictions; by reintroducing Spencer's approach,[24] Malinowski reintroduced two important ideas from Spencer: (1) the notion of system levels and (2) the concept of different and multiple system needs at each level. In making these two additions, Malinowski made functional analysis more appealing to twentieth-century sociological theorists.

Malinowski's scheme has three system levels: the biological, the social structural, and the symbolic.[25] At each level we can discern basic needs or survival requisites that must be met if biological health, social-structural integrity, and cultural unity are to exist. Moreover, these system levels constitute a hierarchy, with biological systems at the bottom, social-structural arrangements next, and symbolic systems at the highest level. Malinowski stressed that the way in which needs are met at one system level sets constraints on how they are met at the next level in the hierarchy. Yet, he did not advocate a reductionism of any sort; indeed, he thought that each system level reveals its own distinctive requisites and processes meeting these needs. In addition, he argued that the important system levels for sociological or anthropological analysis are the structural and symbolic. And in his actual discussion, the social-structural level receives the most attention. Table 2.1 lists the requisites or needs of the two most sociologically relevant system levels.

In analyzing the structural system level, Malinowski stressed that institutional analysis is necessary. For Malinowski, institutions are the general and relatively stable ways in which activities are organized to meet critical requisites.

Table 2.1 Requisites of System Levels in Malinowski's Scheme

CULTURAL (SYMBOLIC) SYSTEM LEVEL	STRUCTURAL (INSTRUMENTAL) SYSTEM LEVEL
1. Requisites for systems of symbols that provide information necessary to adjust to the environment.	1. The requisite for production and distribution of consumer goods.
2. Requisites for systems of symbols that provide a sense of control over people's destiny and over chance events.	2. The requisite for social control of behavior and its regulation.
3. Requisites for systems of symbols that provide members of a society with a sense of a "communal rhythm" in their daily lives and activities.	3. The requisite for education of people in traditions and skills.
	4. The requisite for organization and execution of authority relations.

All institutions, he felt, have certain universal properties or "elements" that can be listed and then used as dimensions for comparing different institutions. These universal elements are

1. *Personnel:* Who and how many people will participate in the institution?
2. *Charter:* What is the purpose of the institution? What are its avowed goals?
3. *Norms:* What are the key norms that regulate and organize conduct?
4. *Material apparatus:* What is the nature of the tools and facilities used to organize and regulate conduct in pursuit of goals?
5. *Activity:* How are tasks and activities divided? Who does what?
6. *Function:* What requisite does a pattern of institutional activity meet?

By describing each institution along these six dimensions, Malinowski believed that he had provided a common analytical yardstick for comparing patterns of social organization within and between societies. He even constructed a list of universal institutions as they resolve not just structural but also biological and symbolic requisites.

In sum, Malinowski's functional approach opened new possibilities for sociologists who had long forgotten Spencer's similar arguments. Malinowski suggested to sociologists that attention to system levels is critical in analyzing requisites; he argued that there are universal requisites for each system level; he forcefully emphasized that the structural level is the essence of sociological analysis; and, much like Spencer before him and Talcott Parsons a decade later (see Chapter 3), Malinowski posited four universal functional needs at this level—economic adaptation, political authority, educational socialization, and social control—that were to be prominent in subsequent functional schemes. Moreover, he provided a clear method for analyzing institutions as they operate to meet functional requisites. It is fair to say, therefore, that Malinowski drew the rough contours for modern sociological functionalism.

ROBERT MERTON'S CRITIQUE
OF GRAND FUNCTIONAL SCHEMES

In the late 1930s, a unique convergence of ideas and individuals occurred at Harvard University. Robert K. Merton (1910–), then a graduate student, conducted several seminars with fellow graduate students and young instructors, one of whom was Talcott Parsons who became the preeminent functionalist of the twentieth century. Although Parsons had studied briefly with Bronislaw Malinowski in England, it is likely that Parsons and others who became well-known functional theorists[26] received their first intense exposure to A. R. Radcliffe-Brown's and Bronislaw Malinowski's functionalism through Robert K. Merton. Both Merton and Parsons became the preeminent functionalists of the midcentury, but they took very different directions in their views about how to conduct functional analysis. Merton emphasized the importance of a functionalism that is empirical and that avoids the tendency to construct grand analytical schemes into which the flow of empirical events is pushed and shoved, whereas Parsons constructed a great analytical edifice (see next chapter)—an edifice that Merton sought, at least implicitly, to tear down. Merton's goal was to keep functional assumptions to a minimum, whereas Parsons' intent was to build a functional analytical scheme that could explain all reality. At the heart of Merton's criticism of Malinowski's analytical scheme building and, later, of Parsons' as well was the contention that concern for developing an all-encompassing system of concepts would prove both futile and sterile. To Merton, the search for "a total system of sociological theory, in which observations about every aspect of social behavior, organization, and change promptly find their preordained place, has the same exhilarating challenge and the same small promise as those many all-encompassing philosophical systems which have fallen into deserved disuse."[27]

Merton believed grand theoretical schemes are premature because the theoretical and empirical groundwork necessary for their completion has not been performed. Just as Einsteinian theory did not emerge without a long, cumulative research foundation and theoretical legacy, so sociological theory will have to wait for its Einstein, primarily because "it has not yet found its Kepler—to say nothing of its Newton, Laplace, Gibbs, Maxwell, or Planck."[28]

In the absence of this foundation, what passes for sociological theory, in Merton's view, consists of "general orientations toward data, suggesting types of variables which theorists must somehow take into account, rather than clearly formulated, verifiable statements of relationships between specified variables."[29] Strategies advocated by those such as Malinowski and Parsons are not really theory but philosophical systems, with "their varied suggestiveness, their architectonic splendor, and their sterility."[30] Pursuing the opposite strategy of constructing inventories of low-level empirical propositions will prove equally sterile, however, thus suggesting to Merton the need for "theories of the middle range" in sociology.

Merton argued that grand functional schemes tend to fall into several intellectual traps. One is the problem of assuming "functional unity." Theorists such as Durkheim and Radcliffe-Brown had assumed that social integration is the primary requisite of society; this assumption is easily translated into a belief that a high degree of integration is necessary for system survival. But the level of integration actually varies, and to assume that it must exist at a high degree simply begs the more interesting empirical questions about what levels of integration under what conditions exist for varying system parts. A related problem is the issue of "functional universality." It is easy to assume that because a part exists in a system, it serves some positive function, whereas in fact, the opposite can be the case. Indeed, when examined empirically, it becomes evident that parts can have positive, negative, or no consequences for functional integration of the larger social whole. Finally, there is the question of "functional indispensability." Merton argues that functionalists assume that all systems have needs or requisites that must be met and that certain structures are critical or indispensable in meeting these needs. It can be questioned, however, if there are universal functional requisites and if certain structures are always involved in meeting these requisites.

Merton thus anticipated many of the criticisms that would be leveled at functional theory as it emerged in the 1950s. Merton proposed an alternative functionalism [which is reviewed on the Web page for this book (www .sociology.wadsworth.com)]. Despite his early attack, functionalism became the dominant theoretical orientation during the mid-twentieth century.

CONCLUSION

Often coupled with evolutionary theorizing (examined in Part II of this book), functionalism was sociology's first theoretical perspective. By visualizing societies as systemic wholes with basic requisites necessary for survival in the environment, functional theory provided a way to examine complex social systems. Each part of a society was seen to have a "function" or effect on one of the basic survival requisites; thus, by exploring just how a part had this effect, the reason for the part's existence and operation was presumed to be explained. There are many problems with this kind of theoretical explanation (this explanation is reviewed on the Wadsworth Web site for this book), but at the very least, functionalism gave analysts a procedure for describing large and complex systems.

By the midpoint of the twentieth century, functionalism became sociology's dominant theoretical perspective. Talcott Parsons was the most important of these functional theorists, and we will examine his work in the next chapter. But the hegemony of functionalism was never complete, nor was it long-lived. By the 1970s, functional theory was in full retreat as its deficiencies became ever more evident.[31] Still, contemporary sociological theory cannot be understood without the recognition that functionalism was sociology's first theoretical perspective and, if only for a brief period, the only approach that came close to dominating the discipline.[32]

NOTES

1. Auguste Comte, *The Course of Positive Philosophy* (1830–1842). References are to the more commonly used edition that Harriet Martineau condensed and translated, *The Positive Philosophy of Auguste Comte,* vols. 1, 2, and 3 (London: Bell & Sons, 1898; originally published in 1854).

2. Auguste Comte, *System of Positive Polity or Treatise on Sociology* (London: Burt Franklin, 1875; originally published in 1851), pp. 239–240.

3. Ibid., pp. 241–242.

4. Herbert Spencer, *Social Statics* (New York: Appleton, 1870; originally published in 1850) was only one volume, but it became a much larger work near the end of Spencer's career when he wrote *Principles of Ethics* (New York: Appleton, 1879–1893).

5. Herbert Spencer, *The Principles of Biology* (New York: Appleton, 1864–1867).

6. Herbert Spencer, *The Principles of Psychology* (New York: Appleton, 1898; originally published 1855).

7. These are contained in his *First Principles* (New York: A. C. Burt, 1880; originally published in 1862).

8. Herbert Spencer, *The Principles of Sociology* (1874–1896). This work has been reissued in varying volume numbers. References in this chapter are to the three-volume edition (the third edition) issued by Appleton, New York, in 1898. When you read this long work, it is much more critical to note the parts (numbered I through VII) than the volumes, because pagination can vary with editions.

9. See Jonathan H. Turner, *Herbert Spencer: Toward a Renewed Appreciation* (Beverly Hills, CA: Sage, 1985), Chapter 4. See also Spencer's *Principles of Sociology,* vol. I, part II, pp. 449–457. The bulk of Spencer's organicism is on these few pages of a work that spans more than 2,000 pages; yet, the organismic analogy is what we most remember about Spencer.

10. Spencer, *Principles of Sociology,* part II, pp. 451–462.

11. Spencer's theory of symbolism is commonly ignored by contemporary sociologists who simply accept Durkheim's critique. Part I of *Principles* contains a very sophisticated analysis of symbols.

12. Spencer, *Principles of Sociology,* part II, p. 477.

13. Ibid, p. 478.

14. Émile Durkheim, *The Division of Labor in Society* (New York: Macmillan, 1933; originally published in 1893). Durkheim tended to ignore the similarity between Spencer's organismic analogy and his own organic formulations as well as the close correspondence between their theories of symbols. For more details about this argument, see Jonathan H. Turner, "Émile Durkheim's Theory of Social Organization," *Social Forces* 68 (3, 1990), pp. 1–15, and "Spencer's and Durkheim's Principles of Social Organization," *Sociological Perspectives* 27 (January 1984), pp. 21–32.

15. Émile Durkheim, *The Rules of the Sociological Method* (New York: Free Press, 1938, originally published in 1895), p. 96.

16. Ibid., p. 97.

17. Ibid., p. 35. For a more detailed analysis, see Jonathan H. Turner and Alexandra Maryanski, *Functionalism* (Menlo Park, CA: Benjamin/ Cummings, 1979). See also Percy S. Cohen, *Modern Social Theory* (New York: Basic Books, 1968), pp. 35–37.

18. Robert A. Nisbet, *Émile Durkheim* (Englewood Cliffs, NJ: Prentice-Hall, 1965), pp. 9–102.

19. For basic references on Malinowski's functionalism, see his "Anthropology," *Encyclopedia Britannica,* supplementary

vol. 1 (London and New York, 1936); *A Scientific Theory of Culture* (Chapel Hill: University of North Carolina Press, 1944); and *Magic, Science, and Religion and Other Essays* (Glencoe, IL: Free Press, 1948). For basic references on A.R. Radcliffe-Brown's functionalism, see his "Structure and Function in Primitive Society," *American Anthropologist* 37 (July–September, 1935), pp. 58–72; *Structure and Function in Primitive Society* (Glencoe, IL: Free Press, 1952); and *The Andaman Islanders* (Glencoe, IL: Free Press, 1948). See also Turner and Maryanski, *Functionalism* (cited in note 17).

20. Radcliffe-Brown, "Structure and Function in Primitive Society" (cited in note 19), p. 68. This statement is, of course, incorrect, because the organismic analogy was far more developed in Spencer's work.

21. Radcliffe-Brown, *Structure and Function in Primitive Society* (cited in note 19), pp. 31–50. For a secondary analysis of this example, see Arthur L. Stinchcombe, "Specious Generality and Functional Theory," *American Sociological Review* 26 (December, 1961), pp. 929–930.

22. See, for example, Radcliffe-Brown, *Structure and Function in Primitive Society* (cited in note 19).

23. A perceptive critic of an earlier edition of this manuscript provided an interesting way to visualize the problems of tautology:

When do you have a surviving social system?

When certain survival requisites are met.

How do you know when certain survival requisites are met?

When you have a surviving social system.

24. Don Martindale, *The Nature and Types of Sociological Theory* (Boston: Houghton Mifflin, 1960), p. 459.

25. Bronislaw Malinowski, *A Scientific Theory of Culture and Other Essays* (London: Oxford University Press, 1964), pp. 71–125; see also Turner and Maryanski, *Functionalism* (cited in note 17), pp. 44–57.

26. For example, Wilbert Moore, Kingsley Davis, and Marion J. Levy were all exposed to functionalism at this time. Early functionalist theories, such as Davis' and Moore's famous "Some Principles of Stratification," *American Sociological Review* 10 (1945), pp. 242–247, was, no doubt, influenced by Merton's teachings, as was the functional slant of Kingsley Davis' *Human Societies* (New York: Macmillan, 1948). Other early functional statements, such as David F. Aberle, Albert K. Cohen, A. K. Davis, Marion J. Levy, and F. Y. Sutton's "The Functional Requisites of Society," *Ethics* 55 (1950), pp. 100–111, came from participants in these seminars. For further details, see Jonathan H. Turner and Alexandra Maryanski, *Functionalism* (cited in note 17).

27. Robert K. Merton, "Discussion of Parsons' 'The Position of Sociological Theory,'" *American Sociological Review* 13 (1948), pp. 164–168.

28. Ibid. Most of Merton's significant essays on functionalism have been included, and frequently expanded, in Robert K. Merton, *Social Theory and Social Structure* (Glencoe, IL: Free Press, 1949). The quotation is from page 45 of the 1968 edition of this classic work. Most subsequent references will be made to the articles incorporated into this book. For more recent essays on Merton's work, see *The Idea of Social Structure,* ed. Lewis A. Coser (New York: Free Press, 1975). For excellent overviews of Merton's sociology, see Piotr Sztompka, *Robert K. Merton: An Intellectual Profile* (New York: St. Martin's, 1986); and Charles Crothers, *Robert K. Merton* (London: Tavistock, 1981).

29. Merton, *Social Theory and Social Structure* (cited in note 28), p. 47.

30. Ibid., p. 42.

31. In many ways, the decline of functionalism was unfortunate because theorists often "threw the baby out with the bathwater." As is explored on this book's Web site, Jeffrey Alexander was the first to recognize this fact, and he proposed a "neofunctionalism" that sought to retain the strong points of functionalism, while eliminating its weak points. More recently, I have sought to do much the same, but in a somewhat different way than Alexander did. See my *Macrodynamics: Towards a Theory on the Organization of Human Populations* (New Brunswick, NJ: Rutgers University Press, 1995). See also my and others' essays in J. Trevino, ed., *The Sociological Theories of Talcott Parsons: Essays in Socio-Historical Context* (New York: Greenwood, 2002).

32. For a more thorough analysis of the historical legacy of functionalism, see Don Martindale's *The Nature and Types of Sociological Theory* (cited in note 24) and his "Limits of and Alternatives to Functionalism in Sociology," in *Functionalism in the Social Sciences,* American Academy of Political and Social Science Monograph, no. 5 (Philadelphia, 1965), pp. 144–162; see also Ivan Whitaker, "The Nature and Value of Functionalism in Sociology," also in *Functionalism in the Social Sciences,* pp. 127–143.

3

Analytical Functionalism: Talcott Parsons

alcott Parsons (1902–1979) was probably the most prominent theorist of his time, and it is unlikely that any one theoretical approach will so dominate sociological theory again. In the years between 1950 and the late 1970s, Parsonian functionalism was clearly the focal point around which theoretical controversy raged. Even those who despised Parsons' functional approach could not ignore it. Even now, years after his death and more than two decades since its period of dominance, Parsonian functionalism is still the subject of controversy.[1] To appreciate Parsons' achievement in bringing functionalism to the second half of the twentieth century, it is best to start at the beginning, in 1937, when he published his first major work, *The Structure of Social Action*.[2]

THE STRUCTURE OF SOCIAL ACTION

In *The Structure of Social Action*, Parsons advocated using an "analytical realism" to build sociological theory. Theory in sociology must use a limited number of important concepts that "adequately 'grasp' aspects of the external world . . . These concepts do not correspond to concrete phenomena, but to elements in them that are analytically separable from other elements."[3] Thus, first, theory must involve the development of concepts that abstract from empirical reality, in all its diversity and confusion, common analytical elements. In this way, concepts will isolate phenomena from their embeddedness in the complex relations that constitute social reality.

The unique feature of Parson's analytical realism is the insistence on how these abstract concepts are to be employed in sociological analysis. Parsons did not advocate the immediate incorporation of these concepts into theoretical statements but, rather, advocated their use to develop a "generalized system of concepts." This use of abstract concepts would involve their ordering into a coherent whole that would reflect the important features of the "real world." What is sought is an organization of concepts into analytical systems that grasp the salient and systemic features of the universe without being overwhelmed by empirical details. This emphasis on systems of categories represents Parsons' application of Max Weber's ideal-type strategy for analytically accentuating salient features of the world. Thus, much like Weber, Parsons believed that theory should initially resemble an elaborate classification and categorization of social phenomena that reflects significant features in the organization of these social phenomena. This strategy was evident in Parsons' first major work, where he developed the "voluntaristic theory of action."[4]

Parsons believed that the "voluntaristic theory of action" represented a synthesis of the useful assumptions and concepts of utilitarianism, positivism, and idealism. In reviewing the thought of classical economists, Parsons noted the excessiveness of their utilitarianism: unregulated and atomistic actors in a free and competitive marketplace rationally attempting to choose those behaviors that will maximize their profits in their transactions with others. Parsons believed such a formulation of the social order presented several critical problems: Do humans always behave rationally? Are they indeed free and unregulated? How is order possible in an unregulated and competitive system? Yet, Parsons saw as fruitful several features of utilitarian thought, especially the concern with actors as seeking goals and the emphasis on the choice-making capacities of human beings who weigh alternative lines of action. Stated in this minimal form, Parsons felt that the utilitarian heritage could indeed continue to inform sociological theorizing. In a similar critical stance, Parsons rejected the extreme formulations of radical positivists, who tended to view the social world as observable cause-and-effect relationships among physical phenomena. In so doing, he felt, they ignored the complex symbolic functionings of the human mind. Furthermore, Parsons saw the emphasis on observable cause-and-effect relationships as too easily encouraging a sequence of infinite reductionism: Groups were reduced to the causal relationships of their individual members; individuals were reducible to the cause-and-effect relationships of their physiological processes; these were reducible to physicochemical relationships, and so on, down to the most basic cause-and-effect connections among particles of physical matter. Nevertheless, despite these extremes, radical positivism draws attention to the physical parameters of social life and to the deterministic impact of these parameters on much—but of course not all—social organization. Finally, in assessing idealism, Parsons saw as useful the conceptions of "ideas" that circumscribe both individual and social processes,

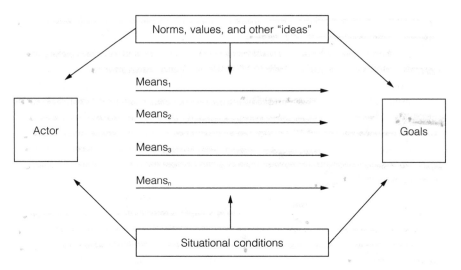

FIGURE 3.1 The Units of Voluntaristic Action

although all too frequently these ideas are seen as detached from the ongoing social life they were supposed to regulate.

The depth of scholarship in Parsons' analysis of these traditions is impossible to communicate. More important than the details of his analysis is the weaving of selected concepts from each of these traditions into a voluntaristic theory of action. At this starting point, in accordance with his theory-building strategy, Parsons began to construct a functional theory of social organization. In this initial formulation, he conceptualized voluntarism as the subjective decision-making processes of individual actors, but he viewed such decisions as the partial outcome of certain kinds of constraints, both normative and situational. Voluntaristic action therefore involves these basic elements: (1) Actors, who at this point in Parsons' thinking, are individual persons. (2) Actors are viewed as goal seeking. (3) Actors also possess alternative means to achieve the goals. (4) Actors are confronted with a variety of situational conditions, such as their own biological makeup and heredity as well as various external ecological constraints, that influence the selection of goals and means. (5) Actors are governed by values, norms, and other ideas such that these ideas influence what is considered a goal and what means are selected to achieve it. (6) Action involves actors making subjective decisions about the means to achieve goals, all of which are constrained by ideas and situational conditions.

Figure 3.1 represents this conceptualization of voluntarism. The processes diagrammed are often termed the *unit act,* with social action involving a succession of such unit acts by one or more actors. Parsons chose to focus on such basic units of action for at least two reasons. First, he felt it necessary to synthesize the historical legacy of social thought about the most basic social process and to dissect it into its most elementary components. Second, given his position on what

FIGURE 3.2 Parsons' Conception of Action, Interaction, and Institutionalization

theory should be, the first analytical task in the development of sociological theory is to isolate conceptually the systemic features of the most basic unit from which more complex processes and structures are built.

Once these basic tasks were completed, Parsons began to ask: How are unit acts connected to each other, and how can this connectedness be conceptually represented? Indeed, near the end of *The Structure of Social Action,* he recognized that "any atomistic system that deals only with properties identifiable in the unit act . . . will of necessity fail to treat these latter elements adequately and be indeterminate as applied to complex systems."[5] However, only the barest hints of what was to come were evident in those closing pages.

THE SOCIAL SYSTEM

Figure 3.2 summarizes the transition from unit acts to social system.[6] This transition occupies the early parts of Parsons' next significant work, *The Social System.*[7] Drawing inspiration from Weber's typological approach to this same topic,[8] Parsons viewed actors as "oriented" to situations by motives (needs and readiness to mobilize energy) and values (conceptions about what is appropriate). There are three types of motives: (1) cognitive (need for information), (2) cathectic (need for emotional attachment), and (3) evaluative (need for assessment). Also, there are three corresponding types of values: (1) cognitive (evaluation by objective standards), (2) appreciative (evaluation by aesthetic standards), and (3) moral (evaluation by absolute rightness and wrongness). Parsons called these *modes of orientation.* Although this discussion is somewhat vague, the general idea seems to be that the relative salience of these motives and values for any actor creates a composite type of action, which can be one of three types: (1) instrumental (action oriented to realize explicit goals efficiently), (2) expressive (action directed at realizing emotional satisfactions), and (3) moral (action concerned with realizing standards of right and wrong). That is, depending on which modes of motivational and value orientation are strongest, an actor will act in one of these basic ways. For example, if cognitive motives are strong and cognitive values most salient, then action will be primarily instrumental, although the action will also have expressive and moral content. Thus, the various combinations and permutations of the modes of orientation—that is, motives and values—produce action geared in one of these general directions.

"Unit acts" therefore involve motivational and value orientations and have a general direction as a consequence of the combination of values and motives that prevails for an actor. Thus far Parsons had elaborated only on his conceptualization of the unit act. The critical next step, which was only hinted at in the closing pages of *The Structure of Social Action:* As variously oriented actors (in the configuration of motivational and value orientations) interact, they develop agreements and sustain patterns of interaction, which become "institutionalized." Such institutionalized patterns can be, in Parsons' view, conceptualized as a social system. Such a system represents an emergent phenomenon that requires its own conceptual edifice. The normative organization of status-roles becomes Parsons' key to this conceptualization; that is, the subject matter of sociology is the organization of status, roles, and norms. Yet, Parsons recognized that the actors who are incumbent in status-roles are motivationally and value oriented; thus, as with patterns of interaction, the task now becomes one of conceptualizing these dimensions of action in systemic terms. The result is the conceptualization of action as composed of three "interpenetrating action systems": the cultural, the social, and the personality. That is, the organization of unit acts into social systems requires a parallel conceptualization of motives and values that become, respectively, the personality and cultural systems. The goal of action theory now becomes understanding how institutionalized patterns of interaction (the social system) are circumscribed by complexes of values, beliefs, norms, and other ideas (the cultural system) and by configurations of motives and role–playing skills (the personality system). Later Parsons added the organismic (subsequently called behavioral) system, but let us not get ahead of the story. At this stage of conceptualization, analyzing social systems involves developing a system of concepts that, first, captures the systemic features of society at all its diverse levels and, second, points to the modes of articulation among personality systems, social systems, and cultural patterns.

In his commitment to developing concepts that reflect the properties of all action systems, Parsons was led to a set of concepts denoting some of the variable properties of these systems. Termed *pattern variables,* they simultaneously allow the categorization of the modes of orientation in personality systems, the value patterns of culture, and the normative requirements in social systems. The variables are phrased as polar dichotomies that, depending on the system under analysis, allow a rough categorization of decisions by actors, the value orientations of culture, or the normative demands on status roles.

1. *Affectivity/affective neutrality* concerns the amount of emotion or affect that is appropriate in a given interaction situation. Should a great deal or little affect be expressed?

2. *Diffuseness/specificity* denotes the issue of how far-reaching obligations in an interaction situation are to be. Should the obligations be narrow and specific, or should they be extensive and diffuse?

3. *Universalism/particularism* points to the problem of whether evaluation of others in an interaction situation is to apply to all actors, or should all actors be assessed by the same standards?

4. *Achievement/ascription* deals with the issue of how to assess an actor, whether by performance or by inborn qualities, such as sex, age, race, and family status. Should an actor treat another in a certain way because of achievements or ascriptive qualities that are unrelated to performance?

5. *Self-collectivity* denotes the extent to which action is to be oriented to self-interest and individual goals or to group interests and goals. Should actors consider their personal or self-related goals over those of the group or large collectivity in which they are involved?[9]

Some of these concepts, such as self-collectivity, were later dropped from the action scheme, but others, such as universalism-particularism, assumed greater importance. The intent of the pattern variables remained the same, however: to categorize dichotomies of decisions, normative demands, and value orientations. In *The Social System,* however, Parsons was inclined to view them as value orientations that circumscribe the norms of the social system and the decisions of the personality system. Thus, the structure of the personality and social systems reflects the dominant patterns of value orientations in culture. This implicit emphasis on the impact of cultural patterns on regulating and controlling other systems of action became ever more explicit in his later work.

By 1951, Parsons had already woven a complex conceptual system that emphasizes the process of institutionalization of interaction into stabilized patterns called social systems, which are penetrated by personality and circumscribed by culture. The profile of institutionalized norms, of decisions by actors in roles, and of cultural value orientations can be typified by concepts—the pattern variables—that capture the variable properties in each of these action components.

Having built this analytical edifice, Parsons then returned to a question, first raised in *The Structure of Social Action,* that guided all his subsequent theoretical formulations: How do social systems survive? More specifically, why do institutionalized patterns of interaction persist? Such questions raise the issue of system imperatives or requisites. Parsons was asking how systems resolve their integrative problems. The answer is provided by the elaboration of additional concepts that point to how personality systems and culture are integrated into the social system, thereby providing some degree of normative coherence and a minimal amount of commitment by actors to conform to norms and play roles. Figure 3.3 delineates the key ideas in Parsons' reasoning.

Just how are personality systems integrated into the social system, thereby promoting equilibrium? At the most abstract level, Parsons conceptualized two

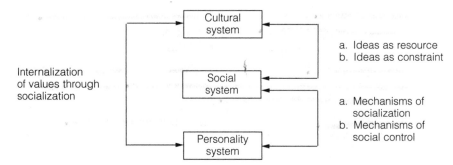

FIGURE 3.3 Parsons' Early Conception of Integration among Systems of Action

mechanisms that integrate the personality into the social system: (1) mechanisms of socialization and (2) mechanisms of social control.

1. *Mechanisms of socialization* are the means through which cultural patterns—values, beliefs, language, and other symbols—are internalized into the personality system, thereby circumscribing its need structure. Through this process, actors are made willing to deposit motivational energy in roles (thereby willing to conform to norms) and are given the interpersonal and other skills necessary for playing roles. Another function of socialization mechanisms is to provide stable and secure interpersonal ties that alleviate much of the strain, anxiety, and tension associated with acquiring proper motives and skills.

2. *Mechanisms of social control* involve those ways in which status-roles are organized in social systems to reduce strain and deviance. There are numerous specific control mechanisms, including (a) institutionalization, which makes role expectations clear and unambiguous while segregating in time and space contradictory expectations; (b) interpersonal sanctions and gestures, which actors subtly employ to mutually sanction conformity; (c) ritual activities, in which actors act out symbolically sources of strain that could prove disruptive while they reinforce dominant cultural patterns; (d) safety-valve structures, in which pervasive deviant propensities are segregated in time and space from normal institutional patterns; (e) reintegration structures, which are specifically charged with bringing deviant tendencies back into line; and, finally, (f) institutionalizing the capacity to use force and coercion into some sectors of a system.

These two mechanisms resolve one of the most persistent integrative problems facing social systems. The other major integrative problem facing social systems concerns how cultural patterns contribute to the maintenance of social order and equilibrium. Again at the most abstract level, Parsons visualized two ways in which this occurs: (1) Some components of culture, such as language, are basic resources necessary for interaction to occur. Without symbolic resources, communication and, hence, interaction would not be possible.

Thus, by providing common resources for all actors, interaction is made possible by culture. (2) A related but still separable influence of culture on interaction is exerted through the substance of ideas contained in cultural patterns (values, beliefs, ideology, and so forth). These ideas can provide actors with common viewpoints, personal ontologies, or, to borrow from W. I. Thomas, a common "definition of the situation." These common meanings allow interaction to proceed smoothly with minimal disruption.

Naturally, Parsons acknowledged that the mechanisms of socialization and social control are not always successful, hence allowing deviance and social change to occur. But clearly the concepts developed in *The Social System* weight analysis in the direction of looking for processes that maintain the integration and, by implication, the equilibrium of social systems.

THE TRANSITION
TO FUNCTIONAL IMPERATIVISM

In collaboration with Robert Bales and Edward Shils, Parsons published *Working Papers in the Theory of Action* shortly after *The Social System*. In *Working Papers,* conceptions of functional imperatives dominated the general theory of action,[10] and by 1956, with Parsons and Neil Smelser's publication of *Economy and Society,* the functions of structures for meeting system requisites were well institutionalized into action theory.[11]

During this period, systems of action were conceptualized to have four survival problems, or requisites: adaptation, goal attainment, integration, and latency. *Adaptation* involves securing sufficient resources from the environment and then distributing these throughout the system. *Goal attainment* refers to establishing priorities among system goals and mobilizing system resources for their attainment. *Integration* denotes coordinating and maintaining viable interrelationships among system units. *Latency* embraces two related problems: pattern maintenance and tension management. Pattern maintenance pertains to how to ensure that actors in the social system display the appropriate characteristics (motives, needs, role-playing, and so forth). Tension management concerns dealing with the internal tensions and strains of actors in the social system.

All these requisites were implicit in *The Social System,* but they tended to be viewed under the general problem of integration. In Parsons' discussion of integration within and between action systems, problems of securing facilities (adaptation), allocation and goal seeking (goal attainment), and socialization and social control (latency) were conspicuous. Thus, the development of the four functional requisites—abbreviated A, G, I, and L—was not so much a radical departure from earlier works as an elaboration of concepts implicit in *The Social System.*

With the introduction of A, G, I, and L, however, a subtle shift away from the analysis of structures to the analysis of functions occurs. Structures are now evaluated explicitly by their functional consequences for meeting the four

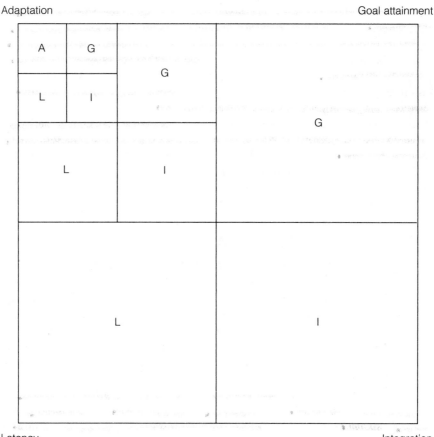

FIGURE 3.4 Parsons' Functional Imperativist View of Social System

requisites. Interrelationships among specific structures are now analyzed by how their interchanges affect the requisites that each must meet.

As Parsons' conceptual scheme became increasingly oriented to function, social systems are divided into sectors, each corresponding to a functional requisite—that is, A, G, I, or L. In turn, any subsystem can be divided into these four functional sectors. Then, each subsystem can be divided into four functional sectors, and so on. This process of "functional sectorization," to invent a word to describe it, is illustrated for the adaptive requisite in Figure 3.4.

Of critical analytical importance in this scheme are the interchanges among systems and subsystems. It is difficult to comprehend the functioning of a designated social system without examining the interchanges among its A, G, I, and L sectors, especially because these interchanges are affected by exchanges among constituent subsystems and other systems in the environment. In turn, the functioning of a designated subsystem cannot be understood without examining internal interchanges among its adaptive, goal attainment, integrative, and latency sectors, especially because these interchanges are influenced by exchanges with other subsystems and the more inclusive system of which it is a subsystem. Thus, at this juncture, as important interchanges among the functional sectors of systems and subsystems are outlined, the Parsonsian scheme begins to resemble an elaborate mapping operation.

THE INFORMATIONAL HIERARCHY
OF CONTROL

Toward the end of the 1950s, Parsons turned his attention toward interrelationships *among* (rather than *within*) what were then four distinct action systems: culture, social structure, personality, and organism. In many ways, this concern represented an odyssey back to the analysis of the basic components of the unit act outlined in *The Structure of Social Action*. But now each element of the unit act is a full-fledged action system, each confronting four functional problems to resolve: adaptation, goal attainment, integration, and latency. Furthermore, although individual decision making is still a part of action as personalities adjust to the normative demands of status-roles in the social system, the analytical emphasis has shifted to the input/output connections among the four action systems.

At this juncture, Parsons began to visualize an overall action system, with culture, social structure, personality, and organism composing its constituent subsystems.[12] Each of these subsystems is seen as fulfilling one of the four system requisites—A, G, I, L—of the overall action system. The organism is considered to be the subsystem having the most consequences for resolving adaptive problems because it is ultimately through this system that environmental resources are made available to the other action subsystems. As the goal-seeking and decision-making system, personality is considered to have primary consequences for resolving goal-attainment problems. As an organized network of status-norms integrating the patterns of the cultural system and the needs of personality systems, the social system is viewed as the major integrative subsystem of the general action system. As the repository of symbolic content of interaction, the cultural system is considered to have primary consequences for managing tensions of actors and ensuring that the proper symbolic resources are available to maintain institutional patterns (latency).

After viewing each action system as a subsystem of a more inclusive, overall system, Parsons explored the interrelations among the four subsystems. What emerged is a hierarchy of informational controls, with culture informationally circumscribing the social system, social structure informationally regulating the personality system, and personality informationally regulating the organismic system. For example, cultural value orientations would be seen as circumscribing or limiting the range of variation in the norms of the social system; in turn, these norms, as translated into expectations for actors playing

Overall function	System level	Interrelations among system levels
Latency	Cultural system	Informational controls
Integration	Social system	
Goal attainment	Personality system	
Adaptation	Organismic system	Energic conditions

FIGURE 3.5 Parsons' Cybernetic Hierarchy of Control

roles, would be viewed as limiting the kinds of motives and decision-making processes in personality systems; these features of the personality system would then be seen as circumscribing biochemical processes in the organism. Conversely, each system in the hierarchy is also viewed as providing the "energic conditions" necessary for action at the next higher system. That is, the organism provides the energy necessary for the personality system, the personality system provides the energic conditions for the social system, and the organization of personality systems into a social system provides the conditions necessary for a cultural system. Thus, the input/output relations among action systems are reciprocal, with systems exchanging information and energy. Systems high in information circumscribe the utilization of energy at the next lower system level, and each lower system provides the conditions and facilities necessary for action in the next higher system. This scheme has been termed a *cybernetic hierarchy* of control and is diagrammed in Figure 3.5.

GENERALIZED MEDIA OF EXCHANGE

Until his death, Parsons maintained his interest in the intra- and inter-systemic relationships of the four action systems. Although he never developed the concepts fully, he had begun to view these relationships as *generalized symbolic media of exchange*.[13] In any interchange, generalized media are employed—for example, money is used in the economy to facilitate the buying and selling of goods. What typifies these generalized media, such as money, is that they are really symbolic modes of communication. The money is not worth much by itself; its value is evident only for what it says symbolically in an exchange relationship.

Thus, what Parsons proposed is that the links among action components are ultimately informational. This means that transactions are mediated by symbols. Parsons' emphasis on information is consistent with a cybernetic hierarchy of control. Informational exchanges, or cybernetic controls, are seen as operating in at least three ways. First, the interchanges or exchanges *among* the four subsystems of the overall action system are carried out by different types of symbolic media—that is, money, power, influence, or commitments.

Second, the interchanges *within* any of the four action systems are also carried out by distinctive symbolic media. Finally, the system requisites of adaptation, goal attainment, integration, and latency determine the type of generalized symbolic media used in an inter- or intra-systemic exchange.

Within the social system, the adaptive sector uses money as the medium of exchange with the other three sectors; the goal-attainment sector employs power—the capacity to induce conformity—as its principal medium of exchange; the integrative sector of a social system relies on influence—the capacity to persuade; and the latency sector uses commitments—especially the capacity to be loyal. The analysis of interchanges of specific structures within social systems should thus focus on the input/output exchanges using different symbolic media.

Among the subsystems of the overall action system, a similar analysis of the symbolic media used in exchanges should be undertaken, but Parsons never clearly described the nature of these media.[14] What he appeared to be approaching was a conceptual scheme for analyzing the basic types of symbolic media, or information, linking systems in the cybernetic hierarchy of control.[15]

PARSONS ON SOCIAL CHANGE

In the last decade of his career, Parsons became increasingly concerned with social change. Built into the cybernetic hierarchy of control is a conceptual scheme for classifying the locus of such social change. What Parsons visualized was that the information and energic interchanges among action systems provide the potential for change within or between the action systems. One source of change can be excesses in either information or energy in the exchange among action systems. In turn, these excesses alter the informational or energic outputs across systems and within any system. For example, excesses of motivation (energy) would have consequences for the enactment of roles and perhaps ultimately for the reorganization of these roles or the normative structure and eventually of cultural value orientations. Another source of change comes from an insufficient supply of either energy or information, again causing external and internal readjustments in the structure of action systems. For example, value (informational) conflict would cause normative conflict (or anomie), which in turn would have consequences for the personality and organismic systems. Thus, concepts that point to the sources of both stasis and change are inherent in the cybernetic hierarchy of control.[16]

To augment this new macro emphasis on change, Parsons used the action scheme to analyze social evolution in historical societies. In this context, the first line of *The Structure of Social Action* is of interest: "Who now reads Spencer?" Parsons then answered the question by delineating some of the reasons why Spencer's evolutionary doctrine had been so thoroughly rejected by 1937. Yet, after some forty years, Parsons chose to reexamine the issue of societal evolution that he had so easily dismissed in the beginning. And in so doing, he reintroduced Spencer's and Durkheim's evolutionary models back into functional theory.

In drawing heavily from Spencer's and Durkheim's insights into societal development, Parsons proposed that the processes of evolution display the following elements:

1. Increasing differentiation of system units into patterns of functional interdependence
2. Establishment of new principles and mechanisms of integration in differentiating systems
3. Increasing adaptive capacity of differentiated systems in their environments

From the perspective of action theory, then, evolution involves (a) increasing differentiation of the personality, social, cultural, and organismic systems from one another; (b) increasing differentiation within each of these four action subsystems; (c) escalating problems of integration and the emergence of new integrative structures; and (d) the upgrading of the survival capacity of each action subsystem, as well as of the overall action system, to its environment.

Parsons then embarked on an ambitious effort in two short volumes to outline the pattern of evolution in historical systems through primitive, intermediate, and modern stages.[17] In contrast with *The Social System,* where he stressed the problem of integration between social systems and personality, Parsons drew attention in his evolutionary model to the inter- and intra-differentiation of the cultural and social systems and to the resulting integrative problems. Each stage of evolution is seen as reflecting a new set of integrative problems between society and culture as each of these systems has become more internally differentiated as well as differentiated from the other. Thus, the concern with the issues of integration within and among action systems, so evident in earlier works, was not abandoned but applied to the analysis of specific historical processes.

Even though Parsons was vague about the causes of evolutionary change, he saw evolution as guided by the cybernetic hierarchy of controls, especially the informational component. In his documenting of how integrative problems of the differentiating social and cultural systems have been resolved in the evolution of historical systems, the informational hierarchy is regarded as crucial because the regulation of societal processes of differentiation must be accompanied by legitimation from cultural patterns (information). Without such informational control, movement to the next stage of development in an evolutionary sequence will be inhibited.

Thus, the analysis of social change is an attempt to use the analytical tools of the general theory of action to examine a specific process, the historical development of human societies. What is of interest in this effort is that Parsons developed many propositions about the sequences of change and the processes that will inhibit or accelerate the unfolding of these evolutionary sequences. It is of more than passing interest that tests of these propositions indicate that, on the whole, they have a great deal of empirical support.[18]

PARSONS ON "THE HUMAN CONDITION"

Again in a way reminiscent of Spencer's grand theory, Parsons attempted to extend his analytical scheme to all aspects of the universe.[19] In this last conceptual addition, it is ironic that Parsons' work increasingly resembled Spencer's. Except for the opening line in *The Structure of Social Action*—"Who now reads Spencer?"—Parsons ignored Spencer. Indeed, he may not have realized how closely his analyses of societal evolution and his conceptualization of the "human condition" resembled Spencer's effort of 100 years earlier. At any rate, this last effort was more philosophy than sociology. Yet, it represents the culmination of Parsons' thought. Parsons began in 1937 with an analysis of the smallest and most elementary social unit, the act. He then developed a requisite functionalism that embraced four action systems: the social, cultural, personality, and what he called "the behavioral" in later years (he had earlier called this the organismic). Finally, in this desire to understand basic parameters of the human condition, he viewed these four action systems as only one subsystem within the larger system of the universe. This vision is portrayed in Figure 3.6.

As can be seen in Figure 3.6, the universe is divided into four subsystems, each meeting one of the four requisites—that is, A, G, I, or L. The four action systems resolve integrative problems, the organic system handles goal-attainment problems, the physicochemical copes with adaptation problems, and the telic ("ultimate" problems of meaning and cognition) deals with latency problems.

Each subsystem employs its own media for intra- and intersubsystem activity. For the action subsystem, the distinctive medium is symbolic meanings; for the telic, it is transcendental ordering; for the organic, it is health; and for the physicochemical, it is empirical ordering (lawlike relations of matter, energy, and so forth). There are double interchanges of these media among the four A, G, I, L sectors, with "products" and "factors" being reciprocally exchanged. That is, each subsystem of the universe transmits a product to the others, while it provides a factor necessary for the operation of other subsystems. This can be illustrated with the L (telic) and I (action) interchange. At the product level, the telic system provides "definitions of human responsibility" to the action subsystems and receives "sentiments of justification" from the action subsystem. At the factor level, the telic provides "categorical imperatives" and receives "acceptance of moral obligations." These double interchanges are, of course, carried out with the distinctive media of the I and A subsystems—that is, transcendental ordering and symbolic meaning, respectively.

The result of this analysis was a grand metaphysical vision of the universe as it impinges on human existence. Parsons' analysis represents an effort to categorize the universe into systems, subsystems, system requisites, generalized media, and exchanges involving these media. As such, this analysis is no longer sociology but philosophy or, at best, a grand meta-theoretical vision. Parsons had indeed come a long way since the humble unit act made its entrance in 1937.

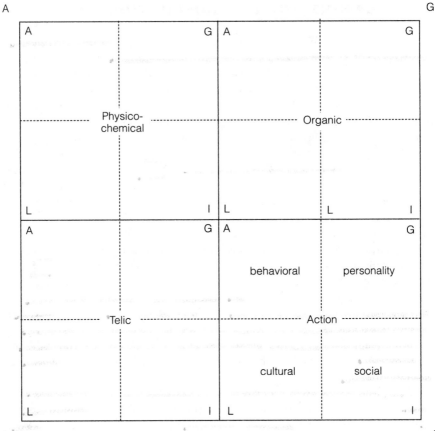

FIGURE 3.6 The Subsystems of the Human Condition

NOTES

1. Although few appear to agree with all aspects of Parsonian theory, rarely has anyone quarreled with the assertion that he has been the dominant sociological figure of this century. For documentation of Parsons' influence, see Robert W. Friedrichs, *A Sociology of Sociology* (New York: Free Press, 1970), and Alvin W. Gouldner, *The Coming Crisis of Western Sociology* (New York: Basic Books, 1970).

2. Talcott Parsons, *The Structure of Social Action* (New York: McGraw-Hill, 1937); the most recent paperback edition (New York: Free Press, 1968) will be used in subsequent footnotes.

3. Ibid., p. 730.

4. For useful analyses of Parsons' work in relation to the issues he raised in *The Structure of Social Action,* see Leon Mayhew, "In Defense of Modernity: Talcott Parsons and the Utilitarian Tradition," *American Journal of Sociology* 89 (1984), pp. 1273–1306; and Jeffrey C. Alexander, "Formal and Substantive Voluntarism in the Work of Talcott Parsons: A Theoretical Reinterpretation," *American Sociological Review* 13 (1978), pp. 177–198.

5. Parsons, *Structure of Social Action* (cited in note 2), pp. 748–749.

6. See also Jonathan H. Turner, "The Concept of 'Action' in Sociological Analysis," in *Analytical and Sociological Theories of Action,* eds. G. Seeba and Raimo Toumea (Dordrecht, Holland: Reidel, 1985).

7. Talcott Parsons, *The Social System* (New York: Free Press, 1951).

8. Max Weber, *Economy and Society,* vol. I (Totowa, NJ: Bedminster, 1968), pp. 1–95.

9. These pattern variables were developed in collaboration with Edward Shils and were elaborated in *Toward a General Theory of Action* (New York: Harper & Row, 1951), pp. 76–98, 203–204, 183–189. Again, Parsons' debt to Max Weber's concern with constructing ideal types can be seen in his presentation of the pattern variables.

10. Talcott Parsons, Robert F. Bales, and Edward A. Shils, *Working Papers in the Theory of Action* (Glencoe, IL: Free Press, 1953).

11. Talcott Parsons and Neil J. Smelser, *Economy and Society* (New York: Free Press, 1956). These requisites are the same as those enumerated by Malinowski. See Chapter 2 in this work, Table 2-1.

12. Talcott Parsons, "An Approach to Psychological Theory in Terms of the Theory of Action," in *Psychology: A Science,* ed. S. Koch, vol. 3 (New York: McGraw-Hill, 1958), pp. 612–711. By 1961, these ideas were even more clearly formulated; see Talcott Parsons, "An Outline of the Social System," in *Theories of Society,* eds. T. Parsons, E. Shils, K.D. Naegele, and J.R. Pitts (New York: Free Press, 1961), pp. 30–38. See also Jackson Toby, "Parsons' Theory of Social Evolution," *Contemporary Sociology* 1 (1972), pp. 395–401.

13. Parsons' writings on this topic are incomplete, but see "On the Concept of Political Power," *Proceedings of the American Philosophical Society* 107 (1963), pp. 232–262; "On the Concept of Influence," *Public Opinion Quarterly* 27 (Spring 1963), pp. 37–62; and "Some Problems of General Theory," in *Theoretical Sociology: Perspectives and Developments,* eds. J.C. McKinney and E.A. Tiryakian (New York: Appleton-Century-Crofts, 1970), pp. 28–68. See also Talcott Parsons and Gerald M. Platt, *The American University* (Cambridge, MA: Harvard University Press, 1975).

14. For his first attempt at a statement, see Parsons, "Some Problems of General Theory" (cited in note 13), pp. 61–68.

15. For a more readable discussion of these generalized media, see T.S. Turner, "Parsons' Concept of Generalized Media of Social Interaction and Its Relevance for Social Anthropology," *Sociological Inquiry* 38 (Spring 1968), pp. 121–134.

16. For a fuller discussion, see Alvin L. Jacobson, "Talcott Parsons: A Theoretical and Empirical Analysis of Social Change and Conflict," in *Institutions and Social Exchange: The Sociologies of Talcott Parsons and George C. Homans,* eds. H. Turk and R. L. Simpson (Indianapolis: Bobbs-Merrill, 1970).

17. Talcott Parsons, *Societies: Evolutionary and Comparative Perspectives* and *The System of Modern Societies* (Englewood Cliffs, NJ: Prentice-Hall, 1966, 1971, respectively). The general stages of development were first outlined in Talcott Parsons, "Evolutionary Universals in Society," *American Sociological Review* 29 (1964), pp. 339–357.

18. See Gary L. Buck and Alvin L. Jacobson, "Social Evolution and Structural-Functional Analysis: An Empirical Test," *American Sociological Review* 33 (June 1968), pp. 343–355; A. L. Jacobson, "Talcott Parsons: Theoretical and Empirical Analysis" (cited in note 16).

19. Talcott Parsons, *Action Theory and the Human Condition* (New York: Free Press, 1978). See the last chapter in this book and my analysis in "Parsons on the Human Condition," *Contemporary Sociology* 9 (1980), pp. 380–383.

4

Systems Functionalism: Niklas Luhmann

The grand architecture of the Parsonian functional scheme, as it evolved over a forty-year period at the midcentury, inspired a great amount of criticism, both inside and outside the functionalist perspective. Within the functionalist camp, Robert Merton criticized the Parsonian conceptual edifice for being too abstract and detached from empirical reality. Unlike Merton, however, other functionalists were not so willing to abandon high-level abstractions in favor of empirical assessments of functional needs. Rather, the alternative was to reduce the complexity and rigidity of the conceptual edifice, while maintaining a broad scheme at a high level of abstraction. As can be seen on the Web site for this book, neofunctionalists such as Jeffrey C. Alexander downplayed the notion of functional requisites, although he sustained an interest in the substantive problems raised by Talcott Parsons. Others continued to build on Parsons' approach, focusing on the same substantive questions as Parsons did and sustaining a commitment to analyzing these problems within the four-functions paradigm.[1]

In this chapter, we will examine the work of Niklas Luhmann (1927–1998), who took the criticisms about the analytical complexity of Parsons' four functions approach seriously and dropped many particulars of this scheme itself but not the goal of producing abstract frameworks for analyzing social reality. Luhmann studied for a time with Parsons, but he eventually criticized Parsonian action theory for being "overly concerned with its own architecture." Luhmann considers himself a systems theorist more than a functionalist, and in recent years the systems aspects of his scheme have been given increasing emphasis.[2] But he is still a functionalist because he tends to analyze system processes by how they meet one master functional requisite: reduction of environmental complexity.[3]

LUHMANN'S GENERAL SYSTEMS APPROACH

System and Environment

Luhmann employs a *general systems* approach to emphasize that human action becomes organized and structured into systems. When the actions of several people become interrelated, a social system can be said to exist. The basic mechanism by which actions become interrelated to create social systems is communication via symbolic codes, such as words and other media. All social systems exist in multidimensional environments, posing potentially endless complexity with which a system must deal. To exist in a complex environment, therefore, a social system must develop mechanisms for reducing complexity, lest the system simply merge with its environment. These mechanisms involve selecting ways and means for reducing complexity. Such selection creates a boundary between a system and its environment, thereby allowing the system to sustain patterns of interrelated actions.

The basic functional requisite in Luhmann's analysis is thus the need to reduce the complexity of the environment in relation to a system of interrelated actions. All social processes are analyzed with respect to their functions for reducing complexity in relation to an environment. Processes that function in this way are typically defined as *mechanisms* in a manner reminiscent of Parsons' early discussion in *The Social System*[4] (see pp. 40–45 in Chapter 3). Indeed, the bulk of Luhmann's sociology revolves around discussions of such mechanisms—differentiation, ideology, law, symbolic media, and other critical elements of his scheme.

Dimensions of the Environment

The complexity of the environment is reduced by these mechanisms along three basic dimensions: (1) a temporal dimension, (2) a material dimension, and (3) a symbolic dimension. More than most social theorists, Luhmann is concerned with time as a dimension of the social universe. Time always presents complexity for a system because it reaches into the past, because it embodies complex configurations of acts in the present, and because it involves the vast horizons of the future. Thus, a social system must develop mechanisms for reducing the complexity of time. The system must find a way to order this dimension by developing procedures to orient actions to the past, present, and future.[5]

Luhmann is also concerned with the material dimension of the environment—that is, with all the possible relations among actions in potentially limitless physical space. Luhmann always asks these questions: What mechanisms are developed to order interrelated actions in physical space? What is the structure and form of such ordering of relations?

Luhmann visualizes the third dimension of human systems as the symbolic. Of all the complex symbols and their combinations that humans can conceivably generate, what mechanisms select some symbols over others and organize them in some ways instead of the vast number of potential alternatives? What kinds of symbolic media are selected and used by a social system to organize social actions?

Thus, the mechanisms of a social system that reduce complexity and thereby maintain a boundary between the system and the environment function along three dimensions, the temporal, material, and symbolic. The nature of a social system—its size, form, and differentiations—will be reflected in the mechanisms that the system uses to reduce complexity along these dimensions.

Types of Social Systems

A social system exists any time the actions of individuals are "meaningfully interrelated and interconnected," thereby setting them off from the temporal, material, and symbolic environment by virtue of the selection of functional mechanisms. From such processes come three basic types of social systems: (1) interactional systems, (2) organizational systems, and (3) societal systems.[6]

Interaction Systems An interaction system emerges when individuals are co-present and perceive each other. The very act of perception is a selection mechanism that sorts from a much more complex environment, creating a boundary and setting people off as a system. Such systems are elaborated by the use of language in face-to-face communication, thereby reducing complexity even further along the temporal, material, and symbolic dimensions. For example, Luhmann would ask: How does the language and its organization into codes shape people's perceptions of time? Who is included in the conversation? And what codes and agreements guide conversation and other actions?

Interaction systems reveal certain inherent limitations and vulnerabilities, however. First, only one topic can be discussed at a time, lest the system collapse as everyone tries to talk at once (which, of course, frequently occurs). Second, the varying conversational resources of participants often lead to competition over who is to talk, creating inequalities and tensions that can potentially lead to conflict and system disintegration. Third, talk and conversation are time-consuming because they are sequential; as a result, an interaction system can never be very complex.

Thus, interaction systems are simple because they involve only those who can be co-present, perceived, and talked to; they are vulnerable to conflict and tension; and they consume a great deal of time. For a social system to be larger and more complex, additional organizing principles beyond perceptions of co-presence and sequential talk are essential.

Organization Systems These systems coordinate the actions of individuals with respect to specific conditions, such as work on a specific task in exchange for a specific amount of money. Organizational systems typically have entry and exit rules (for example, come to work for this period of time and leave with this much money), and their main function is to "stabilize highly 'artificial' modes of behavior over a long stretch of time." They resolve the basic problem of reconciling the motivations and dispositions of individuals and the need to get certain tasks done. An organization does not depend on the moral commitment of individuals; nor does it require normative consensus. Rather, the entrance and exit rules specify tasks in ways that allow individuals to do what is required without wholly identifying with the organization.

Organization systems are thus essential to a complex social order. They reduce environmental complexity by organizing people (1) *in time* by generating entrance and exit rules and by ordering activities in the present and future; (2) *in space* by creating a division of labor, which systems of authority coordinate; and (3) *in symbolic terms* by indicating what is appropriate, what rules apply, and what media, such as money or pay, are to guide action. In his delineation of organization systems, Luhmann stresses that complex social orders do not require consensus on values, beliefs, or norms to be sustained; they can operate quite effectively without motivational commitments of actors. The very strength of complex social orders—flexibility and adaptability to changing environmental conditions—depends on delimited and situational commitments of actors, along with neutral media of communication, such as money.[7]

Societal Systems These systems cut across interaction and organization systems. A societal system is a "comprehensive system of all reciprocally accessible communication actions."[8] Historically, societal systems have been limited by geopolitical considerations, but today Luhmann sees a trend toward one world society. Luhmann's discussion on the societal system is rather vague, but the general idea can be inferred from his analysis of more specific topics: Societal systems use highly generalized communication codes, such as money and power, to reduce the complexity of the environment. In so doing, they set broad limits on how and where actions are to be interrelated into interaction and organization systems. These systems also organize how time is perceived and how actions are oriented to the past, present, and future.

System Differentiation, Integration, and Conflict

These three systems—interaction, organization, and societal—cannot be totally separated because "all social action obviously takes place in society and is ultimately possible only in the form of interaction."[9] Indeed, in very simple societies these systems are fused together, but, as societies become larger and more complex, these systems become clearly differentiated from and irreducible to one another. Organizations become distinctive with respect to (1) their functional domains (government, law, education, economy, religion, science), (2) their entrance and exit rules, and (3) their reliance on distinctive media of communication (money, truth, power, love, and so on). As a consequence, organizations cannot be reduced to a societal system. Interaction systems follow their own laws, for rarely do people strictly follow the guidelines of organizations and society in their conversations.

The differentiation of these systems poses problems for the more inclusive system. First is the problem of what Luhmann calls "bottlenecks." Interaction systems are slow, sequentially organized patterns of talk, and they follow their own dynamics as people use their resources in conversations. As a result, interaction systems often prevent organizations from operating at high levels of efficiency. As people interact, they develop informal agreements and take their time, with the specific tasks of the organization going unperformed or underperformed. Similarly, as organization systems develop their own structures and programs, their interests often collide, and they become "bottlenecks" to action requirements at the societal level. Second is the problem of conflict in differentiated systems. Interactants may disagree on topics; they may become jealous or envious of those with conversational resources. Because interaction systems are small, they cannot become sufficiently complex "to consign marginals to their borders or to otherwise segregate them." At the organizational level, diverse organizations can pursue their interests in ways that are disruptive to both the organization and the more inclusive societal system.

Yet, countervailing these disruptive tendencies are processes that maintain social integration. One critical set of processes is the "nesting" of system levels inside each other. Actions within an interactive system are often nested within an organization system, and organizational actions are conducted within a societal system. Hence, the broader, more inclusive system can promote integration in two ways: (1) It provides the temporal, material, and social premises for the selection of actions, and (2) it imposes an order or structure on the proximate environment around any of its subsystems. For example, an organizational system distributes people in space and in an authority hierarchy; it orients them to time; it specifies the relevant communication codes; and it orders the proximate environment (other people, groupings, offices, and so on) of any interaction system. Similarly, the functional division of a society into politics, education, law, economy, family, religion, and science determines the substance of an organization's action, while it orders the proximate environment of any particular organization. For example, societal differentiation of a distinctive economy delimits what any economic organization can do. Thus, a corporation in a capitalist economy will use money as its distinctive communications media; it will articulate with other organizations concerning market relations; it will organize its workers into bureaucratic organizations with distinctive entrance and exit rules ("work for money"); and it will be oriented to the future, with the past as only a collapsed framework to guide present activity in the pursuit of future outcomes (such as profits and promotions).

In addition to these nesting processes, integration is promoted by the deflection of people's activities across different organizations in diverse functional domains. When many organizations exist in a society, none consumes an individual's sense of identity and self because people's energies are dispersed across several organization systems. As a consequence of their piecemeal involvement, members are unlikely to be emotionally drawn into conflict among organization systems, and, when individual members cannot be pulled emotionally into a conflict, its intensity and potential for social disruption are lessened. Moreover, because interaction systems are distinct from the more inclusive organization, the rank and file often sees any conflict between organizations as distant and remote to their interests and concerns; it is something "out there" in the environment of their interaction systems, and hence, it is not very involving.

Yet another source of conflict mitigation are the entrance and exit rules of an organization. As these become elaborated into hierarchies, offices, established procedures, salary scales, and the like, these rules reduce the relevance of members' conflicts outside the organization—for example, race and religion. Such outside conflicts are separated from those within the organization, and as a result, their salience in the broader societal system is reduced.

Finally, once differentiation of organizations is an established mechanism in a society, specific social control organizations—law, police, courts—can be easily created to mitigate and resolve conflicts. That is, the generation of distinct organizations that are functionally specific represents a new "social technology"; once this technology has been used in one context, it can be applied to additional contexts. Thus, the integrative problems created by the differentiation and proliferation of organizations create the very conditions that can resolve these problems—the capacity to create organizations to mediate among organizations.

And so, although differentiation of three system levels creates problems of integration and conditions conducive to conflict, it also produces countervailing forces for integration. In making this argument, Luhmann emphasizes that, in complex systems, order is not sustained by consensus on common values, beliefs, and norms. On the contrary, there is likely to be considerable disagreement about these, except perhaps at the most abstract level. This point of emphasis is an important contribution of Luhmann's sociology, for it distinguishes his theoretical approach from that of Parsons, who overstressed the need for value consensus in complex social systems. In addition, Luhmann stresses that individuals' moral and emotional attachment to the social fabric is not essential for social integration. To seek a romantic return to a cohesive community, as Émile Durkheim, Karl Marx, and others have, is impossible in most spheres of a complex society. And, rather than viewing this as a pathological state—as concepts like alienation, egoism, and anomie connote—the impersonality and neutrality of many encounters in complex systems can be seen as normal and analyzed less evaluatively. Moreover, people's lack of emotional embeddedness in complex systems gives them more freedom, more options, and more flexibility.[10] This also liberates them from the constraints of tradition, the restrictions of dependency on others, and the indignities of surveillance by the powerful that are so typical of less complex societies.

Communications Media, Reflexivity, and Self-Thematization

Luhmann's system theory stresses the relation of a system to its environment and the mechanisms used to reduce its complexity. All social systems are based on communication among actors as they align their respective modes of conduct. Because action systems are built from commnication, Luhmann devotes considerable attention to *communications theory*, as he defines it. He stresses that human communications become reflexive and that this reflexiveness leads to self-thematization. Luhmann thus develops a communications theory revolving around communication codes and media as well as around reflexiveness and self-thematization. We will explore each of these elements in his theory briefly.

Communication and Codes   Luhmann waxes philosophically and metaphorically about these concepts, but in the end he concludes that communication occurs through symbols that signal actors' lines of behavior, and such symbols constitute a code with several properties.[11] First, the organization of symbols into a code guides the selection of alternatives that reduce the complexity of the environment. For example, when someone in an interaction system says that he or she wants to talk about a particular topic, these symbols operate as a code that reduces the complexity of the system in an environment (its members will now discuss this topic and not all the potential alternatives). Second, codes are binary and dialectical in that their symbols imply their opposite. For example, the linguistic code "be a good boy" also implicitly signals its opposite—that is, what is not good and what is not male. As Luhmann notes, "language makes negative copies available" by its very nature. Third, in implying their opposite, codes create the potential for the opposite action— for instance, "to be a bad boy." In human codes, then, the very process of selecting lines of action and reducing complexity with a code also expands potential options (to do just the opposite or some variant of the opposite). This makes the human system highly flexible because the communications codes used to organize the system and reduce complexity also contain implicit messages about alternatives.

Communications Media   Communication codes stabilize system responses to the environment (while implying alternative responses). Codes can organize communication into distinctive media that further order system responses. As a society differentiates into functional domains, distinctive media are used to organize the resources of systems in each domain.[12] For example, the economy uses money as its medium of communication, which guides interactions within and among economic organizations. Thus, in an economy, relations among organizations are conducted in money terms (buying and selling in markets), and intraorganizational relations among workers are guided by entrance and exit rules structured by money (pay for work at specified times and places). Similarly, power is the distinctive communications medium of the political domain; love is the medium of the family; truth, the medium of science; and so on for other functional domains.[13]

Several critical generalizations are implicit in Luhmann's analysis of communications media. First, the differentiation of social systems into functional domains cannot occur without the development of a distinctive medium of communication for that domain. Second, media reduce complexity because they limit the range of action in a system.[14] (For example, love as a medium limits the kinds of relations that are possible in a family system.) Third, even in reducing complexity, media imply their opposite and thus expand potential options, giving systems flexibility (for instance, money for work implies its opposite, work without pay; the use of power implies its opposite, lack of compliance to political decisions).

Reflexivity and Self-Thematization   The use of media allows for *reflexivity*, or the capacity to examine the process of action as a part of the action itself. With communications media structuring action, we can use these media to think about or reflect on action. Social units can use money to make money; they employ power to decide how power is to be exercised; they can analyze love to decide what is true love; they can use truth to specify the procedures to get at truth; and so on. Luhmann sees this reflexivity as a mechanism that facilitates adaptation of a system to its environment. Reflexivity does so by ordering responses and reducing complexity, while providing actors in a system with the capacity to think about new options for action. For example, it becomes possible to mobilize power to think about new and more adaptive ways to exercise power in political decisions, as is the case when a society's political elite create a constitutional system based on a separation of powers.

As communications media are used reflexively, they allow for what Luhmann terms *self-thematization*. Using media, a system can conceptualize itself and relations with the environment as a "perspective" or "theme." Such self-thematization reduces complexity by providing guidelines for dealing with the temporal, material, and symbolic dimensions of the environment. It becomes possible to have a guiding perspective about how to orient to time, to organize people in space, and to order symbols into codes. For example, money and its reflexive use for self-thematization in a capitalist economy create a concern with the future, an emphasis on rational organization of people, and a set of codes that emphasize impersonal exchanges of services and commodities. The consequence of these self-thematizations is that economic organizations reduce the complexity of their environments and, thereby, coordinate social action more effectively.

Luhmann's Basic Approach

In sum, Luhmann's general systems approach revolves around the system versus environment distinction. Systems need to reduce the complexity of their environments in their perceptions about time, their organization of actors in space, and their use of symbols. Processes that reduce complexity are conceptualized as functional mechanisms. There are three types of systems: interaction, organization, and societal. All system processes occur through communications that can develop into distinctive media and allow reflexivity and self-thematization in a system.

LUHMANN'S CONCEPTION
OF SOCIAL EVOLUTION

Because Luhmann's substantive discussions are cast into an evolutionary framework, it is wise to begin by extracting from his diverse writings the key elements of this evolutionary approach. Like other evolutionary theorists,

Luhmann views evolution as the process of increasing differentiation of a system in relation to its environment.[15] Such increased differentiation allows a system to develop more flexible relations to its environment and, as a result, to increase its level of adaptation. As systems differentiate, however, there is the problem of integrating diverse subsystems; as a consequence, new kinds of mechanisms emerge to sustain the integration of the overall system. But, unlike most evolutionary theorists, Luhmann uses this general image of evolution in a way that adds several new twists to previous evolutionary approaches.

The Underlying Mechanisms of Evolution

Luhmann is highly critical of the way traditional theory has analyzed the process of social differentiation.[16] First, traditional theories—from Marx and Durkheim to Parsons—all imply that there are limits to how divided a system can be; so they all postulate an end to the process, which, in Luhmann's view, is little more than an evaluative utopia. Second, traditional theories overstress the importance of value consensus as an integrating mechanism in differetiated systems. Third, these theories see many processes, such as crime, conflict, dissensus about values, and impersonality, as deviant or pathological; however, they are inevitable in differentiated systems. Fourth, previous theories have great difficulty handling the persistence of social stratification, viewing it as a source of evil or as a perpetual conflict-producing mechanism.

Luhmann's alternative to these evolutionary models is to use his systems theory to redirect the analysis of social differentiation. Like most functionalists, he analogizes to biology but not to the physiology of an organism; rather, his analogies are to the processes delineated in the theory of evolution. Thus, he argues for an emphasis of those processes that produce (1) variation, (2) selection, and (3) stabilization of traits in societal systems.[17] The reasoning here is that sociocultural evolution is like other forms of biological evolution. Social systems have mechanisms that are the functional equivalents of those in biological evolution. These mechanisms generate variation in the structure of social systems, select those variations that facilitate adaptation of a system, and stabilize these adaptive structures.[18]

Luhmann argues that the "mechanism for variation" inheres in the process of communication and in the formation of codes and media. All symbols imply their opposite; so there is always the opportunity to act in new ways (a kind of "symbolic mutation"). The very nature of communication permits alternatives, and at times people act on these alternatives, thereby producing new variations. Indeed, the capacity of human systems for variation is much greater than in biological systems.

The "mechanism for selection" can be found in what Luhmann terms *communicative success*. The general idea behind this concept is that certain new forms of communication facilitate increased adjustment to an environment by reducing its complexity while allowing more flexible responses to the environment. For example, the creation of money as a medium greatly facilitated adaptation of systems and subsystems to the environment, as did the development of power as a medium to coordinate activity in systems. And, because these communication forms facilitated survival and adaptation, they were retained in the structure of the social organism.

The "stabilization mechanism" resides in the very process of system formation. That is, new communication codes and media are used to order social actions among subsystems, and, in so doing, they create structures, such as political systems and economic orders that regularize for a time the use of the new communications media. For example, once money is used, it creates an economic order revolving around markets and exchange that, in turn, feeds back and encourages the extension of money as a medium of communication. From this reciprocity ensues some degree of continuity and stability in the economic system.

Evolution and Social Differentiation

Luhmann believes that sociocultural evolution involves differentiation in seven senses.

1. *Evolution is the increasing differentiation of interaction, organization, and societal systems from one another.* That is, interaction systems increasingly become distinct from organization systems, which in turn are more clearly separated from societal systems. Although these system levels are nested in each other, they also have their unique dynamics.

2. *Evolution involves the internal differentiation of these three types of systems.* Diverse interaction systems multiply and become different from one another (for example, compare conversations at work, at a party, at home, and at a funeral). Organization systems increase in number and specialize in different activities (compare economic with political organizations, or contrast different types of economic organizations, such as manufacturing and retail organizations). And the societal system becomes differentiated from the organization and interaction systems that it comprises. Moreover, there is an evolutionary trend, Luhmann claims, toward a one-world society.

3. *Evolution involves the increasing differentiation of societal systems into functional domains, such as economy, polity, law, religion, family, science, and education.* Organization subsystems within these domains are specialized to deal with a limited range of environmental contingencies, and, in being specialized, subsystems can better deal with contingencies. The overall result for a societal system is increased adaptability and flexibility in its environment.

4. *Functional differentiation is accompanied by (and is the result of) the increasing use of distinctive media of communication.* For example, organization systems in the economy employ money, those in the polity or government exercise power, those in science depend on truth, and those in the family domain use love.

5. *There is a clear differentiation during evolution among the persons, roles, programs, and values.* Individuals are entities separated from the roles and organizations in which they participate. One plays many roles, and each

involves only a segment or part of a person's personality and sense of self; many roles are played with little or no investment of oneself in them. Moreover, most roles persist whether or not any one individual plays them, thereby emphasizing their separation from the person. Such roles are increasingly grouped together into an ever-increasing diversity of what Luhmann calls programs (work, family, play, politics, consumption, and so on) that typically exist inside different kinds of organization systems operating in a distinctive functional domain. In addition, these roles can be shuffled around into new programs, emphasizing the separation of roles and programs. Finally, societal values become increasingly abstract and general, with the result that they do not pertain to any one functional domain, program, role, or individual.[19] They exist as very general criteria that can be selectively invoked to help organize roles into programs or to mobilize individuals to play roles; however, their application to roles and programs is made possible by additional mechanisms such as ideologies, laws, technologies, and norms. By themselves, societal values are too general and abstract for individuals to use in concrete situations. Indeed, one of the most conspicuous features of highly differentiated systems is the evolution of mechanisms to attach abstract values to concrete roles and programs.

6. *Evolution involves the movement through three distinctive forms of differentiation: (a) segmentation, (b) stratification, and (c) functional differentiation.*[20] That is, the five processes outlined earlier have historically created, Luhmann believes, only three distinctive forms of differentiation. When the simplest societies initially differentiate, they do so segmentally in that they create like and equal subsystems that operate very much like the ones from which they emerged. For example, as it initially differentiates, a traditional society will create new lineages, or new villages, that duplicate previous lineages and villages. But segmentation limits a society's complexity and, hence, its capacity to adapt to its environment. And so, alternative forms of differentiation are selected during sociocultural evolution. Further differentiation creates stratified systems in which subsystems vary in their power, wealth, and other resources. These subsystems are ordered hierarchically, and this new form of structure allows more complex relations with an environment but imposes limitations on how complex the system can become. As long as the hierarchical order must be maintained, the options of any subsystem are limited by its place in the hierarchy.[21] Thus, pressures build for a third form of differentiation, the functional. Here, communication processes are organized around the specific function to be performed for the societal system. Such a system creates inequalities because some functions have more priority for the system (for example, economics over religion). This inequality is, however, fundamentally different from that in hierarchically ordered or stratified systems. In a functionally differentiated society, the other subsystems are part of the environment of any given subsystem—for example, organizations in the polity, law, education, religions, science, and family domains

are part of the environment of the economy. And although the economy might have functional priority in the society, it treats and responds to the other subsystems in its environment as equals. Thus, inequality in functionally differentiated societies does not create a rigid hierarchy of subsystems; as a consequence, differentiation allows more autonomy of each subsystem, which in turn gives them more flexibility in dealing with their respective environments. The overall consequence of such subsystem autonomy is increased flexibility of the societal system to adjust and adapt to its environment.

7. *Evolutionary differentiation increases the complexity of a system and its relationship with the environment.* In so doing, differentiation escalates the risks, as Luhmann terms the matter, of making incorrect and maladaptive decisions about how to relate to an environment. With increased complexity comes an expanded set of options for a system, but there is a corresponding chance that the selection of options will be dysfunctional for a system's relationship to an environment. For example, any organization in the economy must make decisions about its actions, but there are increased alternatives and escalated unknowns, resulting in expanded risks. In Luhmann's view, the ever-increasing risk level that accompanies evolutionary differentiation must be accompanied by mechanisms to reduce risk, or at least by the perception or sense that risk has been reduced. Thus, evolution always involves an increase in the number and complexity of risk-reducing mechanisms. Such mechanisms also decrease the complexity of a system's environment because they select some options over others. For example, a conservative political ideology is a risk-reducing mechanism because it selects some options from more general values and ignores others. In essence, an ideology assures decision makers that accepting the goals of the ideology reduces the risks.[22]

Before proceeding further, we should review these elements of Luhmann's view of evolution and how they change a society's and its constituent subsystem's relation to the temporal, material, and symbolic dimensions of the environment. Temporally, Luhmann argues that social evolution and differentiation lead to efforts at developing a chronological metric, or a standardized way to measure time (clocks, for example). Equally fundamental is a shift in people's perspective from the past to the future. The past becomes highly generalized and lacks specific dictates of what should be done in the present and the future. For, as systems become more complex, the past cannot serve as a guide to the present or future because there are too many potential new contingencies and options. The present sees time as ever more scarce and in short supply; thus, people become more oriented to the future and to the consequences of their present actions. Materially, social differentiation involves (1) the increasing separation of interaction, organization, and societal systems; (2) the compartmentalization of organization systems into functional domains; (3) the growing separation of person, role, program, and values; and (4) the movement toward functional differentiation and away from segmentation and stratification.

Symbolically, communication codes become more complex and organized as distinctive media for a particular functional domain. Moreover, they increasingly function as risk-reducing mechanisms for a universe filled with contingency and uncertainty.

Luhmann has approached the study of specific organizational systems from this overall view of sociocultural evolution and differentiation. As he has consistently argued, an analytical framework is only as good as the insights into empirical processes that it can generate. Luhmann's framework is much more complex than he contends such a framework should be, and it is often more metaphorical than analytical. Yet, this framework allows him to analyze political, legal, and economic processes in functionally differentiated societies in very intriguing ways.

THE FUNCTIONAL DIFFERENTIATION OF SOCIETY

Politics as a Social System

As societies grow more complex, new structures emerge for reducing complexity. Old processes, such as appeals to traditional truths, mutual sympathy, exchange, and barter, become ever more inadequate. A system that reaches this point of differentiation, Luhmann argues, must develop the "capacity to make binding decisions." Such capacity is generated from the problems of increased complexity, but this capacity also becomes an important condition for further differentiation.

To make binding decisions, the system must use a distinctive medium of communication: power.[23] Power is defined by Luhmann as "the possibility of having one's own decisions select alternatives or reduce complexity for others." Thus, whenever one social unit selects alternatives of action for other units, power is being employed as the medium of communication.

The use of power for making binding decisions functions to resolve conflicts, to mitigate tensions, and to coordinate activities in complex systems. Societies that can develop political systems capable of performing these functions can better deal with their environments. Several conditions, Luhmann believes, facilitate the development of this functional capacity. First, there must be time to make decisions; the less time an emerging political system is allowed, the more difficulty it will have in becoming autonomous. Second, the emerging political system must not confront a single power block in its environment, such as a powerful church. Rather, it requires an environment of multiple subsystems whose power is more equally balanced. So, the more the power in the political subsystem's environment is concentrated, the more difficult is its emergence as an autonomous subsystem. Third, the political system must stabilize its relations with other subsystems in the environment in two distinctive ways: (1) at the level of diffuse legitimacy, so that its decisions are accepted as its proper function; and (2) at the level of daily transactions among individuals and subsystems.[24] That is, the greater the problems of a political system are in gaining diffuse support for its right to make decisions for other subsystems and the less salient the decisions of the political system are for the day-to-day activities, transactions, and routines of system units, then the greater will be its problems in developing into an autonomous subsystem.

Thus, to the extent that a political system has time to develop procedures for making decisions, confront multiple sources of mitigated power, and achieve diffuse legitimacy as well as relevance for specific transactions, then the more it can develop into an autonomous system and the greater will be a society's capacity to adjust to its environment. In so developing, the political system must achieve what Luhmann calls *structural abstraction*, or the capacity to (1) absorb multiple problems, dilemmas, and issues from a wide range of system units and (2) make binding decisions for each of these. Luhmann sees the political system as "absorbing" the problems of its environment and making them internal to the political system. Several variables, he argues, determine the extent to which the political system can perform this function: (1) the degree to which conflicts are defined as political (instead of moral, personal, and so forth) and therefore in need of a binding decision, (2) the degree of administrative capacity of the political system to coordinate activities of system units, and (3) the degree of structural differentiation within the political system itself.

This last variable is the most crucial in Luhmann's view. In response to environmental complexity and the need to absorb and deal with problems in this environment, the political system must differentiate along three lines: (1) the creation of a stable bureaucratic administration that executes decisions, (2) the evolution of a separate arena for politics and the emergence of political parties, and (3) the designation of the public as a relevant concern in making binding decisions. Such internal differentiation increases the capacity of the political system to absorb and deal with a wide variety of problems; as a consequence, it allows greater complexity in the societal system.

This increased complexity of the political and societal systems also increases the risks of making binding decisions that are maladaptive. As complexity increases, there are always unknown contingencies. Therefore, not only do political systems develop mechanisms such as internal differentiation for dealing with complexity, but they also develop mechanisms for reducing risk or the perception of risk. One mechanism is the growing reflexiveness of the political process—that is, its increased reflection on itself. Such reflection is built into the nature of party politics where the manner and substance of political decisions are analyzed and debated. Another mechanism is what Luhmann calls the *positivation of law*, or the creation of a separate legal system that makes "laws about how to make laws" (more on this in the next section). Yet another mechanism is ideology or symbolic codes that select which values are relevant for a particular set of decisions. A related mechanism is the development of a political code that typifies and categorizes political decisions into a simple typology.[25] For example, the distinction between progressive and conservative politics is, Luhmann argues, an important political code in differentiated societies. Such a code is

obviously very general, but this is its virtue because it allows very diverse political acts and decisions to be categorized and interpreted with a simple
dichotomy, thereby giving political action a sense of order and reducing perceptions of risk. Luhmann even indicates that it is a system's capacity to develop
a political code, more than consensus of values, that leads to social order. For in
interpreting actions in terms of the code, a common perspective is maintained,
but it is a perspective based on differences—progressive versus conservative—
rather than on commonality and consensus. Thus, complex social orders are sustained by their very capacity to create generalized and binary categories for
interpreting events rather than by value consensus.

Still another mechanism for reducing risks is arbitrary decision making by
elites. However, although such a solution achieves order, it undermines the
legitimacy of the political system in the long run because system units start to
resent and to resist arbitrary decision making. A final mechanism is invocation
of a traditional moral code (for example, fundamentalistic religious values)
that, in Luhmann's terms, "remoralizes" the political process. But when such
remoralization occurs, the political system must de–differentiate because strict
adherence to a simple moral code precludes the capacity to deal with complexity (an example of this process would be Iran's return to a theocracy from
its previously more complex political system).

In sum, then, it is fair to say that Luhmann uses his conceptual metaphor
to analyze insightfully specific institutional processes, such as government. Yet,
he does not use his scheme in a rigorous deductive sense; much like Parsons
before him, he employs the framework as a means for denoting and highlighting particular social phenomena. Although much of his analysis of political system differentiation is "old wine in new bottles," there is a shift in emphasis and,
as a result, some intriguing but imprecise insights. In a similar vein, Luhmann
analyzes the differentiation of the legal system and the economy.

The Autonomy of the Legal System

Luhmann visualizes social evolution as involving a separation of persons, roles,
programs, and values. For him, differentiation of structure occurs at the level
of roles and programs. Consequently, there is the problem of how to integrate
values and persons into roles organized into programs within organization
systems. The functional mechanism for mobilizing and coordinating individuals to play roles is law, whereas the mechanism for making values relevant to
programs is ideology.[26] Thus, because law regulates and coordinates people's
participation in roles and programs and because social differentiation must
always occur at the roles level, it becomes a critical subsystem if a society is to
differentiate and evolve. That is, a society cannot become complex without the
emergence of an autonomous legal system to specify rights, duties, and obligations of people playing roles.[27]

A certain degree of political differentiation must precede legal differentiation because there must be a set of structures to make decisions and enforce
them. But political processes often impede legal autonomy, as is the case when
political elites have used the law for their own narrow purposes. For legal

autonomy to emerge, therefore, political development is not enough. Two additional conditions are necessary: (1) "the invocation of sovereignty," or references by system units to legal codes that justify their communications and actions; and (2) "lawmaking sovereignty," or the capacity of organizations in the legal system to decide just what the law will be.

If these two conditions are met, then the legal system can become increasingly reflexive. It can become a topic unto itself, creating bodies of procedural and administrative law to regulate the enactment and enforcement of law. In turn, such procedural laws can themselves be the subject of scrutiny. Without this reflexive quality, the legal system cannot be sufficiently flexible to change in accordance with shifting events in its environment. Such flexibility is essential because only through the law can people's actions be tied to the roles that are being differentiated. For example, without what Luhmann calls the "positivization of law," or its capacity to change itself in response to altered circumstances, new laws and agencies (for example, workers' compensation, binding arbitration of labor and management disputes, minimum wages, health and safety) could not be created to regulate people's involvement in roles (in this case, work roles in a differentiating economy).

Thus, positivization of the law is a critical condition for societal differentiation. It reduces complexity by specifying relations of actors to roles and relegating cooperation among social system units. But it reduces complexity in a manner that presents options for change under new circumstances; thus, it becomes a condition for the further differentiation of other functional domains, such as the economic.

The Economy as a Social System

Luhmann defines the economy as "deferring a decision about the satisfaction of needs while providing a guarantee that they will be satisfied and so utilizing the time thus acquired."[28] The general idea seems to be that economic activity—production and distribution of goods and services—functions to satisfy basic or primary needs for food, clothing, and shelter as well as derived or secondary needs for less basic goods and services. But this happens in a way not fully appreciated in economic analysis: The economic activity restructures humans' orientation to time because economic action is oriented to the satisfaction of future needs. Present economic activity is typically directed at future consumption; so, when a person works and a corporation acts in a market, they are doing so to guarantee that their future will be unproblematic.

Luhmann's definition of the economic subsystem is less critical than is his analysis of the processes leading to the creation of an autonomous economic system in society. In traditional and undifferentiated societies, Luhmann argues, only small-scale solutions are possible with respect to doing something in the present to satisfy future needs. One solution is stockpiling of goods, with provisions for the redistribution of stocks to societal members or trade with other societies.[29] Another solution is mutual assistance agreements among individuals, kin groups, or villages. But such patterns of economic organization are very limited because they merge familial, political, religious, and community activity. Only with the differentiation of distinctly economic roles can more complexity and flexibility be structured into economic action. The first key differentiation along these lines is the development of markets with distinctive roles for buyers and sellers.

A market performs several crucial functions. First, it sets equivalences or the respective values of goods and services. Second, it neutralizes the relevance of other roles—for instance, the familial, religious, and political roles of parties in an exchange. Value is established by the qualities of respective goods, not by the positions or characteristics of the buyers and sellers.[30] Third, markets inevitably generate pressures for a new medium of communication that is not tied to other functional subsystems. This medium is money, and it allows quick assessments of equivalences and value in an agreed-on metric. In sum, then, markets create the conditions for the differentiation of distinctly economic roles, for their separation and insulation from other societal roles, and for the creation of a uniquely economic medium of communication.

Money is a very unusual medium, Luhmann believes, because it "transfers complexity." Unlike other media, money is distinctive because it does not reduce complexity in the environment. For example, the medium of power is used to make decisions that direct activity, thereby reducing the complexity of the environment. The medium of truth in science is designed to simplify the understanding of a complex universe. And the medium of love in the family circumscribes the actions and types of relations among kindred and, in so doing, reduces complexity. In contrast, money is a neutral vehicle that can always be used to buy and sell many different things. It does not limit; it opens options and creates new opportunities. For example, to accept money for a good or for one's work does not reduce the seller's or worker's options. The money can be used in many different ways, thereby preserving and even increasing the complexity of the environment. Money thus sets the stage for—indeed it encourages—further internal differentiation in the economic subsystem of a society.

In addition to transferring complexity, Luhmann sees money as dramatically altering the time dimension of the environment. Money is a liquid resource that is always "usable in the future." When we have money, it can be used at some future date—whether the next minute or the following year. Money thus collapses time because it is to be used in the future, hence making the past irrelevant, and the present is defined by what will be done with money in the future. However, this collapsing of time can come about only if (1) money does not inflate over time, and (2) it is universally used as the medium of exchange (that is, barter, mutual assistance, and other traditional forms of exchange do not still prevail).[31]

Like all media of communication, money is reflexive. It becomes a goal of reflection, debate, and action itself. We can buy and sell money in markets; we can invest money to make more money; we can condemn money as the root of evil or praise it as a goal that is worth pursuing; we can hoard it in banks or spread it around in consumptive activity. This reflexive quality of money, coupled with its capacity to transfer complexity and reorient actors to time, is what allows money to become an ever-more dominant medium of communication in complex societies. Indeed, the economy becomes the primary subsystem of complex societies because its medium encourages constant increases in complexity and growth in the economic system. As a consequence, the economy becomes a prominent subsystem in the environment of other functional subsystems—that is, science, polity, family, religion, and education. The economy becomes something that must always be dealt with by these other subsystems.

This growing complexity of the economic subsystem increases the risks in human conduct. The potential for making a mistake in providing for a person's future needs or a corporation's profits increases because the number of unknown contingencies dramatically multiplies. Such escalated risks generate pressures, Luhmann argues, for their reduction through the emergence of specific mechanisms. The most important of these mechanisms is the tripart internal differentiation of the economy around (1) households, (2) firms, and (3) markets.[32] There is a "structural selection" for this division, Luhmann believes, because these are structurally and functionally different. Households are segmental systems (structurally the same) and are the primary consumption units. Firms are structurally diverse and the primary productive units. And markets are not as much a unit as a set of processes for distributing goods and services. Luhmann is a bit vague on this point, but it seems that there is strength in this correspondence of basically different structures with major economic functions. Households are segmented structurally and are functionally oriented to consumption; firms are highly differentiated structurally and are functionally geared to production; and markets are processually differentiated by their function to distribute different types of goods and services. Such differentiation reduces complexity, but at the same time it allows flexibility: Households can change consumption patterns, firms can alter production, and markets can expand or contract. Because they are separated from one another, each has the capacity to change and redirect its actions, independently of the others. This flexibility is what allows the economic system to become so prominent in modern industrial societies.

Yet, Luhmann warns, the very complexity of the economy and its importance for other subsystems create pressures for other risk-reducing mechanisms. One of these is intervention by government so that power is used to make binding decisions on production, consumption, and distribution as well as on the availability of money as a medium of communication. The extensive use of this mechanism, Luhmann believes, reduces risk and complexity in the economy at the expense of its capacity to meet needs in the future and to make flexible adjustments to the environment.

NOTES

1. For the best of these efforts, see Richard Münch's work: *Theory of Action: Towards a New Synthesis Going Beyond Parsons* (London: Routledge, 1988); *Die Struktur der Moderne* (Frankfurt am Main: Suhrkamp, 1984).

2. See, for example, Niklas Luhmann, *Systems Theory* (Stanford, CA: Stanford University Press, 1995).

3. Luhmann has published extensively, but most of his work is in German. The best sample of his work in English is *Systems Theory* (cited in note 2) and *The Differentiation of Society,* trans. S. Holmes and C. Larmore (New York: Columbia University Press, 1982).

4. Talcott Parsons, *The Social System* (New York: Free Press, 1951).

5. Luhmann, *The Differentiation* (cited in note 3), Chap. 12.

6. Ibid., pp. 71–89.

7. In making this assertion, Luhmann directly attacks Parsons. Luhmann, *The Differentiation,* Chapter 3 (cited in note 3).

8. Ibid., p. 73.

9. Ibid., p. 79.

10. Here Luhmann takes a page from Georg Simmel's *The Philosophy of Money,* trans. T. Bottomore and D. Frisby (Boston: Routledge & Kegan Paul, 1978).

11. Luhmann, *The Differentiation* (cited in note 3), p. 169.

12. Obviously Luhmann is borrowing Parsons' idea about generalized media. See Chapter 3.

13. Much like Parsons, this analysis of communications media is never fully explicated or systematically discussed for all functional domains.

14. We will see shortly, however, that money is the sole exception here.

15. This is essentially Parsons' definition (see Chapter 4). It was Spencer's and Durkheim's as well (see Chapter 2).

16. Luhmann, *The Differentiation* (cited in note 3), pp. 256–257.

17. Luhmann's interpretation of the synthetic theory of evolution in biology is, at best, loose and inexact.

18. Luhmann, *The Differentiation* (cited in note 3), p. 265. Luhmann seems completely unaware that Herbert Spencer in his *The Principles of Sociology* (New York: Appleton, 1885; originally published in 1874) performed a similar, and more detailed, analysis 100 years ago.

19. Luhmann is borrowing here from Émile Durkheim's analysis in *The Division of Labor in Society* (New York: Free Press, 1949; originally published in 1893) as well as from Talcott Parsons' discussion of "value generalization." See Chapter 4.

20. Luhmann, *The Differentiation* (cited in note 3), pp. 229–254.

21. Ibid., p. 235.

22. Ibid., p. 151.

23. Ibid., p. 151.

24. Ibid., pp. 143–144.

25. Ibid., pp. 168–189.

26. Ibid., pp. 90–137.

27. This is essentially the same conclusion Parsons reached in his description of evolution in *Societies: Evolutionary and Comparative Perspectives* and *The System of Modern Societies* (Englewood Cliffs, NJ: Prentice-Hall, 1966 and 1971, respectively).

28. Luhmann, *The Differentiation* (cited in note 3), p. 194.

29. Ibid., p. 197.

30. Luhmann fails to cite the earlier work of Georg Simmel on these matters. See Simmel's *The Philosophy of Money* (cited in note 10).

31. Luhmann, *The Differentiation* (cited in note 3), p. 207.

32. Ibid., p. 216.

✳

PART II

Evolutionary Theorizing

5

Early
Evolutionary Theory

Social thought from the 1700s to the nineteenth century was filled with
visions of social progress. Particularly in France, Enlightenment thinkers
viewed society as progressing to an ever-better state of social organization.
It should not be surprising, therefore, that virtually all the early sociologists
developed their ideas within an evolutionary framework, in which stages of
societal development were postulated. For most, each stage of development
also represented a marked movement in human progress. Table 5.1 summarizes
some of the more prominent schemes. Only Max Weber appears to have hes-
itated in proclaiming the inexorable movement of society; yet, even he posited
the spread of rational-legal authority as the trend for modern societies, but he
clearly did not view this trend as progress. Thus, from its very beginnings sociological theory conceptualized the movement of society through evolutionary
stages.

At the same time that stage models of evolution were gaining prominence
in sociology during the nineteenth century, alternative views of evolution were
being developed in the natural sciences. These revolved around trying to
account for the diversity of species to be found on the planet. The Linnean classification system had provided a way to classify species; now the task was to
explain the mechanisms by which the diversity of species was created and the
patterns of evolution in the distribution of species. At first, Lamarkian interpretations (that is, acquired characteristics are passed on to offspring) dominated

Note: This chapter is coauthored with Alexandra Maryanski.

Table 5.1 Evolutionary Thinking in Early Sociology

Theorist	Stages of Evolution					Driving Force of Evolution
Auguste Comte	*Theological*	*Metaphysical*	*Positivistic*			Movement of ideas toward science
Herbert Spencer	*Simple* (hunting/gathering)	*Compound* (horticuture)	*Double Compound* (agrarian)	*Treble Compound* (industrial)		Differentiation along four axes: production, reproduction, regulation, and distribution
Karl Marx	*Primitive communism* (hunting/gathering)	*Slavery* (horticulture/agrarian)	*Feudalism* (horticulture/agrarian)	*Capitalism* (industrial)	*Communism*	Inequalities and exploitation
Émile Durkheim	*Mechanical* (hunting/gathering)		*Organic* (industrial)			Differentiation and problems of integration

explanations for speciation, but by the midpoint of the nineteenth century, new mechanisms were sought to explain how species emerged and became differentiated from each other. This search culminated in Alfred Wallace's and Charles Darwin's theories, which changed the way that scholars viewed evolution forever.[1]

Although seemingly very different, stage model theories of societal development in sociology and efforts to explain speciation in biology often converged. Sociological theory generally saw evolution as a process of differentiation, or specialization, of activities and functions; this point of emphasis is analogous to speciation among plants and animals (the words *specialization* and *speciation* have the same Latin roots). Moreover, drawing inspiration from biological theories, Herbert Spencer and Émile Durkheim explicitly emphasized the basic force behind evolution as competition for resources—an idea that parallels Darwin's theory of natural selection as the driving force of biological evolution.[2] As stage models of evolution converged with notions of competition and selection, ecological theories in sociology were born. These theories emphasized that increasing specialization or differentiation is driven by competition for resources, with those less fit to occupy a resource niche moving to, or creating, a new resource niche.

EARLY ECOLOGICAL MODELS

Herbert Spencer's Evolutionary Theory

Almost a decade before Darwin published *On the Origin of Species,* Spencer coined the phrase "survival of the fittest."[3] He used this phrase in a moral and philosophical sense, arguing that the best forms of social organization emerge with unregulated competition among humans, which allows the most fit to survive, thereby elevating the level of society. Obviously, this moral philosophy is highly flawed, but nonetheless, Darwin acknowledged Spencer in the preface to his famous book, in which the basic idea of natural selection as the driving force of speciation is developed. This acknowledgment was perhaps only a courtesy to a well-known social philosopher who was friends with many of Darwin's supporters. Thus, even though Spencer's original phrasing of the argument of evolution as survival of the fittest preceded Darwin's formulation, at least in print, it had little direct impact on the reemergence of biologically inspired thinking in the second half of the twentieth century.[4] Like Auguste Comte before him, Spencer had made the connection between biology and sociology[5]; unlike Comte, Spencer developed a sophisticated mode of biological reasoning.[6]

One of these modes of reasoning is, of course, functional theory in which system parts are analyzed with respect to their functions for the larger social whole. Spencer conceived of relations among organisms as superorganisms, and he argued that these organisms must adapt to the physical, organic, and social environment. As they do so, they will tend to differentiate (or specialize) along three main axes: (1) *operation* or production and reproduction, (2) *regulation* or the use of power and symbols to coordinate and control, and (3) *distribution* or the movement of information, people, and resources. As societies differentiate, then, they do so along these axes. Simple societies of hunters and gatherers reveal very little differentiation along these axes, although those with a head or leader reveal the beginnings of distinctive regulatory structures. As societies compound into horticultural systems, however, clear differentiation between regulatory (political) and operative (productive and reproductive) structures is evident; then, as they doubly compound into agrarian societies, they differentiate distinctive distributive systems such as markets, ports, and roads. Finally, with treble compounding into industrial societies, complex patterns of differentiation between and within these axes are evident. As societies differentiate, they become more adapted to their environments.

The force driving differentiation is competition, often erupting into war between societies. Spencer argued that as societies engage in war, the more fit is more likely to win. Because the winner is usually more complex and differentiated, successive conquests slowly increased the overall level of differentiation in societies. Moreover, competition for resources within societies allows those most fit to survive, while those who are less fit must find resources elsewhere or die. Although Spencer was rather moralistic about these processes, he was the first social scientist to develop an ecological perspective of social evolution: Societies find themselves in competition with their neighbors, whereas members of societies are in competition with each other for resources. Out of this intra- and inter-societal competition, societies evolve into ever-more complex forms.

Émile Durkheim's Evolutionary Theory

Today, we tend to forget how important a figure Spencer was, not just in the nineteenth century in Europe but also in America well into the twentieth century. Today, we see Durkheim as a far more imposing figure, and we often give him credit for ideas that, in reality, come from Spencer.[7] But Durkheim made the connection between the Darwinian idea of evolution by natural selection and societal evolution more explicit than had Spencer. Thus, as bio-ecological theorizing and evolutionary theory were developing in the early twentieth century, Durkheim became as significant a contributor to the ecological model of human evolution.

Durkheim's first major work was *The Division of Labor in Society*,[8] and, as we saw in Chapter 2, it served as an inspiration for functional theorizing. In analyzing the causes of the division of labor—that is, what forces increase specialization of activities (or social "speciation")—Durkheim began to draw from his reading of Darwin:

> Thus, Darwin says that in a small area, opened to immigration, and where, consequently, the conflict of individuals must be acute, there is always to be seen a very great diversity in the species inhabiting it.[9]

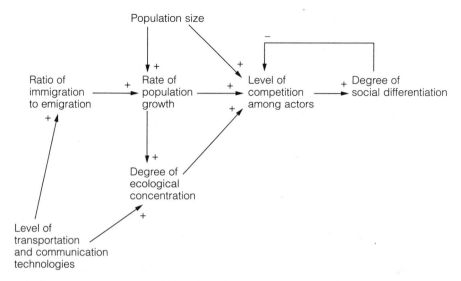

FIGURE 5.1 Durkheim's Ecological Model of Social Differentiation

Durkheim then noted that such diversity made the survival of each species less problematic and, indeed, contributed to the well-being of each species. And so, Durkheim posited,

> Men submit to the same law. In the same city, different occupations can coexist without being obliged mutually to destroy one another, for they pursue different objects. The soldier seeks military glory, the priest moral authority, the statesman power, the businessman riches, the scholar scientific renown. Each of them can attain this end without preventing the others from attaining theirs.[10]

Durkheim was seeking an answer to a question that had vexed all social theory since the time of Adam Smith (who, in the eighteenth century, created the basic utilitarian ideas that so dominate economics today): If societies are differentiating, what force is to hold them together? Durkheim's answer became part of his functionalism, but in the previous passage, we can see his effort to paint the division of labor in a benign light. For our purposes here, Durkheim's ecological model on the causes of the division of labor is more important than his ultimate answer about what holds society together. In this model, Durkheim argues that those forces that increase the *material density* of a population—forces such as immigration, population growth, and ecological barriers—and those that reduce the "social space" between individuals—forces like improved transportation and communication technologies—all increase *competition*. Such competition, in turn, leads to *social speciation* or the division of labor, which, Durkheim felt, reduced competition and increased cooperation as individuals in different social niches went their own ways while exchanging resources with each other. Durkheim's argument is outlined in Figure 5.1.

In a manner more explicit than Spencer's, then, Durkheim argued that population density increases competition for resources, which then leads to social differentiation, but like Spencer, Durkheim viewed competition as the force behind social evolution of society from simple to more complex forms. That is, as populations grow or the social space among members is reduced by new technologies, competition escalates; from competition comes social differentiation and increased societal complexity.

CHARLES DARWIN
AND NATURAL SELECTION

We have alluded to Darwin, but let us review how his ideas set the framework not only for nineteenth century evolutionary theorizing but, more significantly, for the revival of evolutionary theory in the twentieth century. Like Spencer, Darwin was greatly influenced by Thomas Malthus' essay on population,[11] especially Malthus' "notion of a natural elimination mechanism." In his early notebooks,[12] for example, Darwin considered the power of the Malthusian force when he wrote that "no structure will last . . . without it(s) . . . adaptation to *whole* life . . . it will decrease and be driven outwards in the grand crush of population" and ". . . there is a contest . . . and a grain of sand turns the balance." Coupled with Darwin's observations as the naturalist on the famous voyage of the *Beagle,* where it became clear to him that somewhat different environments create new variants of species, Darwin was led to the concept of *natural selection.* Originally, this concept was to be the title of his book, but he later settled on the more controversial title *On the Origin of Species.*[13] Darwin held the idea of natural selection for twenty years before he published his treatise; only when Wallace,[14] who had also been inspired by Malthus, came up with a similar idea to explain evolution did Darwin begin to publish his ideas. Darwin's and Wallace's initial papers were read jointly at the Royal Society, and both argued that the natural world reveals a "struggle" among species and that this competition "selects" for survival those organisms that are better equipped to adapt to the conditions imposed by an environment. As a result, these organisms are more likely than less fit organisms to produce offspring. Thus, the basic assumptions of Darwin's (and Wallace's) model are as follows:

1. Members of any given species reveal variations in their physical and behavioral traits.
2. Members of any given species tend to produce more offspring than can be supported by an environment.
3. Members of any given species must therefore compete with one another and with other species for resources in an environment.
4. Members of a given species revealing those traits that enable them to compete and secure resources will be more likely to survive and produce

offspring, whereas those members evidencing traits that are unsuited to competition or ability to secure resources will be less likely to survive and produce offspring.

Thus, the environment "selects" those traits of organisms that enable them to compete, secure resources, survive, and reproduce. This process of natural selection drives evolution, as the environment successively selects varying traits of organisms that promote fitness. In this argument, an important distinction must be emphasized: Selection operates on an *individual organism,* whereas evolution involves a *population of organisms.* That is, the individual organism survives and reproduces, or fails to do so, but the population as a whole evolves. This population consists of all those individual organisms that possess those traits that enabled them to survive and reproduce. This distinction is critical for understanding modern evolutionary theory. We must remember, then, that as different individual organisms revealing varying traits are "selected for" by the conditions of the environment, the overall composition of the population of organisms changes, or evolves.

We can see an affinity of these ideas to Spencer's famous phrase "survival of the fittest," but the most direct source of inspiration for modern evolutionary theory in the social sciences was the blending of Darwin's discovery of the mechanism of natural selection with Gregor Mendel's overlooked insights into the mechanisms of inheritance. For, despite the power of the concept of natural selection to explain evolution, Darwin's portrayal could not answer some basic questions: What is the source of those variations in organisms that are the objects of natural selection? How are traits passed on from one organism to another? What is the mechanism of inheritance? The answers to these questions sat for thirty-five years in dusty academic journals in the form of Mendel's short manuscripts on the inheritance of characteristics in garden peas.[15] Not until 1900 was the science of genetics born with the rediscovery of Mendel's work and its independent confirmation by Karl Correns in Germany, Hugo de Vries in Holland, and Erich Tschermak in Austria. This synthesis of the notions of natural selection and genetic variation was coupled with additional insights into the forces of evolution in what is now called the "modern synthesis." This initial synthesis was, as we will see, crucial to reconnecting biology and sociology in the twentieth century.

CONCLUSION

Biological reasoning in sociology has come and gone in several distinct waves, each time resurfacing in a somewhat new guise. There have, in essence, been three basic theoretical approaches in sociology that have derived inspiration from biology. One is ecological and emphasizes the process of competition among social actors for limited resources. Another is based more on genetics and emphasizes the effects of genic selection on the nature of human behavior and social organization. The third overlaps with functional theories of evolution and stresses that the long-term trend in human societies has been for increased complexity and differentiation. More significantly, as will be examined in Chapter 7, a fourth wave of theorizing seeks to use the accumulated knowledge of social and biological evolution to develop sophisticated models.

This last effort at synthesis is the future of evolutionary sociology in the twenty-first century, where, as in the nineteenth century, a revolution in biology—in this case, the biotechnologies that come with genetic engineering—will make biology once again the dominant science. Biological thinking can expand the explanatory power of sociological theories. In a sense, this is just what Spencer and Durkheim sought to do, and, after a century of grappling with bio-ecological processes and their implications for patterns of social organization, sociology is poised to take these earlier efforts much further.

NOTES

1. Charles Darwin, *On the Origin of Species* (New York: New American Library, 1958; originally published 1859).

2. Alexandra Maryanski, "The Pursuit of Human Nature in Sociobiology and Evolutionary Sociology," *Sociological Perspectives* 37 (1994), pp. 375–390; see also Jonathan H. Turner and Alexandra Maryanski, "The Biology of Human Organization," *Advances in Human Ecology* 2 (1993), pp. 1–33.

3. Herbert Spencer, *Social Statics; or the Conditions Necessary for Human Happiness Specified, and First of Them Developed* (New York: Appleton, 1888; originally published in 1852). Spencer had used the phrase earlier when writing articles for newspapers.

4. Richard Hofstader, *Social Darwinism in American Thought* (Boston: Beacon, 1955).

5. Auguste Comte, *The Course of Positive Philosophy* (originally published in serial form between 1830 and 1842). More accessible is Harriet Martineau's translation and condensation, published under the title, *The Positive Philosophy of August Comte,* 3 volumes (London: Bell & Sons, 1898; originally published 1854).

6. Herbert Spencer, *The Principles of Sociology,* 3 volumes (New York:

Appleton, 1898; originally published in serial form between 1874 and 1896).

7. For the details of this argument, see Jonathan H. Turner, "Durkheim's and Spencer's Principles of Social Organization," *Sociological Perspectives* 27 (1984), pp. 21–32.

8. Émile Durkheim, *The Division of Labor in Society* (New York: Free Press, 1933; originally published in 1893).

9. Ibid., p. 266.

10. Ibid., p. 267.

11. Thomas R. Malthus, *An Essay on the Principle of Population as It Affects the Future Improvement of Society* (London: Oxford University Press, 1798).

12. *Charles Darwin's Notebooks, 1836–1844: Geology, Transmutation of Species, Metaphysical Enquiries.* Notebook E, transcribed and edited by David Kohn (British Museum, New York: Cornell University Press), p. 395.

13. In a letter to Asa Gray on September 5, 1857, Darwin wrote the following: "I think it can be shown that there is such an unerring power at work in *Natural Selection* (the title of my book) which selects exclusively for the good of each organic being." See George Gaylord Simpson, *The Book of Darwin*

(New York: Washington Square, 1982), p. 24. Also see Charles Darwin, *On the Origin of Species* (New York: New American Library, Mentor Books, 1958; originally published in 1859).

14. See Charles Darwin and Alfred Russell Wallace, *Evolution by Natural Selection* (Cambridge: Cambridge University Press, 1958).

15. Gregor Mendel, "Versuche über pflanzen-hybriden," translated into English in the *Journal of the Rural Horticulture Society* 26 (1901), originally published in 1865. For the still definitive account of Mendel's discoveries, see W. Bateson, *Mendel's Principles of Heredity* (Cambridge: Cambridge University Press, 1909).

6

Ecological Theory:
Amos Hawley

E cological arguments were downsized during early and middle portions of the twentieth century. Scholars first analyzed urban areas as ecosystems in which various actors competed for living space. Later, theorists began to apply ecological ideas to populations of organizations, viewing them as competing for resources in various niches (see the Wadsworth Web site for this book for overviews of these ecological theories). In the 1980s, Amos Hawley, who had been instrumental in developing these downsized ecological theories,[1] took theorizing back up to the macro level in a manner highly reminiscent of Herbert Spencer's and Émile Durkheim's approaches.[2]

THE BASIC ASSUMPTIONS

Amos Hawley's theory of ecological processes begins with three basic assumptions[3]:

1. Adaptation to environment proceeds through the formation of a system of interdependencies among the members of a population.

2. System development continues, other things being equal, to the maximum complexity afforded by the existing facilities for transportation and communication.

3. System development is resumed with the introduction of new information that increases the capacity for movement of materials, people, and messages and continues until that capacity is fully used.

Hawley terms these assumptions, respectively, the *adaptive, growth,* and *evolution* "propositions." These assumptions resurrect in altered form ideas developed by Spencer[4] and Durkheim.[5] To survive and adapt in an environment, human populations become differentiated and integrated by a system of mutual interdependencies. The size of a population and the complexity of social organization for that population are limited by its knowledge base, particularly with respect to transportation and communication technologies. Populations cannot increase in size, nor elaborate the complexity of their patterns of organization, without expansion of knowledge about (1) communication and (2) movement of people and materials. Hawley conceptualized the combined effects of transportation and communication technologies as *mobility costs.*

Linked to transportation and communication technologies is another variable, *productivity.* Curiously, in his most recent theoretical essay,[6] this variable is somewhat subordinate, whereas it is highlighted in earlier statements. No great contradiction or dramatic change in conceptualization occurs in this more recent statement; so we can merely reintroduce the productivity variable in more explicit terms. Basically, a reciprocal set of relations exists between production of materials, information, and services, on the one side, and the capacity of a system to move these products to other system units, on the other side. The development of new transportation and communication technologies encourages expanded production, whereas the expansion of production burdens existing capacities for mobility and thereby stimulates a search for new technologies. There is also a more indirect linkage among productivity, growth, and evolution because productivity "constitutes the principal limiting condition on the extent to which a system can be elaborated, on the size of the population that can be sustained in the system, and on the area or space that the system can occupy."[7] Thus, to support a larger, more differentiated, population in a more extended territory requires the capacity to (1) produce more goods and services and (2) distribute these goods and services through transportation and communication technologies. If productivity cannot be increased or if the mobility costs of transportation and communication cannot be reduced, then there is an upper limit on the size, scale, and complexity of the system.

THE ENVIRONMENT

An ecosystem is "an arrangement of mutual dependencies in a population by which the whole operates as a unit and maintains a viable environmental relationship."[8] The environment is the source of energy and materials for productivity, but the environment reveals more than a biophysical dimension. There is also an "ecumenic" dimension composed of the "ecosystems or cultures possessed by peoples in adjacent areas and beyond."[9] Moreover, in Hawley's view, ecological analysis "posits an external origin of change" because "a thing cannot cause itself"[10]; thus, in examining a population as a whole in its physical, social, or biological environment, Hawley's approach emphasizes that change comes more from these environmental systems than from processes internal to organization of a population.[11]

FUNCTIONS AND KEY FUNCTIONS

In Hawley's approach, the arrangement of mutual dependencies of a population in an environment is conceptualized as classes or types of *units* that form *relations* with one another with respect to *functions*.[12] Functions are defined as "repetitive activity that is reciprocated by another or other repetitive activities." Of particular importance are *key functions,* which are repetitive activities "directly engaged with the environment." As such, key functions transmit environmental inputs (materials and information) to other "contingent functions" (or repetitive activities joining units in a relation).[13] Hawley visualizes that a relatively small number of key functions exists, and "to the extent that the principle of key functions does not obtain, the system will be tenuous and incoherent."[14] A system is thus composed of functional units, a few of which have direct relations with the environment and perform key functions. Most other units, therefore, must "secure access to the environment indirectly through the agency of the key function."[15]

For example, production is a key function, and in earlier essays Hawley seemed to see productivity as *the* primary key function. Yet, there are obviously other key functions—political, military, and perhaps ideological—that also influence the flow of resources to and from the environment. As a result, other functional units gain access to the environment only through their interconnections with those units engaged in these various key functions. Thus, the relations of units that form the structure of a population are conceptualized as functions and key functions, or classes of reciprocated repetitive activities that join units together. This is, of course, another way of denoting specialization and differentiation of various types in clusters of activity. Just why Hawley proposes this particular terminology is unclear, but, in doing so, Hawley transforms the ecology perspective into a more functional form of analysis.

Indeed, slipping into Hawley's analysis is a stronger version of the term *function*. In part, this stronger notion of function is implied by the concept of "key function." A key function regulates inputs of energy, materials, and information into the system, and it is not hard to see how the next step on the road to functionalism is made: Certain key functions are necessary for adaptation and survival. Hawley himself takes this step when he notes,

> We might suppose, for purposes of illustration, that every instance of collective life is sustained by a mix of activities that produce sustenance and

Table 6.1 Hawley's General Propositions on Functions in Ecosystems

I. The more a function (recurrent and reciprocated activity) mediates critical environmental relationships (key function), the more it determines the conditions under which all other functions are performed.

II. The more proximate is a function to a key function, the more the latter constrains the other, and vice versa.

III. The more a function is a key function, the greater is the power of those actors and units involved in this function, and vice versa.

IV. The more differentiated are functions, the greater is the proportion of all functions indirectly related to the environment.

V. The greater the number of units using the products of a function and the less the costs of the skills used in the function, the greater is the number of units in the population engaged in this function.

VI. The greater the mobility costs (for communication and transportation) associated with a function, the more stable are the number of, and the Interrelations among, units implicated in this function.

VII. The more stable the number of, and interrelations among, units implicated in functions, the more a normative order corresponds to the functional order.

related materials, distribute the production among the participants, maintain the number of units required to produce and distribute the products, and exercise the controls needed to assure an uninterrupted performance of all tasks with a minimum of friction.[16]

Indeed, these requisites look very much like those proposed by Spencer—production, reproduction, regulation, and distribution.

Whatever the merits or defects in such functionalism, Hawley translated his ideas into a series of "hypotheses." Table 6.1 restates in somewhat modified form some of the most critical propositions that can be pulled from his analysis thus far.[17] These propositions represent abstract "laws" from which Hawley's many hypotheses can be derived. The basic ideas in the propositions of Table 6.1 are these: Key functions, or those that mediate exchanges with the environment, disproportionately influence other functions and hold power over these other functions (for example, units involved in key economic or political functions in a society usually hold more power and influence than do others, because they are engaged in interchanges, respectively, with the physical and social environment); the more proximate a function is to a key function, the greater this influence is; conversely, the more remote a function is from a key function, the less influence this function has on a key function. Differentiation of key functions decreases other functions' direct access to the environment because such access is now mediated by units involved in key functions (for example, most people do not grow their own food or provide their own military defense in highly differentiated societies). As mobility costs for personnel and materials needed for functions increase, the functions' number and relations stabilize; under these conditions, a normative order can develop to regulate the internal relations of functions, as well as their interrelations.

EQUILIBRIUM AND CHANGE

An ecosystem is thus a population organized to adapt to an environment, with change in this system being defined by Hawley as "a shift in the number and kinds of functions or as a rearrangement of functions in different combinations."[18] In contrast with change, growth is "the maturation of a system through the maximization of the potential for complexity and integration implicit in the technology for movement and communication possessed at a given point in time,"[19] whereas evolution is "the occurrence of new structural elements from environmental inputs that lead to synthesis of new with old information and a consequent increase in the scope of the accessible environment."[20] This series of definitions presents a picture of ecosystem dynamics as revolving around (1) the internal rearrangement of functions, (2) the increase of complexity to the maximum allowed by an existent level of communication and transportation technologies, and (3) the receipt of environmental inputs, especially new information that expands transportation and communication (or capacity for mobility) and that, as a consequence, increases the scale and complexity of the ecosystem (to the limits imposed by the new technologies).

There is an image, then, of a system in equilibrium that is then placed into disequilibrium by new knowledge about production as it influences mobility (of people, materials, and information). Somewhat less clear is where this new information comes from. Must it be totally exogenous (from other societies, migrants, changes in biophysical forces that generate new knowledge)? Or can the system itself generate the new information through a particular array of functions? It would appear that both can be the source of change, yet, the imagery of Hawley's model[21] connotes a system that must be disrupted from the outside if it is to evolve and develop new levels of structural complexity. Internal dialectical processes, or self-transforming processes that increase technology, seem to be underemphasized as crucial ecosystem dynamics. Table 6.2 summarizes the more abstract "laws" that can be culled from Hawley's hypotheses on these dynamics.[22]

These propositions reinforce the emphasis in human ecology that the source of change is exogenous, residing particularly in the "ecumenic" environment. From this environment, new knowledge will come and then become "synthesized" with the existing knowledge base. Such synthesized knowledge will then change production, transportation, and communication in ways that allow the system to increase its complexity, size, and territory. Yet, new knowledge can introduce change only to a point. If some technologies lag behind others, the rate of change will be pulled down by the lower technology. Eventually the maximal size, scale, and complexity of the system will be reached, unless new technologies are inserted into the system from the environment. Thus, systems that have grown to the maximum size, scope, and complexity allowed by production, transportation, and communication technologies will achieve an *equilibrium*. New knowledge from the environment can disrupt the equilibrium when such knowledge is used to achieve increases

Table 6.2 Hawley's General Propositions, Change, Growth, and Evolution in Ecosystems

I. The greater the exposure of an ecosystem to the ecumenic environment (other societies or cultures of other societies), the greater is the probability of new information and knowledge penetrating the system and, hence, the greater is the probability of change, growth, and evolution.

II. The more new information increases the mobility of people, materials, and information, as well as production, the more likely it is that change will be cumulative, or evolutionary to the limits of complexity allowed by the new information as it is translated into technologies for production, transportation, and communication.

III. The more new information improves various mobility and productive processes at differential rates, the more the slower rate of technology will impose limits on the faster-changing technology.

IV. The more a system approaches the scale and complexity allowed by technologies, the slower the rate of change, growth, and evolution is and the more likely the system is to achieve a state of closure (equilibrium) in its ecumenic environment.

in productivity and mobility. But each technology has limits on how much growth and evolution it can facilitate; when this limit is reached, the system will tend to re-equilibrate.

The concept of *equilibrium* is most problematic, although Hawley employs it only as a heuristic device. Hawley means the notion of equilibrium to connote "the balance of nature, denoting a tendency toward stabilization of the relative numbers of diverse organisms within the web of life and their several claims on the environment. . . ."[23] Yet, Hawley recognizes that "equilibrium . . . is a logical construct"[24] and connotes that ecological systems tend toward stability, although he also employs terms like "partial equilibrium" to connote only a tendency toward some degree of instability.

EVOLUTION

The most interesting portions of ecological theory are those dealing with growth and evolution—that is, increasing size, scale, scope, and complexity of the systematic whole in its environment. This analysis builds on the propositions in Tables 6.1 and 6.2, but it extends them in creative ways and, as a result, goes considerably beyond the early formulations of Spencer and Durkheim.

In Figure 6.1, Hawley's model is redrawn in a way that makes the causal dynamics more explicit. Starting on the far left of the model, Hawley believes that an expanded knowledge base must come from the ecumenical environment. As the model shows, new knowledge causes growth and change when it increases the level of communication and transportation technologies, either

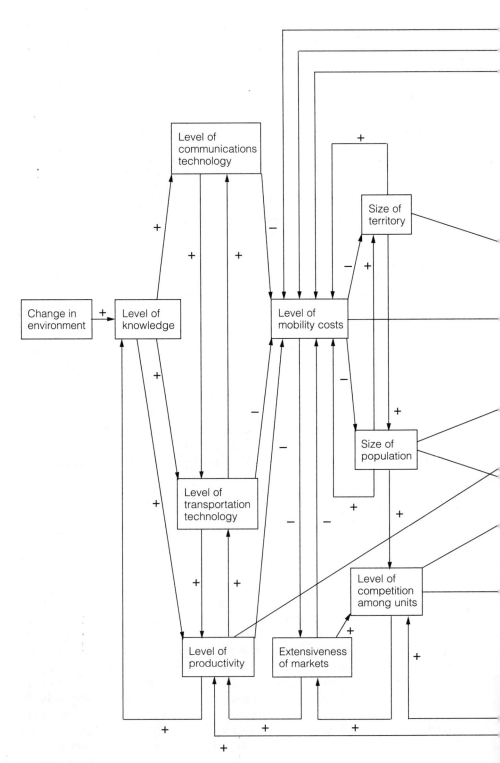

FIGURE 6.1 Elaboration of Hawley's Model

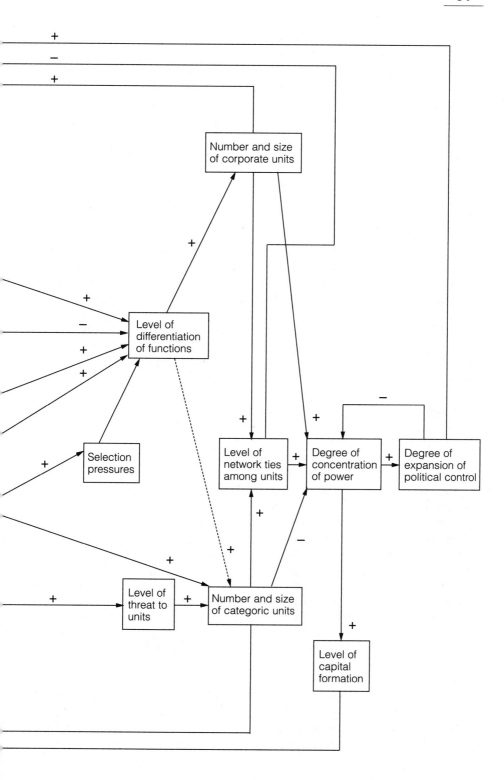

directly or indirectly, through increasing production (which then causes expansion of these technologies). A critical variable in Hawley's scheme is *mobility costs;* for any given technology, a cost (time, energy, money, materials) is associated with the movement of information, materials, and people. As these costs reach their maximum—that is, the system cannot "pay" for them without degenerating—they impose a limit on the scale of the system: the size of its population, the extent of its territory, the level of its productivity, and the level of complexity. Conversely, as the feedback arrows in the model indicate, the size of territory and population will, as they expand and grow, begin to impose higher mobility costs. Eventually these costs will increase to a point at which the population cannot grow or expand its territory—*unless* new communication and transportation technologies that reduce costs are discovered.

Much as Spencer and Durkheim argued, population and territorial size, as these are influenced by mobility costs, cause specialization of functions—what is termed *differentiation* in the model. As Hawley notes, however, the relationship between population size and differentiation is not unambiguous, but it does create "conditions that foster, if not necessitate, increases in the sizes of subsystems" and the number of such subsystems serving various functions. Thus, Hawley believes, "the greater the size, the greater the probable support for units with degrees of specialization." As he adds, "Other pertinent conditions are the rate or volume of intersystem communications, scope of a market, and amount of stability in intersystem relations."[25]

These causal connections are not clearly delineated by Hawley, so the model involves making many causal inferences. The causal paths moving from level of productivity through extensiveness of markets and level of competition to selection pressures and differentiation of functions represent the old Spencerian and Durkheimian argument: Expansion of markets increases the level of competitiveness among units and, at the same time, increases the capacity to distribute goods and services because these are constrained by mobility costs (note the arrows connecting markets and mobility costs); competition under conditions of increased production and population size allows—indeed encourages—specialization as actors seek their most viable niche. Similarly, the causal arrows moving from communication and transportation technologies through mobility costs, size of territory, and size of population to level of differentiation of functions restate Spencer's, but more particularly Durkheim's, argument in a more sophisticated form: Changes in communication and transportation technologies reduce mobility costs and allow population growth and territorial expansion; all these forces together create selective pressures to adjust and adapt varying attributes and competencies, especially under conditions of intense competition for resources.

Hawley believed that differentiation of subunits engaged in various functions occurs along two axes: (1) corporate and (2) categoric.[26] Corporate units are constructed from "symbiotic relations" of mutual dependence among differentiated actors, whereas categoric units are composed of "commensalistic" relations among actors who reveal common interests and who pool their activities

Table 6.3 A Typology of System Units

Unifying principle	Relational Structure	
	Corporate	**Categoric**
Familial	Household-producing and personal service unit	Kin, clan, and tribe
Territorial	Village, city, and ecumene	Polity, neighborhood, ethnic, enclave, ghetto
Associational	Industry, retail, store, school, government	Caste, class, sect, guild, club, union, professional organization

to adapt more effectively to their environments. Table 6.3 delineates these types of units along an additional dimension—their "unifying principle."[27] Thus, as differentiation increases, an ecosystem will represent a complex configuration of corporate and categoric units along various "unifying principles": familial, territorial, associational. It is not clear if Hawley meant this typology to be exhaustive or merely illustrative. Nonetheless, the typology is provocative.

The dynamics of these two types of units are very different. Corporate units form around functions, or sets of related activities, and are engaged in interchanges with other corporate units. Because of this contact, corporate units tend to resemble one another, especially those that engage in frequent interchanges or are closely linked to corporate units engaged in key functions (interchanges with the environment). Moreover, as they engage in interchanges, corporate units tend toward closure of structure and establishment of clear boundaries. The size and number of such corporate units depend, of course, on the size of the population, the inter- and intra-unit mobility costs associated with communication and transportation technologies, the capacity for production and distribution in markets (as constrained by mobility costs), and the level of competition among units.

In contrast, categoric units involve interdependencies that develop "on the basis of similarities among the members of a population"[28]; their number and size are related to the size of the population and territory as well as to the level of threat imposed by their environment. As Hawley noted, the nature of the threat can vary—a "task too large for the individual to accomplish in a limited time, such as the harvesting of a crop . . ."; "losing land to an invader"; "possible destruction of a road or other amenity"; "a technological shift that might render an occupation obsolete"; and so on. If a threat is persistent, the actors in a categoric unit will form a more "lasting association," and, if similar units are in competition (say, rival labor unions or ideologically similar political parties), the costs and destructiveness of such competition will eventually lead to their consolidation into a larger categoric unit. Moreover, those categoric units that persist will develop a corporate core to sustain the flow and coordination of resources necessary to deal with the persisting or recurring threat. Categoric units can also get much larger than corporate units because their membership criteria—mere possession of certain characteristics (ethnic, religious, occupational, ideological)—are much more lax than are those of corporate units, which recruit members to perform certain specialized and interdependent activities or functions. Of course, the size and number of categoric units are still circumscribed by the size and complexity of the ecosystem and, to a lesser extent than with corporate units, by the mobility costs associated with communication and transportation technologies.

As is indicated in the right portion of Figure 6.1, differentiation of categoric and corporate units leads to the consolidation of units into networks, which create larger subsystems. Such regularization of ties among units engaged in similar and symbiotic activities or functions reduces mobility costs, thereby facilitating growth of the ecosystem (note the feedback arrow to mobility costs).

Differentiation of units and their consolidation into larger networks also have consequences for the concentration of power. Categoric unit formation, and the consolidation of such units into larger networks and subsystems, tend to reduce concentrations of power because various confederations of categoric units will pose a check on one another. In contrast, corporate units are more likely to cause the concentration of power. This concentration is directly related to the capacity of some units to perform key functions and thereby dictate the conditions under which interrelated functions must operate. This control is facilitated by consolidation of networks into subsystems because such networks connect outlying and remote corporate units, via configurations of successive network ties, to those engaged in key functions. Such connections among corporate units, as they facilitate the concentration of power, enable political control to expand to the far reaches of the ecosystem; political and territorial boundaries tend to become coterminous in ecosystems. Yet, centralization of power and extension of control can increase mobility costs as rules and regulations associated with efforts at control escalate, which sets limits on how complex the ecosystem can become without a change in communication and transportation technologies (hence the long feedback arrow at the top of Figure 6.1).

We can add a variable to the model that is implicit but crucial: capital formation. Hawley does not address this issue extensively, so we are clearly adding it to his model. Nonetheless, it is important to recognize that concentration of power also consolidates the flow of resources, facilitating capital formation. If not squandered on maintenance of control, defense, or offensive efforts at military expansion, this capital can be used to expand productivity and, indirectly, to change the knowledge and technological base of the system (note the long feedback arrows at the bottom of Figure 6.1).

As with Tables 6.1 and 6.2, Table 6.4 extracts the most crucial hypothesis from Hawley's many hypotheses. As territory and population size increase, because of new knowledge about production, transportation, and communication, it is possible and perhaps necessary to differentiate units around specific functions. This is particularly true for corporate units, which represent clusters of interdependencies revolving around a particular function. Categoric units

Table 6.4 Basic Propositions of Patterns of Ecosystem Differentiation

I. The greater the size of a population and its territory and the greater the selection pressure stemming from competition among members of the population, the greater will be the differentiation of functions and the number and size of corporate units, to the maximum allowed by mobility costs.	IV. The greater the number of relations among units and the higher the costs of mobility, the more likely are differentiated units to establish networks and combine into more inclusive subsystems, thereby reducing mobility costs.
II. The greater the size of a population and the greater the threats posed by competition and environmental change to actors in similar situations, the greater will be the number and size of categoric units, to the maximum allowed by mobility costs.	V. The more differentiated corporate units, the more centralized is power around those units and subsystems performing key functions, whereas, the more differentiated categoric units are and the greater is their size, the less centralized is power.
III. The greater the number and size of categoric and corporate units, the more the potential number of relations increases as a geometric rate and the greater is the amount of time and energy allocated to mobility.	V. The more concentrated is power, the more prominent are networks and subsystems, the more extensive is political regulation of units in the ecosystem.

form in response to threats, which ultimately stem from the competition that results from increases in population size, productivity, and markets. As the number of differentiated units in a system increases, the number of relations increases at an exponential rate, increasing mobility costs. Corporate and categoric units both tend to consolidate into larger networks, forming subsystems and reducing mobility costs. But the effects of corporate and categoric unit differentiation and consolidation on the concentration of power vary. Corporate units consolidate, centralize, and extend power and regulation, whereas categoric units form power blocks that diffuse power in a system of checks and balances.

As with the other propositions, the many specific hypotheses in Hawley's scheme can be deduced from these and from the scenario delineated.[29] Thus, the propositions in Tables 6.1, 6.2, and 6.4 do not do full justice to the depth and extent of Hawley's scheme. They are intended more as abstract statements rather than as the many "hypotheses" that punctuate Hawley's theory.

CONCLUSION

In sum, then, Hawley's ecological theory retains some important ideas of early sociology. One of these ideas is the obvious but often-ignored view that "society" represents an adaptation of the human species to its environment. Another related idea is that it is not possible to understand human social organization without reference to the interchanges between environment and internal social structure. Yet another crucial idea is that the basic dynamics of a society revolve around (1) aggregation of actors in physical space, competition, and differentiation; and (2) integration through subsystem formation and centralization of power. Still another useful point is the emphasis on population size, territory, productivity, communication and transportation technologies, and competition as important causes of those macro structural processes—differentiation, conflict, class formation, consolidation of power, and the like—that have long interested sociologists. Finally, a significant, though problematic, idea is that the altered flow of resources—energy, information, materials—into the system is the ultimate source of social system growth and evolution.

At the same time that ecological theories have flourished in sociology (see the Wadsworth Web site, www.sociology/wadsworth.com, for more theories), a revival of older evolutionary questions surfaced again in sociology. Questions about human evolution, human nature, and societal development have become blended with ecological models from biology, producing what we will term for convenience a new type of "evolutionary sociology." This new evolutionary theorizing is an eclectic mix of theoretical ideas from biology, genetics, developmental notions about increasing complexity from functionalism, bio-ecology, and more sociologically oriented ecology. There is little coherence to this new evolutionary theory, but it goes beyond mere analogies and uses biological and ecological concepts to explain patterns of human behavior and social organization.

In a very real sense, this newer approach has little in common with the theory presented in this chapter, despite the common view that a science of human ecology should draw concepts from its biological counterpart. Yet, as we will come to appreciate, this newer approach is not nearly as developed or coherent as the ecological models. Thus, ecologically oriented evolutionary sociology represents one of the emerging trends in evolutionary theorizing.

NOTES

1. Amos H. Hawley, *Human Ecology: A Theory of Community Structure* (New York: Ronald, 1950).

2. Amos H. Hawley, "The Logic of Macrosociology," *Annual Review of Sociology* 18 (1992), pp. 1–14. The following list of titles from Hawley's work reviews this progression of thinking that culminated in the last reference at the end of this note. "Human Ecology," in *International Encyclopedia of the Social Sciences,* ed. D.C. Sills (New York: Crowell, Collier and Macmillan, 1968); *Urban Society: An Ecological Approach* (New York: Ronald, 1971 and 1981); "Human Ecology: Persistence and Change," *American Behavioral Scientist* 24 (3, January 1981), pp. 423–444; "Human Ecological and Marxian Theories," *American Journal of Sociology* 89 (1984), pp. 904–917; "Ecology and Population," *Science* 179 (March 1973), pp. 1196–1201; "Cumulative Change in Theory and History," *American Sociological Review* 43 (1978), pp. 787–797; "Spatial Aspects of Populations: An Overview," in *Social Demography,* eds. K.W. Taueber, L.L. Bumpass, and J.A. Sweet (New York:

Academic, 1978); "Sociological Human Ecology: Past, Present and Future," in *Sociological Human Ecology,* eds. M. Micklin and H.M. Choldin (Boulder, CO: Westview, 1980); and, most significantly, *Human Ecology: A Theoretical Essay* (Chicago: University of Chicago Press, 1986).

3. Hawley, "Human Ecological and Marxian Theories" (cited in note 2), p. 905.

4. Herbert Spencer, *The Principles of Sociology,* 3 volumes (New York: Appleton, 1898; originally published in serial form between 1874 and 1896).

5. Émile Durkheim, *The Division of Labor in Society* (New York: Free Press, 1933; originally published in 1893).

6. Hawley, *Human Ecology: A Theoretical Essay* (listed in note 2).

7. Hawley, "Human Ecology" (cited in note 2).

8. Hawley, *Human Ecology: A Theoretical Essay* (cited in note 2).

9. Ibid., p. 13.

10. Hawley, "Human Ecological and Marxian Theories" (cited in note 2).

11. Ibid.

12. Hawley, "Human Ecology," and *Human Ecology: A Theoretical Essay,* p. 32 (both cited in note 2).

13. Hawley, *Human Ecology: A Theoretical Essay* (cited in note 2), p. 34.

14. Hawley, "Human Ecology" (cited in note 2), p. 332.

15. Ibid.

16. Hawley, *Human Ecology: A Theoretical Essay* (cited in note 2), p. 32.

17. Ibid., pp. 43–44.

18. Ibid., p. 46.

19. Ibid., p. 52.

20. Ibid.

21. Ibid., p. 59. Hawley "boxes" lists of variables and then draws arrows among the boxes, but not among the variables within each box. Hence, detailed causal arguments need to be inferred.

22. Ibid., pp. 85–87.

23. Hawley, "Human Ecology" (cited in note 2), p. 329.

24. Ibid., p. 334.

25. Hawley, *Human Ecology: A Theoretical Essay* (cited in note 2), pp. 80–81.

26. Ibid., pp. 68-73, and "Human Ecology" (cited in note 2), pp. 331–332.

27. Hawley, *Human Ecology: A Theoretical Essay* (cited in note 2), p. 74.

28. Ibid., p. 70.

29. Ibid., pp. 106–108, 123–124.

7

New Evolutionary
Theories

As we saw in the last chapter, the most prominent form of biologically inspired theorizing in sociology has been ecological. Alongside ecological approaches, developmental theories of societal evolution from simple to more complex forms have also persisted. At the same time, from the modern synthesis of evolutionary theory in biology, a new form of biologically inspired theory—sociobiology—emphasizes genes as the driving force behind not only the evolution of populations of organisms but also the evolution of social forms. This new interest in biology has also inspired a revival of what at one time were called "instinct" theories of human behavior, although today these are much more sophisticated and more attuned with developments in biology. There is, then, a revival of interest in evolution in sociological theory, and this rethinking of how evolutionary theory can be used in sociology takes theorizing in a number of directions.

In this chapter, we will review some of the more promising types of evolutionary sociology. None of these approaches dominates, but each attempts to reconnect biology and sociology in new and creative ways. Moreover, each of the theories draws inspiration from different aspects of the modern evolutionary synthesis in biology. What emerges is a rather eclectic mix of innovative theoretical leads rather than mature theories. Yet, these leads might well develop into more coherent theoretical orientations that could become more

Note: This chapter is coauthored with Alexandra Maryanski.

prominent, perhaps rivaling the ecological theories that dominated biologically inspired theorizing in sociology for most of the twentieth century.

Although all theories in evolutionary sociology rest on the modern synthesis, these theories can be sorted and grouped into four distinctive, though overlapping traditions: (1) theories working within the sociobiology framework, (2) theories of cross species comparisons, (3) theories employing biological ideas in evolutionary stage models, and (4) theories on the biological nature of humans. We will begin with sociobiology and then examine the rather eclectic mix of theories within a comprehensive evolutionary-ecological framework.

SOCIOBIOLOGICAL THEORY

Pierre van den Berghe has consistently been among the most prolific advocates of a biological perspective on human affairs. Van den Berghe believes it "is high time that we seriously look at ourselves as merely one biological species among many. . . ." Until this shift away from what he calls "species-wide anthropocentrism" is accomplished, sociology will remain stagnant, for there can be no doubt that biological forces shape and constrain patterns of human organization.[1] In his early advocacy, van den Berghe proposed a "biological" approach that corresponded to the instinct approach of some early sociologists and several contemporary thinkers, whereas in his later works, van den Berghe fully adopted the sociobiological approach and, since then, has consistently used sociobiology theory to interpret a variety of social behaviors among humans. Van den Berghe began his turn to sociobiology by posing the question: Why are humans "social" in the first place? His answer is that the banding together of animals in cooperative groups increases their reproductive fitness by (1) protecting them against predators and (2) providing advantages in locating, gathering, and exploiting resources. Such fitness allows the alleles of those who are social to stay in the gene pool (for a review of the origins of sociobiology, see the Web site for this book).

Three sociobiological mechanisms produce the sociality that promotes reproductive fitness:[2] (1) kin selection or what is sometimes termed "inclusive fitness" in sociobiology (see the Web site, www.sociology.wadsworth.com), (2) reciprocity, or what is often labeled "reciprocal altruism," and (3) coercion. Because each of these mechanisms promotes reproductive fitness of individuals, these mechanisms lie at the base of sociocultural phenomena. Let us examine each mechanism separately and then see how van den Berghe generates theoretical explanations with them.

Kin Selection

In van den Berghe's view, *kin selection* (that is, a propensity to favor kin) is the oldest mechanism behind sociality. He sees this mechanism, as with all modern human sociobiological arguments, as operating at the genetic level, for "the gene is the ultimate unit of natural selection, (although) each gene's reproduction can be modified by cultural forces and, overall, is dependent on what Robert Dawkins terms its 'survival machine,' the organism in which it happens to be at any given time."[3]

This "survivor machine" carrying genetic material in its genotype need not be consciously aware of how natural selection in the distant past has created "replicators" or genes in its body that seek to survive and to be immortal. But selection clearly favored those replicators that could pass themselves on to new and better survival machines. One early survivor machine was the body of individual organisms, and a later one has been the development of cooperative arrangements among bodies sharing alleles in their genotypes. In van den Berghe's words,

> Since organisms are survival machines for genes, by definition those genes that program organisms for successful reproduction will spread. To maximize their reproduction, genes program organisms to do two things: successfully compete against . . . organisms that carry alternative alleles . . . , and successfully cooperate with (and thereby contribute to the reproduction of) organisms that share the same alleles of the genes.[4]

So, in van den Berghe's terms, individuals are *nepotistic* and favor kin over nonkin, and close kin over distant kin, for the simple reason that close kin will share genetic material (in their genotypes):

> Each individual reproduces its genes directly through its own reproduction and indirectly through the reproduction of its relatives, to the extent that it shares genes with them. In simple terms, each organism may be said to have a 100 percent genetic interest in itself, a 50 percent interest in its parents, offspring, and full-siblings, a 25 percent interest in half-siblings, grandparents, grandchildren, uncles, aunts, nephews, and nieces, a 12½ percent interest in first cousins, half-nephews, great-grandchildren, and so on.[5]

The degree of "altruism" for kin or "nepotism" will vary with the amount of genetic material shared with a relative *and* with the ability of that relative to reproduce this material. For van den Berghe, then, "blood is thicker than water" for a simple reason: reproductive fitness, or the capacity to help those "machines" carrying one's genetic material to survive and reproduce.

Van den Berghe is careful, however, to emphasize that these biologically based propensities for nepotism, or kin selection, are elaborated and modified by both environmental and cultural variations. Yet, clearly a biological factor operates in the overwhelming tendency of humans to be nepotistic. One cannot, van den Berghe insists, visualize such nepotism as a purely cultural process.

Reciprocity

When individuals exchange assistance, they create a bond of *reciprocity.* Such reciprocity increases the "fitness" of genes carried by the organisms (and organizations of organisms) involved; that is, if organisms help each other or can be relied on to reciprocate for past assistance, the survival of genetic material is increased for both organisms. Such exchange, or what sociobiologists sometimes term "reciprocal altruism,"[6] greatly extends cooperation beyond nepotism, or "inclusive fitness" and "kin selection" in sociobiological jargon. Thus, reciprocal exchange is not a purely social product; it is a behavioral tendency programmed by genes. Such programming occurred in the distant past as natural selection favored those genes that could create new kinds of survivor machines beyond an individual's physical body and social groupings of close kin. Those genes that could lodge themselves in nonkin groupings organized around bonds of exchange and reciprocity were more likely to survive; today the descendants of these genes provide a biological push for creating and sustaining such bonds of reciprocity.

At this point, van den Berghe reveals the affinity of such arguments with utilitarianism by introducing the problem of "free-riding" or, as he terms it, "free-loading." That is, what guarantee does an individual (and its genotype) have that others will indeed reciprocate favors and assistance? Here van den Berghe appears to argue that this problem of free-riding created selection pressures for greater intelligence so that our protohuman ancestors could remember and monitor whether or not others reciprocated past favors. But, ironically, intelligence also generated greater capacities for sophisticated deceit, cheating, and free-riding, which in turn escalated selection pressures for the extended intelligence to "catch" and "detect" such concealed acts of nonreciprocation

There is, then, a kind of selection cycle operating: Reciprocity increases fitness, but it also leads to cheating and free-riding. Hence, once reciprocity is a mechanism of cooperation, it can generate its own selection pressures for greater intelligence to monitor free-riding, but, ironically, increased intelligence enables individuals to engage in more subtle and sophisticated deceptions to hide their free-riding; to combat this tendency, there is increased pressure for greater intelligence, and so on. At some point culture and structure supplant this cycle by creating organizational mechanisms and cultural ideas to limit free-riding (see the discussion of rational choice theory in Chapter 20 for a discussion of what these sociocultural mechanisms might be).

Van den Berghe does not pursue this discussion, however, except to point out that this cycle eventually produces "self-deceit." Van den Berghe believes that the best way to deceive is to believe one's own lies and deceptions, and in this way one can sincerely make and believe verbal pronouncements that contradict, at least in some ways, one's actual behavior. Religion and ideology, van den Berghe posits, are "the ultimate forms of self-deceit" because religion "denies mortality" and ideology facilitates "the transmission of credible, self-serving lies."[7] This conceptual leap from free-riding to religion and ideology is, to say the least, rather vague, but it does provide a sense of what sociobiology tries to do: connect what might be considered purely "cultural" processes—religion and ideology—to a fundamental biological process—in this case, reproductive fitness through reciprocity.

Coercion

There are limits to social organization for reciprocal exchanges, van den Berghe argues, because each party has to perceive that it receives benefits in the relationship.[8] Such perceptions of benefit can, of course, be manipulated by ideologies and other forms of deceit that hide the asymmetry of the relationship, but there are probably limits to the manipulation of perceptions. Power is an alternative mechanism to both kin selection and reciprocal exchanges because its mobilization allows some organisms to dominate others in their access to resources that promote fitness. *Coercion* thus enables some to increase their fitness at a cost to others. Although this mechanism is hardly unique to our species, humans "hold pride of place in their ability to use to good effect conscious, collective, organized, premeditated coercion in order to establish, maintain, and perpetuate systems of intraspecific parasitism."[9] Coercion allows the elaboration of the size and scale of human organization (states, classes, armies, courts, and so forth), but it is nonetheless tied to human biology as this was molded by selection. That is, genes that could use coercion to create larger and more elaborate social structures as their survival machines were more likely to survive and reproduce.

In sum, then, sociality or cooperation and organization are the result of natural selection because it preserved genes that could produce better survival machines through nepotism (kin selection and inclusive fitness), reciprocity (or reciprocal altruism), and coercion (or territorial and hierarchical patterns of dominance). The linkages between biology, on the one side, and culture and society, on the other, are complex and often indirect, even after we recognize that these linkages occur along the three basic dimensions or axes of nepotism, reciprocity, and coercion. Certainly there have been complex interactions between ecological and genetic factors to produce patterns of human (and many other animal) organization; once initiated, selection processes producing greater intelligence allow culture, as "an impressive bag of tricks," to operate as a force of human evolution.

Conceptualizing Cultural Processes

From van den Berghe's vantage point, culture is created and transmitted in humans through mechanisms fundamentally different from those involved in genetic natural selection. Actually, van den Berghe portrays cultural evolution in Lamarkian rather than Darwinian terms: "Acquired cultural characteristics, unlike . . . genetic evolution, can be transmitted, modified, transformed, or eliminated through social learning." In recent years, van den Berghe has come to see culture in some ways as "an emergent phenomenon" that provides humans with another method of adaptation. For van den Berghe, the issue is not the genes versus culture but their interface, for both are intimately intertwined. Although culture is an outgrowth of biological evolution, it now has an autonomy, he says, that provides humans with the ability to modify their own genotypes, making the intricate feedbacks between nature and nurture more complex than ever.[10] Thus, culture is not a *separate* entity; it is yet one more product and process of biological evolution driven by natural selection as it produced genes trying to maximize their fitness by nesting themselves in better and better survival machines.

Explanations of Social Phenomena with Sociobiology

At various times, van den Berghe has used the concepts of sociobiology to explain such empirical phenomena as kinship systems, incest taboos, ethnicity, skin color, sexual selection, and classes. Probably his two most detailed empirical analyses are on (1) kinship systems and (2) ethnicity. Each of these will be briefly summarized.

1. *Kinship*. In one of his early sociobiological articles, van den Berghe and David Barash endeavored to explain various features of kinship systems by the behavioral strategies males and females pursue to maximize their fitness (that is, keep their alleles in the gene pool). Because the details of their suggestive arguments can be complex, just one example of the kinds of arguments that they make will be summarized.[11]

   The widespread preference in human societies for polygyny (males with the option for multiple wives), hypergamy (females marrying males of higher-ranking kin groups), and double standards of sexual morality (males being given more latitude than females) can be explained by reproductive fitness strategies. Women have comparatively fewer eggs to offer in their lifetime, have intervals when they are infertile (for example, during lactation), and, even in the most liberal or egalitarian societies, have to spend more time than do men raising children. Hence, a female will seek a reproductive strategy that will ensure the survival of her less abundant genetical material, and the most maximizing strategy is to marry a male with the resources and capacity to ensure the survival of her offspring (and, thereby, one-half of her genotype). Thus, a woman will seek to "marry up" (hypergamy) in the sense of securing a man who has more resources than her kinship group has.

   On the male side, men produce an uninterrupted and large supply of sperm and have fewer child-care responsibilities; they can thus afford to be more promiscuous with little cost (and they will derive some benefit from the fitness that comes with spreading their genes around). Although men have an interest in ensuring that as many women as possible bear children with one-half their genes, a male cannot know that a female is bearing his child if she is promiscuous, and so men also have an interest in restricting female sexual activity through polygyny to ensure that their genes are indeed contained in the genotype of the children born to a female (creating limits of female sexuality outside marriage). Thus, what are commonly viewed as purely cultural phenomena—the preference for polygyny in human societies (or monogamy with promiscuity), hypergamy ("marrying up"), and sexual double standards (favoring male promiscuity)—can be explained as the result of varying fitness strategies for males and females.

2. **Ethnicity**. Turning to another empirical example, van den Berghe has sought to apply sociobiology to what has always been his main area of research, ethnicity.[12] Again, kin selection is his starting point, but he extends this idea beyond family relatives helping one another (to maximize their fitness) to a larger subpopulation. Historically, larger kin groups (composed of lineages) constituted a breeding population of close and distant kin who would sustain trust and solidarity with one another while mistrusting other breeding populations. Van den Berghe coined the term *ethny* for "ethnic group" and views an ethny as extended nepotism of these more primordial breeding populations. An ethny is a cluster of kinship circles that is created by endogamy (intermarriage of its members) and territoriality (physical proximity of its members and relative isolation from nonmembers). An ethny represents a reproductive strategy for maximizing fitness beyond the narrower confines of kinship because, by forming an ethny—even a very large one of millions of people—individuals create bonds with those who can help preserve their fitness, whether by actually sharing genes or, more typically, by reciprocal acts of altruism to fellow "ethnys." An ethny is, therefore, a manifestation of more basic "urges" for helping "those like oneself." Whereas ethnys become genetically diluted as their size increases and become subject to social and cultural definitions, the very tendency to form and sustain ethnys is the result of natural selection as it produced nepotism. Van den Berghe's argument is, of course, much more complicated and sophisticated, but we can get at least a general sense for how a supposedly emergent phenomenon—ethnic groups—is explained by reduction to a theoretical perspective built on the principles of genetic evolution.

In summary, the sociobiology models developed by van den Berghe emphasize the interactive effects among genes, culture, and environment. Individuals are viewed as "selfish maximizers" who seek to maximize their own inclusive fitness. To accomplish this goal, different reproductive strategies are employed, and variations in reproductive strategies between populations are mostly the result of different cultural adaptations to particular environmental conditions. In recent years, however, van den Berghe and collaborators have highlighted the power of culture in overriding the reproductive consequences of human actions, thereby subverting the genes' game of reproducing themselves. Van den Berghe[13] now says that this subversion of the genes is especially evident in industrial societies where many individuals "are no longer maximizing fitness" because the contraceptive technology and the comforts and security of material affluence have separated the hedonistic rewards of the "good life" from reproductive efforts. Thus, in modern societies, van den Berghe suggests that a more complex model is necessary to assess the quality versus quantity of offspring and the balance between human needs for luxury goods versus reproductive investment.

CROSS-SPECIES COMPARISONS
OF SOCIAL FORMS

Richard Machalek has applied modern evolutionary theory to traditional sociological problems.[14] Machalek would like to see a truly comparative sociology or one that crosses species lines. His approach is to search for the foundations and development of "sociality" wherever it is found, in both human and nonhuman species. By identifying the elementary forms of social life among human and nonhuman organisms, information can be gleaned about how the organizational features among species are assembled. In this effort to create a truly comparative sociology, Machalek outlines a four-step protocol for conducting a sociological analysis of generic social forms "with a priority on sociality, not the organism."[15]

1. Identify and describe a social form that is distributed across two or more species lines.
2. Identify the "design problems" that might constrain the evolution of his social form. In other words, what prerequisites are necessary for a particular social form to come into existence?
3. Identify the processes that generate a social form.
4. Identify those benefits and beneficiaries of a social form that will help explain the persistence and proliferation of certain social forms over other forms.

In applying this protocol, Machalek focused on the evolution of macro societies, a social form that first appeared in human social evolution about 5,000 years ago. He asked this: What makes human macro societies possible? Machalek suggests that we cannot just look at agrarian and industrial societies to answer this question, but, rather, we must subordinate the study of human macro-level societies to the study of macro societies as a general social form. If we take a cross-species comparative approach, it is evident that "macro sociality" is rare and exists in only two taxonomic orders: insects and primates.

Machalek describes a macro society as a society with hundreds of millions of members with distinct social classes and a complex division of labor. Among social insects, this social form is very old, but in humans it is very recent, beginning about 5,000 years ago with the emergence of agrarian societies. Obviously, humans and insects are remote species, separated by at least 600 million years of divergent evolution; hence, they cannot be compared by individual biological characteristics. Indeed, humans and insects are separated by major anatomical differences that include "six orders of magnitude in brain size," which means that intelligence did not play a role in the evolution of insect macro societies. Instead, insect and human macro-societal social forms must be compared strictly for their "social structural design" features in what appears to be a case of convergent evolution.

In considering the fundamental similarities between the organization of human and insect macro societies, Machalek maintains that "whatever the species, all social organisms confront the same basic problems of organizational design and regulation if they are to succeed in evolving a macro society."[16] When looked at this way, the existence of this social form in two such distinctive and biologically remote taxa allows us to address such questions as this: What constraints must be surmounted before a species can evolve a macro society?

Machalek suggests that macro societies are rare because the evolution of this social form requires successful solutions to a series of difficult and complex problems. Machalek suggests that only insects and humans have managed to push aside or overcome (1) organismic constraints, (2) ecological constraints, (3) cost-benefit constraints, and (4) sociological constraints. Each of these will be briefly examined.

Organismic Constraints In detailing the organismic constraints that must be overcome before complex cooperative behavior can evolve, Machalek highlights the morphology of a species as an important factor that can either promote or inhibit the ability of a species to evolve a macro society. For example, aquatic social species such as whales, who are extremely intelligent and who clearly enjoy a "social life," are hopelessly constrained by their enormous "body plans," a constraint that makes it difficult for them to engage in "diverse forms of productive behavior."[17] And, when a body plan constrains the variety of cooperative behaviors possible, it "also constrains the evolution of a complex and extensive division of labor."[18]

Ecological Constraints In addition to organismic constraints, the ecological niche of a species sets limits on both the population size and complexity of a society. An ecosystem's physical properties can vary in the number of predators, competition for resources like food and shelter, diversity of other species, and mortality rates because of disease. All these can become factors in limiting population size for a given species. Social insects are more likely than humans to find a habitat with ample resources to support their macro societies because they are such very small creatures.

Cost-Benefit Constraints In addition to organismic and ecological constraints, the evolution of a macro society will depend on economic factors or various "costs and benefits" that accompany any macro society. Although the evolution of a macro society would seem to be beneficial to any social species, a society with complex and extensive cooperation has both costs and benefits. Using the logic of cost-benefit analysis, a particular evolved trait can be analyzed for the ratio of its costs to benefits. Among social insects like ants, costs (which include such problems as social parasitism where alien species expropriate labor or food from unsuspecting ants) do not exceed benefits. This is because social insects greatly benefit from a complex division of labor that allows them to compensate for the small size of each individual "and thus increase their ergonomic efficiency and effectiveness."[19]

Sociological Constraints Of all the constraints, this is the most important. Even if all other constraints are overcome, the evolution of a macro society requires a unique form of social interaction that is rare in nature and beyond the capacity of most organisms. Essentially, an organism must overcome three large sociological problems to evolve a macro society[20]:

1. The individuals must be able to engage in impersonal cooperation.
2. The labor of members must be divided among distinct social categories.
3. The division of labor among members must be integrated and coordinated.

In considering these critical "design problems" that must be surmounted before a macro society can evolve, we should ask why it is that only the social insects and humans have been able to generate a rare and complex form of sociality. If we turn to other social species for clues, we find that the fundamental mechanism underlying social organization in most animals is kinship or genetic relatedness. Machalek argues that kinship bonds effectively restrict the number of individuals within a particular cooperative group, making it very difficult for most species to evolve a macro society. Machalek notes that the general principle that links kinship to social behavior among animals can be stated as follows: "The greater the degree of genetic relatedness among individuals, the higher the probability that they will interact cooperatively."[21] In other words, natural selection has seemingly favored social species with the basic capacity to distinguish individual kin from nonkin, and this makes kinship networks possible. Thus, kinship connections based on individual recognition of relatives are the basis for social cooperation for most social species.

In social insects, however, kin are distinguished from nonkin largely through remote chemical communication, for there is no evidence that "blood relatives" recognize each other as individuals. Thus, in ant societies, members interact with five or six *types* of ants—not millions of individual ants. Ants treat each other as members of distinct categories or castes. In turn, social categories or castes are occupationally specialized, allowing task specialization (that is, foraging, brood-tending, nest-repair, defense, and so on) and leading to a complex division of labor. Caste types are recognized by olfactory cues, the dominant mechanism behind the organization of ants. Machalek notes that humans often link a complex division of labor to human intelligence, culture, and technological development, but this social form clearly exists outside the range of human intelligence.

In contrast, despite selection for language and culture, human societies were small and based on face-to-face individualized kinship relations for most of human evolutionary history. Yet, in agrarian times, full-blown hierarchical stratification evolved, leading to the question: How were humans able to escape the constraining influences of personalized kinship relations and their highly evolved capacity for individual recognition? Following Machalek,

> Humans have evolved macro societies because they are empowered by culture to form highly cooperative patterns of behavior with "anonymous others." Thus, for the social insects, a state of permanent personal anonymity enables them to form large, complex societies comprising

purely impersonal cooperation among members of different castes. Humans, on the other hand, are capable of forming cooperative social systems based either upon personal relationship or impersonal status–role attributes.[22]

Thus, chemical communication allows insects to convert individuals into social types, whereas humans employ "cognitive culture" and socially constructed typifications. This capacity allows humans to interact cooperatively not as individuals but as personal strangers, dividing individuals into types of social categories. Machalek believes "it is impersonal cooperation that lies at the very foundation of macrosociality."[23] Social insects and humans have thus "used different but functionally analogous strategies to achieve the capacity for close cooperation among anonymous others, thereby facilitating the evolution of macrosociety."[24] In addition, this impersonality specifies and limits the rights and obligations between (or among) parties to an interaction, for as Machalek notes, status–role constructs "are the evolutionary convergent human analogue to the chemical and tactile typification processes among social insects upon which caste systems are built."[25] Essentially, status–role constructs allow humans to ignore the unique and distinctive qualities of persons, thereby increasing the economy of a cooperative interaction. Unlike social insects, however, humans can also move between personal and impersonal attributes in organizing their social lives.

In sum, then, only in insects and humans has macro sociality become a reality, primarily because of the design problems in creating macro societies. Machalek emphasizes that sociologists have long struggled to understand the elementary forms of social behavior, but this quest has been limited because of a general reluctance by sociologists to expand their perspectives to include inquiry into nonhuman social species. It is important, Machalek argues, to see how particular social traits are spread across species. The ability to research questions such as the emergence of a complex division of labor and why it is found in only a few societies can help us discover how it evolved in human societies. In addition, if we compare sociality forms across species by consequences, "we can enhance our understanding of the adaptive value of sociality as a response to ecological challenges."[26] Finally, beginning with the social form and then selecting for observation those species in which that form appears would also allow us to better understand the emergent properties of social systems, the adaptive value and processes that generate particular social forms, and the essential design features that might represent a solution to common problems facing diverse species.

STAGE THEORIES OF EVOLUTION

In the 1960s, sociologists turned once again to a view of societal evolution as involving movement from simple to more complex forms of social organization. Earlier theorists, such as Herbert Spencer and Émile Durkheim, had been the first to conceptualize long-term historical processes as revolving around increasing differentiation of the structure and culture organizing a population. Much of the spirit of these earlier approaches was recaptured in the 1960s, but with considerably more anthropological detail and conceptual sophistication. As we saw in Chapters 3 and 4 on functional theorizing, most macro-level theorists in this tradition—theorists such as Talcott Parsons and Niklas Luhmann—addressed the question of differentiation. Yet, by far the most sophisticated conceptualization in the 1960s came from outside functionalism in the form of Gerhard Lenski's more conflict view of societal stratification.

In *Power and Privilege: A Theory of Social Stratification,*[27] Lenski examined what he termed "distributive systems" or the mechanisms by which power, prestige, and material wealth are dispersed among the members of a population. What made this analysis evolutionary was Lenski's emphasis on distribution of power and privilege in distinct societal types that were seen as stages in humans' long-term evolutionary history: (1) hunting and gathering societies, (2) simple horticultural societies, (3) advanced horticultural societies, (4) agrarian societies, and (5) industrial societies. Other types of societies, such as those revolving around herding and fishing were seen as variants of horticultural types, but the critical point was that human societies have moved through conspicuous stages and that different types of societies have revealed varying degrees of inequality. The driving force behind each type of society was the level and nature of technology for economic production, which, in turn, generated varying degrees of economic surplus that was then distributed unequally. The basic finding in this early work by Lenski was that technology, production, and surplus were curvilinearly related to inequality; that is, low technology-production-surplus in hunting and gathering societies displayed the most equality; then through horticultural and agrarian societies inequality increased, but with high technology-production-surplus in industrial societies, redistribution lowered inequality somewhat but not to the level of hunter-gatherers.

Later in work[28] with his wife, Jean Lenski,[29] and then in productive collaboration with Patrick Nolan,[30] Lenski's scheme moved away from a concern with stratification processes, per se, toward a macro-level theory of social organization in general. During the course of this transition to a more macro-level theory of societal organization, concepts from evolutionary theory in biology became increasingly prominent, as did the use of field studies from the Human Area Relations Files[31] (which represent an effort to code and catalogue data gathered from the many ethnographies that anthropologists and others have conducted on diverse types of societies). Other theorists, such as Stephen K. Sanderson[32] and Lee Freese,[33] similarly began to employ concepts from evolutionary biology and ecology to examine the path of human history through various societal types. In this section, we will examine these three stage-model theories of evolution—the Lenski, Nolan, and Lenski approach, the Sanderson framework, and finally, the Freese biosociocultural model.

Gerhard Lenski, Patrick Nolan,
and Jean Lenski's Evolutionary Theory

As Lenski, Nolan, and Lenski added biological theorizing to their stage model of societal development from hunting and gathering to modern industrial systems, they sought to highlight the similarities and differences between biological and social evolution. Both biological and social evolution are, first, "based on records of experience that are preserved and transmitted from generation to generation in the form of coded systems of information" and, second, on "processes that involve random variation and selection" of those traits that promote adaptation to the environment.[34] Yet, there are some important differences between biological and social evolution. One is that in organic evolution the genes are the preservers of the informational codes, whereas in social evolution, cultural "symbol systems are the functional equivalents of the genetic alphabet."[35] Another difference revolves around the way that information is transmitted. In biological evolution, genetic information can be transmitted only through the reproduction of new organisms; moreover, diverse species cannot interbreed, so the transmission of information is limited to one species. In contrast, cultural information is more readily and broadly transmitted, moving from one type of society to another. The result is that in biological evolution, speciation leads to ever-new patterns of differentiation and diversification, whereas in social evolution, the movement of information across societal types "is likely to eventuate in ever fewer and less dissimilar societies than exist today."[36] A related difference is that in biological evolution, both simple and complex species can continue to exist in their respective resource niches, whereas in social evolution, simpler societal types tend to be extinguished by more complex types. Still another difference is that acquired traits can be transmitted through socialization, whereas in biological evolution, such Lamarkian processes do not occur. An outcome of this difference is that genetic change in biological evolution is slow (because selection processes have to sort out genes across many generations), whereas cultural evolution can be very rapid (because new traits can be created, learned, transmitted, and diffused within one generation).

These similarities and differences lead to the recognition that human societies are part of the natural world and subject to selection forces from both their biophysical and sociocultural environments, that humans like any other animal are influenced by their genetic heritage, and that only humans are the creators of their cultural heritage or the informational codes guiding behavior and social organization. The basic model of human social evolution developed by Lenski, Nolan, and Lenski is summarized in Figure 7.1. A given society has social structural and cultural (symbolic) characteristics that, for analytical purposes, can be divided into (1) its population size and characteristics, (2) its culture or systems of symbols, particularly technologies, (3) its material products generated by the application of its technology to productive processes, (4) its organizational forms that structure activities, and (5) its institutional systems that combine (1) through (4) into systems addressing basic problems of survival

FIGURE 7.1 Ecological-Evolutionary Forces Shaping the Characteristics of a Society

Adapted from G. Lenski, P. Nolan, and J. Lenski, *Human Societies: An Introduction to Macrosociology*, 7th edition (New York: McGraw-Hill, 1995), pp. 21, 23–55.

and adaptation for individuals and the society as a whole. These five components of a society influence, while being influenced by, the other forces delineated in Figure 7.1: a society's biophysical environment, its social environment of other societies and their respective cultures, and the genetic heritage of humans as a species, namely an evolved ape. In addition to these reciprocal influences, the prior social and cultural characteristics of a society always constrain the internal operation of a society and its adaptation to the external environment.

When we approach the analysis with the orientation diagrammed in Figure 7.1, we can see that Gerhard Lenski's earlier emphasis on technologies as the driving force of social evolution is retained, but the argument is recast into a more evolutionary framework. As Lenski recently remarked, "It seems no exaggeration to say that advances in subsistence technology are functionally equivalent to adaptive changes in a population's gene pool; new energy resources and new materials enable populations to do things that they could not do before."[37]

Social evolution is a cumulative process in the sense that new technologies that prove more adaptive alter the pattern of social organization, generally toward larger and more complex forms of organization. Two basic forces drive change in human societies[38]: (1) *innovation* where new information and social structural patterns are created, whether by chance or conscious intent, and (2) *extinction* where old cultural and structural patterns are abandoned.

Innovations in sociocultural evolution cause more rapid change than do forces in biological evolution, because (a) humans have conscious capacities to develop new informational codes; (b) humans have "needs and desires" that are potentially "limitless" and, under certain conditions, drive them to make new discoveries as old needs are satisfied and new ones emerge; (c) humans can adopt the information of other societies through diffusion; (d) humans can force another society to adopt their informational codes through conquest and repression of older cultural and structural patterns, especially when larger and more complex societies conquer or co-opt smaller and less complex ones; (e) humans can institutionalize innovation in such structural forms as science, thereby creating a set of cultural codes and social structures specifically geared to constant innovation; and (f) humans can create complex interconnections among systems of information that force changes in other elements as changes in another occur.

Yet, Lenski, Nolan, and Lenski stress that there are also forces operating to sustain continuity in the cultural systems that guide the organization of a population.[39] One force for continuity is socialization, in which older patterns are transmitted to each new generation. Another force is ideology, which preserves cultural systems and guides the transmission of culture from one generation to another. Still another force is the systemic nature of human sociocultural systems, which resist change in one element because so many other elements will be forced to change (although, as noted earlier, once change in one element does occur, it has a cascading effect and actually accelerates change). Another force is vested interests, especially of the powerful in stratified societies who have the power to suppress innovations when changes threaten status quo interests. Another force is inertia, where past practices appear to promote adaptation and sufficient satisfaction for individuals who resist adopting new practices whose impact cannot be fully known.

Despite these forces promoting continuity, however, the long-term historical record confirms that societal evolution has involved change, fueled by technological innovations, toward larger and more complex societies. Societies vary, of course, in their rates of innovation; Lenski, Nolan, and Lenski believe these rates vary because of several important forces. First, the amount of information already possessed by a society greatly influences its capacity to create and adopt more information. Second, the size of a population is another important factor because larger populations have more individuals who hold ideas and who can potentially generate new ideas. Third, the stability and nature of a society's environment, both social and biophysical, is another force of change; the more the environment changes, the more likely a society is to be innovative or adopt the innovations of another. Fourth, the nature of the innovations, per se, is a very significant factor; some innovations are fundamental and pave the way for additional innovations (for example, the discovery of metallurgy or new sources of energy stimulated even more innovations). And fifth, the ideology of a society greatly circumscribes the creation or adoption of innovations; powerful and conservative ideologies make it difficult for individuals to be innovative while discouraging the diffusion of innovations from other societies.

Over the long course of societal development, however, productive technologies are the most important driving force of evolution.[40] In the end, technological innovations can overcome the forces promoting continuity, even the ideologies and the vested interests of the powerful. The reason for this significance of technology is that those societies that can better gather, produce, and distribute resources will generate an economic surplus that can support a larger population and its differentiation into new organizational forms and institutional systems. Eventually, their technologies diffuse to other societies, and particularly so when larger, more complex societies conquer, co-opt, or outcompete smaller and less complex societies. Thus, a kind of "group selection" operates in the history of human societies, as more powerful societies (with better technologies, productive capacities, and organizational forms) impose their cultural systems and structural patterns on others through conquest, provide models and incentives for less developed societies to adopt their cultural and structural systems, or take the resources on which less developed societies depend for their survival. Indeed, selection processes have favored an emerging world system of societies.

Stephen K. Sanderson's Evolutionary Approach to Social Transformations

During the last decade, Stephen K. Sanderson has sought to bring biological concepts into sociological theory.[41] In his most recent efforts, Sanderson has produced a description of long-term historical *transformations* that is similar to Lenski, Nolan, and Lenski's stage model, but with rather different points of emphasis and with a very different presentation style.[42] The goal, however, remains much the same: to portray long-term historical development as a series of societal stages analyzed by concepts adopted from evolutionary theory in biology.

Sanderson posits that the major point of similarity between biological and social evolution is that both involve adaptational processes that produce sequences of change.[43] Unlike Lenski, Nolan, and Lenski, however, Sanderson does not argue for group selection; instead, he believes the basic unit of selection is the individual person. Indeed "adaptation is a process pertaining to individuals and never to any social unit larger than the individual."[44] Social structures cannot be the units of adaptation because they are "only abstractions," and only "concrete, flesh-and-blood individuals can be adaptational units, because only they have needs and wants."[45] Indeed, individuals are viewed as "egoistic" beings who are highly motivated to satisfy their own needs and wants, and they "seek to behave adaptively by maximizing the benefits and minimizing the costs of any course of action (or at least generating more benefits than costs)."[46] This egoistic and adaptive behavior must be the focus of evolutionary analysis, although it should also be stressed that "individuals acting in their own interests create social structures and systems that are the sum total and product of these socially oriented individual actions."[47] Moreover, there can also be a kind of "superstructural feedback" in which, once created, systems of symbols can become causal agents, forcing individuals to adopt and adapt to them. But still, in social evolutionary analysis, a social pattern must be viewed as adaptational only because it promotes adaptation for all, or nearly all, individuals within various social structures or the society as a whole.

Although the individual is the unit of adaptation and, hence, selection, only societies evolve. This line of reasoning draws from evolutionary biology stressing individual organisms (and underlying genotype) as the unit of selection but the population of organisms (and the underlying gene pool) as the unit of evolution. Thus, individual humans are the units of adaptation and selection, creating or adopting sociocultural traits because these meet their needs; in this process, the structure and culture of societies can be transformed. Such adaptations by individuals represent adaptive responses to "either the physical environment, the social environment, or both."[48]

Still, much like Lenski, Nolan, and Lenski, Sanderson stresses that "the principle causal factors in social evolution are the material conditions of human existence, that is demographic, ecological, technological, and economic forces at work in social life."[49] Demographic forces are variations in human populations, particularly their size and rates of growth because these put pressure on resources. Ecological factors are all those dimensions of the natural or physical environment that force members of a population to adapt, particularly as these factors interact with demographics and technology. Technological factors are those revolving around knowledge, tools, and techniques available to members of a society as means for adapting to their environment. And economic factors are the modes of social organization that enable people to produce, distribute, and exchange goods and services.[50] These basic "material conditions" of human life have causal significance because they influence "human needs concerning the production of subsistence and the reproduction of human life."[51] How these basic conditions play out is, however, highly variable depending on the empirical conditions in which individuals find themselves. Yet, "different types of social systems in different historical epochs and at different evolutionary stages embody different 'evolutionary logics.'"[52]

Also, much like Lenski, Nolan, and Lenski, Sanderson recognizes that these "material conditions of human existence" point to differences between biological and social evolution. First, in biological evolution, divergence of species is more likely than in human evolution where there is much more convergence of societal types. Second, in biological evolution, genetic variations are a random process on which selection can work, whereas in social evolution the variation on which selection operates is often deliberately and purposefully created by conscious thought and action by individuals. Third, social evolution has a much more predictive direction than biological evolution does, for if human evolution started over again, the same sequence of societal types that have appeared during the last 100,000 years would again emerge, whereas such would not be the case for the biological evolution of species. Fourth, because humans can consciously create the variations on which selection works, social evolution is much more rapid than biological evolution is, even when we factor in punctuated evolutionary leaps in the process of speciation. Fifth, in social evolution, traits diffuse across societies in a manner that has no counterpart in biological evolution through natural selection on genetic variations. And sixth, natural selection operates in social evolution, but it is not the actual cause of evolution because causality ultimately resides in the behavioral adaptations of motivated and conscious individuals who create cultural and social structural traits. So, Sanderson concludes, "the differences between social and biological evolution are great enough to require that social evolution be studied as a process in its own right, and not merely along the lines of an analogy with biological evolution."[53]

Social evolution, when viewed from the perspective of world history, evidences "social transformation and directional trends of sufficient generality such that topologies of social forms can be fruitfully constructed."[54] Yet, despite these patterns and directionality to social forms or societal types like hunting and gathering, horticulture, agrarianism, industrialism, and world system development, other forces such as social stasis, de-evolution back to simpler forms, and extinction of social structures are basic facts of world history; these too must be part of any evolutionary analysis of world history. Still, there is a directional trend to human history, but not one with a grand teleological design; rather, as individuals have adapted to their environments, they have created cultural and social systems that are similar. For example, Sanderson notes that the "Neolithic Revolutions," where individuals began to plant and harvest food, occurred independently in at least eight major regions of the world—Southwest Asia, Southeast Asia, Africa, China, Europe, Mesoamerica, South America, and North America—as well as in subregions within these major regions of the world. And these transformations all occurred within relatively similar times, within a few thousand years of each other. Similarly, the rise of the state is another case of such parallel evolution, emerging independently in several parts of the world. Even a third great evolutionary transformation—the emergence of capitalism—was not unique to Europe, as is generally argued, but occurred in Japan as well. Only an evolutionary analysis can explain these great transformations, Sanderson argues, because they did not emerge because of diffusion but rather as independent adaptations of individuals creating social structures and culture.

Of course, once created, these adaptations can spread, or force others to adopt them to survive. The spread of capitalism across the world, creating a world system, is an excellent example of how a major social transformation can force members of other societies to adopt the structures and culture of capitalism to remain viable in their environment. Indeed, there is always the potential for a "superstructural feedback" in which, once created, systems like the culture of capitalism become one of the conditions to which individuals must adapt, thereby accelerating the spread of particular cultural systems and the social forms that these symbols regulate and legitimate.

Lee Freese's Model of Biosociocultural Regimes

Lee Freese has, in recent years, sought to develop a more ecologically oriented approach to long-term development of human societies.[55] Freese believes traditional accounts of social evolution are flawed because they make analogies to biological theory, while employing stage models of human development from simple to complex forms. The problem with this approach, Freese argues, is that it tends to focus almost exclusively on sociocultural phenomena as the basic evolving unit, whether this unit is a pattern of organization, a system of symbols, or a whole society. Analogies are then drawn to biological evolution, although, as we have seen for the stage theories examined thus far, there is always a list of differences between biological and sociocultural evolution. But Freese argues even more strongly that such differences are fundamental to how we theorize about patterns of human organization.

In biological evolution, genes are the unit of inheritance and are subject to selection forces that determine whether or not they will be transmitted to the next generation. In human social systems, symbolic information is not the analogue of genes, Freese says, for several reasons. First, cultural information and social structural patterns regulated by culture cannot make exact copies of themselves, as can genes. Second, unlike genetic material, cultural symbols are not discrete or particulate but, rather, are diffuse, often blending, fusing, differentiating, and disappearing in ways not typical of genetic codes. Third, as all stage theories also emphasize, inheritance is not Darwinian in the sense of being guided by the transmission of genetically coded information across generations, but instead, sociocultural evolution is Lamarkian, with innovations in one generation being used and then passed on, and perhaps modified or expanded on by subsequent generations. And fourth, because of the Lamarkian character of sociocultural evolution, change in human social systems can become much more rapid than the evolution of biological species. Thus, Freese contends, we should not even consider sociocultural systems or their respective parts as undergoing any type of evolution that is analogous to biological evolution. Instead, stage models of evolution like those developed by Lenski, Nolan, and Lenski and Sanderson are, in reality, developmental models describing the increasing complexity of societal social systems. How, then, do we account for these changes over the long run of human history?

Freese argues that to answer this question, it is necessary to reemphasize the effects of ecological parameters. In particular, we need to view sociocultural phenomena as responding to environmental pressures at both the individual person and group level. Sociocultural phenomena are, in the end, adaptations to two primary habitat conditions: (1) the rate and extent of human mortality, and (2) the resource potential of a habitat. These two habitat conditions exert a "push and pull" on human culture and patterns of social organization, with the resource potential of a habitat generally moving upward (as new technologies for exploiting resources are developed) and with rates of mortality waxing and waning over the course of human history.

As sociocultural systems seek to extract resources from the environment and reduce mortality, the complex interplay between the biophysical and sociocultural becomes crucial to understanding the nature, types, and extent of social organization. Social systems are always seeking to extract resources and control mortality; thus the nature of such sociocultural systems will reflect the degree of success in adapting to the biophysical parameters of human existence. Reciprocally, the biophysical environment is changed as a result of sociocultural adaptations used to seek resources and regulate death rates. Essentially, Freese views a sociocultural system as resting on and adapting to a biophysical system. However, once these systems are in interaction, several internal self-generating dynamics are set into motion as biophysical and sociocultural assemblies connect, interact, organize, and reorganize in response to the challenges initiated by the other. This self-organizing and self-renewing process with its complex and mutual interdependencies, in turn, gives rise to a "biosociocultural system" or, when viewed from a point in time, a "biosociocultural regime." The unit of evolution for understanding societal change and complexity, then, is the biosociocultural regime, although Freese maintains that Darwinian processes of "transmission" and "inheritance" do not operate in this perspective. Instead, Freese entertains the theoretical possibility of a "descent with modification" as regimes—through self-generating, cumulative, and normally irreversible processes—proceed through time fashioning new material structures with a greater potential for energy capture and transfer, which modify and in some cases totally replace the existing assemblies involved in a biosociocultural regime.

Thus, biosociocultural regimes are the evolving unit. Here, natural selection is still operative but it is not the causal force of change. Instead, matter-energy forms and flow cycles initiate the complex interactions between biophysical-sociocultural assemblies.[56] In turn, the degree of capacity for greater energy capture and resource transfer reflects and influences the size of a population, its level of technology, and its division of labor, shaping in turn the nature and evolution of the biosociocultural regime. Over time as regimes are assembled for energy capture to sustain activities through self-organization, the result is larger and more complex regimes, as sociocultural development takes on a cumulative character toward ever more complexity and, ultimately, toward macro societies. Freese states "selection will tend to favor populations whose energy capture and resource exploitation are maximized relative to alternative populations that are competing for resources derived from the same matter-energy cycle."[57]

With this shift in emphasis from analogies to biological evolution toward a more ecological approach, revolving around the assembling of biosociocultural regimes that self organize to capture energy from the environment for economic production, Freese hopes to broaden the very nature of sociological theory. Rather than adopting biological concepts and theories, then modifying them because of the obvious differences between sociocultural and biological evolution, it is better to begin anew with a broad ecological framework in which sociocultural systems seeking to extract resources and control mortality are seen as parts of biosociocultural regimes. Then, once again a connection can be made among culture, society, and the ecological necessities humans had to confront in the development of complex human societies.

THE RETURN TO THEORIZING
ABOUT HUMAN NATURE

Early sociologists, indeed all early social thought, had a conception about the basic nature of humans. Most of this theorizing disappeared by the turn into the twentieth century, only to be revived again over the last fifty years. Sociobiology represented one effort to get back to the question of the biological forces underlying human behavior, and it did so with more biological sophistication than earlier "instinct" approaches. More recently, sociologists have made new efforts to bring considerations of humans' biological propensities into the mainstream of sociological theory. These efforts have stayed outside sociobiology, but they also evidence a level of biological sophistication that early "instinct" approaches lacked. Among the many potential theoretical approaches,[58] we will examine two in this closing section of the chapter: the approaches of Richard Udry and Alexandra Maryanski.

J. Richard Udry's Gender Theory

Richard Udry is a strong proponent for bringing biology back into sociology, arguing that humans have basic predispositions that can be divided into two broad categories: (1) predispositions unique to individuals, and (2) predispositions shared by all *Homo sapiens.* Udry maintains that it is now well accepted (even by sociologists) that human bodies and brains have evolved through natural selection; yet, understanding of behavior is still considered by most sociologists to reside outside the realm of evolutionary forces.[59] To document his advocacy for a biologically informed sociology, Udry has proposed a theory of "gendered behaviors" within and between the sexes.[60] Udry argues that most sociologists assume that all gendered behaviors are human inventions, the combined result of (1) gender roles and norms assigned to each sex in a given society, (2) diverse gender-specific socialization experiences, and (3) differential social opportunities for males and females. Although everyone recognizes that males and females differ in many ways, all notions of biological influences are rejected or considered trivial in sociological models and theories.[61] Yet, as Udry points out, there now exists outside sociology an active area of research on "sexual dimorphisms," or those characteristics that distinguish males and females. In addition, the hormones that control dimorphism are linked in all mammals with "sex-dimorphic body structures" and "sex-dimorphic reproductive behaviors," which, says Udry, lie "at the heart of gender."[62] Humans, and higher primates, have the same hormonal structure. In nonhuman primates, sex-dimorphic (or gendered behaviors) have been linked to two stages in the life cycle of primates: (1) a stage in mid-pregnancy when the testicles of a male fetus produce large amounts of testosterone for the genitals as well as for the neural structure of the brain; and (2) a stage of puberty when the sex hormones for all individuals trigger those changes in body morphology and neurology of the brain that produce adult sex-dimorphic behaviors.[63] If the sex hormones influence higher primate behavior, it is plausible that these sex hormones in humans create a gendered blueprint for human behaviors as well. Indeed, these hormonal and reproductive systems operate in humans much the same way they do in other primates, and particularly so for those reproductive mechanisms linked to infant survival, thereby making them likely candidates for preservation during human evolution.[64]

In an exploratory test of his hypothesis, Udry applied his primate-hormonal model to predict within-sex patterns of gendered behaviors among a sample of 250 adult women. From this study, Udry noted that "we were able to confirm several very specific hypotheses concerning the specific hormones involved prenatally, the trimester of effects of prenatal hormones, the specific hormones involved in adulthood, and the interaction of adult with prenatal hormones."[65] His successful predictions in this early study led him to conclude that "individual women differ in their biological propensity to sex-typed behavior."

Based on this early research, Udry proposed the following: "Those processes which affect within-sex variance in gendered behaviors are the same processes as cause between-sex differences. . . . We can also infer that males and females differ from one another in their average biological propensity to the same behaviors. . . . Gender has biological foundations."[66] In an effort to support this conclusion, Udry performed a thought experiment: Imagine a hypothetical society where both males and females *have gendered predispositions that are panhuman and universal to all human societies.* Let us also assume that this hypothetical society sequentially adopts three distinct socially constructed gender ideologies: (1) a traditional gender-segregated society with sex-typed normative rules for males and females, followed by (2) a single gender society supported by a "unisex" gender ideology, and (3) with institutional changes over time, a permissive society where males and females could follow their own gender proclivities. In a longitudinal examination of this society, what would the behavioral distributions for males and females look like for each structure?

Udry's theoretical model would predict the following patterns over time: In the traditional society, the strong normative sanctions for strictly segregated gender roles would push aside any individual predispositions that conflicted with socially constructed gender norms. In the "antigender" phase, the restrictive norms against divergent gender norms would also push males and females away from their biological inclinations toward conformity to a unisex standard. Finally, in the gender-permissive phase, where everyone could choose their gender preferences, individuals' gendered roles would mirror their biologically based predispositions. The important point here is that for all three ideologies, a "gender structure" would be clearly evident, but only in the gender-permissive society would gendered behaviors prevail "without the gender norms supporting the gendered structure."[67]

Yet, in the absence of a biosocial theory of gender, social scientists would conclude that all three ideologies, including the one advocating a gender-permissive society, were socially constructed. The reason for this conclusion is that sociologists think it impossible for a behavior to have biological foundations, in part because of the social change in ideologies guiding behavior. As this thought experiment demonstrates, however, ideological changes over time are always driven by purely social forces. What is constant in each phase is biologically based gendered predispositions. But only in the gender-permissive phase would gendered proclivities be allowed the potential of their fullest expression because of the absence of socially constructed gender roles.

In addition to this example, Udry maintains that his gender theory will help us better understand a variety of sexual differences between males and females that cannot be explained by purely sociological theories. These include such questions as the following:

1. Why do male and female behaviors vary so dramatically in some instances and not in others?

2. Why do these variations in behaviors show such cross-cultural commonalities, despite major societal and cultural differences?

3. Why do some males act much more masculine than other males?

4. Why do some females act much more feminine than other females?

Udry feels the challenge for the social sciences is to learn how to integrate biological variables into normal social sciences. He emphasizes that only "social scientists imagine that if a behavior is under biological influence, there is nothing we can do about it. . . ." The nature of social arrangements can override or alter any human predispositions.[68]

Finally, Udry offers the following propositions: The higher the level of social constraints in a society, the less is the variance in the behavior that is controlled by biological differences. In contrast, the more choices individuals are permitted, the more their behavior will be controlled by biological forces. Thus, biological forces influence behavior most when individual choice is broad. In complex societies, some people have more choice than others do; hence, biological forces will exert more influence on those portions of the population that are less constrained by social forces. For Udry, an advanced industrial society represents a natural experiment in which to study the range of women's biologically based behaviors because modern women have more choice than they did previously about such matters as childbearing, occupation, contraception, marriage, and abortion. But the biological factors, Udry argues, will be invisible to most sociologists because in sociological models nobody is looking for biological factors. When societies provide gender-neutral opportunities, the naturally occurring variation in gender predispositions among individuals allows them to take advantage of these opportunities. The result will not be a "degendered" society, but rather one in which the range variation in biologically driven behaviors will be more evident in the actual role behaviors of males and females. He notes that work on the biology of genes has just begun, with his work as just one small step. He encourages replication of his exploratory work and also continued research on both males and females to see which behaviors are sensitive to hormonal influences.

Alexandra Maryanski's Cross-Species Comparative Analysis on the Origins of Human Sociality

In recent years, Alexandra Maryanski, in conjunction with sometime collaborator Jonathan Turner, has approached the question of human nature by examining the social network ties of humans' closest living relatives, the apes.[69] As is well known, humans share more than 98 percent of their genetic material with chimpanzees (Pan); indeed, chimpanzees might be closer to humans than they are to gorillas (Gorilla). And both chimpanzees and gorillas who are African apes are certainly closer to humans than they are to orangutans (Pongo) or gibbons (Hylobates), the other two genera who are Asian apes. In fact, humans and chimpanzees came from the same animal only about five million years ago, according to the latest fossil and molecular data.[70]

Long-term field studies have documented that primates are highly intelligent, slow to mature, undergo a long period of socialization, and live a long time, and the majority of primates are organized into year-round societies that require the integration of a wide variety of age and sex classes, not just adult males and females. In addition, primates have clear-cut social bonding patterns that vary widely among the 187 species of primates.

Using a historical comparative technique, which is termed cladistic analysis in biology, Maryanski began by examining the social relational data on present-day ape genera—that is, chimpanzees, gorillas, gibbons, and orangutans.[71] Following this procedure, Maryanski first identified a limited group of entities—in this case one crucial property of ape social structure, the strength of social bonds between and among age and sex classes in all ape genera—to see if there were structural regularities in the patterning of relations. If phyletically close species living in different environments reveal characteristic traits in common, then it can be assumed that their Last Common Ancestor (LCA) also had similar relational features. For this exercise, Maryanski undertook a comprehensive review of bonding propensities for apes living under natural field conditions in an effort to profile their social network structures with the idea of uncovering a blueprint of the LCA population to present-day apes and humans.

To assess the validity of these relational patterns, she followed the procedures of cladistic analysis by including an "outgroup lineage"—a sample of Old World monkey social networks—for comparison. She also subjected her data set to two fundamental assumptions associated with this comparative technique: (1) the *relatedness hypothesis*, which indirectly assesses whether or not the shared patterns of social relations are caused by chance, and (2) the *regularity hypothesis*, which indirectly assesses whether the modifications from the ancestral to descendant forms evidence a systematic bias and are not randomly acquired. Both hypotheses provided strong empirical support for her reconstruction of hominoid (that is, apes and humans) LCA patterns.[72]

Maryanski's analysis led to a striking conclusion: Like the contemporary apes phyletically closest to humans, the LCA population evidenced a fluid organizational structure, consisting of a relatively low level of sociality and a lack of intergenerational group continuity over time. The proximal reasons for this structure are a combination of several forces that are still found in all living ape social networks: (a) a systematic bias toward female (and usually male) transfer from the natal unit at puberty, which is the opposite trend from monkeys where only males transfer and females stay to form intergenerational matrilines; (b) a promiscuous mating pattern that makes paternity difficult to establish; and (c) an abundance of weak social ties and few strong ties among most adults. In addition, the Regularity Hypothesis that was used to assess the modifications from the LCA social structure suggested that after descendants separated from the ancestral population, the future trend in hominoid evolution (that is, ape and human) involved selection pressures for heightened sociality, seemingly to increase hominoid survival and reproductive success. Indeed, it is an established fact in the fossil record that about 18 million years ago, a huge number of ape species underwent a dramatic decline and extinction, just when species of monkeys suddenly proliferated and, according to the fossil record, moved into the former ape niches, perhaps because monkeys developed a competitive, dietary edge over apes. Whatever the explanation, the fossil record confirms that, when ape niches were being usurped by monkeys, apes began to undergo anatomical modifications to a marginal niche that required a peculiar locomotion pattern that involves hand-over-hand movement in the trees through space along with other novel skeletal features that characterize the anatomy of both apes and humans today.[73] Today, monkeys remain the dominant primates, and apes are a distinct and tiny minority; moreover, with the exception of humans, the few remaining nonhuman hominoids—that is, chimpanzee, gorilla, orangutan, and gibbon—are now considered "evolutionary failures" and "evolutionary leftovers" because of their small numbers and specialized and restricted niches.

The significance of this finding is important for thinking about human nature. If humans' closest relatives reveal a tendency for relatively weak social ties, then humans are also likely to have this social tendency as part of their genetic coding. What, however, is meant by weak and fluid ties?[74] Maryanski confirmed in her review of the data that monkeys have lots of strong ties and high-density matri-focal networks. In monkey societies, males at puberty disperse to other groups, whereas females remain behind, forming as many as four generations of strongly tied matrilines (that is, composed of grandmothers, mothers, sisters, and daughters). These extended female-bonds provide intergenerational continuity and are the backbone of most monkey societies. In contrast, females in ape societies evidence the rare pattern of dispersal at puberty with migration typically within a larger regional or community population. In addition, males in ape societies (with the exception of the chimpanzee) also depart. Thus, with both sexes dispersing at puberty, most kinship ties are broken (certainly matri-focal ties in all apes), intergenerational continuity is lost, and the result is a relatively fluid social structure with adult individuals moving about as a shifting collection of individuals within a larger regional population. In Asia, adult orangutans are nearly solitary, rarely interacting with others purely for social reasons. Mothers with their dependent young are the only stable social unit. In Africa, chimpanzees and gorillas are more socially inclined, with gorillas living together peacefully in small groups, but individuals are so self-contained that it is uncommon to observe any overt social interactions between adults. Among our closest chimpanzee relatives, adult females are also self-contained, spending most of their days traveling about alone with their dependent offspring. Adult chimpanzee males, in contrast, are relatively more social and are likely to have a few individual "friendships" with other males. A mother and son also form strong ties. But, except for mother and her young offspring, there are no stable groupings in chimpanzee societies. Thus, chimpanzee males are still highly individualistic and self-reliant, preferring to move about independently in space within a large and fluid regional population.

Thus, if humans' closest African ape relatives evidence behavioral propensities for individualism, autonomy, mobility, and weak social ties, Maryanski argues that these genetically coded propensities are probably part of human nature as well. Indeed, if we examine the societal type within which humans as a species evolved—that is, hunting and gathering—it is clear that it approximates the pattern among the Great Apes, especially African apes: There is considerable mobility within a larger home range of bands; there is a high degree of individualism and personal autonomy; and, except for married couples, relatively loose and fluid social ties are evident. At a biological level, then, Maryanski argues that humans might not have the powerful biological urges for great sociality and collectivist-style social bonding that sociologists, and indeed social philosophy in general, frequently impute to our nature.[75]

In collaborative work with Jonathan Turner, Maryanski has described the implications in a review of the stages of societal development. Hunting and gathering is the stage in which human's basic human biological coding evolved; these societies of small, wandering bands within a territory evidence rather loose and fluid social ties, high individual autonomy, self-reliance, and mobility from band to band.[76] Yet, as human populations grew in size and were forced to adopt first horticulture and then agriculture to sustain themselves, they settled down to cultivate land, and, in the process, they "caged" themselves in sociocultural forms that violated basic needs for freedom, some degree of individual autonomy, and fluid ties within a larger community of local groups.

Thus, sociocultural evolution began to override the basic nature of humans. As Maryanski and Turner conclude, market-driven systems of the present industrial and post-industrial era are, despite their many obvious problems, closer than horticulture and agrarianism to the original societal type in which humans evolved biologically, at least in this sense: They offer more choices; they allow and indeed encourage individualism; they are structured in ways that make most social ties fluid and transitory; and they limit strong ties beyond family for many. Maryanski and Turner note that, for many sociologists of the past and today, the very features of human behavior required by market-driven societies are viewed as pathologies that violate humans' basic nature. Maryanski and Turner believe that societal evolution has, since hunting and gathering was left behind, just begun to create conditions more compatible with humans' basic hominoid nature as an evolved ape.

Although many of these conclusions are obviously somewhat speculative, the point of Maryanski's analysis is clear: If we use evolutionary approaches from biology, such as cladistic analysis and cross-species comparison with humans' close evolutionary relatives, we can make informed inferences about human nature. Then, we can use these inferences to determine whether sociocultural evolution has been compatible or incompatible with humans' primate legacy. From this analysis, it is possible to examine basic institutional systems, such as kinship, polity, religion, and economy to determine how and why they evolved in the first societal type—that is, hunting and gathering—and how they have interacted with humans' basic nature as an evolved ape during the various stages of societal development.

CONCLUSION

In this long chapter, we have reviewed a variety of approaches to developing a brand of sociological theorizing that is informed by biology, or at least biologically inspired modes of thinking. In many ways, these new evolutionary sociologies represent an odyssey back to sociology's very beginnings in the early nineteenth century, where the connection between sociology and biology was first made explicit. As is evident, the strategy for developing evolutionary sociology is highly varied, and perhaps with the exception of stage models of societal development, none of these approaches rivals the influence of the ecological perspective.

Yet, in the twenty-first century, these newer perspectives might rival the ecological approaches that have so dominated biologically inspired theorizing for most of the twentieth century. For it is now clear, and should have been all through the development of sociology, that humans are animals with an evolutionary history; we evolved like any animal and we must, like all species, adapt to the environment. Concepts from bio-ecology might prove increasingly useful. But, perhaps more important, sociological theory requires a mental set that forces a simple recognition: Human beings and their sociocultural creations are still subject to the basic problem of how to adjust and adapt to the environment. Theory in sociology should reflect this simple recognition.

NOTES

1. Pierre van den Berghe, *Age and Sex in Human Societies: A Biosocial Perspective* (Belmont, CA: Wadsworth, 1973), p. 2. See also his *Man in Society: A Biosocial View* (New York: Elsevier, 1975); "Territorial Behavior in a Natural Human Group," *Social Science Information* 16 (1977), pp. 421–430; "Bringing Beasts Back In: Toward a Biosocial Theory of Aggression," *American Sociological Review* 39 (1974), pp. 777–788; "Why Most Sociologists

Don't (And Won't) Think Evolutionarily," *Sociological Forum* 5 (1990), pp. 173–185; and "Once More with Feeling: Genes, Mind and Culture," *Behavioral and Brain Sciences* 14 (1991), pp. 317–318.

2. van den Berghe, "Bridging the Paradigms" *Society* 15 (1977–1978), pp. 42–49; *The Ethnic Phenomenon* (New York: Elsevier, 1981); and *Human Family Systems* (Prospect Heights, IL: Waveland, 1990), pp. 14ff.

3. van den Berghe, "Bridging the Paradigms," p. 46, and *Human Family Systems,* p. 15 (both cited in note 2).

4. van den Berghe, *The Ethnic Phenomenon* (cited in note 2), p. 7. See also Pierre van den Berghe and Joseph Whitmeyer, "Social Class and Reproductive Success," *International Journal of Contemporary Sociology* 27 (1990), pp. 29–48.

5. van den Berghe, "Bridging the Paradigms," pp. 46–47, and *Human Family Systems,* pp. 19–20 (both cited in note 2).

6. See discussion of sociobiology on this book's Web site (www.sociology/wadsworth.com).

7. van den Berghe, *The Ethnic Phenomenon,* p. 9, and "Bridging the Paradigms," p. 48 (both cited in note 2).

8. van den Berghe, "Bridging the Paradigms" (cited in note 2).

9. van den Berghe, *The Ethnic Phenomenon,* p. 10 (cited in note 2). See van den Berghe and Whitmeyer, "Social Class and Reproductive Success" (cited in note 4), pp. 31–32.

10. van den Berghe, *The Ethnic Phenomenon,* p. 6, and *Human Family Systems,* p. 220 (both cited in note 2).

11. Pierre van den Berghe and David Barash, "Inclusive Fitness and Family Structure," *American Anthropologist* 79 (1977), pp. 809–823.

12. van den Berghe, *The Ethnic Phenomenon* (cited in note 2), and also see van den Berghe, "Heritable Phenotypes and Ethnicity," *Behavioral and Brain Sciences* 12 (1989), pp. 544–545.

13. van den Berghe, "Once More with Feeling: Genes, Mind and Culture," *Behavioral and Brain Sciences* 14 (1991), (cited in note 1), pp. 317–318. See van den Berghe and Whitmeyer, "Social Class and Reproductive Success" (cited in note 4), pp. 41–44.

14. Richard Machalek, "Why Are Large Societies Rare?" *Advances in Human Ecology* 1 (1992), pp. 33–64.

15. Richard Machalek, "Crossing Species Boundaries: Comparing Basic Properties of Human and Nonhuman Societies." (Unpublished manuscript.)

16. Machalek, "Why Are Large Societies Rare?" (cited in note 14), p. 35.

17. Ibid., p. 42.

18. Ibid.

19. Ibid., p. 44.

20. Ibid., p. 45.

21. Ibid., p. 46.

22. Ibid., p. 47.

23. Ibid., p. 48.

24. Ibid., p. 50.

25. Ibid.

26. Ibid., p. 61.

27. Gerhard Lenski, *Power and Privilege: A Theory of Social Stratification* (New York: McGraw-Hill, 1966).

28. Gerhard Lenski, *Human Societies: An Introduction to Macrosociology* (New York: McGraw-Hill, 1970).

29. In subsequent editions of *Human Societies,* Lenski began to collaborate with Jean Lenski.

30. More recent editions of *Human Societies* are coauthored with Patrick Nolan. See, for the most recent edition, Gerhard Lenski, Patrick Nolan, and Jean Lenski, *Human Societies: An Introduction to Macrosociology,* 7th ed. (New York: McGraw-Hill, 1995).

31. See, for a recent discussion on their use, Patrick Nolan, *Annual Review of Sociology,* (Menlo Park, CA: Annual Reviews, 1997).

32. Stephen K. Sanderson, *Social Transformations: A General History of Historical Development* (Cambridge, MA: Blackwell, 1995).

33. Lee Freese, *Evolutionary Connections* (Greenwich, CT: JAI, 1997).

34. Lenski, Nolan, and Lenski, *Human Societies* (cited in note 30), p. 75.

35. Ibid.

36. Ibid., pp. 75–76.

37. Gerhard Lenski, "Societal Taxonomies: Mapping the Social Universe," *Annual Review of Sociology* 20 (1994), p. 23.

38. Lenski, Nolan, and Lenski, *Human Societies* (cited in note 30), pp. 57–58.

39. Ibid.

40. Ibid., p. 84.

41. See, for example, Stephen K. Sanderson, *Social Evolutionism: A Critical History* (Oxford, England: Blackwell, 1990).

42. Stephen K. Sanderson, *Social Transformations* (cited in note 32). See also his *Macrosociology: An Introduction to Human Societies* (New York: HarperCollins, 1991).

43. Sanderson, *Social Transformations* (cited in note 32).

44. Ibid., pp. 10–11.

45. Ibid., p. 11.

46. Ibid., pp. 12–13.

47. Ibid., p. 13.

48. Ibid., p. 11.

49. Stephen Sanderson, "Evolutionary Materialism: A Theoretical Strategy for the Study of Social Evolution," *Sociological Perspectives* 37 (1994), pp. 47–73; see page 52 for quote.

50. Ibid., p. 53.

51. Ibid., p. 53.

52. Ibid.

53. Ibid., pp. 50–53.

54. Ibid., p. 52.

55. Ibid., p. 50.

56. Lee Freese, *Evolutionary Connections* (cited in note 33). See also Lee Freese, "Evolution and Sociogenesis. Part I: Ecological Origins; Part II: Social Continuities" in *Advances in Group Processes*, vol. 5, ed. E. J. Lawler and B. Markovsky (Greenwich, CT: JAI, 1988), pp. 53–118.

57. In assuming evolution by self-organization, Freese adopts Alfred Lotka's law as the force driving evolution in biosociocultural regimes. This principle states, "Natural selection will so operate as to increase the total flux through the system, so long as there is presented an unutilized residue of matter and available energy" (quoted in Freese, *Evolutionary Connections,* cited in note 33). The underlying assumption here is that acting entities always generate change.

58. Freese, *Evolutionary Connections* (cited in note 33).

59. For instance, see William Catton, "Separation versus Unification in Sociological Human Ecology" in *Advances in Human Ecology,* vol 1, ed. L. Freese (Greenwich, CT: JAI, 1992), pp. 65–99; Walter Gove, "Why We Do What We Do: A Biopsycho-social Theory of Human Motivation," *Social Forces* 73 (1994), pp. 363–394; Walter Gove and G. Carpenter, *The Fundamental Connection Between Nature and Nurture* (Toronto: Lexington, 1982); Warren TenHouten, "Cerebral-Lateralization Theory and the Sociology of Knowledge," *The Dual Brain,* eds. D. F. Benson and E. Zaidel (New York: Guilford, 1985), pp. 341–355; Warren TenHouten, "Into the Wild Blue Yonder: On the Emergence of the Ethnoneuro-logies—the Social Science-Based Neurologies and the Philosophy-Based Neurologies," *Journal of Social and Biological Structures* 14 (1991), pp. 381–408; John Baldwin and Janice Baldwin, *Beyond Sociobiology* (New York: Elsevier, 1981); Marvin Olsen, "A Socioecological Perspective on Social Evolution" in *Advances in Human Ecology,* ed. L. Freese (London: JAI, 1993), vol. 2, pp. 69–92; Thomas Dietz and Tom Burns, "Human Agency and the Evolutionary Dynamics of Culture," *Acta Sociologica* 35 (1992), pp. 187–200; Thomas Dietz, Tom Burns, and F. Buttel, "Evolutionary Theory in Sociology: An Examination of Current Thinking," *Sociological Forum* 5 (1990), pp. 155–185; Theodore Kemper,

Social Structure and Testosterone (New Brunswick, NJ: Rutgers University Press, 1990); Eugene Rosa, "Sociology, Biosociology or Vulgar Biologizing?" *Sociological Symposium* 27 (1979), pp. 28–45.

60. J. Richard Udry, "Sociology and Biology: What Biology Do Sociologists Need to Know?," *Social Forces* 73 (1995), pp. 1267–1278; J. Richard Udry, "The Nature of Gender," *Demography* 31 (1994), pp. 561–573.

61. Ibid., p. 562.

62. Ibid.

63. Ibid., p. 568.

64. Udry, "Sociology and Biology" (cited in note 60), p. 1274.

65. Udry, "The Nature of Gender" (cited in note 60), p. 570.

66. Ibid., p. 571.

67. Ibid., p. 565.

68. Ibid., p. 572.

69. A. Maryanski, "The Last Ancestor: An Ecological Network Model on the Origins of Human Sociality," *Advances in Human Ecology,* ed. L. Freese, vol. 1 (Greenwich, CT: JAI, 1992), pp. 1–32; A. Maryanski and Jonathan Turner, *The Social Cage* (Stanford, CA: Stanford University Press, 1992); and A. Maryanski, "African Ape Social Structure: Is There Strength in Weak Ties?" *Social Networks* 9 (1987), pp. 191–215.

70. See Charles G. Sibley, John A. Comstock, and Jon E. Ahlquist, "DNA Hybridization Evidence of Hominoid Phylogeny: A Reanalysis of the Data," *Journal of Molecular Evolution* 30 (1990), pp. 202–236; M. Goodman, D. A. Tagle, D. H. A. Fitch, W. Bailey, J. Czelusnak, B. F. Koop, P. Benson, and J. L. Slightom, "Primate Evolution at the DNA Level and a Classification of Hominids," *Journal of Molecular Evolution* 30 (1990), pp. 260–266.

71. This technique is a standard tool for reconstruction in such fields as comparative biology, historical linguistics, and textual criticism. Essentially, the basic procedure is to identify a set of characters believed to be the end points or descendants of an evolutionary or developmental process, with the idea that an "original" or common ancestor can be reconstructed through the detection of shared diagnostic characters.

72. For discussions of this methodology, see R. Jeffers and I. Lehiste, *Principles and Methods for Historical Linguistics* (Cambridge, MA: MIT Press, 1979); M. Hass, "Historical Linguistics and the Genetic Relationship of Languages," *Current Trends in Linguistics* 3 (1966), pp. 113–153; and N. Platnick and H. D. Cameron, "Cladistic Methods in Textual, Linguistic, and Phylogenetic Analysis," *Systematic Zoology* 26 (1977), pp. 380–385.

73. For discussions, see P. Andrews, "Species Diversity and Diet in Monkeys and Apes during the Miocene" in *Aspects of Human Evolution,* ed. C. B. Stringer (London: Taylor and Francis, 1981), pp. 25–61; J. Temerin and J. Cant, "The Evolutionary Divergence of Old World Monkeys and Apes," *American Naturalist* 122 (1983), pp. 335–351; and R. Ciochon and R. Corruccini, eds., *New Interpretations of Ape and Human Ancestry* (New York: Plenum, 1983).

74. To array social tie patterns, affective ties were assessed on the basis of mutually reinforcing and friendly interactions. Degrees of attachment were described along a simple scale of tie strength: null ties, weak ties, moderate ties, strong ties. Individuals without ties (for example, father-daughter where paternity cannot be known) or who rarely, if ever, interact have null ties; those who interact in a positive manner on an occasional basis have weak ties; those who affiliate closely for a time but without endurance over time (at least for adults) have moderate ties; and those who exhibit extensive nonsexual physical contact with much observable affect (for example, reciprocal grooming), have very high interactional rates, and show mutual support

with stable and long-term relations over time have strong ties. Scaling tie strength for primates is a straightforward procedure because age and sex classes have clear-cut social tendencies that have been documented by field researchers during the last fifty years. Also see Maryanski, "The Last Ancestor," and Maryanski and Turner, *The Social Cage* (both cited in note 69), for detailed discussions about how the network analysis of primate social ties was conducted. For general references on network analysis, see Chapter 30 on social network analysis in this book.

75. See for example M. G. Bicchieri, *Hunters and Gatherers Today* (New York: Holt, Rinehart & Winston,

1972) for a study of eleven food-collecting societies. Also see Margaret Power, *The Egalitarians—Human and Chimpanzee: An Anthropological View of Social Organization* (Cambridge: Cambridge University Press, 1991), pp. xviii, 290; Robert C. Bailey and Robert Aunger, "Humans as Primates: The Social Relationships of Efe Pygmy Men in Comparative Perspective," *International Journal of Primatology,* Vol. 11, No. 2 (1990), pp. 127–145, which details some of the similarities between chimpanzee and human hunter-gatherer societies.

76. Maryanski and Turner, *The Social Cage* (cited in note 69), Chapter 4, pp. 69–90.

PART III

✳

Conflict Theorizing

8

Early Conflict Theory

A long with functionalism, conflict theory was sociology's first theoretical orientation. Even some early functional theorists, such as Herbert Spencer,[1] developed conceptualizations of conflict; yet, over the years, these functional approaches increasingly came under attack for underemphasizing conflict and change.[2] In seeking "the function" of sociocultural forces for meeting needs for integration and other requisites, functionalists tended to underemphasize the effects of inequality in systematically generating conflict, disintegration, and change.

Conflict theory in sociology began with Karl Marx (1818–1883), but the development of the approach owes a debt to two other early German sociologists, Max Weber (1864–1920) and Georg Simmel (1858–1918). Weber and Simmel also articulated conflict theories, but they were suspicious of Marx's polemics and, as a result, added necessary qualifications and refinements to Marx's ideas. Taken together, Marx, Weber, and Simmel provided the core ideas that still inspire contemporary conflict approaches. Despite the genius of these early masters, conflict theory remained recessive during the first half of the twentieth century, although considerable research and limited theorizing was performed on particular instances of conflict, such as ethnic tensions or colonialism. The ideas of Marx, Weber, and Simmel on conflict began to resurface in America and assume a central place in sociological theory during the 1950s in the works of two German-born sociologists, Ralf Dahrendorf and Lewis Coser. Although others were also involved in the development of the new conflict approach, Dahrendorf and Coser set the tone for this revival in the United States. In Europe, conflict sociology had always been more prominent, and so, it should not be surprising that Europeans sparked interest in conflict theorizing. In this chapter, we will first explore the key insights of Marx, Weber, and Simmel and then we will review Dahrendorf's and Coser's ideas. From this conceptual base, conflict theory has gone in many interesting directions during the last fifty years, as we will see in Chapters 9 through 11.

KARL MARX AND CONFLICT THEORY

We will encounter Marx's work in analyzing several theoretical perspectives in present-day sociology; here, it is not necessary to present his entire theoretical corpus here. For the present, the goal is to describe the more general, abstracted model of conflict that is packaged between the polemics of the Marxian scheme. Table 8.1 summarizes Marx's assumptions about the social world and the key forces behind conflict and change in societies.[3] As shown in Proposition I, Marx argued that the degree of inequality in the distribution of resources generates inherent conflicts of interest between those who have and those who do not have valued resources. Proposition II then emphasizes that when members of subordinate segments of the society become aware of their true interests in redistributing resources and, thereby, reducing inequality, they will begin to question the legitimacy of the system. Next, Proposition III specifies the conditions that facilitate subordinates' awareness of their true conflict of interest. Propositions III-A, B, C, and D deal, respectively, with the disruption in the social situation of deprived populations, the amount of alienation people feel as a result of their situation, the capacity of members of deprived segments to communicate with one another, and their ability to develop a unifying ideology that codifies their true interests. Marx saw these conditions as factors that increase and heighten awareness of subordinates' collective interests and, hence, decrease their willingness to accept as legitimate the right of superordinates to command a disproportionate share of resources.

In turn, some of these forces heightening awareness are influenced by such structural conditions as ecological concentration (III-C-1), educational opportunities (III-C-2), the availability of ideological spokespeople (III-D-1), and the control of socialization processes and communication networks by superordinates (III-D-2). Marx hypothesized (shown in Proposition IV) that the increasing awareness by deprived classes of their true interests and the resulting questioning of the legitimacy of resource distribution increases the likelihood that the disadvantaged strata will begin to organize collectively their opposition against the dominant segments of a system. This organization is seen as especially likely under several conditions: disorganization among the dominant segments with respect to articulating their true interests (IV-A), sudden escalation of subordinates' sense of deprivation as they begin to compare their situation with that of the privileged (IV-B), and mobilization of political leadership to carry out the organizational tasks of pursuing conflict (IV-C). Marx emphasized (shown in Proposition V) that, once deprived groups possess

Table 8.1 Marx's Abstracted Propositions on Conflict Processes

[handwritten: ev: parking at BYUL]

I. The more unequal is the distribution of scarce resources in a society, the greater is the basic conflict of interest between its dominant and subordinate segments.

II. The more subordinate segments become aware of their true collective interests, the more likely they are to question the legitimacy of the existing pattern of distribution of scarce resources.

III. Subordinates are more likely to become aware of their true collective interests when

   A. Changes wrought by dominant segments disrupt existing relations among subordinates. *[handwritten: draws attention to it.]*

   B. Practices of dominant segments create alienative dispositions. *[handwritten: A parked in B]* *[handwritten: when "A" spots are empty]*

   C. Members of subordinate segments can communicate their grievances to one another, which, in turn, is facilitated by

      1. The ecological concentration among members of subordinate groups. *[handwritten: close proximity]*

      2. The expansion of educational opportunities for members of subordinate groups. *[handwritten: knowledge of other groups]*

   D. Subordinate segments can develop unifying ideologies, which, in turn, is facilitated by *[handwritten: all parking should be =]* *[handwritten: ideology: all men are equal]*

      1. The capacity to recruit or generate ideological spokespeople.

      2. The inability of dominant groups to regulate socialization processes and communication networks among subordinates. *[handwritten: if they don't have a good justification]*

IV. The more that subordinate segments of a system become aware of their collective interests and question the legitimacy of the distribution of scarce resources, the more likely they are to join in overt conflict against dominant segments of a system, especially when *[handwritten: (revolt)]*

   A. Dominant groups cannot clearly articulate, nor act in, their collective interests.

   B. Deprivations of subordinates move from an absolute to a relative basis, or escalate rapidly. *[handwritten: no more "B" parking]*

   C. Subordinate groups can develop a political leadership structure. *[handwritten: organization]*

V. The greater is the ideological unification of members of subordinate segments of a system and the more developed is their political leadership structure, the more likely are the interests and relations between dominant and subjugated segments of a society to become polarized and irreconcilable.

VI. The more polarized are the dominant and subjugated, the more will the conflict be violent. *[handwritten: opposite]*

VII. The more violent is the conflict, the greater is the amount of the structural change within a society and the greater is the redistribution of scarce resources.

---

a unifying ideology and political leadership, their true interests begin to take on clear focus and their opposition to superordinates begins to increase—polarizing the interests and goals of superordinates and subordinates. As polarization increases, the possibilities for reconciliation, compromise, or mild conflict decrease because the deprived are sufficiently alienated, organized, and unified to press for a complete change in the pattern of resource distribution. As Proposition VI underscores, subordinates begin to see violent confrontation as the only way to overcome the inevitable resistance of superordinates. Finally, Marx noted (shown in Proposition VII) that violent conflict will cause great changes in patterns of social organization, especially its distribution of scarce resources. The propositions in Table 8.1 are stated much more abstractly than

Marx would have considered appropriate,[4] but his ideas began to filter back into contemporary sociology in this form. As theorists sought explanations for the forces generating conflict and change, they implicitly drew from Marx this image of society as filled with conflicts of interests in the distribution of scarce resources, with inequality in the distribution of valued resources setting into motion the mobilization of the subordinates to pursue conflict against superordinates. Yet, few borrowed only from Marx; as conflict theories came to the forefront in sociology during the 1950s and 1960s, both Max Weber and Georg Simmel were also consulted.

MAX WEBER AND CONFLICT THEORY

Max Weber was implicitly critical of Marx's theory of conflict, arguing that the unfolding of history is contingent on specific empirical conditions. Conflicts of interests do not, Weber believed, inexorably cause the revolutionary crescendo described by Marx. Yet, like Marx, Weber developed a theory of conflict, and despite a convergence in their theories, Weber saw conflict as highly contingent on the emergence of "charismatic leaders" who could mobilize subordinates. Unlike Marx, Weber saw the emergence of such leaders as far from inevitable, and hence, revolutionary conflict would not always be produced in systems of inequality. Nonetheless, when Weber's implicit propositions shown in Table 8.2 are compared with those of Marx in Table 8.1, considerable overlap is evident.

Most of the principles in Table 8.2 can be found in Weber's discussion of the transition from societies based on traditional authority to those organized around rational-legal authority.[5] In societies where the sanctity of tradition legitimates political and social activity, the withdrawal of legitimacy from these traditions is a crucial condition of conflict, as is emphasized in Proposition I of Table 8.2. What, then, causes subordinates to withdraw legitimacy? As indicated in Proposition II-A, one cause is a high degree of correlation among power, wealth, and prestige or, in Weber's terms, among positions of political power (party), occupancy in advantaged economic positions (class), and membership in high-ranking social circles (status groups). When economic elites, for example, are also social and political elites, and vice versa, then those who are excluded from power, wealth, and prestige become resentful and receptive to conflict alternatives. Another condition (Proposition II-B) is dramatic discontinuity in the distribution of rewards, or the existence of large gaps in social hierarchies that give great privilege to some and very little to others. When only a few hold power, wealth, and prestige and the rest are denied these rewards, tensions and resentments exist. Such resentments become a further inducement for those without power, prestige, and wealth to withdraw legitimacy from those who hoard these resources. A final condition (Proposition II-C) is low rates of social mobility. When those of low rank have little chance to move up social hierarchies or to enter a new class, party, or status group, then resentments accumulate. Those denied opportunities to increase their

Table 8.2 Weber's Abstracted Propositions on Conflict Processes

[handwritten annotations: "Students/Have Nots" ... "university/Haves"]

I. Subordinates are more likely to pursue conflict with superordinates when they withdraw legitimacy from political authority. *(not giving their support)*

II. Subordinates are more likely to withdraw legitimacy from political authority when

    A. The correlation among memberships in class, status group, and political hierarchies is high. *[position] [power]*

    B. The discontinuity or degrees of inequality in the resource distributions within social hierarchies is high. *high vs. low*

    C. Rates of social mobility up social hierarchies of power, prestige, and wealth are low.

III. Conflict between superordinates and subordinates becomes more likely when charismatic leaders can mobilize resentments of subordinates.

IV. When charismatic leaders are successful in conflict, pressures mount to routinize authority through new systems of rules and administration. *the beginnings of "change"*

V. As a system of rules and administrative authority is imposed, the more likely are conditions II-A, II-B, and II-C to be met, and hence, the more likely are new subordinates to withdraw legitimacy from political authority and to pursue conflict with the new subordinates, especially when new traditional and ascriptive forms of political domination are imposed by elites.

---

access to resources become restive and unwilling to accept the system of traditional authority.

As stressed in Proposition III in Table 8.2, the critical force that galvanizes the resentments inhering in these three conditions is charisma. Weber felt that whether or not charismatic leaders emerge is, to a great extent, a matter of historical chance, but if such leaders do emerge to challenge traditional authority and to mobilize resentments caused by the hoarding of resources by elites and the lack of opportunities to gain access to wealth, power, or prestige, then conflict and structural change can occur.

When successful, however, such leaders confront organizational problems of consolidating their gains. As stated in Proposition IV, one result is that charisma becomes routinized as leaders create formal rules, procedures, and structures for organizing followers after their successful mobilization to pursue conflict. And, as is emphasized in Proposition V, if routinization creates new patterns of ascription-based inequalities, thus erecting a new system of traditional authority, renewed conflict can be expected as membership in class, status, and party becomes highly correlated, as the new elites hoard resources, and as social mobility up hierarchies is blocked. Yet, if rational-legal routinization occurs, authority is based on equally applied laws and rules, and performance and ability become the basis for recruitment and promotion in bureaucratic structures. Under these conditions, conflict potential will be mitigated.

Unlike Marx, who tended to overemphasize the economic basis of inequality and to argue for a simple polarization of societies into propertied and nonpropertied (exploited) classes, Weber's Propositions I and II show more theoretical options. Weber believed that variations in the distribution of power, wealth, and prestige and the extent to which holders of one resource control the other resources become critical. Unlike Marx, who saw this correlation as inevitable, Weber saw more diverse relations among class, status, and party. Moreover, the degree of discontinuity in the distribution of these resources— in other words, the extent to which there are clear gaps and lines demarking privilege and nonprivilege—can also vary. Unlike Marx, Weber did not see the complete polarization of superordinates and subordinates as inexorable. Finally, the degree of mobility—the chance to gain access to power, wealth, and prestige—becomes a crucial variable in generating the resentments and tensions that make people prone to conflict; unlike Marx, Weber did not see a drop in mobility rates as always accompanying inequality.

In addition to the propositions in Table 8-2, which pertain primarily to *intra*-societal conflict processes, Weber developed theoretical ideas on *inter*-societal processes.[6] Because conflict between societies is, as Herbert Spencer recognized early in his work, a basic condition of human societies that have settled in territories and developed political leadership, it is not surprising that Weber also analyzed intersocietal conflict, or the "geopolitics" between societies. This emphasis has been a prominent theme in the dramatic revival of historical sociology in both its neo-Marxian[7] and neo-Weberian[8] forms and will be explored in later chapters. Weber believed the degree of legitimacy accorded political authority within a system very much depends on that authority's capacity to generate prestige in the wider geopolitical system, or what today we might term "world system." Thus, withdrawal of legitimacy is not just the result of conditions II-A, B, and C in Table 8.2; legitimacy also depends on the "success" and "prestige" of a state in relation to other states.[9]

Political legitimacy is a precarious situation because it relies on the capacity of political authority to meet the needs among system members for defense and attack against external enemies, even during periods of relative peace. Without this sense of "threat" and a corresponding "success" in dealing with this threat, legitimacy lessens. Weber did not argue that legitimacy is always necessary for superordinates to dominate; indeed, there are periods of apathy among members of a population, supported by tradition and routine. There can also be periods of coercive force by superordinates to quell potential rebellion. Nor did Weber argue that "external enemies" must always be present to keep legitimacy revved up; rather, internal conflicts that pose threats can also give legitimacy to political authority. Thus, the very processes that might lead some to withdraw legitimacy and initiate conflict under charismatic leadership can sometimes bolster the legitimacy of political authority, *if* enough other groupings in a society feel threatened. Indeed, Weber argued, political authorities often stir up internal or external "enemies" as a ploy for increasing their legitimacy and power to control the distribution of resources.

But the attention of those with political authority to the external system is not always political. Prestige, per se, can motivate some groupings to encourage military and other forms of contact with other societies. More important, however, are economic interests. Those economic interests—colonial and booty capitalists, privileged traders, financial dealers, arms exporters, and the like—who rely on the state to sustain their viability encourage foreign military

Table 8.3 Weber's Abstracted Propositions on Geopolitics and Conflict

I. The capacity of political authority to dominate a society depends on its legitimacy.

II. The more those with power can sustain a sense of prestige and success in relations with external societies, the greater will be the capacity of leaders to be viewed as legitimate.

III. When productive sectors of a society depend on political authority for their viability, they encourage political authority to engage in military expansion to augment their interests. When successful, such expansion increases the prestige and, hence, the legitimacy of political authority.

IV. When productive sectors do not depend on the state for their viability, they encourage political authority to rely on co-optation rather than on military expansion, and when successful, such co-optation increases prestige and, hence, the legitimacy of political authority.

V. The more those with power can create a sense of threat from external forces, the greater is their capacity to be viewed as legitimate.

VI. The more those with power can create a sense of threat among the majority by internal conflict with a minority, the greater is their capacity to be viewed as legitimate.

VII. When political authority cannot sustain a sense of legitimacy, it becomes vulnerable to outbreaks of internal conflict, and when political authority loses prestige in the external system, it loses legitimacy and becomes more vulnerable to internal conflict.

---

expansion, whereas those economic interests that rely on market dynamics and free trade will usually resist military expansionism because it can hurt domestic productivity, or profits in external markets. Instead, these interests will encourage co–optive efforts through trade relations and market dependencies of external populations on commodities and services provided by these interests.

Table 8.3 presents Weber's argument in more abstract terms; these propositions supplement those in Table 8.2 where Weber sees the loss of legitimacy as increasing the likelihood of conflict. The essential point is not so much that Weber developed a mature theory but, rather, that he stimulated a conflict approach that examined the relationship between internal and external conflict processes.

GEORG SIMMEL AND CONFLICT THEORY

Georg Simmel was committed to developing theoretical statements that captured the *form of basic social processes,* an approach he labeled *formal sociology.* Primarily through his own observations, Simmel sought to extract the essential properties from processes and events in a wide variety of empirical contexts. In turn, abstract statements about these essential properties could be articulated.

Much like Marx, Simmel viewed conflict as ubiquitous and, hence, subject to analysis in formal terms. In his most famous essay on conflict, Simmel devoted considerable effort to analyzing the positive consequences of conflict for the maintenance of social wholes and their subunits.[10] Simmel recognized, of course, that an overly cooperative, consensual, and integrated society would show "no life process," but his analysis of conflict is still loaded in the direction of how conflict promotes solidarity and unification. Thus, unlike Marx, who saw conflict as ultimately becoming violent and revolutionary and leading to the structural change of the system, Simmel quite often analyzed the opposite phenomena—less intense and violent conflicts that promote the solidarity, integration, and orderly change.[11]

Simmel's key ideas on the violence of conflict are summarized in Table 8.4. Proposition I-A somewhat overlaps those developed by Marx. Like Marx, Simmel emphasized that violent conflict is the result of emotional arousal. Such arousal is particularly likely when conflict groups possess a great deal of internal solidarity. As shown in Proposition I-B, Simmel indicated that, coupled with emotional arousal, the extent to which members see the conflict as transcending their personal aims and self-interests increases the likelihood of violent conflict. Proposition II is Simmel's most important because it contradicts Marx's hypothesis that objective consciousness of interests will lead to organization for violent conflict. Simmel argued that the more clearly articulated are the interests of conflict parties, the more clear-cut and focused are their goals; with clearly articulated goals, less combative means, such as bargaining and compromise, are more likely to be used to meet the specific objectives of the group. Thus, for Simmel, consciousness of common interests can, under unspecified conditions, lead to highly instrumental and nonviolent conflict. In the context of labor-management relations, for example, Simmel's proposition is more accurate than Marx's prediction because violence has more often accompanied labor-management disputes in the initial formation of unions, when interests and goals are not well articulated. As interests become clarified, violent conflict has been increasingly replaced by less violent forms of social negotiation.[12]

The consequences of conflict for (1) the conflict parties and (2) the systemic whole in which the conflict occurs are summarized in Propositions III and IV. Propositions III-A, B, C, and D summarize Simmel's ideas about the functions of conflict for the respective parties to the conflict. Conflict increases the formation of clear-cut group boundaries, the centralization of authority, the control of deviance and dissent, and the enhancement of social solidarity within conflict parties.

Proposition IV, on the consequences of conflict for the social whole, provides an important qualification to Marx's analysis. Marx visualized initially mild conflicts as intensifying as the combatants become increasingly polarized, ultimately resulting in violent conflict that would lead to radical social change in the system. In contrast, Simmel argued that conflicts of low intensity and high frequency in systems of high degrees of interdependence do not necessarily intensify or lead to radical social change. On the contrary, these conflicts release tensions and become normatively regulated, thereby promoting stability

Table 8.4 Simmel's Abstracted Propositions on Conflict Processes

I. The level of violence in conflict increases when
   A. The parties to the conflict have a high degree of emotional involvement, which, in turn, is related to the respective levels of solidarity among parties to the conflict.
   B. The membership of each conflict party perceives the conflict to transcend their individual self-interests, which, in turn, is related to the extent to which the conflict is about value-infused issues. *principle of the matter above & beyond justome.*
II. The level of violence in conflict is reduced when the conflict is instrumental and perceived by the conflict parties to be a means to clear-cut and delimited goals.
III. Conflict will generate the following among the parties to a conflict:
   A. Clear group boundaries.
   B. Centralization of authority and power.
   C. Decreased tolerance of deviance and dissent.
   D. Increased internal solidarity among memberships of each party, but particularly for members of minority parties and for groups engaged in self defense.
IV. Conflict will have integrative consequences for the social whole when
   A. Conflict is frequent, low in intensity, and low in violence, which, in turn, allows disputants to release hostilities. *let off steam* *(ex: letters to editors in Strol)*
   B. Conflict occurs in a system whose members and subunits reveal high levels of functional interdependence, which, in turn, encourages the creation of normative agreements to regulate the conflict so that the exchange of resources is not disrupted.
   C. Conflict produces coalitions among various conflicting parties. *alliances*

Brings society together

in social systems. Further, with the increasing organization of the conflicting groups, and the formation of coalitions among conflict groups, violence will decrease as their goals become better articulated. The consequence of such organization and articulation of interests will be a greater disposition to initiate milder forms of conflict, involving competition, bargaining, and compromise.

THE RE-EMERGENCE OF CONFLICT THEORY IN THE TWENTIETH CENTURY

Ralf Dahrendorf's Dialectical Theory

For the first half of the twentieth century, the conflict ideas contained in the German masters had not been explicitly incorporated into the mainstream of sociological theory, especially in America. Marxist scholarship was particularly recessive, being repressed in America by the anti–communism of the Cold War era. The reinvigoration of conflict theory was couched as a critique of the excesses of functionalism, which was often accused of being a conservative and supportive ideology of the status quo.

In the late 1950s, Ralf Dahrendorf persistently argued that the Parsonian scheme, and functionalism in general, presented an overly consensual, integrated, and static vision of society—in his words a "utopia."[13] In Dahrendorf's view, society has two faces—one of consensus, the other of conflict. It was time, Dahrendorf asserted, to begin analysis of society's ugly face and abandon the utopian image created by functionalism.

The model that emerged from this theoretical calling is a dialectical conflict perspective, which still represents one of the best efforts to incorporate the insights of Marx and (to a lesser extent) Weber and Simmel into a coherent set of theoretical propositions. Dahrendorf believed that the process of institutionalization involves the creation of *imperatively coordinated associations* (hereafter referred to as *ICAs*) that, in criteria not specified, represent a distinguishable organization of roles. This organization is characterized by power relationships, with some clusters of roles having power to extract conformity from others. Dahrendorf was somewhat vague on this point, but it appears that any social unit—from a small group or formal organization to a community or an entire society—could be considered an ICA for analytical purposes if an organization of roles displaying power differentials exists. Furthermore, although power denotes the coercion of some by others, these power relations in ICAs tend to become legitimated and can therefore be viewed as authority relations in which some positions have the "accepted" or "normative right" to dominate others. Dahrendorf thus conceived of the social order as maintained by processes creating authority relations in the various types of ICAs existing throughout all layers of social systems.[14]

At the same time, however, power and authority are the scarce resources over which subgroups within a designated ICA compete and fight. They are thus the major sources of conflict and change in these institutionalized patterns. This conflict is ultimately a reflection of where clusters of roles in an ICA stand in relation to authority, because the "objective interests" inherent in any role are a direct function of whether that role possesses authority and power over other roles. However, even though roles in ICAs possess varying degrees of authority, any particular ICA can be typified as just two basic types of roles, ruling and ruled. The ruling cluster of roles has an interest in preserving the status quo, and the ruled cluster has an interest in redistributing power, or authority. Those who are ruled constitute only a *quasi group* because they are not fully aware of their interests to challenge the system of authority, nor are they organized to pursue conflict with those in authority.

Under certain specified conditions, however, awareness of these contradictory interests increases, with the result that ICAs polarize into two conflict groups, each now aware of its objective interests, which then engage in a contest for authority. The resolution of this contest or conflict involves the redistribution of authority in the ICA, thus making conflict the source of change in social systems. In turn, the redistribution of authority represents the institutionalization of a new cluster of ruling and ruled roles that, under certain conditions, polarize into two interest groups that initiate another contest for authority. Social reality is thus typified by this unending cycle of conflict over authority within the various types of ICAs that constitute the social world.

In Dahrendorf's theoretical scheme, the key variables are (1) the degree of conflict-group formation, (2) the degree of intensity of the conflict, (3) the degree of violence of the conflict, (4) the degree of change of social structure, and (5) the rate of such change. As is evident in Table 8.5,[15] Dahrendorf's propositions appear to be an elaboration of those developed by Marx, but with some important qualifications. Like Marx, Dahrendorf saw conflict as related to subordinates' growing awareness of their interests and formation into conflict groups (Proposition I). Such awareness and group formation are a positive function of the degree to which (a) the technical conditions (leadership and unifying ideology), (b) the political conditions (capacity to organize), and (c) the social conditions (ability to communicate) are met. These ideas clearly come from Marx's discussion. However, as shown in Proposition II, Dahrendorf borrows from Simmel and contradicts Marx, emphasizing that if groups are *not* well organized—that is, if the technical, political, and social conditions are not met—then conflict is likely to be emotionally involving. Then Dahrendorf borrowed from Weber (Proposition III) by stressing that the superimposition of rewards—that is, the degree of correlation among those who enjoy privilege (power, wealth, and prestige)—also increases the emotional involvement of subordinates who pursue conflict. Proposition IV shows that Dahrendorf also takes as much from Weber as from Marx. Dahrendorf believed that the lack of mobility into positions of authority escalates the emotional involvement of subordinates. Proposition V is clearly from Simmel and contradicts Marx, in that the violence of conflict is related to the lack of organization and clear articulation of interests. But in Proposition VI, Dahrendorf returns to Marx's emphasis that sudden escalation in people's perception of deprivation—that is, relative deprivation—increases the likelihood of violent conflict. In Proposition VII, however, Dahrendorf returns to Simmel and argues that violence is very much related to the capacity of a system to develop regulatory procedures for dealing with grievances and releasing tensions. And in Propositions VIII and IX, Dahrendorf moves again to Marx's emphasis on how conflict produces varying rates and degrees of structural change in a social system.

Dahrendorf was not the first conflict theorist of the midcentury, but he soon became the most influential. Primarily because of his attack on Parsonian functionalism, he gained wide notoriety and, hence, a receptive audience for his reanalysis of Marx, which incorporated important qualifications from Simmel and Weber. Orthodox Marxists were very critical of Dahrendorf's abstract and analytical approach because in their view Dahrendorf had taken much of the substance out of Marx's analysis. Dahrendorf had stripped Marx, in their view, of the very concepts that made Marx's approach so important—concepts like proletariat, bourgeoisie, capitalism, exploitation, value theory of labor, and the like. Still, Dahrendorf did liberate conflict theory from Marxian parochialism, making it appealing to a wider sociological audience. At the same

Table 8.5 Dahrendorf's Abstract Propositions

I. Conflict is likely to occur as members of quasi groups in ICAs can become aware of their objective interests and form a conflict group, which, in turn, are related to

   A. The *technical* conditions of organization which, in turn, depend on

      1. The formation of a leadership cadre among quasi groups.

      2. The codification of an idea system, or charter.

   B. The *political* conditions of organization, which are dependent on dominant groups permitting organization of opposed interests.

   C. The *social* conditions of organization, which, in turn, are related to

      1. Opportunities for members of quasi groups to communicate.

      2. Opportunities for recruiting members.

II. The less the technical, political, and social conditions of organization are met, the more intense the conflict will be.

III. The more the distribution of authority and other rewards are associated with each other (superimposed), the more intense the conflict will be.

IV. The less the mobility between super- and subordinate groups, the more intense the conflict will be.

V. The less the technical, political, and social conditions or organizations are met, the more violent the conflict will be.

VI. The more the deprivation of the subjugated in the distribution of rewards shifts from an absolute to a relative basis, the more violent the conflict will be.

VII. The less is the ability of conflict groups to develop regulatory agreements, the more violent the conflict will be.

VIII. The more intense is the conflict, the more will be the degree of structural change and reorganization.

IX. The more intense is the conflict, the more will be the degree of structural change and reorganization.

---

time that Marxists were criticizing Dahrendorf, another conflict theorist—Lewis Coser—with more sympathy for functional sociology was proposing a less extreme alternative to dialectical approaches. Drawing more from Simmel than Marx, Coser proposed a functional theory of conflict.

Lewis Coser's Conflict Functionalism

Lewis Coser published a major work on conflict before Ralf Dahrendorf did. Yet, because this work had a functional flavor and borrowed from Simmel more than Marx, it was not initially seen as a devastating critique of functionalism in quite the same way as Dahrendorf's early polemic. Still, in his more functional version of conflict theory, Coser launched what became the standard polemic against functionalism: Conflict is not given sufficient attention, and related phenomena such as deviance and dissent are too easily viewed as "pathological" for the equilibrium of the social system.[16] Although Coser consistently maintained that functional theorizing "has too often neglected the dimensions of power and interest," he did not follow either Marx's or Dahrendorf's emphasis on the disruptive consequences of violent conflict.

Table 8.6 Coser's Propositions on the Causes of Conflict

I. Subordinate members in a system of inequality are more likely to initiate conflict as they question the legitimacy of the existing distribution of scarce resources, which, in turn, is caused by

   A. Few channels for redressing grievances.

   B. Low rates of mobility to more privileged positions.

II. Subordinates are most likely to initiate conflict with superordinates as their sense of relative deprivation and, hence, injustice increases, which, in turn, is related to

   A. The extent to which socialization experiences of subordinates do not generate internal ego constraints.

   B. The failure of superordinates to apply external constraints on subordinates.

Rather, Coser sought to correct Dahrendorf's analytical excesses by emphasizing the integrative and "adaptability" functions of conflict for social systems.[17] Thus, Coser justified his efforts by criticizing functionalism[18] for ignoring conflict and by criticizing conflict theory for underemphasizing the functions of conflict. In so doing, he turned to Georg Simmel's view of conflict as promoting social integration of the social systems, or at least of some of its critical parts.

Coser's analysis then proceeded as follows: (1) Imbalances in the integration of system parts lead to (2) the outbreak of varying types of conflict among these parts, which in turn causes (3) temporary reintegration of the system, which leads to (4) increased flexibility in the system's structure, increased capability to resolve future imbalances through conflict, and increased capacity to adapt to changing conditions. Coser executed this approach by developing, at least implicitly in his discursive argument, a variety of propositions that are extracted and presented in Tables 8.6 through 8.10. He began with the causes of conflict (Table 8.6), turned to the issue of violence in conflict (Table 8.7), moved next to the duration of conflict (Table 8.8), and finally explored the functions of conflict (Tables 8.9 and 8.10).

Much like Weber, Coser emphasized (shown in Proposition I of Table 8.6) that the withdrawal of legitimacy from an existing system of inequality is a critical precondition for conflict.[19] In contrast, dialectical theorists such as Dahrendorf tended to view the causes of conflict as residing in "contradictions" or "conflicts of interest." In such dialectical theories, as subordinates become aware of their interests, they pursue conflict; hence, the major theoretical task is to specify the conditions raising levels of awareness. But Coser argued that conflicts of interest are likely to be exposed only after the deprived withdraw legitimacy. Coser emphasized that the social order is maintained by some degree of consensus over existing sociocultural arrangements and that "disorder" through conflict occurs only when conditions decrease this consensus. Two such conditions are specified in Propositions I-A and I-B of Table 8.6, both of which owe their inspiration more to Weber than to Marx. When channels for expressing grievances do not exist and when the deprived's desire

Table 8.7 Coser's Propositions on the Violence of Conflict

   I. When groups engage in conflict over realistic issues (obtainable goals), they are more likely to seek compromises over the means to realize their interests, and hence, the less violent the conflict will be.

  II. When groups engage in conflict over nonrealistic issues, the greater is the level of emotional arousal and involvement in the conflict, and hence, the more violent the conflict will be, especially when

   A. Conflict occurs over core values.

   B. Conflict endures over time.

 III. When functional interdependence among social units is low, the less available are the institutional means for absorbing conflicts and tensions, and hence, the more violent the conflict will be.

---

for membership in higher ranks is thwarted, the withdrawal of legitimacy becomes more likely.

As Proposition II in Table 8.6 indicates, the withdrawal of legitimacy, in itself, is not likely to result in conflict. People must first become emotionally aroused. The theoretical task then becomes one of specifying the conditions that translate the withdrawal of legitimacy into emotional arousal, instead of some other emotional state such as apathy and resignation. Here Coser drew inspiration from Marx's notion of relative deprivation. For, as Marx observed and as several empirical studies have documented, absolute deprivation does not always foster revolt.[20] When people's expectations for a better future suddenly begin to exceed perceived avenues for realizing these expectations, only then do they become sufficiently aroused to pursue conflict. The level of arousal will, in turn, be influenced by their commitments to the existing system, by the degree to which they have developed strong internal constraints, and by the nature and amount of social control in a system. Such propositions, for example, lead to predictions that, in systems with absolute dictators who ruthlessly repress the masses, revolt by the masses is less likely than in systems where some freedoms have been granted and where the deprived have been led to believe that things will be getting better. Under these conditions the withdrawal of legitimacy can be accompanied by released passions and emotions.

Coser's most important propositions on the level of violence in a conflict are presented in Table 8.7.[21] As most functional theorists emphasized, Coser's Proposition I in Table 8.7 is directed at specifying the conditions under which conflict will be less violent. In contrast, dialectical theorists, such as Marx, often pursued just the opposite: specifying the conditions under which conflict will be more violent. Yet, the inverse of Coser's first proposition can indicate a condition under which conflict will be violent. The key concept in this proposition is "realistic issues." Coser reasoned that realistic conflict involves the pursuit of specific aims against real sources of hostility, with some estimation of the costs to be incurred in such pursuit. As noted earlier, Simmel

Table 8.8 Coser's Propositions on the Duration of Conflict

I. Conflict will be prolonged when
   A. The goals of the opposing parties to a conflict are expansive.
   B. The degree of consensus over the goals of conflict is low.
   C. The parties in a conflict cannot easily interpret their adversary's symbolic points of victory and defeat.
II. Conflict will be shortened when
   A. Leaders of conflicting parties perceive that complete attainment of goals is possible only at very high costs, which, in turn, is related to
      1. The equality of the power between conflicting groups.
      2. The clarity of indexes of defeat or victory in a conflict.
   B. Leaders' capacity to persuade followers to terminate conflict, which, in turn, is related to
      1. Centralization of power in conflict parties.
      2. Integration within conflict parties.

recognized that, when clear goals are sought, compromise and conciliation are likely alternatives to violence. Coser restated this proposition (shown in Proposition II in Table 8.7) on conflict over "nonrealistic issues," such as ultimate values, beliefs, ideology, and vaguely defined class interests. When nonrealistic, the conflict will be violent. Such nonrealism is particularly likely when conflict is about core values, which emotionally mobilize participants and make them unwilling to compromise (Proposition II-A). Moreover, if conflict endures for a long time, it becomes increasingly nonrealistic as parties become emotionally involved, as ideologies become codified, and as "the enemy" is portrayed in increasingly negative terms (Proposition II-B). Proposition III shows a more structural variable to the analysis of conflict violence. In systems in which there are high degrees of functional interdependence among actors—that is, where there are mutual exchanges and cooperation—conflict is less likely to be violent.

As shown in the propositions of Table 8.8, Coser underscored that conflicts with a broad range of goals or with vague goals will be prolonged.[22] When goals are limited and articulated, it is possible to know when they have been attained. With perception of attainment, the conflict can be terminated. Conversely, with a wide variety or long list of goals, a sense of attainment is less likely to occur—thus prolonging the conflict. Coser also emphasized that knowledge of what would symbolically constitute victory and defeat will influence the length of conflict. If the parties do not have the ability to recognize defeat or victory, conflict is likely to be prolonged to a point where one party destroys the other. Leadership has important effects on conflict processes; the more leaders can perceive that complete attainment of goals is not possible and the greater their ability is to convince followers to terminate conflict, the less prolonged the conflict will be.

Table 8.9 Coser's Propositions on the Functions of Conflict for the Respective Parties

I. The more violent or intense is the conflict, the more the conflict will generate
  A. Clear-cut boundaries for each conflict party.
  B. Centralized decision-making structures for each conflict party, especially when these parties are structurally differentiated.
  C. Structural and ideological solidarity among members of each conflict party, especially when the conflict is perceived to affect the welfare of all segments of the conflict parties.
  D. Suppression of dissent and deviance within each conflict party as well as forced conformity to norms and values.

II. The more conflict between parties leads centers of power to force conformity within conflict groups, the greater is the accumulation of hostilities and the more likely is internal group conflict to surface in the long run.

Coser divided his analysis of the functions of conflict along lines similar to those by Simmel: the functions of conflict for (1) the respective parties to the conflict, and (2) the systemic whole in which the conflict occurs. In the propositions listed in Table 8.9, the intensity of conflict—that is, people's involvement in and commitment to pursue the conflict—and its level of violence increase the demarcation of boundaries (Proposition I-A), centralization of authority (Proposition I-B), structural and ideological solidarity (Proposition I-C), and suppression of dissent and deviance (Proposition I-D) within each of the conflict parties.[23] Conflict intensity is presumably functional because it increases integration, although centralization of power as well as the suppression of deviance and dissent create malintegrative pressures in the long run (see Proposition II). Thus, there appears to be an inherent dialectic in conflict-group unification—one that creates pressures toward disunification. Unfortunately, Coser did not specify the conditions under which these malintegrative pressures are likely to surface. In focusing on positive functions—that is, forces promoting integration—the analysis ignored a promising area of inquiry. This bias becomes even more evident when Coser shifts attention to the functions of conflict for the systemic whole within which the conflict occurs. These propositions are listed in Table 8.10.[24]

Coser's propositions are not presented in their full complexity in Table 8.10, but the essentials of his analysis are clear. In Proposition I, complex systems that have a large number of interdependencies and exchanges are more likely to have frequent conflicts that are less emotionally involving and violent than conflicts in those systems that are less complex and in which tensions accumulate. The nature of interdependence, Coser argued, causes conflicts to erupt frequently, but, because they emerge periodically, emotions do not build to the point that violence is inevitable. Conversely, systems in which there are low degrees of functional interdependence will often polarize into hostile camps; when conflict does erupt, it will be intense and violent. In Proposition II, frequent conflicts of low intensity and violence are seen to have certain

Table 8.10 Coser's Propositions on the Functions of Conflict for the Social Whole

---

I. The more differentiated and functionally interdependent are the units in a system, the more likely is conflict to be frequent but of low degrees of intensity and violence.

II. The lower are the intensity and violence of conflicts, the more likely are conflicts to

   A. Increase the level of innovation and creativity of system units.

   B. Release hostilities before they polarize system units.

   C. Promote normative regulation of conflict relations.

   D. Increase awareness of realistic issues.

   E. Increase the number of associative coalitions among social units.

III. The more conflict promotes II-A through II-E, the greater will be the level of internal social integration of the system whole and the greater will be its capacity to adapt to its external environment.

---

positive functions. First, such frequent and low-intensity conflicts will force those in conflict to reassess and reorganize their actions (Proposition II-A). Second, these conflicts will release tensions and hostilities before they build to a point where adversaries become polarized around nonrealistic issues (Proposition II-B). Third, frequent conflicts of low intensity and violence encourage the development of normative procedures—laws, courts, mediating agencies, and the like—to regulate tensions (Proposition II-C). Fourth, these kinds of conflicts also increase a sense of realism over what the conflict is about. That is, frequent conflicts in which intensity and violence are kept under control allow conflict parties to articulate their interests and goals, thereby allowing them to bargain and compromise (Proposition II-D). Fifth, conflicts promote coalitions among units that are threatened by the action of one party or another. If conflicts are frequent and have low intensity and violence, such coalitions come and go, thereby promoting flexible alliances (Proposition II-E). If conflicts are infrequent and emotions accumulate, however, coalitions often polarize threatened parties into ever more hostile camps, with the result that, when conflict does occur, it is violent. And Proposition III simply states Coser's functional conclusion that, when conflicts are frequent and when violence and intensity are reduced, conflict will promote flexible coordination within the system and increased capacity to adjust and adapt to environmental circumstances. This increase in flexibility and adaptation is possible because of the processes listed in Proposition II-A through II-E.

Coser borrowed and extended Georg Simmel's initial insights. In its time, Coser's functionalism represented an important corrective to more Marxian-inspired dialectical approaches. None of Coser's ideas needed to be expressed in the language of functionalism, but the tactic was successful and enabled Coser to postulate an alternative to Marxian sociology. Today, Coser's and Simmel's ideas are incorporated into views of conflict processes that have abandoned the language of functionalism, and it is difficult to see an explicitly functional emphasis in any contemporary conflict theory.

CONCLUSION

Dahrendorf's critique of Talcott Parsons's functional approach was, for its time, a classic. Coser's more functional approach, borrowing from Simmel, has had a less enduring impact. But both Coser's and Dahrendorf's work indicated that theorizing in sociology was about to change. In particular, Dahrenforf's critique signaled the beginning of the end to the dominance of functional theorizing, and it ushered in a new era of conflict theorizing. For a time, virtually all theorizing seemed to call itself a "conflict" approach, and indeed, conflict theory in the 1970s and 1980s seemed to become almost as hegemonic as functionalism had been in the 1950s and 1960s. All this overemphasis on conflict eventually receded, but from this exuberance about rediscovering that the social world is filled with conflict, several important streams of theorizing emerged. We will focus primarily on trends inspired by Marx and Weber, whose work still informs all theorizing in sociology. In the area of conflict sociology, this influence is even more dramatic.

NOTES

1. Herbert Spencer, *The Principles of Sociology* (New York: Appleton, 1898; originally published in serial form between 1874–1896). Spencer argued that war between populations had been an important evolutionary force because the better-organized society usually won and "selected out" the weaker one or at least brought it to the level of organization of the victor. This kind of geopolitical analysis became, in the latter half of the twentieth century, an ever-more prominent form of conflict theorizing.

2. See, for example, David Lockwood, "Some Remarks on 'The Social System,'" *British Journal of Sociology* 7 (1956), pp. 134–146; Ralf Dahrendorf, "Out of Utopia: Toward a Reorientation of Sociological Analysis," *American Journal of Sociology* 744 (1958), pp. 115–127.

3. In Karl Marx's and Friedrich Engels's *The Communist Manifesto* (New York: International, 1971; originally published in 1847) are the key ideas in these propositions. Further amplification of these ideas came with Marx's *Capital: A Critical Analysis of Capitalist Production,* vol. 1 (New York:

International, 1967; originally published in 1867). The critical and polemical substance of these and other works will be explored in Chapter 12 on the emergence of critical theory.

4. For criticism of efforts of such abstract renderings of Marx, see Richard P. Appelbaum, "Marx's Theory of the Falling Rate of Profit: Towards a Dialectical Analysis of Structural Social Change," *American Sociological Review* 43 (February 1978), pp. 64–73.

5. For a fuller discussion, see Jonathan H. Turner, Leonard Beeghley, and Charles Powers, *The Emergence of Sociological Theory* (Belmont, CA: Wadsworth, 1998), pp. 213–229. For original sources, see Max Weber, *Economy and Society* (New York: Bedminster, 1968).

6. Weber, *Economy and Society* (cited in note 5), pp. 901–1372, especially pp. 901–920.

7. For example, see Immanuel Wallerstein, *The Modern World System,* 3 volumes (New York: Academic, 1974–1989).

8. For example, see Randall Collins, *Weberian Sociological Theory* (Cambridge: Cambridge University Press, 1986); Michael Mann, *The Sources of Social Power,* vol. 1 (New York: Cambridge University Press, 1986); Theda Skocpol, *States and Social Revolutions* (New York: Cambridge University Press, 1979). The last work combines the analysis of internal revolution and geopolitics, describing the former as a potential consequence of failed policies in the latter.

9. Ibid. (all references in note 8).

10. All subsequent references to this work are taken from Georg Simmel, *Conflict and the Web of Group Affiliation,* trans. K.H. Wolff (Glencoe, IL: Free Press, 1956).

11. Pierre van den Berghe has argued that a dialectical model of conflict is ultimately one in which unification, albeit temporary, emerges out of conflict. Yet, the differences between Marx and Simmel have inspired vastly different theoretical perspectives in contemporary sociology. See Pierre van den Berghe, "Dialectic and Functionalism: Toward a Theoretical Synthesis," *American Sociological Review* 28 (1963), pp. 695–705.

12. Admittedly, Marx's late awareness of the union movement in the United States forced him to begin pondering this possibility, but he did not incorporate this insight into his theoretical scheme.

13. Ralf Dahrendorf, "Out of Utopia: Toward a Reorientation of Sociological Analysis," *American Journal of Sociology* 64 (1958), p. 127.

14. Ralf Dahrendorf, "Toward a Theory of Social Conflict," *Journal of Conflict Resolution* 2 (1958), pp. 170–183; *Class and Class Conflict in Industrial Society* (Stanford, CA: Stanford University Press, 1959), pp. 168–169; *Gesellschaft un Freiheit* (Munich: R. Piper, 1961); *Essays in the Theory of Society* (Stanford, CA: Stanford University Press, 1967).

15. The propositions listed in the table differ from those in a list provided by Dahrendorf, *Class and Class Conflict* (cited in note 14), pp. 239–240, in two respects: (1) They are phrased consistently as statements of covariance, and (2) they are phrased somewhat more abstractly without reference to "class," which in this particular work was Dahrendorf's primary concern.

16. Lewis A. Coser, *The Functions of Social Conflict* (London: Free Press, 1956).

17. A listing of some of Coser's prominent works, to be used in subsequent analysis, reveals the functional flavor of his conflict perspective: *Functions of Social Conflict* (cited in note 16); "Some Social Functions of Violence" *Annals of the American Academy of Political and Social Science* 364 (1960), pp. 1–15; "Some Functions of Deviant Behavior and Normative Flexibility," *American Journal of Sociology* 68 (1962), pp. 172–181; and "The Functions of Dissent," in *The Dynamics of Dissent* (New York: Grune & Stratton, 1968), pp. 158–170. Other prominent works with less revealing titles but critical substance include "Social Conflict and the Theory of Social Change," *British Journal of Sociology* 8 (1957), pp. 197–207; "Violence and the Social Structure," in *Science and Psychoanalysis,* ed. J. Masserman, vol. 7 (New York: Grune & Stratton, 1963), pp. 30–42. These and other essays are collected in Coser's *Continuities in the Study of Social Conflict* (New York, Free Press, 1967). One should also consult his *Masters of Sociological Thought* (New York: Harcourt Brace Jovanovich, 1977).

18. Lewis Coser, "Durkheim's Conservatism and Its Implications for His Sociological Theory," in *Émile Durkheim, 1858–1917: A Collection of Essays,* ed. K.H. Wolff (Columbus: Ohio State University Press, 1960); also reprinted in Coser's *Continuities in the Study of Social Conflict* (cited in note 18).

19. The propositions in Table 8.6 are extracted from *Functions of Social Conflict* (cited in note 16), pp. 8–385; "Social Conflict and the Theory of Social Change" (cited in note 17), pp. 197–207; and "Violence and Social Structure" (cited in note 17).

20. James Davies, "Toward a Theory of Revolution," *American Journal of Sociology* 27 (1962), pp. 5–19; Ted Robert Gurr, *Why Men Rebel* (Princeton, NJ: Princeton University Press, 1970); and "Sources of Rebellion in Western Societies: Some Quantitative Evidence," *Annals of American Academy of Political and Social Science* 38 (1973), pp. 495–501.

21. These propositions are taken from Coser's *Functions of Social Conflict* (cited in note 16), pp. 45–50. Again, they have been made more formal than Coser's more discursive text.

22. These propositions come from Coser, "The Termination of Conflict," in *Continuities* (cited in note 17), pp. 37–52; and *Functions of Social Conflict* (cited in note 16), pp. 20, 48–55, 59, 128–133.

23. These propositions are taken from Coser, *Functions of Social Conflict* (cited in note 16), pp. 37–38, 45, 69–72, 92–95.

24. Ibid., pp. 45–48. See the following works cited in note 16: "Social Conflict and the Theory of Social Change," "Some Social Functions of Violence," and "The Functions of Dissent."

9

Neo-Weberian Conflict Theory: Randall Collins

D uring the last thirty years, Randall Collins has consistently employed a conflict approach, emphasizing that inequalities inevitably set into motion conflict processes, some of which are relatively mild and routinized, but many of which can become more violent. As with any theorist committed to science, Collins sees the goal of a sociological theory of conflict as using a few key ideas to generate propositions explaining the full range of social processes in human interaction and organization. In this chapter, we will emphasize Collins's early Weberian thrust; in later chapters, his use of other theoretical traditions will be highlighted.

THE MICRO BASIS
OF SOCIAL ORGANIZATION

Randall Collins has developed a conflict approach[1] that, at its core, is Weberian but that adds elements from Émile Durkheim's analysis of rituals, Erving Goffman's dramaturgy (Chapter 24), conversation analysis within ethnomethodology (Chapter 25), and other micro-level theoretical perspectives. Collins's argument is that macro-level phenomena are, ultimately, created and sustained by micro encounters among individuals.[2] In essence, large and long-term social structures are built from what he terms *interaction rituals* that have been strung together over time in complex patterns. If true understanding of social reality is to be achieved by sociological theorizing, what transpires in face-to-face interaction must be examined, even if this examination only involves sampling of interaction rituals within a macrostructure.[3]

Interaction rituals occur when individuals are physically co-present, when these individuals reveal a common focus of attention, when they develop a common emotional mood, and when they represent their common focus and mood with symbols (words, objects, phrases, speech styles, and the like) and develop a sense of moral righteousness about these symbols. The dynamics of these interaction rituals revolve around several elements. First, individuals bring to a face-to-face encounter *cultural capital,* or resources that they command in the broader society (for example, power and authority, knowledge, education, network ties and alliances, experiences) or that they accumulated in past interactions of a particular type (for example, memories, information, knowledge, or other resources that they can use again when an interaction is reconstituted). Second, individuals bring a level of *emotional energy* to the interaction, which, in turn, is related to (a) the level of cultural capital they possess, (b) the power and prestige or status that they enjoy in the interaction situation, and (c) their memories about the levels of positive emotions or enhanced cultural capital received from the previous time the interaction occurred. Third, individuals monitor situations along several lines: (a) the respective resources of other actors relative to self; (b) the number of others present in a situation; (c) the number of alternative options to the present interaction that are available to self and others; (d) the amount of work-practical, ceremonial, and social content of the interaction; and most important, (e) the payoffs in the amount of positive emotional energy and augmentation of cultural capital likely to be gained from a person's assessment of the inequalities in resources, the alternatives that might be pursued, the number of others presently monitoring the situation, the nature of the situation (as social, work-practical, or ceremonial), and the experiences (emotional energy and cultural capital received) in previous interactions of this nature.

These micro-level concepts have been extended during the last several decades into a more robust theory of emotions and interaction (see Chapter 26), but in his first major work, *Conflict Sociology,* Collins's approach was Weberian in two senses. First, he moved rapidly from the analysis of micro social processes to meso-level social forces, such as stratification and organizations, and then to truly macro-level processes operating at the societal and intersocietal level. Second, although his intent was to retain elements of the micro sociology, the key concepts Collins used to explain the dynamics of interaction rituals become ever more recessive as analysis became ever more macro. The result is a creative neo-Weberian theory of conflict processes.

CONFLICT SOCIOLOGY

In *Conflict Sociology,* Collins proposed the following steps for building social theory. First, examine typical real-life situations in which people encounter one another. Second, focus on the material arrangements that affect interaction—

the physical layout of situations, the means and modes of communication, and the available tools, weapons, and goods. Third, assess the relative resources that people bring to, use in, or extract from encounters. Fourth, entertain the general hypotheses that those with resources press their advantage, that those without resources seek the best deal they can get under the circumstances, and that stability and change are to be explained through the lineups and shifts in the distribution of resources. Fifth, assume that cultural symbols—ideas, beliefs, norms, values, and the like—are used to represent the interests of those parties who have the resources to make their views prevail. Sixth, look for the general and generic features of particular cases so that more abstract propositions can be extracted from the empirical particulars of a situation.

Collins is particularly concerned with the encounter, with the distribution of individuals in physical space, with their respective capital or resources to use in exchanges, and with inequalities in resources. The respective resources of individuals are critical: *Power* is the capacity to coerce or to have others do so on one's behalf, *material resources* are wealth and the control of money as well as property or the capacity to control the physical setting and people's place in it, and *symbolic resources* are the respective levels of linguistic and conversational resources as well as the capacity to use cultural ideas, such as ideologies, values, and beliefs, for one's purposes.

A central consideration in all Collins's propositions is *social density,* or the number of people co-present in a situation where an encounter takes place. Social density is, of course, part of the macrostructure because it is typically the result of past chains of interaction. But it can also be a "material resource" that some individuals can use to their advantage. Thus, the interaction in an encounter will be most affected by the participants' relative resources and the density or number of individuals co-present. These variables influence the two underlying micro dynamics in Collins's scheme, talk and ritual.

Talk and Ritual

Collins sees talk as the emission of verbal and nonverbal gestures that carry meaning and that are used to communicate with others and to sustain (or create) a common sense of reality.[4] Talk is one of the key symbolic resources of individuals in encounters, and much of what transpires among interacting individuals is talk and the use of this cultural capital to develop their respective lines of conduct. As can be seen in Proposition I in Table 9.1, the likelihood that people will talk is related to their sheer co-presence: If others are near, a person is likely to strike up a conversation. More important sociologically are conversations that are part of a "chain" of previous encounters. If people felt good about a past conversation, they will usually make efforts to have another; if they perceive each other's resources, especially symbolic or cultural but also material ones, as desirable, then they will seek to talk again. And if they have developed ritualized interaction that affirms their common group membership, they will be likely to enact those rituals again. As Proposition II indicates, conversations among equals who share common levels of resources will be more personal, flexible, and long-term because people feel comfortable with

Table 9.1 Key Propositions on Conditions Producing Talk and Conversation

I. The likelihood of talk and conversational exchanges among individuals is a positive and additive function of (a) the degree of their physical co-presence, (b) the emotional gratifications retained from their previous conversational exchanges, (c) the perceived attractiveness of their respective resources, and (d) their level of previous ritual activity.

II. The greater the degree of equality and similarity that exists in the resources of individuals, the more likely conversational exchanges are to be (a) personal, (b) flexible, and (c) long-term.

III. The greater the level of inequality that exists in the resources of individuals, the more likely conversational exchanges are to be (a) impersonal, (b) highly routinized, and (c) short-term.

IV. The greater the amount of talk among individuals, especially among equals, the more likely are (a) strong, positive emotions; (b) sentiments of liking; (c) common agreements, moods, outlooks, and beliefs; and (d) strong social attachments sustained by rituals.

such conversations. As a result, the encounter raises their levels of emotional energy and increases their cultural capital. That is, they are eager to talk again and to pick up where they left off. However, the nature of talk in an encounter changes dramatically when there is inequality in the resources of the participants. As shown in Proposition III, subordinates will try to avoid wasting or losing emotional energy and spending their cultural capital by keeping the interaction brief, formal, and highly ritualized with trite and inexpensive words. Yet, as Proposition IV indicates, even under conditions of inequality and even more when equality exists, people who interact and talk in repeated encounters will tend, over time, to develop positive sentiments and will have positive emotional feelings. Moreover, they will also converge in their definitions of situations and develop common moods, outlooks, beliefs, and ideas. And, finally, they will be likely to develop strong attachments and a sense of group solidarity, which is sustained through rituals.

Thus, the essence of interaction is talk and ritual as mediated by an exchange dynamic; as chains of encounters are linked together over time, conversations take on a more personal and also a ritualized character that results from and at the same time reinforces the growing sense of group solidarity among individuals. Such is the case because the individuals have "invested" their cultural capital (conversational resources) and have derived positive feelings from being defined as group members. Collins's intent is thus clear: to view social structure as the linking together of encounters through talk and ritual. This basic view of the micro reality of social life pervades all Collins's sociological theory, especially as he began the analysis of inequalities in social life.

Deference and Demeanor

Inequality and stratification are structures only in the sense of being temporal chains of interaction rituals and exchanges among varying numbers of people with different levels of resources. Thus, to understand these structures, we must examine what people actually do across time and in space. One thing that people do in interaction is exhibit deference and demeanor. Collins and co-author Joan Annett define *deference* as the process of manipulating gestures to show respect to others, or, if one is in a position to command respect, the process of gesture manipulation is to elicit respect from others.[5] The actual manipulation of gestures is termed *demeanor.* Deference and demeanor are, therefore, intimately connected to each other. They are also tied to talk and rituals because talk involves the use of gestures and because deference and demeanor tend to become ritualized. Hence, deference and demeanor can be visualized as one form of talk and ritual activity—a form that is most evident in those interactions that create and sustain inequalities among people.

As would be expected, Collins visualizes several variables as central to understanding deference and demeanor:

1. Inequality in resources, particularly wealth and power.
2. Social density variables revolving around the degree to which behaviors are under the "surveillance of others" in a situation.
3. Social diversity variables revolving around the degree to which communications networks are "cosmopolitan" (that is, not restricted to only those who are co-present in a situation).

In Table 9.2 these variables are incorporated into a few abstract propositions that capture the essence of Collins's and Annett's numerous propositions and descriptions of the history of deference and demeanor.[6] In these propositions, Collins and Annett argue that rituals and talk revealing deference and demeanor are most pronounced between people of unequal status, especially when their actions are observable and when communication outside the situation is restricted. Such density and surveillance are, of course, properties of the macrostructure as it distributes varying numbers of people in space. As surveillance decreases, however, unequals avoid contact or perform deference and demeanor rituals in a perfunctory manner. For example, military protocol will be much more pronounced between an officer and enlisted personnel in public on a military base than in situations where surveillance is lacking (for example, off the base). Moreover, Collins and Annett stress that inequalities and low mobility between unequal groups create pressures for intragroup deference and demeanor rituals, especially when communications outside the group are low (for example, between new army recruits and their officers or between prison inmates and guards). But as communication outside the group increases or as surveillance by group members decreases, then deference and demeanor will decrease.

Class Cultures

These exchange processes revolving around talk, ritual, deference, and demeanor explain what are often seen as more macro processes in societies. One such process is variation in the class cultures. That is, people in different social classes tend to exhibit diverging behaviors, outlooks, and interpersonal styles. These differences can be seen in two main variables:

Table 9.2 Key Propositions on Deference and Demeanor

I. The visibility, explicitness, and predictability of deference and demeanor rituals and talk among individuals increase with

  A. Inequality in resources among individuals, especially with respect to

    1. Material wealth.

    2. Power.

  B. Surveillance by others of behaviors, and surveillance increases with

    1. Co-presence of others.

    2. Homogeneity in outlook of others.

  C. Restrictiveness of communication networks (low cosmopolitanism), and restrictiveness decreases with

    1. Complexity in communications technologies.

    2. Mobility of individuals.

II. The greater is the degree of inequality among individuals and the lower is the level of surveillance, the more likely behaviors are to be directed toward

  A. Avoidance of contact and emission of deference and demeanor by individuals.

  B. Perfunctory performance of deference and demeanor by individuals when avoidance is not possible.

III. The greater the degree of inequality among individuals and the lower the level of cosmopolitanism among individuals, the more likely behaviors are to be directed toward simplified but highly visible deference and demeanor.

IV. The greater is the degree of inequality among individuals, and the less is the degree of mobility among groups with varying levels of resources, the more visible, explicit, and predictable are deference and demeanor rituals and talk within these groups.

V. The greater is the equality among individuals, and the greater is the degree of cosmopolitanism and/or the less is the level of surveillance, the less compelling are deference and demeanor talk and rituals.

---

1. The degree to which one possesses and uses the capacity to coerce, to materially bestow, and to symbolically manipulate others so that one can give orders in an encounter and have these orders followed.

2. The degree to which communication is confined to others who are physically co-present in a situation or, conversely, the degree to which communication is diverse, involving the use of multiple modes of contact with many others in different situations.

Using these two variables, as well as several less central variables such as wealth and physical exertion on the job, Collins describes the class cultures of American society. More significant for theory building, he also offers several abstract propositions that stipulate certain important relationships among power, order-giving, communication networks, and behavioral tendencies among individuals. These relationships are restated in somewhat altered form in Table 9.3.[7] With these principles, Collins explains variations in the behaviors, outlooks, and interpersonal styles of individuals in different occupations and status groups. For example, those occupations that require order giving, that reveal high co-presence of others, and that involve little physical exertion will generate behaviors that are distinctive and that circumscribe other activities, such as

Table 9.3 Key Propositions on Class Cultures

  I. Giving orders to others in a situation increases with the capacity to mobilize and use coercive, material, and symbolic resources.

 II. The behavioral attributes of self-assuredness, the initiation of talk, positive self-feelings, and identification with the goals of a situation are positively related to the capacity to give orders to others in that situation.

III. The behavioral attributes of toughness and courage increase as the degree of physical exertion and danger in that situation escalates.

IV. The degree of behavioral conformity exhibited in a situation is positively related to the degree to which people can communicate only with others who are physically co-present in that situation and is negatively related to the degree to which people can communicate with a diversity of others who are not physically co-present.

 V. The outlook and behavioral tendencies of an individual are an additive function of those spheres of life—work, politics, home, recreation, community—where varying degrees of giving or receiving orders, physical exertion, danger, and communication occur.

whom one marries, where one lives, what one values, and what activities one pursues in various spheres of life. Giving different weights to these variables would cause varying behavioral tendencies in individuals. Thus, from the processes delineated in the propositions of Table 9.3, understanding of such variables as class culture, ethnic cultures, lifestyles, and other concerns of investigators of stratification is achieved. But such understanding is anchored in the recognition that these class cultures are built and sustained by interaction chains in which deference and demeanor rituals have figured prominently. Thus, a class culture is not mere internalization of values and beliefs or simple socialization (although this is no doubt involved); rather, a class culture is the result of repeated encounters among unequals under varying conditions imposed by the macrostructure as it has been built from past chains of interaction.

Organizational Processes

Like Max Weber before him, Collins also uses an extensive analysis of organizations and develops a rather long inventory of propositions on organizational properties and dynamics.[8] These propositions overlap, to some degree, with those on stratification because an organization is typically a stratified system with a comparatively clear hierarchy of authority. Table 9.4 lists three groups of propositions from Collins's analysis. These revolve around processes of organizational control, the administration of control, and the general organizational structure.

In the propositions shown in Table 9.4, control within an organization increases with the concentration of coercive, material, and symbolic resources. The pattern of control varies, however, with the particular type of resource—whether coercive, material, or symbolic—that is controlled and with the configuration among these resources, as is summarized in Propositions III, IV, and V. Control within an organization must be administered, and the pattern of such administrative control varies with the nature of the resources used to gain control. Collins extends Weber's analysis of organizations, and Propositions VI

Table 9.4 Key Propositions on Class Cultures

Processes of Organizational Control

I. Control in patterns of organizations is a positive and additive function of the concentration among individuals of (a) coercive resources, (b) material resources, and (c) symbolic resources.

II. The form of control in organizations depends on the configuration of resources held by those individuals seeking to control others.

III. The more control is sought through the use of coercive resources, the more likely those subject to the application of these resources are to (a) seek escape, (b) fight back, if escape is impossible, (c) comply if (a) and (b) are impossible and if material incentives exist, and (d) sluggishly comply if (a), (b), and (c) do not apply.

IV. The more control is sought through the use of material resources, the more likely those subject to the manipulation of material incentives are to (a) develop acquisitive orientations and (b) develop a strategy of self-interested manipulation.

V. The more control is sought through the use of symbolic resources, the more likely those subject to the application of such resources are to (a) experience indoctrination into values and beliefs, (b) be members of homogeneous cohorts of recruits, (c) be subject to efforts to encourage intra-organizational contact, (d) be subject to efforts to discourage extra-organizational contact, (e) partici- pate in ritual activities, especially those involving rites of passage, and (f) be rewarded for conformity with upward mobility.

Administration of Control

VI. The more those in authority employ coercive and material incentives to control others, the greater is the reliance on surveillance as an administrative device to control.

VII. The more those in authority use surveillance to control, the greater are (a) the level of alienation by those subject to surveillance, (b) the level of conformity in only higher visible behaviors, and (c) the ratio of supervisory to nonsupervisory individuals.

VIII. The more those in authority employ symbolic resources to control others, the greater is their reliance on systems of standardized rules to achieve control.

IX. The greater is the reliance on systems of standardized rules, the greater are (a) the impersonality of interactions, (b) the standardization of behaviors, and (c) the dispersion of authority.

Organizational Structure

X. Centralization of authority is a positive and additive function of (a) the concen- tration of resources, (b) the capacity to mobilize the administration of control through surveillance, material incentives, and systems of rules; (c) the capacity to control the flow of information; (d) the capacity to control contingencies of the environment; and (e) the degree to which the tasks to be performed are routine.

XI. The bureaucratization of authority and social relations is a positive and additive function of (a) record-keeping technologies, (b) nonkinship agents of socialization of potential incumbents, (c) money markets, (d) transportation facilities, (e) non- personal centers of power, and (f) diverse centers of power and authority.

---

through IX summarize various patterns in the administration of control. In the end, Collins sees the profile of an organization's structure as reflecting the nature and concentration of resources, as well as how these are used to admin- ister control. Propositions X and XI review Collins's basic argument.

Table 9.5 Key Propositions on the State, Economy, and Ideology

I. The size and scale of political organization are a positive function of the productive capacity of the economy.

II. The productive capacity of the economy is a positive and additive function of (a) level of technology, (b) level of natural resources, (c) population size, and (d) efficiency in the organization of labor.

III. The form of political organization is related to the levels of and interactive effects among (a) size of territories to be governed, (b) the absolute numbers of people to be governed, (c) the distribution and diversity of people in a territory, (d) the organization of coercive force (armies), (e) the distribution (dispersion or concentration) of power and other resources among a population, and (f) the degree of symbolic unification within and among social units.

IV. The stability of the state is a negative and additive function of

   A. The capacity for political mobilization by other groups, which is a positive function of

      1. The level of wealth.

      2. The capacity for organization as a status group.

   B. The incapacity of the state to resolve periodic crises.

The State and Economy

As did Weber, Collins eventually moves to the analysis of the state, which, though a type of complex organization, still controls and regulates the entire society. As the propositions in Table 9.5 summarize,[9] the size and scale of the state depend on the productive capacity of the economy; in the end, the state can only be supported by a large economic surplus. In turn, as is summarized in Proposition II, the productive capacity of the economy is related to technologies, natural resources, the number of people who must be supported, and the efficiency with which the division of labor is organized. The particular form of state power varies enormously, but these forms vary under the impact of basic forces summarized in Proposition III. The stability of the state is also a crucial variable, especially for a conflict theory. As Proposition IV summarizes, the state must be able to prevent mobilization by groups pursuing counter-power, and it must be able to resolve periodic crises. When it cannot, the state becomes unstable. Like Weber before him, Collins recognizes that much of the state's viability depends on the relation of the state to surrounding societies. No society exists in isolation; it almost always finds itself in competition with other societies. The ability of the state to prevail in this world of geopolitics often determines its form, viability, and stability.

Geopolitics

Borrowing from Weber but adding his own ideas, Collins argues that there are sociological reasons for the historical facts that only certain societies can form stable empires and that societies can extend their empires only to a maximal size of about three to four million square miles.[10] When a society has a resource

Table 9.6 Key Propositions on Geopolitics

I. The possibility of winning a war between nation-states is a positive and additive function of
   A. The level of resource advantage of one nation-state over another, which is a positive function of
      1. The level of technology.
      2. The level of productivity
      3. The size of the population.
      4. The level of wealth formation.
   B. The degree of *marchland advantage* of one nation-state over another, which is a positive and additive function of
      1. The extent to which the borders of a nation-state are peripheral to those of other nation-states.
      2. The extent to which a nation-state has enemies on only one border.
      3. The extent to which a nation-state has natural buffers (mountains, oceans, large lakes, and so on) on most of its borders.
II. The likelihood of an empire is a positive function to the extent to which a march land state has resource advantages over neighbors and uses these advantages to wage war
III. The size of an empire is a positive and additive function of the dominant nation-states' capacity to
   A. Avoid showdown war with the empire of other marchland states.
   B. Sustain a marchland advantage.
   C. Maintain territories with standing armies.
   D. Maintain logistical capacity for communications and transportation, which is a positive function of levels of communication, transportation, and military technologies and a negative and additive function of
      1. The size of a territory.
      2. The distances of borders from the home base.
   E. Diffusion of technologies to potential enemies.
IV. The collapse of an empire is a positive and additive function of
   A. The initiation of war between two empires.
   B. The overextension of an empire beyond its logistical capacity.
   C. The adoption of its superior technologies by enemy nation-states.

(money, technology, population base) and marchland advantage (no enemies on most of its borders), it can win wars, but eventually it will (a) extend itself beyond its logistical capacities, (b) bump up against another empire, (c) lose its marchland advantage as it extends its borders and becomes ever more surrounded by enemies, and (d) lose its technological advantages as enemies adopt them. The result of these forces is that empires begin to stall at a certain size, as each of these points of resistance is activated. These processes indicate that internal nation-states will not build long-term or extensive empires because they are surrounded by enemies, increasingly so as they extend territory. Rather, marchland states, with oceans, mountains, or unthreatening neighbors at their backs, can move out and conquer others, because they have to fight a war on only one front. But eventually they overextend, confront another marchland empire, lose their technological advantage, and acquire enemies on a greater proportion of their borders (thereby losing the marchland advantage and, in effect, becoming an internal state that must now fight on several borders). Sea and air powers can provide a kind of marchland advantage, but the logistical loads of distance from home bases and maintenance of sophisticated technologies make such empires vulnerable. Only when it encounters little resistance can an empire be maintained across oceans and at great distances by air; as resistance mounts, the empire collapses quickly as its supply lines are disrupted. Table 9.6 summarizes these ideas more formally.

CONCLUSION

It is not hard to see what makes Collins's approach to conflict processes neo-Weberian. Like Weber, Collins begins with a conceptualization of micro processes—in Weber's case, types of meaningful action, and in Collins's theory, interaction rituals. Then, their analysis shifts to the meso-level, examining patterns of stratification and forms of complex organizations. Finally, both Weber and Collins move to the analysis of the state and geopolitics. In all these levels of analysis, their concern is with inequalities of resources and how these inequalities generate tension and potential conflict.

NOTES

1. Randall Collins, *Conflict Sociology: Toward an Explanatory Science* (New York: Academic, 1975).

2. Randall Collins, "On the Micro-Foundation of Macro-Sociology," *American Journal of Sociology* 86 (1981), pp. 984–1014.

3. Randall Collins, "Micro-Translation as a Theory of Building Strategy," in *Advances in Social Theory and Methodology: Toward an Integration of Micro- and Macro-Sociology,* eds. K. Knorr-Cetina and A. V. Cicourel (London: Routledge, 1981), pp. 84–96.

4. Collins, *Conflict Sociology* (cited in note 1), pp. 114–131.

5. Randall Collins and Joan Annett, "A Short History of Deference and

Demeanor," in *Conflict Sociology* (cited in note 1), pp. 161–224.

6. Ibid., pp. 216–219.

7. Collins, *Conflict Sociology* (cited in note 1), pp. 49–88.

8. Ibid., pp. 286–347.

9. Ibid., pp. 348–413.

10. See Randall Collins, *Weberian Sociological Theory* (Cambridge: Cambridge University Press, 1986), pp. 167–212; "Long-Term Social Change and the Territorial Power of States," in his *Sociology Since Midcentury: Essays in Theory Cumulation* (New York: Academic, 1981).

10

Neo-Marxian
Conflict Theories

In the review of Karl Marx's theory of conflict in Chapter 8, much of the substance of Marx's ideas about the dynamics of capitalist societies was left out. Instead, we abstracted Marx's substantive categories to produce a general theory of conflict in systems of inequality. As Marx's ideas were used during the middle decades of the twentieth century, this more abstract approach to building on Marx was typical, as we saw in the work of Ralf Dahrendorf in Chapter 8. Yet, Marx considered himself to be a revolutionary[1], and his life's work was to develop a theoretical system that could explain the self-destructive dynamics of capitalism and the emergence of communism.[2] This more substantive and emancipatory thrust of Marx's work was never lost during the midcentury, but the theory had to be revised because the revolution by the proletariat did not occur and because the communist systems of the twentieth century were hardly emancipatory. As we will see in Chapter 12, this failure of Marxian predictions led to the emergence of critical theory in a rather pessimistic guise. In this chapter, however, we will review some theories that sustain both the substantive thrust of Marx's ideas and the view that the contradictions of capitalism will, perhaps, open the doors for new, more emancipatory forms of social organization.

A BRIEF REVIEW OF MARX'S
SUBSTANTIVE ARGUMENT

To appreciate the creative directions that Marx's ideas have taken during the last two decades, we need to review, if only briefly, some substantive points of emphasis in Marx's analytical scheme. Marx believed the analytical goal was to explain the contradictions in capitalist modes of economic production and how these would lead to the conflict processes that would usher in communism. His predictions were wrong, perhaps because of some fatal errors in his logic, but his analysis is still useful, as we will see when we turn to more contemporary theories.

For Marx, capitalism is an economic system where those who own and control the means of production seek to make profits from the goods that they sell in competitive markets. In such a system, labor must sell itself as a commodity to capitalists and must do so under unfavorable circumstances where the supply of workers is high relative to demand, thereby driving the wages of labor down (and, hence, reducing the costs of labor for capitalists). The key to profits for capitalists is to make labor work beyond the actual labor time needed to make the goods that pay their wages; the difference is *surplus value* or profit for capitalists. The greater this surplus value is, the more workers are *exploited* by capitalists who, in essence, appropriate the surplus value of the goods produced by workers for their own gain. So, in Marx's view, labor power is the ultimate source of value of products as well as the source of profits for capitalists. Capitalism is thus sustained by exploitation.

But capitalists face a dilemma: They must compete with each other in markets, and hence, the price that they can get for products is driven down to the point where it becomes difficult to make a profit. As businesses fail, laborers are thrown out of work, which in turn means that they do not have wages to buy goods in markets. As a result, demand for goods declines; with this decline in demand, profits of capitalists also decline. Capitalists seek to get around this *declining rate of profit* by using more productive technologies and machinery in place of labor, thereby putting more laborers out of work and lessening demand for the goods produced by capitalists. Although such efforts by capitalists can give them a short-term advantage over their competitors and, thereby, increase their profits for a time, competitors soon copy technologies and machinery. As a consequence, a new round of competition over price occurs. This new round of competition, however, must confront the lessened capacity of unemployed labor to purchase goods in markets where prices are coming down.

In this process of declining profits, many capitalists go under, and indeed, their competitors might buy them out, creating oligopolies and monopolies that can better manipulate prices when they do not have to compete. But they must do so in conditions of lessening demand in markets where labor does not have wages to buy goods. Moreover, the many capitalists who have lost out in the competition are without money to buy goods and services, and indeed, many are driven into the proletariat. Eventually, even as monopolies gain control of key productive sectors, they have trouble making a profit; goods can go unsold because there is not enough money in the hands of workers and displaced bourgeoisie to buy them. As goods remain unsold, capitalists reduce production, but as workers are laid off, cutting back production only decreases the buying power of workers in markets. Thus, Marx felt that capitalism would, in the end, move toward a situation where profits and production were declining while unemployment and monopoly control of production were increasing.

From this situation would come the mobilization by the proletariat for revolution. Such revolutionary efforts had to confront, however, the power of capitalists to control the state and ideological system. But, as crises of unemployment deepen, mobilization by the proletariat can overcome the power of the state to control coercively and the capacity of ideology to impart *false consciousness* (see the propositions in Table 8.1 on page 133 for an overview of the conditions producing mobilization for conflict). Such mobilization is facilitated by the very acts of capitalists in concentrating workers so that they can communicate their grievances, in making them appendages to machines and thereby increasing their sense of alienation, and in subjecting them to a decline in, or uncertainty about, their living standards. All these acts of capitalists lead workers to question the legitimacy of political authority and the appropriateness of dominant ideologies.

This brief summary does not capture the depth, texture, or subtlety of Marx's analysis of capitalism, but it gives us the tools to place into context the two basic directions of theorizing that Marx's work continues to inspire. One prominent direction is revising Marx's conception of exploitation and its effects on class processes in modern societies. The other direction has been to move beyond the nation-state as a unit of analysis to a world system level where, it is argued, the contradictions of capitalism will ultimately emerge. We will begin with neo-Marxian class analysis and then explore world systems theorizing.

NEO-MARXIAN CLASS ANALYSIS:
ERIK OLIN WRIGHT

In the twentieth century, Marxist theory has confronted several problems. First, the predicted collapse of capitalism has not occurred, despite the Great Depression and periodic recessions. Second, the projected polarization of capitalist societies into bourgeoisie and proletarians has been muted by the growth of a large and varied middle class of managers, experts, small business operators, skilled manual workers, and others who do not seem highly disadvantaged and who do not see themselves as exploited. Third, capitalism has appeared to emerge, at least in recent history, as the clear victor in the contest between capitalism and communism, although state-managed societies operating under the ideological banner of communism were hardly what Marx had in mind. Nonetheless, the historical predictions of Marx and the trajectory of capitalism into socialism and communism have not occurred.

Yet, despite these troubling issues, Marxism has remained a viable intellectual tradition, driven perhaps by an emancipatory zeal emphasizing the elimination of exploitation of the disadvantaged by the advantaged. Still, Marxist intellectual circles have been in crisis for more than a decade, as many former Marxists have moved to other forms of radical thinking or have become critical theorists and postmodernists—perspectives that are explored in the chapters of Part IV. Although some still cling to the orthodox picture of Marx, briefly summarized earlier, most Marxists have changed Marx's core ideas to fit current historical realities. Among these Marxists are several important scholars,[3] but in an effort to summarize the issues with which they have had to deal, we will focus on the work of Erik Olin Wright who has, in his words, sought to do more than merely draw from the Marxian tradition but, instead, to contribute to "the reconstruction of Marxism." Wright has termed his and fellow travelers' approach "analytical Marxism." But before discussing the basic concepts in Wright's scheme, let us set the stage with his more metatheoretical assertions.

Erik Olin Wright's Analytical Marxism

The goal of analytical Marxism is to shed some of the baggage of orthodox Marxist analysis while retaining the core ideas that make Marx's theory unique.[4] Analytical Marxism retains the emancipatory thrust of Marx, stressing that the goal is to reduce, if not eliminate, inequalities and exploitation. Indeed, emphasis is on constructing scientific theory about how socialism can emerge from the dynamics inhering in capitalist exploitation. But this emancipatory thrust does not abandon a commitment to the conventional norms of science in which theoretical ideas are assessed against empirical observations. Moreover, the goal is to produce abstract formulations that specify the "mechanisms" generating empirical regularities in the world, and for the analytical Marxist, particular concern is with the mechanisms flowing from social class structures.

Social Class, Emancipation, and History

Marxist theory posits an historical trajectory: feudalism to capitalism, then capitalism to communism. In this historical trajectory, class inequalities will be eliminated, and communism will usher in a classless society. In this trajectory and outcome, class is the pivotal dynamic, mobilizing individuals to seek alternative social relations in which exploitation is eliminated. Wright believes that these three basic orienting assumptions—that is, historical trajectory, class emancipation, and class as the driving force of history—need to be mitigated somewhat.[5] Emphasis should be on how the dynamics of capitalism present possibilities for new, less exploitive social arrangements rather than on the inevitability of the forces driving human society toward communism. In this vein, emphasis on class emancipation should not blindly pursue the goal of a classless society but, rather, present a critique of existing social relations to reduce class inequalities and exploitation. Moreover,

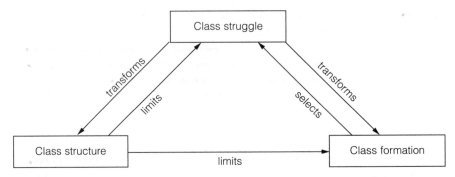

FIGURE 10.1 Wright's General Model of Class Analysis

emphasis on class as the driving force of history must be tempered by a recognition that class is one of many forces shaping the organization of a society, both in the present and future.

Wright's theoretical work stresses this last consideration: What mechanisms revolving around social class generate what outcomes? As a Marxist, Wright views the *class structure* of a society as limiting the nature of *class formation* (the organization of individuals) and *class struggle* (the use of organization to transform class structures). He posits a simple model, as delineated in Figure 10.1.[6] In this model, class struggle transforms the nature of class formations and class structure, whereas class formations select or channel class struggle in certain directions depending on the nature of organization of class members. The key dynamic in Wright's program, however, is class structure; as the model outlines, class structure limits the nature of class formation and class struggle. The goal of a reconstituted Marxian analysis must, therefore, examine the properties of class structure in capitalist societies if class formations and emancipatory class struggles are to be understood.

Micro-Level versus Macro-Level Class Analysis

In Wright's view, Marxian class analysis must confront two impulses. One is to retain Marx's vision of the class structure in society as ultimately polarizing into two conflictual classes—in the capitalist historical epoch, these are the bourgeoisie who own the means of production versus the proletariat who are exploited. The other impulse is to explore "the complexity of the class structural concept itself in the hope that such complexity will more powerfully capture the explanatory mechanisms embedded in class relations."[7] Wright argues that this complexity is not as evident when analysis stays at the macro-level, focusing on the global characteristics of capitalism as composed ultimately of owners and workers. However, when research moves to the micro-level of the individual and seeks to understand the locations of individuals in the class system, a much more varied, complex, and contradictory picture emerges. If the causal effects of class relations are to be understood, then, it is necessary to explore class processes at the micro level.

Wright's basic strategy has been to examine the jobs that people hold because in their jobs individuals connect to the system of production and the class relations that inhere in this system. For most of his work in the 1970s and 1980s,[8] Wright sought to construct a "relational map of locations of individuals" in the class system, but by the 1990s, he had recognized that "the simple linkage of individuals-in-jobs to classes" must be modified in several important ways: Individuals can occupy more than one job; they can have indirect and mediated relations to a job (as is the case with children and others who do not directly participate in the system of formal employment); they can move about jobs and cross class locations during the course of a career; and they can have contradictory locations in the class system.[9] In essence, as we will see shortly, Wright's conceptual scheme has tried to deal with these kinds of complexities that a micro-level analysis exposes; indeed, his conceptualizations have changed during the course of the last twenty years as he has confronted both data[10] and conceptual criticisms.[11]

When class analysis turns micro, the vagueness of much macro-level Marxian theory is revealed. Wright argues that it is important in a reconstructed Marxian analysis to be specific about the mechanisms involved in generating class formation and class struggle effects. He illustrates the differences between a macro-level and micro-level view of class mechanisms by summarizing the three ways in traditional Marxism that class structure is seen to exert effects on class formation and struggle[12]: (1) material interests, (2) lived experiences, and (3) collective capacities. We will examine each of these.

(1) *Material interests.* The first mechanism by which class structure exerts causal effects on class formation and struggle is through individuals' *material interests.* There are two basic types of material interests: (a) *economic welfare* or "the total package of toil-leisure-incomes available to a person,"[13] with people having an interest in reducing their toil and in increasing their leisure and consumption; and (b) *economic power* or the capacity to control how surplus products are distributed, with surplus product being defined as "that part of the total social product that is left over after all the inputs into production (both labor power and physical capital) have been reproduced."[14] Thus, the material interests of individuals are determined by their economic welfare and economic power.

The concept of *exploitation* ties these two types of material interests together. Those with economic power can use this power to appropriate productive surplus from those without power. In so doing, they increase their economic welfare at the expense of those whose surplus product they take. In Marxian class analysis, then, the material interests of classes are not just different; they are opposed in a kind of zero-sum game.

The material interests of individuals circumscribe their options. Depending on their respective material interests, people make different choices, employ diverse strategies, and make varying trade-offs. When individuals share material interests, their choices, strategies, and trade-offs should converge because they face similar dilemmas as they pursue economic welfare and economic power. In Marx's macro-level approach, social systems polarize around two classes with different material interests, fueled by exploitation. In a more micro-level approach to material interests, a more complex and, at times, contradictory picture emerges of individuals with diverse perceptions about what they should do in pursuing their economic welfare and in seeking economic power. Moreover, the lived experiences of individuals as they make choices and pursue strategies can also diverge, or at a minimum, individuals do not perceive that they have common material interests (a problem that Marx dismissed, perhaps too quickly, as "false consciousness").

(2) *Lived experiences.* In Marxian theory, common material interests as dictated by class location lead to common experiences. Those who do not own capital are seen to have similar subjective understandings of the world because they are forced to sell their labor, because they are dominated and bossed around, and because they are unable to control the surplus products of their labor. When individuals are exploited this way, they are also *alienated,*[15] and together, these forces give alienated individuals a common experience that, Marx felt, would lead to their collective mobilization.[16] Yet, a more micro-level approach reveals that individuals might not have similar experiences, or at the very least, they do not see their lived experiences as similar because they occupy somewhat different jobs that locate them at different points in the class system.

(3) *Collective capacities.* The third class force in traditional Marxian analysis flows from the first two: People with common material interests and lived experiences possess a capacity for collective action. Moreover, as Marx emphasized, capitalists are forced by their own material interests to create many of the conditions that facilitate collective mobilization, such as concentrating workers in factories and urban areas, making them appendages to machine technologies, disrupting their life routines through lay-offs, providing literacy and media access, and encouraging other forces that shape class formation and struggle. This kind of scenario has a certain plausibility when examined at the macro level, but on the individual level, the contradictory locations of individuals in jobs and their differentiation across an array of middle-class locations make collective mobilization more problematic. Individuals do not see that they have common material interests or that they share common lived experiences, with the result that they do not naturally organize collectively. Even alliances and coalitions among individuals who see that they share some interests become problematic, although once formed these alliances have strength (because the costs of compromises have already been incurred).[17]

Thus, in Wright's micro approach, the three class forces in Marxian analysis do not reveal the same degree of coherence as when they are examined from a more macro level. Moreover, microanalysis shows that, in contrast with traditional Marxism, these forces are not necessarily correlated with each other. When analysis moves to the micro level, "there is no longer necessarily a simple coincidence of material interests, lived experience, and collective capacity."[18] People who might seem to have common material interests do not perceive this to be the case, nor do they reveal a driving need to mobilize collectively. In a micro approach to understanding class mechanisms, then, the complexity of the class system makes traditional macro-level Marxian causal forces too global and crude to account for the specifics of class formation and struggle.

The Problem of the Middle Class

Wright's entry into Marxist analysis began with the question of how to account for the emergence and proliferation of jobs in the middle classes,[19] and although he has sought to move in different directions, this question is still at the core of his theoretical formulations. In his effort to build a "map of the class structure," Wright recognizes that the array of middle-class positions posed the biggest challenge to traditional Marxian class analysis. If class structures are to be seen as relevant to the class formation and to the struggle by classes for social emancipation, then a more fine-grained analysis of this structure is necessary. Wright's analytical project has thus involved an effort to isolate the mechanisms being generated by this more complex class system. Through his empirical and theoretical work during the last two decades, he has proposed several ways to conceptualize class structures and the mechanism for class formation and struggle that inhere in these structures. Some of these have been rejected, others retained, and most modified and integrated in new ways by Wright. In contrast with orthodox Marxism, Wright has been willing to change his mind and to develop, elaborate, and qualify ideas in his effort to isolate the causal mechanisms of class structures in advanced capitalist societies. He has, in essence, proposed several models of class structures, the basic elements of which are briefly summarized here.

Contradictory Class Locations Wright's first attempt at conceptualizing the middle classes in Marxian terms led him to develop the idea of *contradictory class locations*.[20] Individuals can occupy a class location that is contradictory because it puts people into different classes, presumably giving them contradictory material interests and diverse lived experiences and collective capacities. These locations are contradictory because, for example, many managers, semi-autonomous wage earners, professionals and experts, and small-scale employers can reveal varying amounts and combinations of (a) owning the means of their production, (b) purchasing the labor of others, (c) controlling and managing the labor of others, and (d) selling their labor. To illustrate, a manager sells labor to an owner of a business, but at the same time this manager will be involved in hiring and controlling the labor of others. Similarly a skilled consultant sells labor, but might own the facilities by which this labor is organized. Such variations can put individuals in contradictory class locations in the sense that they are neither owners of the means of production nor helpless sellers of their labor; they have an element of both, and, hence, they have contradictory material interests and, no doubt, lived experiences and collective capacities. They might not see themselves as exploiters or as exploited; indeed, they can be both in varying proportions.

This approach made Wright a prominent Marxist theorist, but it also brought criticism that, in turn, led Wright to pursue an alternative conceptualization. One problem was that domination (telling others what to do) and exploitation (extracting surplus product) were somewhat decoupled. For example, managers could give orders but they did not directly enjoy the economic welfare of appropriated surplus (this went to owners of the means of production). Another problem revolved around employment in the state or government. Are those employed by the state workers in the means of economic production? If not, then their status is unclear: They are paid labor, but their products are not directly appropriated by capitalists. They are managers and hence can direct not only each other but perhaps workers and even owners in the economy. These conceptual problems, coupled with the difficulties that Wright encountered in measuring contradictory locations of individuals, led him to propose a new conceptualization of the middle classes.[21]

Multiple Exploitation   Adopting ideas from John Roemer,[22] Wright's second solution to the problem of the middle classes was to posit an *exploitation nexus* that varies by the kinds of assets that individuals possess and their degree of ownership or control of these assets. The four assets are (a) *labor power assets,* (b) *capital assets,* (c) *organization assets,* and (d) *skill or credential assets.* Each of these leads to a particular type of exploitation: Individuals who only have labor assets are likely to be exploited because they depend on those who have the economic power to appropriate the surplus value of their labor; capital assets can be used to invest in equipment and labor as a means of extracting the surplus product generated by technology and labor; organization assets can be used to manage and control others in ways that extract surplus products; and skills or educational credentials can be employed to extract extra resources beyond the resources it took to acquire and maintain these skills and credentials.

This approach allowed Wright to address the issue of the middle class by re-coupling the concepts of exploitation (of surplus) and domination (through control or order-giving). In essence what had been domination was translated into a new type of exploitation by those with organization assets, highly valued skills, and educational credentials. At the same time, the exploitation envisioned by Marx—extraction by capitalists of surplus value from workers—could remain close to Marx's original formulation. A particular society could then be typified by the combinations and configurations of these various types of exploitation.

Wright preferred this conceptualization of the middle classes to the contradictory class location formulation because it allowed him to put exploitation back as the central mechanism by which economic welfare and economic power are connected, thereby making his scheme more consistent with Marx's original formulation.[23] Moreover, it allowed him to conceptualize managers in the state, professionals, and other skilled workers with some degree of autonomy through Marxian-inspired class dynamics: They too are exploiters, just like capitalists, but they use different assets to extract surplus value and product from others.

This approach also came under heavy criticism, leading Wright to back down from some of the assertions in this model.[24] First, those with skills and credentials are not so much exploiters of the less skilled as advantaged workers who can prevent capitalists from exploiting them as much as their less-skilled counterparts are exploited (because capitalists value and need their skills and credentials). Second, managers inside government as well as in the private capitalist sector can move up the organizational hierarchy and use their higher salaries to buy into the capitalist sector (via purchase of stocks, bonds, and so on), thereby confusing just what their material interests would be. Third, the location of individuals in the state bureaucracy would determine the mix of assets; for example, those higher in the state might possess more capital assets or at least a mix of organization and capital assets, whereas those lower in the hierarchy would possess only organization assets, and those lower still would possess only labor assets to be exploited. Coupled with the problems of measuring these various types of assets and documenting empirically how they led to different forms of exploitation caused Wright to shift his scheme yet again.[25]

The Emerging Scheme As Wright has dealt with the conceptual and empirical problems of measuring class locations at the micro level, he has responded to criticisms by elaborating new concepts or, perhaps more accurately, reformulating older ideas in a new guise. These new conceptualizations still revolve primarily around the problem of the middle classes, but they reveal a more eclectic character. Some of the key ideas are reviewed in the following discussion.[26]

One idea is the notion of *multiple locations*. Like most traditional Marxists, Wright had originally assumed that individuals had one class location, even if this location was contradictory and placed a person into classes with different material interests. But, people often have more than one job and, hence, can actually have several class locations. For example, a person can have a salaried day job, then operate a small business at night or on weekends, thereby making this individual both a proletarian and capitalist.

Another idea deals with *mediated locations*. Individuals are often connected to a class via networks to others who hold a job or own capital. Children, wives, and husbands can all have a mediated relation to a class location of a parent or spouse, and these mediated relations can become complicated. For example, if a female manager is married to a carpenter, each has a mediated relation to the other's class location, and their children, if they have any, will bear mediated relations to both classes. Wright proposes the notion of an *overall class interest* in these situations, which is a "weighted combination of these direct and mediated locations," that may or may not be contradictory.

Still another idea in Wright's evolving scheme is a concern with *temporal locations*. Careers might not significantly change a person's class location, but often careers do involve movement across class locations, as when individuals move up government and corporate hierarchies, when a small business gets large, when workers begin to form companies, and when students move from school to job, and into a career track. People's class locations can thus change over time, giving them different material interests, lived experiences, and collective capacities.

Yet another idea is a conceptualization of distinct *strata* within classes. The argument is that within basic classes such as owners and workers, there are distinctive strata whose members might have somewhat different material interests and most likely have very different lived experiences and collective capacities. These strata can take a number of forms. For example, professionals and experts with skills and credentials can be seen as able to collect *rents* on their skills and credentials, which make them a distinct strata within the working class (they are still part of the working class because they must sell their labor power). Temporal mobility in a career can often increase these rents; if the rents are sufficiently high, they can be invested as capital, thereby giving a person a position within a stratum of the capitalist class as well as the working class. Similarly, managers or manual workers can translate their skills and career mobility into rents that can then become capital. All these workers are in contradictory locations because they are, on the one hand, workers who are paid a salary and, on the other hand, investors in businesses that hire workers. Thus, the basic classes envisioned by Marx—workers and owners of the means of production—can be re-conceptualized by distinct strata within these broad classes, with the incumbents in various strata potentially having a contradictory class location as both workers and capitalists.

The issue of state employment can be translated into a *state mode of production*. Rather than view high-level state workers as organization exploiters, it is better to visualize the state as producing goods and services of a particular kind and, hence, as revealing distinct classes (and perhaps strata within these classes). The dominant class would be those who direct the appropriation and allocation of surplus productivity that the state acquires to support itself (in forms such as taxes, fees, tariffs, and the like). The subordinate class would be those who actually perform the services and produce the goods provided by the state. Within the state mode of production could be various combinations of contradictory positions. For example, a state manager can control the actions of other workers but be controlled by elite decision makers in the dominant class of the state; a state manager who can command a high salary can invest this rent in the private sector, thereby placing this individual in both the economic and state modes of production. Relations in the state mode of production can also be mediated, as when high-level members of the dominant class have relations with corporations doing business with government or being regulated by government. Moreover, the career path of many incumbents in both the economic and government modes of production can involve movement back and forth between these modes, thereby shifting the class location of individuals.

A further set of ideas developed in Wright's evolving project moves beyond the problem of the middle classes. The existence of an unemployable and often welfare-dependent segment of a population has led Wright to introduce a distinction between "non-exploitive economic oppression" and "exploitive economic oppression." In *exploitive economic oppression,* one group's economic welfare is increased by virtue of the exploitation of another whose welfare declines because the latter's surplus products are appropriated by the former. This situation is oppressive not just because of exploitation, per se, but because the exploiting group often uses morally sanctioned and legitimated coercion to get its way. Yet, even under these oppressive conditions of exploitation, the exploited have some power because their exploiters depend on them; so, the exploitation often involves implicit negotiation and consent. In *nonexploitive economic oppression*, there is no transfer of surplus productivity to an exploiter. Instead, the economic welfare of exploiters depends on the exclusion of the oppressed from access to valued resources being consumed by oppressors. Under these conditions, Wright argues, genocide can occur because the goal of exploiters is to get rid of those who might seek access to resources that they have, or covet. Yet, even here, the non-exploited oppressed have a resource: the capacity to disrupt efforts at consumption by exploiters. Thus, the non-exploited oppressed can often force exploiters to provide some resources (as happens with those who pay for the welfare of those who are kept out of the economy).

The Overall Marxian Project

At this writing, Wright's scheme continues to evolve. Thus, analytical Marxism is constantly changing in an effort to come to grips with the complexity of the class systems of advanced capitalist societies. The great asset of this theory program is the coherence that comes from efforts to conceptualize class mechanisms as exploitation and to sustain a common emancipatory vision. Thus, even as theorists and researchers argue and develop alternative schemes, the dialogue and debate stay within the extended boundaries of Marxian analysis.

This strength is also a weakness in at least one sense: It is hard to engage in the theoretical debate without buying into the key notion that at the core of class dynamics are not just differences in interests but material interests fueled by exploitation. Very different theorists share similar emancipatory goals—that is, to reduce inequalities—but if one follows the Marxian approach, emancipation can only come with reduction in exploitation. Yet, if another analyst does not see market systems distributing variously skilled labor to different jobs with varying degrees of remuneration as exploitative, then theoretical and emancipatory discussion will hit an impasse.

Wright's work has had wide appeal beyond Marxist circles not so much for the Marxism that, despite its flexibility and creativity, is just that: a Marxist analysis of stratification. Rather, the broader appeal has come from the carefully executed and comparative empirical work on class structures; this empirical work has proven useful to Marxists and non-Marxists alike. Moreover, Wright's insistence that Marxist analyses be subject to the same test of evidence as other scientific projects has added to the general appeal of Wright's and other analytical Marxists' work. Yet, such work will always be constrained by the desire to sustain, as much as is possible, basic Marxian categories of analysis—refined to be sure, but still squarely in the Marxian tradition—and by the need to orient theory to an ultimate emancipatory goal or, alternatively, to emancipatory possibilities. These concerns will bias inquiry, perhaps no more than other commitments by other theorists, but these biases will limit interchange with other theoretical perspectives.

NEO-MARXIAN WORLD
SYSTEMS ANALYSIS

In the 1970s, Marx-inspired theory began to shift the unit of analysis from nation-states to relations among societies. Capitalism was viewed as a dynamic engine of transformation that would create a world-level economy. This world-capitalist economy, in turn, would reveal many of the same contradictions that Marx had predicted for capitalism within a particular society. The study of empires and imperialism had, of course, long been a major topic in a variety of disciplines—history, political science, economics, and sociology. Some of the flavor of what world system analysts would argue was captured early by the British economist, J. A. Hobson,[27] in his view that capitalist nations need to conquer and exploit other nations to stave off many of the problems predicted by Marx. But, Immanuel Wallerstein[28] codified Marxist ideas into a coherent conceptual scheme for the analysis of the world system. His work, in turn, has stimulated much further theoretical and empirical effort. We will concentrate on Wallerstein's scheme, but add conceptual points from others as we proceed.

Immanuel Wallerstein's Analysis of World Systems

World Empires and World Economy Wallerstein begins his historical analysis on the emergence of a capitalist world system by distinguishing between two basic forms of interconnection among societies: (1) world empires and (2) world economy. A *world empire* is created by military conquest or threats of such conquest, then extraction of resources, usually in the form of tribute, from those populations that have been defeated or threatened. Often these conquered societies can retain considerable autonomy as long as they pay the tribute demanded by their conquerors. Whether through direct appropriation, taxation, or tribute, dominant nations can accumulate wealth and use their wealth to finance the privilege of elites and the military activities of the polity. Military empires are thus built around a strong state that administers the flow of taxes, franchises, and tributary wealth, while financing and coordinating the military for war-making and conquest. Wallerstein argues that this was, historically, the dominant form of societal interconnection among societies before the 1400s when the capitalist revolution had begun, although many debate this point and emphasize that trade-based and empire-based systems of domination existed long before modern European capitalism.[29] Moreover, many argue that imperial and trade forms of world system domination had come and gone in various cycles many times in history,[30] long before the modern world system began to develop in the 1400s. Nonetheless, the important point is that one form of connection among nations is through state-based imperialism. Indeed, this form has persisted for most of the twentieth century, as the Soviet Union before its breakup can attest.

Wallerstein, as well as other historical sociologists (whose theories are examined in on the Web site for this book), emphasizes the structural dilemma for imperial forms of governance: sustaining the resource levels necessary to support privilege of elites and a large military and administrative bureaucracy despite resentful peasants and the need to control conquered populations. Corruption and graft only aggravate these problems, but in the end, the state leaders face fiscal crises and must confront a variety of enemies within and outside their homeland borders. Eventually, the empire collapses, often because two imperial empires come to a showdown conflict, as Collins emphasized in his analysis of geopolitics (see Table 9.6 on page 160).

In contrast with an empire, a *world economy* reveals a different structure composed of (a) multiple states at its core, some of which have approximately equal military power; (b) competition among these core states in both the military and economic arena, with the latter being dominated by markets; and (c) peripheral states whose cheap labor and raw resources are extracted through trade, but trade that is vastly unequal because of the military power and economic advantages of the core states in market transactions.

Core, Periphery, and Semiperiphery Wallerstein's distinction among the core and periphery at the world-system level parallels in a rough way Marx's notion of capitalists and proletarians at the societal level. Core nations correspond to capitalist class at the societal level and, like the capitalist class, extract surplus through exploitation. The *core areas* of the world system are the great military powers of their time. Since military power ultimately rests on the economy's ability to support the use of coercive force, these military powers are also leading economic powers. There are *external areas* to the core, and these become the *periphery* when a core state decides to colonize them or engage in exploitive trade. The periphery consists of less developed countries whose resources are needed and, with threats of potential or actual military intervention, are taken in exploitive market transactions. Wallerstein also distinguishes what is termed the *semiperiphery*, which comprises (a) minor nations in the core area and (b) leading states in the periphery. These semiperipheral states have a higher degree of economic development and military strength than the periphery, but not as much as the core states; they are often used as intermediaries in trade between core and periphery.[31]

The semiperiphery can also be the origin of mobility among states, and, at times, areas of the periphery can become semiperipheral and, perhaps, even part of the core area (as with the history of the United States and Japan). Similarly, much of Southeast Asia is moving today from either semiperipheral (China, for example) or even peripheral (India, for instance) to the core. Japan is clearly at the core in the current world system, whereas India and other parts of Asia are still somewhat semiperipheral but clearly capable of moving to a new core.

The basic connection that drives the world economy, however, is the relationship between the core and periphery. The core has a large consumer market for both basic and luxury goods, a well-paid labor force (at least relative to the labor force in the periphery), a comparatively low rate of taxation enabling the accumulation of private wealth, a high level of technology (both economic and military) coupled with market-driven needs to sustain technological innovation, and a set of large-scale firms that engage in trade with peripheral states. The periphery has resources that consumers in the core states desire, and because states in the periphery are at a trading disadvantage (because of their lack of military strength and their lack of technology and capital to develop their own resources), each exchange between core and periphery in a market transfers wealth to the core. This exploitation by the core perpetuates the problems of development in the periphery because peripheral states do not receive sufficient money from the core to finance infrastructural development (roads, transportation, and communication) or to afford educational and other welfare-state needs.[32] Moreover, because of the lack of economic development and the high degree of economic uncertainty in peripheral nations, population growth places even greater burdens on the state as individual citizens view children as their only potential source of economic security in the future. As a consequence, peripheral states not only remain poor and underdeveloped, they are typically politically unstable, a situation that only sustains their problems of development and their dependence on core states for trade.

The Dynamics of the World Economy A world economy reveals its own dynamics, some of which are much the same as in empires, but others of which are unique to capitalism. What the core states have all had in common with older forms of empire building is their constant wars with each other, especially over conquest and control of the periphery. Moreover, they encounter many of the same fiscal problems of empires in trying to sustain wealth, profits, and well-being at home along with a large military and administrative system to wage war and to control their own citizens and dissidents in their conquered or dominated territories. Indeed, core states are often just ahead of problems, as they colonize ever more territory to sustain the costs of their prosperity while financing the administrative and coercive basis of control at home and abroad. When these competing powers begin to fight closer to home, they often ruin their respective economies through the costs of financing war and then maintaining control. Such wars make core states vulnerable enough that new powers can move into the core and supplant them (as has occurred with, for example, Spain and Portugal).

Another dynamic, Wallerstein argues, is the cyclical tendencies of the world economy. Wallerstein emphasizes what are termed *Kondratieff waves,* which are long-term oscillations[33] in the world system, running approximately 150 years. At the beginning of a Kondratieff wave, the demand within core states for goods is high, which increases production and the need for ever more raw materials. This need for raw materials leads to the expansion of the core states into external areas, making the latter peripheral suppliers of resources to the core. The next step in the Kondratieff wave occurs when the supplies of raw materials and the production of goods exceeds demands for them, leading core states to reduce geographical expansion but, equally important, for businesses to reduce production and, thereby, set off the down cycle emphasized by Marx: lowered domestic demand, decreased production, intense competition for market share driving profits down, increased unemployment as production declines, and, consequently, even less demand for goods, further reductions in production, business failures, and growth of monopolies and oligopolies.

This concentration of capital, however, sets the stage for the next point in the wave: High unemployment generates class conflict as workers demand better working conditions and wages; such demands eventually lead to higher wages for workers as the state responds to political pressures and large corporations give in; concentrated capital meantime seeks new technologies and ever more efficient means of production to lower costs; with more wages, economic demand increases, and, with new technologies and capital investment, a new period of higher profits and relative prosperity ensues, leading to increased demand for raw materials from peripheral states. But eventually, this new round of prosperity falls victim to the forces predicted by Marx: Market saturation of goods, intense competition over price, increased unemployment, decreased demand, further decreases in production, increases in business failures, and crisis bring to a close this long 150-year wave.

Other Cyclical Dynamics in the World Economy Within these long waves are shorter cycles that have been extensively studied by not only conventional economists but world-system analysts as well.[34] These all operate much as Marx had predicted, but without the great revolution at their end. The classic business cycle, sometimes termed the *Juglar cycle,* appears to last from five to seven years. Production expands to increased market demand, unemployment declines, demand in markets increases further, production expands more, then oversupply of goods in relation to demand starts a recession. Some have argued that part of this cycle reflects the replacement costs of new machinery, which tends to wear out about every eight years, forcing new capital investments that can drive market demand, but once this demand is met, it can also set into motion the declining demand for capital goods. Such capital demand is especially important in high technology core nations where much employment revolves around making equipment and providing services for other businesses. Capital demand can become as significant, or more so, as household consumer demand for goods and services.[35]

Another cycle is what is termed the *Kuznet cycle;* these operate over a twenty-five-year period in core and semiperipheral states.[36] Just why these cycles occur is unknown, although there are several hypotheses. One is related to generational turnover, in which about every twenty years, demand for basic household purchases such as houses and other buildings declines—and, hence, decreases production and employment—until the next generation has sufficient money to drive up demand for these goods, thereby setting off another wave of prosperity.

Hegemonic Sequences As Wallerstein argued,[37] but as others have developed further, there are oscillations in the degree of centralization among the core nations of the world system. Before capitalism,[38] these oscillations revolved around the rise and fall of empires through war, conquest, tribute, and collapse. With capitalism, however, the nature of the oscillation changes. Hegemonic core states seek to control trade, particularly trade across oceans, and thereby connect core and periphery in an exploitive trade arrangement. The dominant state or states can prevent military empires from encroaching on this trade and can force empires to act as capitalists in the system of world trade (as with the former Soviet Union and as is occurring in China today).

Thus, the cycle of centralization revolves around the rise and fall of hegemonic core states that have been able to dictate the terms of trade in the world system. Shifts in this domination by a core state can come with wars, but unlike pre-capitalist empire building, the domination that ensues is oriented toward dictating the terms of trade as much as toward outright conquest of territory or extraction of tribute in response to military threats. The rise of a new hegemonic state gives the state greater access to the resources of other peripheral and semiperipheral states, while enabling it to dominate other core states (as has been the case, for example, with the United States in the post–World War II period, at least to this point).

In addition to war, hegemonic states often rise because of new economic or military technology that gives them advantages. Under these conditions, states can charge "rents" for their innovations, or use them to control trade and, in the case of military technology, to make threats that improve the terms of trade. As these innovations are copied, however, the advantages can be lost or neutralized, setting the stage for another potential hegemonic state to emerge because of new technologies and other productive or military advantages.

The End of Capitalism?

Wallerstein and many other world-system analysts still accept Marx's vision that capitalism will collapse, but for world systems theory, capitalism must first penetrate the entire world for its contradictions to emerge. As long as peripheral states exist to be exploited by the core, capitalism can sustain itself by relying on the resources and the cheap labor of less developed countries. But once capitalism exists everywhere, there is no longer an escape from the processes outlined by Marx. The problems endemic to capitalism—saturation of markets, decreased demand, lowered production, and further decreases in demand—will lead to the collapse of capitalist modes of production, a period of conflict between old-line capitalists (along with their allies in the state) and the broader population that seeks a better way to distribute resources fairly. In the wake of these crises will come world-level socialism, and perhaps even world government. Although the details of this ultimate scenario vary among analysts, the emancipatory thrust of Marx's predictions remains. Whether these predictions are any more accurate than Marx's remains to be seen, but regardless of their accuracy, world-systems theory has provided important insights into basic dynamics of human organization.[39]

CONCLUSION

Varieties of analytical class analysis along with diverse approaches to world-systems analysis attest to the continued viability of Marxian–inspired sociological theory. Indeed, class and world-systems analyses retain much of the substantive flavor of Marx's theory and extend this substance in useful and creative ways. The key dynamic remains exploitation, whether by those who control capital within a society or by those nations who dominate other nations militarily and economically. Moreover, although a certain caution and moderation is evident, the emancipatory thrust of Marx is retained: In the long run, it is supposed, the contradictions of capitalism will indeed lead to a revolution in which there is less inequality in the distribution of resources among people within societies and between societies.

What makes these neo-marxian approaches appealing is their willingness to confront data and to use empirical studies to modify, qualify, and change theoretical statements. This is not to say, however, that these theorists' emancipatory ideology does not make them reluctant to accept findings that might contradict the emphasis on exploitation as the central mechanism within and between societies, but at least there is a willingness to move outside the narrow confines of Marx's original formulation. In this way, they keep Marx alive as a viable source of theoretical development.

NOTES

1. Karl Marx and Friedrich Engels, *The Communist Manifesto* (New York: International, 1978; originally published in 1848).

2. Karl Marx, *Capital,* 3 volumes (New York: International, 1967; originally published in 1867, 1885, and 1894).

3. For example, Perry Anderson, *Considerations on Western Marxism* (London: New Left Review, 1976); Michael Buraway, *The Politics of Production* (London: Verso, 1985); Sam Bowles and Herbert Gintis, *Democracy and Capitalism* (New York: Basic Books, 1986); G. A. Cohen, *History of Labor and Freedom: Themes from Marx* (Oxford: Clarendon, 1988) and *Karl Marx's Theory of History: A Defense* (Princeton, NJ: Princeton University Press, 1978); John Elster, *Making Sense of Marx* (Cambridge: Cambridge University Press, 1978); Barry Hindess and Paul Q. Hirst, *Capital and Capitalism Today* (London: Routledge, 1977); Claus Offe,

Disorganized Capitalism: Contemporary Transformations of Work and Politics (Cambridge: Cambridge University Press, 1985); Adam Przeworski, *Capitalism and Social Democracy* (Cambridge: Cambridge University Press, 1985); John A. Roemer, *A General Theory of Exploitation and Class* (Cambridge, MA: Harvard University Press, 1982) and *Analytical Foundations of Marxian Economic Theory* (Cambridge: Cambridge University Press, 1981).

4. Erik Olin Wright, "What Is Analytical Marxism?" *Socialist Review* 19 (1989), pp. 35–56.

5. Erik Olin Wright, "Class Analysis, History and Emancipation," *New Left Review* 202 (1993), pp. 15–35.

6. Ibid., p. 28.

7. Erik Olin Wright, "Rethinking, Once Again, the Concept of Class Structure," in *The Debate on Classes,* ed. E. O. Wright (London: Verso, 1989), p. 269.

8. See, in particular, Erik Olin Wright, *Class, Crisis and the State* (London: Verso, 1978), *Class Structure and Income Distribution* (New York: Academic, 1979), and *Classes* (London: Verso, 1985); Erik Olin Wright and Luca Perrone, "Marxist Class Categories and Income Inequality," *American Sociological Review* 42 (1977), pp. 32–55.

9. Wright, "Rethinking, Once Again, the Concept of Class Structure" (cited in note 7).

10. See, for examples, Wright's own comparative survey research on class structures, which can be found in "The Comparative Project on Class Structures and Class Consciousness: An Overview," *Acta Sociologica* 32 (1989), pp. 3–22; *Class Structure and Income Distribution* (cited in note 8); *Classes* (cited in note 8); and Wright and Perrone, "Marxist Class Categories and Income Inequality" (cited in note 8).

11. See the chapters in Wright, *The Debate on Classes* (cited in note 7).

12. Wright, "Rethinking, Once Again, the Concept of Class Structure" (cited in note 7).

13. Ibid., p. 281.

14. Ibid., p. 282.

15. Marx conceived of *alienation* as the result of workers' inability to determine what they produce, how they produce, and to whom the products of their labor are sold.

16. See propositions in Table 8.1 on p. 133 for a list of these conditions.

17. Wright, "Class Analysis, History and Emancipation" (cited in note 5).

18. Wright, "Rethinking, Once Again, the Concept of Class Structure" (cited in note 7), p. 296.

19. Wright and Perrone, "Marxist Class Categories"; Wright, *Classes* and *Class, Crisis and the State* (all cited in note 8).

20. Wright, *Class, Crisis and the State* and *Class Structure and Income Distribution* (both cited in note 8).

21. Wright, *Classes* (cited in note 8).

22. Roemer, *A General Theory of Exploitation and Class* (cited in note 3).

23. Wright, "Rethinking, Once Again, the Concept of Class Structure" (cited in note 7).

24. Wright, "Class Analysis, History and Emancipation" (cited in note 5).

25. His most recent major effort is Erik Olin Wright, *Class Counts* (Cambridge: Cambridge University Press, 1997), but for a more recent statement, see Michael Burawoy and Erik Olin Wright, "Sociological Marxism" in *Handbook of Sociological Theory,* edited by J. H. Turner (New York: Plenum, 2002).

26. For brief reviews of the ideas presented here, see Wright, "Rethinking, Once Again, the Concept of Class Structure" (cited in note 7), and "Class Analysis, History and Emancipation" (cited in note 5).

27. John Atkinson Hobson, *Capitalism and Imperialism in South Africa* (London: Contemporary Review, 1900); *The Conditions of Industrial Peace* (New York: Macmillan, 1927); *Confessions of an Economic Heretic* (London: Allen and Unwin, 1938); *The Economics of Distribution* (London: Macmillan, 1900).

28. Immanuel Wallerstein, *The Modern World System,* 3 volumes (New York: Academic, 1974, 1980, 1989). Earlier work by scholars such as Andre Gunder Frank on "dependency theory" anticipated much of what Wallerstein was to argue: Underdeveloped societies, especially those in Latin America, could not go through the stages to modernization because they were economically dependent on advanced economies, and this dependency and the corresponding exploitation by advanced industrial powers kept them from becoming fully industrialized and modern. See for example, Frank's *Capitalism and Underdevelopment in Latin America* (New York: Monthly Review Press, 1967). See also his later

work, *Dependent Accumulation* (New York: Monthly Review Press, 1979). Also, historians such as Fernand Braudel had conducted analyses of world-system processes (for his overview, see *Civilization and Capitalism,* 3 volumes (New York: Harper & Row, 1964).

29. For a review, see Christopher Chase-Dunn and Peter Grimes, "World-Systems Analysis," *Annual Review of Sociology,* 21 (1995), pp. 387–417. See also Albert J. Bergesen, ed., *Studies of the Modern World System* (New York: Academic Press, 1980).

30. See Christopher Chase-Dunn and T. D. Hall's edited collection of essays on *Core/Periphery Relations in Precapitalist Worlds* (Boulder, CO: Westview, 1991). See also Andre Gunder Frank and B. K. Gills, eds., *The World System: Five Hundred Years or Five Thousand?* (London: Routledge, 1993).

31. For a somewhat different analysis, see Christopher Chase-Dunn, *Global Formation* (Cambridge: Blackwell, 1989). See also Volker Bornschier and Christopher Chase-Dunn, *Transnational Corporations and Under-development* (New York: Praeger, 1985).

32. This was the essential point of dependency theorists; cited in note 28.

33. See Chase-Dunn and Grimes, "World Systems Analysis" (cited in note 29) for a brief overview of wave analysis. For a short but very clear summary of Wallerstein's argument, see Randall Collins, *Theoretical Sociology* (New York: Harcourt Brace Jovanovich, 1988), pp. 96–97.

34. See Chase-Dunn and Grimes, "World Systems Analysis" (cited in note 29) for a brief review of empirical and conceptual work on these cycles.

35. Ibid., p. 404.

36. Ibid., pp. 404–405.

37. Wallerstein, *The Modern World System* (cited in note 28).

38. See Chase-Dunn and Grimes, "World Systems Analysis" (cited in note 29), pp. 411–414, for a useful review.

39. For a recent test of the world system model, see Ronan Van Rossem, "The World System Paradigm As General Theory of Development: A Cross-National Test," *American Sociological Review* 61 (1996), pp. 508–527.

11

Feminist Conflict Theory

In the 1960s and early 1970s, the obvious gender bias of sociological inquiry was exposed. Both theory and research in sociology had focused on males and, in a very real sense, contributed to patterns of gender inequality. Indeed, if one looks to the early masters of sociological theory, they were conspicuously quiet about gender issues, despite the fundamental facts that roughly one-half of the human population is female and that all patterns of social organization have historically revealed a gender-based division of labor. When sociological theorizing turned to gender questions, however, theorizing itself became confrontational and conflictual. As will be explored in Chapter 15, critical feminist thinking tended to reject science and "male modes" of thinking about the world in general, offering a variety of new ways to analyze social reality. Yet, many critical feminists stayed within the scientific fold, preferring to conceptualize gender processes in more neutral theoretical terms. In particular, those in this scientific camp worked within a conflict-theory approach, analyzing gender inequalities as yet another form of conflict-producing stratification. Most of these theorists sought to explain why women have experienced discrimination, and how this discrimination has placed them in disadvantaged positions in the stratification system. In this chapter, we will examine two prominent examples of feminist theorizing that remain committed to developing scientific laws: Rae Lesser Blumberg and Janet Chafetz.

RAE LESSER BLUMBERG'S GENDER STRATIFICATION THEORY

Rae Lesser Blumberg developed a theory emphasizing women's degree of control of the means of production and the distribution of economic surplus.[1] Blumberg's theory is based on a broad empirical knowledge of diverse societal types, ranging from hunting and gathering through horticultural and agrarian systems to industrial societies. Her theory thus explains the position of women relative to men in all types of societies, from the earliest to the most complex societies of the late twentieth century. (See Table 11.1.)

Sexual stratification, Blumberg argues, is ultimately driven by the degree to which, relative to men, women control the means of production and the allocation of productive surplus or, in Marxian terms, "surplus value." Such control gives women *economic power* that, in turn, influences their level of political power, prestige, and other stratifying resources. In Blumberg's view, sexual inequalities are "nested" at diverse levels: Male-female relations are nested in households; households are nested in local communities; and if a society is sufficiently large to reveal a coercive state and a system of class stratification, household and community are nested inside of the class structure that, in turn, is lodged within a larger state-managed society. This nesting is important because women's control of economic resources can be located at different levels, and the level at which their economic power is strongest influences the power that women can command at the other levels of social organization.

Nesting of economic power is marked by what Blumberg calls a *discount rate* in which women's economic power will be reduced or enhanced depending on the level at which it is concentrated. If women's relative economic power is at the micro level of the household (for example, women work and contribute to family income), women will not have household authority proportionate to their economic contribution if males control more macro social spheres. Male control at these more macro levels "discounts" or reduces the power that women should have in the household. Conversely, if women possess power at more macro levels, then the discount rate turns positive and will enhance women's power at the more micro, household level. Thus, as a general proposition, the more women have economic power at macro levels of social organization, the more they will be able to gain access to other forms of power—political, coercive, ideological—and the more their economic contributions at the micro level will be appreciated and increase their authority within the household and their influence within a community.

Blumberg emphasizes that during times of transition, when women's economic power relative to men is growing, men are likely to perceive such changes as a threat and to repress physically and politically women's efforts to gain equal power. Yet, as women's relative economic power increases, this increase will translate into political influence: If women's economic power and political influence become consolidated, then political policies working against

Table 11.1 Abbreviated Summary of Blumberg's Gender Stratification Theory

I. The degree of gender stratification is inversely related to the level of economic power women can mobilize, and conversely, the less economic power women can mobilize, the more likely are they to be oppressed physically, politically, and ideologically.

II. The level of economic power that women can mobilize is a positive and additive function of

    A. The ability to participate in economic production.

    B. The ability to control the distribution of their economic production.

    C. The ability to mitigate the "discount rate" for their labor which, in turn, is positively related to the degree to which they exert influence at macro levels of social organization.

    D. The strategic indispensability of their economic activities, which, in turn, is a positive and additive function of

        1. The demand for their labor relative to the supply.

        2. The comparability of their productive labor with reproductive obligations and options.

        3. The degree to which their labor is seen as important.

        4. The extent to which women control technical expertise.

        5. The degree to which women can work autonomously from male supervision.

        6. The size, scale, and level organization in women's work groups.

        7. The degree to which women can organize on their own behalf and pursue their interests.

        8. The degree to which women can avoid competition from other sources of labor.

    E. The extent to which the kinship systems facilitate the acquisition of property by women that, in descending order of importance, depends on

        1. Rules of inheritance allowing women to inherit property.

        2. Rules of residence giving females kin allies.

        3. Rules of descent favoring the female side of the kinship system in passing property, power, and authority.

III. The greater women's economic power is relative to that enjoyed by men, the greater women's control of their own lives will be for

    A. Their fertility.

    B. Their marriages and divorces.

    C. Their premarital, marital, and extramarital sexual activities.

    D. Their household authority and duties.

    E. Their educational achievements.

    F. Their freedom to pursue diverse opportunities.

IV. The greater women's economic power is relative to men's and the more women control their own lives, the greater their access will be to other sources of value in stratified social systems, especially honor and prestige, political power, and ideological support for their rights.

women will recede, male-supremacist ideologies will decline, and male violence against women will be punished.

Thus, gaining control of economic power—that is, the control of their
means of production and the allocation of the fruits of their production—is the
critical condition influencing women's position in the stratification system of
a society. What, then, determines when and how women gain economic
power? For Blumberg, the key variable is the *demand* for labor performed by
women, especially the *strategic indispensability* of their labor. In simple societies
without class stratification, women's participation in production is a function
of (1) the demand for their labor relative to the supply of labor and (2) the
degree of compatibility of this productive labor with the reproductive (especially breast feeding) labor that women must also perform. In class-stratified
systems, the demand for labor becomes more important as other arrangements
can be made for child care. In these complex systems, women can begin to
move into male-dominated positions when there is a shortage of men to perform the activity (such as when men are at war, or the demographics of war
have created a shortage of men in the population) or when the economic
activity of women is sufficiently valuable for traditional norms about the sexual division of labor to change.

Thus, the *strategic indispensability* of women's labor becomes one of the
most important determinants of women's access to economic power. When
women's activities are defined as important, their indispensability increases,
but other conditions influence indispensability: (a) the extent to which
women control technical expertise, (b) the degree to which women can work
autonomously from male supervision, (c) the size, scale, and level of organization in women's work groups, (d) the degree to which women can organize on their own behalf and pursue their interests, and (e) the degree to
which women can avoid competition from workers (other groups of women,
slaves, immigrants, and the like) who can be used as substitutes for women's
labor.

The kinship system also influences women's capacity to gain economic
power. Blumberg sees inheritance rules as the most critical: That is, can
women inherit and control property? If so, then they can exercise economic
power. Next most important is the residence rule of kinship: Does a bride
continue to reside with or near her kin in their community? If so, then she can
control domestic property and secure necessary support and coercive backup
from her local family. Another influence from kinship comes from the descent
rule: Is the system matrilineal (with property and power passing through the
female's side of the family) or patrilineal (with property and power coming
from the male's side)? If the system is matrilineal, women retain more power
(even though much of the property and power goes through her male kin who
will, nonetheless, provide support in dealings with her husband).

In addition to strategic indispensability and kinship rules, an important factor influencing women's economic power is the way surplus and other
resources are distributed. When communal relations of production prevail,

where men and women equally share work and its outputs, women will have more economic power than in systems where men control the means of production and distribution of its surplus. Such male control increases with class stratification; inequalities are high along every front, including the distribution of power, prestige, property, and opportunities for the respective sexes. Under these conditions, especially if women cannot inherit or control property, their ability to gain economic power is dramatically reduced. In these stratified systems, however, those at the bottom of the stratification ladder will have virtually no property, creating a situation where men and women will share their misery more equally. Conversely, as one moves up the class ladder in such systems, inequalities between the sexes increase, and females are denied access to economic power.

Without economic power, Blumberg argues, women are denied honor and prestige, and more important, they have less control over such basic matters as their fertility patterns (when and how many children to have), their marriages (when, if, and with whom), their rights to seek a divorce, their premarital sex, their access to extramarital sex, their household activities, their levels and types of education, and their freedom to move about and pursue diverse interests and opportunities. Thus, economic power has important consequences for what women can, or cannot, do in a society. And, Blumberg emphasizes, it is not just women's economic participation that matters; rather, does such economic participation translate into *control of one's own productive activities and the distribution of the outputs from this productive activity?* If women's work is strategically indispensable, if kinship facilitates their inheritance and acquisition of property, and if stratification at the macro level does not so blatantly favor men, then women can gain economic power. Without such economic power, sexual stratification will be high, but with this economic power, the degree gender inequality will decline. Table 11.1 summarizes Blumberg's main argument in propositional form somewhat shorter than her longer list of propositions or hypotheses.

JANET SALTZMAN CHAFETZ'S GENDER EQUITY THEORY

Janet Chafetz has been one of the most prominent feminist theorists committed to developing scientific explanations of gender stratification. Her most ambitious effort, *Gender Equity: An Integrated Theory of Stability and Change,*[2] presents a set of models and propositions to explain both the forces maintaining a system of gender inequality as well as a theory of how such a system can be changed. As she emphasizes, the two are interrelated because "a theory of the maintenance and reproduction of gender systems is a theory of change targets, because it identifies the critical variables that sustain the status quo and, therefore, must be changed."[3]

The Maintenance of Gender Stratification

Chafetz argues that two types of forces sustain a system of gender inequality: (1) those that are coercive and (2) those that are voluntaristic acts by individuals. The two are interrelated, but Chafetz initially theorizes about them as separate forces.

Coercive Bases of Gender Inequality Gender stratification, Chafetz contends, is ultimately related to the macro-level division of labor in a society. If this division of labor is gendered—that is, work is defined and distributed based on a person's sex—males will typically receive more resources than will women, and this material resource advantage will translate into differences in power between men and women at the micro, interpersonal level. The more males have a material and power advantage over their wives stemming from the gendered division of labor, the more men will use this power in their relations with wives, and as a result, the more likely are wives to defer to, and comply with, the demands of their husbands.[4] Thus, once there is a macro-level division of labor that favors men, this system gives men power advantages for interpersonal demands and, as a result, makes them less likely to contribute to family and domestic work. Wives thus become burdened with domestic chores, even when they work, which makes it increasingly difficult for them to compete with men for resource-generating work outside the home—a situation that, in turn, sustains the macro-level gendered division of labor.

When men have advantages in the macro-level division of labor, they are also more likely to be incumbents in those elite societal positions to which power resources accrue. The more males control these elite power positions, the more likely the distribution of opportunities in both power and work roles outside the home will favor men over women.[5] Once this situation exists, the attitudes and behaviors in work roles will continue to give men advantages, because these roles will be viewed as attributes favoring men over women. Indeed, the attributes of women will often be negatively evaluated, thereby perpetuating the advantage of men in competition with women for those positions generating material and power resources.

These definitional processes at the macro level filter down not only to micro-level interactions between men and women, especially between husbands and wives, but to virtually all inter-gender interactions as well. As men control material and power resources, while using this resource advantage to define and, hence, ideologically control the work situation, men can use this same definitional power to regulate micro encounters between men and women. If women accept their male interaction partners' definitions of reality, they are more likely to defer to men and to play gender-traditional domestic roles that, in turn, support the macro-level bias in the division of labor.

This process is exacerbated because men control elite positions in the broader society and can, therefore, perpetuate definitions of worth that favor men; these definitions typically lead to the devaluation of the work that women perform, inside and outside of the domestic sphere. For example, domestic family work of a wife goes unpaid and, hence, undervalued, whereas traditional work roles for women, such as secretary, are underpaid because they are not valued as highly as are roles performed by men.

Gender social definitions become, in Chafetz's model, a critical link between macro- and meso-level coercive processes and voluntaristic processes that operate more typically at the personal, decision-making level. Chafetz distinguishes among three types of gender definitions: (1) *gender ideology* or beliefs about the basic and, typically, presumably biological differences in the natures of men and women; (2) *gender norms* or expectations about the appropriate and proper ways for men and women to behave; and (3) *gender stereotypes* or accentuation of the differences between men and women in how they will generally respond in situations. For Chafetz, the greater the level of consensus is among members of a population on these gender definitions and the more the gendered differences are presumed by individuals to be the way the sexes are, the more power these definitions have to influence both macro- and micro-level social processes sustaining gender inequality. In general, Chafetz argues, the gender ideology sets the constraints for gender norms that then contribute to gender stereotyping about the differences between men and women.

All these definitional processes legitimate the distribution of opportunities for men and women in the division of labor, in positions of power and authority, and in micro encounters between men and women inside and outside of the home. These interrelated forces will, in turn, influence what Chafetz terms *engenderment* or the processes whereby men and women, but especially women, accept "voluntarily" their position in the system of gender stratification.

Voluntaristic Bases of Gender Inequality The more the economic division of labor, the distribution of incumbents in elite positions, and the cultural definitions of a society reveal a gender bias, the more likely members of the adult generation are to evidence gender differentiation in their work and home activities. As a result, adults become both role models and active socializing agents for engendering the next generation in their behaviors, expectations for their future, and definitions of what is real and appropriate. To the extent that this engenderment occurs via family and other socialization forces, individuals "voluntarily" act in ways sustaining macro-level division of labor and cultural definitions about differences between men and women, while reproducing these gender differences in micro-level encounters between men and women.

These basic ideas, which Chafetz presents as a systematic list of propositions and as a series of causal models, constitute the core of her argument about the maintenance of gender inequality and stratification. Table 11.2 presents the core propositions in highly abbreviated form.

As Chafetz emphasizes, however, once the forces maintaining a system are understood, the critical targets for change are also identified. Much of her approach involves an effort to use understanding of the maintenance forces to

Table 11.2 Abbreviated Summary of Chafetz's Theory on the Maintenance of Gender Stratification

I. The maintenance of a system of gender stratification is a joint function of the following conditions:

  A. The degree to which males have coercive power that, in turn, successively increases when

    1. The macro-level division of labor is gendered.

    2. The gendered division of labor gives males material resource advantages.

    3. The material resource advantages of men are used in micro encounters with women to extract compliance that, in turn, will

      a. Burden women in domestic and reproductive chores.

      b. Decrease their ability to compete with men in the macro-level division of labor.

    4. The macro-level and micro-level resource advantages of men translates into their control of elite positions in the broader society, which, in turn, leads to

      a. Distribution of opportunities in work, political, and other spheres favoring men over women.

      b. Definitions of positive and negative attributes in work, political, and other spheres favoring men over women.

    5. The definitions of men's and women's attributes are

      a. Accepted consensually by all members of a society.

      b. Organized into an integrated and hierarchical system of distinctions between men and women comprising

        1. Gender ideologies.

        2. Gender norms.

        3. Gender stereotypes.

      c. Used to legitimate the distribution of opportunities in

        1. The division of labor.

        2. The system of power.

        3. The micro encounters between men and women.

  B. The degree to which the coercive advantages of males, enumerated in I-A, cause engenderment or the voluntaristic acceptance of gender distinctions, which, in turn, is additively increased by

    1. Gendered division of domestic and nondomestic labor by adults in family settings.

    2. Gendered adult role models in family settings.

    3. Gender-biased socialization by adults in family settings.

construct what she terms "gender system change."[6] From the theory, the obvious targets for changing a system of gender inequality are (1) the gender division of labor, (2) the resulting superior resource power of men, (3) the social definitions comprising gender ideologies, norms, and stereotypes, and (4) the engenderment processes that differentiate the orientations, expectations, and behaviors of men and women.

Changing Systems of Gender Inequality
and Stratification

Many of the processes generating changes in gender stratification, whether long-term change in the distribution of resources or shorter-term oscillations in the opportunities for women, are external to the gender system itself. Forces such as technological changes, demographic shifts in the age and composition of the population, changes in the structure of the economy, and geopolitical forces like war and migration can all exert pressures on the system of gender inequality. Chafetz conceptualizes these as "unintentional change processes," and her argument runs as follows:

Demographic Variables Expansion of the working-age population will tend to decrease the opportunities for women, holding steady the number of actual work roles available in a society, whereas a decline in the working-age population will increase opportunities for women in the economic division of labor. Sex ratios also have much the same effects: As the sex ratio of men to women drops below parity, opportunities for women increase; if the reverse is true and the proportion of men relative to women increases, opportunities for women will decline.

Technological Variables Changes in technology have important effects on gender stratification. Technology can alter, Chafetz argues, the strength requirements, the mobility required, and the capacity to work outside the home and its domestic responsibilities. The greater is the amount of change along these variables, the greater will be the effects of technology on gender stratification. In general, when technologies reduce the strength requirements of work outside the home (which, as Chafetz emphasizes, are typically exaggerated by males anyway), when less physical mobility is required, and when the obligations of child rearing and household can be overcome by technology, then opportunities for women will increase, thereby reducing the effects of the gendered division of labor on gender inequality. Conversely, when strength requirements, mobility, and domestic burdens are all high, or perceived to be so by virtue of gender definitions, then opportunities for women decline. Moreover, technological change that renders obsolete the skills of any gender, whether the male or female, will work against women because men will enjoy a competitive advantage in seeking new resource-generating work roles.

Economic Variables Structural changes in the economy, typically driven by both demographic and technological transformations, will also influence gender stratification. An expanding economy will help women gain access to resource-generating work roles, as long as men are fully employed. The reverse is also true: A retracting economy will decrease opportunities for women. De-skilling of jobs is an important form of economic change, as technologies (particularly information systems but mechanical ones as well) are used to perform tasks that once required skill. Because of men's favored position of power in the division of labor, their jobs will be less likely to be de-skilled than will those occupied by women, or at the very least, men's jobs will be de-skilled less rapidly.

Political Variables   Conflicts in the political arena can be external or internal. Chafetz argues that, regardless of the case, conflict will tend to strengthen traditional gender definitions. Internal conflict is especially likely to do so, and the more prolonged the conflict, the more likely this is to be the case. Even when women can assume traditional male roles during a conflict, as when men are gone to war, Chafetz argues that traditional gender definitions will still be strengthened and that the opportunities presented to women because the sex ratio has dropped below parity will be only temporary. When men return from war women will be displaced, or, if a large number of men have been killed, women will be displaced as the pool of male labor is replenished and engendered.

These demographic, technological, economic, and political forces are, as Chafetz stresses, often unintended; they simply occur as the world economy and technologies on which it runs change, as the political and the international politics among nations are altered, and as the international migration of populations unfolds over time. Yet, much change in gender stratification is intentional, involving deliberate acts to alter the distribution of resources among men and women.

One source of intended change is, at first glance, not easily predicted: elite males who control key positions actively seeking to change gender stratification. Chafetz argues that two conditions cause this kind of elite-initiated change to occur: (1) when elites perceive that gender inequality threatens their incumbency as elites or thwarts their plans for the society; and (2) when competing factions of elites need to recruit women to their side to prevail in a conflict. Under these conditions, elites will attempt to mobilize women's support in exchange for promises to ameliorate women's disadvantages in the division of labor and in the system of gender definitions.

Whether or not initiated by such top-down efforts by elites, women's mobilization to pursue their interests is influenced by other forces, especially industrialization, urbanization, and expansion of the middle classes. When these events occur, middle-class women might begin to seek expanded opportunities outside their domestic responsibilities, and they are more likely to have the resources (material, educational, and symbolic-ideological) to pursue opportunities. As they do so, however, they confront the existing system of gender stratification, which creates role dilemmas. As women overcome these dilemmas, they acquire a sense of efficacy and begin to change their frames of reference in ways counter to dominant gender definitions. As women pursue interests outside the domestic sphere with this changed frame of reference, especially if they do so in a context where other women are also in proximity pursuing the same goals, they will experience an escalated sense of deprivation as they encounter the gendered division of labor and the distribution of power. For now, they interpret these obstacles in light of a sense that they deserve more than old gender definitions allowed, and their sense of deprivation

Table 11.3 Abbreviated Summary of Chafetz's Theory on Change in Gender Stratification

I. Change in systems of gender stratification is determined by the following conditions:

  A. Unintended change processes stemming from

    1. Demographic changes in

      a. Work-age population relative to number of available jobs.

      b. Sex ratio.

    2. Technological innovations that cause changes in

      a. Strength requirements (or perceptions about such requirements) for resource-generating roles.

      b. Physical mobility requirements for resource-generating roles.

      c. Domestic requirements of women so that they can pursue nondomestic resource-generating roles.

    3. Structural economic changes in

      a. Rate of economic growth and number of resource-generating work roles.

      b. De-skilling of work roles performed by men and women.

    4. Political conflicts causing a change in

      a. Salience of traditional gender definitions.

      b. Demographic shifts in sex ratio.

  B. Intentional change processes stemming from

    1. Efforts by elites to support changes in gender inequality when

      a. They perceive that gender stratification threatens their position as elites.

      b. They believe that gender stratification thwarts their societal plans and goals.

      c. They find themselves in competition with other factions of elites and require women as allies.

    2. Efforts by women to mobilize and pursue their interests in breaking down gender stratification, with such mobilization being a positive and additive function of

      a. Industrialization as it increases nondomestic roles.

      b. Urbanization as it congregates and concentrates women.

      c. Expansion of middle classes as it expands the pool of less domestically burdened women.

      d. Sense of efficacy and escalated expectations experienced by women with nondomestic options.

      e. Sense of relative deprivation as escalated expectations confront barriers in existing system of gender stratification.

      f. Experience of deprivation collectively by women.

      g. Ideological ferment that changes public gender definitions toward moderate positions.

      h. Support from societal elites.

  C. Unintentional and intentional change processes in a system of gender stratification threaten interest groups that mobilize counter-change movements, with such movements gaining power when

    1. A large proportion of women are engendered within traditional gender definitions.

    2. A large proportion of men-dominated roles are threatened.

    3. A high degree of internal conflict within the women's movement has alienated former supporters.

increases relative to their dramatically escalated expectations for what is possible, or what should be possible.

When women experience these sentiments collectively and in proximity, they begin to form women's movement organizations to pursue the interests of women in eliminating or at least mitigating gender inequality. Even if these movements split into diverse factions, the ideological and political ferment created will begin to erode old gender definitions and to instill those of the more moderate organizations of the women's movement. As public support increases for these moderate definitions, more expansive efforts to change the gender-biased division of labor, the system of gender ideology, norms, and stereotypes, and the distribution of power can proceed. And, if elites begin to support these efforts, the women's movement will proceed more rapidly and successfully.

Yet, Chafetz emphasizes, successful mobilization of women inevitably generates a sense of threat among powerful interest groups in a society. The greater this sense of threat is, the more likely those threatened are to lobby against efforts of the women's movement. Such threat need not always come from threatened males, but can also come from women who are committed to traditional gender roles and definitions. Such efforts to thwart the goals of women's movements can be influenced by the internal conflicts within the movement and its ideologies. Internal conflict, per se, consumes resources that could be mobilized to pursue the goals of the movement. Equally important, conflict creates alienation and disaffection from some part of the movement, giving anti-feminist men and women potential allies.

The basic ideas from Chafetz's propositions on change are summarized in abbreviated form in Table 11.3. These dynamics of conflict mobilization appear within a broader cultural, political, technological, economic, and demographic context. Thus, political conflict, whether internal and external to the nation, produces cultural conservatism that, in turn, strengthens traditional gender definitions in ways that can work against efforts by women to mobilize. If gender definitions are highly conservative and biased against women, mobilization will encounter resistance, regardless of whether or not the movement occurs within the context of political conflict. Economic and demographic forces, described earlier, can also work against a movement; if the economy contracts, if technologies de-skill, or if migration alters the supply of male workers or sex ratios, these forces can work against women's efforts to change gender definitions and the division of labor, as well as the distribution of power.

CONCLUSION

These two theories are representative of more scientifically oriented feminist approaches.[7] Gender inequalities will exist when men control disproportionate resources, and conversely, they will decline as women gain economic, political, and ideological resources. To gain access to these resources requires, however, mobilization by women and their allies, and here other conditions influence how effective this mobilization can be. This kind of theorizing tries to cast gender inequality in a more comparative light, viewing patterns of gender stratification in all types of societies—past, present, and future. Such theories seek the universal dimensions of gender inequality and stratification; as a comparison with theories in Chapter 15 on critical theories reveals, these feminist conflict theorists try to remain objective, avoiding ideological critique in the name of explanatory power.

NOTES

1. Rae Lesser Blumberg, "A General Theory of Gender Stratification," *Sociological Theory* 2 (1984), pp. 23–101.

2. Janet Saltzman Chafetz, *Gender Equity: An Integrated Theory of Stability and Change* (Newbury Park, CA: Sage, 1990). See also her *Sex and Advantage: A Comparative Macro-Structural Theory of Sexual Stratification* (Totowa, NJ: Rowman and Allanheld, 1984).

3. Chafetz, *Gender Equity* (cited in note 24), p. 17.

4. Ibid., p. 48.

5. Ibid., p. 54.

6. Ibid., pp. 99–220.

7. For an effort to reconcile both Blumberg's and Chafetz's theories with others in the conflict tradition, see Randall Collins, Janet Saltzman Chafetz, Rae Lesser Blumberg, Scott Coltrane, and Jonathan H. Turner, "Toward an Integrated Theory of Gender Stratification," *Sociological Perspectives* 36 (3, 1993), pp. 185–216.

PART IV

Critical Theorizing

12

Early Critical Theory

Virtually all early sociologists were influenced by a broad intellectual movement, often termed "The Enlightenment," which grew out of both the Renaissance and, later, the Age of Science in the seventeenth century.[1] The Enlightenment still inspires thinkers, in at least two respects. First, the social universe has often been seen as "progressing," moving from one stage of development to another. To be sure, theorists have disagreed about the stages, and many have had doubts about the notion of "progress," but it would be hard to deny that sociologists see directional movement of society or world systems as a central theme. A second legacy from The Enlightenment has been the belief that science can be used to further social progress. As with the idea of progress, this faith in science has not been universal, but even those who have doubted that science is the key to social progress still tend to believe that analysis of the human condition and its pathologies can be used for human betterment.

These two points of emphasis from The Enlightenment were part of a more general effort to come to terms with what is often termed "modernity" or the transformations associated with the rise of commerce and industrial capitalism from the debris of the old feudal order. Indeed, the central problem for all early sociologists was to understand the dramatic transformations of the social order being caused by the expansion of commerce and markets, the industrialization of production, the urbanization of labor, the decline of cohesive and local communities, the rise of the bureaucratic state, the decreasing salience of sacred symbols as a result of expanding secular law and science, the conflicts among new social classes, and many other disruptive transformations. These were changes that early theorists sought to comprehend. Some were pessimistic and worried about what was occurring; others were optimistic about the new modern age; still others believed that things would get better after the current turmoil subsided. But no one who was considered a serious social thinker could ignore "modernity."

Critical theorizing in all its forms enters this old debate about modernity from a number of different directions. As the name implies, most theorists in this "critical" tradition view industrial capitalism in negative terms, and some have even posited a new stage of history, "postmodernity," which is similarly viewed in a negative light. Almost all critical theorists disparage the optimism of The Enlightenment, seeing the use of science for constructing a better society as naive, as pursuit of an illusion, or even as harmful. For most, science is part of a broader culture of commerce and capitalism, which, critical theorists believe, are the cause of the problems in the modern or postmodern era, rather than part of their solution. Yet, ironically, these very same critics often appear to be figures of The Enlightenment because they address the very same problems of the earlier Enlightenment-inspired theorists, because they use analysis and reason to pronounce the problems of the modern or postmodern era, and because they often propose solutions to the ills of the current era even as they drown their pronouncements in pessimism. True, most critical theorists maintain a hearty disdain for science and the implicit Enlightenment projects of theories examined in earlier chapters, but they have not escaped the mood, tone, and problematic issues of The Enlightenment.

CRITICAL STRAINS IN MARX'S THOUGHT

In 1846, Karl Marx and Friedrich Engels completed *The German Ideology*, which was initially turned down by the publisher.[2] Much of this work is an attack on the "Young Hegelians," who were advocates of the German philosopher Georg Hegel (1770–1831), and is of little interest today. Yet this attack contained certain basic ideas that have served as the impetus behind "critical theory," or the view that social theory must be critical of oppressive arrangements and propose emancipatory alternatives. This theme exists, of course, in all of Marx's work,[3] but the key elements of contemporary critical theory are most evident in this first statement.

Marx criticized the Young Hegelians severely because he had once been one of them and was now making an irrevocable break. Marx saw the Hegelians as hopeless idealists, in the philosophical sense. That is, they saw the world as reflective of ideas, with the dynamics of social life revolving around consciousness and other cognitive processes by which "ideal essences" work their magic on humans. Marx saw this emphasis on the "reality of ideas" as nothing more than a conservative ideology that supports people's oppression by the material forces of their existence. His alternative was "to stand Hegel on his head," but in this early work there is still an emphasis on the relation between consciousness and self-reflection, on the one hand, and social reality, on the other. This dualism became central to contemporary critical theory.

Actually, Marx's "standing of Hegel on his head" has been reversed by some contemporary theorists who, in essence, have put Hegel back on his feet. Indeed, for many who commented on the condition of modernity or post-modernity near the close of the twentieth century, the world has been trans-formed into a sea of symbols that have lost anchorage in material conditions and that have, as a result, changed the very nature of society from one driven by control of the means of material production to one dominated by signs and texts symbolizing little but themselves. For critical theorists schooled in the Marxian tradition, even those who call themselves postmodernists, such arguments go too far, but there can be little doubt that Marx's dismissal of Hegel and the Young Hegelians was not the final word on the place of ideas, symbols, and signs in societal evolution.

Marx was a modernist, not a postmodernist; so he went a different direction than the Young Hegelians. Marx believed humans are unique by virtue of their conscious awareness of themselves and their situation; they are capable of self-reflection and, hence, assessment of their positions in society. Such consciousness arises from people's daily existence and is not a realm of ideas that is somehow independent of the material world, as much German philosophy argued or as later versions of postmodernism implied. According to Marx, people produce their ideas and conceptions of the world because of social structures in which they are born, raised, and live.

The essence of people's lives is the process of production, because, for Marx, human "life involves, before anything else, eating and drinking, a habitation, clothing, and many other material things."[4] To meet these contingencies of life, production is necessary, but, as production satisfies one set of needs, new needs arise and encourage alterations in the ways that productive activity is organized. The elaboration of productive activity creates a division of labor, which, in the end, is alienating because it increasingly deprives humans of their capacity to control their productive activities. Moreover, as people work, they are exploited in ways that generate private property and capital for those who enslave them. Thus, as people work as alienated cogs in the division of labor, they produce that which enslaves them: private property and profits for those who control the modes and means of production. Marx provided a more detailed discussion of the evolution of productive forces to this capitalist stage, and like any Enlightenment thinker, he argued that this capitalist stage would lead to a new era of human organization.

Marx believed that the capacity to use language, to think, and to analyze their conditions would enable humans to alter their environment. People do not merely have to react to their material conditions in some mechanical way; they can also use their capacities for thought and reflection to construct new material conditions and corresponding social relations. Indeed, the course of history involved such processes as people actively restructured the material conditions of their existence. The goal of social theory, Marx implicitly argued, is to use humans' unique facility to expose those oppressive social relations and to propose alternatives. Marx's entire career was devoted to this goal, and this emancipatory aspect of Marx's thought forms the foundation for critical theory, even in some of its postmodern manifestations.

Marx used the somewhat ambiguous term "praxis" to describe this blending of theory and action. The basic notion is that action to change social conditions generates increased knowledge that can then be used to mount more effective change-producing action. Thus, the interplay between action and theoretical understanding can eventually lead individuals to a better social life. Although those with power can impose their ideologies on subordinates and, thereby, distort the latter's perceptions of their true interests, Marx had typical Enlightenment-inspired faith that subordinates possessed the capacity for praxis and that they would eventually use their capacities for agency to change the nature of modernity.

Today, contemporary critical theorists appear somewhat divided on the question of whether analysis of modernity and postmodernity can be used to improve the human condition. As we will see shortly, many confronted Max Weber's pessimism about the ever tightening "cage" of rational-legal authority and state domination. Others sustained the emancipatory faith of Marx's belief in praxis.

Still others emphasized an inherent force articulated in Marx's analysis of capitalism—the capacity of money-driven markets to "commodify" all things, symbols, and ideals—as a basis for a renewed pessimism about the human condition. To *commodify* means that symbols, signs, objects, cultures, relationships, and virtually anything can be turned into a marketable thing, to be bought and sold for a price stated in monetary terms. Hence, as capitalists seek profits, they buy and sell not just the material objects necessary for human survival, but they produce and sell symbols and signs that, as commodities, lose their power to provide meaning to human life. Coupled with information technologies that Marx could never have visualized, as well as markets for services and cultural symbols that Marx did not fully anticipate, the social world is now dominated by the production and distribution of signs, symbols, texts, and other cultural commodities. This transformation has changed the very nature of humans' capacities to understand and respond to their conditions.

WEBER'S PESSIMISM:
THE BASIC DILEMMA
FOR EARLY CRITICAL THEORISTS

Max Weber was concerned with the historical transition to modern capitalist societies, and his description and explanation of this transition represent a devastating critique of Marx's optimism about revolutionary movements toward a new utopian society. Weber's analysis is complex, and the historical detail that he presented to document his case is impressive, but his argument is captured by the concept of *rationalization*.[5] Weber argued that the rationality that defines modern societies is "means/ends rationality" and, hence, involves a search for the most efficient means to achieve a defined end. The process of rationalization, Weber felt, involves the ever-increasing penetration of means/ends rationality into more spheres of life, thereby destroying older traditions. As bureaucracies expand in the economic and governmental sphere, and as markets allow individuals to pursue their personal ends rationally, the traditional moral fabric is broken. Weber agreed with Georg Simmel that this rationalization of life brings individuals a new freedom from domination by religious dogmatism, community, class, and other traditional forces, but in their place it creates a new kind of domination by impersonal economic forces, such as markets and corporate bureaucracies, and by the vast administrative apparatus of the ever-expanding state. Human options were, in Weber's view, becoming ever more constrained by the "iron cage" of rational and legal authority. Unlike Marx, Weber did not see such a situation as rife with revolutionary potential; rather, he saw the social world as increasingly administered by impersonal bureaucratic forces.

This pessimistic view seemed, by the early 1930s, to be a far more reasonable assessment of modernity than was Marx's utopian dream. Indeed, the communist revolution in Russia had degenerated into Stalinism and bureaucratic totalitarianism by the Communist Party; in the West, particularly the United States, workers seemed ever more willing to sell themselves in markets and work in large-scale organizations; and political fascism in Germany and Italy was creating large authoritarian bureaucracies. How, then, was the first generation of critical theorists to reconcile Weber's more accurate assessment of empirical trends with Marx's optimistic and emancipatory vision? This became the central question of early critical theory.

THE FRANKFURT SCHOOL

The first generation of critical theorists, who are frequently referred to as the Frankfurt School because of their location in Germany and their explicit interdisciplinary effort to interpret the oppressive events of the twentieth century,[6] confronted a real dilemma: how to reconcile Marx's emancipatory dream with the stark reality of modern society as conceptualized by Max Weber. Indeed, when the Frankfurt Institute for Social Research was founded in 1923, there seemed little reason to be optimistic about developing a theoretically informed program for freeing people from unnecessary domination. The defeat of the left-wing working-class movements, the rise of fascism in the aftermath of World War I, and the degeneration of the Russian Revolution into Stalinism had, by the 1930s, made it clear that Marx's analysis needed drastic revision. Moreover, the expansion of the state, the spread of bureaucracy, and the emphasis on means/ends rationality through the application of science and technology all signaled that Weber's analysis had to be confronted.

The members of the Frankfurt School wanted to maintain Marx's views on praxis—that is, a blending of theory and action or the use of theory to stimulate action, and vice versa. And they wanted theory to expose oppression in society and to propose less constrictive options. Yet, they were confronted with the spread of political and economic domination of the masses. Thus, modern critical theory in sociology was born in a time when there was little reason to be optimistic about realizing emancipatory goals.

Three members of the Frankfurt School are most central: György Lukács, Max Horkheimer, and Theodor Adorno.[7] Lukács' major work appeared in the 1920s,[8] whereas Horkheimer[9] and Adorno[10] were active well into the 1960s. In many ways, Lukács was the key link in the transition from Marx and Weber to modern critical theory because Horkheimer and Adorno were reacting to much of Lukács' analysis and approach.

All these scholars are important because they directly influenced the intellectual development and subsequent work of Jürgen Habermas, the most prolific contemporary critical theorist, whose work is examined in the next chapter.[11]

György Lukács

György Lukács (1885–1971) blended Marx and Weber together by seeing a convergence of Marx's ideas about commodification of social relations through money and markets with Weber's thesis about the penetration of rationality into ever more spheres of modern life. Borrowing from Marx's analysis of the "fetishism of commodities," Lukács employed the concept of *reification* to denote the process by which social relationships become "objects" that can be manipulated, bought, and sold. Then, reinterpreting Weber's notion of "rationalization" to mean a growing emphasis on the process of "calculation" of exchange values, Lukács combined Weber's and Marx's ideas. As traditional societies change, he argued, there is less reliance on moral standards and processes of communication to achieve societal integration; instead, there is more use of money, markets, and rational calculations. As a result, relations are coordinated by exchange values and by people's perceptions of one another as "things."[12]

Lukács painted himself into a conceptual corner, however. If indeed such is the historical process, how is it to be stopped? Lukács' answer was to resurrect a contrite Hegel; that is, rather than look to contradictions in material conditions or economic and political forces, one must examine the dialectical forces inherent in human consciousness. There are limits, Lukács argued, to how much reification and rationalization people will endure. Human subjects have an inner quality that keeps rationalization from completely taking over.[13]

This emphasis on the process of consciousness is very much a part of critical theory that borrows much from the early Marx[14] and that, at the Frankfurt School, had a heavy dose of Sigmund Freud and psychoanalytic theory. As a result, unlike its sources of inspiration, Marx and Weber, early critical theory was subjectivist and failed to analyze intersubjectivity, or the ways people interact through mutually shared conscious activity. Emphasizing the inherent resistance of subjects to their total reification, Lukács could only propose that the critical theorist's role is to expose reification at work by analyzing the historical processes that have dehumanized people. As a consequence, Lukács made critical theory highly contemplative, emphasizing that the solution to the problem of domination resides in making people more aware and conscious of their situation through a detailed, historical analysis of reification.

Max Horkheimer and Theodor Adorno

Both Max Horkheimer (1895–1973) and Theodor Adorno (1903–1964) were highly suspicious of Lukács' Hegelian solution to the dilemma of reification and rationalization. These processes do not imply their own critique, as Hegel would have suggested. Subjective consciousness and material reality cannot be separated. Consciousness does not automatically offer resistance to those material forces that commodify, reify, and rationalize. Critical theory must, therefore, actively (1) describe historical forces that dominate human freedom and (2) expose ideological justifications of these forces. Such is to be achieved through interdisciplinary research among variously trained researchers and theorists who confront one another's ideas and use this dialogue to analyze concrete social conditions and to propose courses of ameliorative action. This emphasis on praxis—the confrontation between theory and action in the world—involves developing ideas about what oppresses and what to do about it in the course of human struggles. As Horkheimer argued, "[The] value of theory is not decided alone by the formal criteria of truth . . . but by its connection with tasks, which in the particular historical moment are taken up by progressive social forces."[15] Such critical theory is, Horkheimer claimed, guided by a "particular practical interest" in the emancipation of people from class domination.[16] Thus, critical theory is tied, in a sense that Marx might have appreciated, to people's practical interests.

As Adorno and Horkheimer interacted and collaborated, their positions converged (although by the late 1950s and early 1960s, Horkheimer had seemingly rejected much of his earlier work). Adorno was more philosophical and, yet, research oriented than Horkheimer; Adorno's empirical work on "the authoritarian personality" had a major impact on research in sociology and psychology, but his theoretical impact came from his collaboration with Horkheimer and, in many ways, through Horkheimer's single-authored work.[17] Adorno was very pessimistic about the chances of critical theory making great changes, although his essays were designed to expose patterns of recognized and unrecognized domination of individuals by social and psychological forces. At best, his "negative dialectics" could allow humans to "tread water" until historical circumstances were more favorable to emancipatory movements. The goal of negative dialectics was to sustain a constant critique of ideas, conceptions, and conditions. This critique could not by itself change anything, for it operates only on the plane of ideas and concepts. But it can keep ideological dogmatisms from obscuring conditions that might eventually allow emancipatory action.

Both Horkheimer and Adorno emphasized that humans' "subjective side" is restricted by the spread of rationalization. In conceptualizing this process, they created a kind of dualism between the subjective world and the realm of material objects, seeing the latter as oppressing the former. From their viewpoint, critical theory must expose this dualism, and it must analyze how this "instrumental reason" (means/ends rationality) has invaded the human spirit. In this way, some resistance can be offered to these oppressive forces.

Within the Frankfurt School, then, the idealism of Lukács had been brought partially back into a more orthodox Marxian position, but not completely so. The damage had been done to pure Marxian materialism, and outside the narrow confines of Frankfurt, critical theory once again turned to idealism, even among those critical Marxists who had immigrated to America from Frankfurt during the rise of Nazism.[18]

THE CULTURAL TURN IN CRITICAL THEORY

Antonio Gramsci's Theory of Ideological Hegemony

Antonio Gramsci (1891–1937) was an Italian Marxist who, obviously, cannot be considered part of the Frankfurt School. Yet, he is a key figure in continuing what the Frankfurt School emphasized: Criticism acknowledging that the capitalist systems of the twentieth century's midpoint were generating prosperity and that the working classes in these systems did not seem particularly disposed to revolution. Gramsci completed the turning of Marx's ideas back into a more Hegelian mode.[19] That is, rather than view ideas as reflections of the material structure of society, much greater prominence is given to cultural forces in determining material relations in society.

Marx believed that ideology and the "false consciousness" of workers were ideological obfuscations created and maintained by those who controlled the material (economic) "substructure." Marx had argued that those who control the means and modes of production also control the state that, in turn, generates ideologies justifying this control and power. In this way, the proletariat is kept, for a time until the full contradictions of capitalism are manifest, from becoming a class "for themselves" ready to pursue revolutionary conflict with their oppressors. Gramsci simply turned this argument around: The "superstructure" of state and ideology drives the organization of society and the consciousness of the population.

Gramsci believed the ruling social class is *hegemonic,* controlling not only property and power, but ideology as well. Indeed, the ruling class holds onto its power and wealth by virtue of its ability to use ideologies to manipulate workers and all others. The state is no longer a crude tool of coercion, nor an intrusive and insensitive bureaucratic authority; it has become the propagator of culture and the civic education of the population, creating and controlling key institutional systems in more indirect, unobtrusive and, seemingly, inoffensive ways. Thus, the views of capitalists become the dominant views of all, with workers believing in the appropriateness of the market-driven systems of competition; the commodification of objects, signs, and symbols; the buying and selling of their labor; the use of law to enforce contracts favoring the interests of the wealthy; the encouragement of private charities, the sponsorship of clubs and voluntary organizations; the state's conceptions of a "good citizen"; the civics curriculum of the schools; and virtually all spheres of institutional activity that are penetrated by the ideology of the state. Culture and ideology are, in Albert Bergesen's words,[20] "no longer the thing to be explained but . . . now a thing that does the explaining." A dominant material class rules, to be sure, but it does so by cultural symbols, and the real battle in capitalist societies is over whose symbols will prevail. Or, more accurately, can subordinates generate alternative ideologies to those controlled by the state?

This view of critical theory takes much of the mechanical menace out of Weber's "iron cage" metaphor because the state's control is now "soft" and "internal." It has bars that bend flexibly around those whose perceptions of the world it seeks to control. The Marxian view of emancipation is still alive in Gramsci's theories because the goal of "theory" is to expose the full extent to which ideology has been effectively used to manipulate subordinates. Moreover, the recognition that systems of symbols become the base of society is a theme that resonated well with later postmodernists (see Chapter 14) and structuralists (see Chapter 29) who began to conceptualize modernity as the production of signs and symbols.

Louis Althusser's Structuralism

Initially, Louis Althusser (1918–1990) seems more strictly orthodox in his Marxism than does Gramsci[21]; yet he was also a French scholar in a long line of structuralists whose emphasis is on the logic of the deeper, underlying structure of surface empirical reality.[22] Althusser remains close to Marx in this sense: The underlying structure and logic of the economy is ultimately determinative. But, having said this, he then developed a theory of "The Ideological State Apparatus"[23] which gave prominence to the state's use of ideology to sustain control within a society.

For Althusser, economic, political, and ideological systems reveal their own structures, hidden beneath the surface and operating by their own logics. The economic might be the dominant system, circumscribing the operation of political and ideological structures, but these latter have a certain autonomy. History is, in essence, a reshuffling of these deep structures, and the individual actor becomes merely a vessel through which the inherent properties of structures operate. Individual actions, perceptions, beliefs, emotions, convictions, and other states of consciousness are somehow "less real" than the underlying structure that cannot be directly observed. To analogize the structuralist theories from which Althusser drew inspiration, social control comes from individuals perceiving that they are but words in a grammatical system generated by an even more fundamental structure. Each actor is at a surface place in the economic and political structures of a society, and their perceptions of these places also put them within an ideological or cultural sphere. But these places and spheres are only one level of reality; people also see themselves as part of a deeper set of structures that, in essence, defines who and what they are. Under these conditions, ideology has even more power because it is doing much more than blinding the subjects to some other reality, such as their objective class interests. Ideology is also defining actors' places in a reality beyond their direct control and a reality operating by its own logic of structure.

Thus, unlike Marx or Gramsci who believe ideology is a tool—an invidious and insidious one—used by those in power, Althusser sees the Ideological State Apparatus as more controlling because it is perceived not just as conventions, rules, mores, traditions, and beliefs, but instead as the essence of order and persons' place in this order. The subject is thus trapped in the deeper logics of economic, political, and ideological systems that erode human capacities for praxis and agency.

CONCLUSION

By the middle of the twentieth century, Marx's emancipatory project had been turned into something very different than he had visualized. His and Engel's *The Communist Manifesto* was a call to arms, based on a view of the inherent contradictions in the nature of capitalist systems. Within one hundred years of this call, critical theory had become decidedly more philosophical. Indeed, Marx's dismissal of the "Young Hegelians" in *The German Ideology* had apparently not worked; they were back in different forms and guises, but they increasingly dominated critical theorizing in the twentieth century. The "Young Hegelians" so viciously criticized by Marx and Engels had considered themselves revolutionaries, but Marx saw them as more concerned with ideas about reality than with reality itself. They were accused of "blowing theoretical bubbles" about ideals and essences, and it could be imagined that he and Engels might make the very same criticisms of the critical theories that developed in the second half of the twentieth century, especially as these theories began to merge with postmodernism. Nonetheless, critical theory in both its material and cultural formulations now represents one of the more prominent theoretical approaches in sociology.[24]

NOTES

1. Jonathan H. Turner, "Founders and Classics: A Canon in Motion" in *The Student Sociologist's Handbook,* ed. C. Middleton, J. Gubbay, and C. Ballard (Oxford: Blackwell, 1997).

2. Karl Marx and Friedrich Engels, *The German Ideology* (New York: International, 1947; written in 1846).

3. Karl Marx, *Capital: A Critical Analysis of Capitalist Production,* volume 1

(New York: International, 1967; originally published in 1867); Karl Marx and Friedrich Engels, *The Communist Manifesto* (New York: International, 1971; originally published in 1848).

4. Marx and Engels, *The German Ideology* (cited in note 2), p. 15.

5. Max Weber, *Economy and Society,* trans. G. Roth (Berkeley: University of California Press, 1978).

6. For descriptions of this activity, see Martin Jay, *The Dialectical Imagination* (Boston: Little, Brown, 1973), and "The Frankfurt School's Critique of Marxist Humanism," *Social Research* 39 (1972), pp. 285–305; David Held, *Introduction to Critical Theory* (Berkeley: University of California Press, 1980), pp. 29–110; Robert J. Antonio, "The Origin, Development, and Contemporary Status of Critical Theory," *Sociological Quarterly* 24 (Summer 1983), pp. 325–351; Phil Slater, *Origin and Significance of The Frankfurt School* (London: Routledge & Kegan Paul, 1977).

7. Other prominent members included Friedrich Pollock (economist), Erich Fromm (psychoanalyst, social psychologist), Franz Neumann (political scientist), Herbert Marcuse (philosopher), and Leo Loenthal (sociologist). During the Nazi years, the school relocated to the United States, and many of its members never returned to Germany.

8. György Lukács, *History and Class Consciousness* (Cambridge, MA: MIT Press, 1968; originally published in 1922).

9. Max Horkheimer, *Critical Theory: Selected Essays* (New York: Herder and Herder, 1972), is a translation of essays written in German in the 1930s and 1940s; *Eclipse of Reason* (New York: Oxford University Press, 1947; reprinted by Seabury in 1974) was the only book by Horkheimer originally published in English. It takes a slightly different turn than earlier works, but it does present ideas that emerged from his association with Theodor Adorno. See also Horkheimer, *Critique of Instrumental Reason* (New York: Seabury, 1974). See David Held, *Introduction to Critical Theory* (cited in note 6), pp. 489–491, for a more complete listing of Horkheimer's works in German.

10. Theodor W. Adorno, *Negative Dialectics* (New York: Seabury, 1973; originally published in 1966), and, with Max Horkheimer, *Dialectic of Enlightenment* (New York: Herder and Herder, 1972; originally published in 1947). See Held, *Introduction to Critical Theory* (cited in note 6), pp. 485–487, for a more complete listing of Adorno's works.

11. "From Lukács to Adorno: Rationalization as Reification," pp. 339–399 in Jürgen Habermas, *The Theory of Communicative Action,* vol. 1 (Boston: Beacon, 1984), contains Habermas' critique of Lukács, Horkheimer, and Adorno.

12. Lukács, *History and Class Consciousness* (cited in note 8).

13. Ibid., pp. 89–102. In a sense, Lukács becomes another "Young Hegelian" whom Marx would have criticized. Yet, in Marx's own analysis, he sees alienation, per se, as producing resistance by workers to further alienation by the forces of production. This is the image that Lukács seems to take from Marx.

14. Karl Marx and Friedrich Engels, *The German Ideology* (cited in note 2).

15. Max Horkheimer, "Zum Rationalismusstreit in der gegenwartigen Philosophie," originally published in 1935; reprinted in *Kritische Theorie,* vol. 1, ed. A. Schmidt (Frankfurt: Fischer Verlag, 1968), pp. 146–147. This and volume 2, by the way, represent a compilation of many of the essays Horkheimer wrote while at the Institute in Frankfurt.

16. Habermas used this idea, but he extended it in several ways.

17. Theodor W. Adorno, Else Frenkel-Brunswick, Daniel Levinson, and R.

Nevitt Sanford, *The Authoritarian Personality* (New York: Harper & Row, 1950).

18. See note 7.

19. Antonio Gramsci, *Selections from the Prison Notebooks* (New York: International, 1971; originally published in 1928).

20. Albert Bergesen, "The Rise of Semiotic Marxism," *Sociological Perspectives* 36 (1993), p. 5.

21. Louis Althusser, *For Marx* (New York: Pantheon, 1965); *Lenin and Philosophy* (New York: Monthly Review Press, 1971); Louis Althusser and Etienne Balabar, *Reading Capital* (London: New Left, 1968).

22. See Chapters 27 and 29 for examples of this French lineage of structuralism.

23. "Ideology and Ideological Status Apparatus" in Althusser, *Lenin and Philosophy* (cited in note 21).

24 See, for examples of critical theorizing today, David Hoy and Thomas McCarthy, *Critical Theory* (Oxford: Blackwell, 1994), or Stephen Regan, ed., *The Year's Work in Critical and Cultural Theory* (Oxford: Blackwell, 1995). Earlier reviews and analyses of critical theory and sociology include Paul Connerton, ed., *Critical Sociology* (New York: Penguin, 1970); Raymond Geuss, *The Idea of a Critical Theory* (New York: Cambridge University Press, 1981); David Held, *Introduction to Critical Theory* (Berkeley: University of California Press, 1980); Trent Schroyer, *The Critique of Domination: The Origins and Development of Critical Theory* (New York: Braziller, 1973); Albrecht Wellmer, *Critical Theory of Society* (New York: Seabury, 1974); Ellsworth R. Fuhrman and William E. Snizek, "Some Observations on the Nature and Content of Critical Theory," *Humboldt Journal of Social Relations* 7 (Fall–Winter 1979–1980), pp. 33–51; Zygmunt Bauman, *Towards a Critical Society* (Boston: Routledge & Kegan Paul, 1976); Robert J. Antonio, "The Origin, Development and Contemporary Status of Critical Theory," *Sociological Quarterly* 24 (Summer 1983), pp. 325–351; Jim Faught, "Objective Reason and the Justification of Norms," *California Sociologist* 4 (Winter 1981), pp. 33–53.

13

Critical Theory:
Jürgen Habermas

The German philosopher-sociologist, Jürgen Habermas, has been the most prolific descendant of the original Frankfurt School. As with the earlier generation of Frankfurt School social theorists, Habermas's work revolves around several important questions: (1) How can social theory develop ideas that keep Karl Marx's emancipatory project alive, yet, at the same time, recognize the empirical inadequacy of his prognosis for advanced capitalist societies? (2) How can social theory confront Max Weber's historical analysis of rationalization[1] in a way that avoids his pessimism and thereby keeps Marx's emancipatory goals at the center of theory? (3) How can social theory avoid the retreat into subjectivism of earlier critical theorists, such as György Lukács, Max Horkheimer, and Theodor Adorno, who increasingly focused on states of subjective consciousness *within individuals* and, as a consequence, lost Marx's insight that society is constructed from, and must therefore be emancipated by, the processes that sustain *social relations among* individuals? (4) How can social theory conceptualize and develop a theory that reconciles the forces of material production and political organization with the forces of intersubjectivity among reflective and conscious individuals in such a way that it avoids (*a*) Weber's pessimism about the domination of consciousness by rational economic and political forces, (*b*) Marx's naive optimism about inevitability of class consciousness and revolt, and (*c*) early critical theorists' retreat into the subjectivism of Georg Hegel's dialectic, where oppression mysteriously mobilizes its negation through increases in subjective consciousnesses and resistance?

At different points in his career, Habermas has focused on one or another of these questions, but all four have always guided his approach, at least implicitly. Habermas has been accused of abandoning the critical thrust of his earlier works, but this conclusion is too harsh. For, in trying to answer these questions, he has increasingly recognized that mere critique of oppression is not enough. Such critique becomes a "reified object itself." Although early critical theorists knew this, they never developed conceptual schemes that accounted for the underlying dynamics of societies. For critique to be useful in liberating people from domination, it is necessary, Habermas seems to say, for the critique to discuss the fundamental processes integrating social systems. In this way the critique has some possibility of suggesting ways to create new types of social relations. Without theoretical understanding about how society works, critique is only superficially debunking and becomes an exercise in futility. This willingness to theorize about the underlying dynamics of society, to avoid the retreat into subjectivism, to reject superficial criticism and instead to base critique on reasoned theoretical analysis, and to incorporate ideas from many diverse theoretical approaches make Habermas's work theoretically significant.[2]

HABERMAS'S ANALYSIS OF "THE PUBLIC SPHERE"

In his first major publication, *Structural Transformation of the Public Sphere,* Habermas traced the evolution and dissolution of what he termed *the public sphere.*[3] This sphere is a realm of social life where people can discuss matters of general interest; where they can discuss and debate these issues without recourse to custom, dogma, and force; and where they can resolve differences of opinion by rational argument. To say the least, this conception of a public sphere is rather romanticized, but the imagery of free and open discussion that is resolved by rational argumentation became a central theme in Habermas's subsequent approach. Increasingly throughout his career, Habermas came to see emancipation from domination as possible through "communicative action," which is a reincarnation of the public sphere in more conceptual clothing.

In this early work, however, Habermas appeared more interested in history and viewed the emergence of the public sphere as occurring in the eighteenth century, when various forums for public debate—clubs, cafés, journals, newspapers—proliferated. He concluded that these forums helped erode the basic structure of feudalism, which is legitimated by religion and custom rather than by agreements that have been reached through public debate and discourse. The public sphere was greatly expanded, Habermas argued, by the extension of market economies and the resulting liberation of the individual from the constraints of feudalism. Free citizens, property holders, traders, merchants, and members of other new sectors in society could now be actively concerned about the governance of society and could openly discuss and debate issues.

But, in a vein similar to Weber's analysis of rationalization, Habermas argued that the public sphere was eroded by some of the very forces that stimulated its expansion. As market economies experience instability, the powers of the state are extended in an effort to stabilize the economy; with the expansion of bureaucracy to ever more contexts of social life, the public sphere is constricted. And, increasingly, the state seeks to redefine problems as technical and soluble by technologies and administrative procedures rather than by public debate and argumentation.

The details of this argument are less important than the fact that this work established Habermas's credentials as a critical theorist. All the key elements of critical theory are there—the decline of freedom with the expansion of capitalism and the bureaucratized state as well as the seeming power of the state to construct and control social life. The solution to these problems is to resurrect the public sphere, but how is this to be done given the growing power of the state? Thus, in this early work, Habermas had painted himself into the same conceptual corner as his teachers in the Frankfurt School. The next phase of his work extended this critique of capitalist society, but he also tried to redirect critical theory so that it does not have to retreat into the contemplative subjectivism of Lukács, Horkheimer, and Adorno. Habermas began this project in the late 1960s with an analysis of knowledge systems and a critique of science.

THE CRITIQUE OF SCIENCE

In *The Logic of the Social Sciences*[4] and *Knowledge and Human Interest,*[5] Habermas analyzes systems of knowledge in an effort to elaborate a framework for critical theory. The ultimate goal of this analysis is to establish the fact that science is but one type of knowledge that exists to meet only one set of human interests. To realize this goal, Habermas posits three basic types of knowledge that encompass the full range of human reason: (1) There is empirical/analytic knowledge, which is concerned with understanding the lawful properties of the material world. (2) There is hermeneutic/historical knowledge, which is devoted to the understanding of meanings, especially through the interpretations of historical texts. (3) There is critical knowledge, which is devoted to uncovering conditions of constraint and domination. These three types of knowledge reflect three basic types of human interests: (1) a technical interest in the reproduction of existence through control of the environment, (2) a practical interest in understanding the meaning of situations, and (3) an emancipatory interest in freedom for growth and improvement. Such interests reside not in individuals but in more general imperatives for reproduction, meaning, and freedom that presumably are built into the species as it has become organized into societies. These three interests create, therefore, three types of knowledge. The interest in material reproduction has produced science or empirical/analytic knowledge; the interest in understanding of meaning has led to the development of hermeneutic/historical knowledge; and the interest in freedom has required the development of critical theory.

These interests in technical control, practical understanding, and emancipation generate different types of knowledge through three types of media: (1) "work" for realizing interests in technical control through the development of empirical/analytic knowledge, (2) "language" for realizing practical interests in understanding through hermeneutic knowledge, and (3) "authority" for realizing interests in emancipation through the development of critical theory. There is a kind of functionalism in this analysis: needs for "material survival and social reproduction," for "continuity of society through interpretive understanding," and for "utopian fulfillment" create interests. Then, through the media of work, language, and authority, these needs produce three types of knowledge: the scientific, hermeneutical, and critical.

This kind of typologizing is, of course, reminiscent of Weber and is the vehicle through which Habermas makes the central point: Positivism and the search for natural laws constitute only one type of knowledge, although the historical trend has been for the empirical/analytic to dominate the other types of knowledge. Interests in technical control through work and the development of science have dominated the interests in understanding and emancipation. And so, if social life seems meaningless and cold, it is because technical interests in producing science have dictated what kind of knowledge is permissible and legitimate. Thus Weber's "rationalization thesis" is restated with the typological distinction among interest, knowledge, and media. Table 13.1 summarizes Habermas's argument.

This typology allowed Habermas to achieve several goals. First, he attacked the assumption that science is value free because, like all knowledge, it is attached to a set of interests. Second, he revised the Weberian thesis of rationalization in such a way that it dictates a renewed emphasis on hermeneutics and criticism. These other two types of knowledge are being driven out by empirical/analytic knowledge, or science. Therefore it is necessary to reemphasize these neglected types of knowledge. Third, by viewing positivism in the social sciences as a type of empirical/analytic knowledge, Habermas associated it with human interests in technical control. He therefore visualized social science as a tool of economic and political interests. Science thus becomes an ideology; actually, Habermas sees it as the underlying cause of the legitimation crises of advanced capitalist societies (more on this shortly). In dismissing positivism in this way, he oriented his own project to hermeneutics with a critical twist. That is, he visualized the major task of critical theory as the analysis of those processes by which people achieve interpretative understanding of one another in ways that give social life a sense of continuity. Increasingly, Habermas came to focus on the communicative processes among actors as the theoretical core for critical theorizing. Goals of emancipation cannot be realized without knowledge about how people interact and communicate. Such an emphasis represents a restatement in a new guise of Habermas's early analysis of the public sphere, but now the process of public discourse and debate is viewed as the essence of human interaction in general. Moreover, to understand interaction, it is

Table 13.1 Types of Knowledge, Interests, Media (and Functional Needs)

Functional Needs	Interests	Knowledge	Media
Material survival and social reproduction generate pressures for	technical control of the environment, which leads to the development of	empirical/analytic knowledge, which is achieved through	work
Continuity of social relations generates pressures for	practical under-standing through interpretations of other's subjective states, which leads to the development of	hermeneutic and historical knowledge, which is achieved through	language
Desires for utopian fulfillment generate pressures for	emancipation from unnecessary domination, which leads to the development of	critical theory, which is achieved through	authority

necessary to analyze language and linguistic processes among individuals. Knowledge of these processes can, in turn, give critical theory a firm conceptual basis from which to launch a critique of society and to suggest paths for the emancipation of individuals. Yet, to justify this emphasis on hermeneutics and criticism, Habermas must first analyze the crises of capitalist societies through the overextension of empirical/analytic systems of knowledge.

LEGITIMATION CRISES IN SOCIETY

As Habermas had argued in his earlier work, there are several historical trends in modern societies: (1) the decline of the public sphere, (2) the increasing intervention of the state into the economy, and (3) the growing dominance of science in the service of the state's interests in technical control. These ideas are woven together in *Legitimation Crisis*.[6]

The basic argument in *Legitimation Crisis* is that, as the state increasingly intervenes in the economy, it also seeks to translate political issues into "technical problems." Issues thus are not topics for public debate; rather, they represent technical problems that require the use of technologies by experts in bureaucratic organizations. As a result, there is a "depoliticization" of practical issues by redefining them as technical problems. To do this, the state propagates a "technocratic consciousness" that Habermas believed represents a new kind of ideology. Unlike previous ideologies, however, it does not promise a future utopia; but, like other ideologies, it is seductive in its ability to veil problems, to simplify perceived options, and to justify a particular way of organizing social life. At the core of this technocratic consciousness is an emphasis on "instrumental reason," or what Weber termed *means/ends rationality*. That is, criteria of the efficiency of means in realizing explicit goals increasingly guide evaluations of social action and people's approach to problems. This emphasis on instrumental reason displaces other types of action, such as behaviors oriented to mutual understanding. This displacement occurs in a series of stages: Science is first used by the state to realize specific goals; then, the criterion of efficiency is used by the state to reconcile competing goals of groupings; next, basic cultural values are themselves assessed and evaluated for their efficiency and rationality; finally, in Habermas's version of *Brave New World,* decisions are completely delegated to computers, which seek the most rational and efficient course of action.

This reliance on the ideology of technocratic consciousnesses creates, Habermas argues, new dilemmas of political legitimation. Habermas believes capitalist societies can be divided into three basic subsystems: (1) the economic, (2) the politico-administrative, and (3) the cultural (what he later calls *lifeworld*). From this division of societies into these subsystems, Habermas then posits four points of crises: (1) an "economic crisis" occurs if the economic subsystem cannot generate sufficient productivity to meet people's needs; (2) a "rationality crisis" exists when the politico-administrative subsystem cannot generate a sufficient number of instrumental decisions; (3) a "motivation crisis" exists when actors cannot use cultural symbols to generate sufficient meaning to feel committed to participate fully in the society; and (4) a "legitimation crisis" arises when actors do not possess the "requisite number of generalized motivations" or diffuse commitments to the political subsystem's right to make decisions. Much of this analysis of crises is described in Marxian terms but emphasizes that economic and rationality crises are perhaps less important than either motivational or legitimation crises. For, as technocratic consciousness penetrates all spheres of social life and creates productive economies and an intrusive state, the crisis tendencies of late capitalism shift from the inability to produce sufficient economic goods or political decisions to the failure to generate (a) diffuse commitments to political processes and (b) adequate levels of meaning among individual actors.

Legitimation Crisis contains an early form of what becomes an important distinction: "Systemic" processes revolving around the economy and the politico-administrative apparatus of the state must be distinguished from "cultural" processes. This distinction will later be conceptualized as *system* and *lifeworld*, respectively, but the central point is this: In tune with his Frankfurt School roots, Habermas is shifting emphasis from Marx's analysis of the economic crisis of production to crises of meaning and commitment; if the problems or crises of capitalist societies are in these areas, then critical theory must focus on the communicative and interactive processes by which humans generate understandings and meanings among themselves. If instrumental reason, or means/ends rationality, is driving out action based on mutual understanding and commitment, then the goal of critical theory is to expose this trend and to suggest ways of overcoming it, especially because legitimation and motivational crises make people aware that something is missing from their lives and, therefore, receptive to more emancipatory alternatives.

So the task of critical theory is to develop a theoretical perspective that allows the restructuring of meaning and commitment in social life. This goal will be realized, Habermas argues, by further understanding of how people communicate, interact, and develop symbolic meanings.

EARLY ANALYSES OF SPEECH AND INTERACTION

In 1970, Habermas wrote two articles that marked a return to the idea of the public sphere, but with a new, more theoretical thrust. They also signaled an increasing emphasis on the process of speech, communication, and interaction. In his "On Systematically Distorted Communication," Habermas outlined the nature of undistorted communication.[7] True to Habermas's Weberian origins, this outline is an ideal type. The goal is to determine the essentials and essence of undistorted communication so that those processes that distort communication, such as domination, can be better exposed. What, then, are the features of undistorted communication? Habermas lists five: (1) expressions, actions, and gestures are noncontradictory; (2) communication is public and conforms to cultural standards of what is appropriate; (3) actors can distinguish between the properties of language, per se, and the events and processes that are described by language; (4) communication leads to, and is the product of, intersubjectivity, or the capacity of actors to understand one another's subjective states and to develop a sense of shared collective meanings; and (5) conceptualizations of time and space are understood by actors to mean different things when externally observed and when subjectively experienced in the process of interaction. The details of his analysis on the distortion of communication are less essential than the assertions about what critical theory must conceptualize. For Habermas the conceptualization of undistorted communication is used as a foil for mounting a critique against those social forces that make such idealized communication difficult to realize. Moreover, as his subsequent work testifies, Habermas emphasizes condition 4, or communication and intersubjectivity among actors.

This emphasis became evident in his other 1970 article, "Toward a Theory of Communicative Competence."[8] The details of this argument are not as critical as the overall intent, especially because his ideas undergo subsequent modification. Habermas argues that, for actors to be competent, they must know more than the linguistic rules of how to construct sentences and to talk; they must also master "idealogue-constitutive universals," which are part of the "social linguistic structure of society." Behind this jargon is the idea that the meaning of language and speech is contextual and that actors use implicit stores or stocks of knowledge to interpret the meaning of utterances. Habermas then proposes yet another ideal type, "the ideal speech situation," in which actors possess all the relevant background knowledge and linguistic skills to communicate without distortion.

Thus, in the early 1970s, Habermas began to view the mission of critical theory as emphasizing the process of interaction as mediated by speech. But such speech acts draw on stores of knowledge—rules, norms, values, tacit understandings, memory traces, and the like—for their interpretation. These ideals of the speech process represent a restatement of the romanticized public sphere, where issues were openly debated, discussed, and rationally resolved. What Habermas has done, of course, is to restate this view of "what is good and desirable" in more theoretical and conceptual terms, although it could be argued that there is not much difference between the romanticized portrayal of the public sphere and the ideal-typical conceptualization of speech. But with this conceptualization, the goal of critical theory must be to expose those conditions that distort communication and that inhibit realization of the ideal speech situation. Habermas's utopia is thus a society where actors can communicate without distortion, achieve a sense of one another's subjective states, and openly reconcile their differences through argumentation that is free of external constraint and coercion. In other words, he wants to restore the public sphere but in a more encompassing way—that is, in people's day-to-day interactions.

Habermas moved in several different directions in trying to construct a rational approach for realizing this utopia. He borrows metaphorically from psychoanalytic theory as a way to uncover the distortions that inhibit open discourse,[9] but this psychoanalytic journey is far less important than his growing concentration on the process of communicative action and interaction as the basis for creating a society that reduces domination and constraint. Thus, by the mid-1970s, he labels his analysis *universal pragmatics,* whose centerpiece is the "theory of communicative action."[10] This theory will be discussed in more detail shortly, but let us briefly review its key elements. Communication involves more than words, grammar, and syntax; it also involves what Habermas terms *validity claims.* There are three types of claims: (1) those asserting that a course of action as indicated through speech is the most effective and efficient means for attaining ends; (2) those claiming that an action is correct and proper in accordance with relevant norms; and (3) those maintaining that the subjective experiences as expressed in a speech act are sincere and authentic. All speech acts implicitly make these three claims, although a speech act can emphasize one more than the other two. Those responding to communication can accept or challenge these validity claims; if challenged, then the actors contest, debate, criticize, and revise their communication. They use, of course, shared "stocks of knowledge" about norms, means/ends effectiveness, and sincerity to make their claims as well as to contest and revise them. This process (which restates the public sphere in yet one more guise) is often usurped when claims are settled by recourse to power and authority. But if claims are settled by the "giving of reasons for" and "reasons against" the claim in a mutual give-and-take among individuals, then Habermas sees it as "rational discourse." Thus, built into the very process of interaction is the potential for rational discourse that can be used to create a more just, open, and free society. Such discourse is not merely means/ends rationality, for it involves adjudication of two other validity claims: those concerned with normative appropriateness and those concerned with subjective sincerity. Actors thus implicitly assess and critique one another for effectiveness, normative appropriateness, and sincerity of their respective speech acts; so the goal of critical theory is to expose those societal conditions that keep such processes from occurring for *all three types* of validity claims.

In this way, Habermas moves critical theory from Lukács's, Horkheimer's, and Adorno's emphasis on subjective consciousness to a concern with *inter*-subjective consciousness and the interactive processes by which intersubjectivity is created, maintained, and changed through the validity claims in each speech act. Moreover, rather than viewing the potential for liberating alternatives as residing in subjective consciousness, Habermas could assert that emancipatory potential inheres in each and every communicative interaction. Because speech and communication are the basis of interaction and because society is ultimately sustained by interaction, the creation of less restrictive societies will come about by realizing the inherent dynamics of the communication process.

HABERMAS'S RECONCEPTUALIZATION OF SOCIAL EVOLUTION

All critical theory is historical in the sense that it tries to analyze the long-term development of oppressive arrangements in society. Indeed, the central problem of critical theory is to reconcile Marx's and Weber's respective analyses of the development of advanced capitalism. It is not surprising, therefore, that Habermas produces a historical/evolutionary analysis, but, in contrast with Weber, he sees emancipatory potential in evolutionary trends. At the same time, he wants to avoid the incorrect prognosis in Marx's analysis and to retain the emancipatory thrust of Marx's approach. Habermas's first major effort to effect this reconciliation appeared in his *The Reconstruction of Historical Materialism,* parts of which have been translated and appear in *Communication and the Evolution of Society.*[12]

Habermas's approach to evolution pulls together many of the themes discussed earlier, so a brief review of his general argument can set the stage for an analysis of his most recent theoretical synthesis, *The Theory of Communicative Action.*[13] In many ways Habermas reintroduces traditional functionalism into Marx's and Weber's evolutionary descriptions, but with both a phenomenological and a structuralist emphasis.

As have all functional theorists, he views evolution as the process of structural differentiation and the emergence of integrative problems. He also borrows from Herbert Spencer, Talcott Parsons, and Niklas Luhmann when he argues that the integration of complex systems leads to an adaptive upgrading, increasing the capacity of the society to cope with the environment.[14] That is, complex systems that are integrated are better adapted to their environments than are less complex systems. The key issue, then, is this: What conditions increase or decrease integration? For, without integration, differentiation produces severe problems.

Habermas's analysis of system integration argues that contained in the worldviews or stocks of knowledge of individual actors are learning capacities and stores of information that determine the overall learning level of a society. In turn, this learning level shapes the society's steering capacity to respond to environmental problems. At times Habermas refers to these learning levels as *organization principles*. Thus, as systems confront problems of internal integration and external contingencies, the stocks of knowledge and worldviews of individual actors are translated into organization principles and steering capacities, which in turn set limits on just how a system can respond. For example, a society with only religious mythology will be less complex and less able to respond to environmental challenges than a more complex society with large stores of technology and stocks of normative procedures determining its organization principles. But societies can "learn"[15] that, when confronted with problems beyond the capacity of their current organization principles and steering mechanisms, they can draw upon the "cognitive potential" in the knowledge of individuals who reorganize their actions. The result of this learning creates new levels of information that allow the development of new organization principles for securing integration despite increased societal differentiation and complexity.

The basis for societal integration lies in the processes by which actors communicate and develop mutual understandings and stores of knowledge. To the extent that these interactive processes are arrested by the patterns of economic and political organization, the society's learning capacity is correspondingly diminished. One of the main integrative problems of capitalist societies is the integration of the material forces of production (economy as administered by the state), on the one side, and the cultural stores of knowledge that are produced by communicative interaction, on the other side. Societies that differentiate materially in the economic and political realms without achieving integration on a normative and cultural level (that is, shared understandings) will remain unintegrated and experience crises.

Built into these dynamics, however, is their resolution. The processes of "communicative interaction" that produce and reproduce unifying cultural symbols must be given equal weight with the "labor" processes that generate material production and reproduction. At this point, Habermas developed his more-synthetic approach in *The Theory of Communicative Action*.

THE THEORY OF COMMUNICATIVE ACTION

The two-volume *The Theory of Communicative Action* pulls together into a reasonably coherent framework various strands of Habermas's thought.[16] Yet, true to his general style of scholarship, Habermas wandered over a rather large intellectual landscape. In Thomas McCarthy's words, Habermas develops his ideas through "a somewhat unusual combination of theoretical constructions with historical reconstructions of the ideas of 'classical' social theorists."[17] Such thinkers as Marx, Weber, Durkheim, Mead, Lukács, Horkheimer, Adorno, and Parsons are, for Habermas, "still very much alive" and are treated as "virtual dialogue partners."[18] As a consequence, the two volumes meander through selected portions of various thinkers' work critiquing and yet using key ideas. After the dust settles, however, the result is a very creative synthesis of ideas into a critical theory.

Habermas's basic premise is summarized near the end of volume 1:

> If we assume that the human species maintains itself through the socially coordinated activities of its members and that this coordination is established through communication—and in certain spheres of life, through communication aimed at reaching agreement—then the reproduction of the species also requires satisfying the conditions of a rationality inherent in communicative action.[19]

In other words, intrinsic to the process of communicative action, where actors implicitly make, challenge, and accept one another's validity claims, is a rationality that can potentially serve as the basis for reconstructing the social order in less oppressive ways. The first volume of *The Theory of Communicative Action* thus focuses on action and rationality in an effort to reconceptualize both processes in a manner that shifts emphasis from the subjectivity and consciousness of the individual to the process of symbolic interaction. In a sense, volume 1 is Habermas's microsociology, whereas volume 2 is his macrosociology. In the second volume, Habermas introduces the concept of system and tries to connect it to microprocesses of action and interaction through a reconceptualization of the phenomenological concept of lifeworld.

The Overall Project

Let us begin by briefly reviewing the overall argument, and then return to volumes 1 and 2 with a more detailed analysis. There are four types of action: (1) teleological, (2) normative, (3) dramaturgical, and (4) communicative. Only communicative action contains the elements whereby actors reach intersubjective understanding. Such communicative action—which is, actually, *inter*action—presupposes a set of background assumptions and stocks of knowledge, or, in Habermas's terms, a *lifeworld*. Also operating in any society are "system" processes, which revolve around the material maintenance of the species and its survival. The evolutionary trend is for system processes and lifeworld processes to become internally differentiated *and* differentiated from each other. The integration of a society depends on a balance between system and lifeworld processes. As modern societies have evolved, however, this balance has been upset as system processes revolving around the economy and the state (also law, family, and other reproductive structures) have "colonized" and dominated lifeworld processes concerned with mutually shared meanings, understandings, and intersubjectivity. As a result, modern society is poorly integrated.

These integrative problems in capitalist societies are manifested in crises concerning the "reproduction of the lifeworld"; that is, the acts of communicative interaction that reproduce this lifeworld are displaced by "delinguistified media," such as money and power, that are used in the reproduction of system processes (economy and government). The solution to these crises is a rebalancing of relations between lifeworld and system. This rebalancing is to come through the resurrection of the public sphere in the economic and political arenas and in the creation of more situations in which communicative action (interaction) can proceed uninhibited by the intrusion of system's media, such as power and money. The goal of critical theory, therefore, is to document those facets of society in which the lifeworld has been colonized and to suggest approaches whereby situations of communicative action (interaction) can be reestablished. Such is Habermas's general argument, and now we can fill in some of the details.

The Reconceptualization of Action and Rationality

In volume 1 of *The Theory of Communicative Action,* Habermas undertakes a long and detailed analysis of Weber's conceptualization of action and rationalization. Habermas wants to reconceptualize rationality and action in ways that allow him to view rational action as a potentially liberating rather than imprisoning force.[20] In this way, he feels, he can avoid the pessimism of Weber and the retreat into subjectivity of Lukács, Adorno, and Horkheimer. There are, Habermas concludes, several basic types of action:[21]

1. *Teleological action* is behavior oriented to calculating various means and selecting the most appropriate ones to realize explicit goals. Such action becomes strategic when other acting agents are involved in one's calculations. Habermas also calls this action "instrumental" because it is concerned with means to achieve ends. Most important, he emphasizes that this kind of action is too often considered "rational action" in previous conceptualizations of rationality. As he argues, this view of rationality is too narrow and forces critical theory into a conceptual trap: if teleological or means/ends rationality has taken over the modern world and has, as a consequence, oppressed people, then how can critical theory propose rational alternatives? Would not such a rational theory be yet one more oppressive application of means/ends rationality? The answers to these questions lie in recognizing that there are several types of action and that true rationality resides not in teleological action but in communicative action.

2. *Normatively regulated action* is behavior that is oriented to common values of a group. Thus, normative action is directed toward complying with normative expectations of collectively organized groupings of individuals.

3. *Dramaturgical action* is action that involves conscious manipulation of oneself before an audience or public. It is ego-centered in that it involves actors mutually manipulating their behaviors to present their own

intentions, but it is also social in that such manipulation is done in the context of organized activity.

4. *Communicative action* is interaction among agents who use speech and nonverbal symbols as a way of understanding their mutual situation and their respective plans of action to agree on how to coordinate their behaviors.

These four types of action presuppose different kinds of "worlds." That is, each action is oriented to a somewhat different aspect of the universe, which can be divided into the (1) "objective or external world" of manipulable objects; (2) "social world" of norms, values, and other socially recognized expectations; and (3) "subjective world" of experiences. Teleological action is concerned primarily with the objective world; normatively regulated action with the social; and dramaturgical with the subjective and external. But only with communicative action do actors "refer simultaneously to things in the objective, social, and subjective worlds in order to negotiate common definitions of the situation."[22]

Such communicative action is therefore potentially more rational than all of the others because it deals with all three worlds and because it proceeds as speech acts that assert three types of validity claims. Such speech acts assert that (1) statements are true in "propositional content," or in reference to the external and objective world; (2) statements are correct with respect to the existing normative context, or social world; and (3) statements are sincere and manifest the subjective world of intention and experiences of the actor.[23] The process of communicative action in which these three types of validity claims are made, accepted, or challenged by others is inherently more rational than other types of action. If a validity claim is not accepted, then it is debated and discussed in an effort to reach understanding without recourse to force and authority.[24] The process of reaching understanding through validity claims, their acceptance, or their discussion takes place against

> The background of a culturally ingrained pre-understanding. This background remains unproblematic as a whole; only that part of the stock of knowledge that participants make use of and thematize at a given time is put to the test. To the extent that definitions of situations are negotiated by participants *themselves,* this thematic segment of the lifeworld is at their disposal with the negotiation of each new definition of the situation.[25]

Thus, in the process of making validity claims through speech acts, actors use existing definitions of situations or create new ones that establish order in their social relations. Such definitions become part of the stocks of knowledge in their lifeworlds, and they become the standards by which validity claims are made, accepted, and challenged. Thus, in reaching an understanding through communicative action, the lifeworld serves as a point of reference for the adjudication of validity claims, which encompass the full range of worlds—the objective, social, and subjective. And so, in Habermas's eyes, there is more rationality inherent in the very process of communicative interaction than in means/ends or teleological action.[26] As Habermas summarizes,

> We have . . . characterized the rational structure of the processes of reaching understanding in terms of (a) the three world-relations of actors and the corresponding concepts of the objective, social, and subjective worlds; (b) the validity claims of propositional truth, normative rightness, and sincerity or authenticity; (c) the concept of a rationally motivated agreement, that is, one based on the intersubjective recognition of criticizable validity claims; and (d) the concept of reaching understanding as the cooperative negotiation of common definitions of the situation.[27]

Thus, as people communicatively act (interact), they use and at the same time produce common definitions of the situation. Such definitions are part of the lifeworld of a society; if they have been produced and reproduced through the communicative action, then they are the basis for the rational and nonoppressive integration of a society. Let us now turn to Habermas's discussion of this lifeworld, which serves as the "court of appeals" in communicative action.

The Lifeworld and System Processes of Society

Habermas believes the lifeworld is a "culturally transmitted and linguistically organized stock of interpretative patterns." But what are these "interpretative patterns" about? What do they pertain to? His answer, as one expects from Habermas, is yet another typology. There are three different types of interpretative patterns in the lifeworld: There are interpretative patterns with respect to culture, or systems of symbols; there are those pertaining to society, or social institutions; and there are those oriented to personality, or aspects of self and being. That is, (1) actors possess implicit and shared stocks of knowledge about cultural traditions, values, beliefs, and linguistic structures as well as how these are to be used in interaction; (2) actors also know how to organize social relations and what kinds and patterns of coordinated interaction are proper and appropriate; and (3) actors understand what people are like, how they should act, and what is normal or aberrant.

These three types of interpretative patterns correspond, Habermas asserts, to the following functional needs for reproducing the lifeworld (and, by implication, for integrating society): (1) reaching understanding through communicative action transmits, preserves, and renews cultural knowledge; (2) communicative action that coordinates interaction meets the need for social integration and group solidarity; and (3) communicative action that socializes agents meets the need for the formation of personal identities.[28]

Thus, the three components of the lifeworld—culture, society, personality—meet corresponding needs of society—cultural reproduction, social integration, and personality formation—through three dimensions along which communicative action is conducted: reaching understanding, coordinating interaction, and effecting socialization. As Habermas summarizes in volume 2,

> In coming to an understanding with one another about their situation, participants in communication stand in a cultural tradition which they

use and at the same time renew; in coordinating their actions via inter-subjective recognition of "criticizable" validity claims, they rely upon their membership in groupings and at the same time reenforce their integration; through participating in interaction with competent persons, growing children internalize value orientations and acquire generalized capacities for action.[29]

These lifeworld processes are interrelated with system processes in a society. Action in economic, political, familial, and other institutional contexts draws on, and reproduces, the cultural, societal, and personality dimensions of the lifeworld. Yet evolutionary trends are for differentiation of the lifeworld into separate stocks of knowledge with respect to culture, society, and personality and for differentiation of system processes into distinctive and separate institutional clusters, such as economy, state, family, and law. Such differentiation creates problems of integration and balance between the lifeworld and system.[30] And therein reside the dilemmas and crises of modern societies.

Evolutionary Dynamics and Societal Crises

In a sense, Habermas blends traditional analysis by functionalists on societal and cultural differentiation with a Marxian dialectic whereby the seeds for emancipation are sown in the creation of an ever more rationalized and differentiated society. Borrowing from Durkheim's analysis of mechanical solidarity, Habermas argues that "the more cultural traditions predecide which validity claims, when, where, for what, from whom, and to whom must be accepted, the less the participants themselves have the possibility of making explicit and examining the potential groups in which their yes/no positions are based."[31] But "as mechanical solidarity gives way to organic solidarity based upon functional interdependence," then "the more the worldview that furnishes the cultural stock of knowledge is decentered" and "the less the need for understanding is covered *in advance* by an interpreted lifeworld immune from critique," and therefore "the more this need has to be met by the interpretative accomplishments of the participants themselves." That is, if the lifeworld is to be sustained and reproduced, it becomes ever more necessary with growing societal complexity for social actions to be based on communicative processes. The result is that there is greater potential for rational communicative action because less and less of the social order is preordained by a simple and undifferentiated lifeworld. But system processes have reduced this potential, and the task of critical theory is to document how system processes have colonized the lifeworld and thereby arrested this potentially superior rationality inherent in the speech acts of communicative action.

How have system processes restricted this potential contained in communicative action? As the sacred and traditional basis of the lifeworld organization has dissolved and been replaced by linguistic interaction around a lifeworld differentiated along cultural, social, and personality axes, there is a countertrend in the differentiation of system processes. System evolution involves the expansion of material production through the greater use of technologies, science, and "delinguistified steering mechanisms" such as money and power to carry out system processes.[32] These media do not rely on the validity claims of communicative action; when they become the media of interaction in ever more spheres of life—markets, bureaucracies, welfare state policies, legal systems, and even family relations—the processes of communicative action so essential for lifeworld reproduction are invaded and colonized. Thus, system processes use power and money as their media of integration, and in the process they "decouple the lifeworld" from its functions for societal integration.[33] There is an irony here because differentiation of the lifeworld facilitated the differentiation of system processes and the use of money and power,[34] so "the rationalized lifeworld makes possible the rise of growth of subsystems which strike back at it in a destructive fashion."[35]

Through this ironical process, capitalism creates market dynamics using money, which in turn spawn a welfare state employing power in ways that reduce political and economic crises but that increase those cries revolving around lifeworld reproduction. For the new crises and conflicts "arise in areas of cultural reproduction, of social integration and of socialization."[36]

CONCLUSION

Habermas has now circled back to his initial concerns and those of early critical theorists. He has recast the Weberian thesis by asserting that true rationality inheres in communicative action, not teleological (and strategic or instrumental) action, as Weber claimed. And he has redefined the critical theorist's view on modern crises; they are not crises of rationalization, but crises of colonization of those truly rational processes that inhere in the speech acts of communicative action, which reproduce the lifeworld so essential to societal integration. Thus, built into the integrating processes of differentiated societies (*note:* not the subjective processes of individuals, as early critical theorists claimed) is the potential for a critical theory that seeks to restore communicative rationality despite impersonal steering mechanisms. If system differentiation occurs in delinguistified media, like money and power, and if these reduce the reliance on communicative action, then crises are inevitable. Critical theorists can use the resulting collective frustration over the lack of meaning in social life to mobilize people to restore the proper balance between system and lifeworld processes. Thus, crises of material production will not be the impetus for change, as Marx contended. Rather, the crises of lifeworld reproduction will serve as the stimulus to societal reorganization. And returning to his first work, Habermas sees such reorganization as involving (1) the restoration of the public sphere in politics, where relinguistified debate and argumentation, rather than delinguistified power and authority, are used to make political decisions (thus reducing "legitimation crises"), and (2) the extension of communicative action back into those spheres—family, work, and social relations—that have become increasingly dominated by delinguistified steering media (thereby eliminating "motivational crises").

The potential for this reorganization inheres in the nature of societal integration through the rationality inherent in the communicative actions that reproduce the lifeworld. The purpose of critical theory is to release this rational potential.

NOTES

1. That is, the spread of means/end rationality into ever more spheres of life.

2. Jürgen Habermas, *The Theory of Communicative Action* (Boston: Beacon, 1981, 1984). Some useful reviews and critiques of Habermas's work include John B. Thompson and David Held, eds., *Habermas: Critical Debates* (London: Macmillan, 1982); David Held, *An Introduction to Critical Theory* (London: Hutchinson, 1980), chapters 9–12.

3. Jürgen Habermas, *Struckturwandel der Offentlichkeit* (Neuwied, Germany: Luchterhand, 1962).

4. Jürgen Habermas, *Zur Logik der Sozialwissenschaften* (Frankfurt: Suhrkamp, 1970).

5. Jürgen Habermas, *Knowledge and Human Interest,* trans. J. Shapiro (London: Heinemann, 1970; originally published in German in 1968). The basic ideas in *Zur Logik der Sozialwissenschaften* and *Knowledge and Human Interest* were stated in Habermas's inaugural lecture at the University of Frankfurt in 1965 and were first published in "Knowledge and Interest," *Inquiry* 9 (1966), pp. 285–300.

6. Jürgen Habermas, *Legitimation Crisis,* trans. T. McCarthy (London: Heinemann, 1976; originally published in German in 1973).

7. Jürgen Habermas, "On Systematically Distorted Communication," *Inquiry* 13 (1970); pp. 205–218.

8. Jürgen Habermas, "Toward a Theory of Communicative Competence," *Inquiry* 13 (1970), pp. 360–375.

9. Habermas sometimes calls this aspect of his program "depth hermeneutics." The idea is to create a methodology of inquiry for social systems that parallels the approach of psychoanalysis—that is, dialogue, removal of barriers to understanding, analysis of underlying causal processes, and efforts to use this understanding to dissolve distortions in interaction.

10. For an early statement, see "Some Distinctions in Universal Pragmatics: A Working Paper," *Theory and Society* 3 (1976), pp. 155–167.

11. Jürgen Habermas, *Zur Rekonstruktion des Historischen Materialismus* (Frankfurt: Suhrkamp, 1976).

12. Jürgen Habermas, *Communication and the Evolution of Society,* trans. T. McCarthy (London: Heinemann, 1979).

13. For an earlier statement, see Jürgen Habermas, "Towards a Reconstruction of Historical Materialism," *Theory and Society* 2 (3, 1975), pp. 84–98.

14. He borrows from Niklas Luhmann here (see Chapter 4 in this work), although much of Habermas's approach is a reaction to Luhmann.

15. Habermas analogizes here to Jean Piaget's and Lawrence Kohlberg's analysis of the cognitive development of children, seeing societies as able to "learn" as they become more structurally complex.

16. Jürgen Habermas, *The Theory of Communicative Action,* 2 vols. (cited in note 2). The subtitle of volume 1, *Reason and the Rationalization of Society,* gives some indication of its

thrust. The translator, Thomas McCarthy, has done an excellent service in translating very difficult prose. Also, his "Translator's Introduction" to volume 1, pp. v–xxxvii, is the best summary of Habermas's recent theory that I have come across.

17. Thomas McCarthy, "Translator's Introduction" (cited in note 16), p. vii.

18. Ibid.

19. Jürgen Habermas, *The Theory of Communicative Action* (cited in note 2), vol. 1, p. 397.

20. Recall that its subtitle is *Reason and the Rationalization of Society.*

21. Jürgen Habermas, *The Theory of Communicative Action* (cited in note 2), pp. 85–102.

22. Ibid., p. 95.

23. Ibid., p. 99.

24. Recall Habermas's earlier discussion of nondistorted communication and the ideal speech act. This is his most recent reconceptualization of these ideas.

25. Ibid., p. 100. Emphasis in original.

26. Ibid., p. 302.

27. Ibid., p. 137.

28. We are now into volume 2, ibid., pp. 205–240, entitled *System and Lifeworld: A Critique of Functionalist Reason,* which is a somewhat ironic title because of the heavily functional arguments in volume 2. But, as noted earlier, Habermas's earlier work has always had an implicit functionalism.

29. Ibid., p. 208

30. This is the old functionalist argument of "differentiation" producing "integrative problems," which is as old as Spencer and which is Parsons reincarnated with a phenomenological twist.

31. All quotes here are from p. 70 of volume 1.

32. Here Habermas is borrowing from Simmel's analysis in *The Philosophy of Money* (see Chapter 16 of this book) and from Parsons' conceptualization of generalized media (see Chapter 3).

33. Volume 2 of *The Theory of Communicative Action,* pp. 256–276.

34. Habermas appears in these arguments to borrow heavily from Parsons' analysis of evolution (see Chapter 3 of this work).

35. Volume 2, p. 227.

14

Postmodern Theory

Sociology was created as a self-conscious discipline to explain the transformations associated with "modernity," especially the rise of industrial capitalism and the corresponding decline of the agrarian feudal system in Europe and, eventually, elsewhere in the world. Some theorists—indeed, most examined in this book—have taken a scientific stance and have searched for fundamental and basic social forces that operate in all times and places and that, as a consequence, explain social processes in not only the modern era but also the past and future as well. Others have preferred a more restricted time framework and more modest goals, but even these scholars have sought to develop analytical frameworks for, at the very least, interpreting events in the modern world.

Postmodernism, like all critical theories, challenges the scientific and, in some cases, even the analytical pretensions of sociology. The label "postmodern" encompasses many divergent points of view, but the term contains two common themes: (1) a critique of sociology as a science and (2) a decisive break with modernity in which cultural symbols, media-driven images, and other forces of symbolic signification have changed the nature of social organization and the relation of individuals to the social world.

Note: This chapter is coauthored with Kenneth Allan.

THE POSTMODERN CRITIQUE OF SCIENCE

The Age of Science, as it emerged from The Enlightenment, posited that it would be possible to use language to denote key properties of the universe and to communicate among scientists the nature and dynamics of these properties. Indeed, it was believed that, as knowledge accumulated by testing general theories against empirical cases, theorists could use ever more formal languages, such as mathematics, and experimental researchers could develop ever more precise measuring instruments. In this manner, the accumulation of knowledge about properties and dynamics of the universe would accelerate. For such accumulation to occur, the degree of correspondence between theories stated in languages and the actual nature of the universe would have to increase. No scientist assumed, of course, that there could ever be a perfect correspondence, but there was a faith that the use of more precise languages and measuring instruments calibrated for these languages could make representations of the universe increasingly accurate.

This faith in science was one of the cornerstones of "modernism," in at least this sense: Scientific knowledge could be used to forge a better society. As knowledge about the world accumulated, it could be used to increase productivity, democracy, and fairness in patterns of social organization. As with all critical approaches, postmodernism attacks modernity's faith in science. Postmodernism poses three interrelated problems associated with human knowledge.

First, the problem of representation. Postmodernists often question the view that science could be used to demystify the world by discovering and using the law-like principles governing its operation. Undergirding this modern belief was the notion that there is a single best mode—scientific theory and research findings—for expressing "truth" about the world. Postmodernists typically challenge this assumed correspondence between the signs of scientific language and obdurate reality. Does the language of science, or any language, provide a direct window through which we can view reality; that is, does language simply represent reality? Or, is language a social construction that by its very existence distorts the picture of reality? To the degree that language is a social construction, and, thus related to social groups and their interests, the assumption of the direct representation of language is rendered problematic.

Second, the problem of power and vested interests. Though some postmodernists may concede that the physical world might operate by laws, the very process of discovering these laws creates culture that, in turn, is subject to interests, politics, and forms of domination. For example, law-like knowledge in subatomic physics has reflected political interests in war-making or the laws of genetics can be seen to serve the interests of biotechnology firms. What is true of the laws of the physical and organic worlds is even more true of social laws whose very articulation reflects moral, political, economic, and other interests within the social sphere. From a postmodernist's view, "truth" in science, especially social science, is not a correspondence between theoretical statements and the actual social universe, but a cultural production like any other sign system. Science cannot, therefore, enjoy a "privileged voice" because it is like all cultural texts.

Third, the problem of continuity. Postmodernists question the view that knowledge accumulates in ways that increase continuity among understandings about the world and that can be used to advance society. This faith in knowledge was a hallmark of "modernity," but to postmodernists, who see discontinuities in knowledge as tied to shifts in the interests of dominant factions in society, such faith in the progressing continuity of knowledge and culture is not only misguided but also empirically wrong. Postmodernists argue that because there is no truth that exists apart from the ideological interests of humans, discontinuity of knowledge is the norm, and a permanent pluralism of cultures is the only real truth that humans must continually face.

In the end, the postmodern philosophical attack on science denies privileged status to any knowledge system, including its own "because any place of arrival is but a temporary station. No place is privileged, no place better than another, as from no place the horizon is nearer than from any other."[1] Postmodernism emphasizes that, as a human creation, knowledge is relative to, and contingent on, the circumstances in which it was generated. Because knowledge is ultimately a system of signs, or a language of human expression, it is about itself as much as an external world "out there."

Jean-François Lyotard

Jean-François Lyotard built much of his critique of science[2] on a notion borrowed from Ludwig Wittgenstein: language as a game.[3] Wittgenstein had posited an analogous relationship between the manner in which language functions and the way games are played. He argued that language, like a game, is an autonomous creation that requires no justification for its existence other than itself and is subject only to its own rules. With the term *language,* Wittgenstein was denoting not simply words and their syntactical arrangements but, rather, all that is wrapped up in the presentation, reception, and enactment of human expression. And this expression exists for no other reason than itself and is subject to no other rules than its own.

Lyotard, using Wittgenstein's analogy, proposes a comparison between the narrative form of knowledge, on the one side, and the denotative, scientific form of knowledge, on the other. Narrative is a form of expression that is close to the social world of real people; it is expressed within a social circle for the purpose of creating and sustaining this social circle. In this view of narratives, Lyotard means something akin to the oral histories of small familial-based groups, in which there are internal rules concerning who has the right to speak and who has the responsibility to listen. Verification of the knowledge created in such a narrative is reflexive because such verification of the narrative refers to its own rules of discourse.

In contrast, the denotative, scientific form of knowledge does not originate from social bonds, but rather, science proposes to simply represent what is in the physical universe, thereby subjugating the narrative form of knowledge.

Lyotard argues that narrative and tradition are no longer needed in science because theory and research will reveal the true nature of the universe. Yet, there is a problem with science: To be heard, science must appeal to a form of narrative knowledge, in this case a *grand narrative*. This grand narrative is based on The Enlightenment's promise of human emancipation and encompasses the vision of progress most clearly expressed by Georg Hegel. Lyotard maintains that postmodernism is defined by a diffuse sense of doubt concerning any such grand narrative and that this need to appeal to a narrative reveals science to be a language game like any other. Thus, science has no special authority or power to supervise other language games. According to Lyotard's vision, dissension must now be emphasized rather than consensus; heterogeneous claims to knowledge, in which one voice is not privileged over another, are the only true basis of knowledge.

Richard Rorty

The philosopher Richard Rorty[4] pushes the philosophical critique of science further to the extreme—indeed, to the point of appearing to assert that there is no external, obdurate reality "out there." Science argues, of course, that there is a reality "out there," that languages can be used in increasingly precise ways to denote and understand its properties and dynamics, that language can be used to communicate the discoveries of science to fellow scientists and others as well, that truth is the degree of correspondence between theory and data, and that efforts to increase this correspondence make science self-correcting. Hence, science does use language in ways that make it a more "objective" representation of the external world, thereby ensuring that certain languages are more objective than others. But, Rorty asserts, the issue can never be which language is more objective or scientific because the use of language is always directed toward pragmatic ends. Underlying every claim that one language brings a better understanding to a phenomenon than another is the assumption that it is more useful for a particular purpose. As Rorty claims, "vocabularies are useful or useless, good or bad, helpful or misleading, sensitive or coarse, and so on; but they are not 'more objective' or 'less objective' nor more or less 'scientific.'"[5]

In addition, even if there is a true reality and a true language with which to represent that reality, the moment *humans use a language,* it becomes evaluative. Thus, discovering the "true nature" of reality is not the goal of language use, scientific or otherwise, but rather, this use is directed at practical concerns, and such pragmatic concerns are always value based. Social scientists can tell stories that converge and reflect their common value concerns, thereby increasing their sense of solidarity and community as social scientists. Social scientists can also tell stories of power or of forces that divide them, thereby revealing the discordant features of any collective. But these stories are about this community of individuals more than about any "real world out there."

What, then, is left for social analysts? Rorty's answer is typical of many postmodernists: Deconstruct texts produced by communities of individuals using language for some value-laden, practical purpose. *Deconstruction* refers to the process of taking apart the elements of a text, and in Rorty's view, such deconstruction can be (a) critical, exposing the interests and ideology contained in the text, or (b) affirming, revealing elements of a text to enlighten and inform.

As becomes evident, then, Lyotard and Rorty would take sociological theory in a very different direction. Emphasis would be on language and texts,[6] and scientific explanations of an obdurate social reality would be seen as yet another form of text. This new direction—which represents a philosophical assault on scientific sociological theory—can be further appraised with illustrative examples of sociologists who have used the thrust of this philosophical critique in their more explicitly sociological works.

Illustrative Elaborations and Extensions
Within Sociology

Richard Harvey Brown's *Society as Text* Richard Harvey Brown[7] specifically applies the philosophical critique of postmodernism to social science, positing that social and cultural realities, and social science itself, are linguistic constructions. Brown advocates an approach termed *symbolic realism*[8] in which the universe is seen as existing for humans through communicative action. Moreover, each act of communication is based on previously constructed communicative actions—modes and forms of discourse, ideologies, worldviews, and other linguistic forms. Hence, the search for the first or ultimate reality is a fruitless endeavor. Indeed, the "worlds" that are accepted as "true" at any one point in human history are constituted through normative, practical, epistemological, political, aesthetic, and moral practices which, in turn, are themselves symbolic constructions. Symbolic realism is thus a critical approach that seeks to uncover the ideologies surrounding the premises on which knowledge, senses of self, and portrayals of realities are constructed.

In this critical vein, Brown concludes that sociological theories themselves are "practices through which things take on meaning and value, and not merely as representations of a reality that is wholly exterior to them."[9] Theory in sociology ought to be critical and reflexive, with theorists recognizing that their own theories are themselves rhetorical constructions and, thus, texts constructed in time, place, and context as well as through linguistic conventions. This kind of approach to social theory as rhetoric sees its own discourse as not being about society—that is, as an effort to construct "true" representations on the nature of society—but, rather, as being simply part of what constitutes society, particularly its forms of textual discourse and representation.[10]

Charles C. Lemert's Emphasis on Rhetoric For Charles Lemert,[11] all social theory is inherently discursive, stated in loose languages and constructed within particular social circles. What discursive theoretical texts explain—that is, "empirical reality"—is itself a discursive text, constructed like any text and subject to all the distorting properties of any text production. That theoretical texts depend on empirical texts, and vice versa, for their scientific value increases science's discursiveness. Each scientific portrayal of reality—whether from the "theory" or "research findings" side—is a text and, actually, a kind of "text on top of another text." This compounding of texts has implications for social scientific explanations: Social science explanations are often less adequate to understanding reality than are ordinary discursive texts that are less convoluted and compounded.

This understanding of the primacy of language leads to the use of irony in social theory. But the social theorist's use of irony is more than a literary device; it is a position from which the theorist views reality and its relationship to language. The physical universe is known to humans only through representation, culture, or language. Thus, reality shifts in response to different modes of representation. For example, in the eyes of humanity, the earth has shifted from being the center of the universe to being simply one of many planets circling one of a multitude of stars. But this position of the theorist also views language as humanity's certainty: Language is certain, and in that sense real, because the fundamental qualities and meanings of a linguistic system are known, valid, and replicable *within itself*. Because language is certain, theorists can make general statements concerning the properties of the physical universe, but the certitude of those statements rests in language and not in the physical reality or even the assumed relationship between culture and reality. The only position then for a social theorist is an ironic one: General theoretical statements can be made but with a "tongue-in-cheek" attitude because the author of such statements is reflexively aware that the only certitude of the statements rests in the linguistic system and not in the physical or social reality.

Mark Gottdiener's and Steven Seidman's Critiques Steven Seidman[12] adopts Rorty's distinction between enriching and critical forms of text deconstruction. And, along with Mark Gottdiener,[13] and many others as well, Seidman questions any social theory that posits a *foundationalism,* or the view that knowledge accumulates such that one level of knowledge can serve as the base on which ever more knowledge is built. Foundationalism is, of course, at the very core of science, so this critique is truly fundamental for the activities that intellectuals can pursue. For Seidman and Gottdiener, however, foundationalism is just another effort to impose a grand narrative as a privileged voice.

Gottdiener sees foundationalism in sociological theory as an ideology, based on a *logocentrism* where "the classics" in theory are seen as the base on which a theoretical position is built. Such logocentrism is nothing more than a political ploy by established theorists to maintain their privileged position. Thus, sociological theory is about language and power-games among theorists, seeking to construct a grand narrative that also sustains their privilege and authority within an intellectual community.[14]

If such is the case, Seidman argues, the hope of human emancipation through sociological theory must be replaced by "the more modest aspiration of a relentless defense of immediate, local pleasures and struggles for justice."[15] But Gottdiener sees this position as akin to Rorty's concern with the use of vocabularies to sustain communities of scholars. Because of the inherent and ultimate privileging of one morality over another in such communities—not all moralities, even local ones, are commensurable one with another—theory does not become sufficiently critical. Instead, Gottdiener advocates a continuous, critical, and reflexive cycle of evaluation relative to the relationship between power and knowledge for evaluating all theories—postmodern or otherwise—that seek some grand narrative or self-legitimating tradition.

In sum, these representative commentaries offer a sense for the postmodern critique of science. Yet, postmodernism is much more than a philosophical critique. If this were all that postmodernists had to offer, there would be little point in examining these criticisms. Moreover, not all postmodernist theorists accept the philosophical critique just outlined, although most are highly suspicious of the "hard-science" view of sociological theory.[16] Indeed, most are committed to analysis of contemporary societies, especially the effects that dramatic changes in distribution, transportation, and information systems have had on the individual self and patterns of social organization. We can begin with "economic postmodernists" who generally employ extensions of Karl Marx's ideas and who, to varying degrees, still retain some of Marx's emancipatory zeal or, if not zeal, guarded hope that a better future that may lie ahead.

ECONOMIC POSTMODERNISM

Economic postmodernists are primarily concerned with capital, especially its overaccumulation (that is, overabundance) as well as its level of dispersion and rapid movement in the new world system of markets driven and connected by information technologies. Moreover, culture or systems of symbols are seen to emerge from economic processes, but they exert independent effects on not only the economy but also every other facet of human endeavor. Indeed, for some economic postmodernists, advanced capitalism has evolved into a new stage of human history[17] that, like earlier modernity, is typified by a series of "problems," including the loss of a core or essential sense of self, the use of symbolic as much as material means to control individuals, the increased salience of cultural resources as both tools of repression and potential resistance, the emotional disengagement of individuals from culture, and the loss of national identities and a corresponding shift to local and personal identities. This list, and other "pathologies" of the postmodern era, sound much like those that concerned early sociologists when they worried about such matters as anomie and egoism (Émile Durkheim), alienation (Marx), marginal and fractured self (Georg Simmel), ideological control and manipulation by the powerful (Marx and, later, Antonio Gramsci and Louis Althusser), political-ideological mobilization as resistance (Marx), overdifferentiation and fragmentation of social structure (Adam Smith, Herbert Spencer, and Durkheim), rationalization and domination by overconcerns with efficiency (Max Weber), and so on. Thus, economically oriented postmodernists evidence many of the same analytical tendencies as did those who first sought to theorize about modernity.

Fredric Jameson

Among the central figures in economic postmodernism, Fredric Jameson is the most explicitly Marxist.[18] Although his theory is about the complex interplay among multinational capitalism, technological advance, and the mass-media, "the truth of postmodernism . . . [is] the world space of multinational capital."[19] He posits that capitalism has gone through three distinct phases, with each phase linked to a particular kind of technology. Early-market capitalism was linked to steam-driven machinery, mid-monopoly capitalism was characterized by steam and combustion engines, and late-multinational capitalism is associated with nuclear power and electronic machines.

Late-multinational capitalism is the subject of postmodern theory. In particular, the nature of *praxis,* or the use of thought to organize action to change conditions and the use of experiences in action to reexamine thought, is transformed and confounded by the changed nature of signification that comes when the machines of symbolic reproduction—cameras, computers, videos, movies, tape recorders, fax machines—remove the direct connection between human production and its symbolic representation. These machines generate sequences of signs on top of signs that alter the nature of praxis—that is, how can thought guide action on the world, and vice versa, when concepts in such thought are so detached from material conditions?

Drawing from Marx's philosophy of knowledge, Jameson still attempts to use the method of praxis to critique the social construction of reality in postmodernity. Marx argued that reality did not exist in concepts, ideas, or reflexive thought but in the material world of production. Indeed, he broke with the young Hegelians over this issue, seeing them as "blowing theoretical bubbles" about the reality of ideas. But, like the earlier generation of critical theorists in the first decades of the twentieth century, those of the late twentieth century begin to sound even more Hegelian. According to Jameson, the creation of consciousness through production was unproblematically represented by the aesthetic of the machine in earlier phases of capitalism, but in multinational capitalism, electronic machines like movie cameras, videos, tape recorders, and computers do not have the same capacity for signification because they are machines of *reproduction* rather than of production. Thus, the foundation of thought and knowledge in postmodernity is not simply false, as Marx's view of "false consciousness" emphasized, it is nonexistent. Because the machines of late capitalism reproduce knowledge rather than produce it, and because the reproduction itself is focused more on the medium than on the message, the signification chain from object to sign has broken down. Jameson characterizes this breakdown as the schizophrenia of culture. Based on Ferdinand de Saussure's notion that meaning is a function of the relationship between signifiers, the concept of a break in the signification chain indicates that each sign stands alone, or in a relatively loose association with fragmented groups of other signs, and that meaning is free-floating and untied to any clear material reality.

Moreover, in a postmodern world dominated by machines of reproduction, language loses the capacity to ground concepts to place, to moments of time, or to objects, in addition to losing its ability to organize symbols into coherent systems of concepts about place, time, and object. As language loses these capacities, time and space become disassociated. If a sign system becomes detached and free-floating and if it is fragmented and without order, the meaning of concepts in relation to time and space cannot be guaranteed. Indeed, meaning in any sense becomes problematic. The conceptual connection between the "here-and-now" and its relation to the previous "there-and-then" has broken down, and the individual experiences "a series of pure and unrelated presents in time."[20]

Jameson goes on to argue that culture in the postmodern condition has created a fragmented rather than alienated subject. Self is not so much alienated from the failure to control its own productive activities; rather, self is now a series of images in a material world dominated by the instruments of reproduction rather than production. In addition, the decentering of the postmodern self produces a kind of emotional flatness or depthlessness "since there is no longer any self to do the feeling . . . [emotions] are now free-floating and impersonal."[21] Subjects are thus fragmented and dissolved, having no material basis for consciousness or narratives about their situation; under these conditions, individuals' capacity for praxis—using thought to act, and action to generate thought—is diminished. Of course, this capacity for praxis is not so diminished that Jameson cannot develop a critical theory of the postmodern condition, although the action side of Marx's notion of praxis is as notably absent, if not impotent, as it was for the first generation of Frankfurt critical theorists.

David Harvey

In a manner like that of Jameson, David Harvey[22] posits that capitalism has brought about significant problems associated with humans' capacity to conceptualize time and space. Yet, for Harvey, the cultural and perceptual problems associated with postmodernism are not new. Some of the same tendencies toward fragmentation and confusion in political, cultural, and philosophical movements occurred around the turn of the century. And, in Harvey's view, the cultural features of the postmodern world are no more permanent—as many postmodernists imply—than were those of the modernity that emerged in the nineteenth and early twentieth centuries.

Unlike Jameson, Harvey does not see the critical condition of postmodernity as the problem of praxis—of anchoring signs and symbols in a material reality that can be changed through thought and action—but, rather, as a condition of *overaccumulation,* or the modes by which too much capital is assembled and disseminated. All capitalist systems—as Marx recognized—have evidenced this problem of overaccumulation, because capitalism is a system designed to grow through exploitation of labor, technological innovation, and organizational retrenchment. At some point there is overabundance: too many products to sell to nonexistent buyers, too much productive capacity that goes unused, or too much money to invest with insufficient prospects for profits.

This overaccumulation is met in a variety of ways, the most common being the business cycle where workers are laid off, plants close, bankruptcies increase, and money is devalued. Such cycles generally restore macro-level economic controls (usually by government) over money supply, interest rates, unemployment compensation, bankruptcy laws, tax policies, and the like. But Harvey emphasizes another response to overaccumulation: absorption of surplus capital through "temporal" and "spatial" displacement. *Temporal displacement* occurs when investors buy "futures" on commodities yet to be produced, when they purchase stock options in hopes of stock prices rising, when they invest in other financial instruments (mortgages, long-term bonds, government securities), or when they pursue any strategy for using time and the swings of all markets to displace capital and reduce overaccumulation. *Spatial displacement* involves moving capital away from areas of overaccumulation to new locations in need of investment capital. Harvey argues that *displacement* is most effective when both its temporal and spatial aspects are combined, as when money raised in London is sent to Latin America to buy bonds (which will probably be resold again in the future) to finance infrastructural development.

The use of both spatial and temporal displacement to meet the issue of overaccumulation can contribute to the more general problem of time and space displacement. Time and space displacement occurs because of four factors: (1) advanced communication and transportation technologies, (2) increased rationalization of distribution processes, (3) meta- and world-level money markets that accelerate the circulation of money, and (4) decreased spatial concentration of capital in geographical locations (cities, nations, regions). These changes create a perceived sense of time and space compression that must be matched by changes in beliefs, ideologies, perceptions, and other systems of symbols. As technologies combine to allow us to move people and objects more quickly through space—as with the advent of travel by rail, automobile, jet, rocket—space becomes compressed; that is, distance is reduced and space is not as forbidding or meaningful as it was at one time. Ironically, as the speed of transportation, communication, market exchanges, commodity distribution, and capital circulation increases, the amount of available time decreases, because there are more things to do and more ways to do them. Thus, our sense of time and space compresses in response to increases in specific technologies and structural capacities. If these technological and structural changes occur gradually, then the culture that renders the resulting alterations in time and space understandable and meaningful will evolve along with the changes. But, if the changes in structure and technology occur rapidly, as in postmodernity, then the modifications in symbolic categories will not keep pace, and people will be left with a sense of disorientation concerning two primary categories of human existence, time and space. The present response to overaccumulation, "flexible capitalism," helps create a sense of time and space compression as capital is rapidly moved and manipulated on a global scale in response to portfolio management techniques.

In addition, because the new mode of accumulation is designed to move capital spatially and temporally in a flexible and thus ever-changing manner, disorientation ensues as the mode of regulation struggles to keep up with the mode of accumulation. For example, if capital sustaining jobs in one country can be immediately exported to another with lower-priced labor, beliefs among workers about loyalty to the company, conceptions about how to develop a career, commitments of companies to local communities, ideologies of government, import policies, beliefs about training and retraining, conceptions of labor markets, ideologies of corporate responsibility, laws about foreign investment, and many other cultural modes for regulating the flow of capital will all begin to change. Thus, in postmodernity, physical place has been replaced by a new social space driven by the new technologies of highly differentiated and dynamic markets, but cultural orientations have yet to catch up to this pattern of time and space compression.

As with most economic postmodernists, Harvey emphasizes that markets now distribute services as much as they deliver commodities or "hard goods," and many of the commodities and services that are distributed concern the formation of an image of self and identity. Cultural images are now market driven, emphasizing fashion and corporate logos as well as other markers of culture, lifestyle, group membership, taste, status, and virtually anything that individuals can see as relevant to their identity. As boredom, saturation, and imitation create demands for new images with which to define self, cultural images constantly shift—being limited only by the imagination of people, advertisers, and profit-seeking producers. As a result, the pace and volatility of products to be consumed accelerates, and producers for markets as well as agents in markets (such as advertisers, bankers, investors) search for new images to market as commodities or services.

Given a culture that values instant gratification and easy disposability of commodities, people generally react with sensory block, denial, a blasé attitude, myopic specialization, increased nostalgia (for stable old ways), and a search for eternal but simplified truths and collective or personal identity. To the extent that these reactions are the mark of postmodernity, Harvey argues that they represent the lag between cultural responses to new patterns of capital displacement over time and place. Eventually, culture and people's perceptions will catch up to these new mechanisms for overcoming the latest incarnation of capital overaccumulation.

Scott Lash and John Urry

Like David Harvey, Scott Lash and John Urry argue that a *postmodern disposition* occurs with changes in advanced capitalism that shift time and space boundaries.[23] In their view, shifting conceptualizations of time and space are associated with changes in the distribution of capital. Moreover, like most postmodern theorists, Lash and Urry stress that postmodern culture is heavily influenced by the mass media and advertising. Yet, revealing their Marxian roots, they add that the postmodern disposition is particularly dependent on the fragmentation of class experience and the rise of the service class. With its emphasis on capital and the class structure, the focus of Lash and Urry's analysis is thus Marxian, but their method is Weberian: They disavow causal sequences, preferring to speak of preconditions and ideal-types. Thus, they see the postmodernism forms outlined by Lyotard, Jameson, and, as we will see, Jean Baudrillard as an ideal-type against which different systems of culture can be compared.

Like Harvey, Lash and Urry do not see postmodern culture as entirely new, but unlike Harvey, they are less sure that it is a temporary phase waiting for culture to catch up to changed material conditions. Lash and Urry believe that postmodern culture will always appeal to certain audiences with "postmodern dispositions." These dispositions emerge in response to three forces: First, the boundary between reality and image must become blurred as the media, and especially advertising, present ready-made rather than socially constructed cultural images. Second, the traditional working class must be fractured and fragmented; at the same time, a new service class oriented to the consumption of commodities for their symbolic power to produce, mark, and proclaim distinctions in group memberships, taste, lifestyle, preferences, gender-orientation, ethnicity, and many other distinctions must become prominent. And third, the construction of personal and subjective identities must increasingly be built from cultural symbols detached from physical space and location, such as neighborhood, town, or region; as this detachment occurs, images of self become ever more transitory. As these three forces intensify, a postmodern disposition becomes more likely, and these dispositions can come to support a broader postmodern culture where symbols marking difference, identity, and location are purchased by the expanding service class.

Although Lash and Urry are reluctant to speak of causation, they see at least four deciding factors as bringing about these postmodern conditions. The first factor involves the shift from Taylorist or regimented forms of production, such as the old factory assembly line, to more flexible forms of organizing and controlling labor, such as production teams, "flex-time" working hours, reduced hierarchies of authority, and deconcentration of work extending to computer terminals at home. Like Harvey, Lash and Urry believe that these shifts cause, and reflect, decreased spatial concentration of capital and expanded communication and transportation technologies. Spatial dispersion, deconcentration of capital, and rapid movement of information, people, and resources are thus the principle dynamics of change. The second factor concerns large-scale economic changes—the globalization of a market economy, the expansion of industry and banking across national boundaries, and the spread of capitalism into less developed countries. A third factor is increased distributive capacities that accelerate and extend the flow of commodities from the local and national to international markets. This increased scope and speed of circulation can empty many commodities of their ethnic, local, national, and other traditional anchors of symbolic and affective meaning. This rapid circulation of commodities increases the likelihood that many other commodities will be made and purchased for what they communicate aesthetically and cognitively about ever-shifting tastes, preferences, lifestyles, personal statements, and new boundaries of prestige and status group membership. And a fourth factor is really a set of forces that follows from the other factors: (a) the commodification of leisure as yet one more purchased symbolic statement; (b) the breakdown of, and merger among, previously distinct and coherent cultural forms (revolving around music, art, literature, class, ethnic, or gender identity, and other cultural distinctions in modernism); (c) the general collapse of social space, designated physical locations, and temporal frames within which activities are conducted and personal identifications are sustained; and (d) the undermining of politics as tied to traditional constituencies (a time dimension) located in physical places like neighborhoods and social spaces such as classes and ethnic groups.

Together these factors create a spatially fragmented division of labor, a less clear-cut working class, a larger service class, a shift to symbolic rather than material or coercive domination, a use of cultural more than material resources for resistance, and a level of cultural fragmentation and pluralism that erodes nationalism. But Lash and Urry argue, in contrast with Jameson, this emptying out process is not as deregulated as it might appear. They posit that new forms of distribution, communication, and transportation all create networks in time, social spaces, and physical places. Economic governance occurs where the networks are dense, with communications having an increasingly important impact on the difference between core and peripheral sites. Core sites are heavily networked communication sites that function as a "wired village of noncontiguous communities."[24]

All these economic postmodernists clearly have roots in Marxian analysis, both the critical forms that emerged in the early decades of the century and the world-system forms of analysis that arose in the 1970s and continue (see Chapter 10). Early critical theorists had to come to terms with the Weberian specter of coercive and rational-legal authority as crushing emancipatory class activity, but this generation of postmodern critics has had to reconcile their rather muted emancipatory goals to: the spread of world capitalism as the preferred economic system; the prosperity generated by capitalism; the breakdown of the proletariat as a coherent class (much less a vanguard of emancipation); the commodification of everything in fluid and dynamic markets; the production and consumption of symbols more than hard goods (as commodities are bought for their symbolic value); the destruction of social, physical, and temporal boundaries as restrictions of space and time are changed by technologies; the purchase of personal and subjective identities by consumer-driven actors; and the importance of symbolic and cultural "superstructures" as driving forces in world markets glutted with mass-media and advertising images. Given these forced adaptations of the Marxian perspective, it is not surprising that many postmodernists have shifted their focus from the economic base to culture.

CULTURAL POSTMODERNISM

All postmodern theories emphasize the fragmenting character of culture and the blurring of differences marked by symbols. Individuals are seen as caught in these transformations, participating in, and defining self from, an increasing array of social categories, such as race, class, gender, ethnicity, or status, while being exposed to ever increasing varieties of cultural images as potential markers of self. At the same time, individuals lose their sense of being located in stable places and time frames. Many of the forces examined by economic postmodernists can account for this fragmentation of culture, decline in the salience of markers of differences, and loss of identity in time, place, and social space, but cultural postmodernists place particular emphasis on mass media and advertising because these are driven by markets and information technologies.

Jean Baudrillard

The strongest postmodern statement concerning the effects of the media on culture comes from Jean Baudrillard,[25] who sees the task before the social sciences today as challenging the "meaning that comes from the media and its fascination."[26] In contrast with philosophical postmodernism, Baudrillard's theory is based on the assumption that there is a potential equivalence or correspondence between the sign and its object, and based on this proposition, Baudrillard posits four historical phases of the sign. In the first phase, the sign represented a profound reality, with the correlation and correspondence between the sign and the obdurate reality it signified being very high. In the next two phases, signs dissimulated or hid reality in some way: In the second phase, signs masked or counterfeited reality, as when art elaborated or commented on life, whereas in the third phase, signs masked the absence of any profound reality, as when mass commodification produced a plethora of signs that have no real basis in group identity but have the appearance of originating in group interaction. The second phase roughly corresponds to the period of time from the Renaissance to the Industrial Revolution, whereas the third phase came with the Industrial Age, as production and new market forces created commodities whose *sign values* marking tastes, style, status, and other symbolic representations of individuals began to rival the *use value* (for some practical purpose) or *exchange value* (for some other commodity or resource like money) of commodities. In Baudrillard's view, then, the evolution of signs has involved decreasing, if not obfuscating, their connection to real objects in the actual world.

The fourth stage in the evolution of the sign is the present postmodern era. In this age, the sign "has no relation to any reality whatsoever: It is its own pure simulacrum."[27] Signs are about themselves and, hence, are simulations or *simulacrums* of other signs with little connection to the basic nature of the social or material world. Baudrillard's prime example of simulacrum is Disneyland. Disneyland presents itself as a representation of Americana, embodying the values and joys of American life. Disneyland is offered as imagery—a place to symbolically celebrate and enjoy all that is good in the real world. But Baudrillard argues that Disneyland is presented as imagery to hide the fact that it is American reality itself. Life in the surrounding "real" communities, for example, Los Angeles and Anaheim, consists simply of emulations of past realities: People no longer walk as a mode of transportation; rather, they jog or power walk. People no longer touch one another in daily interaction; rather, they go to contact-therapy groups. The essence of life in postmodernity is imagery; behavior is determined by image potential and is thus simply image. Baudrillard depicts Los Angeles as "no longer anything but an immense scenario and a perpetual pan shot."[28] Thus, when Disneyland is presented as a symbolic representation of life in America, when life in America is itself an image or simulation of a past reality, then Disneyland becomes a simulation of a simulation with no relationship to any reality whatsoever, and it hides the nonreality of daily life.

Baudrillard argues that the presentation of information by the media destroys information. This destruction occurs because there is a natural entropy within the information process; any information about a social event is a degraded form of that event and, hence, represents a dissolving of the social. The media is nothing more than a constant barrage of bits of image and sign that have been removed an infinite number of times from actual social events. Thus, the media does not present a surplus of information, but, on the contrary, what is communicated represents total entropy of information and, hence, of the social world that is supposedly denoted by signs organized into information. The media also destroys information because it stages the presentation of information, presenting it in a pre-packaged meaning form. As information is staged, the subject is told what constitutes their particular relationship to that information, thereby simulating for individuals their place and location in a universe of signs about signs.

Baudrillard argues that advertising facilitated the break between reality and the sign. Advertising eventually reduces objects from their use-value to their sign-value; the symbols of advertisements become commodities in and of themselves, image more than information about the commodity is communicated. Thus, advertisements typically juxtapose a commodity with a desirable image—for example, a watch showing one young male and two young females with their naked bodies overlapping one another—rather than providing information about the quality and durability of the commodity. So that what is being sold and purchased is the image rather than the commodity itself. But, further, advertising itself can become the commodity sought after by the consuming public rather than the image of the advertisement. In the postmodern era, the form of the advertisement rather than the advertisement itself becomes paramount. For example, a currently popular form of television commercials is what could be called the "MTV-style." Certain groups of people respond to these commercials not because of the product and not simply because of the images contained within the advertisements, but because they respond to the overall form of the message and not to its content at all. Thus, in postmodernity, the medium is the message, and what people are faced with, according to Baudrillard, is simulations of simulations and an utter absence of any reality.

Further Elaborations of Cultural Postmodernism

Kenneth Gergen   The self is best understood, in Kenneth Gergen's view,[29] as the process through which individuals categorize their own behaviors. This process depends on the linguistic system used in the physical and social spaces that locate the individual at a given time. Because conceptualizations of self are situational, the self generally tends to be experienced by individuals as fragmented and sometimes contradictory. Yet, people are generally motivated to eliminate inconsistencies in conceptualizations, and though Gergen grants that other possible factors influence efforts to resolve inconsistencies, people in western societies try to create a consistent self-identity because they are socialized to dislike cognitive dissonance in much the same way they are taught to reason rationally. Gergen thus sees an intrinsic relationship between the individual's experience of a self and the culture within which that experience takes place, a cultural stand that he exploits in his understanding of the postmodern self.

Gergen argues that the culture of the self has gone through at least three distinct stages—the romantic, modern, and current postmodern phases. During the romantic period, the self as an autonomous individual and agent was stressed as individuals came out from the domination of various institutions including the church and manorial estate; during the modern period, the self was perceived as possessing essential or basic qualities, such as psychologically defined inherent personality traits. But the postmodern self consists only of images, revealing no inherent qualities and, most significantly, has lost the ability as well as desire to create self-consistency. Further, because knowledge and culture are fragmented in the postmodern era, the very concept of the individual self must be questioned and the distinction between the subject and the object dropped. According to Gergen, then, the very category of the self has been erased as a result of postmodern culture.

Thus, like Baudrillard, Gergen sees the self in postmodern culture as becoming saturated with images that are incoherent, communicating unrelated elements in different languages. And corresponding to Baudrillard's death of the subject, Gergen posits that the category of the self has been eradicated because efforts to formulate consistent and coherent definitions of who people are have been overwhelmed by images on images, couched in diverse languages that cannot order self-reflection.

Norman Denzin and Douglas Kellner   In contrast with Baudrillard's claim that television is simply a flow of incessant disjointed and empty images, both Norman Denzin[30] and Douglas Kellner[31] argue that television and other media have formed people's ideas and actions in much the same way as traditional myth and ritual: These media integrate individuals into a social fabric of values, norms, and roles. In the postmodern culture and economy, media images themselves are the basis from which people get their identities—in particular, their identities of race, class, and gender.

In addition, Denzin and Kellner advocate a method of social activism: a critical reading of the texts from media presentations to discover the underlying ideologies, discourses, and meanings that the political economy produces. The purpose of these critical readings is to "give a voice to the voiceless, as it deconstructs those popular culture texts which reproduce stereotypes about the powerless."[32] Both theorists disavow any grand narrative, and like more radical postmodernists, neither advocates a centerpoint, ultimate hope, and grand or totalizing discourse. Yet, like critical theorists before them, they both hold out the hope of forming new solidarities and initiating emancipatory conflicts through the exposé of the political economy of signs.

But Denzin, unlike Kellner, takes issue with Baudrillard's and Jameson's views on self as an incoherent mirage of signs and symbols and as incapable of ordering images into some coherence. Denzin argues that the "lived experience" itself has become the final commodity in the circulation of capital and that the producers of postmodern culture selectively choose which lived experiences will be commodified and marketed to members of a society. Postmodern culture only commodifies those cultures that present a particular aesthetic picture of race, class, and gender relations, but because culture has become centrally important in postmodernity, this process of commodification has a positive value for giving individuals a sense of identity and for enabling them to act in the material world on the basis of this identity.

Mark Gottdiener Like Denzin and Kellner, Gottdiener wants to maintain a critical postmodern stand but also to argue that an objective referent is behind the infinite regress of meaning. In contrast with Denzin and Kellner, Gottdiener sees the effects of media and markets as trivializing the culture of postmodernity.[33] According to Gottdiener, signs in technologically advanced societies can circulate between the levels of lived experience and the level where the sign is expropriated by some center of power, including producers and marketers of symbols.

Capitalizing on Baudrillard's notion of sign-value, Gottdiener argues that there are three separate phases of interaction wherein a sign can be endowed with meaning. In the first stage, economically motivated producers create objects of exchange-value for money and profit, an intent that is decidedly different from the goals of those who purchase the objects for their use-value. In the second stage, these objects become involved in the everyday life of the social groups that use them. During this stage users might "transfunctionalize" the object from its use-value into a sign-value to connect the object to their subgroup or culture (for example, a type of denim jacket is personalized to represent a group, such as the Hell's Angels). The third stage occurs if and when the economic producers and retailers adopt these personalized and transfunctionalized objects and commodify them (for instance, the Hell's Angels' style of jacket can now be bought by any suburban teenager in a shopping mall). This third stage involves a "symbolic leveling" or "trivialization" of the signed object.[34]

Thomas Luckmann Although Thomas Luckmann[35] recognizes the importance of the media and advertising in creating a postmodern culture, he focuses on the process of *de-institutionalization* as it pushes people into the cultural markets found in the mass media. The basic function of any institution, Luckmann argues, is to provide a set of predetermined meanings for the perceived world and, simultaneously, to provide legitimation for these meanings. Religion, in particular, provides a shield of solidarity against any doubts, fears, and questions about ultimate meaning by giving and legitimating an ultimate *meaning set*. Yet, modern structural differentiation and specialization have, Luckmann contends, made the ultimate meanings of religion structurally unstable because individuals must confront a diverse array of secular tasks and obligations that carry alternative meanings. This structural instability has, in turn, resulted in the privatization of religion. This privatization of religion is, however, more than a retreat from secular structural forces; it is also a response to forces of the sacralization of subjectivity found in mass culture.

Because of the effects of structural differentiation, markets, and mass culture, consciousness within individuals is one of immediate sensations and emotions. As a consequence, consciousness is unstable, making acceptance of general legitimating myths, symbols, and dogmas problematic—Lyotard's "incredulity toward grand narratives." Yet, capitalist markets have turned this challenge into profitable business. The individual is now faced with a highly competitive market for ultimate meanings created by mass media, churches and sects, residual nineteenth-century secular ideologies, and substitute religious communities. The products of this market form a more or less systematically arranged meaning set that refers to minimal and intermediate meanings but rarely to ultimate meanings. Under these conditions, a meaning set can be taken up by an individual for a long or short period and combined with elements from other meaning sets. Thus, just as early capitalism and the structural forces that it unleashed undermined the integrative power of religion, so advanced capitalism creates a new, more postmodern diversity of commodified meaning sets that can be mass produced and consumed by individuals in search of cultural coherence that can stave off their anxieties and fears in a structurally differentiated and culturally fragmented social world.

Zygmunt Bauman Like Luckmann, Zygmunt Bauman[36] examines the effects of de-institutionalization on meanings about self in chaotic, often random, and highly differentiated systems. Within these kinds of systems, identity formation consists of self-constitution with no reference point for evaluation or monitoring, no clear anchorage in place and time, and no lifelong and consistent project of self-formation. People thus experience a high degree of uncertainty about their identity, and consequently, Bauman argues, the only visible vehicle for identity formation is the body. Thus, in postmodernity, body cultivation becomes an extremely important dynamic in the process of self-constitution. Because the body plays such an important role in constituting the postmodern-self, uncertainty is highest around bodily concerns, such as health, physique, aging, and skin blemishes; these issues become causes of increased reflexivity, evaluation, and, thus, uncertainty.

Bauman, like Luckmann, argues that the absence of any firm and objective evaluative guide tends to create a demand for a substitute. These substitutes are symbolically created, as other people and groups are seen as "unguarded totemic poles which one can approach or abandon without applying for permission to enter or leave."[37] Individuals use these others as reference points and adopt the symbols of belonging to the other. The availability of the symbolic tokens depends on their visibility, which, in turn, depends on the use of the symbolic token to produce a satisfactory self-construction. In the end, the efficacy of these symbols rests on either expertise in some task or mass following. Bauman also argues that accessibility of the tokens depends on an agent's resources and increasingly is understood as knowledge and information. So, for example, people might adopt the symbols associated with a specific professional athlete—wearing the same type of shoe or physically moving in the same defining manner—or, individuals might assume all the outward symbols and cultural capital associated with a perceived group of computer wizards. The important issue for Bauman is that these symbols of group membership can be taken up or cast off without any commitment or punitive action because the individuals using the symbols have never been an interactive part of these groups or celebrities' lives.

The need for these tokens results in "tribal politics," defined as self-constructing practices that are collectivized.[38] These tribes function as *imagined communities* and, unlike premodern communities, exist only in symbolic form through the shared commitments of their members.[39] For example, a girl in rural North Carolina might pierce various body parts, wear mismatched clothing three sizes too large, have the music of "Biohazard" habitually running through her mind, and see herself as a member of the grunge or punk community but never once interact with group members. Or, an individual might develop a concern for the use of animals in laboratory experiments, talk about it to others, wear proclamations on tee-shirts and bumper stickers, and attend an occasional rally, and, thus, might perceive himself as a group member but not be part of any kind of social group or interaction network. These quasi-groups function without the powers of inclusion and exclusion that earlier groups possessed; indeed, these "neo-tribes" are created only through the repetitive performance of symbolic rituals and exist only as long as the members perform the rituals. Neo-tribes are thus formed through concepts rather than through face-to-face encounters in actual social groups. They exist as imagined communities through self-identification and persist solely because people use them as vehicles for self-definition and as "imaginary sediments." Because the persistence of these tribes depends on the affective allegiance of the members, self-identifying rituals become more extravagant and spectacular. Spectacular displays, such as body scarring or extreme or random violence, are necessary because in postmodernity the true scarce resource on which self and other is based is public attention.

Table 14.1 Comparing Economic and Culture Postmodernism

The Structure of Advanced Capitalism	Consequences of Advanced Capitalism
High volume/velocity/scope markets fueled by advertising	Increasing significance of culture over material social structures
Increased commodification of objects, people, and most important, cultural symbols	Detachment of cultural from local groups, local time, and local space
Rapid movement of capital all over the world, and its de-concentration	Destabilization of cultural symbols and their ability to provide stable meanings for individuals
Compression of time and space due to advances in transportation and communication technologies	Increased salience of the individual over groups
	Increased reflexivity of self
Growing dominance of technologies of reproduction (imaging technologies) over those of production	Decreased viability, stability, and coherence of self conceptions

CONCLUSION

Because postmodern theories are critical of science, it is difficult to assess them by whether or not they are empirically correct or wrong. To impose this criterion uses, in the postmodernists' view, an outmoded epistemology to evaluate postmodern narratives. Nonetheless, it is still reasonable to ask: How plausible are various assertions about the nature of the postmodern world? One way to answer this question is to separate economic and cultural postmodernists. In Table 14.1, the arguments of economic and cultural postmodernists are arrayed. On the left are the empirical assertions of the economic postmodernists, and on the right are those of the cultural postmodernists.

Typically, the economic forces portrayed on the left are viewed as causing the transformations to culture, groups, and self on the right. A cursory examination of the table suggests that the economic arguments are highly plausible. Advanced capitalism and globalization do indeed seem to be operating along the lines portrayed in the table, and so, the real question becomes whether or not these economic trends are changing in fundamental ways the nature of society, culture, and individuals. If we ask if the arguments of the cultural postmodernists ring true, the answer is not as unambiguous as it is for the economic postmodernists. Perhaps it is true that culture is now dominant over material structures, that culture has been commodified and detached from local groups, time and space, that cultural symbols are so destabilized as to be unable to provide stable meanings for individuals, that self is now ascendant over the group, that self is highly reflexive, and that self has lost coherence and stability. But it is equally likely that none of these trends is operating. There are no systematic tests of these assertions, and so it is difficult to know. It appears that, on the surface, the postmodernists who are all ivory-tower academics are arguing that their impressions are actually the way empirical reality is unfolding.

They offer only examples and illustrations, rather than systematically collected data. Of course, they would reject any criticism of the "failed" epistemology of science. Hence, postmodernists conveniently make it impossible to challenge their assertions with evidence that they would be willing to accept.

NOTES

1. Zygmunt Bauman, *Intimations of Postmodernity* (London and New York: Routledge, 1992).

2. Jean-François Lyotard, *The Postmodern Condition* (Minneapolis: University of Minnesota Press, 1979, 1984).

3. Ludwig Wittgenstein, *Philosophical Investigations* (New York: Macmillan, 1936–1949, 1973).

4. Richard Rorty, "Philosophy as a Kind of Writing: An Essay on Derrida," *New Literary History* 10 (1978), pp. 141–160; *Philosophy and the Mirror of Nature* (Princeton, NJ: Princeton University Press, 1979); "Method, Social Science, and Social Hope," in *The Postmodern Turn: New Perspectives on Social Theory,* ed. Steven Seidman (Cambridge: Cambridge University Press, 1994).

5. Rorty, "Method, Social Science, and Social Hope" (cited in note 4), p. 57.

6. For the postmodernist, all cultural expressions are to be understood as language. But the use of linguistic systems as a basis for understanding all social phenomena is not new with postmodernism. For example, this linguistic equivalence model is central to the work of Claude Lévi-Strauss. But postmodernism has, building on the poststructuralist work of Jacques Derrida and Michel Foucault, explicitly made signs, sign systems, and texts human reality *in toto*.

7. Richard Harvey Brown, *Society as Text: Essays on Rhetoric, Reason, and Reality* (Chicago: The University of Chicago Press, 1987); *Social Science as Civic Discourse: Essays on the Invention, Legitimation, and Uses of Social Theory* (Chicago: The University of Chicago Press, 1989); "Rhetoric, Textuality, and the Postmodern Turn in Sociological Theory," *Sociological Theory* 8 (1990), pp. 188–197.

8. Brown, *Social Science as Civic Discourse* (cited in note 7), pp. 49–54.

9. Ibid., p. 188.

10. In the postmodern literature, a distinction is often made between social and sociological theory. Social theory is generally understood to be a text that is self-consciously directed toward improving social conditions through entering the social discourse, whereas sociological theory is a denotative text that is abstracted from social concerns and involvement. In the view of postmodernism, social theory is preferred to sociological theory.

11. Charles C. Lemert, "The Uses of French Structuralisms in Sociology," *Frontiers of Social Theory: The New Syntheses,* ed. George Ritzer (New York: Columbia University Press, 1990), pp. 230–254. Charles C. Lemert, "General Social Theory, Irony, Postmodernism," *Postmodernism and Social Theory,* eds. Steven Seidman and David G. Wagner (Cambridge, MA: Blackwell, 1990), pp. 17–46.

12. Steven Seidman, "The End of Sociological Theory," in *The Postmodern Turn: New Perspectives on Social Theory,* ed. Steven Seidman (Cambridge: Cambridge University Press, 1994), pp. 84–96.

13. Mark Gottdiener, "The Logocentrism of the Classics," *American Sociological Review* 55 (June 1990), pp. 460–463; "Ideology, Foundationalism, and Sociological Theory," *Sociological Quarterly* 34 (1993), pp. 653–671.

14. Gottdiener, "Ideology, Foundationalism, and Sociological Theory" (cited in note 13), p. 667.

15. Seidman, "The End of Sociological Theory" (cited in note 12), p. 120.

16. For example, Lemert (*Sociology After the Crisis,* Boulder, CO: Westview, 1995, p. 78) makes a distinction between radical postmodernism and strategic postmodernism. Radical postmodernists disavow any possibility of truth or reality whereas strategic postmodernists attempt to undercut the authority that modernist knowledge claims while preserving the language and categories that modernist knowledge uses. Strategic postmodernists, according to Lemert, still maintain the modernist hope of emancipation.

17. See, for example, Stephen Crook, Jan Pakulski, and Malcolm Waters, *Postmodernization* (London: Sage International, 1992).

18. Fredric Jameson, *The Postmodern Condition* (Minneapolis: University of Minnesota Press, 1984).

19. Ibid., p. 92.

20. Ibid., p. 72.

21. Ibid., p. 64.

22. David Harvey, *The Conditions of Postmodernity: An Inquiry into the Origins of Cultural Change* (Oxford: Blackwell, 1989).

23. Scott Lash and John Urry, *The End of Organized Capitalism* (Madison: University of Wisconsin Press, 1987); *Economies of Signs and Space* (Newbury Park, CA: Sage, 1994).

24. Lash and Urry, *Economies of Signs and Space* (cited in note 23), p. 28.

25. Jean Baudrillard, *For a Critique of the Political Economy of the Sign* (St. Louis: Telos, 1972, 1981); *The Mirror of Production* (St. Louis: Telos, 1973, 1975); *Simulacra and Simulation* (Ann Arbor: University of Michigan Press, 1981, 1994); *Symbolic Exchange and Death* (Newbury Park, CA: Sage, 1993).

26. Baudrillard, *Simulacra and Simulation* (cited in note 25), p. 84.

27. Ibid., p. 6.

28. Ibid., p. 13.

29. Kenneth J. Gergen, *The Saturated Self* (New York: Basic Books, 1991); *The Concept of Self* (New York: Holt, Rinehart & Winston, 1971).

30. Norman K. Denzin, "Postmodern Social Theory," *Sociological Theory* 4 (1986), pp. 194–204; *Images of Postmodern Society: Social Theory and Contemporary Cinema* (London: Sage International, 1991); *Symbolic Interactionism and Cultural Studies* (Oxford: Blackwell, 1992).

31. Douglas Kellner, "Popular Culture and the Construction of Postmodern Identities," in *Modernity and Identity,* eds. Scott Lash and Jonathan Friedman (Oxford: Blackwell, 1992); *Media Culture: Cultural Studies, Identity and Politics Between the Modern and the Postmodern* (London: Routledge, 1995).

32. Denzin, *Images of Postmodern Society* (cited in note 30), p. 153.

33. Mark Gottdiener, "Hegemony and Mass Culture: A Semiotic Approach," *American Journal of Sociology* 90 (1985), pp. 979–1001; *Postmodern Semiotics: Material Culture and the Forms of Postmodern Life* (Oxford: Blackwell, 1995).

34. Gottdiener, "Hegemony and Mass Culture" (cited in note 33), p. 996.

35. Thomas Luckmann, "The New and the Old in Religion," *Social Theory for a Changing Society,* eds. Pierre Bourdieu and James S. Coleman (Boulder, CO: Westview, 1991).

36. Zygmunt Bauman, *Modernity and Ambivalence* (Ithaca, NY: Cornell University Press, 1991); *Intimations of Postmodernity* (London and New York: Routledge, 1992).

37. Bauman, *Intimations of Postmodernity* (cited in note 36), p. 195.

38. Ibid., pp. 198–199.

39. See Benedict Anderson, *Imagined Communities* (London: Verso, 1983).

15

Feminist Critical Theory

Since the early 1970s, one of the most sustained challenges to "mainstream" sociological theory has come from critical feminist theorists. Appearing shortly after the beginning of the "second wave" of the women's movement in the mid-to-late 1960s, the first feminist critiques focused on the underrepresentation of women and women's experiences within sociology, both as the subjects of research and the producers of theory. Concurrently, feminist theorists examined the construction of gender and sex roles in modern society to demonstrate the existence of a "female world" that sociology had hitherto ignored.[1] Subsequent critiques went further, as feminists used the concepts of gender and patriarchy to reveal masculine (or androcentric) stances in social research methodologies and in sociological theory. These more radical critiques questioned the capacity of sociological research and theory, as a body of knowledge constructed from the experiences of men, to address the experiences of women. Critical feminist theorists proposed alternative methodological approaches, including the construction of a "feminist standpoint" or women's sociology that would begin with the social universe of women and reflect women's perspectives on society.[2] In the past decade, several radical feminist theorists have also used the epistemological issues inherent in feminist methodologies to critique the

Note: This chapter is coauthored with P. R. Turner.

249

"positivistic" foundations of sociological understanding and to lay the groundwork for a "feminist epistemology."[3]

The feminist critique, like much of sociological theory at present, does not form a coherent paradigm. There is little consensus among critical feminist theorists about what constitutes "the feminist critique" or about how sociological understandings should be restructured to obviate the criticisms of feminists. Nevertheless, several common threads distinguish the feminist position from other forms of critical theory. The critical feminist theorists discussed in this chapter share with their more scientifically oriented colleagues examined in Chapter 11 the conviction that gender represents a fundamental form of social division within society. They also share a commitment to analyzing the sources of oppression and inequality for women, the most important being the patriarchal structure of society and its institutions. These two groups differ, however, in their focus, methods, and purpose. Instead of examining gender inequalities as a form of conflict-producing stratification, the feminist theorists examined in this chapter have focused on gender and forms of patriarchy to criticize social research practices and the production of sociological theory itself.[4] In their analyses of theory production as a form of patriarchy, many of these feminist theorists have not felt bound by "positivistic" methods of inquiry that guided the theorists examined in Chapter 11; indeed, they have questioned the legitimacy and objectivity of these methods by exploring the ways in which they embody androcentric (male-oriented) modes of thought. Finally, these critical feminist theorists are often self-consciously aware of the political and practical implications of their attacks for feminist politics and the status of women. As Mary Jo Neitz stated, "the critical questions for feminist scholarship came out of the women's movement, not out of the disciplines."[5] Consequently, most critical feminist theorists want to preserve the emancipatory dimension of feminist theory—that is, its ability to serve, like Marxism, as "both a mode of understanding and a call to action."[6] This self-conscious conflation of theory, method, politics, and praxis, combined with a focus on gender and patriarchy as the primary sources of oppression and inequality, constitute the common denominators distinguishing the feminist critique of sociological theory.

REPRESENTATION OF GENDER:
EARLY CHALLENGES TO SOCIAL SCIENCE

Early feminist critiques of sociological research and theory were concerned primarily with the issue of representation. Kathryn Ward and Linda Grant, in an analysis of more than 700 gender-related articles in sociology journals between 1974 and 1983, asserted that the feminist critique of gender inequities within sociology dealt with the following four issues[7]:

1. Omission and underrepresentation of women as research subjects.

2. Concentration on masculine-dominated sectors of social life.

3. Use of paradigms, concepts, methods, and theories that more faithfully portray men's than women's experiences.

4. Use of men and male lifestyles as the norms against which social phenomena were interpreted.

One of the most influential early works that addressed all of these issues is Ann Oakley's survey of housewives and their opinions of housework. Oakley argued that discrimination against women in society is mirrored by sexism in sociology, and she used the academic neglect of housework as *work* to address the broader issue of sexual bias within sociological research and theory in general.[8] Oakley stated that women's "invisibility" in sociology can be seen in all the major subject areas of sociology. In the subject area of deviance, for example, Oakley argued that until the mid-1970s very little data had been collected on women and that "theories of deviance may include some passing reference to women, but interpretations of female behavior are uncomfortably subsumed under the umbrella of explanation geared to the model of masculine behavior."[9] She also questioned whether or not standard definitions of deviance consider patterns of behavior that are gender-related or associated only with women.[10] With regard to social stratification theory, to take an example from another prominent subject area of sociology, Oakley posited that the following untested assumptions about class membership effectively render women invisible and irrelevant: (1) The family is the unit of stratification; (2) the social position of the family is determined by the status of the man in it; and (3) only in rare circumstances is a woman's social position not determined by the men to whom they are attached by marriage or family of origin.[11] Oakley argued that these assumptions often do not reflect social reality, because many people do not live in families, many families are headed by women, and many husbands and wives do not have identical social status rankings. The problematics of these assumptions would be revealed, according to Oakley, if sociologists recognize the significance of gender as a criterion for social differentiation and stratification. Without such recognition, women's roles and position in the social stratification system would continue to be hidden and misrepresented.[12]

Oakley attributed the inherent sexism in sociological theory and research to the male-oriented attitudes of its "founding fathers,"[13] the paucity of women social researchers and theorists, and the pervasiveness of ideologies advocating gender roles within contemporary societies. The ideology of gender, she argued, contains stereotypical assumptions about women's social status and behavior that are uncritically reproduced within sociology, and these stereotypes will only be overcome if women's experiences are made the focus of analysis and viewed from their perspective.[14]

Most of these early critiques of sociological research and theory share with Oakley two related assumptions about the primacy and construction of gender: First, gender is a fundamental determinant of social relations and behavior, and second, gender divisions in a society shape the experiences and perspectives of each sex, with the result that women's experiences are distinctly different from those of men. Some feminist scholars went further than Oakley and began to argue that society is gendered in ways that segregate men and women into distinct and often exclusionary homosocial worlds. Building on Georg Simmel's insight that "women possess a world of their own which is not comparable with the world of men,"[15] Jessie Bernard argued in *The Female World* that society is divided into "single-sex" worlds. Sociology and other disciplines in the humanities and human sciences have dealt heretofore almost exclusively with the male world. Bernard has sought to correct this imbalance by tracing the historical development of the female world and the uniquely female experiences and perspectives that have emerged from it. She has argued that the female world differs subjectively and objectively from that of men, and hence, the female world must be examined "as an entity in its own right, not as a by-product of the male world."[16] The neglect of the female world and women's experiences by sociology and other disciplines, Bernard has asserted, deprives public debate of perspectives that might provide innovative solutions and approaches to contemporary problems.[17]

Other feminist theorists have used the concept of gendered social spheres to explore more specifically the stratification of sex roles and the social construction of gender. Jean Lipman–Blumen proposed a homosocial theory of sex roles to account for the traditional barriers that restrict women's entry into male spheres—such as politics, military, and major league sports—and that confine women to the domestic sphere.[18] She hypothesized that men are socialized to be attracted to, and to be interested in, other men. This attraction is reinforced and perpetuated by patriarchal social institutions that traditionally value men over women and give to men nearly exclusive control of resources.[19] With the important exceptions of reproductive and sexual needs, men look to men for support, whereas women are forced to transform themselves into sex objects to acquire resources and support from men. Lipman-Blumen argued the preeminence of men in the exchange and protection of resources creates "dominance hierarchies" that persist even when technology eliminates the need for the differentiation and stratification of sex roles.[20]

In her highly influential book, *The Reproduction of Mothering: Psychoanalysis and the Sociology of Gender,* Nancy Chadorow theorized that women's responsibility for childrearing (and the collateral absence of male domestic roles) has profound consequences for the construction of gender identity and the sexual division of labor. Chadorow posits, "all societies are constituted around a structural split, growing out of women's mothering, between the private, domestic world of women and the public, social world of men."[21] This structural split is created by a sexual division of labor that is itself reproduced each generation by gender personality differences between men and women. These behavioral differences or "intrapsychic structures" are not biological; rather, they stem from the distinct social relationships girls and boys develop with their mothers. Girls learn to be women and to mother by identifying with their mothers, whereas boys must develop a masculine gender identification in opposition to their mothers and often in the absence of affective, ongoing relationships to a father figure. This results in different "relational capacities" and "senses of self" in men and women that prepare them "to assume the adult gender roles which situate women primarily within the sphere of reproduction in a sexually unequal society."[22]

A SOCIOLOGY FOR WOMEN: FEMINIST METHODOLOGIES, EPISTEMOLOGIES, AND "STANDPOINT" THEORIES

Efforts in the late 1970s and 1980s to devise a sociology for women arose from a growing conviction among more radical critical feminist theorists that to simply refocus the discipline's theoretical and methodological lenses on gender and women's domains would do little to correct the androcentric (male) biases and patterns of patriarchal thought inhering in sociological work. Because of these biases, traditional forms of explanation within sociology were increasingly seen as fundamentally incapable of representing accurately a social world in which, many feminist critics began to assert, all social relations are gendered.[23] Recognizing the link between feminist thought and politics, John Shotter and Josephine Logan argue that only by finding a "new voice" can feminist scholars and the women's movement as a whole escape the "pervasiveness of patriarchy":

> The women's movement must of necessity develop itself within a patriarchal culture of such a depth and pervasiveness that, even in reacting to or resisting its oppressive nature, the women's movement continually "reinfects" or "contaminates" itself with it. All of us, women and men alike, are "soaked" in it. . . . Patriarchy is enshrined in our social practices, in our ways of positioning and relating ourselves to one another, and in the resources we use in making sense of one another. . . . We must find a different voice, a new place currently unrecognized, from which to speak about the nature of our lives together.[24]

This kind of more-radical attack on the sociology of knowledge was fueled by a growing frustration among feminist critics in general about what they saw as a continued resistance within sociology—and sociological theory in particular—to study gender and to draw out the conceptual and theoretical implications of this research. Grant and Ward, for example, found in their analysis of articles published in ten sociology journals between 1974 and 1983 that the number of theoretical papers, reviews, and critiques focusing on gender in mainstream journals was still relatively small compared with other traditional topics—an indication, they feel, that journal editors continued to view gender as a peripheral in contemporary sociology.[25]

Other feminist critics have echoed Grant and Ward's concerns. Joan Acker's review of stratification literature asserts that, aside from Rae Lesser Blumberg's landmark book (see Chapter 11),[26] stratification texts still do not "successfully integrate women into the analysis and generally evade the problem by including brief descriptions of sex-based inequality generally ungrounded in a conceptualization of societal-wide stratification."[27] Judith Stacey and Barrie Thorne conclude that although feminist scholars have made valuable contributions to numerous traditional branches of sociological research (for example, organizations, occupations, criminology, deviance and stratification), and have pioneered work in many others (for example, sexual harassment, feminization of poverty), they had yet to effect significant conceptual transformations in the field.[28] Feminist scholars in sociology—unlike their counterparts in anthropology, history, and literary criticism—have not succeeded in influencing the discipline to the point where women are being put regularly at the center of analysis. Instead, Stacey and Thorne argue that "feminist sociology seems to have been both co-opted and ghettoized, while the discipline as a whole and its dominant paradigms have proceeded relatively unchanged."[29]

Feminist scholars propose a variety of explanations to account for the "ghettoization" of gender issues within sociological research and theory. In their study of women's involvement in theory production, Ward and Grant emphasize that the relative lack of theorizing on gender might be partly because of the scarcity and low profile of women theorists. Compared with their male colleagues, Ward and Grant found that women sociologists (1) affiliate with the ASA theory section less, (2) self-identify as theorists less, (3) write fewer textbooks and journal articles, (4) receive less visibility in textbooks and popular teaching materials, and (5) serve less frequently as editors or board members of theory journals.[30] As possible explanations for the "peculiar eclipsing" of women as theorists Ward and Grant cite (1) the comparatively high status of theory production which, in turn, can lead to higher barriers against the entry of women, and (2) the fragmentation of contemporary sociological theory into multiple and competing paradigms that can restrict the spread of feminist thought.

Ward and Grant also speculate that differences in how women sociologists approach their research subjects might decrease the likelihood of their work on gender being accepted for publication. They have found that there are "systematic links" between gender and methods within sociology, with women scholars publishing in major sociological journals employing qualitative methods more often than their male colleagues.[31] Many feminist theorists argue that qualitative methods (for example, intensive interviews and participant observation) are more appropriate for exploring gender and women's issues, which tend to be more private, context-bound, and hence, less easily quantifiable.[32] Yet Grant and Ward have failed to find a correlation between gender and methods in published research on gender among mainstream sociological journals. In gender articles, both sexes preferred quantitative methods, leading them to speculate that "qualitative papers on gender might have presented double nonconformity, reducing the likelihood of acceptance for publication."[33] Finally, Ward and Grant also refer to Judith A. Howard's contention that the influence of feminist perspectives is limited by "the inability of extant social theories (including Marxism) to conceptualize gender as a major organizing principle of society and culture and by the predominance of positivist epistemological traditions that encourage emphasis on gender as a variable rather than a concept."[34]

Acker takes a different tack, suggesting that sociological theory "continues in a prefeminist mode" because of both institutional resistance within the discipline and the underdevelopment of feminist alternatives to mainstream theoretical concepts and methodologies.[35] Sociology, Acker argues, shares with other academic disciplines

> A particular connection to power in society as a whole or to the relations of ruling: The almost exclusively male domain of academic thought is associated with abstract, intellectual, textually mediated processes through which organizing, managing and governing are carried out. . . . The perspectives that develop their concepts and problematics from within what is relevant to the relations of ruling are successful.[36]

Acker questions whether critical feminist theories can ever effect a paradigm shift within sociological theory as long as societal institutions remain patriarchally structured and power relations continue to be dominated by men.[37] Yet, Acker also holds feminist theory accountable for its relative lack of influence within mainstream sociological theory. Feminist scholars, she argues, "have not, as yet, been able to suggest new ways of looking at things that are obviously better than the old ways for comprehending a whole range of problems. . . ."[38] Acker outlines her vision of a feminist paradigm capable of competing with or supplanting established theoretical positions. Such a paradigm would

1. Provide a better understanding of class structure, the state, social evolution, and militarism, as well as a better understanding of the sex segregation of labor, male dominance in the family, and sexual violence.

2. Place women and their lives in a central place in understanding social relations as a whole, while creating a more accurate and comprehensive account of industrial, capitalist society.

3. Contain a methodology that produces knowledge *for* rather than *of* women in all their diverse situations.[39]

Implicit in Acker's proposal for a feminist paradigm is a radical critique of the very concepts, methodologies, and epistemological assumptions that form the foundation of sociological understandings of the social universe. As espoused by feminist theorists such as Dorothy Smith, Sandra Harding, and Evelyn Fox Keller, feminist theorists have failed thus far to transform prevailing mainstream theoretical paradigms because the underlying epistemologies and methodologies give privilege to the male experience.[40] Smith, one of the first feminist critical theorists to call for a "woman-centered" sociology, asserts that sociological thought has been "based on and built up within the male social universe,"[41] and as a consequence, sociology contains unexamined androcentric (male) modes of thought that serve the interests of men and that are by definition gender biased and exclusionary of women's perspectives.[42] Smith argues that as long as feminist scholars work within forms of thought made or controlled by men, women will be constrained to view themselves not as subjects but as the "other" and their experience will be marginalized accordingly.[43] It is not enough, she claims,

> To supplement an established sociology by addressing ourselves to what has been left out, overlooked, or by making sociological issues of the relevances of the world of women. That merely extends the authority of the existing sociological procedures and makes of a women's sociology an addendum.[44]

This radical feminist critique has taken three main forms. First, it criticizes standard methodological practices and proposes to replace them with feminist methodologies. Second, it questions the epistemological assumptions of "positivistic" science because science, like the broader society, is gendered, and, therefore, new epistemologies need to be developed that eliminate gender bias while recognizing the primacy of gender and its implications for knowledge production. Finally, radical feminist theorists propose the construction of an independent feminist "standpoint" that can avoid both the androcentric biases inherent in social research practices and the "positivistic" epistemological foundations of mainstream sociological theory.[45]

One of the first detailed feminist critiques of contemporary social methodology was a volume of essays edited by sociologists Marcia Millman and Rosabeth Moss Kanter.[46] Viewing the various critiques collectively, Millman and Kanter identify six standard methodological practices that can lead to gender bias in social research. During the past twenty years, these practices have remained central to the feminist critique of social methodology:

1. The use of conventional field-defining models that overlook important areas of social inquiry.

2. The focus by sociologists on public, official, visible role players to the neglect of unofficial, supportive, private, and invisible spheres of social life and organization that are equally important.

3. The assumption in sociology of a "single society," in which generalizations can be made that will apply equally to men and women.

4. The neglect in numerous fields of study of sex as an important explanatory variable.

5. The focus in sociology on explaining the status quo, which tends to provide rationalizations for existing power relations.

6. The use of certain methodological techniques, often quantitative, and research situations that might systematically prevent the collection of certain kinds of data.[47]

First, Millman and Kanter argue that sociologists' reliance on models of social structure and action has led to a "systematic blindness to crucial elements of social reality."[48] For example, they assert that the sociological focus on Weberian rationality as an explanation for human action and social organization effectively removes the equally important element of emotion from consideration. They also question the veracity of sociological models that do not focus on the individual and his or her subjective experience as the center of analysis and instead emphasize issues of agency.[49] Bernard had earlier made a distinction between "agency," which emphasizes variables, and "communion," which focuses on individuals:

> Agency operates by way of mastery and control; communion with naturalistic observation, sensitivity to qualitative patterning, and greater personal participation by the investigator. . . . The specific processes involved in agentic (sic) research are typically male preoccupations. . . . The scientist using this approach creates his own controlled reality. He can manipulate it. He is master. He has power. The communal approach is much humbler. It disavows control, for control spoils the results. Its value rests precisely on the absence of controls.[50]

Millman and Kanter make the point that research based exclusively on "agentic" quantitative methods fails to represent accurately crucial segments of the social world.[51]

Second, sociology overlooks important arenas of social life by focusing only on "official actors and actions," and ignoring private, unofficial and local social structures where women often predominate.[52] Millman, for example, posits that research on deviance and social control often emphasizes locations such as courtrooms and mental hospitals, but fails to recognize "the importance of studying everyday, interpersonal social control and the subtle, continuous series of maneuvers that individuals use to keep each other in line during ordinary mundane activities."[53]

Third, the assumption by sociologists that all humans inhabit a "single society" runs counter to evidence collected by feminist sociologists such as Bernard and Oakley that men and women often inhabit their own social worlds.[54] Focusing on a more narrow issue, Thelma McCormack posits that voting studies have erroneously assumed that men and women inhabit a single political culture, with the result that women tend to appear more conservative or apathetic.[55]

Fourth, Millman and Kanter cite several studies that demonstrate the failure of social researchers to consider sex as an explanatory variable. They include Sarah Lightfoot's analysis of the sociology of education, in which she asserts that researchers do not consider issues raised by the fact that most teachers are women.[56]

Fifth, Millman and Kanter argue that by seeking to explain the status quo, sociologists need to be more sensitive to the ways in which their research might also legitimate existing social relations and institutions. They argue that researchers should focus more attention on social transformation.[57] Arlene Daniels goes further to assert that research on women should not only concern itself with revealing the sources of women's oppression but should also engage in exploring the concrete ways in which their status and lives can be improved.[58]

Finally, Millman and Kanter point out that unquestioned methodological assumptions and techniques can adversely affect findings and conclusions. They cite David Tresemer's analysis of statistical studies of sex differences. Tresemer asserts that most of these studies are misleading because they improperly use bipolar, unidimensional continuous, normal distributions that have the effect of exaggerating differences.[59] Although this particular problem might best be corrected by adopting another less-biased quantitative method, Millman and Kanter claim that in many cases qualitative techniques might be more suitable and yield more balanced results than do the standard quantitative approaches.[60]

Critical feminist theorists have developed several methodological approaches designed to address the topic of gender asymmetry and to avoid the possible gender biases in standard sociological practices. Judith Cook and Mary Fonow assert that feminist methodologies frequently employ the following seven research strategies and techniques[61]:

1. Visual techniques, such as photography and videotaping to collect or elicit data.
2. Triangulation, or the use of more than one research technique simultaneously.
3. The use of linguistic techniques in conversational analysis.
4. Textual analysis as a means to identify gender bias.
5. Refined quantitative approaches to measure phenomena related to sexual asymmetry and women's worlds.
6. Collaborative strategies or collective research models to enhance feedback and promote cooperative, egalitarian relations among researchers.
7. Situation-at-hand research practices that use an already existing situation as a focus for sociological inquiry or as a means of collecting data.

Cook and Fonow stress that none of these techniques is explicitly or exclusively feminist; however, their innovative character is revealed in their application and in the degree to which they incorporate and are informed by five basic principles that govern the production of feminist knowledge.[62] Cook and Fonow identify these principles as follows:

1. The necessity of continuously and reflexively attending to the significance of gender relations as a basic feature of social life, including the conduct of research.
2. The centrality of consciousness-raising as a specific methodological tool and as a "way of seeing."
3. The need to challenge the norm of "objectivity" that assumes a dichotomy between the subject and object of research.

4. The concern for the ethical implications of research.

5. An emphasis on the transformation of patriarchy and the empowerment of women.[63]

Feminist standpoint theories, as espoused by Dorothy Smith, Hilary Rose, Nancy Hartsock, and others, build on these epistemological and methodological principles by explicitly focusing on women and their direct experience as the center of analysis. *Standpoint theorists* argue that they can use women's experiences to analyze social relations in ways that overcome the androcentric dichotomies of Enlightenment "positivism"—such as culture versus nature, rational mind versus irrational emotions, objectivity versus subjectivity, public versus private—that have structured knowledge production in the social and natural sciences.[64] Smith asserts that "women's perspective discredits sociology's claim to constitute an objective knowledge independent of the sociologist's situation."[65]

Feminist standpoint theorists articulate a feminist methodology that at once privileges the feminist standpoint as more inherently objective, challenges "mainstream" sociological inquiry, and provides a paradigmatic alternative. Smith disputes that such a paradigm shift would entail a "radical transformation of the subject matter"[66]; rather, she argues that what is involved is the restructuring of the relationship between the sociologist and the object of her research:

> What I am suggesting is more in the nature of a re-organization which changes the relation of the sociologist to the object of her knowledge and changes also her problematic. This re-organization involves first placing the sociologist where she is actually situated, namely at the beginning of those acts by which she knows or will come to know; and second, making her direct experience of the everyday world the primary ground of her knowledge.[67]

Critical theorists also suggest that a feminist standpoint methodology rooted in women's experience would elucidate the epistemological connections among the production of knowledge, everyday experiences, and political praxis that "positivistic" epistemologies often deny. Rose asserts in "Women's Work: Women's Knowledge" that human knowledge and consciousness "are not abstract or divorced from experience or 'given' by some process separate from the unitary material reality of the world. Human knowledge . . . comes from practice, from working on and changing the world."[68]

Viewed collectively, feminist empiricism—in the form of feminist methodologies, epistemologies, and standpoints—challenges key tenets of traditional empiricism embodied in "positivistic" science. Harding argues that feminist empiricism specifically questions three central assumptions:

1. The assumption that the social identity of the observer is irrelevant to the "goodness" of the results of research, asserting that the androcentrism of science is both highly visible and damaging. It argues that women *as a*

social group are more likely than men *as a social group* to select problems for inquiry that do not distort human social experience.

2. The assumption that science's methodological and sociological norms are sufficient to eliminate androcentric biases by suggesting that the norms themselves appear to be biased insofar as they have been incapable of detecting androcentrism.

3. The assumption that science must be protected from politics. Feminist empiricism argues that *some* politics—the politics of movement for emancipatory social change—can increase the objectivity of science.[69]

CHALLENGES TO CRITICAL FEMINIST THEORY

Feminist methodologies, epistemologies, and standpoint theories have received their own share of criticism. The most formidable of these have come from feminist critics themselves, who use feminist concepts and positions to, in effect, critique the "critique." What links many of these counter critiques is an emphasis on the role of ideology in the structuring of feminist theory, epistemology, and practice.

The foundation for all critical feminist theory is the belief in the primacy of gender as a fundamental division that structures social relations. Sarah Matthews questions the importance of gender dichotomy, arguing "this dichotomy does not match social reality as closely as assumed."[70] The existence of gender identities coded masculine and feminine does not, she asserts, necessarily mean that gender is the critical variable determining social behavior[71]:

> All of these [feminist] critiques have in common as their beginning point the assumption that distinguishing between two genders is the appropriate foundation from which to build research questions and theory. To say that women have been excluded from sociological research; that research on women must be done to parallel research on men; that different methodologies must be utilized to understand women in society; that boys and girls are socialized differently; and that women as a group are oppressed, is to accept and to re-enforce the taken-for-granted assumption that there are in fact two gender categories into which it is important to sort all human beings.[72]

Matthews goes on to argue that gender or sex is not "an immutable fact" and that feminist research and theory can be interpreted as supportive of this position. That this support has not been acknowledged, she asserts, is due to the ideological basis of feminism that is committed to seeing two genders.[73] She concludes by positing that sociologists can overcome sexual bias in research by developing paradigms "that do not include gender as having *a priori* significance."[74]

Attempts to construct feminist methods that espouse a privileged position for an independent "women's standpoint" have also been criticized by feminist critics such as Elizabeth Spelman. Spelman sees the phrase "as a woman" as "the Trojan horse of feminist ethnocentrism" because it embodies the assumption that "gender identity exists in isolation from race and class identity."[75] She argues that the feminist perspective or standpoint "obscures the heterogeneity of women"[76] and hence serves as little more than a methodological means of privileging white, middle-class women's experience. Spelman, in particular, challenges the following five assumptions inherent in feminist discussions of gender[77]:

1. Women can be talked about "as women."
2. Women are oppressed "as women."
3. Gender can be isolated from other elements of identity that affect one's social, economic, and political position such as race, class, ethnicity; hence, sexism can be isolated from racism and classism.
4. Women's situation can be contrasted with men's.
5. Relations between men and women can be compared with relations between other oppressor/oppressed groups, and, hence, it is possible to compare the situation of women with the situation of blacks, Jews, the poor, and others.

Like Matthews, Spelman attributes the current feminist research agenda, with its emphasis on a unitary concept of "woman," to an ideology within feminism that asserts "the possibility of a coherent feminist politics seems to require a singleness of voice and purpose."[78]

CONCLUSION

Like all critical theories, it is difficult to assess feminist critical theory by the criterion of science. Gender as a force of human organization had been ignored by sociology, and especially scientific sociology; thus, it is not surprising that the feminist critique of science has hit a responsive cord. The question is, however, where can critical feminist theory go as pure critique? One tract has been to formulate feminist analyses in various theoretical traditions, such as Marxism, postmodernism, rational choice theory, and even Parsonian functionalism (see the Wadsworth Web site for this book for illustrations). Still, we might conclude this chapter with words from Donna Haraway as they pose the challenge to critical feminist theory:

We wanted a way to go beyond showing bias in science . . . and beyond separating the good scientific sheep from the bad goats of bias and misuse. It seemed promising to do this by the strongest possible constructionist argument that left no cracks for reducing the issues to bias versus objectivity, use versus misuse, science versus pseudo-science. We unmasked the doctrines of objectivity . . . and we ended up with one more excuse for not learning any post-Newtonian physics and one more reason to drop the old feminist self-help practices of repairing our own cars. They're just texts anyway, so let the boys have them back. . . . Our problem is how to have *simultaneously* an account of radical historical contingency for all knowledge claims . . . , a critical practice for recognizing our own "semiotic technologies" for making meanings, *and* a no-nonsense commitment to faithful accounts of a "real world. . . ."[79]

NOTES

1. Jessie Bernard, *The Female World* (New York: Free Press, 1981); Ann Oakley, *The Sociology of Housework* (New York: Pantheon, 1974).

2. Dorothy Smith, "Women's Perspective as a Radical Critique of Sociology," *Sociological Inquiry* 44 (1974), pp. 7–15; "Sociological Theory: Methods of Writing Patriarchy" in *Feminism and Sociological Theory* (Newbury Park, CA: Sage, 1989), pp. 34–64; *The Everyday World as Problematic: A Feminist Sociology* (Boston: Northeastern University Press, 1987). Also Nancy Hartsock, *Money, Sex, and Power* (New York: Longman, 1983).

3. For example, see Chris Weedon, *Feminist Practice & Poststructuralist Theory* (New York: Blackwell, 1987); Judith Butler, "Contingent Foundations: Feminism and the Question of Post-Modernism" in *The Postmodern Turn: New Perspectives on Social Theory* (Cambridge: Cambridge University Press, 1994), pp. 152–170; Susan Hekman, *Gender and Knowledge: Elements of a Postmodern Feminism* (Boston: Northeastern University Press, 1990); Sondra Farganis, "Postmodernism and Feminism" in *Postmodernism and Social Inquiry* (New York: Guilford, 1994); and Thomas Meisenhelder, "Habermas and Feminism: The Future of Critical Theory" in *Feminism and Sociological Theory*, ed. Ruth A. Wallace (Newbury Park, CA: Sage, 1989), pp. 119–134.

4. This has led some to question whether many feminist critiques should properly be called "theory." See Mary Jo Neitz, "Introduction to the Special Issue Sociology and Feminist Scholarship," *American Sociologist* 20 (1989), p. 5.

5. Ibid., p. 4.

6. Sondra Farganis, "Social Theory and Feminist Theory: The Need for Dialogue," *Social Inquiry* 56 (1986), p. 56.

7. Kathryn Ward and Linda Grant, "The Feminist Critique and a Decade of Published Research in Sociology Journals," *Sociological Quarterly* 26 (1985), p. 140. On the issue of inadequate representation of women as the subjects of research, see Arlie Russell Hochschild, "A Review of Sex Role Research," *American Journal of Sociology* 78 (1973), pp. 1011–1029; and Cynthia Fuchs Epstein, "A Different Angle of Vision: Notes on the Selective Eye of Sociology," *Social Science Quarterly* 55 (1974), pp. 645–656. Critiques on the neglect of female-dominated social sectors include Ann Oakley, *Sociology of Housework* (cited in note 1), and Jessie Bernard, "My Four Revolutions: An Autobiographical History of the ASA," *American Journal of Sociology* 78 (1973), pp. 773–791. For early critiques of sociological methods and their failure to reflect women's experiences and perspectives, see Dorothy Smith, "Women's Perspective as a Radical Critique of Sociology," *Sociological Inquiry* 44 (1974), pp. 7–15; and Arlie Russell Hochschild, "The Sociology of Feeling and Emotion:

Selected Possibilities" in *Another Voice: Feminist Perspectives on Social Life and Social Science,* eds. Marcia Millman and Rosabeth Moss Kanter (New York: Octagon, 1976), pp. 280–307. Finally, among the early feminist theorists to criticize the use of men and their lifestyles as "normative" were Joan Acker, "Women and Social Stratification: A Case of Intellectual Sexism," *American Journal of Sociology* 78 (1973), pp. 936–945; and Jessie Bernard, "Research on Sex Differences: An Overview of the State of the Art" in *Women, Wives, Mothers* (Chicago: Aldine, 1975), pp. 7–29.

8. Oakley, *Sociology of Housework* (cited in note 1), p. 2.

9. Ibid., p. 5.

10. Ibid., p. 8.

11. Ibid., pp. 8–9. In a similar critique of social stratification literature, Joan Acker adds two additional assumptions: "(a) Women determine their own social status only when they are not attached to a man; and (b) women are unequal to men in many ways, are differentially evaluated on the basis of sex, but this is irrelevant to the structure of stratification systems." See Acker, "Women and Social Stratification: A Case of Intellectual Sexism," (cited in note 7), p. 937.

12. Ann Oakley, *Sociology of Housework* (cited in note 1), pp. 12–13.

13. Ibid., p. 21. Oakley argues that of the five "founding fathers" of sociology—Marx, Comte, Spencer, Durkheim and Weber—only two, Marx and Weber, had "emancipated views" about women. Terry Kandal, in a more recent analysis of the "woman question" in classical sociological theory, offers a less condemnatory accounting, asserting that there were "complex and contradictory variations in the writings about women by different classical theorists." *The Woman Question in Classical Sociological Theory* (Miami: Florida International University Press, 1988), p. 245.

14. Ann Oakley, *Sociology of Housework* (cited in note 1), pp. 21–28.

15. As quoted in opening epigraphs in Jessie Bernard's *The Female World* (cited in note 1).

16. Ibid., p. 3.

17. Ibid., pp. 12–15.

18. See, for example, Jean Lipman-Blumen, "Toward a Homosocial Theory of Sex Roles: An Explanation of the Sex Segregation of Social Institutions," *Signs* (1976), pp. 15–31.

19. Ibid., p. 16.

20. Ibid., p. 17.

21. Nancy Chadorow, *The Reproduction of Mothering: Psychoanalysis and the Sociology of Gender* (Berkeley: University of California Press, 1978), pp. 173–174.

22. Ibid., p. 173.

23. Joan Acker, "Making Gender Visible" in *Feminism and Sociological Theory,* ed. R.A. Wallace (Newbury Park, CA: Sage, 1989), p. 73.

24. John Shotter and Josephine Logan, "The Pervasiveness of Patriarchy: On Finding a Different Voice" in *Feminist Thought and the Structure of Knowledge* (New York: New York University Press, 1988), pp. 69–70.

25. Linda Grant and Kathryn Ward, "Is There an Association Between Gender and Methods in Sociological Research?" *American Sociological Review* 52 (1987), p. 861.

26. Rae Lesser Blumberg, *Stratification: Social, Economic and Sexual Inequality* (Dubuque, IA: William C. Brown, 1978).

27. Joan Acker, "Women and Stratification: A Review of Recent Literature," *Contemporary Sociology* 9 (1980), p. 26.

28. Judith Stacey and Barrie Thorne, "The Missing Feminist Revolution in Sociology," *Social Problems* 32 (1985), pp. 301–316.

29. Ibid., p. 302.

30. Kathryn Ward and Linda Grant, "On a Wavelength of Their Own? Women and Sociological Theory," *Current Perspectives in Social Theory* 11 (1991), p. 134.

31. Grant and Ward, "Is There an Association Between Gender and Methods in Sociological Research?" (cited in note 25), pp. 856–862.

32. See Marlene Mackie, "Female Sociologists' Productivity, Collegial Relations, and Research Style Examined through Journal Publications," *Sociology and Social Research* 69 (1985), pp. 189–209; Ellen Carol Dubois, ed., *Feminist Scholarship: Kindling in the Groves of Academe* (Urbana: University of Illinois Press, 1985); and Rhoda Unger, "Through the Looking Glass: No Wonderland Yet! The Reciprocal Relationship between Methodology and Models of Reality," *Psychology of Women Quarterly* 8 (1983), pp. 9–32.

33. Linda Grant and Kathryn Ward, "Is There an Association Between Gender and Methods in Sociological Research?" (cited in note 25), p. 861.

34. See J. A. Howard, "Dilemmas in Feminist Theorizing: Politics and the Academy," *Current Perspectives in Social Theory* 8 (1987), pp. 279–312.

35. Joan Acker, "Making Gender Visible" (cited in note 23), pp. 65–81.

36. Ibid., pp. 68–69. As Acker readily acknowledges, her analysis of sociology's relationship to ruling power structures owes much to Dorothy Smith. See note 2: Smith, *The Everyday World as Problematic.*

37. Ibid., Acker, p. 78.

38. Ibid., Acker, p. 72.

39. Ibid., Acker, p. 67.

40. Dorothy Smith, *The Everyday World as Problematic* (cited in note 2). Also see Sandra Harding, *The Science Question in Feminism* (Ithaca, NY: Cornell University Press, 1986); Evelyn Fox Keller, "Feminism and Science," *Signs* 7 (1982), pp. 589–602.

41. Dorothy Smith, "Women's Perspective" (cited in note 2), p. 7.

42. Judith Stacey and Barrie Thorne, "The Missing Revolution" (cited in note 28), p. 309.

43. Dorothy Smith, *The Everyday World as Problematic* (cited in note 2), p. 52.

44. Smith, "Women's Perspective" (cited in note 2), p. 7. Liz Stanley and Sue Wise make a similar criticism in their book *Breaking Out: Feminist Consciousness and Feminist Research* (London: Routledge, 1983), p. 28.

45. John Shotter and Josephine Logan, "The Pervasiveness of Patriarchy" (cited in note 24), pp. 69–86. Also see Dorothy Smith, "A Sociology for Women" in *The Prism of Sex* (Madison: University of Wisconsin Press, 1979), pp. 135–188.

46. Marcia Millman and Rosabeth Moss Kanter, eds., *Another Voice: Feminist Perspectives on Social Life and Social Science* (New York: Octagon, 1976).

47. Ibid., pp. ix–xvii.

48. Ibid., p. ix.

49. See Arlie Russell Hochschild's essay "The Sociology of Feeling and Emotion: Selected Possibilities" (cited in note 7), pp. 280–307.

50. Jessie Bernard, "My Four Revolutions" (cited in note 7), p. 785. For more discussion of agency and communion approaches to research see David Bakan, "Psychology Can Now Kick the Science Habit," *Psychology Today* 5 (1972), pp. 26, 28, 86–88; and Rae Carlson, "Sex Differences in Ego Functioning: Exploratory Studies of Agency and Communion," *Journal of Consulting and Clinical Psychology* 37 (1971), pp. 267–277.

51. Marcia Millman and Rosabeth Moss Kanter, eds., *Another Voice* (cited in note 46), p. x.

52. Ibid., p. xi.

53. Ibid.

54. Ibid. See also note 1: Bernard, *The Female World,* and Oakley, *The Sociology of Housework.*

55. Marcia Millman and Rosabeth Moss Kanter, eds., *Another Voice* (cited in note 46), p. xiii. Also Thelma McCormack, "Toward a Nonsexist

Perspective on Social and Political Change," *Another Voice* (cited in note 46), pp. 1–33.

56. Marcia Millman and Rosabeth Moss Kanter, eds., *Another Voice* (cited in note 46), p. xiv.

57. Ibid., p. xv.

58. Ibid. Also see Arlene Daniels, "Feminist Perspectives in Sociological Research," *Another Voice* (cited in note 46), pp. 340–380.

59. Marcia Millman and Rosabeth Moss Kanter, eds., *Another Voice* (cited in note 46), p. xv. See also David Tresemer, "Assumptions Made About Gender Roles," *Another Voice* (cited in note 46), pp. 308–39.

60. Marcia Millman and Rosabeth Moss Kanter, eds., *Another Voice* (cited in note 46), p. xvi.

61. Judith Cook and Mary Fonow, "Knowledge and Women's Interests: Issues of Epistemology and Methodology in Feminist Sociological Research," *Sociological Inquiry* 56 (1986), pp. 2–29.

62. Ibid., p. 14.

63. Ibid., p. 2.

64. Sandra Harding, *The Science Question in Feminism* (Ithaca, NY: Cornell University Press, 1986), pp. 136–162.

65. Dorothy Smith, "Women's Perspective" (cited in note 2), p. 11.

66. Ibid.

67. Ibid.

68. Hilary Rose, "Women's Work: Women's Knowledge" in *What is Feminism,* eds. Juliet Mitchell and Ann Oakley (New York: Pantheon, 1986), p. 161.

69. Sandra Harding, *The Science Question in Feminism* (cited in note 64), p. 162.

70. Sarah Matthews, "Rethinking Sociology through a Feminist Perspective," *American Sociologist* 17 (1982), p. 29.

71. Ibid.

72. Ibid., p. 30.

73. Ibid., p. 29.

74. Ibid.

75. Elizabeth Spelman, *Inessential Woman: Problems of Exclusion in Feminist Thought* (Boston: Beacon, 1988), p. x.

76. Ibid., p. ix.

77. Ibid., p. 165.

78. Ibid., p. 161.

79. 135. Donna Haraway, *Simians, Cyborgs and Women* (New York: Routledge, 1991), pp. 186–187.

PART V

✳

Exchange Theorizing

16

Early Exchange Theory

From its very beginnings, sociological theory focused on the market forces that were transforming the modern social world. Adam Smith[1] was, of course, the first to formulate the "laws of supply and demand," but what is often forgotten is that Smith also presented to sociology one of the key questions that guided all nineteenth century sociological theory: What force or forces are to hold modern societies together as they differentiate and as actors pursue their narrow and specialized interests? His answer was a combination of moral and symbolic forces along with the "invisible hand of order" that comes when rational actors pursue their self-interests in open and free markets.

Much of early sociology represented an effort to elaborate on this answer, or to formulate an alternative. In either case, social scientists of the nineteenth and twentieth centuries soon found themselves developing exchange-theoretic ideas.

EXCHANGE THEORY
IN CLASSICAL ECONOMICS

Given Smith's influence on sociology, and the impact of other British Isle thinkers, most of whom were Scottish, on nineteenth century social thought, it is perhaps best to begin with the ideas that come from this tradition. All these early classical economists considered themselves "moralists" and, hence, were concerned with broad ethical issues like justice, freedom, and fairness.[2] The label, utilitarianism, was meant to capture the broader moral concerns of these early moralists, but the term now tends to be associated with narrow economic models of the marketplace that have filtered into social theory. Today, these classical economic theorists portray humans as rational persons who seek to maximize their material benefits, or utility, from transactions or exchanges with others in a free and competitive marketplace. Free in the marketplace, people have access to necessary information; they can consider all available alternatives, and, on the basis of this consideration, rationally select the course of activity that will maximize material benefits. Entering into these rational considerations are calculations of the costs involved in pursuing various alternatives, with such costs being weighed against material benefits in an effort to determine which alternative will yield the maximum payoff or profit (benefits less costs). This view of the early utilitarians is narrow and ignores their concerns with morality, but this portion of their ideas endures today and inspires theory in economics and political science as well as in sociology.

With the emergence of sociology as a self-conscious discipline, there was considerable borrowing, revision, and reaction to this conception of humans. In the end, many sociologists muted extreme utilitarian assumptions in the ways enumerated here:

1. Humans do not seek to maximize profits, as utilitarians argued, but they nonetheless attempt to make some profit in their social transactions with others. *works out well for me.*

2. Humans are not perfectly rational, but they do engage in calculations of costs and benefits in social transactions.

3. Humans do not have perfect information on all available alternatives, but they are usually aware of at least some alternatives, which form the basis for assessments of costs and benefits.

4. Humans always act under constraints, but they still compete with one another in seeking to make a profit in their transactions.

5. Humans always seek to make a profit in their transactions, but they are limited by the resources that they have when entering an exchange relation.

In addition to these alterations of utilitarian assumptions, exchange theory removes human interaction from the limitations of material transactions in an economic marketplace, requiring two more additions to the previous list:

6. Humans do engage in economic transactions in clearly defined marketplaces in all societies, but these transactions are only special cases of more general exchange relations occurring among individuals in virtually all social contexts.

7. Humans do pursue material goals in exchanges, but they also mobilize and exchange nonmaterial resources, such as sentiments, services, and symbols.

Aside from this revised substantive legacy, some forms of modern exchange theory have also adopted the strategy of the utilitarians for constructing social theory. In assuming humans to be rational, utilitarians argued that exchanges among people could also be studied by a rational science, one in which the "laws of human nature" would stand at the top of a deductive system of explanation. Thus utilitarians borrowed the early physical-science conception of theory as a logico-deductive system of axioms or laws and various layers of lower-order propositions that could be rationally deduced from the laws of "economic man." Most exchange theories are thus presented in a propositional format, as we will appreciate when more contemporary approaches are reviewed.

EXCHANGE THEORY IN ANTHROPOLOGY

Sir James Frazer

In 1919, Sir James Frazer (1854–1941), in his second volume of *Folklore in the Old Testament,* conducted what was probably the first explicit exchange-theoretic analysis of social institutions.[3] In examining a wide variety of kinship and marriage practices among primitive societies, Frazer was struck by the clear preference of Australian aborigines for cross-cousin over parallel-cousin marriages: "Why is the marriage of cross-cousins so often favored? Why is the marriage of ortho-cousins [that is, parallel cousins] so uniformly prohibited?"[4]

Although the substantive details of Frazer's descriptions of the aborigines' practices are fascinating in themselves (if only for their inaccuracy), the form of explanation marks his theoretical contribution. In a manner clearly indebted to utilitarian economics, Frazer launched an economic interpretation of the predominance of cross-cousin marriage patterns. In this explanation Frazer invoked the "law" of "economic motives": By having "no equivalent in property to give for a wife, an Australian aborigine is generally obliged to get her in exchange for a female relative, usually a sister or daughter."[5] Thus, the material or economic motives of individuals in society (lack of property and desire for a wife) explain various social patterns (cross-cousin marriages). Frazer went on to postulate that, once a particular pattern emanating from economic motives becomes established in a culture, it constrains other social patterns that can potentially emerge.

Frazer believed that the social and structural patterns that typify a particular culture reflect economic motives in humans, who, in exchanging commodities, attempt to satisfy their basic economic needs. Although Frazer's specific explanation was found to be sadly wanting by subsequent generations of anthropologists, especially Bronislaw Malinowski and Claude Lévi-Strauss, modern exchange theory in sociology invokes a similar conception of social organization:

1. Exchange processes are the result of efforts by people to realize basic needs.

2. When yielding payoffs for those involved, exchange processes lead to the patterning of interaction.

3. Such patterns of interaction not only serve the needs of individuals but also constrain the kinds of social structures that can subsequently emerge.

In addition to anticipating the general profile of modern explanations about how elementary exchange processes create more complex patterns in a society, Frazer's analysis also foreshadowed another concern of contemporary exchange theory: social systems' differentiation of privilege and power. Much as Karl Marx had done a generation earlier, Frazer noted that those who possess resources of high economic value can exploit those who have few such resources, thereby enabling the former to possess high privilege and presumably power. Hence, the exchange of women among the aborigines was observed by Frazer to lead to the differentiation of power and privilege in at least two separate ways. First, "since among the Australian aboriginals women had a high economic and commercial value, a man who had many sisters or daughters was rich and a man who had none was poor and might be unable to procure a wife at all." Second, "the old men availed themselves of the system of exchange in order to procure a number of wives for themselves from among the young women, while the young men, having no women to give in exchange, were often obliged to remain single or to put up with the cast-off wives of their elders."[6] Thus, at least implicitly, Frazer supplemented the conflict theory contribution with a fourth exchange principle:

4. Exchange processes differentiate groups by their relative access to valued commodities, resulting in differences in power, prestige, and privilege.

As provocative and seemingly seminal as Frazer's analysis appears, it had little direct impact on modern exchange theory. Rather, contemporary theory remains indebted to those in anthropology who reacted against Frazer's utilitarianism.

Bronislaw Malinowski and Nonmaterial Exchange

Despite Malinowski's close ties with Frazer, Malinowski developed an exchange perspective that radically altered the utilitarian slant of Frazer's analysis of cross-cousin marriage. Indeed, Frazer himself, in his preface to Malinowski's *Argonauts of the Western Pacific,* recognized the importance of Malinowski's contribution to the analysis of exchange relations.[7] In his now-famous ethnography of the Trobriand Islanders—a group of South Seas Island cultures—Malinowski observed an exchange system termed the *Kula Ring,* a closed circle of exchange relations among tribal peoples inhabiting a wide ring of islands. What was distinctive in this closed circle, Malinowski observed, was the predominance of exchange of two articles—armlets and necklaces—that the inhabitants constantly exchanged in opposite directions. Armlets traveling in one direction around the Kula ring were exchanged for necklaces moving in the opposite direction around the ring. In any particular exchange between individuals, then, an armlet would always be exchanged for a necklace.

In interpreting this unique exchange network, Malinowski distinguished material or economic from nonmaterial or symbolic exchanges. In contrast with the utilitarians and Frazer, who did not conceptualize nonmaterial exchange relations, Malinowski recognized that the Kula was not only an economic or material exchange network but also a symbolic exchange, cementing a web of social relationships: "One transaction does not finish the Kula relationship, the rule being 'once in the Kula, always in the Kula,' and a partnership between two men is a permanent and lifelong affair."[8] Although purely economic transactions did occur within the rules of the Kula, the ceremonial exchange of armlets and necklaces was observed by Malinowski to be the Kula's principal function.

The natives themselves, Malinowski emphasized, recognized the distinction between purely economic commodities and the symbolic significance of armlets and necklaces. However, to distinguish economic from symbolic commodities does not mean that the Trobriand Islanders failed to assign graded values to the symbolic commodities; indeed, they made gradations and used them to express and confirm the nature of the relationships among exchange partners as equals, superordinates, or subordinates. But, as Malinowski noted, "in all forms of [Kula] exchange in the Trobriands, there is not even a trace of gain, nor is there any reason for looking at it from the purely utilitarian and economic standpoint, since there is no enhancement of mutual utility through the exchange."[9] Rather, the motives behind the Kula were social psychological, for the exchanges in the ring were viewed by Malinowski to have implications for the needs of both individuals and society (recall from Chapter 2 that Malinowski was also a founder of functional theory). From his functionalist framework, he interpreted the Kula to mean "the fundamental impulse to display, to share, to bestow [and] the deep tendency to create social ties."[10] Malinowski, then, considered an enduring social pattern such as the Kula Ring to have positive functional consequences for satisfying individual psychological needs and societal needs for social integration and solidarity.

This form of functional analysis presents many logical difficulties (see the Wadsworth Web site on functionalism). Nevertheless, Malinowski's analysis made several enduring contributions to modern exchange theory:

1. In Malinowski's words, "the meaning of the Kula will consist in being instrumental to dispel [the] conception of a rational being who wants nothing but to satisfy his simplest needs and does it according to the economic principle of least effort."[11]

2. Psychological rather than economic needs are the forces that initiate and sustain exchange relations and are therefore critical in the explanation of social behavior.

3. Exchange relations can also have implications beyond two parties, for, as the Kula demonstrates, complex patterns of indirect exchange can maintain extended and protracted social networks.

4. Symbolic exchange relations are the basic social process underlying both differentiation of ranks in a society and the integration of society into a cohesive and solitary whole.

With this emphasis, Malinowski helped free exchange theory from the limiting confines of utilitarianism. By stressing the importance of symbolic exchanges for both individual psychological processes and patterns of social integration, he anticipated the conceptual base for two basic types of exchange perspectives, one emphasizing the importance of psychological processes and the other stressing the significance of emergent cultural and structural forces on exchange relations.

Marcel Mauss and the Emergence
of Exchange Structuralism

Reacting to what he perceived as Malinowski's tendency to overemphasize psychological instead of social needs, Marcel Mauss (1872–1950) reinterpreted Malinowski's analysis of the Kula.[12] In this effort he formulated the broad outlines of a "collectivistic," or structural-exchange, perspective.[13] Mauss believed the critical question in examining an exchange network as complex as that of the Kula was, "In primitive or archaic types of societies, what is the principle whereby the gift received has to be repaid? What force is there in the thing which compels the recipient to make a return?"[14] The "force" compelling reciprocity was, Mauss believed, society or the group. As he noted, "It is groups, and not individuals, which carry on exchange, make contracts, and are bound by obligations."[15] The individuals actually engaged in an exchange represent the moral codes of the group. Exchange transactions among individuals are conducted in accordance with the rules of the group, thereby reinforcing these rules and codes. Thus, for Mauss, utilitarians' overconcern with individuals' self-interests and Malinowski's overemphasis on psychological needs are replaced by a conception of individuals as representatives of social groups. In the end, exchange relations create, reinforce, and serve a group morality that is an entity *sui generis,* to borrow a famous phrase from Mauss's mentor, Émile Durkheim. Furthermore, in a vein similar to that of Frazer, once such a morality emerges and is reinforced by exchange activities, it regulates other activities in the social life of a group, beyond particular exchange transactions.

Mauss's work has received scant attention from sociologists, but he was the first to forge a reconciliation between the exchange principles of utilitarianism and the structural, or collectivistic, thought of Durkheim. In recognizing that exchange transactions give rise to and, at the same time, reinforce the normative structure of society, Mauss anticipated the structural position of some contemporary exchange theories. Mauss's influence on modern theory has been indirect, however. The French collectivist tradition of Durkheim and Mauss has influenced the exchange perspectives of contemporary sociological theory through Lévi-Strauss's structuralism.

Claude Lévi-Strauss and Structuralism

In 1949, Lévi-Strauss launched an analysis of cross-cousin marriage in his classic work, *The Elementary Structures of Kinship*.[16] In restating Durkheim's objections to utilitarians, Lévi-Strauss took exception to Frazer's utilitarian interpretation of cross-cousin marriage patterns. And, similar to Mauss's opposition to Malinowski's emphasis on psychological needs, Lévi-Strauss developed a sophisticated structural-exchange perspective.

In rejecting Frazer's interpretation of cross-cousin marriage, Lévi-Strauss first questioned the substance of Frazer's utilitarian conceptualization. Frazer, he noted, "depicts the poor Australian aborigine wondering how he is going to obtain a wife since he has no material goods with which to purchase her, and discovering exchange as the solution to this apparently insoluble problem: 'men exchange their sisters in marriage because that was the cheapest way of getting a wife.'" In contrast, Lévi-Strauss emphasizes, "it is the exchange which counts and not the things exchanged." For Lévi-Strauss, exchange must be viewed by its functions for integrating the larger social structure. Lévi-Strauss then attacked Frazer's and the utilitarians' assumption that the first principles of social behavior are economic. Such an assumption contradicts the view that social structure is an emergent phenomenon that operates according to its own irreducible laws and principles.

Lévi-Strauss also rejected psychological interpretations of exchange processes, especially the position advocated by behaviorists (see next section). In contrast with psychological behaviorists, who see little real difference in the laws of behavior between animals and humans, Lévi-Strauss emphasized that humans possess a cultural heritage of norms and values that separates their behavior and societal organization from that of animal species. Human action is thus qualitatively different from animal behavior, especially in social exchange. Animals are not guided by values and rules that specify when, where, and how they are to carry out social transactions. Humans, however, carry with them into any exchange situation learned definitions of how they are to behave—thus ensuring that the principles of human exchange will be distinctive.

Furthermore, exchange is more than the result of psychological needs, even those that have been acquired through socialization. Exchange cannot be understood solely through individual motives because exchange relations are a reflection of patterns of social organization that exist as an entity, *sui generis*. Exchange behavior is thus regulated from without by norms and values, resulting in processes that can be analyzed only by their consequences, or functions, for these norms and values.

In arguing this view, Lévi-Strauss posited several fundamental exchange principles. First, all exchange relations involve costs for individuals, but, in contrast with economic or psychological explanations of exchange, such costs are attributed to society—to those customs, rules, laws, and values that require behaviors incurring costs. Thus, individuals do not assign the costs to themselves, but to the "social order." Second, for all those scarce and valued resources in society—whether material objects, such as wives, or symbolic resources, like esteem and prestige—their distribution is regulated by norms and values. As long as resources are in abundant supply or are not highly valued in a society, their distribution goes unregulated, but, once they become scarce and highly valued, their distribution is soon regulated. Third, all exchange relations are governed by a norm of reciprocity, requiring those receiving valued resources to bestow on their benefactors other valued resources. In Lévi-Strauss's conception of reciprocity are various patterns of reciprocation specified by norms and values. In some situations, norms dictate "mutual" and direct rewarding of one's benefactor, whereas in other situations the reciprocity can be "univocal," involving diverse patterns of indirect exchange in which actors do not reciprocate directly but only through various third (fourth, fifth, and so forth) parties. Within these two general types of exchange reciprocity—mutual and univocal—numerous subtypes of exchange networks can be normatively regulated.

Lévi-Strauss believed that these three exchange principles offer a more useful set of concepts to describe cross-cousin marriage patterns because these patterns can now be viewed by their functions for the larger social structure. Particular marriage patterns and other features of kinship organization no longer need be interpreted merely as direct exchanges among individuals but can be conceptualized as univocal exchanges between individuals and society. In freeing exchange from the analysis of only direct and mutual exchanges, Lévi-Strauss offered a tentative theory of societal integration and solidarity. His explanation extended Durkheim's provocative analysis and indicated how various subtypes of direct and univocal exchange both reflect and reinforce different patterns of societal integration and organization.

This theory of integration is, in itself, of theoretical importance, but it is more significant for our present purposes to stress Lévi-Strauss's impact on current sociological exchange perspectives. Two points of emphasis strongly influenced modern sociological theory.

1. Various forms of social structure, rather than individual motives, are the critical variables in the analysis of exchange relations.

2. Exchange relations in social systems are frequently not restricted to direct interaction among individuals but are protracted into complex networks of indirect exchange. On the one hand, these exchange processes are caused by patterns of social integration and organization; on the other hand, they promote diverse forms of such organization.

Lévi-Strauss's work represents the culmination of a reaction to economic utilitarianism as Frazer originally incorporated it into anthropology. Malinowski recognized the limitations of Frazer's analysis of only material or economic motives in direct exchange transactions. As the Kula Ring demonstrates, exchange can be generalized into protracted networks involving noneconomic motives that have implications for societal integration. Mauss drew explicit attention to the significance of social structure in regulating exchange processes and to the consequences of such processes for maintaining social structure. Finally, in this intellectual chain of events in anthropology, Lévi-Strauss began to indicate how different types of direct and indirect exchange are linked to different patterns of social organization. This intellectual heritage has influenced both the substance and the strategy of exchange theory in sociology, but it has done so only after considerable modification of assumptions and concepts by a particular strain of psychology: behaviorism.

PSYCHOLOGICAL BEHAVIORISM
AND EXCHANGE THEORY

As a psychological perspective, behaviorism began from insights derived from observations of an accident. The Russian physiologist Ivan Petrovich Pavlov (1849–1936) discovered that experimental dogs associated food with the person bringing it.[17] He observed, for instance, that dogs on whom he was performing secretory experiments would salivate not only when presented with food but also when they heard their feeder's footsteps approaching. After considerable delay and personal agonizing, Pavlov undertook a series of experiments on animals to understand such "conditioned responses."[18] From these experiments he developed several principles that were later incorporated into behaviorism. These include the following:

(1) A stimulus consistently associated with another stimulus producing a given physiological response will, by itself, elicit that response. (2) Such conditioned responses can be extinguished when gratifications associated with stimuli are no longer forthcoming. (3) Stimuli that are similar to those producing a conditioned response can also elicit the same response as the original stimulus. (4) Stimuli that increasingly differ from those used to condition a particular response will decreasingly be able to elicit this response. Thus, Pavlov's experiments exposed the principles of conditioned responses, extinction, response generalization, and response discrimination. Although Pavlov clearly recognized the significance of these findings for human behavior, his insights came to fruition in America under the tutelage of Edward Lee Thorndike (1874–1949) and John B. Watson (1978–1958)—the founders of behaviorism.

Thorndike conducted the first laboratory experiments on animals in America. During these experiments, he observed that animals would retain response patterns for which they were rewarded.[19] For example, in experiments on kittens placed in a puzzle box, Thorndike found that the kittens would engage in trial-and-error behavior until emitting the response that allowed them to escape. And, with each placement in the box, the kittens would engage in less trial-and-error behavior, indicating that the gratifications associated with a response allowing the kittens to escape caused them to learn and retain this response. From these and other studies, which were conducted at the same time as Pavlov's, Thorndike formulated three principles or laws: (1) the "law of effect," which holds that acts in a situation producing gratification will be more likely to occur in the future when that situation recurs; (2) the "law of use," which states that the situation-response connection is strengthened with repetitions and practice; and (3) the "law of disuse," which argues that the connection will weaken when practice is discontinued.[20]

These laws converge with those presented by Pavlov, but there is one important difference. Thorndike's experiments involved animals engaged in free trial-and-error behavior, whereas Pavlov's work was on the conditioning of physiological—typically glandular—responses in a tightly controlled laboratory situation. Thorndike's work could thus be seen as more directly relevant to human behavior in natural settings.

Watson was only one of several thinkers to recognize the significance of Pavlov's and Thorndike's work, but he soon became the dominant advocate of what was becoming explicitly known as behaviorism.[21] Watson's opening shot for the new science of behavior was fired in an article entitled "Psychology as the Behaviorist Views It":

> Psychology as the behaviorist views it is a purely objective experimental branch of natural science. Its theoretical goal is the prediction and control of behavior. Introspection forms no essential part of its methods, nor is the scientific value of its data dependent upon the readiness with which they lend themselves to interpretation in terms of consciousness. The behaviorist, in efforts to get a unitary scheme of animal response, recognizes no dividing line between man and brute.[22]

Watson thus became the advocate of the extreme behaviorism against which many vehemently reacted.[23] For Watson, psychology is the study of stimulus-response relations, and the only admissible evidence is overt behavior. Psychologists are to stay out of the "Pandora's box" of human consciousness and to study only observable behaviors as they are connected to observable stimuli.[24]

In many ways, behaviorism is similar to utilitarianism because it operates on the principle that humans are reward-seeking organisms pursuing alternatives that will yield the most reward and the least punishment. Rewards are simply another way of phrasing the economist's concept of "utility," and "punishment" is somewhat equivalent to the notion of "cost." For the behaviorist, reward is any behavior that reinforces or meets the needs of the organism, whereas punishment denies rewards or forces the expenditure of energy to avoid pain (thereby incurring costs).

Modern exchange theories have borrowed the notion of reward from behaviorists and used it to reinterpret the utilitarian exchange heritage. In place of utility, the concept of reward has often been inserted, primarily because it allows exchange theorists to view behavior as motivated by psychological needs. However, the utilitarian concept of cost appears to have been retained in preference to the behaviorist's formulation of punishment because the notion of cost allows exchange theorists to visualize more completely the alternative rewards that organisms forego in seeking to achieve a particular reward.

Despite these modifications of the basic concepts of behaviorism, its key theoretical generalizations have been incorporated with relatively little change into some forms of sociological exchange theory:

1. In any given situation, organisms will emit those behaviors that will yield the most reward and the least punishment.

2. Organisms will repeat those behaviors that have proved rewarding in the past.

3. Organisms will repeat behaviors in situations that are similar to those in the past in which behaviors were rewarded.

4. Present stimuli that on past occasions have been associated with rewards will evoke behaviors similar to those emitted in the past.

5. Repetition of behaviors will occur only as long as they continue to yield rewards.

6. An organism will display emotion if a behavior that has previously been rewarded in the same or similar situation suddenly goes unrewarded.

7. The more an organism receives rewards from a particular behavior, the less rewarding that behavior becomes (because of satiation) and the more likely the organism is to emit alternative behaviors in search of other rewards.

These principles were discovered in laboratory situations where experimenters typically manipulated the environment of the organism; so, it is difficult to visualize the experimental situation as interaction. The experimenter's tight control of the situation precludes the possibility that the animal will affect significantly the responses of the experimenter. This has forced modern exchange theorists using behaviorist principles to incorporate the utilitarian's concern with transactions, or exchanges. In this way, humans can be seen as mutually affecting one another's opportunities for rewards. In contrast with animals in a Skinner box or some similar laboratory situation, humans exchange rewards. Each person represents a potentially rewarding stimulus situation for the other.

As sociological exchange theorists have attempted to apply behaviorist principles to the study of human behavior, they have inevitably confronted the problem of the black box: Humans differ from laboratory animals in their greater ability to engage in a wide variety of complex cognitive processes. Indeed, as the utilitarians were the first to emphasize, what is distinctly human is the capacity to abstract, to calculate, to project outcomes, to weigh alternatives, and to perform a wide number of other cognitive manipulations. Furthermore, in borrowing behaviorists' concepts, contemporary exchange theorists have also had to introduce the concepts of an introspective psychology and structural sociology. Humans not only think in complex ways; their thinking is emotional and circumscribed by many social and cultural forces (first incorporated into the exchange theories of Mauss and Lévi-Strauss). Once it is recognized that behaviorist principles must incorporate concepts denoting both internal psychological processes and constraints of social structure and culture, it is also necessary to visualize exchange as frequently transcending the mutually rewarding activities of individuals in direct interaction. The organization of behavior by social structure and culture, coupled with humans' complex cognitive abilities, allows protracted and indirect exchange networks to exist.

When we review the impact of behaviorism on some forms of contemporary exchange theory, the vocabulary and general principles of behaviorism are evident, but concepts have been redefined and the principles altered to incorporate the insights of the early utilitarians as well as the anthropological reaction to utilitarianism. The result has been that proponents of an exchange perspective employing behaviorist concepts and principles have abandoned much of what made behaviorism a unique perspective as they have dealt with the complexities introduced by human cognitive capacities and their organization into sociocultural groupings.

THE SOCIOLOGICAL TRADITION
AND EXCHANGE THEORY

The vocabulary of exchange theory clearly comes from utilitarianism and behaviorism. Anthropological work forced the recognition that cultural and social dynamics need to be incorporated into exchange theory. When we look at early sociological work, however, the impact of early sociological theorists on modern exchange theory is difficult to assess for several reasons. First, much sociological theory represented a reaction against utilitarianism and extreme behaviorism and, therefore, has been reluctant to incorporate concepts from these fields. Second, the most developed of the early exchange theories—that provided by Georg Simmel in his *The Philosophy of Money*—was not translated into English until the 1970s.[25] (German-reading theorists, such as Peter Blau and Talcott Parsons, were to some degree influenced by Simmel's ideas.) Third, the topics of most interest to many sociological exchange theorists—differentiations of power and conflict in exchanges—have more typically been conceptualized as conflict theory than as exchange theory. But, as will become evident, sociological theories of exchange converge with those on conflict processes, and Marx's and Max Weber's ideas exerted considerable influence on sociologically oriented exchange theories.

Karl Marx's Theory of Exchange and Conflict

Most contemporary theories of exchange examine situations where actors have unequal levels of resources with which to bargain. Those with valued resources are in a position to strike a better bargain, especially if others who value their resources do not possess equally valued resources to offer in exchange. This fact of social life is the situation described in Marx's conflict theory.[26] Capitalists have the power to control the distribution of material rewards, whereas all that workers have is their labor to offer in exchange. Although the capitalist values labor, it is in plentiful supply, and thus no one worker is in a position to bargain effectively with an employer. As a consequence, capitalists can get labor at a low cost and can force workers to do what the capitalists want. As capitalists press their advantage, they create the very conditions that allow workers to develop resources—political, organizational, ideological—that workers can then use to strike a better bargain with capitalists and, in the end, to overthrow them.

Granted, this is simplifying Marx's implicit exchange theory, but the point is clear: Dialectical conflict theory is a variety of exchange theory. Let us list some of these exchange dynamics more explicitly:

1. Those who need scarce and valued resources that others possess but who do not have equally valued and scarce resources to offer in return will be dependent on those who control these resources.

2. Those who control valued resources have power over those who do not. That is, the power of one actor over another is directly related to (a) the capacity of one actor to monopolize the valued resources needed by other actors and (b) the inability of those actors who need these resources to offer equally valued and scarce resources in return.

3. Those with power will press their advantage and will try to extract more resources from those dependent on them in exchange for fewer (or the same level) of the resources that they control.

4. Those who press their advantage in this way will create conditions that encourage those who are dependent on them to (a) organize in ways that increase the value of their resources or, failing this, to (b) organize in ways that enable them to coerce those on whom they are dependent.

If the words *capitalist* and *proletarian* are inserted at the appropriate places in the previous list, Marx's exchange model becomes readily apparent. Dialectical conflict theory is thus a series of propositions about exchange dynamics in systems in which the distribution of resources is unequal. And, as will become evident in the next chapters, sociological exchange theories have emphasized these dynamics that inhere in the unequal distribution of resources. Such is Marx's major contribution to exchange theory.

Georg Simmel's Exchange Theory

In *The Philosophy of Money*,[27] Simmel analyzed Marx's "value theory of labor"[28] and, in its place, provided a clear exposition of exchange theory. *The Philosophy of Money* is, as its title indicates, about the impact of money on social relations and social structure. For Simmel, social exchange involves the following:

1. The desire for a valued object that one does not have.

2. The possession of the valued object by an identifiable other.

3. The offer of an object of value to secure the desired object from another.

4. The acceptance of this offer by the possessor of the valued object.[29]

Contained in this portrayal of social exchange are several additional points that Simmel emphasized. First, value is idiosyncratic and is, ultimately, tied to an individual's impulses and needs. Of course, what is defined as valuable is typically circumscribed by cultural and social patterns, but how valuable an object is will be a positive function of (a) the intensity of a person's needs and (b) the scarcity of the object. Second, much exchange involves efforts to manipulate situations so that the intensity of needs for an object is concealed and the availability of an object is made to seem less than what it actually is. Inherent in exchange, therefore, is a basic tension that can often erupt into other social forms, such as conflict. Third, to possess an object is to lessen its value and to increase the value of objects that one does not possess. Fourth, exchanges will occur only if both parties perceive that the object given is less valuable than the one received. Fifth, collective units as well as individuals participate in exchange relations and hence are subject to the four processes listed. Sixth, the more liquid the resources of an actor are in an exchange—that is, the more that resources can be used in many types of exchanges—the greater that actor's options and power will be. For if an actor is not bound to exchange with any other and can readily withdraw resources and exchange them with another, then that actor has considerable power to manipulate any exchange.

Economic exchange involving money is only one case of this more general social form, but it is a very special case. When money becomes the predominant means for establishing value in relationships, the properties and dynamics of social relations are transformed. This process of displacing other criteria of value, such as logic, ethics, and aesthetics, with a monetary criterion is precisely the long-term evolutionary trend in societies. This trend is both a cause and effect of money as the medium of exchange. Money emerged to facilitate exchanges and to realize even more completely humans' basic needs. But, once established, money has the power to transform the structure of social relations in society.

Thus, the key insight in *The Philosophy of Money* is that the use of different criteria for assessing value has an enormous impact on the form of social relations. As money replaces barter and other criteria for determining values, social relations are fundamentally changed. Yet, they are transformed in accordance with some basic principles of social exchange, which are never codified by Simmel but are very clear. In Table 16.1, these ideas are summarized as abstract exchange principles.

CONCLUSION

Curiously, despite Adam Smith's influence on sociological theory in the nineteenth century, and behaviorists' impact on early social psychology, a clear sociological approach to exchange theory did not emerge until the 1960s.

Table 16.1 Georg Simmel's Exchange Principles

I. *Attraction Principle:* The more actors perceive as valuable one another's respective resources, the more likely an exchange relationship is to develop among these actors.

II. *Value Principle:* The greater is the intensity of an actor's needs for a resource of a given type, and the less available is that resource, the greater is the value of that resource to the actor.

III. *Power Principles:*

   A. The more an actor perceives as valuable the resources of another actor, the greater is the power of the latter over the former.

   B. The more liquid are an actor's resources, the greater will be the exchange options and alternatives and, hence, the greater will be the power of that actor in social exchanges.

IV. *Tension Principle:* The more actors in a social exchange manipulate the situation in an effort to misrepresent their needs for a resource or conceal the availability of resources, the greater is the level of tension in that exchange and the greater is the potential for conflict.

When it finally arrived, this approach has remained prominent within the sociological canon since the midcentury, and today, it is one of the most important perspectives within sociological theorizing. In the next group of chapters, we see how economic and behaviorist ideas were brought back into sociological theory and blended with the discipline's concern with social structure, power, and inequality. In particular, we can emphasize the two surviving variants of this midcentury burst of creative activity, primarily the exchange network approaches (Chapter 19) and rational choice theories (Chapter 20).

NOTES

1. Adam Smith, *An Inquiry into the Nature and Causes of the Wealth of Nations* (London: Davis, 1805; originally published in 1776).

2. Charles Camic, "The Utilitarians Revisited," *American Journal of Sociology* 85 (1979), pp. 516–550.

3. Sir James George Frazer, *Folklore in the Old Testament,* vol. 2 (New York: Macmillan, 1919); see also his *Totemism and Exogamy: A Treatise on Certain Early Forms of Superstition and Society* (London: Dawsons of Pall Mall, 1968; originally published in 1910); and his Preface to Bronislaw Malinowski's *Argonauts of the Western Pacific* (London: Routledge & Kegan Paul, 1922), pp. vii–xiv.

4. Frazer, *Folklore* (cited in note 3), p. 199.

5. Ibid., p. 198.

6. Ibid., pp. 200–201 for this and immediately preceding quote.

7. Bronislaw Malinowski, *Argonauts of the Western Pacific* (cited in note 3), p. 81.

8. Ibid., pp. 82–83.

9. Ibid., p. 175.

10. Ibid.

11. Ibid., p. 516.

12. Marcel Mauss, *The Gift,* trans. I. Cunnison (New York: Free Press, 1954; originally published as *Essai sur le don en sociologie et anthropologie* [Paris: Presses universitaires de France, 1925]). It should be noted that Mauss

rather consistently misinterpreted Malinowski's ethnography, but through such misinterpretation he came to visualize a "structural" alternative to "psychological" exchange theories.

13. In Peter Ekeh's excellent discussion of Mauss and Lévi-Strauss, *Social Exchange Theory and the Two Sociological Traditions* (Cambridge, MA: Harvard University Press, 1975), pp. 55–122, the term *collectivist* is used in preference to *structural* and is posited as the alternative to *individualistic* or psychological exchange perspectives. I prefer the terms *structural* and *psychological;* thus, although I am indebted to Ekeh's discussion, these terms will be used to make essentially the same distinction. My preference for these terms will become more evident in subsequent chapters because, in contrast with Ekeh's analysis, I consider Peter M. Blau and George C. Homans to have developed, respectively, structural and psychological theories. Ekeh considers the theories of both Blau and Homans to be individualistic, or psychological.

14. Mauss, *The Gift* (cited in note 12), p. 1.

15. Ibid., p. 3.

16. Claude Lévi-Strauss, *The Elementary Structures of Kinship* (Boston: Beacon, 1969). This is a translation of Lévi-Strauss's 1967 revision of the original *Les structures élémentaires de la parenté* (Paris: Presses universitaires de France, 1949).

17. See, for relevant articles, lectures, and references, I. P. Pavlov, *Selected Works,* ed. K. S. Kostoyants, trans. S. Belsky (Moscow: Foreign Languages Publishing House, 1955); and *Lectures on Conditioned Reflexes,* 3rd ed., trans. W. H. Grant (New York: International, 1928).

18. I. P. Pavlov, "Autobiography," in *Selected Works* (cited in note 17), pp. 41–44.

19. Edward L. Thorndike, "Animal Intelligence: An Experimental Study of the Associative Processes in Animals," *Psychological Review Monograph,* Supplement 2 (1989).

20. See Edward L. Thorndike, *The Elements of Psychology* (New York: Seiler, 1905), *The Fundamentals of Learning* (New York: Teachers College Press, 1932), and *The Psychology of Wants, Interests, and Attitudes* (New York: Appleton, 1935).

21. Others who recognized their importance included Max F. Meyer, *Psychology of the Other-One* (Columbus, OH: Missouri Book, 1921); and Albert P. Weiss, *A Theoretical Basis of Human Behavior* (Columbus, OH: Adams, 1925).

22. J. B. Watson, "Psychology as the Behaviorist Views It," *Psychological Review* 20 (1913), pp. 158–177. For other basic works by Watson, see *Psychology from the Standpoint of a Behaviorist,* 3rd ed. (Philadelphia: Lippincott, 1929); *Behavior: An Introduction to Comparative Psychology* (New York: Henry Holt, 1914).

23. For example, in *Mind, Self, and Society* (Chicago: University of Chicago Press, 1934), George Herbert Mead has eighteen references to Watson's work.

24. For a more detailed discussion of the emergence of behaviorism, see Jonathan H. Turner, Leonard Beeghley, and Charles Powers, *The Emergence of Sociological Theory,* 5th ed. (Belmont, CA: Wadsworth, 2002).

25. Georg Simmel, *The Philosophy of Money,* trans. T. Bottomore and D. Frisby (Boston: Routledge & Kegan Paul, 1978; originally published in 1907).

26. Karl Marx and Frederick Engels, *The Communist Manifesto* (New York: International, 1971; originally published 1848); Karl Marx, *Capital: A Critical Analysis of Capitalist Production,* vol. 1 (New York: International, 1967; originally published in 1867).

27. See note 25.

28. Karl Marx, *Capital* (cited in note 26).

29. Georg Simmel, *The Philosophy of Money* (cited in note 25), pp. 85–88.

17

Behavioristic Exchange Theory: George C. Homans

eorge Homans's (1910–1989) exchange scheme first surfaced in a polemical reaction to Claude Lévi-Strauss's structural analysis of cross-cousin marriage patterns. In collaboration with David Schneider, Homans previewed what become prominent themes in his writings: (1) a skeptical view of any form of functional theorizing, (2) an emphasis on psychological principles as the axioms of social theory, and (3) a preoccupation with exchange-theoretic concepts.[1] In their assessment of Lévi-Strauss's exchange functionalism, Homans and Schneider took exception to virtually all that made Lévi-Strauss's theory. First, they rejected the conceptualization of different forms of indirect, generalized exchange. In so conceptualizing exchange, Lévi-Strauss "thinned the meaning out of it." Second, Lévi-Strauss's position that different forms of exchange symbolically reaffirm and integrate different patterns of social organization was questioned, for an "institution is what it is because it results from the drives, or meets the immediate needs, of individuals or subgroups within a society."[2] The result of this rejection of Lévi-Strauss's thought was that Homans and Schneider argued that exchange theory must initially emphasize face-to-face interaction, focus primarily on limited and direct exchanges among individuals, and recognize that social structures are created and sustained by the behaviors of individuals.

With this critique of the anthropological tradition, Homans resurrected the utilitarians' concern with individual self-interest in the conceptual trappings of psychological behaviorism. Indeed, as Homans and Schneider emphasized, "We may call this an individual self-interest theory, if we remember that interests may be other than economic."[3] By the early 1960s, this self-interest theory was recast in the behaviorist language of B. F. Skinner. Given Homans's commitment to axiomatic theorizing and his concern with face-to-face interaction among individuals, it was perhaps inevitable that he would look toward Skinner and, indirectly, to the early founders of behaviorism—I. P. Pavlov, Edward Lee Thorndike, and J. B. Watson. But Homans borrowed directly from Skinner's reformulations of early behaviorist principles.[4] Stripped of its subtlety, Skinnerian behaviorism states as its basic principle that, if an animal has a need, it will perform activities that in the past have satisfied this need. A first corollary to this principle is that organisms will attempt to avoid unpleasant experiences but will endure limited amounts of such experiences as a cost in emitting the behaviors that satisfy an overriding need. A second corollary is that organisms will continue emitting certain behaviors only as long as they continue to produce desired and expected effects. A third corollary of Skinnerian psychology emphasizes that, as needs are satisfied by a particular behavior, animals are less likely to emit the behavior. A fourth corollary states that, if in the recent past a behavior has brought rewards and if these rewards suddenly stop, the organism will appear angry and gradually cease emitting the behavior that formerly satisfied its needs. A final corollary holds that, if an event has consistently occurred at the same time as a behavior that was rewarded or punished, the event becomes a stimulus and is likely to produce the behavior or its avoidance.

These principles were derived from behavioral psychologists' highly controlled observations of animals, whose needs could be inferred from deprivations imposed by the investigators. Although human needs are much more difficult to ascertain than those of laboratory pigeons and mice and, despite the fact that humans interact in groupings that defy experimental controls, Homans believed that the principles of operant psychology could be applied to the explanation of human behavior in both simple and complex groupings. One of the most important adjustments of Skinnerian principles to fit the facts of human social organization involved the recognition that needs are satisfied by other people and that people reward and punish one another. In contrast with Skinner's animals, which only indirectly interact with Skinner through the apparatus of the laboratory and which have little ability to reward Skinner (except perhaps to confirm his principles), humans constantly give and take, or exchange, rewards and punishments.

The conceptualization of human behavior as exchange of rewards (and punishments) among interacting individuals led Homans to incorporate, in altered form, the first principle of elementary economics: Humans rationally calculate the long-range consequences of their actions in a marketplace and attempt to maximize their material profits in their transactions. Homans qualified this simplistic notion, however:

> Indeed we are out to rehabilitate the economic man. The trouble with
> him was not that he was economic, that he used resources to some
> advantage, but that he was antisocial and materialistic, interested only in

money and material goods and ready to sacrifice even his old mother to get them.[5]

Thus, to be an appropriate explanation of human behavior, this basic economic assumption must be altered in four ways: (1) People do not always attempt to maximize profits; they seek only to make some profit in exchange relations. (2) Humans do not usually make either long-run or rational calculations in exchanges, for, in everyday life, "the Theory of Games is good advice for human behavior but a poor description of it." (3) The things exchanged involve not only money but also other commodities, including approval, esteem, compliance, love, affection, and other less materialistic goods. (4) The marketplace is not a separate domain in human exchanges, for all interaction involves individuals exchanging rewards (and punishments) and seeking profits.

THE BASIC EXCHANGE PRINCIPLES

In Propositions I through III of Table 17.1, Homansian principles of Skinnerian psychology are restated. The more valuable an activity (III), the more often such activity is rewarded (I), the more a situation approximates one in which activity has been rewarded in the past (II), the more likely a particular activity will be emitted. Proposition IV indicates the condition under which the first three propositions fall into temporary abeyance. In accordance with the reinforcement principle of satiation or the economic law of marginal utility, humans eventually define rewarded activities as less valuable and begin to emit other activities in search of different rewards (again, however, in accordance with the principles enumerated in Propositions I through III). Proposition V introduces a more complicated set of conditions that qualify Propositions I through IV. From Skinner's observation that pigeons reveal anger and frustration when they do not receive an expected reward, Homans reasoned that humans will probably reveal the same behavior.

In addition to these principles, Homans introduces a "rationality proposition," which summarizes the stimulus, success, and value propositions. This proposition is also placed in Table 17.1 because it is so prominent in Homans's actual construction of deductive explanations. To translate the somewhat awkward vocabulary of Principle VI as Homans wrote it: People make calculations about various alternative lines of action. They perceive or calculate the value of the rewards that might be yielded by various actions. But they also temper this calculation through perceptions of how probable the receipt of rewards will be. Low probability of receiving highly valued rewards would lower their reward potential. Conversely, high probability of receiving a lower-valued reward increases their overall reward potential. This relationship can be stated by the following formula:

Action = Value × Probability

Table 17.1 Homans's Exchange Propositions

I. *Success Proposition:* For all actions taken by persons, the more often a particular action of a person is rewarded, the more likely the person is to perform that action.

II. *Stimulus Proposition:* If in the past the occurrence of a particular stimulus or set of stimuli has been the occasion on which a person's action has been rewarded, then, the more similar the present stimuli are to the past ones, the more likely the person is to perform the action or some similar action now.

III. *Value Proposition:* The more valuable to a person the result of his or her action is, the more likely he or she is to perform the action.

IV. *Deprivation/Satiation Proposition:* The more often in the recent past a person has received a particular reward, the less valuable any further unit of that reward becomes for that person.

V. *Aggression/Approval Propositions:*

A. When a person's action does not receive the reward expected or receives punishment that was not expected, he or she will be angry and become more likely to perform aggressive behavior. The results of such behavior become more valuable to that person.

B. When a person's actions receive the reward expected, especially greater reward than expected, or does not receive punishment expected, he or she will be pleased and become more likely to perform approving behavior. The results of such behavior become more valuable to that person.

VI. *Rationality Proposition:* In choosing between alternative actions, a person will choose that one for which, as perceived by him or her at the time, the value of the result, multiplied by the probability of getting that result, is greater.

People are, Homans asserted, rational in the sense that they are likely to emit that behavior, or action, among alternatives in which value on the right side of the equation is largest. For example, if $Action_1$ is highly valued (say, 10) but the probability of getting it by emitting $Action_1$ is low (.20) and if $Action_2$ is less valued (say, 5) but the probability of receiving it is greater (.50) than $Action_1$, then the actor will emit $Action_2$ (because $10 \times .20 = 2$ yields less reward than $5 \times .50 = 2.5$).

As summarized in Table 17.1, Homans believed these basic principles or laws explain, in the sense of deductive explanation, patterns of human organization. As is obvious, these "laws" are psychological in nature. What is more, these psychological axioms are the only general sociological propositions because "there are no general sociological propositions that hold good of all societies or social groups as such." The fact that psychological propositions are the most general, however, does not make any less relevant or important the sociological propositions stating the relationships among group properties or between group properties and those of individuals. On the contrary, these are the very propositions that are to be deduced from the psychological axioms. Thus, sociological propositions will be conspicuous in the deductive system emanating from the psychological principles.

USING THE BASIC PRINCIPLES TO CONSTRUCT EXPLANATIONS

Homans himself never presented a well-developed deductive explanation, even though he championed their development.[6] He tended to simply invoke, in a rather ad hoc fashion, his axioms and to reconcile them in a very loose and imprecise manner with empirical regularities. Or he constructed brief deductive schemes to illustrate his strategy. One of Homans's explanations is reproduced below. Homans recognized that this is not a complete explanation, but he argued that it is as good as any other that exists. Moreover, although certain steps in the deductive scheme are omitted, Homans believed this was the proper way to develop scientific explanations. In this scheme, Homans sought to explain Golden's Law that industrialization and the level of literacy in the population are highly correlated. Such empirical generalizations are often considered to be theory, but, as a theorist, Homans correctly perceived that this "law" is only an empirical regularity that belongs at the bottom of the deductive scheme. Propositions move from the most abstract statement, or the axiom(s),[7] to the specific empirical regularity to be explained. Golden's Law is thus explained in the following manner:

1. Individuals are more likely to perform an activity the more valuable they perceive the reward of that activity to be.
2. Individuals are more likely to perform an activity the more successful they perceive the activity to be in getting that reward.[8]
3. Compared with agricultural societies, a higher proportion of individuals in industrial societies are prepared to reward activities that involve literacy. (Industrialists want to hire bookkeepers, clerks, and persons who can make and read blueprints, manuals, and so forth.)
4. Therefore, a higher proportion of individuals in industrial societies will perceive the acquisition of literacy as rewarding.
5. And [by (1)] a higher proportion will attempt to acquire literacy.
6. The provision of schooling costs money, directly or indirectly.
7. Compared with agricultural societies, a higher proportion of individuals in industrial societies are, by some standard, wealthy.
8. Therefore, a higher proportion of individuals are able to provide schooling (through government or private charity), and a higher proportion of individuals are able to pay for their own schooling without charity.
9. And a higher proportion will perceive the effort to acquire literacy as apt to be successful.
10. And [by (2) as well as by (1)] a higher proportion will attempt to acquire literacy.

11. Because their perceptions are generally accurate, a higher proportion of individuals in industrial societies will acquire literacy. That is, the literacy rate is apt to be higher in an industrial than in an agricultural society.[9]

Propositions 1 and 2 are an earlier statement of the rationality proposition that summarizes the success, stimulus, and value propositions. From these first two propositions, or axioms, others are derived in an effort to explain Golden's Law (Proposition 11 in the previous scheme). Examining some features of this explanation can provide insight into Homans's deductive strategy.

In this example, the transition between Propositions 2 and 3 ignores so many necessary variables that it simply describes in the words of behavioral psychology what Homans perceived to have occurred. Why are people in industrial societies prepared to reward literacy? This statement does not explain; it describes and, thus, opens a large gap in the logic of the deductive system. Homans believed that this statement is a given. It states a boundary condition, for the theory is not trying to explain why people are prepared to reward literacy. Another story is required to explain this event. Thus, Homans argued that "no theory can explain everything" and that it is necessary to ignore some things and assume them to be givens for the purposes of explanation at hand. The issue remains, however: Has not Homans defined away the most interesting sociological issue—what makes people ready to reward literacy in a society's historical development? Homans believed people are just ready to do so.

Another problem in this scheme comes with the placement of the word *therefore*. This transitive is typically used immediately following a statement of the givens that define away important classes of sociological variables. For example, the "therefore" preceding key propositions (4 and 8) begs questions such as the following: Why do people perceive literacy as rewarding? What level of industrialization would make this so? What level of educational development? What feedback consequences does desire for literacy have for educational development? By ignoring the why and what of these questions, Homans could then in Propositions 5 and 10 reinsert the higher order axioms (1 and 2) of the explanation, thereby giving the scheme an appearance of deductive continuity. Answers to the critical sociological questions have been avoided, such as why people perceive as valuable and rewarding certain crucial activities.

Homans's reply to such criticisms is important to note. First, he emphasized that this deductive scheme was just an example or illustrative sketch, leaving out many details. Second, and more important, Homans contended that it is unreasonable for the critic to expect that a theory can and must explain every given condition (Propositions 3 and 7, for example). He offered the example of Newton's laws, which can help explain the movement of the tides (by virtue of gravitational forces of the moon relative to the axis of the earth), but these laws cannot explain why oceans are present and why the earth exists. This latter argument is reasonable, in principle, because deductive theories explain only a delimited range of phenomena. Still, even though Homans did

not need to explain the givens of a deductive scheme, all the interesting sociological questions were contained in those givens. Moreover, these questions
beg for the development of abstract *sociological* laws to explain them (Golden's
Law is not an abstract principle, only an empirical generalization).

FROM BEHAVIOR TO MACROSTRUCTURE

Homans provided many illustrations of how behavioristic principles can
explain research findings in social psychology. One of the most interesting
chapters in *Social Behavior*[10] comes at the end of the book, where he offered a
view of how exchange processes can explain population-level and societal-
level social phenomena. Phrased as a last orgy in his explication, Homans
addressed the issue of how societies and civilizations are, ultimately, built from
the face-to face exchanges of people in groups. His scenario went something
like this:

At points in history, some people have the "capital" to reinforce or provide
rewards for others, whether it comes from their possessing a surplus of food,
money, a moral code, or valued leadership qualities. With such capital, "institutional elaboration" can occur, because some can invest their capital by trying to induce others (through rewards or threats of punishments) to engage in
novel activities. These new activities can involve an "intermeshing of the
behavior of a large number of persons in a more complicated or roundabout
way than has hitherto been the custom." Whether this investment involves con-
quering territory and organizing a kingdom or creating a new form of business organization, those making the investment must have the
resources—whether it be an army to threaten punishment, a charismatic personality to morally persuade followers, or the ability to provide for people's
subsistence needs—to keep those so organized in a situation in which they
derive some profit. At some point in this process, such organizations can
become more efficient and hence rewarding to all when the rewards are clearly
specified as generalized reinforcers, such as money, and when the activities
expended to get their rewards are more clearly specified, such as when explicit
norms and rules emerge. In turn, this increased efficiency allows greater organization of activities. This new efficiency increases the likelihood that generalized reinforcers and explicit norms will be used to regulate exchange relations
and hence increase the profits to those involved. Eventually the exchange networks involving generalized reinforcers and an increasingly complex body of
rules require differentiation of subunits—such as a legal and banking system—
that can maintain the stability of the generalized reinforcers and the integrity
of the norms.

From this kind of exchange process, then, social organization—whether at
a societal, group, organizational, or institutional level—is constructed. The
emergence of most patterns of organization is frequently buried in the recesses
of history, but such emergence is typified by these accelerating processes:

(1) People with capital (reward capacity) invest in creating more complex social relations that increase their rewards and allow those whose activities are organized to realize a profit. (2) With increased rewards, these people can invest in more complex patterns of organization. (3) More complex patterns of organization require, first, the use of generalized reinforcers and then the codification of norms to regulate activity. (4) With this organizational base, it then becomes possible to elaborate further the pattern of organization, creating the necessity for differentiation of subunits that ensure the stability of the generalized reinforcers and the integrity of norms. (5) With this differentiation, it is possible to expand even further the networks of interaction because there are standardized means for rewarding activities and codifying new norms as well as for enforcing old rules.

However, these complex patterns of social organization employing formal rules and secondary or generalized reinforcers can never cease to meet the more primary needs of individuals. Institutions first emerged to meet these needs, and, no matter how complex institutional arrangements become and how many norms and formal rules are elaborated, these extended interaction networks must ultimately reinforce humans' more primary needs. When these arrangements cease meeting the primary needs from which they ultimately sprang, an institution is vulnerable and apt to collapse if alternative actions, which can provide primary rewards, present themselves as a possibility. In this situation, low- or high-status persons—those who have little to lose by non-conformity to existing prescriptions—will break from established ways to expose to others a more rewarding alternative. Institutions might continue to extract conformity for a period, but they will cease to do so when they lose the capacity to provide primary rewards. Thus, complex institutional arrangements must ultimately be satisfying to individuals, not simply because of the weight of culture or norms but because they are constructed to serve people:

> Institutions do not keep going just because they are enshrined in norms, and it seems extraordinary that anyone should ever talk as if they did. They keep going because they have payoffs, ultimately payoffs for individuals. Nor is society a perpetual-motion machine, supplying its own fuel. It cannot keep itself going by planting in the young a desire for these goods and only those goods that it happens to be in shape to provide. It must provide goods that men find rewarding not simply because they are sharers in a particular culture but because they are men.[11]

That institutions of society must also meet primary needs sets the stage for a continual conflict between institutional elaboration and the primary needs of humans. As one form of institutional elaboration meets one set of needs, it can deprive people of other important rewards—opening the way for deviation and innovation by those presenting the alternative rewards that have been suppressed by dominant institutional arrangements. In turn, the new institutional elaborations that can ensue from innovators who have the capital to reward others will suppress other needs, which, through processes similar to its inception, will set off another process of institutional elaboration.

CONCLUSION

In sum, this sketch of how social organization is linked to elementary processes of exchange represents an interesting perspective for analyzing how patterns of social organization are built, maintained, altered, and broken down. Moreover, other exchange theorists repeated the broad contours of this kind of argument as they applied the principles of behaviorism or classical economics to explanations of larger-scale patterns of human organization. Yet, little of Homans's explicit imagery was retained, although the effort to move from micro principles about behavior of individuals to macro-level patterns of organization remained a critical concern in exchange theories.

NOTES

1. George C. Homans and David M. Schneider, *Marriage, Authority, and Final Causes: A Study of Unilateral Cross-Cousin Marriage* (New York: Free Press, 1955).

2. Ibid., p. 15.

3. Ibid.

4. George C. Homans, *Social Behavior: Its Elementary Forms* (New York: Harcourt Brace Jovanovich, 1961; second edition in 1972).

5. Ibid., p. 79.

6. Homans championed this conception of theory in a large number of works; see, for example, Homans, *Social Behavior* (cited in note 4); *The Nature of Social Science* (New York: Harcourt, Brace & World, 1967); "Fundamental Social Processes," in *Sociology*, ed. N. J. Smelser (New York: Wiley, 1967), pp. 27–78; "Contemporary Theory in Sociology," in *Handbook of Modern Sociology*, ed. R. E. L. Faris (Skokie, IL: Rand McNally, 1964), pp. 251–277; and "Bringing Men Back In," *American Sociological Review* 29 (December 1964), pp. 809–818. For an early statement of his position, see George C. Homans, "Social Behavior as Exchange," *American Journal of Sociology* 63 (August 1958), pp. 597–606; "Discovery and the Discovered in Social Theory," *Humboldt Journal of Social Relations* 7 (Fall–Winter 1979–1980), pp. 89–102.

7. The previous uses Homans's vocabulary, but, as emphasized in Chapter 1, "axiomatic" theory for sociology is unrealistic.

8. Note that "axioms" 1 and 2 here are simply an earlier version of Homans's rationality principle (VI) listed in Table 17.1.

9. George C. Homans, "Reply to Blain," *Sociological Inquiry* 41 (Winter 1971), pp. 19–24. Homans wrote this article in response to a challenge by Robert Blain for an explanation of a sociological law: "On Homans's Psychological Reductionism," *Sociological Inquiry* 41 (Winter 1971), pp. 3–25.

10. George C. Homans, *Social Behavior* (cited note 4).

11. Ibid., p. 366.

18

Dialectical Exchange Theory: Peter M. Blau

A few years after George C. Homans' behavioristic approach appeared, another leading sociological theorist—Peter M. Blau—explored exchange theory.[1] Though Blau accepted the behavioristic underpinnings of exchange as a basic social process, he recognized that sociological theory had to move beyond simplistic behavioristic conceptualizations of human behavior. Similarly, crude views of humans as wholly rational had to be modified to fit the realities of human behavior. In the end, he developed a dialectical approach, emphasizing that within the strains toward integration arising from exchange are forces of opposition and potential conflict. Moreover, his analysis has a Simmelian thrust because, much like Georg Simmel, Blau tried to discover the form of exchange processes at both the micro and macro levels, and in so doing, he sought to highlight what was common to exchanges among individuals as well as among collective units of organization.

THE BASIC EXCHANGE PRINCIPLES

Although Blau never listed his principles in quite the same way as Homans did with his "axioms," the principles are nonetheless easy to extract from his discursive discussion. In Table 18.1, the basic principles are summarized. Proposition I, which can be termed the *rationality principle,* states that the frequency of rewards and the value of these rewards increase the likelihood that actions will be emitted. Propositions II-A and II-B on reciprocity borrow from

Table 18.1 Blau's Implicit Exchange Principles

I. *Rationality Principle:* The more profit people expect from one another in emitting a particular activity, the more likely they are to emit that activity.

II. *Reciprocity Principles:*

  A. The more people have exchanged rewards with one another, the more likely are reciprocal obligations to emerge and guide subsequent exchanges among these people.

  B. The more the reciprocal obligations of an exchange relationship are violated, the more disposed deprived parties are to sanction negatively those violating the norm of reciprocity.

III. *Justice Principles:*

  A. The more exchange relations have been established, the more likely they are to be governed by norms of *fair exchange.*

  B. The less norms of fairness are realized in an exchange, the more disposed deprived parties are to sanction negatively those violating the norms.

IV. *Marginal Utility Principle:* The more expected rewards have been forthcoming from the emission of a particular activity, the less valuable the activity is and the less likely its emission is.

V. *Imbalance Principle:* The more stabilized and balanced are one set of exchange relations among social units, the more likely are other exchange relations to become imbalanced and unstable.

Bronislaw Malinowski's and Claude Lévi-Strauss's initial discussion as reinterpreted by Alvin Gouldner.[2] Blau postulated, "the need to reciprocate for benefits received in order to continue receiving them serves as a 'starting mechanism' of social interaction."[3] Equally important, once exchanges have occurred, a "fundamental and ubiquitous norm of reciprocity" emerges to regulate subsequent exchanges. Thus, inherent in the exchange process, per se, is a principle of reciprocity. Over time, and as the conditions of Principle I are met, a social "norm of reciprocity," whose violation brings about social disapproval and other negative sanctions, emerges in exchange relations.

Blau recognized that people establish expectations about what level of reward particular exchange relations should yield and that these expectations are normatively regulated. These norms are termed *norms of fair exchange* because they determine what the proportion of rewards to costs should be in a given exchange relation. Blau also asserted that aggression is forthcoming when these norms of fair exchange are violated. These ideas are incorporated into Principles III-A and III-B and are termed the *justice principles.*[4] Following economists' analyses of transactions in the marketplace, Blau introduced a principle on "marginal utility" (Proposition IV). The more a person has received a reward, the more satiated he or she is with that reward and the less valuable are further increments of the reward.[5] Proposition V on imbalance completes the listing of Blau's abstract laws. For Blau, as for all exchange theorists, established exchange relations are seen to involve costs or alternative rewards foregone. Most actors must engage in more than one exchange relation, and so the balance and stabilization of one exchange relation is likely to create imbalance and strain in other necessary exchange relations. Blau believes that social life is thus filled with dilemmas in which people must successively trade off stability and balance in one exchange relation for strain in others as they attempt to cope with the variety of relations that they must maintain.

ELEMENTARY SYSTEMS OF EXCHANGE

Blau initiated his discussion of elementary exchange processes with the assumption that people enter into social exchange because they perceive the possibility of deriving rewards (Principle I). Blau labeled this perception *social attraction* and postulated that, unless relationships involve such attraction, they are not relationships of exchange. In entering an exchange relationship, each actor assumes the perspective of another and thereby derives some perception of the other's needs. Actors then manipulate their presentation of self to convince one another that they have the valued qualities others appear to desire. In adjusting role behaviors in an effort to impress others with the resources that they have to offer, people operate under the principle of reciprocity, for, by indicating that one possesses valued qualities, each person is attempting to establish a claim on others for the receipt of rewards from them. All exchange operates under the presumption that people who bestow rewards will receive rewards in turn as payment for value received.

Actors attempt to impress one another through competition in which they reveal the rewards they have to offer in an effort to force others, in accordance with the norm of reciprocity, to reciprocate with an even more valuable reward. Social life is thus rife with people's competitive efforts to impress one another and thereby extract valuable rewards. But, as interaction proceeds, it inevitably becomes evident to the parties in an exchange that some people have more valued resources to offer than others, putting them in a unique position to extract rewards from all others who value the resources that they have to offer.

At this point in exchange relations, groups of individuals become differentiated by the resources they possess and the kinds of reciprocal demands they can make on others. Blau then asked an analytical question: What generic types or classes of rewards can those with resources extract in return for bestowing their valued resources on others? Blau conceptualized four general classes of such rewards: money, social approval, esteem or respect, and compliance. Although Blau did not make full use of his categorization of rewards, he offered some suggestive clues about how these categories can be incorporated into abstract theoretical statements.

Blau first ranked these generalized reinforcers by their value in exchange relations. In most social relations, money is an inappropriate reward and hence is the least valuable reward. Social approval is an appropriate reward, but for most humans it is not very valuable, thus forcing those who derive valued services to offer with great frequency the more valuable reward of esteem or

**Table 18.2 Blau's Conditions for the Differentiation of Power
in Social Exchange**

I. The fewer services people can supply in return for the receipt of particularly valued services, the more those providing these particularly valued services can extract compliance.

II. The fewer alternative sources of rewards people have, the more those providing valuable services can extract compliance.

III. The less those receiving valuable services from particular individuals can employ physical force and coercion, the more those providing the services can extract compliance.

IV. The less those receiving the valuable services can do without them, the more those providing the services can extract compliance.

respect to those providing valued services. In many situations, the services offered can command no more than respect and esteem from those receiving the benefit of these services. At times, however, the services offered are sufficiently valuable to require those receiving them to offer, in accordance with the principles of reciprocity and justice, the most valuable class of rewards— compliance with one's requests.

When people can extract compliance in an exchange relationship, they have power. They have the capacity to withhold rewarding services and thereby punish or inflict heavy costs on those who might not comply. To conceptualize the degree of power possessed by individuals, Blau formulated four general propositions that determine the capacity of powerful individuals to extract compliance. These are listed and reformulated in Table 18.2.[6]

These four propositions list the conditions leading to differentiation of members in social groups by their power. To the extent that group members can supply some services in return, seek alternative rewards, potentially use physical force, or do without certain valuable services, individuals who can provide valuable services will be able to extract only esteem and approval from group members. Such groups will be differentiated by prestige rankings but not by power. Naturally, as Blau emphasized, most social groups reveal complex patterns of differentiation of power, prestige, and patterns of approval, but of particular interest to him are the dynamics involved in generating power, authority, and opposition.

Blau believed that, power differentials in groups create two contradictory forces: (1) strains toward integration and (2) strains toward opposition and conflict.

Strains Toward Integration

Differences in power inevitably create the potential for conflict. However, such potential is frequently suspended by a series of forces promoting the conversion of power into authority, in which subordinates accept as legitimate the leaders' demands for compliance. Principles II and III in Table 18-1 denote two processes fostering such group integration: Exchange relations always operate under the presumption of reciprocity and justice, forcing those deriving valued services to provide other rewards in payment. In providing these rewards, subordinates are guided by norms of fair exchange, in which the costs that they incur in offering compliance are to be proportional to the value of the services that they receive from leaders. Thus, to the extent that actors engage in exchanges with leaders and to the degree that the services provided by leaders are highly valued, subordination must be accepted as legitimate in accordance with the norms of reciprocity and fairness that emerge in all exchanges. Under these conditions, groups elaborate additional norms specifying just how exchanges with leaders are to be conducted to regularize the requirements for reciprocity and to maintain fair rates of exchange. Leaders who conform to these emergent norms can usually assure themselves that their leadership will be considered legitimate. Blau emphasized that, if leaders abide by the norms regulating exchange of their services for compliance, norms carrying negative sanctions typically emerge among subordinates stressing the need for compliance to leaders' requests. Through this process, subordinates exercise considerable social control over one another's actions and thereby promote the integration of superordinate and subordinate segments of groupings.

Authority, therefore, "rests on the common norms in a collectivity of subordinates that constrain its individual members to conform to the orders of a superior."[7] In many patterns of social organization, these norms simply emerge from the competitive exchanges among collective groups of actors. Frequently, however, for such "normative agreements" to be struck, participants in an exchange must be socialized into a common set of values that define not only what constitutes fair exchange in a given situation but also the way such exchange should be institutionalized into norms for both leaders and subordinates. Although it is quite possible for actors to arrive at normative consensus in the course of the exchange process itself, an initial set of common values facilitates the legitimation of power. Actors can now enter into exchanges with a common definition of the situation, which can provide a general framework for the normative regulation of emerging power differentials. Without common values, the competition for power is likely to be severe. In the absence of guidelines about reciprocity and fair exchange, considerable strain and tension will persist as definitions of these are worked out. For Blau, then, legitimation "entails not merely tolerant approval but active confirmation and promotion of social patterns by common values, either preexisting ones or those that emerge in a collectivity in the course of social interaction."[8]

With the legitimation of power through the normative regulation of interaction, as confirmed by common values, the structure of collective organization is altered. One of the most evident changes is the decline in interpersonal competition, for now actors' presentations of self shift from a concern about impressing others with their valuable qualities to an emphasis on confirming their status as loyal group members. Subordinates accept their status and manipulate their role behaviors to ensure that they receive social approval from their peers as a reward for conformity to group norms. Leaders can typically assume a lower profile because they no longer must demonstrate their superior qualities in every encounter with subordinates—especially because norms now define when and how they should extract conformity and esteem for providing their valued services. Thus, with the legitimation of power as authority, the interactive processes (involving the way group members define the situation and present themselves to others) undergo a dramatic change, reducing the degree of competition and thereby fostering group integration.

With these events, the amount of direct interaction between leaders and subordinates usually declines, because power and ranking no longer must be constantly negotiated. This decline in direct interaction marks the formation of distinct subgroupings as members interact with those of their own social rank, avoiding the costs of interacting with either their inferiors or their superiors. In interacting primarily among themselves, subordinates avoid the high costs of interacting with leaders, and, although social approval from their peers is not a particularly valuable reward, it can be extracted with comparatively few costs—thus allowing a sufficient profit. Conversely, leaders can avoid the high costs (of time and energy) of constantly competing and negotiating with inferiors regarding when and how compliance and esteem are to be bestowed on them. Instead, by having relatively limited and well-defined contact with subordinates, they can derive the high rewards that come from compliance and esteem without incurring excessive costs in interacting with subordinates—thereby allowing for a profit.

Strains Toward Opposition

Thus far, Blau's exchange perspective is decidedly functional. Social exchange processes—attraction, competition, differentiation, and integration—are analyzed by how they contribute to creating a legitimated set of normatively regulated relations. Yet, Blau was keenly aware that social organization is always rife with conflict and opposition, creating an inevitable dialectic between integration and opposition in social structures.

Blau's exchange principles, summarized in Table 18.1, allow the conceptualization of these strains for opposition and conflict. As Principle II-B on reciprocity documents, the failure to receive expected rewards in return for various activities leads actors to attempt to apply negative sanctions that, when ineffective, can drive people to violent retaliation against those who have denied them an expected reward. Such retaliation is intensified by the dynamics summarized in Principle III-B on justice and fair exchange, because when those in power violate such norms, they inflict excessive costs on subordinates, creating a situation that, at a minimum, leads to attempts to sanction negatively and, at most, to retaliation. Finally, Principle V on the inevitable imbalances emerging from multiple exchange relations emphasizes that to balance relations in one exchange context by meeting reciprocal obligations and conforming to norms of fairness is to put other relations into imbalance. Thus, the imbalances potentially encourage a cyclical process in which actors seek to balance previously unbalanced relations and thereby throw into imbalance currently balanced exchanges. In turn, exchange relations that are thrown into imbalance violate the norms of reciprocity and fair exchange, thus causing attempts at negative sanctioning and, under some conditions, retaliation. Blau posited, then, that sources of imbalance are built into all exchange relationships. When severely violating norms of reciprocity and fair exchange, these imbalances can lead to open conflict among individuals in group contexts.

In Table 18.3, Blau's ideas are summarized as propositions.[9] To appreciate the degree to which these propositions resemble those in conflict theory, we can compare these propositions with those in Tables 8.1 and 8.5 on, respectively, pages 133 and 142. For, in the end, dialectical conflict theory and exchange theory are converging perspectives. It could be argued that conflict theory is a derivative of exchange theory, although many would argue just the reverse. In either case, the perspectives converge.

From the discursive context in which the propositions in Table 18.3 are imbedded comes a conceptualization of opposition. Blau hypothesized that, the more imbalanced exchange relations are experienced collectively, the greater is the sense of deprivation and the greater is the potential for opposition. Although he did not explicitly state the case, Blau appeared to argue that increasing ideological codification of deprivations, the formation of group solidarity, and the emergence of conflict as a way of life—that is, members' emotional involvement in and commitment to opposition to those with power—will increase the intensity of the opposition. These propositions offered a suggestive lead for conceptualizing inherent processes of opposition in exchange relations.[10]

EXCHANGE SYSTEMS
AND MACROSTRUCTURE

Although the general processes of attraction, competition, differentiation, integration, and opposition are evident in the exchange among macrostructures, Blau saw several fundamental differences between these exchanges and those among microstructures.

1. In complex exchanges among macrostructures, the significance of "shared values" increases, for through such values indirect exchanges among macrostructures are mediated.
2. Exchange networks among macrostructures are typically institutionalized. Although spontaneous exchange is a ubiquitous feature of social life, there are usually well-established historical arrangements that circumscribe the basic exchange processes of attraction, competition, differentiation, integration, and even opposition among collective units.
3. Macrostructures are themselves the product of more elementary exchange processes, and so the analysis of macrostructures requires the analysis of more than one level of social organization.[11]

Table 18.3 Blau's Propositions on Exchange Conflict

I. The probability of opposition to those with power increases when exchange relations between super- and subordinates become imbalanced, with imbalance increasing when

   A. Norms of reciprocity are violated by the superordinates.

   B. Norms of fair exchange are violated by superordinates.

II. The probability of opposition increases as the sense of deprivation among subordinates escalates, with this sense of deprivation increasing when subordinates can experience collectively their sense of deprivation. Such collective experience increases when

   A. Subordinates are ecologically and spatially concentrated.

   B. Subordinates can communicate with one another.

III. The more subordinates can collectively experience deprivations in exchange relations with superordinates, the more likely are they to codify ideologically their deprivations and the more likely are they to oppose those with power.

IV. The more deprivations of subordinates are ideologically codified, the greater is their sense of solidarity and the more likely are they to oppose those with power.

V. The greater the sense of solidarity is among subordinates, the more they can define their opposition as a noble and worthy cause and the more likely they are to oppose those with power.

VI. The greater is the sense of ideological solidarity, the more likely are subordinates to view opposition as an end in itself, and the more likely are they to oppose those with power.

Mediating Values

Blau believed that the "interpersonal attraction" of elementary exchange among individuals is replaced by shared values at the macro level. These values can be conceptualized as "media of social transactions" in that they provide a common set of standards for conducting the complex chains of indirect exchanges among social structures and their individual members. Blau views such values as providing effective mediation of complex exchanges because the individual members of social structures have usually been socialized into a set of common values, leading them to accept these values as appropriate. Furthermore, when coupled with codification into laws and enforcement procedures by those groups and organizations with power, shared values provide a means for mediating the complex and indirect exchanges among the macrostructures of large-scale systems. In mediating indirect exchanges among groups and organizations, shared values provide standards for the calculation of (a) expected rewards, (b) reciprocity, and (c) fair exchange.

Thus, because individuals are not the units of complex exchanges, Blau emphasized that, for complex patterns of social organization to emerge and persist, a "functional equivalent" of direct interpersonal attraction must exist. Values assume this function and ensure that exchange can proceed in accordance with the principles presented in Table 18.1. Even when complex exchanges do involve people, their interactions are frequently so protracted and indirect that one individual's rewards are contingent on others who are far removed, requiring that common values guide and regulate the exchanges.

Institutionalization

Whereas values facilitate processes of indirect exchange among diverse types of social units, institutionalization denotes those processes that regularize and stabilize complex exchange processes.[12] As people and various forms of collective organization become dependent on particular networks of indirect exchange for expected rewards, pressures for formalizing exchange networks through explicit norms increase. This formalization and regularization of complex exchange systems can be effective in three minimal conditions: (1) The formalized exchange networks must have profitable payoffs for most parties to the exchange. (2) Most individuals organized into collective units must have internalized through prior socialization the mediating values used to build exchange networks. And, (3) those units with power in the exchange system must receive a level of rewards that moves them to seek actively the formalization of rules governing exchange relations.

Institutions are historical products whose norms and underlying mediating values are handed down from one generation to another, thereby limiting and circumscribing the kinds of indirect exchange networks that can emerge. Institutions exert a kind of external constraint on individuals and various types of collective units, bending exchange processes to fit their prescriptions and proscriptions. Institutions thus represent sets of relatively stable and general norms regularizing different patterns of indirect and complex exchange relations among diverse social units.

Blau stressed that all institutionalized exchange systems reveal a counter-institutional component "consisting of those basic values and ideals that have not been realized and have not found expression in explicit institutional forms, and which are the ultimate source of social change."[13] To the extent that these values remain unrealized in institutionalized exchange relations, individuals who have internalized them will derive little payoff from existing institutional arrangements and will therefore feel deprived, seeking alternatives to dominant institutions. These unrealized values, even when codified into an opposition ideology advocating open revolution, usually contain at least some of the ideals and ultimate objectives legitimated by the prevailing culture. This indicates that institutional arrangements "contain the seeds of their potential destruction" by failing to meet all the expectations of reward raised by institutionalized values.

Blau did not enumerate the conditions for mobilization of individuals into conflict groups, but his scheme explicitly denoted the source of conflict and change: Counter-institutional values whose failure of realization by dominant institutional arrangements creates deprivations that can lead to conflict and change in social systems. Such tendencies for complex exchange systems to generate opposition can be explained by the basic principles of exchange. When certain mediating values are not institutionalized in a social system, exchange relations will not be viewed as reciprocated by those who have internalized these values. Thus, in accordance with Blau's principles on reciprocity (see Table 18.1), these segments of a collectivity are more likely to feel deprived and to seek ways of retaliating against the dominant institutional arrangements, which, from the perspective dictated by their values, have failed to reciprocate. For those who have internalized values that are not institutionalized, it is also likely that perceptions of fair exchange have been violated, leading them, in accordance with the principles of justice, to attempt to sanction negatively those arrangements that violate alternative norms of fair exchange. Finally, in institutionalized exchange networks, the balancing of exchange relations with some segments of a collectivity inevitably creates imbalances in relations with other segments (the imbalance principle in Table 18.1), thereby violating norms of reciprocity and fairness and setting into motion forces of opposition.

Unlike direct interpersonal exchanges, however, opposition in complex exchange systems is between large collective units of organization, which, in their internal dynamics, reveal their own propensities for integration and opposition. This requires that the analysis of integration and opposition in complex exchange networks be attuned to various levels of social organization. Such analysis needs to show, in particular, how exchange processes among macrostructures, whether for integration or for opposition, are partly influenced by the exchange processes occurring among their constituent substructures.

Levels of Social Organization

Blau believes the "dynamics of macrostructures rest on the manifold interdependences between the social forces within and among their substructures."[14] Blau simplifies the complex analytical tasks of examining the dynamics of substructures by positing that organized collectivities, especially formal organizations, are the most important substructures in the analysis of macrostructures. Thus, the theoretical analysis of complex exchange systems among macrostructures requires that primary attention be drawn to the relations of attraction, competition, differentiation, integration, and opposition among various types of complex organizations. In emphasizing the pivotal significance of complex organizations, Blau posited a particular image of society that should guide the ultimate construction of sociological theory.

Organizations in a society must typically derive rewards from one another, thus creating a situation in which they are both attracted to, and in competition with, one another. Hierarchical differentiation between successful and less successful organizations operating in the same sphere emerges from this competition. Such differentiation usually creates strains toward specialization in different fields among less successful organizations as they seek new sources of resources. To provide effective means for integration, separate political organizations must also emerge to regulate their exchanges. These political organizations possess power and are viewed as legitimate only as long as they are

MICROEXCHANGE

FIGURE 18.1 Blau's Image of Social Organization

considered by individuals and organizations to follow the dictates of shared cultural values. Typically, political organizations are charged with several objectives: (1) regulating complex networks of indirect exchange by the enactment of laws; (2) controlling through law competition among dominant organizations, thereby ensuring the latter of scarce resources; and (3) protecting existing exchange networks among organizations, especially those with power, from encroachment on these rewards by organizations opposing the current distribution of resources.

Blau believes that differentiation and specialization occur among macrostructures because of the competition among organizations in a society. Although mediating values allow differentiation and specialization among organizations to occur, it is also necessary for separate political organizations to exist and regularize, through laws and the use of force, existent patterns of exchange among other organizations. Such political organizations will be viewed as legitimate as long as they normatively regulate exchanges that reflect the tenets of mediating values and protect the payoffs for most organizations, especially the most powerful. The existence of political authority inevitably encourages opposition movements, however, for now opposition groups have a clear target—the political organizations—against which to

MACROEXCHANGE

FIGURE 18.1 continued

address their grievances. As long as political authority remains diffuse, opposition organizations can only compete unsuccessfully against various dominant organizations. With the legitimation of clear-cut political organizations charged with preserving current patterns of organization, opposition movements can concentrate their energies against one organization, the political system.

In addition to providing deprived groups with a target for their aggressions, political organizations inevitably must aggravate the deprivations of various segments of a population because political control involves exerting constraints and distributing resources unequally. Those segments of the population that must bear the brunt of such constraint and unequal distribution usually experience great deprivation of the principles of reciprocity and fair exchange, which, under various conditions, creates a movement against the existing political authorities. To the extent that this organized opposition forces redistribution of rewards, other segments of the population are likely to feel constrained and deprived, leading them to organize into an opposition movement. The organization of political authority ensures that, in accordance with the principle of imbalance, attempts to balance one set of exchange relations among organizations throw into imbalance other exchange relations, causing the formation of opposition organizations. Thus, built into the structure of political authority in a society are inherent forces of opposition that give society a dialectical and dynamic character.

BLAU'S IMAGE OF SOCIAL ORGANIZATION

Figure 18.1 summarizes Blau's view of social organization at the micro level and the macro-organizational level. Clearly, the same processes operate at both levels of exchange: (1) social attraction, (2) exchange of rewards, (3) competition for power, (4) differentiation, (5) strains toward integration, and (6) strains toward opposition. Thus, the Simmelian thrust of Blau's effort is clear because he sees the basic form of exchange as much the same, regardless of whether the units involved in the exchange are individuals or collective units of organization. There are, of course, some differences between exchange among individuals and organizational units, and these are noted across the bottom of the figure.

CONCLUSION

Despite Blau's effort to synthesize elements of functional and conflict theory, his approach did not endure. Indeed, even Blau himself increasingly believed that the isomorphism between micro-level and macro-level exchange processes was forced. And in the end, he abandoned the exchange approach at the macro-structural level (his alternative theory is presented on the Web site for this book), but still, more than any theorist of the time, Blau recognizes that exchange and conflict theory converge. Exchange processes produce both institutionalized patterns and forces of opposition to these patterns, primarily because exchange generates inequalities in power. But subsequent theorists—who drew more from either network theory or more purely economic approaches—never followed these leads. Let us now turn to the profile of these approaches.

NOTES

1. Peter M. Blau's major exchange work is *Exchange and Power in Social Life* (New York: Wiley, 1964). This formal and expanded statement on his exchange perspective was anticipated in earlier works. For example, see Peter M. Blau, "A Theory of Social Integration," *American Journal of* *Sociology* 65 (May 1960), pp. 545–556; and Peter M. Blau, *The Dynamics of Bureaucracy,* 1st and 2nd eds. (Chicago: University of Chicago Press, 1955, 1963). It is of interest to note that George C. Homans in *Social Behavior: Its Elementary Forms* (New York: Harcourt, Brace & World, 1961)

makes frequent reference to the data summarized in this latter work. For a more recent statement of Blau's position, see Peter M. Blau, "Interaction: Social Exchange," in *International Encyclopedia of the Social Sciences,* vol. 7 (New York: Macmillan, 1968), pp. 452–458.

2. Alvin W. Gouldner, "The Norm of Reciprocity," *American Sociological Review* 25 (April 1960), pp. 161–178.

3. Peter M. Blau, *Exchange and Power* (cited in note 1), p. 92.

4. See Peter M. Blau, "Justice in Social Exchange," in *Institutions and Social Exchange: The Sociologies of Talcott Parsons and George C. Homans,* eds. H. Turk and R. L. Simpson (Indianapolis: Bobbs-Merrill, 1971), pp. 56–68. See also: Blau, *Exchange and Power* (cited in note 1), pp. 156–157.

5. Peter M. Blau, *Exchange and Power* (cited in note 1), p. 90.

6. Ibid.

7. Ibid., p. 208.

8. Ibid., p. 221.

9. Ibid., pp. 224–252.

10. Peter M. Blau, "Dialectical Sociology: Comments," *Sociological Inquiry* 42 (Spring 1972), p. 185. This article was written in reply to an attempt to document Blau's shift from a functional to a dialectical perspective; see Michael A. Weinstein and Deena Weinstein, "Blau's Dialectical Sociology," *Sociological Inquiry* 42 (Spring 1972), pp. 173–182.

11. Peter M. Blau, "Contrasting Theoretical Perspectives," in *The Micro-Macro Link,* eds. J. C. Alexander, B. Gisen, R. Münch, and N. J. Smelser (Berkeley: University of California Press, 1987), pp. 253–311.

12. Peter M. Blau, *Exchange and Power* (cited in note 1), pp. 273–280.

13. Ibid., p. 279.

14. Ibid., p. 284.

19

Exchange
Network Theory

I n the early 1960s, Richard M. Emerson followed Georg Simmel's lead in seeking a formal sociology of basic exchange processes. In essence, Emerson asked this: Could exchange among individual and collective actors be understood by the same basic principles? Emerson provided a creative answer to this question by synthesizing behaviorist psychology and sociological network analysis. The psychology gave him the driving force behind exchanges, whereas the network sociology allowed him to conceptualize the form of social relations among both individual and collective actors in the same terms. What emerged was exchange network analysis[1] that, after Emerson's early death, was carried forward by colleagues and students, particularly Karen S. Cook.

Emerson borrowed the basic ideas of behaviorist psychology, but unlike many working in this tradition, he became more concerned with the form of relationships among the actors rather than the properties and characteristics of the actors themselves. This simple shift in emphasis profoundly affected how he built his exchange theory. The most significant departure from earlier exchange theories is the concern with why actors entered an exchange relationship in the first place given their values and preferences[2] was replaced by an emphasis on the existing exchange relationship and what is likely to transpire in this relationship in the future. Emerson believed that if an exchange relationship exists, this means that actors are willing to exchange valued resources, and the goal of theory is not so much to understand how this relationship originally came about but, instead, what will happen to it over time.

Thus, the existing exchange relationship between actors—rather than the actors themselves—becomes the unit of sociological analysis. In Emerson's eye, then, social structure is composed of exchanges among actors seeking to enhance the value of their resources. And so behaviorism, which posited a dynamic but atomized actor, was blended with network sociology, which conceptualized structure without dynamic actors.

RICHARD EMERSON'S CORE IDEAS

The key dynamics in Emerson's theory are (1) power, (2) power use, and (3) balancing. Actors have *power* to the extent that others depend on them for resources; hence, the power of Actor A over actor B is determined by the dependence of B on A for a resource that B values, and vice versa. *Dependence,* which is the ultimate source of power in Emerson's scheme, is determined by the degree to which (a) resources sought from other actors are highly valued and (b) alternatives for these resources are few or too costly to pursue. Under these conditions, where B values A's resources and where no attractive alternatives are available, the B's dependence on A is high; hence, the power of A over B is high. Conversely, where B has resources that A values and where alternatives for A are limited, B has power over A. Thus, both actors can reveal a high degree of mutual dependence, giving each *absolute power* over the other and, thereby, increasing *structural cohesion* because of the high amounts of *total* or *average power* in the exchange relationship.[3]

When one actor has more power than an exchange partner, however, this actor will engage in *power use* and exploit its exchange partner's dependence to secure additional resources or to reduce the costs it must incur in getting resources from this dependent partner. If A has power over B because of B's dependency on A, then A has the *power advantage* and will use it.

Such relations are *power imbalanced,* and Emerson felt that imbalance and power use would activate what he termed *balancing* operations. In a situation where A has a power advantage over B, B has four options:

1. Actor B can value less the resources provided by A.
2. B can find alternative sources for the resources provided by A.
3. B can increase the value of the resources it provides A.
4. B can find ways to reduce A's alternatives for the resources that B provides.

All these balancing mechanisms are designed to reduce dependency on A, or alternatively, to increase A's dependency on B in ways that balance the exchange relationship and give it a certain equilibrium.

Exchange in networks can be of two general types:[4] (1) those where actors negotiate and bargain over the distribution of resources; and (2) those where actors do not negotiate but, instead, sequentially provide resources with the expectation that these rewards will be reciprocated. This distinction between what can be termed *negotiated exchanges* and *reciprocal exchanges* is important because it reflects different types of exchanges in the real world. When actors negotiate, they try to influence each other before the resources are divided, as when labor and management negotiate a contract or when individuals argue about whether to go to the movies or to the beach. The dynamics of negotiated exchange are distinctive because they typically take longer to execute, because they generally involve considerably more explicit awareness and calculation of costs and benefits, and because they are often part of conflicts among parties who seek a compromise acceptable to all. In contrast, reciprocal exchanges involve the giving of resources unilaterally by one party to another with, of course, some expectation that valued resources will be given back, as occurs when a person initiates affection with the intent that the other will respond with the same emotion. Reciprocal exchanges are thus constructed in sequences of contingent rewarding, whereas as negotiated exchanges unfold in a series of offers and counter-offers before resources are distributed.

These seminal ideas form the core of Emerson's theoretical scheme. Before his untimely death, Emerson had been collaborating with Karen Cook and their mutual students to test the implications of these ideas for different types of networks. The basic goal was to determine how the structure of the network—that is, the pattern of connections among actors—influences, and is influenced by, the distribution of power, power use, and balancing.

STRUCTURE, NETWORKS, AND EXCHANGE

Emerson's portrayal of social networks will be simplified; for our purposes here the full details of his network terminology need not be addressed. Although Emerson followed the conventions of graph theory and developed a number of definitions, only two definitions are critical:

Actors: Points A, B, C, . . . , n in a network of relations. Different letters represent actors with different resources to exchange. The same letters—that is, A_1, A_2, A_3, and so forth—represent different actors exchanging similar resources.

Exchange relations: A—B, A—B—C, A_1—A_2, and other patterns of ties that can connect different actors to each other, forming a network of relations.

The next conceptual task was to visualize the forms of networks that could be represented with these two definitions. For each basic form, new corollaries and theorems were added as Emerson documented the way in which the basic processes of dependence, power, and balance operate. His discussion was only preliminary, but it illustrated his perspective's potential.

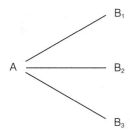

FIGURE 19.1 A Unilateral Monopoly

Several basic social forms are given special treatment: (a) unilateral monopoly, (b) division of labor, (c) social circles, and (d) stratification.

Unilateral Monopoly

In the network illustrated in Figure 19.1, actor A is a source of valuable resources for actors B_1, B_2, and B_3. Actors B_1, B_2, and B_3 provide rewards for A, but, because A has multiple sources for rewards and the Bs have only A as a source for their rewards, the situation is a unilateral monopoly.

Such a structure often typifies interpersonal as well as intercorporate units. For example, A could be a female date for three different men, B_1, B_2, and B_3. Or A could be a corporation that is the sole supplier of raw resources for three other manufacturing corporations, B_1, B_2, and B_3. Or A could be a governmental body and the Bs could be dependent agencies. An important feature of the unilateral monopoly is that, by Emerson's definitions, it is imbalanced, and thus, its structure is subject to change.

Emerson developed additional corollaries and theorems to account for the various ways this unilateral monopoly can change and become balanced. For instance, if no A_2, A_3, . . . , A_n exist and the Bs cannot communicate with each other, the following proposition would apply (termed by Emerson *Exploitation Type I*):

> The more an exchange relation between A and multiple Bs approximates a unilateral monopoly, the more additional resources each B will introduce into the exchange relation, with A's resource utilization remaining constant or decreasing.

Emerson saw this adaptation as short-lived because the network will become even more unbalanced. If the Bs can survive as an entity without resources from A, then a new proposition applies (termed by Emerson *Exploitation Type II*):

> The more an exchange relation between A and multiple Bs approximates a unilateral monopoly, the less valuable to Bs are the resources provided by A across continuing transactions.

This proposition thus predicts that balancing operation 1—a decrease in the value of the reward for those at a power disadvantage—will balance a unilateral monopoly where no alternative sources of rewards exist and where Bs cannot effectively communicate.

Other balancing operations are possible if other conditions exist. If Bs can communicate, they might form a coalition (balancing operation 4) and require A to balance exchanges with a united coalition of Bs. If one B can provide a resource not possessed by the other Bs, then a division of labor among Bs (operations 3 and 4) would emerge. Or if another source of resources, A_2, can be found (operation 2), then the power advantage of A_1 is decreased. Each of these possible changes will occur under varying conditions, but these propositions provide a reason for the initiation of changes—a reason derived from basic principles of operant psychology (the details of these derivations are not discussed here).

Division of Labor

The emergence of a division of labor is one of many ways to balance exchange relations in a unilateral monopoly. If each of the Bs can provide different resources for A, then they are likely to use these in the exchange with A and to specialize in providing A with these resources. This decreases the power of A and establishes a new type of network. For example, in Figure 19.2, the unilateral monopoly at the left is transformed to the division of labor form at the right, with B_1 becoming a new type of actor, C, with its own resources; with B_2 also specializing and becoming a new actor, D; and with B_3 doing the same and becoming actor E.

Emerson developed an additional proposition to describe this kind of change, in which each B has its own unique resources:

> The more resources are distributed *non*uniformly across Bs in a unilateral monopoly with A, the more likely is each B to specialize and establish a separate exchange relation with A.

Several points should be emphasized. First, the units in this transformation can be individual or collective actors. Second, the change in the structure or form of the network is described as a proposition systematically derived from operant principles, corollaries, and other theorems. The proposition could thus apply to a wide variety of micro and macro contexts. For example, it could apply to workers in an office who specialize and provide A with resources not available from others. This proposition could also apply to a division in a corporation that seeks to balance its relations with the central authority by reorganizing itself in ways that distinguish it, and the services it can provide, from other divisions. Or this proposition could apply to relations between a colonial power (A) and its colonized nations (B_1, B_2, B_3), which specialize (become C, D, and E) in their predominant economic activities in order to establish a less dependent relationship with A.

FIGURE 19.2 Transformation of Unilateral Monopoly to Division of Labor

Social Circles

Emerson emphasized that some exchanges are intercategory and others intracategory. An intercategory exchange is one in which one type of resource is exchanged for another type—money for goods, advice for esteem, tobacco for steel knives, and so on. The networks discussed thus far have involved *inter*category exchanges between actors with different resources (A, B, C, D, E). An *intra*category is one in which the same resources are being exchanged—affection for affection, advice for advice, goods for goods, and so on. As indicated earlier, such exchanges are symbolized in Emerson's graph approach by using the same letter—A_1, A_2, A_3, and so forth—to represent actors with similar resources. Emerson then developed another proposition to describe what will occur in these intracategory exchanges:

> The more an exchange approximates an intracategory exchange, the more likely are exchange relations to become closed.

Emerson defined "closed" either as a circle of relations (diagrammed on the left in Figure 19.3) or as a balanced network in which all actors exchange with one another (diagrammed on the right in Figure 19.3). Emerson offered the example of tennis networks to illustrate this balancing process. If two tennis players of equal ability, A_1 and A_2, play together regularly, this is a balanced intracategory exchange—tennis for tennis. However, if A_3 enters and plays with A_2, then A_2 now enjoys a power advantage, as is diagrammed in Figure 19.4.

This is a unilateral monopoly, but, unlike those discussed earlier, it is an intracategory monopoly. A_1 and A_3 are dependent on A_2 for tennis. This relation is unbalanced and sets into motion processes of balance. A_4 might be recruited, creating either the circle or balanced network diagrammed in Figure 19.3. Once this kind of closed and balanced network is achieved, it resists entry by others, A_5, A_6, A_7, . . . , A_n, because, as each additional actor enters, the

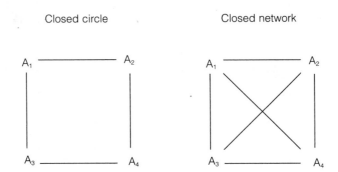

FIGURE 19.3 Closure of Intracategory Exchanges

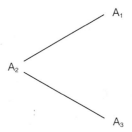

FIGURE 19.4 Imbalanced Intracategory Exchange

network becomes unbalanced. Such a network, of course, is not confined to individuals; it can apply to nations forming a military alliance or common market, to cartels of corporations, and to other collective units.

Stratified Networks

The discussion about how intracategory exchanges often achieve balance through closure can help us understand processes of stratification. If, for example, tennis players A_1, A_2, A_3, and A_4 are unequal in ability, with A_1 and A_2 having more ability than A_3 and A_4, an initial circle might form among A_1, A_2, A_3, and A_4, but, over time, A_1 and A_2 will find more gratification in playing each other, and A_3 and A_4 might have to incur too many costs in initiating invitations to A_1 and A_2. An A_1 and A_3 tennis match is unbalanced; A_3 will have to provide additional resources—the tennis balls, praise, esteem, self-deprecation. The result will be for two classes to develop:

Upper social class A_1—A_2

Lower social class A_3—A_4

Moreover, A_1 and A_2 might enter into new exchanges with A_5 and A_6 at their ability level, forming a new social circle or network. Similarly, A_3 and A_4 might form new tennis relations with A_7 and A_8, creating social circles and

Upper social class   Lower social class

   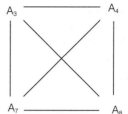

FIGURE 19.5 Stratification and Closure Exchanges

networks with players at their ability level. The result is stratification that reveals the pattern in Figure 19.5.

Emerson's discussion of stratification processes was tentative, but he developed a proposition to describe these stratifying tendencies:

> The more resources are equally valued and the more resources are unequally distributed across a number of actors, the more likely is the network to stratify by resource magnitudes and the more likely are actors with a given level of resources to form closed exchange networks.

Again, this theorem can apply to corporate units as well as to individuals. Nations become stratified and form social circles, as is the case with the distinctions between the developed and underdeveloped nations and the alliances among countries within these two classes. Or this theorem can apply to traditional sociological definitions of class, because closed networks tend to form among members within, rather than across, social classes.

KAREN S. COOK'S
THEORETICAL PROGRAM

Many of the problems of concern among network-exchange theorists were formulated by Karen Cook in collaboration with Richard Emerson and, later, with students working with either or both of them. At the same time, alternative exchange network programs were also developing.[5] The topics pursued by Cook and her collaborators vary, but several stand out: (1) the conditions under which actors in exchange networks develop commitments to partners; (2) the effects of centrality in networks on the distribution of power; (3) the relations among power use, equity, and justice considerations; and (4) the dynamics of restricted and generalized exchanges. Each of these areas of research is briefly examined in the following pages, where the important generalizations emerging from experimental studies will be emphasized.[6]

Commitment Processes in Networks

In Emerson's original formulation, imbalanced power would lead the advantaged partner in an exchange to use this power to extract more resources from another actor, to the point where balancing operations push the exchange toward equilibrium. In early work with Emerson, Cook examined the process of commitment for its effects on power use, and vice versa. The reason for studying this topic is that from a network perspective, actors do not operate in a perfectly free and competitive market; rather they have connections to each other and, by virtue of these connections, they engage in exchange. *Commitment* to an exchange occurs when actors choose their current partners over potential alternatives, and in the case of extreme commitment, when they remain with partners who can give them less beneficial payoffs than alternative partners.[7]

From the perspective of a rational and calculating actor, it would be irrational for a more powerful actor to develop commitments to others because this commitment would decrease exploration of alternatives and the resulting ability to increase their payoffs from dependent actors. Conversely, on the surface, it would seem irrational for disadvantaged actors to develop attachments to those who are using their power to extract ever more resources from them. And yet, this is exactly what appears to happen. The early finding was that power use was inversely related to commitment: actors who develop commitments were less likely to use their power advantages against their less advantaged partners.[8] One early explanation for this tendency was that commitments reduce uncertainty; hence, as actors engage in frequent exchanges, they become more committed to the ratio of payoffs and, thereby, reduce the uncertainty inherent in exchange. Moreover, commitment tempers the use of power by the advantaged because power-advantaged actors become less likely to seek alternatives, thereby enabling payoffs for power-disadvantaged actors to be regularized at predictable costs. A subsequent interpretation by Cook[9] emphasizes that efforts to entice commitment from power-advantaged actors is a balancing strategy to decrease power use by these advantaged actors.

Later, Peter Kollock[10] argued that under conditions of risk and uncertainty in receiving payoffs, both partners to the exchange could see commitment as a "profit-maximizing" strategy. By establishing commitments, each actor lowers the costs associated with risk and uncertainty. Moreover, commitment itself becomes a positively valued resource that increases each actor's resource payoffs.[11] In particular, commitment can be seen as a power-balancing strategy in which lower-power actors offer a new resource—commitment—to reduce power use by advantaged actors. (This point will be explored in the review of Edward J. Lawler's work on the Web site for this book).

Centrality in Networks and the Distribution of Power

In Figure 19.6, Actor A-1 is in a position of centrality in relation to actors A-2, A-3, and A-4. Centrality can be measured and conceptualized in several ways (see Chapter 30 on network theory), but the basic theoretical idea is

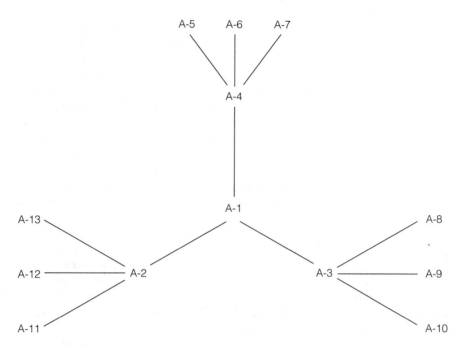

FIGURE 19.6 Power and Centrality in Exchange Networks

relatively straightforward: Some positions in a network mediate the flow of resources by virtue of being in the middle of ties to other points. Thus, in Figure 19.6, Actor A-1 mediates the flow of resources among Actors A-2, A-3, and A-4; hence, in this network, A-1 is in a position of high centrality. Similarly, further out on the network, actors A-2, A-3, and A-4 are also central between the peripheral actors at the ends of the network (A-5 through A-13) and the most central actor, A-1. For example, A-4 is central with respect to A-1, on the one side, and A-5, A-6, and A-7, on the other. The same is true for the other peripheral As connected to A-3 and A-4. Cook, Emerson, and their coauthors then argued that in such a network, power would decentralize toward those actors who possess the highest degree of access to resources.[12] In the network in Figure 19.6, resources are flowing from actors A-5 through A-13 to A-4, A-3, and A-2, and then, on to A-1. Power-dependence theory predicts that this network will have a tendency to collapse around those actors who can control direct access to resources—in this case, Actors A-2, A-3, and A-4. Why should this be so?

The answer resides in the power advantage A-2, A-3, and A-4 have over the respective As from whom they are getting resources. A-5 through A-13 have no other source for resources than A-2, A-3, and A-4, whereas each of these more central As has alternative sources for resources. Thus, those actors at the edges of the network depend on A-2, A-3, and A-4; indeed, each of these three As enjoys what Emerson termed *unilateral monopoly.* They have, therefore, the most direct access to resources, and they enjoy a power advantage because they can play the dependent As (that is, A-5 through A-13) off against each other. A-1 ultimately depends on A-2, A-3, and A-4; hence, if the latter are willing to trade with A-1, then A-1 must have resources that they value. If not, the network will collapse into its three unilateral monopolies revolving around A-2, A-3, and A-4. For this network to remain stable, therefore, A-1 actually has to possess another resource that A-2, A-3, and A-4 value highly and that they cannot get readily elsewhere (hence, in the conventions of network diagrams, A-1 actually becomes B or some other letter indicating that it is providing different resources to As).

Let us put some empirical content into these network dynamics. Let B represent the king in a feudal system, and A-2, A-3, and A-4 the lords of the king's realm. These lords provide resources to the king through their unilateral monopoly over peasants on their estates, and so, they pass on to the king some portion of the resources ultimately generated by peasants. What, then, does the king give back in exchange for this flow of resources? The answer is almost always problematic for kings, and this is why feudal systems tend to collapse—because the lords of the realm are closer to the material resources that sustain the king. Typically, the king provides the coordination of armies and other necessary activities among the lords (who are often feuding amongst themselves) for defense of the realm. This capacity to organize a kingdom is the resource that the king gives back to lords.

Many network structures approximate this one. The important point is that they are inherently unstable because those who enjoy the unilateral monopolies eventually become resentful that they have to pass on resources to a more central actor, and if they begin to perceive that this actor does not provide enough in return, they break off the exchange, and thereby change the distribution of power in the network. More recent work in networks, even in networks where actors are less likely to break off exchange, also found that the locus of power shifted toward the sources of supply of resources that were most highly valued.[13]

Equity and Justice in Exchange Networks

In their early collaborative work, Emerson and Cook had discovered that concerns about *equity*—or the distribution of outcomes from bargaining in accordance with each actor's respective contribution to the outcome—became interwoven with power dynamics.[14] If actors had knowledge of each other's payoffs and if equity considerations became salient, then power use by advantaged actors was curtailed somewhat. This finding was consistent with other research on the issue of justice in exchange—a consideration that was at the center of exchange theory from the beginning.[15]

In subsequent work with others, primarily Karen A. Hegtvedt, Cook has examined the role of justice in social exchange.[16] One of the most important conceptual distinctions highlighted by Cook and Hegtvedt is between distributive justice and procedural justice. *Distributive justice* denotes the norms or rules by which the allocation of resources among actors occurs. There are several types of such rules, including *equality* or the allocation of the same shares to all, *equity* or the distribution of resources relative to the respective inputs and contributions of actors to an outcome, or *need* or the distribution of resources to those who require them most. *Procedural justice* refers to the perceived fairness of the process of bargaining itself, rather than to the distributive outcomes that emerge from negotiations. Actors' sense of fairness in the procedures influences how they will respond to each other, thereby shaping the kinds of tactics and strategies that they will employ in bargaining.

How, then, does power influence considerations of justice? The findings are somewhat mixed, but several generalizations emerge from Cook's and Hegtvedt's experimental work as well as from their efforts to summarize the large literature on justice. One generalization is that more power-advantaged actors are, in general, likely to view the distribution of resources as fair, and these perceptions of fairness are related to their ratio of inputs to outcomes (that is, they see themselves as getting back an appropriate return on their investments and costs). Power-advantaged actors have, however, a tendency to constrain their power use when they know that their advantage rests with their structural position rather than with their abilities and talents as negotiators. In contrast, power-disadvantaged actors often tend to see situations as less fair and to bargain harder to overcome their low relative power.

Perceptions of equity, or the sense that payoffs correspond to one's contributions, have a somewhat greater effect on attributions of why one receives a payoff than does actual power advantage.[17] Individuals who see themselves as treated fairly are likely to have positive sentiments, and they are likely to attribute their fair outcomes to their personal characteristics (to maintain their identity in the situation) as well as to their partner's characteristics. Yet, this process of attribution is altered somewhat because those who have a power advantage (and correctly perceive that they have this advantage) are likely to attribute their success more to their personal characteristics and to the situation that gives them a power advantage than to the characteristics of their exchange partners. When weaker partners are not fully aware of their structurally based power disadvantage, they will bargain harder to overcome their lower outcomes. If they enjoy success in their efforts, they are likely to attribute this success to their personal characteristics.

The relationship between distributive justice or the allocation of benefits, on the one hand, and procedural justice, on the other hand, is far from clear. But Cook and Hegtvedt extract several generalizations from the literature.[18] One is that perceptions of unfair outcomes are usually accompanied by perceptions that the procedures leading to these outcomes were also unfair. Yet, unfair procedures do not produce a corresponding sense of unjust outcomes as long as actors receive what they believe as a fair outcome. Thus, people tend to judge procedures by outcomes: When outcomes are high or perceived as fair, people are less likely to be critical of procedures, even when they are clearly unfair; whereas, if outcomes are low or perceived as unfair, procedures are almost always seen as unjust, even if they are fair.

Considerable work is yet to be done on this line of research, but it is a central dynamic in power. Perceptions of justice and fairness influence how power processes operate: If power use generates a sense of justice, or if it is used in accordance with accepted norms of distributive and procedural justice, then power use will produce more balanced exchanges. If power imbalance leads to actions by the advantaged actor that violate rules of justice, or if behaviors generate a perception of injustice, then power use will perpetuate imbalance, and disadvantaged actors will seek new strategies to rebalance the exchange, if they can.

Generalized Exchange Networks

In rational choice theories (see next chapter), the basic problem of order is defined as the problem or dilemma of *free-riding*. That is, when cooperating with others in the production of a joint good or outcome, it is rational for actors who are trying to maximize benefits and minimize costs to avoid contributing to the production of a joint good. For example, if a set of actors is to produce a product, such as a group-written term paper that will receive a grade, it is rational for each actor to avoid the costs of contributing to the production of the paper but to enjoy the benefits that a good grade bestows, or in other words, it is rational to *free-ride* on the labor of others. The dilemma, of course, is that if everyone free-rides, the joint good will not be produced, and no one will receive the benefits of the jointly produced good. Rational choice theorists argue that under conditions of free-riding, actors create systems of norms, monitoring procedures, and sanctioning systems for controlling the negative results of free-riding, thereby ensuring the production of the joint good.

In her more recent work, Cook,[19] along with Toshio Yamagishi,[20] who has long worked "social dilemma" problems (like free-riding), have approached the same topic as rational choice theorists but from a different angle. Emerson made a distinction between (1) *elementary exchange* where actors directly give and take resources to enhance each actor's individual calculation of personal benefits, and (2) *productive exchange* where actors exchange resources to produce more benefits from the combination of their respective resources. But Emerson's portrayal did not capture a more fundamental distinction between (1) direct exchange and (2) generalized exchange. Most studies of exchange in networks focus on *direct exchanges* in which actors pass resources back and forth in a network that, ultimately, can be seen as a series of dyadic exchanges. Indeed, most studies producing the theoretical ideas summarized in this chapter come from experiments using direct, dyadic exchanges among partners. But, as we saw in Chapter 16 on the history of exchange theory, anthropologists have long been interested in *generalized exchange* systems in which actors give resources to others but do not receive resources directly back; rather, they acquire resources indirectly via actors who are a part of a pool of actors who feel obligated to pass resources on. For example, when a person offers to help someone whose car has broken down, this helpful person might receive positive rewards like thanks and gratitude directly, but also a more generalized exchange is operating: Helpful persons expect that others will help them when they have car trouble. The early anthropologists, such as Marcel Mauss and Claude Lévi-Strauss, had assumed that such generalized exchange systems created chains of social solidarity. Peter Ekeh,[21] in reviewing these early studies reached a similar conclusion, but more important, he made a useful distinction between types of generalized exchanges that Cook and Yamagishi were to explore further. One basic type of generalized exchange is *group-generalized exchange,* in which group members pool their resources to receive the beneficial outcomes from this pooling. Another type is what Cook and Yamagishi prefer to label *network-generalized exchange,* in which each actor provides resources to another who, in turn, provides benefits for yet another actor and so on for however many actors are in the network; the original actor eventually receives resources back from one of these other actors in the network.

The group-generalized exchange comes closest to approximating what rational choice theorists postulate as the kind of situation that generates free-riding, which, in turn, leads to the emergence of norms and other systems of social control. It is rational for actors to avoid contributions of their share to the pooled resources, while enjoying the benefits of group production. If all members free-ride, however, no one receives benefits, and under these conditions, systems of norms, monitoring, sanctioning, and trust and other mechanisms emerge to limit free-riding. Yet, as Cook and Yamagishi point out, network-generalized exchange systems also present potential dilemmas for free-riding. If one person in the chain of resource flows takes resources from one party but does not pass the appropriate resources on to the next person in the chain, then the original actor and perhaps all those in between the defector and the first actor in the chain receive no benefits. Hence, the network collapses. Yet, because there are direct connections among actors in network exchange, Cook and Yamagishi argue that participants are more likely to cooperate in a network-generalized exchange system than in a group-generalized exchange.

The reason for this difference is that in a group-generalized exchange, where actors pool resources, the temptation to free-ride is high because each actor does not have a direct responsibility to pass resources on to a designated actor, but equally important, as the group gets larger, any one actor's decision not to participate is less consequential and perhaps less noticeable to the total group product, thereby diffusing the responsibility for each actor's noncontribution. This same tendency occurs in generalized-network exchanges as they become large, especially if the networks overlap and intersect in ways that make the chains complex and somewhat redundant, but control is still exercised because at least one actor will know if another did not make the appropriate contribution.

As a consequence, trust is more likely to evolve in the network-generalized system. Built into the nature of the network is a certain monitoring, and because of this, actors come to expect that each will exchange in the appropriate manner. This expectation becomes translated into trust; such trust creates a normative climate for participation and cooperation in the generalized exchange of resources. This tendency for trust and cooperation is greater in network-generalized exchanges than in group-generalized exchanges, but, as we will see in the review of rational choice theories in the next chapter, free-riding can generate additional mechanisms beyond trust to ensure cooperation in group-generalized exchanges. However, these mechanisms increase the costs of producing a joint good.

CONCLUSION

Since Emerson's pioneering work, network exchange theory has gone in many directions. Two additional approaches within Emerson's tradition are reviewed in the Web site for this book (see the theories of Linda D. Molm and Edward Lawler). Emerson's key insight was borrowed from Georg Simmel: Study the nature of social relations because these are driven by exchange forces. This insight has allowed theorists to talk about social structures—conceptualized as social networks—while still referring to the psychological forces that drive actors in these networks. Moreover, because the actors can be individual people or collective actors such as corporations or nations, the micro-macro problem of connecting people to structure is obviated. Work in exchange networks continues and represents one of the leading edges of theorizing in sociology.

NOTES

1. For a review of elementary concepts in network analysis, see Chapter 30.

2. The core of Emerson's approach is found in a few seminal articles: "Power-Dependence Relations," *American Sociological Review* 17 (February 1962), pp. 31–41; "Power-Dependence Relations: Two Experiments," *Sociometry* 27 (September 1964), pp. 282–298; "Exchange Theory, Part I: A Psychological Basis for Social Exchange" and "Exchange Theory, Part II: Exchange Relations and Network Structures," in *Sociological Theories in Progress,* eds. J. Berger, M. Zelditch, and B. Anderson (New York: Houghton Mifflin, 1972), pp. 38–87; "Operant Psychology and Exchange Theory," in *Behavior*

Sociology, eds. R. Burgess and D. Bushell (New York: Columbia University Press, 1969); "Social Exchange Theory," *Annual Review of Sociology* 2 (1976), pp. 535–562. See also John F. Stolte and Richard M. Emerson, "Structural Inequality: Position and Power in Network Structures," in *Behavioral Theory in Sociology,* ed. R. Hamblin (New Brunswick, NJ: Transaction, 1977).

3. The notions of "absolute," "structural cohesion," "total," and "average" power are terms that others adopt for their respective schemes (see the Wadsworth Web site for this book), although the meanings of the terms vary somewhat from Emerson's original usage.

4. Richard M. Emerson, "Social Exchange Theory," in *Social Psychology: Sociological Perspectives,* eds. M. Rosenberg and R. H. Turner (New York: Basic Books).

5. For examples see David Willer, "The Basic Concepts of the Elementary Theory," in *Networks, Exchange and Coercion,* eds. D. Willer and B. Anderson (New York: Elsevier, 1981); "Property and Social Exchange," *Advances in Group Processes* 2 (1985), pp. 123–142; and *Theory and the Experimental Investigation of Social Structures* (New York: Gordon and Breach, 1986); David Willer, Barry Markovsky, and Travis Patton, "Power Structures: Derivations and Applications of Elementary Theory," in *Sociological Theories in Progress: New Formulations,* eds. J. Berger, M. Zelditch, and B. Anderson (Newbury Park, CA: Sage, 1989); David Willer and Barry Markovsky, "Elementary Theory: Its Development and Research Program," in *Theoretical Research Programs: Studies in the Growth of Theory,* eds. J. Berger and M. Zelditch, Jr. (Stanford, CA: Stanford University Press, 1993); Philip Bonacich, "Power and Centrality: A Family of Measures," *American Journal of Sociology* 92 (1987), pp. 1170–1082; Elisa Jayne Bienenstock and Philip Bonacich, "The Core as a Solution to Exclusionary Networks," *Social Networks* 14 (1992), pp. 231–243.

6. For overviews of both the Emerson-Cook and various alternative exchange network programs, see Linda D. Molm and Karen S. Cook, "Social Exchange and Exchange Networks," in *Sociological Perspectives on Social Psychology,* eds. K. S. Cook, G. A. Fine, and J. S. House (Boston: Allyn & Bacon, 1995); see also Karen S. Cook, Linda D. Molm, and Toshio Yamagishi, "Exchange Relations and Exchange Networks: Recent Developments in Social Exchange Theory" along with David Willer and Barry Markovsky, "Elementary Theory: Its Developments and Research Program," in *Theoretical*

Research Programs: Studies in the Growth of Theory, eds. J. Berger and M. Zelditch (Stanford, CA: Stanford University Press, 1993).

7. It should be emphasized that most of this work and, until recently, virtually all work by Cook and most exchange theorists has been on *negatively connected networks* in which exchange with one actor precludes exchanging with another.

8. Karen S. Cook and Richard M. Emerson, "Power, Equity, and Commitment in Exchange Networks," *American Sociological Review* 43 (1978), pp. 721–739; Karen S. Cook and Richard M. Emerson, "Exchange Networks and the Analysis of Complex Organizations," *Research on the Sociology of Organizations* 3 (1984), pp. 1–30.

9. Ibid. (refer to both works in previous note).

10. Peter Kollock, "The Emergence of Exchange Structures: An Experimental Study of Uncertainty, Commitment and Trust," *American Journal of Sociology* 100 (1994), pp. 315–345.

11. See James Coleman's discussion in Chapter 20 on similar processes in his analysis of solidarity.

12. Karen S. Cook, Richard M. Emerson, Mary R. Gillmore, and Toshio Yamagishi, "The Distribution of Power in Exchange Networks: Theory and Experimental Results," *American Journal of Sociology* 87 (1983), pp. 275–305. More recently, Yamagishi, Gillmore, and Cook have sought to extend this line of work to positively connected networks where beneficial exchange with one partner does not preclude exchanges with others. Many of the same dynamics are revealed but with some modification: The value of resources becomes the only consideration in positively connected networks, and the locus of power shifts toward the source of supply of valued resources. See their "Network Connections and the Distribution of Power in Exchange

Networks," *American Journal of Sociology* 93 (1988), pp. 833–851. For a more recent effort to theorize on these processes, see also Kazuo Yamaguchi, "Power in Networks of Substitutable and Complementary Exchange Relations: A Rational-Choice Model and An Analysis of Power Centralization," *American Sociological Review* 61 (1996), pp. 308–332. For rivals to the Cook program, also see John Skvoretz and David Willer, "Exclusion and Power: A Test of Four Theories of Power in Exchange Networks," *American Sociological Review* 58 (1993), pp. 801–818.

13. See text in previous footnote.

14. Karen S. Cook and Richard M. Emerson, "Power, Equity and Commitment in Exchange Networks" (cited in note 8).

15. See Chapters 17 and 18, respectively, on the work of George Homans and Peter Blau in the 1960s.

16. Karen A. Hegtvedt and Karen S. Cook, "The Role of Justice in Conflict Situations," *Advances in Group Processes* 4 (1987), pp. 109–136; Karen S. Cook and Karen A. Hegtvedt, "Distributive Justice, Equity, and Equality," *Annual Review of Sociology* 9 (1983), pp. 217–241; Karen Hegtvedt, Elaine Thompson, and Karen S. Cook, "Power and Equity: What Counts in Attributions for Exchange Outcomes," *Social Psychology Quarterly* 56 (1993), pp. 100–119.

17. Karen Hegtvedt, Elaine Thompson, and Karen S. Cook, "Power and Equity" (cited in note 16).

18. Karen A. Hegtvedt and Karen S. Cook, "The Role of Justice in Conflict Situations"; and Cook and Hegtvedt, "Distributive Justice, Equity, and Equality" (cited in note 16); for a review of the justice and injustice literature, see also Karen Hegtvedt and Barry Markovsky, "Justice and Injustice," in *Sociological Perspectives on Social Psychology,* eds. K. S. Cook, G. A. Fine, and J. S. House (Boston: Allyn & Bacon, 1995).

19. Toshio Yamagishi and Karen S. Cook, "Generalized Exchange and Social Dilemmas," *Social Psychology Quarterly* 56 (1993), pp. 235–249.

20. For relevant works by Yamagishi, see "The Provision of a Sanctioning System in the United States and Japan," *Social Psychology Quarterly* 51 (1988), pp. 267–270; "Seriousness of Social Dilemmas and the Provision of a Sanctioning System," *Social Psychology Quarterly* 51 (1988), pp. 32–42; "Unintended Consequences of Some Solutions to the Social Dilemmas Problem," *Sociological Theory and Method* 4 (1989), pp. 21–47.

21. Peter P. Ekeh, *Social Exchange Theory: The Two Traditions* (Cambridge, MA: Harvard University Press, 1974).

20

Rational Choice Theory

dam Smith, who formulated the basic laws of supply and demand for
free markets, is often viewed as the founder of utilitarian economics.
In Smith's formulation, actors are conceptualized as rational and as
seeking to maximize their utilities, or benefits.[1] Yet, his utilitarian ideas also led
Smith to formulate the basic question guiding much sociological theory in the
nineteenth century: What forces are to hold society together in a world where
market-driven production and consumption lead individuals into ever more
specialized social niches? What, then, was to keep specialization from splitting
society apart? Adam Smith had two answers: (1) the laws of supply and demand
in markets would operate as a kind of "invisible hand of order" in matching
people's needs to production and in controlling fraud, abuse, and exploitation;
and (2) differentiated societies would develop sentiments appropriate to the
new social order being created by markets.[2]

Through the midpoint of this century, sociologists were suspicious of the
first answer, wondering how social order could emerge from rational actors
pursuing their own self-interests in markets operating by profit and greed. The
second answer—an emphasis on moral codes—was more appealing but sociologists soon forgot that Adam Smith had recognized the importance of cultural
codes as an essential force of social organization. As a result, for more than half
the twentieth century, sociologists were critical of the utilitarians' views. In
essence, they asked this: how could selfish, resource-maximizing actors ever
create the moral codes and modes of cooperation so necessary for an orderly

society? Their answer was that such utilitarian theories could not explain the emergent forces holding societies together.

Yet, by midcentury, exchange theories were becoming a prominent part of the sociological canon. Some of these theories were couched in behavioristic psychology, others in the utilitarian terminology of classical economics. In either case, the goal was to demonstrate how reward- or utility-seeking and rational actors could construct sociocultural systems. In effect, these new theorists took the challenge that had been presented by sociology's distrust of utilitarianism: Demonstrate how a model of an individualistic, rational, self-interested, and utility-maximizing actor can create the social and cultural forces that bind the members of society together. In this chapter, we will review two such efforts to meet this challenge through the theoretical approach that is now known as rational choice theorizing.[3]

MICHAEL HECHTER'S THEORY
OF GROUP SOLIDARITY

Michael Hechter's theory of group solidarity seeks to explain how rational, resource-maximizing actors create and remain committed to the normative structure of groups.[4] Table 20.1 summarizes his utilitarian assumptions, but the basic ideas are straightforward: Individuals reveal preferences or hierarchies of utility (value); they seek to maximize these preferences; and under certain conditions, it is rational for them to construct cultural and social systems to maximize utilities. Most theories of culture and social structure, Hechter argues, simply assume the existence of emergent sociocultural phenomena but do not explain how and why they would ever emerge in the first place. Rational choice theory can, he believes, offer this explanation for why actors construct and then abide by the normative obligations of groups. And, if such a fundamental process as group solidarity can be explained by rational choice assumptions, virtually all emergent social phenomena can be similarly understood.

The Basic Problem of Order
in Rational Choice Theorizing

In many situations, especially those of interest to sociologists, individuals depend on others in a group context for those resources, or goods, that will maximize utilities. That is, these individuals cannot produce the good for themselves and, hence, must rely on others to produce it for them or join others in its production. For example, if companionship and affection are high preferences, this "good" can be attained only in interaction with others, usually in groups; if money is a preference, then this good can usually be attained in modern settings through work in an organizational context. Thus, the "goods" that meet individual preferences can often be secured only in a group;

Table 20.1 Assumptions of Rational Choice Theory

I. Humans are purposive and goal oriented.

II. Humans have sets of hierarchically ordered preferences or utilities.

III. In choosing lines of behavior, humans make rational calculations about

    A. The utility of alternative lines of conduct with reference to the preference hierarchy.

    B. The costs of each alternative in terms of utilities foregone.

    C. The best way to maximize utility.

IV. Emergent social phenomena—social structures, collective decisions, and collective behavior—are ultimately the result of rational choices made by utility-maximizing individuals.

V. Emergent social phenomena that arise from rational choices constitute a set of parameters for subsequent rational choices of individuals in the sense that they determine

    A. The distribution of resources among individuals.

    B. The distribution of opportunities for various lines of behavior.

    C. The distribution and nature of norms and obligations in a situation.

groups are conceptualized in rational choice theory as existing to provide or produce "goods" for their members.

Those goods that are produced by the activities of group members can be viewed as *joint goods* because they are produced jointly in the coordinated activities of group members. Such joint goods vary along a critical dimension: their degree of "publicness." A highly *public good* is available not only to the members of the group but also to others outside the group as well. Furthermore, once the good is produced, its use by one person does not diminish its supply for another. For instance, radio waves, navigational aids, and roads are public goods because they can be used by those who did not produce them and because their use by one person does not (at least to a point) preclude use by another. In contrast with public goods are *private goods,* which are produced for consumption by their producers. Moreover, consumption by one person decreases the capacity of others to consume the good. Private goods are thus kept out of the reach of others to ensure that only a person, or persons, can consume them.

The basic problem of order for rational choice theorists revolves around the question of public goods. This problem is described as the *free-rider* dilemma.[5] People are supposed to produce public goods jointly. It is rational to consume public goods without contributing to their production. To avoid the costs of contributing to production is free-riding. If everybody free-rides, then the joint good will never be produced. How, then, is this dilemma avoided?

An answer to this question has been controversial in the larger literature in economics, but the basic thrust of the argument is that, if a good is highly public, people can be coerced (through taxes, for example) to contribute to its production (say, national defense) or they can be induced to contribute by being rewarded (salaries, praise) for their contribution. Another way to prevent free-riding is to exclude those who do not contribute to production from consumption, thereby decreasing the degree of "publicness" of the good. This exclusion can result in a group that "throws out" noncontributing members or does not allow them to join in the first place. A final way to control free-riders is to impose user fees or prices for goods that are consumed.

Thus, for rational choice theory, the basis of social order revolves around creating group structures to produce goods that are consumed in ways that limit free-riding—that is, consumption without contributing in some way, directly or indirectly, to production. The sociologically central problem of social solidarity thus becomes one of understanding how rational egoists go about establishing groups that create normative obligations on their members to contribute and, then, enforcing their conformity—thereby diminishing the problem of free-riding. Solidarity is thus seen as a problem of social control.

The Basis of Social Control:
Dependence, Monitoring, and Sanctioning

In rational choice theory, groups exist to provide joint goods. The more an individual depends on a group for resources or goods that rank high in his or her preference hierarchy, the greater is the potential power of the group over that individual. When people depend on a group for a valued good, it is rational for them to create rules and obligations that will ensure access to this joint good. Such is particularly likely to be the case when the valued joint good is not readily available elsewhere, when individuals lack information about alternatives, when the costs of exiting the group are high, when moving or transfer costs are high, and when personal ties, as unredeemable sunk investments, are strong.

Dependence is thus the incentive behind efforts to create normative obligations to ensure that actors will get a joint good. Groups thus have power over individuals who are dependent on the resources generated by the group; as a result of this power, *the extensiveness of normative obligations in a group is related to the degree of dependence.* Hence, dependence creates incentives not just for norms but for extensive norms that guide and regulate to a high degree.

Hechter is quick to emphasize that "the extensiveness of a group alone . . . has no necessary implications for group solidarity."[6] What is crucial is that group members will comply with these norms. Compliance is related to a group's *control capacity,* which in turn is a function of (1) *monitoring* and (2) *sanctioning.* Monitoring is the process of detecting nonconformity to group norms and obligations, whereas sanctioning is the use of rewards and punishments to induce conformity. When the monitoring capacity of a group is low, then it becomes difficult to ensure compliance to norms because conformity is a cost that rational individuals will avoid, if they can. And, without monitoring, sanctioning cannot effectively serve as an inducement to conformity.

Hechter believes, then, that solidarity is the product of dependence, monitoring, and sanctioning. But solidarity is also related to the nature of the group, which led Hechter to distinguish types of groups by the nature of joint goods produced.

Types of Groups

Hechter views control capacity—that is, monitoring and sanctioning—as operating differently in two basic types of groups. If a grouping produces a joint good for a market and does not itself consume the good, then control capacity can be potentially reduced because the profits from the sale of the good can be used to "buy" conformity. Conformity can be bought, for example, because members are compensated for their labor; if they are highly dependent on a group for this compensation, then it is rational to conform to norms. But, because the same compensation can be achieved in other groups, it is less likely that dependence on the group is high, which thereby reduces the extensiveness of norms. The result is that monitoring and sanctioning must be high in such groups, for it would be rational for the individual to free-ride and take compensation without a corresponding effort to produce the marketable good. Yet, if monitoring and sanctioning are too intrusive and impose costs on individuals, then it is rational to leave the group and seek compensation elsewhere. Moreover, as we will see, extensive monitoring and sanctioning are costly and cut into profits—hence limiting the social control capacity of the group. The control capacity of these *compensatory groups,* as Hechter calls them, is thus problematic and ensures that solidarity will be considerably lower than in *obligatory groups.*

Obligatory groups produce a joint good for their members' own consumption. Under these conditions, it is rational to create obligations for contributions from members; if dependence on the joint good is high, then there is considerable incentive for conformity because there is no easy alternative to the joint good (unlike the case in groups in which a generalized medium like money is employed as compensation). Moreover, monitoring and sanctioning can usually be more efficient because monitoring typically occurs as a by-product of joint production of a good that the members consume and because the ultimate sanction—expulsion from the group—is very costly to members who value this good. As Hechter notes

> Due to greater dependence, obligatory groups have lower sanctioning and monitoring costs. Since every group has one relatively costless sanction at its disposal—the threat of expulsion—then the greater the dependence of group members, the more weight this sanctioning causes. [Moreover,] . . . monitoring and sanctioning are to some extent substitutable. If the value of the joint good is relatively large, the threat of expulsion can partly compensate for inadequate monitoring. The more one has to lose by noncompliance, the less likely one is to risk it. . . . [7]

There is an implicit variable in Hechter's analysis: group size. In general terms, compensatory groups organize larger numbers of individuals to produce marketable goods, whereas obligatory groups are smaller and provide goods for their members that cannot be obtained (or, only at great cost) in a market. Thus, not only will dependence be higher in obligatory groups but monitoring and sanctioning also will be considerably easier, thereby increasing solidarity, which Hechter defines as the extent to which members' private resources are contributed to a collective end. High contributions of private resources can occur only with extensive norms and high conformity—two conditions unlikely to prevail in compensatory groups. In Hechter's terms, then, high solidarity can be achieved only in obligatory groups in which dependence on a jointly produced and consumed good is high, in which monitoring is comparatively easy because of small size and because members can observe one another's production and consumption of the good, and in which sanctioning is built into the very nature of the good (that is, receiving a good is a positive sanction, whereas expulsion or not receiving the good is a very costly negative sanction). Under these conditions, people will commit their private resources—time, energy, and self—to the production of the joint good and, in the process, promote high solidarity.

For Hechter, then, high degrees of solidarity are possible only in obligatory groups, in which dependence, monitoring, and sanctioning are high. Figure 20.1 represents his argument, modified in several respects. First, group size is added as a crucial variable. As obligatory groups get large, their monitoring and sanctioning capacity decreases. Second, on the far left is added a variable that is perhaps more typical of many human groupings: the ratio of consumption to compensation. That is, many groupings involve a mixture of extrinsic compensation for the production of goods consumed by others *and* goods consumed by members. For example, groups composed of members working for a salary in an organization often develop solidarity because they also produce joint goods—friendship, approval, assistance, and the like. Indeed, at times solidarity develops around obligations that run counter to the official work norms of the organization. We need to conceptualize groups not so much as two polar types but, rather, as mixtures of (1) external compensation for goods jointly produced by and consumed by others and (2) internal consumption of goods jointly produced and consumed by members. The greater the proportion of compensation is to internal consumption, the less likely are the processes depicted in Figure 20.1 to operate; conversely, the less the ratio of compensation to internal consumption is, the more likely these processes are to be activated in ways that produce solidarity. This proposition does not violate the intent of Hechter's typology because he argues that control capacity of compensatory groups increases if such groups also produce a joint good for their members' own consumption.

A larger-scale social system, such as a community or society, is a configuration of obligatory and compensatory groups. Solidarity will be confined mostly to obligatory groups, whereas the problems of free-riding will be most evident in compensatory groups, unless they also develop joint goods that are highly valued and consumed by group members. Hechter thus turns back to the basic distinctions that dominated early sociological theory—*gemeinschaft* versus *geselleschaft,* primary versus secondary groups, mechanical versus

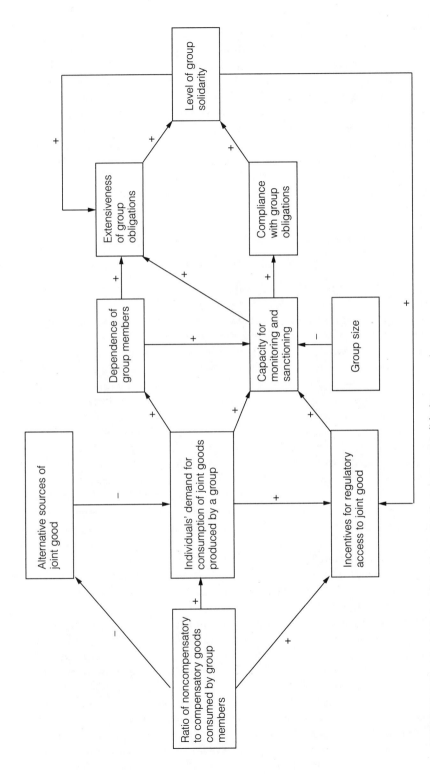

FIGURE 20.1 Hechter's Model of the Forces Producing Group Solidarity

organic solidarity, traditional versus rational authority, folk versus urban—and has sought to explain these distinctions as the production of joint goods and the nature of the control process that stems from whether a joint good is consumed by members or produced for a market in exchange for extrinsic compensation. Hechter believes the nature of the joint good determines the level of dependence of individuals on the group and the control capacity of the group. High dependence and control are most likely when joint goods are consumed, and hence solidarity is high under these conditions. A society with only compensatory groups will, therefore, reveal low solidarity. What is distinctive about Hechter's conceptualization is that it is tied to a utilitarian theory in which both high and low levels of solidarity follow from rational choices of individuals.

Patterns of Control in Compensatory and Obligatory Groups

In a vein similar to classical sociological theory, Hechter examines the process of formalization.[8] As groups get larger, informal controls become inadequate, even in obligatory groups. Of course, if compensatory groups proliferate or grow in size, the process of creating formal controls escalates to an even greater degree. There is, however, a basic dilemma in this process: Formal monitoring and sanctioning are costly because they involve creating special agents, offices, procedures, and roles, thereby cutting into the production of goods. Obligatory groups can put off the process of formal controls because of high dependence and control that comes from joint consumption of a good that is valued, but when obligatory groups get too large, more formal controls become necessary. Compensatory groups can try to keep formal controls to a minimum, especially if they can create consumption of joint goods that reinforce the production norms for those goods that will be externally consumed; however, if they get too large, then they must also increase formal monitoring and sanctioning. In all these cases, it is rational for actors in groups to resist imposing formal controls because they are costly and cut into profits or joint consumption. But if free-riding becomes too widespread and cuts into production, then it is rational to begin to impose formal controls.

To some extent the implementation of formal controls can be delayed, or mitigated, by several forces. One is common socialization, and groups often seek members who share similar outlooks and commitments to reduce the risks of free-riding and cut the costs of monitoring. Another is selection for altruism, especially in obligatory groups, in which unselfish members are recruited. Yet there clearly are limits on how effective these forces can be in maintaining social control, especially in compensatory groups but also in obligatory groups as they get larger.

The result of this basic dilemma between the costs of free-riding, on the one side, and formalization of control, on the other, is for groups to seek "economizing" measures for monitoring and sanctioning.[9] These are particularly visible in compensatory groups in which formal social control is more essential to production, but elements of these "economizing tactics" can be seen in obligatory groups as they get larger or as they produce a joint good that creates problems of free-riding.

Hechter listed a number of monitoring economies. One way to decrease monitoring costs is to increase the visibility of individuals in the group through a variety of techniques: designing the architecture of the group so that people are physically visible to one another, requiring members to engage in public rituals to reaffirm their commitments to the group, encouraging group decision making so that individuals' preferences are exposed to others, and administering public sanctions for behavior that exemplifies group norms. Another set of techniques for reducing monitoring costs includes those that have members share the monitoring burden, as is the case when rewards are given to groups rather than individuals (under the assumption that, if your rewards depend on others, you will monitor their activity), when privacy is limited, when informants are rewarded, and when gossip is encouraged. A final economizing technique, which follows from socialization processes, is to minimize errors of interpretation of behavior through recruitment and training of members into a homogeneous culture.

One technique for economizing on sanctions is symbolic sanctioning through the creation of a prestige hierarchy and the differential rewarding of prestige to group members who personify group norms. Another technique is public sanctioning of deviance from group norms. A final sanctioning technique is to increase the exit costs of group members through geographical isolation from other groups, imposition of nonrefundable investments on entry to the group, and limitation of extragroup affiliations.

There are limits to these monitoring and sanctioning economies, however, especially in compensatory groups. The result is that, at some point, a group must create formal agents and offices to monitor and control. Thus, a formal organization always reveals some of the economizing processes listed and the agents charged with monitoring and control—for example, comptrollers, supervisors, personnel offices, quality-control agents, and the like. Such monitoring and sanctioning are extremely costly, so it is not surprising that organizations try to economize here also.

In addition to the more general techniques previously listed, a variety of mechanisms for reducing agent costs, or increasing productive efficiency and hence profitability, can be employed. For example, inside and outside contractors are often used to perform work (and to incur their own monitoring and sanctioning costs) at a set price for an organization; standardization of tools, work flow, and other features of work is another way to reduce the need for monitoring; assessment of only outputs (and ignoring how these are generated) is yet another technique for economizing on at least some phases of monitoring; setting production goals for each stage in production is still another technique; and, perhaps most effective, the creation of an obligatory group within the larger compensatory organization is the most powerful economizing technique, as long as the norms of the obligatory group correspond to those of the more inclusive compensatory organization (sometimes, however, just the opposite is the case, which thereby increases monitoring costs to even higher levels).

The Theory Summarized

Such are the key elements in Hechter's theory. In Table 20.2, the theory is stated in more formal and abstract terms than in Hechter's work. When stated in this way, the theory can be applied to a wide range of empirical processes—social class formation, ethnic solidarity, complex organization, communities, and other social units. The propositions in Table 20.2 must be seen as building on the assumptions delineated in Table 20.1; when this is done, it is clear that Hechter has tried to explain, as he phrases the matter, "the micro foundations of the macro social order."

Macrostructural Implications

Hechter sees the basic ideas of rational choice theory as useful in understanding more macrostructural processes among large populations of individuals. For example, the basic theory as outlined in Figure 20.1 and Tables 20.1 and 20.2 can be used to explain processes within nation-states. A state or government imposes relatively extensive obligations on its citizens—pay your taxes, be loyal, be willing to die in war, and so on. The reason for this capacity is that citizens are often highly dependent on the state for public goods and cannot leave the society easily (because they like where they live, cannot incur the exit and transfer costs, enjoy many benefits from the joint goods produced by the citizenry, and so on). Compliance with the demands of the state involves more than dependence and extensive obligations; compliance also hinges on the state's control capacity. But how is it possible for the state to monitor and sanction all its citizens who are organized into diverse configurations of obligatory and compensatory groups?

The answer to this question, Hechter argues, lies in economies of control. Such economies can be generated *within* and *between* groups. The key process is to get the citizens themselves monitoring and sanctioning one another within groups, then to link these groups together in ways that maximize dependence and control capacity.

JAMES S. COLEMAN'S THEORY
OF GROUP SOLIDARITY

In many articles, James S. Coleman was an early advocate of a rational choice perspective,[10] but not until the 1990s did he produce a general theory of social organization which was based on rational choice principles.[11] This more synthetic theory was published not long before Coleman's tragically early death. Coleman believed that actors have resources and interest in the resources of others; hence, interaction and ultimately social organization revolve around transactions between those who have and those who seek resources. These transactions can occur between individuals directly, they can also occur indirectly through intermediaries or chains of resource transfer, and they can occur

Table 20.2 Hechter's Implicit Principles of Social Structure

I. The more members of a group jointly produce goods for consumption outside the group, the more their productive efforts will depend on increases in the ratio of extrinsic compensation to intrinsic compensation.

II. The more members of a group jointly produce goods for their own consumption, the more their efforts will depend on the development of normative obligations.

III. The power of the group to constrain the decisions and behaviors of its members is positively related to the dependence of these members on the group for a good or compensation, with dependence increasing when

   A. More attractive alternative sources for a good or compensation are not available.

   B. Information about alternative sources for a good or compensation is not readily available.

   C. The costs of exiting the group are high.

   D. The moving or transfer costs to another group are high.

   E. The intensity of personal ties among group members is high.

IV. The more a group produces a joint good for its own consumption and develops normative obligations to regulate productive activity, the more likely are conditions III-A, III-B, III-C, III-D, and III-E to be met; conversely, the more a group produces a joint good for the consumption of others outside the group, the less likely these conditions are to be met.

V. The more a group produces a joint good for its own consumption and develops extensive normative obligations to regulate productive activity, the more likely is social control through monitoring and sanctioning to be informal and implicit and, hence, less costly.

VI. The more a group produces a good for external consumption and must rely on a high ratio of extrinsic over intrinsic compensation for members, the more likely is social control through monitoring and sanctioning to be formal and explicit and, hence, most costly.

VII. The larger is the size of a group, the more likely is social control to be formal and explicit and the greater will be its cost.

VIII. The greater is the cost of social control through monitoring and sanctioning, the most likely are economizing procedures to be employed in a group.

---

in markets where resources are aggragated and bought and sold according to the laws of supply and demand.

Transferring Rights to Act

Coleman conceived of resources as *rights to act*. These rights can be given away in exchange for other rights to act. Thus, for example, authority relations consist of two types: *conjoint* authority where actors unilaterally give control of their rights to act to another because the vesting of others with authority is seen as in the best interests of all actors, and *disjoint* authority where actors give their rights away for extrinsic compensation, such as money. The same is true for norms that, in Coleman's eye, represent the transfer of rights of control to a system of rules that are sanctioned by others. Thus, social structures and cultural norms are ultimately built by virtue of individuals giving up their rights to control resources in exchange for expected benefits. For Coleman, then, the key theoretical questions in understanding social solidarity are (1) What conditions within a larger collectivity of individuals create a *demand* for rational actors to give their rights of control over resources to normative rules and the sanctions associated with these rules; and (2) what conditions make *realization* of effective control by norms and sanctions?

The Demand for Norms and Sanctions

These two questions—(1) the demand for norms and (2) their realization through effective sanctioning—are at the core of Coleman's theory. This theory goes in many directions, but we will confine our analysis to Coleman's discussion of the conditions producing group solidarity, so as to be in a position to compare Coleman's perspective with Hechter's theory of group solidarity. Thus, given the two questions guiding his approach, Coleman asked this: What basic conditions increase the demand for social norms and what makes them effective? In his answer, Coleman demonstrated how a view of actors as rational, self-interested, calculating, and resource-maximizing can explain emergent phenomena such as norms and group solidarity.

What conditions, then, increase the demand for norms? One is that actors are experiencing *negative externalities,* or harmful consequences in a particular context. Another is that actors cannot successfully bargain tit-for-tat or make offers or threats back and forth to reach agreements that reduce the negative externalities. Another condition is that there are too many actors involved for successful tit-for-tat bargaining, making bargaining cumbersome, difficult, and time consuming. And the most important condition is free-riding, where some actors do not contribute to the production of a joint good, and where tit-for-tat bargaining cannot resolve the problem. Such free-riding, Coleman argued, is most likely in those groupings using disjoint authority or extrinsic compensation for productive activity (what Hechter termed a "compensatory group"). But, ultimately in Coleman's model, negative externalities give actors an *interest* in elaborating social structure and cultural systems. They begin to see that by giving up some of their rights of control over their resources and behaviors, they can reduce negative externalities and, thereby, increase their utilities. Free-riding can become a negative externality, to the degree that it imposes costs and harm on others. As we will see, free-riding became an important dynamic in Coleman's model of solidarity. But, there can be other sources of negative externalities—threats, conflict, abusive use of authority, or any source of punishment or costly action by others. Generally, actors will first engage in tit-for-tat bargaining to resolve a problem creating negative externalities. For example, a threat might be met by a counter-threat followed by an agreement to let the matter pass. But as the size of the group increases, this kind of bargaining becomes less viable: Pairwise bargaining among larger sets of actors to reduce negative externalities becomes difficult because of time and energy consumed; bargaining can create new negative externalities for actors who must constantly negotiate and for those who are left out of bargains.

Coleman argued that the creation of markets represents one solution to problems of pairwise, tit-for-tat bargaining among larger numbers of actors. As the volume of resources to be exchanged increases, and the number of buyers and sellers expands, markets determine the price of the resources that one must give up to get another valued resource, with price being determined by the relative supply and demand for resources, Yet, markets generate their own negative externalities associated with cheating, failure to meet obligations, unavailability of credit, and many other problems, and like all negative externalities, they can create demand for norms to regulate transactions.

Thus, wherever norms emerge (and other features of social systems like authority), they do so because actors have an interest in giving up certain rights to eliminate negative externalities and, thereby, to increase their utilities. Systems of norms, trust, and authority all represent ways to organize actors when tit-for-tat bargaining is difficult or unsuccessful, when the number of people involved grows beyond the capacity to bargain face-to-face, and when markets are no longer "frictionless" and begin to create their own negative externalities.

Under these conditions, actors will then bestow some of their rights to control resources to create *proscriptive norms,* or rules that prohibit certain types of behavior, and they will impose *negative sanctions* on those who violate these proscriptions or prohibitions. Such proscriptions and negative sanctions represent a solution by rational actors to the *first-order free-riding* problem, where actors are not contributing to the production of a jointly produced good. But, this solution to free-riding creates a *second-order free-rider* problem: Monitoring and sanctioning others are costly in time and energy, to say nothing of emotional stress and other negatives involved; hence, rational individuals are likely to engage in free-riding on the monitoring and administration of sanctions. The solution to first-order free-riding can, therefore, generate a new set of negative externalities associated with the costs and problems of sanctioning conformity to prohibitions.

The solution to this second-order free-rider problem is to create *prescriptive norms,* or norms that indicate what is supposed to be done (rather than what cannot be done, or is prohibited), coupled with positive sanctioning for conformity. Such positive sanctions can become, in themselves, a joint good and a source of positive externalities; indeed, receipt of positive sanctions (approval, support, congratulatory statements, esteem, and the like) increases the utilities that rational actors experience. And so, as the costs or negative externalities of the first-order free-rider problem create a demand for prescriptive norms and positive sanctions, actors can enjoy enhanced benefits and reduced costs when they give up their control of some resources and behavioral alternatives to normative prescriptions. Actors thus develop an interest in prescriptive normative control, and it becomes rational for them to do so.

The problem with systems of prescriptive norms and positive sanctions is that they are only viable in relatively small groupings and dense networks where monitoring and sanctioning can be part of the normal interaction among actors as they pursue a common goal or produce a joint good.

Otherwise, the admission of positive sanctions becomes costly, as does the monitoring of conformity. High degrees of solidarity are thus only possible, Coleman argued, when relatively small numbers of actors give up control over their resources to prescriptive norms and rely heavily on positive sanctions that, themselves, become positive externalities that increases the utilities for actors.

PRINCIPLES OF GROUP SOLIDARITY:
SYNTHESIZING HECHTER'S
AND COLEMAN'S THEORIES

Coleman's theory arrives at the same place as Hechter's rational choice approach to solidarity does. This convergence of perspectives can perhaps best be appreciated by bringing the two theories together in composite form, as is done in the principles enumerated in Table 20-3. In this table,[12] the respective vocabularies of Hechter's and Coleman's schemes are mixed together in ways that emphasize the original contributions of each. What is true for solidarity, both would argue, is true for other emergent social and cultural phenomena. But let us concentrate on the four principles of solidarity.

Proposition I simply states Coleman's and Hechter's views on what causes actors to have an interest in creating norms. The key conditions are commonly experienced negative externalities, high rates of free-riding, and dependence of actors on each other for the production of a joint good that gives them utility. Under these conditions, actors will give up some of their rights of control. Proposition II summarizes the conditions that, in Hechter's terms, create extensive regulatory norms where actors relinquish a wide range of rights of control to group norms. The basic conditions under which such extensive norms emerge include interests in creating norms (which are activated by the conditions listed in Proposition I), the ratio of "consumption of" to "extrinsic compensation for" the production of a joint good (that is, the more members themselves consume the joint good, the greater their interest is in creating extensive norms), the dependence of actors on the utilities offered by the joint good is high, the proportion of actors who receive utilities from the production of a joint good is high, and rates of communication among actors are high (with such rates being negatively related to the number of actors involved and positively related to the density of their networks).

Proposition III then addresses the issue of the amount of proscriptive versus prescriptive content of the norms that actors create under the conditions specified in Propositions I and II. The fundamental forces increasing *prescriptive* content are the ability of actors to monitor each others' activities during the normal course of producing a joint good (which, in turn, is related to group size and density of networks), and the capacity to use positive instead of negative sanctions (which is related to the ability to use informal means of sanctioning).

Table 20.3 Principles of Social Solidarity

I. The level of interest in creating norms among actors who are producing a joint good increases with
   A. The intensity of negative externalities that they collectively experience.
   B. The rate of free-riding in the production of the joint good.
   C. The level of actors' dependence on the production of the joint good.
II. The extensiveness of the norms created by actors with an interest in regulating the production of a joint good increases with
   A. The actors' level of dependence on the production of the joint good.
   B. The degree to which actors consume the joint good that they produce.
   C. The proportion of all actors receiving utilities for the production of the joint good.
   D. The rates of communication among members engaged in the production of a joint good which, in turn, is
      1. Negatively related to the size of the group.
      2. Positively related to the density of network ties among members of the group.
III. The ratio of prescriptive to proscriptive content of norms regulating the production of a joint good increases with
   A. The capacity to lower the costs of monitoring conformity to normative obligations, which, in turn, is positively related to
      1. Rates of communication among actors.
      2. Density of network ties.
      3. Ratio of informal to formal monitoring.
      4. Ratio of informal to formal sanctioning.
      5. Ratio of positive to negative sanctioning.
   B. The ratio of positive to negative sanctioning, which, in turn, is positively related to the ratio of informal to formal sanctioning.
IV. The level of solidarity among actors producing a joint good is, therefore, likely to increase when
   A. The actors' dependence on the production of the joint good is high.
   B. The extensiveness of normative obligations is great.
   C. The ratio of prescriptive to proscriptive content of norms is high.
   D. The ratio of positive to negative sanctions is high.
   E. The costs for monitoring and sanctioning are low.
   F. The proportion of actors receiving utilities from the production of the joint good is high.

And finally, Proposition IV summarizes how the conditions stated in the first three propositions all come together to increase social solidarity. The basic conclusion is when the actors' dependence on the production of the joint good is high, when they develop extensive norms, when the ratio of prescriptive to proscriptive content of such norms is high, when the ratio of positive to negative sanctions is also high, and when the proportion of actors receiving utilities is high, then social solidarity will increase.

CONCLUSION

Rational choice theories connect sociology to economic theory and seek to do what early sociologists felt was impossible: to conceptualize emergent social forms and structures through the behaviors of rational, self-interest actors. The two theories examined in this chapter are among the best in meeting the challenge that sociology has posed for theories that begin with assumptions of individual rationality. Just whether or not their answer is satisfactory depends on whether one is receptive to the view that humans always behave in terms of utilities and rewards and that social organization can only be fully understood in these terms.

The two theorists examined in this chapter have been part of a broad, worldwide effort to use economic theory to explain cultural and social processes. Indeed, these rational choice approaches influence not just sociology but political science as well, and there is little doubt that they are here to stay. Sociology in the twenty-first century has reembraced what it had rejected at the beginning of the twentieth century.

NOTES

1. Adam Smith, *An Inquiry into the Nature and Causes of the Wealth of Nations* (Indianapolis: Liberty Fund, 1981; originally published in 1775–1776).

2. Adam Smith, *The Theory of Moral Sentiments* (Indianapolis: Liberty Fund, 1974; originally published in 1759, and later revised in light of the questions raised in *The Wealth of Nations*).

3. This approach has different names in other disciplines but the core ideas come from the models presented on the Web site for this book, where the incorporation of economic and game-theoretical models was introduced.

4. Michael Hechter, *Principles of Group Solidarity* (Berkeley: University of California Press, 1987); "Rational Choice Foundations of Social Order," in *Theory Building in Sociology,* ed. J.H. Turner (Newbury Park, CA: Sage, 1988).

5. Mancur Olson, *The Logic of Collective Action* (Cambridge, MA: Harvard University Press, 1965).

6. Hechter, *Principles of Group Solidarity* (cited in note 4), p. 49.

7. Ibid., p. 126.

8. Ibid., pp. 59–77, 104–124.

9. Ibid., pp. 126–146.

10. See, for examples of his earlier essay, James S. Coleman, *Individual Interests and Collective Action: Selected Essays* (Cambridge: Cambridge University Press, 1986).

11. James S. Coleman, *Foundations of Social Theory* (Cambridge, MA: Belknap, 1990).

12. See also Jonathan H. Turner, "The Production and Reproduction of Social Solidarity: A Synthesis of Two Rational Choice Theories," *Journal for the Theory of Social Behavior* 22 (1993), pp. 311–328.

＊

PART VI

Interactionist
Theorizing

21

Early Interactionist and Phenomenological Theory

The first sociological theorists in Europe were concerned primarily with macro-level phenomena, but with the beginning of the twentieth century, theorists in Europe and America turned to the analysis of micro-level processes. They began to understand that the structure of society is, in some ultimate sense, created and maintained by the actions and interactions of individuals; so increasingly, they sought to discover the fundamental processes of interaction among people. This burst of creative activity generated a wide range of micro-level theories that will, for the sake of simplicity, be labeled "interactionism." The rise of interactionism also marks the beginning of American theory as an active contributor to the theoretical canon of sociology. Hence, it is appropriate that we begin with the American contribution to interactionism, turning later to the European micro-oriented tradition that emerged in the early decades of this century.

EARLY AMERICAN INSIGHTS
INTO INTERACTION

A philosopher at the University of Chicago, George Herbert Mead (1863–1931), made the great breakthrough in understanding the basic properties of human social interaction. His was not a blazing new insight but, rather, a synthesis of ideas that had been developed by others. Yet, without his synthesis, the study of interaction would have been greatly retarded. To appreciate Mead's genius, let us first review those from whom he drew inspiration, then explore how he pieced their ideas into a model of interaction that still serves as the basic framework for most interactionist theories.

William James's Analysis of "Self"

The Harvard psychologist William James (1842–1910) was perhaps the first social scientist to develop a clear concept of self. James recognized that humans have the capacity to view themselves as objects and to develop self-feelings and attitudes toward themselves. Just as humans can (a) denote symbolically other people and aspects of the world around them, (b) develop attitudes and feelings toward these objects, and (c) construct typical responses toward objects, so they can denote themselves, develop self-feelings and attitudes, and construct responses toward themselves. James called these capacities *self* and recognized their importance in shaping the way people respond in the world.

James developed a typology of selves: the "material self," which includes those physical objects that humans view as part of their being and as crucial to their identity; the "social self," which involves the self-feelings that individuals derive from associations with other people; and the "spiritual self," which embraces the general cognitive style and capacities typifying an individual.[1] This typology was never adopted by subsequent interactionists, but James' notion of the social self became a part of all interactionists' formulations.

James's concept of the social self recognized that people's feelings about themselves arise from interaction with others. As he noted, "a man has as many social selves as there are individuals who recognize him."[2] Yet, James did not carry this initial insight very far. He was, after all, a psychologist who was more concerned with internal psychological functioning of individuals than with the social processes from which the capacities of individuals arise.

Charles Horton Cooley's Analysis of Self

Charles Horton Cooley (1864–1929) offered two significant extensions in the analysis of self.[3] First, he refined the concept, viewing self as the process in which individuals see themselves as objects, along with other objects, in their social environment. Second, he recognized that self emerges from communication with others. As individuals interact with each other, they interpret each other's gestures and thereby see themselves from the viewpoint of others. They imagine how others evaluate them, and they derive images of themselves or self-feelings and attitudes. Cooley termed this process *the looking glass self:* The gestures of others serve as mirrors in which people see and evaluate themselves, just as they see and evaluate other objects in their social environment.

Cooley also recognized that self arises from interaction in group contexts. He developed the concept of "primary group" to emphasize that participation in front of the looking glass in some groups is more important in the genesis and maintenance of self than participation in other groups. Those small groups in which personal and intimate ties exist are the most important in shaping people's self-feelings and attitudes.

Cooley thus refined and narrowed James's notion of self and forced the recognition that it arises from symbolic communication with others in group contexts. These insights profoundly influenced Mead.

John Dewey's Pragmatism

John Dewey (1859–1952) was, for a brief period, a colleague of Cooley's at the University of Michigan. But more important was Dewey's enduring association with Mead, whom he brought to the University of Chicago. As the chief exponent of a school of thought known as *pragmatism,* Dewey stressed the process of human adjustment to the world, in which humans constantly seek to master the conditions of their environment. Thus, the unique characteristics of humans arise from the *process* of adjusting to their life conditions.

What is unique to humans, Dewey argued, is their capacity for thinking. Mind is not a structure but a process that emerges from humans' efforts to adjust to their environment. Mind for Dewey is the process of denoting objects in the environment, ascertaining potential lines of conduct, imagining the consequences of pursuing each line, inhibiting inappropriate responses, and, then, selecting a line of conduct that will facilitate adjustment. Mind is thus the process of thinking, which involves deliberation:

> Deliberation is a dramatic rehearsal (in imagination) of various competing possible lines of action. . . . Deliberation is an experiment in finding out what the various lines of possible action are really like. It is an experiment in making various combinations of selected elements . . . to see what the resultant action would be like if it were entered upon.[4]

Dewey's conception of mind as a process of adjustment, rather than as a thing or entity, was critical in shaping Mead's thoughts. Much as Cooley had done for the concept of self, Dewey demonstrated that mind emerges and is sustained through interactions in the social world.

Mead's Thought on Pragmatism, Darwinism, and Behaviorism

At the time that Mead began to formulate his synthesis, the convergence of several intellectual traditions was crucial because it appears to have influenced the direction of his thought. Mead considered himself a behaviorist, but not of the mechanical stimulus/response type. Many of his ideas actually were intended as a refutation of such prominent behaviorists as John B. Watson. Mead accepted the basic premise of behaviorism—that is, the view that reinforcement guides and directs action. However, he used this principle in a novel way. Moreover, he rejected as untenable the methodological presumption of early behaviorism that it was inappropriate to study the internal dynamics of the human mind. James's, Cooley's, and Dewey's influence ensured that Mead would rework the principle of reinforcement in ways that allowed for the consideration of mind and self.

Another strain of thought that shaped Mead's synthesis is pragmatism, as it was acquired through exposure with Dewey. Pragmatism sees organisms as practical creatures that come to terms with the actual conditions of the world. Coupled with behaviorism, pragmatism offered a new way of viewing human life: Human beings seek to cope with their actual conditions, and they learn those behavioral patterns that provide gratification. The most important type of gratification is adjustment to social contexts.

This argument was buttressed in Mead's synthesis by yet another related intellectual tradition, Darwinism. Mead recognized that humans are organisms seeking a niche in which they can adapt. Historically, this was true of humans as an evolving species; more important, it is true of humans as they discover a niche in the social world. Mead's commitment to behaviorism and pragmatism thus allowed him to apply the basic principle of Darwinian theory to each human: That which facilitates survival or adaptation of the organism will be retained.

In this way, behaviorist, pragmatist, and Darwinian principles blended into an image of humans as attempting to adjust to the world around them and as retaining those characteristics—particularly mind and self—that enable them to adapt to their surroundings. Mind, self, and other unique features of humans evolve from efforts to survive in the social environment. They are thus capacities that arise from the processes of coping, adjusting, adapting, and achieving the ultimate gratification or reinforcement: survival. For this reason, Mead's analysis emphasizes the processes by which the infant organism acquires mind and self as an adaptation to society. But Mead did much more; he showed how society is viable only from the capacities for mind and self among individuals. From Mead's perspective, then, the capacities for mind, self, and society are intimately connected.

George Herbert Mead's Synthesis

The names of James, Cooley, and Dewey figure prominently in the development of interactionism, but Mead brought their related concepts together into a coherent theoretical perspective that linked the emergence of the human mind, the social self, and the structure of society to the process of social interaction.[5] Mead appears to have begun his synthesis with two basic assumptions: (1) the biological frailty of human organisms forces their cooperation with one another in group contexts to survive; and (2) those actions within and among human organisms that facilitate their cooperation, and hence their survival or adjustment, will be retained. Starting from these assumptions, Mead reorganized the concepts of others so that they denoted how mind, the social self, and society arise and are sustained through interaction.

Mind Following Dewey's lead, Mead recognized that the unique feature of the human mind is its capacity to (1) use symbols to designate objects in the environment, (2) rehearse covertly alternative lines of action toward these objects, and (3) inhibit inappropriate lines of action and select a proper course of overt action. Mead termed this process of using symbols or language covertly *imaginative rehearsal,* revealing his conception of mind as a *process* rather than as a structure. Further, Mead viewed the existence and persistence of society, or cooperation in organized groups, as dependent on this capacity of humans to imaginatively rehearse lines of action toward one another and thereby select those behaviors that facilitate cooperation.

Much of Mead's analysis focused not so much on the mind of mature organisms as on how this capacity first develops in individuals. Unless mind emerges in infants, neither society nor self can exist. In accordance with principles of behaviorism, Darwinism, and pragmatism, Mead stressed that mind arises from a selective process in which an infant's initially wide repertoire of random gestures is narrowed as some gestures bring favorable reactions from those on whom the infant depends for survival. Such selection of gestures facilitating adjustment can occur either through trial and error or through conscious coaching by those with whom the infant must cooperate. Eventually, through either of these processes, gestures come to have common meanings for both the infant and those in its environment. With this development, gestures now denote the same objects and carry similar disposition for all the parties to an interaction. Gestures that have such common meanings are termed *conventional gestures* by Mead. These conventional gestures have increased efficiency for interaction among individuals because they allow more precise communication of desires and wants as well as intended courses of action—thereby increasing the capacity of organisms to adjust to one another.

The ability to use and to interpret conventional gestures with common meanings represents a significant step in the development of mind, self, and society. By perceiving and interpreting gestures, humans can now assume the perspective (dispositions, needs, wants, and propensities to act) of those with whom they must cooperate for survival. By reading and then interpreting covertly conventional gestures, individuals can imaginatively rehearse alternative lines of action that will facilitate adjustment to others. Thus, by being able to put oneself in another's place, or to "take the role of the other," to use Mead's concept, the covert rehearsal of action reaches a new level of efficiency, because actors can better gauge the consequences of their actions for others and thereby increase the probability of cooperative interaction.

Thus, when an organism develops the capacity (1) to understand conventional gestures, (2) to employ these gestures to take the role of others, and (3) to imaginatively rehearse alternative lines of action, Mead believed that such an organism possesses "mind."

Self   Drawing from James and Cooley, Mead stressed that, just as humans can designate symbolically other actors in the environment, so they can symbolically represent themselves as objects. The interpretation of gestures, then, facilitates human cooperation and serves as the basis for self-assessment and evaluation. This capacity to derive images of oneself as an object of evaluation in interaction depends on the processes of mind. What Mead saw as significant about this process is that, as organisms mature, the transitory "self-images" derived from specific others in each interactive situation eventually become crystallized into a more or less stabilized "self-conception" of oneself as a certain type of object. With these self-conceptions, individuals' actions take on consistency because they are now mediated through a coherent and stable set of attitudes, dispositions, or meanings about oneself as a certain type of person.

Mead chose to highlight three stages in the development of self, each stage marking not only a change in the kinds of transitory self-images an individual can derive from role taking but also an increasing crystallization of a more stabilized self-conception. The initial stage of role taking in which self-images can be derived is termed *play*. In play, infant organisms are capable of assuming the perspective of only a limited number of others, at first only one or two. Later, by virtue of biological maturation and practice at role taking, the maturing organism becomes capable of taking the role of several others engaged in organized activity. Mead termed this stage the *game* because it designates the capacity to derive multiple self-images from, and to cooperate with, a group of individuals engaged in some coordinated activity. (Mead typically illustrated this stage by giving the example of a baseball game in which all individuals must symbolically assume the role of all others on the team to participate effectively.) The final stage in the development of self occurs when an individual can take the role of the "generalized other" or "community of attitudes" evident in a society. At this stage, individuals are seen as capable of assuming the overall perspective of a community, or general beliefs, values, and norms. This means that humans can both (1) increase the appropriateness of their responses to others with whom they must interact and (2) expand their evaluative self-images from the expectations of specific others to the standards and perspective of the broader community. Thus, it is this ever-increasing capacity to take roles with an ever-expanding body of others that marks the stages in the development of self.

Society Mead believed society or institutions represent the organized and patterned interactions among diverse individuals.[6] Such organization of interactions depends on mind. Without the capacities of mind to take roles and imaginatively rehearse alternative lines of activity, individuals could not coordinate their activities. Mead emphasized,

> The immediate effect of such role-taking lies in the control which the individual is able to exercise over his own response. The control of the action of the individual in a co-operative process can take place in the conduct of the individual himself if he can take the role of the other. It is this control of the response of the individual himself through taking the role of the other that leads to the value of this type of communication from the point of view of the organization of the conduct in the group.[7]

Society also depends on the capacities of self, especially the process of evaluating oneself from the perspective of the generalized other. Without the ability to see and evaluate oneself as an object from this community of attitudes, social control would rest solely on self-evaluations derived from role taking with specific and immediately present others—thus making coordination of diverse activities among larger groups extremely difficult.[8]

Although Mead was vitally concerned with how society and its institutions are maintained and perpetuated by the capacities of mind and self, these concepts also allowed him to view society as constantly in flux and rife with potential change. That role taking and imaginative rehearsal are ongoing processes among the participants in any interaction situation reveals the potential these processes give individuals for adjusting and readjusting their responses. Furthermore, the insertion of self as an object into the interactive process underscores that the outcome of interaction will be affected by the ways in which self-conceptions alter the initial reading of gestures and the subsequent rehearsal of alternative lines of behavior. Such a perspective thus emphasizes that social organization is both perpetuated by and altered through the adjustive capacities of mind and the mediating impact of self:

> Thus, the institutions of society are organized forms of group or social activity—forms so organized that the individual members of society can act adequately and socially by taking the attitudes of others toward these activities. . . . [But] there is no necessary or inevitable reason why social institutions should be oppressive or rigidly conservative, or why they should not rather be, as many are, flexible and progressive, fostering individuality rather than discouraging it.[9]

This passage contains a clue to Mead's abiding distaste for rigid and oppressive patterns of social organization. He viewed society as a *constructed* phenomenon that arises from the adjustive interactions among individuals. As such, society can be altered or reconstructed through the processes denoted by the concepts of mind and self. However, Mead went one step further and stressed that change is frequently unpredictable, even by those emitting the change-inducing behavior. To account for this indeterminacy of action, Mead used two concepts first developed by James, the "I" and the "me."[10] For Mead, the "I" points to the impulsive tendencies of individuals, and the "me" represents the self-image of behavior after it has been emitted. With these concepts Mead emphasized that the "I," or impulsive behavior, cannot be predicted because the individual can only "know in experience" (the "me") what has actually transpired and what the consequences of the "I" have been.

In sum, then, Mead believed society represents those constructed patterns of coordinated activity that are maintained by, and changed through, symbolic interaction among and within actors. Both the maintenance and the change of society, therefore, occur through the processes of mind and self. Although Mead views many of the interactions causing both stability and change in groups as predictable, the possibility for spontaneous and unpredictable actions that alter existing patterns of interaction is also likely.

This conceptual legacy had a profound impact on a generation of American sociologists after the posthumous publication of Mead's lectures in

1934. Yet, despite the suggestiveness of Mead's concepts, they failed to address some important theoretical issues.

The most important of these issues concerns the vagueness of his concepts in denoting the nature of social organization or society and the precise points of articulation between society and the individual. Mead viewed society as organized activity, regulated by the generalized other, in which individuals make adjustments and cooperate with one another. Such adjustments and the cooperation are seen as possible by virtue of the capacities of mind and self. Whereas mind and self emerged from existent patterns of social organization, the maintenance or change of such organization was viewed by Mead as a reflection of the processes of mind and self. Although these and related concepts of the Meadian scheme point to the mutual interaction of society and the individual and although the concepts of mind and self denote crucial processes through which this dependency is maintained, they do not allow the analysis of variations in social organization and in the ways that individuals are implicated in these patterns.

Conceptualizing Structure and Role

Though Mead's synthesis provided the initial conceptual breakthrough, it did not satisfactorily resolve the problem of how participation in the *structure* of society shapes individual conduct, and vice versa. In an effort to resolve this vagueness, sociological inquiry began to focus on the concept of role. Individuals were seen as playing roles associated with positions in larger networks of positions. With this vision, efforts to understand more about social structures and how individuals are implicated in them intensified during the 1920s and 1930s. This line of inquiry became known as *role theory.*

Robert Park's Role Theory   Robert Park (1864–1944), who came to the University of Chicago near the end of Mead's career, was one of the first to extend Mead's ideas through an emphasis on roles. As Park observed, "everybody is always and everywhere, more or less consciously, playing a role."[11] But Park stressed that roles are linked to structural positions in society and that self is intimately linked to playing roles within the confines of the positions of social structure:

> The conceptions which men form of themselves seem to depend upon their vocations, and in general upon the role they seek to play in communities and social groups in which they live, as well as upon the recognition and status which society accords them in these roles. It is status, i.e., recognition by the community, that confers upon the individual the character of a person, since a person is an individual who has status, not necessarily legal, but social.[12]

Park's analysis stressed that self emerges from the multiple roles that people play.[13] In turn, roles are connected to positions in social structures. This kind of analysis shifts attention to the nature of society and how its structure influences the processes outlined in Mead's synthesis.

Jacob Moreno's Role Theory Inspired in part by Mead's concept of role taking and by his own earlier studies in Europe, Jacob Moreno (1892–1974) was one of the first to develop the concept of role playing. In *Who Shall Survive* and in many publications in the journals that he founded in America, Moreno began to view social organization as a network of roles that constrain and channel behavior.[14] In his early works, Moreno distinguished different types of roles: (a) "psychosomatic roles," in which behavior is related to basic biological needs, as conditioned by culture, and in which role enactment is typically unconscious; (b) "psychodramatic roles," in which individuals behave in accordance with the specific expectations of a particular social context; and (c) "social roles," in which individuals conform to the more general expectations of various conventional social categories (for example, worker, Christian, mother, and father).

Despite the suggestiveness of these distinctions, their importance comes not so much from their substantive content as from their intent: to conceptualize social structures as organized networks of expectations that require varying types of role enactments by individuals. In this way, analysis can move beyond the vague Meadian conceptualization of society as coordinated activity regulated by the generalized other to a conceptualization of social organization as various *types* of interrelated role enactments regulated by varying *types* of expectations.

Ralph Linton's Role Theory Shortly after Moreno's publication of *Who Shall Survive,* the anthropologist Ralph Linton (1893–1953) further conceptualized the nature of social organization, and the individual's embeddedness in it, by distinguishing among the concepts of role, status, and individuals:

> A status, as distinct from the individual who may occupy it, is simply a collection of rights and duties. . . . A *role* represents the dynamic aspect of status. The individual is socially assigned to a status and occupies it with relation to other statuses. When he puts the rights and duties which constitute the status into effect, he is performing a role.[15]

This passage contains several important conceptual distinctions. Social structure reveals several distinct elements: (a) a network of positions, (b) a corresponding system of expectations, and (c) patterns of behavior that are enacted for the expectations of particular networks of interrelated positions. In retrospect, these distinctions might appear self-evident and trivial, but they made possible the subsequent elaboration of many interactionist concepts:

1. Linton's distinctions allow us to conceptualize society as clear-cut variables: the nature and kinds of interrelations among positions and the types of expectations attending these positions.

2. The variables Mead denoted by the concepts of mind and self can be analytically distinguished from both social structure (positions and expectations) and behavior (role enactment).

3. By conceptually separating the processes of role taking and imaginative rehearsal from both social structure and behavior, the points of articulation

between society and the individual can be more clearly marked, because role taking pertains to covert interpretations of the expectations attending networks of statuses and role denotes the enactment of these expectations as mediated by self.

Thus, by offering more conceptual insight into the nature of social organization, Park, Moreno, and Linton provided a needed supplement to Mead's suggestive concepts. Now, it would be possible to understand more precisely the interrelations among mind, self, and society.

THE RISE OF SYMBOLIC INTERACTIONISM

The first well-developed theoretical perspective to emerge from Mead's synthesis was "symbolic interactionism," a term coined by Herbert Blumer (1900-1987) who took over Mead's social psychology course after Mead's death and who for some fifty years championed a particular interpretation of Mead's ideas. Blumer's advocacy did not go unchallenged, however, and an alternative school of thought emerged at the State University of Iowa, a challenge led by several scholars but principally by Manford Kuhn. The poles around which these two and their allies debated have been labeled the Iowa and Chicago Schools of symbolic interactionism.[16] These labels are misleading because Blumer had left Chicago by midcentury, and Kuhn died shortly thereafter. Moreover, much of the Iowa School tradition had shifted to symbolic interactionists at Indiana University by the 1960s, and so the Iowa-Chicago School dichotomy is more a label of convenience than a real indication of *where* the debate occurred. Still, in the 1950s and 1960s, the debate about how to develop theoretical explanations among those who identified with Mead's legacy was intense, if somewhat dispersed among universities. Indeed, today this very same debate has been replicated by new protagonists.

Despite points of disagreement, all symbolic interactionists share a common legacy of assumptions taken from Mead. These points of convergence are what make symbolic interactionism a distinctive theoretical perspective.[17]

Humans as Symbol Users Symbolic interactionists, as their name implies, place enormous emphasis on the capacity of humans to create and use symbols. In contrast with other animals, whose symbolic capacities are limited or nonexistent, the very essence of humans and the world that they create flows from their ability to symbolically represent one another, objects, ideas, and virtually any phase of their experience. Without the capacity to create symbols and to use them in human affairs, patterns of social organization among humans could not be created, maintained, or changed. Humans have become, to a very great degree, liberated from instinctual and biological programming and thus must rely on their symbol-using powers to adapt and survive in the world.

Symbolic Communication Humans use symbols to communicate with one another. By virtue of their capacity to agree on the meaning of vocal and bodily gestures, humans can effectively communicate. Symbolic communication is, of course, extremely complex, because people use more than word or language symbols in communication. They also use facial gestures, voice tones, body countenance, and other symbolic gestures that have common meaning and understanding.

Interaction and Role Taking By reading and interpreting the gestures of others, humans communicate and interact. They become able to mutually read each other, to anticipate each other's responses, and to adjust to each other. Mead termed this basic capacity "taking the role of the other," or role taking— the ability to see the other's attitudes and dispositions to act. Interactionists still emphasize the process of role taking as the basic mechanism by which interaction occurs. For example, the late Arnold Rose, who was one of the leaders of contemporary interactionism, indicated that role taking "means that the individual communicator imagines—evokes within himself—how the recipient understands that communication."[18] Or, as another modern interactionist, Sheldon Stryker, has emphasized, role taking is "anticipating the responses of others with one in some social act."[19] And, as Alfred Lindesmith and Anselm Strauss stressed, role taking is "imaginatively assuming the position or point of view of another person."[20]

Without the ability to read gestures and to use these gestures as a basis for putting oneself in the position of others, interaction could not occur. And, without interaction, social organization could not exist.

Interaction, Humans, and Society Just as Mead emphasized that mind, self, and society are intimately connected, so symbolic interactionists analyzed the relation between the genesis of "humanness" and patterns of interaction. What makes humans unique as a species and enables each individual to possess distinctive characteristics is the result of interaction in society. Conversely, what makes society possible are the capacities that humans acquire as they grow and mature in society.

Symbolic interactionists tended to emphasize the same human capacities as Mead: the genesis of mind and self. Mind is the capacity to think—to symbolically denote, weigh, assess, anticipate, map, and construct courses of action. Although Mead's term, *mind,* is rarely used today, the processes that this term denotes are given great emphasis. As Rose indicated, "Thinking is the process by which possible symbolic solutions and other future courses of action are examined, assessed for their relative advantages and disadvantages in terms of the values of the individual, and one of them chosen for action."[21]

Moreover, the concept of mind has been reformulated to embrace what W. I. Thomas (1863–1947) termed the *definition of the situation.*[22] With the capacities of mind, actors can name, categorize, and orient themselves to constellations of objects—including themselves as objects—in all situations. In this way they can assess, weigh, and sort out appropriate lines of conduct.[23]

compare w/ gender roles...

Table 21.1 Covergence and Divergence in the Chicago and Iowa Schools of Symbolic Interactionism

Theoretical Issues	Convergence of Schools
The nature of ~~humans~~ *gender roles*	Humans create and use symbols to denote aspects of the world around them. What makes humans unique are their symbolic capacities. Humans are capable of symbolically denoting and invoking objects, which can then shape their definitions of social situations and, hence, their actions. Humans are capable of self-reflection and evaluation. They see themselves as objects in most social situations.
The nature of interaction	Interaction depends on people's capacities to emit and interpret gestures. Role taking is the key mechanism of interaction because it enables actors to view the other's perspective, as well as that of others and groups not physically present. Role taking and mind operate together by allowing actors to use the perspectives of others and groups as a basis for their deliberations, or definitions of situations, before acting. In this way, people can adjust their responses to each other and to social situations.
The nature of social organization	Social structure is created, maintained, and changed by processes of symbolic interaction. It is not possible to understand patterns of social organization—even the most elaborate—without knowledge of the symbolic processes among individuals who ultimately make up this pattern.
The nature of sociological methods	Sociological methods must focus on the processes by which people define situations and select courses of action. Methods must focus on individual persons.
The nature of sociological theory	Theory must be about processes of interaction and seek to isolate out the conditions under which general types of behaviors and interactions are likely to occur.

**Table 21.1 Covergence and Divergence in the Chicago
and Iowa Schools of Symbolic Interactionism** *(continued)*

Divergence of Schools Chicago School	Convergence of Schools Iowa School
Humans with minds can introject any object into a situation.	Humans with minds can define situations, but there tends to be consistency in the objects that they introject into situations.
Although self is an important object, it is not the only object.	Self is the most important object in the definition of a situation.
Humans weigh, assess, and map courses of action before action, but humans can potentially alter their definitions and actions.	Humans weigh, assess, and map course of action but they do so through the prisms of their core self and the groups in which this self is anchored.
Interaction is a constant process of role taking with others and groups.	Interaction depends on the process of role taking.
Others and groups thus becomes objects that are involved in people's definitions of situations.	The expectations of others and norms of the situation are important considerations in arriving at definitions of situations.
Self is another important object that enters into people's definitions.	People's core self is the most important consideration and constraint on interaction.
People's definitions of situations involve weighing and assessing objects and then mapping courses of action.	
Interaction involves constantly shifting definitions and changing patterns of action and interaction.	Interaction most often involves actions that conform to situational expectations as mitigated by the requirements of the core self.
Social structure is constructed by actors adjusting their responses to each other.	Social structures are composed of networks of positions with attendant expectations or norms.
Social structure is one of many objects that actors introject into their definitions of situations.	Although symbolic interactions create and change structures, once these structures are created they constrain interaction.
Social structure is subject to constant realignments as actors' definitions and behaviors change, forcing new adjustments from others.	Social structures are thus relatively stable, especially when people's core self is invested in particular networks of positions.
Sociological methods must penetrate the actors' mental world and see how they construct courses of action.	Sociological methods must measure with reliable instruments actors' symbolic processes.
Researchers must be attuned to the multiple, varied, ever-shifting, and often indeterminate influences on definitions of situations and actions.	Research should be directed toward defining and measuring those variables that causally influence behaviors.
Research must therefore use observational, geographical, and unstructured interview techniques if it is to penetrate people's definitional processes and consider changes in these processes.	Research must therefore use structured measuring instruments, such as questionnaires, to get reliable and valid measures of key variables.
Only sensitizing concepts are possible in sociology.	Sociology can develop precisely defined concepts with clear empirical measures.
Deductive theory is thus not possible in sociology.	Theory can thus be deductive, with a limited number of general propositions subsuming lower-order propositions and empirical generalizations on specific phases of symbolic interaction.
At best, theory can offer general and tentative descriptions and interpretations of behaviors and patterns of interaction.	Theory can offer abstract explanations that can allow predictions of behavior and interactions.

As the concept of the definition of the situation underscores, self remains the key concept in the interactionist literature. Emphasis in the interactionist orientation is on (a) the emergence of self-conceptions—relatively stable and enduring conceptions that people have about themselves—and (b) the ability to derive self-images—pictures of oneself as an object in social situations. Self is thus a major object that people inject into their definitions of situations. It shapes much of what people see, feel, and do in the world around them.

Society, or relatively stable patterns of interaction, is seen by interactionists as possible only by virtue of people's capacities to define situations and, most particularly, to view themselves as objects in situations. Society can exist by virtue of human capacities for thinking and defining as well as for self-reflection and evaluation.

In sum, these points of emphasis constitute the core of the interactionist approach. Yet, there are many points of disagreement among symbolic interactions with respect to not only substantive issues but methodological and theoretical ones as well. In Table 21.1, the points of agreement are listed in the second column on the left, and the points of disagreement are delineated in the two right columns. For the most part, those leaning toward the Iowa pole see social structures of positions and roles as more constraining than do those at the Chicago pole. Along with this emphasis on constraints of social structure, the other major arena of disagreement is over the nature of methods and theory, where some emphasize more precise methods and formal theory while others stress more observational methods using sensitizing concepts to offer descriptions of events.

EARLY EUROPEAN INSIGHTS

Georg Simmel's Analysis of Interaction

Georg Simmel was perhaps the first European sociologist to begin a serious exploration of interaction, or "sociability" as he called it. In so doing, he elevated the study of interaction from the taken-for-granted.[24] For Simmel, as for the first generation of American sociologists in Chicago, the macrostructures and processes studied by functional and some conflict theories—class, the state, family, religion, evolution—are ultimately reflections of the specific interactions among people. These interactions result in emergent social phenomena, but considerable insight into the latter can be attained by understanding the basic interactive processes that first give and then sustain their existence.

In Chapter 8, Simmel's analysis of the forms of conflict were summarized, and in Chapter 16, his exchange theory was summarized. But Simmel's study of interaction extends beyond just the analysis of conflict and exchange—he was concerned with understanding the forms and consequences of many diverse types of interactions. Some of his most important insights, which influenced American interactionists, concern the relationship between the individual and society. In his famous essay on "the web of group affiliations," for example, Simmel emphasized that human personality emerges from, and is shaped by, the particular configuration of a person's group affiliations.[25] What people are—that is, how they think of themselves and are prepared to act—is circumscribed by their group memberships. As he emphasized, "the genesis of the personality [is] the point of intersection for innumerable social influences, as the end-product of heritages derived from the most diverse groups and periods of adjustment."[26]

Although Simmel did not analyze the emergence of human personality in great detail, his "formal sociology" did break away from the macro concerns of early German, French, and British sociologists. He began a mode of analysis in Europe that became the prime concern of the first generation of American sociologists. Simmel thus could be considered one of the first European interactionists.

Émile Durkheim's Metamorphosis

In *Division of Labor in Society,* Émile Durkheim portrayed social reality as an emergent phenomenon, *sui generis,* and as not reducible to the psychic states of individuals. Yet, in his later works, such as *The Elementary Forms of the Religious Life,* Durkheim began to ask, How does society rule the individual? How is it that society "gets inside" individuals and guides them from within? Why do people share common orientations and perspectives?[27] Durkheim never answered these questions effectively because his earlier emphasis on social structures prevented him from seeing the micro reality of interactions among individuals as created in macro social structures. But it is significant that the most forceful advocate of the sociologistic position became intrigued with the relationship between the individual and society. Two critical lines of interactionist thought emerged from *Elementary Forms:* (1) the analysis of ritual and (2) the concern with categories of thought.

1. As Durkheim became interested in the ultimate basis of social solidarity, he turned to the analysis of religion in simple societies. From his reading of secondary accounts on aborigines in Australia, he concluded in *Elementary Forms* that religious worship is, actually, the worship of society, a worship that is sustained by imputing a sacredness to the force of society as it constrained members and that is emotionally charged by the enactment of rituals. Thus, the basic behavioral mechanism by which solidarity is created and sustained, Durkheim argued, is the enactment of rituals that focus people's attention, arouse emotions, and create a common sense of solidarity. Durkheim never pursued the implications of this insight for the study of interaction, but later theorists began to recognize that interpersonal rituals are a key mechanism for creating and sustaining patterns of interaction. And some even asserted that the ultimate bases of macrostructures are chains of interaction rituals.[28]

2. The concern with thought in *Elementary Forms* also influenced social theory. Durkheim emphasized that "the collective conscience" is not "entirely outside us" and that people's definitions of, and orientations to,

situations are related to the organization of subjective consciousness. The categories of this consciousness, however, reflect the structural arrangements of society. Hence, varying macro structures generate different forms of thought and perception of the world. Such forms feed back and reinforce social structures.

The first line of thought exerted considerable influence in interactionist thinking, whereas the second formed the core idea behind much "structuralist" social theory (see Part VII). Although Durkheim's ideas on ritual and categories of thought were never as rigorously or systematically developed as his earlier work on macro processes (see Chapter 2 on the emergence of functionalism), these were perhaps his most original ideas.

Max Weber's Analysis of "Social Action"

Max Weber was also becoming increasingly concerned with the micro social world, although his most important insights were in macro and historical sociology. Yet, Weber's definition of sociology was highly compatible with the flourishing American school of interactionism. For Weber, sociology is "that science which aims at the interpretative understanding of social behavior in order to gain an explanation of its causes, its course, and its effects."[29] Moreover, the behavior to be studied by sociology is seen by Weber as social action that includes

> All human behavior when and insofar as the acting individual attaches a subjective meaning to it. Action in this sense may be overt, purely inward, or subjective; it may consist of positive intervention in a situation, of deliberately refraining from such intervention, or passively acquiescing in the situation. Action is social insofar as by virtue of the subjective meaning attached to it by the acting individual (or individuals), it takes account of the behavior of others and is thereby oriented in its course.[30]

Thus, Weber recognized that the reality behind the macrostructures of society—classes, the state, institutions, and nations—are the meaningful and symbolic interactions among people. Moreover, Weber's methodology stresses the need for understanding macrostructures and processes "at the level of meaning." In the real world, actors interpret and give meaning to the reality around them and act on the basis of these meanings. Yet, despite this key insight, Weber's actual analysis of social structures—class, status, party, change, religion, bureaucracy, and the like—rarely follows his own methodological prescriptions. As with other European thinkers, he tended to focus on social and cultural *structures* and the impact of these structures on one another. The interacting and interpreting person is often lost amid Weber's elaborate taxonomies of structures and analyses of historical events. This failing attracted the attention of Alfred Schutz (1899–1959), who, more than any other European thinker, translated phenomenology into a perspective that could be incorporated into interactionist theory.

European Phenomenology

Phenomenology[31] began as the project of the German philosopher Edmund Husserl (1859–1938). In his hands, this project showed few signs of being anything more than an orgy of subjectivism.[32] The German social thinker Schutz, however, took Husserl's concepts and transformed them into an interactionist analysis that has exerted considerable influence on modern-day interactionism. Schutz's migration to the United States in 1939 facilitated this translation, especially as he was exposed to American interactionism, but his most important ideas were formulated before he came. His subsequent work in America involved an elaboration of basic ideas originally developed in Europe.

Edmund Husserl's Project Husserl's ideas have been selectively borrowed and used in ways that he would not have condoned to develop modern phenomenology and various forms of interactionist thought. In reviewing Husserl's contribution, therefore, it is best to focus more on what was borrowed than on the details of his complete philosophical scheme. With this goal in mind, several features of his work can be highlighted: (1) the basic philosophical dilemma, (2) the properties of consciousness, (3) the critique of naturalistic empiricism, and (4) the philosophical alternative to social science.[33]

1. Basic questions confronting all inquiry are these: What is real? What actually exists in the world? How is it possible to know what exists? For the philosopher Husserl, these were central questions that required attention. Husserl reasoned that humans know about the world only through experience. All notions of an external world, "out there," are mediated through the senses and can be known only through mental consciousness. The existence of other people, values, norms, and physical objects is always mediated by experiences as these register on people's conscious awareness. One does not directly have contact with reality; contact is always indirect and mediated through the processes of the human mind.

   Because the process of consciousness is so important and central to knowledge, philosophic inquiry must first attempt to understand how this process operates and how it influences human affairs. This concern with the process of consciousness—of how experience creates a sense of an external reality—became the central concern of phenomenology.

2. Husserl initially referred to the "world of the natural attitude." Later he used the phrase *lifeworld*. In either case, with these concepts he emphasized that humans operate in a taken-for-granted world that permeates their mental life. It is the world that humans sense to exist and is composed of the objects, people, places, ideas, and other things that people see and perceive as setting the parameters for their existence, for their activities, and for their pursuits.

   This lifeworld or world of the natural attitude *is* reality for humans. Two features of Husserl's conception of natural attitude influenced modern interactionist thought: (a) The lifeworld is taken for granted. It is rarely the topic of reflective thought, and yet it structures and shapes the way people act and think. (b) Humans operate on the presumption that they experience the same world. Because people experience only their own consciousness, they have little capacity to directly determine if this presumption is correct. Yet people act *as if* they experienced a common world.

Human activity, then, is conducted in a lifeworld that is taken for granted and that is presumed to be experienced collectively. This brought Husserl back to his original problem: How do humans break out of their lifeworld and ascertain what is real? If people's lifeworld structures their consciousness and their actions, how is an objective science of human behavior and organization possible? These questions led Husserl to criti-cize what he termed *naturalistic science.*

3. Science assumes that a factual world exists, independent of, and external to, human senses and consciousness. Through the scientific method, this factual world can be directly known. With successive efforts at its measurement, increasing understanding of its properties can be ascertained. But Husserl challenged this vision of science: If one can know only through consciousness and if consciousness is structured by an implicit lifeworld, then how can objective measurement of some external and real world be possible? How can science measure objectively an external world when the only world that individuals experience is the lifeworld of their consciousness?

4. Husserl's solution to this problem is a philosophical one. He advocated what he termed the search for the *essence of consciousness.* To understand social events, the basic process through which these events are mediated—that is, consciousness—must be comprehended. The substantive *content* of consciousness, or the lifeworld, is not what is important; the abstract processes of consciousness, per se, are to be the topic of philosophic inquiry.

Husserl advocated what he termed the *radical abstraction of the individual* from interpersonal experience. Investigators must suspend their natural attitude and seek to understand the fundamental processes of consciousness, per se. One must discover, in Husserl's words, "Pure Mind." To do this, it is necessary to perform "epoch"—that is, to see if the substance of one's lifeworld can be suspended. Only when divorced from the substance of the lifeworld can the fundamental and abstract properties of consciousness be exposed and understood. With understanding of these properties, real insight into the nature of reality would be possible. If all that humans know is presented through consciousness, it is necessary to understand the nature of consciousness in abstraction from the specific substance or content of the lifeworld.

Husserl was not advocating Weber's method of *verstehen,* or sympathetic introspection into an investigator's own mind. Nor was Husserl suggesting the unstructured and intuitive search for people's definitions of situations. These methods would, he argued, only produce data on the substance of the lifeworld and would be no different than the structured measuring instruments of positivism. Rather, Husserl's goal was to create an abstract theory of consciousness that bracketed out, or suspended, any presumption of "an external social world out there."

Not surprisingly, Husserl's philosophical doctrine failed. He never succeeded in developing an abstract theory of consciousness, radically abstracted from the lifeworld. But his ideas set into motion a new line of thought that became the basis for modern phenomenology and for its elaboration into ethnomethodology and other forms of theory.

Alfred Schutz's Phenomenological Interactionism Schutz migrated to the United States in 1939 from Austria, after spending a year in Paris. With his interaction in American intellectual circles and the translation of his early works into English, Schutz's contribution to sociological theorizing has become increasingly recognized.[34]

This contribution resided in his ability to blend Husserl's radical phenomenology with Weber's action theory and American interactionism. This blend, in turn, stimulated the further development of phenomenology, the emergence of ethnomethodology, and the refinement of other interactionist theoretical perspectives.

Schutz's work began with a critique of his compatriot Weber, who employed the concept of social action in his many and varied inquiries.[35] Social action occurs when actors are consciously aware of each other and attribute meanings to their common situation. For Weber, then, a science of society must seek to understand social reality "at the level of meaning." Sociological inquiry must penetrate people's consciousness and discover how they view, define, and see the world. Weber advocated the method of *verstehen,* or sympathetic introspection. Investigators must become sufficiently involved in situations to be able to get inside the subjective world of actors. Causal and statistical analysis of complex social structures would be incomplete and inaccurate without such *verstehen* analysis.

Schutz's first major work addressed Weber's conception of action. Schutz's analysis is critical and detailed, and need not be summarized here except to note that the basic critique turns on Weber's failure to use his *verstehen* method and to explore *why,* and through what processes, actors come to share common meanings. In Schutz's eye, Weber simply assumed that actors share subjective meanings, leading Schutz to ask, Why and how do actors come to acquire common subjective states in a situation? How do they create a common view of the world? This is the problem of "intersubjectivity," and it is central to Schutz's intellectual scheme.

Schutz departed immediately from Husserl's strategy of holding the individual in radical abstraction and of searching for Pure Mind or the abstract laws of consciousness. He accepted Husserl's notion that humans hold a natural attitude and lifeworld that is taken for granted and that shapes who they are and what they will do. He also accepted Husserl's notion that people perceive that they share the same lifeworld and act *as if* they lived in a common world of experiences and sensations. Moreover, Schutz acknowledged the power of Husserl's argument that social scientists cannot know about an external social world out there independently of their own lifeworld.[36]

Having accepted these lines of thought from Husserl, however, Schutz advocated Weber's strategy of sympathetic introspection into people's consciousness. Only by observing people in interaction, rather than in radical abstraction, can the processes whereby actors come to share the same world be discovered. Social science cannot understand how and why actors create a common subjective world independently of watching them do so. This abandonment of Husserl's phenomenological project liberated phenomenology from philosophy and allowed sociologists to study empirically what Schutz considered the most important social reality: the creation and maintenance of intersubjectivity—that is, a common subjective world among pluralities of interacting individuals.[37]

Unfortunately, Schutz died just as he was beginning a systematic synthesis of his ideas; as a result, only a somewhat fragmented but suggestive framework is evident in his collective work. But his early analysis of Weber, Husserl, and interactionism led to a concern with some key issues: (1) How do actors create a common subjective world? (2) What implications does this creation have for how social order is maintained?

All humans, Schutz asserted, carry in their minds rules, social recipes, conceptions of appropriate conduct, and other information that allows them to act in their social world. Extending Husserl's concept of lifeworld, Schutz views the sum of these rules, recipes, conceptions, and information as the individual's "stock knowledge at hand." Such stock knowledge gives people a frame of reference or orientation with which they can interpret events as they pragmatically act on the world around them.

Several features of this stock knowledge at hand are given particular emphasis by Schutz:

1. People's reality *is* their stock knowledge. For the members of a society, stock knowledge constitutes a "paramount reality"—a sense of an absolute reality that shapes and guides all social events. Actors use this stock knowledge and sense of reality as they pragmatically seek to deal with others in their environment.

2. The existence of stock knowledge that bestows a sense of reality on events gives the social world, as Schutz agreed with Husserl, a taken-for-granted character. The stock knowledge is rarely the object of conscious reflection but, rather, an implicit set of assumptions and procedures that are silently used by individuals as they interact.

3. Stock knowledge is learned. It is acquired through socialization within a common social and cultural world, but it becomes *the* reality for actors in this world.

4. People operate under a number of assumptions that allow them to create a sense of a "reciprocity of perspectives." That is, others with whom an actor must deal are considered to share an actor's stock knowledge at

hand. And, although these others might have unique components in their stock knowledge because of their particular biographies, they can be ignored by actors.

5. The existence of stock knowledge, its acquisition through socialization, and its capacity to promote reciprocity of perspectives all give actors in a situation a *sense* or *presumption* that the world is the same for all and that it reveals identical properties for all. What often holds society together is this presumption of a common world.

6. The presumption of a common world allows actors to engage in the process of typification. Action in most situations, except the most personal and intimate, can proceed through mutual typification as actors use their stock knowledge to categorize one another and to adjust their responses to these typifications.[38] With typification, actors can effectively deal with their world; every nuance and characteristic of their situations do not have to be examined. Moreover, typification facilitates entrance into the social world; it simplifies adjustment because humans can treat each other as categories, or as "typical" objects of a particular kind.

These points of emphasis in Schutz's thought represented a blending of ideas from European phenomenology and American interactionism. The emphasis on stock knowledge is clearly borrowed from Husserl, but it is highly compatible with Mead's notion of the generalized other. The concern with the taken-for-granted character of the world as it is shaped by stock knowledge is also borrowed from Husserl but is similar to early interactionists' discussions of habit and routine behaviors. The emphasis on the acquired nature of stock knowledge coincides with early interactionists' discussions of the socialization process. The concern with the reciprocity of perspectives and with the process of typification owes much to Husserl and Weber but is compatible with Mead's notion of role taking, by which actors read one another's role and perspective.

But the major departure from much interactionist theory should also be emphasized: Actors operate on an unverified *presumption* that they share a common world, and this *sense* of a common world and the practices that produce this sense are crucial in maintaining social order. In other words, social organization might be possible not so much by the substance and content of stock knowledge, by the reciprocity of perspectives, or by successful typification as by the presumption actors share intersubjective states. Schutz did not carry this line of inquiry far, but he inspired new avenues of phenomenological inquiry.

CONCLUSION

Given its diverse sources, interactionist theorizing diverged in many directions by the twentieth century's end, although the poles of this divergence and diversity were at one time labelled the Chicago and Iowa Schools of symbolic interactionism, as was summarized in Table 21.1 on page 354–355. At first, however, those who extended Mead's synthesis and those who expanded on the idea of role stayed within the broad parameters of Mead's views, but by the 1960s, new lines of interactionist thinking began to emerge, inspired more by the European masters than by Mead and those who had followed Mead in America. Thus, as interactionism matured at the midcentury, it might have exhausted the Meadian legacy, and, to a degree, purely Meadian microsociology began to stagnate. Indeed, actual theorizing began to take a back seat to debates on the methodology of inquiry, particularly about whether or not a science of interaction was appropriate. At the same time, however, those following the Meadian tradition conducted interesting empirical work. Nonetheless, new theory within the strictly Meadian framework became increasingly hard to find in the literature.

As Mead-inspired interactionism stagnated, however, new alternatives emerged and reinvigorated the study of interaction. Today, it would be hard to visualize a coherent interactionist orientation. New micro-level ideas and interesting extensions and elaborations of old ones are still emerging, as we will see, but the midcentury coherence in the study of interaction has been lost. Yet, by the beginning of the new century, it would be reasonable to conclude that the process of interaction is probably the best-understood dimension of the social universe. So what might seem like stagnation could, actually, be the natural slowdown that occurs whenever more complete knowledge of a phenomenon is achieved.

NOTES

1. William James, *The Principles of Psychology* (New York: Henry Holt, 1890), vol. 1, pp. 292–299.

2. Ibid., p. 294.

3. Charles Horton Cooley, *Human Nature and the Social Order* (New York: Scribner's, 1902) and *Social Organization: A Study of the Larger Mind* (New York: Scribner's, 1916).

4. John Dewey, *Human Nature and Human Conduct* (New York: Henry Holt, 1922), p. 190. For an earlier statement of these ideas, see John Dewey, *Psychology* (New York: Harper & Row, 1886).

5. Mead's most important sociological ideas can be found in the published lecture notes of his students. His most important exposition of interactionism is found in his *Mind, Self, and Society*, ed. C.W. Morris (Chicago: University

of Chicago Press, 1934). Other useful sources include George Herbert Mead, *Selected Writings* (Indianapolis: Bobbs-Merrill, 1964); and Anselm Strauss, ed., *George Herbert Mead on Social Psychology* (Chicago: University of Chicago Press, 1964). For excellent secondary sources on the thought of Mead, see Tamotsu Shibutani, *Society and Personality: An Interactionist Approach* (Englewood Cliffs, NJ: Prentice-Hall, 1962); Anselm Strauss, *Mirrors and Masks: The Search for Identity* (Glencoe, IL: Free Press, 1959); Bernard N. Meltzer, "Mead's Social Psychology," in *The Social Psychology of George Herbert Mead* (Ann Arbor, MI: Center for Sociological Research, 1964), pp. 10–31; Jonathan H. Turner, "Returning to Social Physics: Illustrations from George Herbert

Mead," *Perspectives in Social Theory* 2 (1981), and *A Theory of Social Interaction* (Stanford, CA: Stanford University Press, 1988); also see Jonathan H. Turner, Leonard Beeghley, and Charles Powers, *The Emergence of Sociological Theory* (Belmont, CA: Wadsworth, 1998). For a more global overview of Mead's ideas, see John D. Baldwin, *George Herbert Mead: A Unifying Theory for Sociology* (Beverly Hills, CA: Sage, 1986).

6. For a more detailed analysis, see Jonathan H. Turner, "A Note on G. H. Mead's Behavioristic Theory of Social Structure," *Journal for the Theory of Social Behavior* 12 (July 1982), pp. 213–222.

7. George Herbert Mead, *Mind, Self, and Society* (cited in note 5), p. 254.

8. Ibid., pp. 256–257.

9. Ibid., pp. 261–262.

10. See William James, *Principles of Psychology* (cited in note 1), pp. 135–176.

11. Robert E. Park, "Behind Our Masks," *Survey Graphic* 56 (May 1926), p. 135. For a convenient summary of the thrust of early research efforts in role theory, see Ralph H. Turner, "Social Roles: Sociological Aspects," *International Encyclopedia of the Social Sciences* (New York: Macmillan, 1968).

12. Robert E. Park, *Society* (New York: Free Press, 1955), pp. 285–286.

13. Indeed, Park studied briefly with Georg Simmel in Berlin and apparently acquired insight into Simmel's study of the individual and the web of group affiliations (see later discussion). Coupled with his exposure to William James at Harvard, who also stressed the multiple sources of self, it is clear that Mead's legacy was supplemented by Simmel and James through the work of Robert Park.

14. Jacob Moreno, *Who Shall Survive* (Washington, DC, 1934); rev. ed. (New York: Beacon House, 1953).

15. Ralph Linton, *The Study of Man* (Appleton-Century-Crofts, 1936), p. 28.

16. Bernard N. Meltzer and Jerome W. Petras, "The Chicago and Iowa Schools of Symbolic Interactionism," in *Human Nature and Collective Behavior*, ed. T. Shibutani (Englewood Cliffs, NJ: Prentice-Hall, 1970).

17. For examples, consult Larry T. Reynolds, *Interactionism: Exposition and Critique*, 2nd ed. (Dix Hills, NY: General Hall, 1990); Jerome G. Manis and Bernard N. Meltzer, eds., *Symbolic Interaction: A Reader in Social Psychology* (Boston: Allyn & Bacon, 1972); J. Cardwell, *Social Psychology: A Symbolic Interactionist Approach* (Philadelphia: F. A. Davis, 1971); Alfred Lindesmith and Anselm Strauss, *Social Psychology* (New York: Holt, Rinehart & Winston, 1968); Arnold Rose, ed., *Human Behavior and Social Process* (Boston: Houghton Mifflin, 1962); Tamotsu Shibutani, *Society and Personality* (Englewood Cliffs, NJ: Prentice-Hall, 1961); C. K. Warriner, *The Emergence of Society* (Homewood, IL: Dorsey, 1970); Gregory Stone and H. Farberman, eds., *Symbolic Interaction: A Reader in Social Psychology* (Waltham, MA: Xerox Learning Systems, 1970); John P. Hewitt, *Self and Society: A Symbolic Interactionist Social Psychology* (Boston: Allyn & Bacon, 1976); Robert H. Laver and Warren H. Handel, *Social Psychology: The Theory and Application of Symbolic Interactionism* (Boston: Houghton Mifflin, 1977); Sheldon Stryker, *Symbolic Interactionism* (Menlo Park, CA: Benjamin/Cummings, 1980); Clark McPhail, "The Problems and Prospects of Behavioral Perspectives," *American Sociologist* 16 (1981), pp. 172–174.

18. Arnold Rose, *Human Behavior* (cited in note 17), p. 8.

19. Sheldon Stryker, "Symbolic Interaction as an Approach to Family Research," *Marriage and Family Living* 2 (May 1959), pp. 111–119. See also his "Role-Taking Accuracy and Adjustment," *Sociometry* 20 (December 1957), pp. 286–296.

20. Alfred Lindesmith and Anselm Strauss, *Social Psychology* (cited in note 17), p. 282.

21. Arnold Rose, *Human Behavior* (cited in note 17), p. 12.

22. W. I. Thomas, "The Definition of the Situation," in *Symbolic Interaction,* eds. J. Manis and B. Meltzer (cited in note 17), pp. 331–336.

23. For clear statements on the concept of "definition of the situation" as it is currently used in interactionist theory, see Alfred Lindesmith and Anselm Strauss, *Social Psychology* (cited in note 17), pp. 280–283.

24. Georg Simmel, "Sociability," in *The Sociology of Georg Simmel,* ed. K. H. Wolff (New York: Free Press, 1950), pp. 40–57. For an excellent secondary account of Simmel's significance for interactionism, see Randall Collins and Michael Makowsky, *The Discovery of Society* (New York: Random House, 1972), pp. 138–142.

25. Georg Simmel, *Conflict and the Web of Group Affiliations,* trans. R. Bendix (Glencoe, IL: Free Press, 1955; originally published in 1922).

26. Ibid., p. 141.

27. Émile Durkheim, *The Elementary Forms of the Religious Life* (New York: Free Press, 1954; originally published in 1912).

28. Randall Collins develops this idea in *Conflict Sociology* (New York: Academic, 1975) and other works. See Chapter 32. But perhaps the most significant adoption of Durkheim's emphasis on ritual was by the late Erving Goffman, the subject of Chapter 30.

29. Max Weber, *Basic Concepts in Sociology* (New York: Citadel, 1964), p. 29.

30. Max Weber, *The Theory of Social and Economic Organization* (New York: Free Press, 1947; originally published after Weber's death), p. 88.

31. For some readable, general references on phenomenology, see George Psathas, ed., *Phenomenological Sociology* (New York: Wiley, 1973); Richard M. Zaner, *The Way of Phenomenology: Criticism as a Philosophical Discipline* (New York: Pegasus, 1970); Peter L. Berger and Thomas Luckman, *The Social Construction of Reality* (Garden City, NY: Doubleday, 1966); Herbert Spiegelberg, *The Phenomenological Movement,* vols. 1 and 2, 2nd ed. (The Hague: Martinus Nijhoff, 1969); Hans P. Neisser, "The Phenomenological Approach in Social Science," *Philosophy and Phenomenological Research* 20 (1959), pp. 198–212; Stephen Strasser, *Phenomenology and the Human Sciences* (Pittsburgh: Duquesne University Press, 1963); Maurice Natanson, ed., *Phenomenology and the Social Sciences* (Evanston, IL: Northwestern University Press, 1973); and Quentin Lauer, *Phenomenology: Its Genesis and Prospect* (New York: Harper Torchbooks, 1965).

32. Zygmunt Bauman, "On the Philosophical Status of Ethnomethodology," *Sociological Review* 21 (February 1973), p. 6.

33. Husserl's basic ideas are contained in the following: *Phenomenology and the Crisis of Western Philosophy* (New York: Harper & Row, 1965; originally published in 1936); *Ideas: General Introduction to Pure Phenomenology* (London: Collier-Macmillan, 1969; originally published in 1913); and "Phenomenology," in *The Encyclopedia Britannica,* 14th ed., vol. 17, col. 699–702, 1929. For excellent secondary analyses, see Helmut R. Wagner, "The Scope of Phenomenological Sociology," in *Phenomenological Sociology,* ed. G. Psathas (cited in note 31), pp. 61–86, and "Husserl and Historicism," *Social Research* 39 (Winter 1972), pp. 696–719; Aron Gurwitsch, "The Common-Sense World as Social Reality," *Social Research* 29 (Spring 1962), pp. 50–72; Robert J. Antonio, "Phenomenological Sociology," in *Sociology: A Multiple Paradigm Science,* ed. G. Ritzer (Boston: Allyn & Bacon, 1975), pp. 109–112; Robert Welsh Jordan, "Husserl's Phenomenology as an 'Historical Science,'" *Social Research* 35 (Summer 1968), pp. 245–259.

34. For the basic ideas of Alfred Schutz, see his *The Phenomenology of the Social World* (Evanston, IL: Northwestern University Press, 1967; originally published in 1932); *Collected Papers,* vols. 1, 2, 3 (The Hague: Martinus Nijhoff, 1964, 1970, and 1971, respectively). For excellent secondary analyses, see Maurice Natanson, "Alfred Schutz on Social Reality and Social Science," *Social Research* 35 (Summer 1968), pp. 217–244.

35. Alfred Schutz, *Phenomenology of the Social World* (cited in note 35).

36. Richard M. Zaner, "Theory of Intersubjectivity: Alfred Schutz," *Social Research* 28 (Spring 1961), p. 76.

37. For references to interactionists, see Alfred Schutz, *Collected Papers* (cited in note 35).

38. Ralph H. Turner's emphasis on role differentiation and accretion is an example of how these ideas have been extended by role theorists. See Chapter 23.

22

Self and Identity Theory

In virtually all interactionist theorizing, the central dynamic of face-to-face relations is self, or the conceptions that individuals have about themselves as objects. Some of the most creative theorizing within both the Iowa and Chicago School traditions during the decades around the midcentury revolved around conceptualizing self in more detailed terms. The notion of "identity" became one prominent way to reconceptualize self. In general terms, self was viewed as a set or series of identities that respond to specific situations. Self was thus constructed from a number of identities, and these were viewed by theorists as arranged into hierarchies of salience and importance. Those identities high in the hierarchy are the most influential in individuals' efforts to organize their behaviors and present themselves in a certain light. At the same time, identities can act as filters of selective perception and interpretation as individuals mutually role-take with one another.

Thus, the effort to develop a more refined theory of self was the major thrust of much interactionist theorizing. In this chapter, we will review three such theories of identity, one by Sheldon Stryker, another by George P. McCall and J. L. Simmons, and a third by Peter J. Burke.

SHELDON STRYKER'S IDENTITY THEORY

Designations and Definitions

In Stryker's view,[2] human social behavior is organized by symbolic designations of all aspects of the environment, both physical and social. Among the most important of these designations are the symbols and associated meanings of the positions that people occupy in social structures. These positions carry with them shared expectations about how people are to enact roles and, in general, to comport themselves in relation to others. As individuals designate their own positions, they call forth in themselves expectations about how they are to behave, and as they designate the positions of others, they become cognizant of the expectations guiding the role behaviors of these others. They also become aware of broader frames of reference and definitions of the situation as these positional designations are made. And most important, individuals designate themselves as objects in relation to their location in structural positions and their perceptions of broader definitions of the situation.

Behavior is, however, not wholly determined or dictated by these designations and definitions. True, people are almost always aware of expectations associated with positions but, as they present themselves to others, the form and content of the interaction can change. The amount of such change will vary with the type of larger social structure within which the interaction occurs; some are open and flexible, whereas others are more closed and rigid. Still, all structures impose limits and constraints on what individuals do when engaged in face-to-face interaction.

Identities and the Salience Hierarchy

Stryker reasoned that identities are "parts" of self, and as such, they are internalized self-designations that are associated with positions that individuals occupy within various social contexts. Identity is thus a critical link between the individual and social structure because identities are designations that people make about themselves in relation to their location in social structures and the roles that they play by virtue of this location. Identities are organized into a *salience hierarchy,* and those identities high in the hierarchy are more likely to be evoked than those lower in this hierarchy. Not all situations will invoke multiple identities, but many do. The salience hierarchy determines those identities that people invoke as they orchestrate their roles and interpret the role behaviors of others. As a general rule, Stryker proposes that when an interaction situation is isolated from structural constraints, or these structural constraints are ambiguous, individuals will have more options in their choice of an identity, and, hence, they will be more likely to evoke more than one identity. But as a situation becomes embedded within social structures, the salience hierarchy becomes a good predictor of what identities will be used in interaction with others.

Commitment and Self

Stryker introduced the idea of *commitment* as a means for conceptualizing the link between social structure and self. Commitment designates the degree to which a person's relationship to others depends on being a certain kind of individual with a particular identity. The greater this dependence is, the more a person will be committed to a particular identity and the higher this identity will be in the person's salience hierarchy. Having an identity that is based on the views of others, as well as on broader social definitions, will tend to produce behaviors that conform to these views and definitions.

When people reveal such commitment to an identity in a situation, their sense of self-esteem becomes dependent on the successful execution of their identity. Moreover, when an identity is established by reference to the norms, values, and other symbols of the broader society, esteem is even more dependent on successful implementation of an identity. In this way, cultural definitions and expectations, social structural location, identity, and esteem associated with that identity all become interwoven. And in this process, social structure constrains behavior and people's perceptions of themselves and others.

The Key Propositions

In the early version of the theory, Stryker developed a series of "hypotheses" about the conditions producing the salience of an identity, the effects of identities high in the salience hierarchy on role behaviors, the influence of commitment on esteem, and the nature of changes in identity. These are rephrased somewhat and summarized in Table 22.1. To state Stryker's argument more discursively, here is what he proposed: The more individuals reveal commitment to an identity, the higher this identity will be in the salience hierarchy. If this identity is positively evaluated through the reactions of others and broader value standards, then this identity will move up a person's hierarchy. When the expectations of others are congruent and consistent, revealing few conflicts and disagreements, individuals will be even more committed to the identity presented to these others because they "speak with the same voice." And finally, when the network of these others on whom one depends for identity is large and extended, encompassing many others rather than just a few, the higher in the salience hierarchy will this identity become.

Once an identity is high in the salience hierarchy of an individual, role performances will become ever more consistent with the expectations attached to this identity. Moreover, when identities are high in the salience hierarchy, individuals will tend to perceive situations as opportunities to play out this identity in roles, and they will actively seek out situations where they can use this identity. In this way, the congruence between those identities high in people's hierarchies and the expectations of situations increases.

This congruence increases commitment because individuals come to see their identities as depending on the continued willingness of others to confirm their identities. As commitment increases, and as individuals become dependent on confirmation of their identities from others, their role performances

Table 22.1 A Revised Formulation of Stryker's Hypotheses on Identity

The Salience of Identity

I. The more individuals are committed to an identity, the higher will this identity be in their salience hierarchy.

II. The degree of commitment to an identity is a positive and additive function of

   A. The extent to which this identity is positively valued by others and broader cultural definitions.

   B. The congruence among expectations of others on whom one depends for an identity.

   C. The extensiveness of the network of individuals on whom one depends for an identity.

   D. The number of persons in a network on whom one depends for an identity.

The Consequences of High Salience

III. The higher in a person's salience hierarchy is an identity, the more likely will that individual

   A. Emit role performances that are consistent with the role expectations associated with that identity.

   B. Perceive a given situation as an opportunity to perform in that identity.

   C. Seek out situations that provide opportunities to perform in that identity.

The Consequences of Commitment to Identity

IV. The greater the commitment to an identity, the greater will be

   A. The effect of role performances on self-esteem.

   B. The likelihood that role performances will reflect institutionalized values and norms.

Changing Commitments to Identity

V. The more external events alter the structure of a situation, the more likely are individuals to adopt new or novel identities.

VI. The more changes in identity reinforce and reflect the value-commitments of the individual, the less the individual resists change in adopting a new identity.

have ever more consequences for their level of self-esteem. Moreover, as people become committed to identities and these identities move up in their salience hierarchy, they come to evaluate their role performances through broader cultural definitions and normative expectations; as people make such evaluations, they become even more committed to their identities.

External events can, however, erode commitments to an identity. When this occurs, people are more likely to adopt new identities, even novel identities. As individuals begin to seek new identities, change is likely to move in the direction of those identities that reflect their values. In this way, cultural values pull the formation of new identities in directions that will increase the congruence between cultural definitions and role performance as individuals develop new identity commitments and as their self-esteem becomes dependent on successful role performance of these identity commitments.

Over the last decade and a half, Stryker has continued to work on this identity theory, as we will see in Chapter 26 on theories of emotion. Yet, the theory remains much the same as reported here. In a sense, theories of identity peaked in the 1960s and 1970s, as did symbolic interactionism as a distinctive theoretical approach. Subsequent developments within interactionist theorizing moved beyond the paradigm provided by George Herbert Mead and carried forward by symbolic interactionists. Alternative micro-level theories, drawing not only from Alfred Schutz but from European founders as well, have become a part of the interactionist theoretical approach, broadly conceived as the dynamics of face-to-face interaction in social settings. Still, before leaving the maturing interactionist tradition, we might examine two, somewhat more elaborate theories of identity than Stryker's.

GEORGE P. MCCALL
AND J. L. SIMMONS'S IDENTITY THEORY

Role Identity and Role Support

In contrast with Stryker's more structural theory, where culture and social structure designate many of the identities held by individuals, McCall and Simmons[3] emphasized that roles are typically improvised as individuals seek to realize their various plans and goals. A *role identity* is, therefore, "the character and the role that an individual devises for himself (herself as well) as an occupant of a particular social position."[4] Role identity constitutes an "imaginative view of oneself" in a position, often a rather idealized view of oneself. Each role identity thus has a conventional portion linked to positions in social structure as well as an idiosyncratic portion constructed in people's imaginations.

Role identities become part of individuals' plans and goals because legitimating one's identity in the eyes of others is always a driving force of human behavior. Moreover, people evaluate themselves through the role performances intended to confirm a role identity. But, as McCall and Simmons emphasized, the most important audiences for a role performance are individuals themselves who assess their performances with respect to their own idealized view of their role identity. Still, people must also seek *role support* from relevant audiences outside their own minds for their role identities. This support involves more than audiences granting a person the right to occupy a position, and it includes more than approval from others for conduct by those in a position. For an individual to feel legitimated in a role, audiences must also approve of the more expressive content—the style, emotion, manner, and tone—of role performances designed to legitimate a role identity.

Because much of a role identity is rather idealized in the individual's mind and because a person must seek legitimation along several fronts, there is always discrepancy and disjuncture between the role identity and the role support received for that identity. People idealize too much, and they must seek support for performances that can be misinterpreted. As a result, there is almost always some dissatisfaction by individuals about how much their role identity has been legitimated by audiences. These points of disjuncture between identity and legitimating support motivate and drive individual behavior. Indeed, for McCall and Simmons, the most distinctive emotion among humans is the "drive to acquire support for (their) idealized conceptions of (themselves)."[5]

The Mechanisms for Maintaining Role Support

To overcome the discrepancy between what people desire and get in role support for an identity, several mechanisms are employed. One is the accumulation of "short-term credit" from interactions where discrepancies have been minimal; these emotional credits can then carry individuals through episodes where the responses from others provide less than whole-hearted role support. A second mechanism is "selective perception of cues" from others where individuals only see those responses confirming an identity. A third mechanism is "selective interpretation" of cues whereby the individual sees the cues accurately but puts "a spin" or interpretation on them that supports a role identity. A fourth mechanism is withdrawing from interactions that do not support an identity and seeking alternative situations where more support can be garnered. A fifth mechanism is switching to a new role identity whose performance will bring more support from others. A sixth mechanism is "scapegoating" audiences, blaming them for causing the discrepancy between performance and support. A seventh mechanism is "disavowing" unsuccessful performances that individuals had hoped to legitimate. And a final defensive mechanism is deprecating and rejecting the audience that withholds support for a role identity. When these mechanisms fail, individuals experience misery and anguish, and through such experiences, people learn to be cautious in committing themselves so openly and fully to particular role performances in front of certain audiences.[6]

The Hierarchy of Prominence

The *cohesiveness* role identities of individuals vary, McCall and Simmons argued, in how the elements of an identity fit together and in the compatibility among various role identities. There is also a *hierarchy of prominence* among role identities; although this hierarchy can shift and change as circumstances dictate, it tends to exist at any given point in an interaction. This prominence reflects the idealized view of individuals, the extent to which these ideals have been supported by audiences, the degree to which individuals have committed themselves to these identities, the extrinsic and intrinsic rewards (to be discussed shortly) associated with an identity, and the amount of previous investment in time and energy that has been devoted to an identity.

From this perspective, interaction revolves around each individual asserting through role performances identities that are high in their prominence hierarchy and that they seek to legitimate, in their own eyes as well as in the eyes of others. At the same time, each individual is interpreting the gestures of others to determine just what identity is high in the prominence hierarchy of others and whether or not the role performances of others are worthy of role support and other rewards. To some degree, the external structure of the situation provides the necessary information about what positions people occupy and what expectations are placed on them by virtue of incumbency in these positions. Yet, for McCall and Simmons, most interactions are to some degree ambiguous and unstructured, allowing alternative role performances and varying interpretations of these performances.

Much of the ambiguity in interaction is eliminated through simple role-taking in a person's *inner forum* or cognitive repertoire of vocabularies, gestures, motives, and other information that marks various identities and role performances. Humans have, therefore, the capacity to construct interpretations in light of the vast amounts of information that they accumulate in their "inner forum" or what Schutz called "stocks of knowledge at hand." This information might have to be assembled in somewhat "different proportions and balances" but humans' capacity for mind and thought enables them to do so with amazing speed and accuracy.

Individuals will often improvise a role, adjusting their identities and role performances in light of how they interpret the roles of others. As such improvisation occurs, various expressive strategies are employed; these strategies revolve around orchestrating gestures to present a certain image of self and to claim a particular identity that is high in the prominence hierarchy. Conversely, individuals read these presentations of others to "altercast" and determine the self that is being claimed by these others. In essence, then, interaction is the negotiation of identities, whereby people make expressive and dramaturgical presentations over identities that are high in their respective prominence hierarchies and that can be supported, or that can go unsupported, on the basis of role performances.

The Underlying Exchange Dynamic

This process of negotiation among individuals is complex and subtle, involving an initial but very tentative agreement to accept each others' claims. In this way, people avoid interrupting the expressive strategies that are being used to impart their respective identities. As this process unfolds, however, it moves into a real exchange negotiation whereby individuals seek the rewards that come with legitimation of their role performances. At this point McCall and Simmons merged their interactionist theory with exchange theory.

They begin by classifying three basic types of rewards: First, there are extrinsic rewards, such as money or other reinforcers that are visible to all. Second, there are intrinsic rewards that provide less visible means of reinforcement for the individual—rewards such as satisfaction, pride, and comfort. Third, and most important, there is role support for an identity, which McCall and Simmons believe is the most valuable of all rewards. Individuals are motivated to seek a profit—rewards less the costs in securing them—in all their interactions. Moreover, there are separate types of calculi for each of these three categories of reward, and there are *rules of the marketplace:* Rewards received by each party to an exchange should be roughly comparable in their type (whether extrinsic, intrinsic, or identity support), and rewards should be received in proportion to the investments individuals incur in receiving them (a principle of "distributive justice").

These negotiations are affected by what McCall and Simmons term the *salience of identities,* which are those identities that, for the immediate interaction at hand, are the most relevant in an individual's hierarchy of prominence. This salience of identities constitutes, in McCall and Simmons' words, a *situated self* that is most pertinent to the present interaction. This situational self determines a person's preferences about which role identities he or she will enact in a given situation, but the preferences of the situational self are fluid and changeable. In contrast, the *ideal self* is more stable than the situated self, while being the highest-order identity in the prominence hierarchy. A person's ideal self will thus influence which identities should be salient in an interaction and how they will be invoked to constitute a situated self. Besides the prominence hierarchy, other factors also influence the formation of a situated identity. The needs that an individual feels for support of an identity, the extrinsic and intrinsic rewards to be received by claiming a situated self, and the opportunity for profitable enactment of a role in relation to a situated self all shape identity formation.

All these factors are, in McCall and Simmons' view, potential reinforcers or payoffs for roles emitted in claiming an identity. These payoffs vary in value, however. Support of the ideal self brings greater rewards than either extrinsic or intrinsic rewards. The patterns of payoffs for rewards can also vary. For extrinsic and intrinsic types of rewards, when payoffs match expectations and desires, needs for them decline somewhat (in accordance with satiation or the principle of marginal utility). If people receive either more or less than they expected or desired of these two types of rewards, then their immediate need for these rewards suddenly escalates. In contrast, the payoff schedule for role support for an identity reveals a more complicated pattern. Role support for what was desired or expected does not increase the desire for further role support of an identity; a moderate discrepancy between the support sought and received increases the desire for support of an identity, but extreme discrepancies operate differently, depending on the sign of the discrepancy: If people receive support that greatly exceeds their expectations, they immediately desire more role support, whereas if they dramatically receive less role support than expected, their desire for this role support drops rapidly.

Because payoffs will almost always, or at least eventually, be less than expected, discrepancies will be chronic even after individuals have employed all the defense mechanisms to reduce discrepancies that were discussed earlier. Hence, people are constantly driven to overcome this discrepancy, but this search to reduce discrepancy is complicated by the payoff schedule for role support. Moderate discrepancies drive people to seek more role support, whereas large ones reduce efforts to secure role support for an identity. And when people have received more support than they expected for an identity, they want even more of this reward, raising this identity in salience and, over time, increasing its prominence in the hierarchy.

PETER J. BURKE'S IDENTITY THEORY

Working squarely within the symbolic interactionist tradition, Peter J. Burke and various colleagues, particularly Jan E. Stets, have developed yet another variant of identity theory.[7] For Burke, individuals carry general views of themselves to all situations, or an *idealized self,* but it is the *working self* or *self image* that guides moment to moment interaction.[8] The idealized self may, of course, influence just how individuals see themselves in a situation, but the key dynamics of self revolve around trying to verify this working self or self image in situations as individuals play roles. At other times,[9] Burke has also conceptualized self as a rough hierarchy. At the more abstract level is a *principle self* in which cultural standards contained in broader values and beliefs become part of how individuals see themselves, but this principle-level self influences behavior in situations through a *program-level identity* consisting of the goals that individuals seek to realize in a concrete situation. In general, the more a program level identity is guided by a principle-level self and the more the goals of the program-level self are realized in a situation, the greater are persons' sense of efficacy, and the more positive are their sentiments toward themselves and the situation.[10] Yet, unlike other identity theories, Burke's approach does not place great emphasis on a "salience" or "prominence" hierarchy. Instead, the theory seeks to explain the internal dynamics of self as individuals play a role in an effort to verify the identity associated with this role.

Role Identities

For Burke, self is an occupant of a role in a situation. This situation is, in turn, typically embedded in a larger social structure and associated cultural meanings. Roles are thus the link between self, on the one side, and social structure and culture, on the other. By virtue of playing a role, individuals incorporate meanings and expectations associated with this role into their identity in the situation. Individuals have diverse experiences and any role has multiple meanings; so the identities associated with a role will vary from person to person. Burke's identity theory, however, is less concerned with the actual content of a role identity than with the dynamics of how this identity is sustained in interaction with others in a situation. This emphasis leads Burke to see identity as a cybernetic control system, as individuals seek to regulate their behaviors that others will verify their identity in a role.

Identity as a Cybernetic Control System

In conceptualizing identity as a cybernetic control system, Burke sees the dynamics of this system as revolving around following elements[11]:

1. An *identity standard* operating as a *comparator* or criterion for assessing whether or not an identity is verified and for directing initial behavior in a role.

2. A set of *inputs* from others who are responding to the behaviors of a person playing a role and asserting an identity.

3. A *comparison* of inputs with the comparator to determine if the responses of others are congruent with the identity standard guiding role behaviors.

4. A set of behavioral *outputs* on the environment guided by the degree to which inputs match the identity standard contained in the comparator.

These elements are delineated in Figure 22.1. Individuals have a set of meanings about their identity in a situation. This identity is translated into a standard that, in turn, becomes a comparator or basis for matching inputs to the standard to see if, indeed, the standard has been realized. As individuals play a role in a situation, they emit outputs of meaningful behavior on the environment, particularly to other individuals in the situation who, in turn, respond to these behavioral outputs. As individuals emitting outputs role-take with others in a situation, they experience "reflected appraisals" that become inputs of self-meanings that are compared to the identity standard. Depending on whether or not the identity standard is met, the next round of behavioral outputs will vary. When the identity standards is realized, individuals will experience more positive emotions, and their subsequent behavioral outputs will revolve around commitments to others in the situation. When inputs from others signal that the identity standard is not realized, people will experience negative emotions, and the next round of behavioral outputs will seek to change the responses of others so that a role identity can be confirmed.

Thus, in Burke's theory, humans are motivated to have inputs match up with identity standards. Behavior is goal directed in the sense that individuals try to elicit from others in a situation responses that match their identity standard. To achieve this result, individuals orchestrate their gestures and use other signs[12] in behavioral performances that, they hope, will allow them to receive inputs that match the identity standard.

In Burke's model, a separate control system is operative for each identity.[13] That is, if multiple identities are presented in a situation, each is guided by the dynamics outlined in Figure 22.1. For example, if a professor seeks to present an identity as both an intellect and a sexually attractive person, then two role identities—intellect and sexy—are revealed in behavioral outputs, and two cybernetic control systems revolving around two comparators (dictated by the two identities), two sets of inputs, two comparisons, and two outputs are operative. However, higher-level identities—or what Burke sometimes terms principle-level identities—often provide more general frames of reference for lower-level or program identities, thereby simplifying the control process. For instance, if a college professor is in the classroom, the higher-level identity revolving around beliefs in the importance of intellectual activity, per se, may provide guidance for how the lower-level, program identity of being sexually attractive is to be orchestrated in role behaviors. In this way, the two identities are not contradictory, and the control systems guiding efforts at confirmation will not work at cross-purposes.

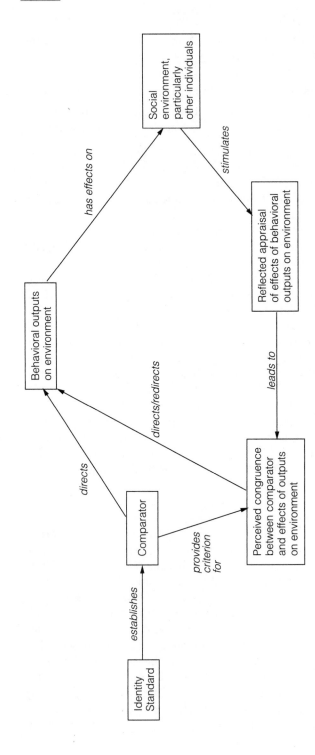

FIGURE 22.1 The Cybernetic Control System in Burke's Theory

Identity and Emotions

Burke and Jan Stets have explored in a number of research projects the effects of verification, or the failure to verify an identity, on people's emotional arousal.[14] When role identities are verified by the responses of others, people will experience positive emotions, and moreover, they will generally have enhanced self-esteem, which can insulate them from the negative efforts of periodic failures to confirm the identity. When a role identity is not verified, people will experience distress, anxiety, and other negative emotions, including lowered self-esteem.

Identity Verification If a role identity is consistently confirmed in interaction with others, individuals will increasingly come to trust these other; they will develop commitments to these others; they will reveal emotional attachments to these others; and they will become more oriented to the group and social structure in which a role identity is confirmed. For example, a person whose identity standard demands that she be considered a "good student" will feel positive emotions toward others, such as professors and follow students, when this identity is confirmed; if this verification consistently occurs in school situations, this person will trust others, develop attachments to them, and become oriented to the intellectual culture of the university community

As a role identity is verified across repeated encounters with others in a situation, not only does the individual trust others and develop commitments and emotional attachments to them and the structure of the situation, the salience to the person of the role identity being presented increases. And the more salient an identity—that is, the more important it is to the individual and the more it guides behavioral outputs—the greater the motivation of the individual to ensure that inputs from the environment do indeed confirm this identity. Thus, a student who has enjoyed success in confirming the role identity of good student will be increasingly motivated to verify this identity as it takes on greater salience.

Failure to Verify Identity More interesting, perhaps, are situations where inputs from others' responses do not match the identity standard. Several conditions produce this outcome. One is where a person's outputs cannot change the situation, no matter how hard he or she tries; under these conditions, a person experiences a loss of efficacy and a greater sense of alienation, disaffection, and estrangement. For instance, a person who cannot match performance with a work identity and, yet, who cannot leave his job will experience this range of negative emotions. Another condition is interference from other identities possessed by a person where confirmation of one role identity does not allow another to be confirmed. For instance, a person who has an identity as a "good student" and a "great athlete" will often discover in college that only one of these two identities can be consistently confirmed. Still another condition is an over-controlled identity in which the elements of a role identity are so rigidly woven together that a person sees a perceived slight to one of these elements as an attack on all elements. Such identities will be difficult to verify, even if most of the elements are accepted by others in the situation, because the individual is simply too rigid in his or her expectations for how others should respond. A final condition increasing the likelihood of failure to verify an identity is where an identity is only episodically played out in a role or only occasionally becomes salient, with the result that the individual is simply out of practice in emitting the behavioral outputs that allow others to verify the identity.

Whatever the source of incongruence between (1) the expectations dictated by an identity standard and (2) the responses of others, the stage is for distressful responses from individuals who experience this inconsistency. Several conditions increase the level of distress experienced. One is the importance to a person of others who have failed to verify a role identity. The more significant to an individual are others whose responses fail to match identity standards, the more intense is the sense of distress, and the more motivated is the individual to adjust behavioral outputs to secure the appropriate responses from these significant others. Another condition is the salience of the role identity itself. The more important to a person the verification of a role identity in a situation, the more distressed that person will become when this identity is not verified. Still another condition is the more that a role identity reflects a commitment to others and the group, the more intense is the sense of distress when others do not verify the identity, especially if this identity is built around principle-level elements or the cultural values and beliefs of the group. Another condition influencing the level of stress is the direction and degree of incongruity between expectations set by a role identity and the nonconfirming responses of others. When the responses of others fall below expectations, individuals will experience distress and be motivated to adjust behavioral outputs to secure verifying responses from others. More complicated is when expectations established by an identity standard are exceeded. Preliminary research indicates that the degree to which expectations are exceeded determines the responses of individuals.[15] The more expectations are exceeded, the more individuals are forced to adjust their identity standards, and as a result, the more they will experience distress, whereas if expectations are exceeded to a more moderate degree, the identity standards does not have to be radically adjusted, and, hence, the person will experience positive emotions.

Failure to verify an identity repeatedly will, over time, cause less intense negative emotions because people begin to adjust their identity standards downward, lowering their expectations for how others will respond.[16] But when an identity standard is not initially verified, individuals will adjust their outputs in an effort to get the identity verified. Thus, for example, a student who has the identity of "good student" will study much harder if he or she does not meet expectations on an examination, although if this individual consistently fails to do well, the role identity and expectations associated with this identity will be adjusted downward, and the student's motivation to study harder will likely decline. Another option when an identity standard is not verified is for the individual to leave the situation, if possible, and thereby avoid the negative emotions that come from incongruities between expectations and responses of others.

In sum, Burke's identity theory generates a number of testable propositions, some of which are summarized in Table 22.2. These and other propositions are

Table 22.2 Key Proposition of Burke's Identity Theory

I. The more salient an identity in a role, the more motivated are individuals to achieve a sense of congruence between the expectations established by the identity standard and the responses of others in a situation.

II. The more the responses of others match the expectations dictated by an identity standard, the more positive are the emotions experienced by individuals and the greater their level of self esteem, and the more enhanced are positive emotions towards self, the more likely are individuals to

A. Develop a sense of trust with others who have verified their identity.

B. Develop emotional attachments to these others.

C. Develop commitments to these others.

D. Become oriented to the standards of the group in which the situation is embedded.

III. The less the responses of others match an identity standard, the more likely are the emotions experienced by individuals to be negative, with the incongruence between expectations set by an identity standard and the responses of others increasing with

A. Multiple and incompatible identity standards from two or more role identities.

B. An overcontrolled self in which the elements of the identity are tightly woven and create inflexible identity standards.

C. A lack of practice in displaying an identity in a role.

D. Efforts to change and/or leave the situation have consistently failed.

IV. The intensity of negative emotions from a failure to verify an identity increases with

A. The salience of an identity in the situation.

B. The significance of the others who have not verified an identity.

C. The degree of incongruity, whether above or below expectations associated with an identity standard.

V. The intensity of negative emotions from the failure to verify an identity will decrease over time as the identity standard is readjusted downward so as to lower expectations.

---

implied by the theory, but equally important, they also come from efforts to test the theory. Although some research has been performed on the other identity theories summarized in this chapter, Burke's theory is subject to ongoing research. The generalizations offered in this chapter have, to varying degrees, been confirmed by research. Moreover, in recent years, efforts have been made to reconcile Burke's identity theory with that offered by Stryker as well as McCall and Simmons,[17] and so, it is likely that in the future various theories of self can become more unified.

CONCLUSION

Drawing from Mead's views, all these theories sought to understand the connection among the person, role behaviors, social structure, and culture. The key dynamic, they all argued, was self and identity. As people plug themselves into social structures and culture, take cognizance of each other, and make roles for themselves, they seek to confirm and reaffirm their self conceptions, typically conceptualized as a series of identities that vary in salience and that are arranged into hierarchies, although Burke's theory underemphasizes hierarchies of identities. Some theorists such as Stryker view culture and social structure as circumscribing these dynamics, whereas others like McCall and Simmons as well as Burke view the individual as exerting more latitude and freedom in constructing identities. But all symbolic interactionists tend to view self as the crucial force behind people's perceptions and actions in interactive situations, organizing and determining the flow of role-playing and role-taking in social contexts composed of others, cultural definitions, and social structural positions.

Along with these interactionist theories of self and identity, a related theoretical orientation emphasizing roles was emerging in the middle decades of the century. Self remained a key dynamic in these theories, but it was not necessarily viewed as the driving dynamic of all role behaviors. Before moving to the more recent directions of interactionist theorizing, then, we need to pause and examine an equally prominent theoretical tradition: role theory (also see the Web site for this book).

NOTES

1. Aside from these figures, others seeking a theory of self and identity include Eugene Weinstein, Mary Glenn Wiley, and William DeVaughn, "Role and Interpersonal Style as Components of Interaction." *Social Forces* 45 (1966), pp. 210–216; Peter J. Burke and Judy C. Tully, "The Measurement of Role/Identity," *Social Forces* 55 (1977), pp. 881–897; Nelson N. Foote, "Identification as the Basis for a Theory of Motivation." *American Sociological Review* 16 (1951), pp. 14–21; Tamotsu Shibutani, *Society and Personality* (Englewood Cliffs, NJ: Prentice-Hall, 1961); Anselm Strauss, *Mirrors and Masks* (Glencoe, IL: Free Press, 1959); Gregory P. Stone, "Appearance and the Self" in *Behavior and Social Processes,* ed. Arnold M. Rose (Boston: Houghton Mifflin, 1962); Jonathan H. Turner, *Face to Face: A Sociological Theory of Interpersonal Behavior* (Stanford, CA: Stanford University Press, 2002). For a review of the history and current profile of identity and self theories, see Viktor Gecas and Peter J. Burke, "Self and Identity," in *Sociological Perspectives on Social Psychology,* eds. Karen S. Cook, Gary Alan Fine and James S. House (Boston: Allyn & Bacon, 1955), pp. 41–67, as well as Jan E. Stets and Peter J. Burke, "A Sociological Approach to Self and Identity," in *Handbook of Self and Identity,* eds. Mark Leary and June Tangney (New York: Guilford, 2002)

2. Sheldon Stryker, *Symbolic Interactionism: A Structural Version* (Menlo Park, CA: Benjamin/Cummings, 1980); "Identity Salience and Role Performance: The Relevance of Symbolic Interaction Theory for Family Research," *Journal of Marriage and the Family* (1968), pp. 558–564; "Fundamental Principles of Social Interaction" in *Sociology,* 2nd ed., Neil J. Smelser, ed. (New York: Wiley, 1973), pp. 495–547. For a more recent version of the theory, see Sheldon Stryker and Richard T. Serpe, "Commitment, Identity Salience, and Role Behavior" in *Personality, Roles, and Social Behavior,*

eds. William Ickes and Eric Knowles (New York: Springer-Verlag, 1982), pp. 199–218; Richard T. Serpe and Sheldon Stryker, "The Construction of Self and the Reconstruction of Social Relationships," *Advances in Group Processes* 4 (1987), pp. 41–66; and Sheldon Stryker, "Exploring the Relevance of Social Cognition for the Relationship of Self and Society" in *The Self-Society Dynamic: Cognition, Emotion, and Action,* eds. Judith Howard and Peter L. Callero (Cambridge: Cambridge University Press, 1991), pp. 19–41.

3. George P. McCall and J. L. Simmons, *Identities and Interactions* (New York: Basic Books, 1960). A second edition of this book was published in 1978, although the theory remained virtually unchanged.

4. Ibid., p. 67.

5. Ibid., p. 75.

6. Ibid., p. 101.

7. Peter J. Burke, "The Self: Measurement Implications from a Symbolic Interactionist Perspective," *Social Psychology Quarterly* 43 (1980), pp. 18–20; "An Identity Model for Network Exchange." *American Sociological Review* 62 (1997), pp. 134–150; "Attitudes, Behavior, and the Self" in *The Self-Society Dynamic,* eds. Judith Howard and Peter L. Callero (cited in note 2), pp. 189–208, "Identity Processes and Social Stress," *American Sociological Review* 56 (1991), pp. 836–849; P. J. Burke and D. C. Reitzes, "An Identity Theory Approach to Commitment," *Social Psychology Quarterly* 54 (1991), pp 239–251; P. J. Burke and Jan E. Stets, "Trust and Commitment through Self

Verification," *Social Psychology Quarterly* 62 (1999), pp. 347–366.

8. Burke, "The Self: Measurement Implications . . ." (cited in note 7)

9. T. Tsushima and P. J. Burke, "Levels, Agency, and Control in Parent Identity," *Social Psychology Quarterly* 62 (1999), pp. 173–189.

10. Ibid. See also Peter J. Burke "Identity Processes and Social Stress" (cited in note 7).

11. Peter J. Burke "Identity Processes and Social Stress" (cited in note 7).

12. Lee Freese and Peter J. Burke, "Persons, Identities, and Social Interaction," in *Advances in Group Processes,* eds. Barry Markovsky, K. Heimer, and Jody O'Brien (Greenwich, CT: JAI, 1994).

13. Peter J. Burke, "Relationships Among Multiple Identities" (Conference in Bloomington, IN: The Future of Identity Theory and Research, 2001).

14. P. J. Burke and Jan E. Sets, "Trust and Commitment through Self Verification" (cited in note 7).

15. Jan E. Stets, "Justice, emotion, and Identity Theory," (Conference in Bloomington, IN: The Future of Identity Theory and Research, 2001); Jan E. Stets and T. M. Tsushima, "Negative Emotion and Coping Responses within Identity Control Theory," *Social Psychology Quarterly* 64 (2001), in press.

16. Ibid (all of those cited in note 15).

17. Jan E. Stets and Peter J. Burke, "A Sociological Approach to Self and Identity Theory" (cited in note 7); Sheldon Stryker and Peter J. Burke, "The Past, Present, and Future of an Identity Theory," *Social Psychology Quarterly* 63 (2000), pp. 284–297.

23

Role Theory:
Ralph H. Turner

y the midcentury, the idea that individuals are connected to larger social structures by virtue of incumbency in status positions and role behaviors pervaded sociological theory. Role was the key concept that linked individuals and social structure, and, as a result of this emphasis, role theorizing became prominent. Yet, much of this role theorizing was, in reality, descriptions of expectations and behaviors in various empirical settings, or at best, more theoretical conceptualizations of a narrow range of role processes.

The thrust of much early role analysis, as it flowed from a mixture of Robert Park's, Georg Simmel's, Jacob Moreno's, Ralph Linton's, and George Herbert Mead's insights, was often captured in the midcentury by quoting a famous passage from Shakespeare's *As You Like It:*

> All the world's a stage
> and all the men and women merely players:
> They have their exits and their entrances;
> And one man in his time plays many parts.
>
> (Act II, scene vii)

The analogy was often drawn between the players on the stage and the actors of society.[1] Just as players have a clearly defined part to play, so actors in society occupy clear positions; just as players must follow a written script, so actors in society must follow norms; just as players must obey the orders of a director, so actors in society must conform to the dictates of those with power or those of importance; just as players must react to each other's performance on the stage, so members of society must mutually adjust their responses to one another; just as players respond to the audience, so actors in society take the role of various audiences or "generalized others"; and just as players with varying abilities and capacities bring to each role their unique interpretations, so actors with varying self-conceptions and role-playing skills have their own styles of interaction.

A general theory of roles never emerged from such metaphors, and during the last decades, efforts to do so appear to have waned. Yet, a great deal was learned about roles in the decades between 1940 and 1980, and the movement of micro-level theory to new topics does not so much reflect the failure of role theory as its success in uncovering many basic dynamics of roles and such related processes as status and expectations. In this chapter, we will examine Ralph H. Turner's approach, which, more than any other role theory, has overcome the problems in earlier theories and which, at the same time, has sought to generate systematic theory (for a more general review of role theory, see the Web site for this book under "role theory.").

During the course of several decades, Turner mounted a consistent line of criticism against what he characterized as structural role theory.[2] This criticism incorporated several lines of attack: (1) Earlier role theory had presented an overly structured vision of the social world, with its emphasis on norms, status positions, and the enactment of normative expectations. (2) Role theory had tended to concentrate an inordinate amount of research and theory-building effort on "abnormal" social processes, such as role conflict and role strain, thereby ignoring the normal processes of human interaction. (3) Role theory was not theory but, rather, a series of disjointed and unconnected propositions and empirical generalizations. (4) Role theory did not recognize Mead's concept of role-taking as its central dynamic. As a corrective to these problems, in the decades around the midcentury Turner offered a conceptualization of roles that emphasized the process of interaction over the dictates of social structures and cultural scripts.[3]

THE ROLE-MAKING PROCESS

Turner used Mead's concept of role-taking to describe the nature of social action. Turner assumed that "it is the tendency to shape the phenomenal world into roles which is the key to the role-taking as the core process in interaction."[4] Turner stressed that actors read gestures or cues—words, bodily countenance, voice inflections, dress, facial expressions, and other gestures—as they interact to "put themselves in the other's role" and, thereby to adjust their lines of conduct in ways that can facilitate cooperation. In emphasizing this point, Turner was simply following Mead's definition of taking the role of the other, or role-taking.

Turner then extended Mead's concept. He first argued that cultural definitions of roles are often vague and even contradictory. At best, they provide a general framework within which actors must construct a line of conduct. Thus, actors *make* their roles and communicate to others *what* role they are playing. Turner then argued that humans act *as if* all others in their environment are playing *identifiable roles.*[5] Humans assume others to be playing a role, and this assumption is what gives interaction a common basis. Operating with this folk assumption, people then read gestures and cues in an effort to determine what roles others are playing.[6] This effort is facilitated by others creating and asserting their roles, with the result that they actively emit cues about what roles they are attempting to play.

Interaction is thus, role-taking and *role making.* Humans make roles in three senses: (1) They are often faced with only a loose cultural framework in which they must make a role to play. (2) They assume others are playing a role and thus make an effort to discover the underlying role behind a person's acts. (3) Humans seek to make a role for themselves in all social situations by emitting cues to others that give them claim on a particular role. Interaction is, therefore, a joint and reciprocal process of role-taking and role making.

THE "FOLK NORM OF CONSISTENCY"

As people interact with one another, Turner argued, they assess behavior less for its conformity to imputed norms or positions in a social structure and more for the consistency of behavior. Humans seek to group one another's behavior into coherent wholes or gestalts, and, by doing so, they can make sense of one another's actions, anticipate one another's behavior, and adjust to one another's responses. If another's responses are inconsistent and not seen as part of an underlying role, then interaction will prove difficult. Thus, there is an implicit "norm of consistency" in people's interactions with one another. Humans attempt to assess the consistency of others' actions to discern the underlying role that is being played.

THE TENTATIVE NATURE OF INTERACTION

For Turner, "interaction is always a tentative process, a process of continuously testing the conception one has of the role of the other."[7] Humans are constantly interpreting additional cues emitted by others and using these new cues to see if they are consistent with those previously emitted and with the imputed roles of others. If they are consistent, then the actor will continue to adjust responses in accordance with the imputed role of the other. But as soon as inconsistent cues are emitted, the identification of the other's role will undergo revision. Thus, the imputation of a particular role to another person will persist only as long as it provides a stable framework for interaction. The tentative nature of the role-making process points to another facet of roles: the process of *role verification.*

THE PROCESS OF ROLE VERIFICATION

Actors seek to verify that behaviors and other cues emitted by people in a situation do indeed constitute a role. Turner argued that such efforts at verification or validation are achieved by applying external and internal criteria. The most often used *internal criterion* is the degree to which an actor perceives a role to facilitate interaction. *External criteria* can vary, but in general they involve assessment of a role by important others, relevant groups, or commonly agreed-on standards. When an imputed role is validated or verified in this way, then it can serve as a stable basis for continued interaction among actors.

SELF-CONCEPTIONS AND ROLE

All humans reveal self-conceptions of themselves as certain kinds of objects. Humans develop self-attitudes and feelings from their interactions with others, but, as Turner and all role theorists emphasized, actors attempt to present themselves in ways that will reinforce their self-conceptions.[8] Because others will always seek to determine an individual's role, it becomes necessary for the individual to inform others, through cues and gestures, about the degree to which self is anchored in a role. Thus, actors will signal one another about their self-identity and the extent to which their roles are consistent with their self-conception. For example, roles not consistent with a person's self-conception will likely be played with considerable distance and disdain, whereas those that an individual considers central to self-definitions will be played much differently.[9]

In sum, Turner's approach maintains much of the dramaturgical metaphor of early role theory, but with an emphasis on the behavioral aspect of roles because actors impute roles to one another through behavioral cues. The notion in early analysis that roles are conceptions of expected behaviors is preserved, for assigning a role to a person invokes an expectation that a certain type and range of responses will ensue. The view that roles are the norms attendant on status positions is given less emphasis than in early theories but not ignored because norms and positions can be the basis for assigning and verifying roles.[10] And the conception in the dramaturgical metaphor of roles as parts that people learn to play is preserved, for people can denote one another's roles by virtue of their prior socialization into a common role repertoire.

TURNER'S STRATEGY
FOR BUILDING ROLE THEORY

Although Turner accepted a process orientation, he was committed to developing interactionism into "something akin to axiomatic theory."[11] He had recognized that role theory was segmented into a series of narrow propositions and hypotheses and that role theorists had been reluctant "to find unifying themes to link various role processes."

Turner's strategy was to use propositions from the numerous research studies to build more formal and abstract theoretical statements. His goal was to maintain a productive dialogue between specific empirical propositions and more abstract theoretical statements. Turner advocated the use of what he termed *main tendency* propositions to link concepts to empirical regularities and to consolidate the thrust of these regularities.[12] What Turner sought was a series of statements that highlight what tends to occur in the normal operation of systems of interaction. To this end, Turner provided a long list of main tendency propositions on (a) roles as they emerge, (b) roles as an interactive framework, (c) roles in relation to actors, (d) roles in organizational settings, (e) roles in societal settings, and (f) roles and the person. The most important of these propositions will be examined.[13]

Emergence and Character of Roles

1. In any interactive situation, behavior, sentiments, and motives tend to be differentiated into units that can be termed roles; once differentiated, elements of behavior, sentiment, and motives that appear in the same situation tend to be assigned to existing roles. (Tendencies for role differentiation and accretion.)

2. In any interactive situation, the meaning of individual actions for ego (the actor) and for any alter (others) is assigned on the basis of the imputed role. (Tendencies for meaningfulness.)

3. In connection with every role, there is a tendency for certain attributes of actors, aspects of behavior, and features of situations to become salient cues for the identification of roles. (Tendencies for role cues.)

4. Every role tends to acquire an evaluation for rank and social desirability. (Tendencies for evaluation.)

5. The character of a role—that is, its definition—will tend to change if there are persistent changes in either the behaviors of those presumed to be playing the role or the contexts in which the role is played. (Tendencies for behavioral correspondence.)

In these five propositions, individuals are seen as viewing the world in terms of roles, as employing a "folk norm" to discover the consistency of behaviors and to assign behavioral elements to an imputed role (role differentiation and accretion), as using roles to interpret and define situations (meaningfulness tendency), as searching roles for signals about the attributes of actors as well as the nature of the situation (role cues), and as evaluating roles for their power, prestige, and esteem, while assessing them for their degree of social desirability and worth (tendency for evaluation). When role behaviors or situations are permanently altered, the definition of role will also undergo change (behavioral correspondence).

Role as an Interactive Framework

6. The establishment and persistence of interaction tend to depend on the emergence and identification of ego and alter roles. (Tendency for interaction in roles.)

7. Each role tends to form as a comprehensive way of coping with one or more relevant alter roles. (Tendency for role complementarity.)

8. There is a tendency for stabilized roles to be assigned the character of legitimate expectations and to be seen as the appropriate way to behave in a situation. (Tendency for legitimate expectations.)

In these three additional propositions, interaction is seen as depending on the identification of roles. Moreover, roles tend to be complements of others—as is the case with wife/husband, parent/child, boss/employee roles—and thus operate to regularize interaction among complementary roles. Finally, roles that prove useful and that allow stable and fruitful interaction are translated into expectations that future transactions will and should occur as in the past.

Role in Relation to Actor

9. Once stabilized, the role structure tends to persist, regardless of changes in actors. (Tendency for role persistence.)

10. There is a tendency to identify a given individual with a given role and a complementary tendency for an individual to adopt a given role for the duration of the interaction. (Tendency in role allocation.)

11. To the extent that ego's role is an adaptation to alter's role, it incorporates some conception of alter's role. (Tendency for role-taking.)

12. Role behavior tends to be judged as adequate or inadequate by comparison with a conception of the role in question. (Tendency to assess role adequacy.)

13. The degree of adequacy in role performance of an actor determines the extent to which others will respond and reciprocate an actor's role performance. (Tendency for role reciprocity.)

Thus, once actors identify and assign one another to roles, the roles persist, and new actors will tend to be assigned to those roles that already exist in a situation. Humans also tend to adopt roles for the duration of an interaction, while having knowledge of the roles that others are playing. In addition, individuals carry with them general conceptions of what a role entails and what constitutes adequate performance. Finally, the adequacy of a person's role performance greatly influences the extent to which the role, along with the rights, privileges, and complementary behaviors that it deserves, will be acknowledged.

Role in Organizational Settings

14. To the extent that roles are incorporated into an organizational setting, organizational goals tend to become crucial criteria for role differentiation, evaluation, complementarity, legitimacy or expectation, consensus, allocation, and judgments of adequacy. (Tendency for organization goal dominance.)

15. To the extent that roles are incorporated into an organizational setting, the right to define the legitimate character of roles, to set the evaluations on roles, to allocate roles, and to judge role adequacy tends to be lodged in particular roles. (Tendency for legitimate role definers.)

16. To the extent that roles are incorporated into an organizational setting, differentiation tends to link roles to statuses in the organization. (Tendency for status.)

17. To the extent that roles are incorporated into an organizational setting, each role tends to develop as a pattern of adaptation to multiple alter roles. (Tendency for role-sets.)

18. To the extent that roles are incorporated into an organizational setting, the persistence of roles is intensified through tradition and formalization. (Tendency for formalization.)

When roles are lodged in an organization, then, its goals and key personnel become important in the role-making process. Moreover, it is primarily within organizations that status and role become merged. In this way, Turner incorporated Linton's and other early theorists' insight that status and role *can* become highly related, but Turner never abandoned Mead's and Herbert Blumer's emphasis that much interaction occurs in contexts where roles are not immersed within networks of clearly defined status positions. Turner also recognized that roles in structured situations develop as ways of adapting to a number of other roles that are typically assigned by role definers or required by organizational goals. Finally, roles within organizations tend to become formalized in that written agreements and tradition develop the power to maintain a given role system and to shape normative expectations.

Role in Societal Setting

19. Similar roles in different contexts tend to become merged and identified as a single role recurring in different relationships. (Tendency for economy of roles.)

20. To the extent that roles refer to more general social contexts and situations, differentiation tends to link roles to social values. (Tendency for value anchorage.)

21. The individual in society tends to be assigned and to assume roles consistent with one another. (Tendency for allocation consistency.)

Many roles are identified, assumed, and imputed in relation to a broader societal context. In the tendencies listed previously, Turner first argued that people tend to group behaviors in different social contexts into as few unifying roles as is possible or practical. Thus, people will identify a role as a way of making sense of disparate behaviors in different contexts. At the societal level, values are the equivalent of goals in organizational settings for identifying, differentiating, allocating, evaluating, and legitimating roles. Finally, all people tend to assume multiple roles in society, but they tend to assume roles that are consistent with one another.

Role and the Person

22. Actors tend to act to alleviate role strain arising from role contradiction, role conflict, and role inadequacy and to heighten the gratifications of high role adequacy. (Tendency to resolve role strain.)

23. Individuals in society tend to adopt a repertoire of role relationships as a framework for their own behavior and as a perspective for interpretation of the behavior of others. (Tendency to be socialized into common culture.)

24. Individuals tend to form self-conceptions by selectively identifying certain roles from their repertoires as more characteristically "themselves" than other roles. (Tendency to anchor self-conception.)

25. The self-conception tends to stress those roles that supply the basis for effective adaptation to relevant alters. (Adaptation of self-conception tendency.)

26. To the extent that roles must be played in situations that contradict the self-conception, those roles will be assigned role distance, and mechanisms for demonstrating lack of personal involvement will be employed. (Tendency for role distance.)

The "person" was a concept employed by Turner to denote "the distinctive repertoire of roles" that an individual enacts in relevant social settings. In these generalizations, Turner emphasized that individuals seek to resolve tensions among roles and to avoid contradictions between self-conceptions and roles. These propositions are, to a very great extent, elaborations of Turner's assumptions about the relationship between self-conceptions and role.

Turner recognized that these and other tendency propositions do not specify the conditions under which the tendency actually would occur. Turner believed that to be true theory, role analysis would have to specify some of these conditions; otherwise, the tendency propositions simply describe what occurs without indicating *when* and *why* these tendencies should be evident. As Turner sought to expand his theory, he began to add explanatory content—that is, to indicate when and why the tendencies exist.

CONCLUSION

Turner began more explanatory efforts by specifying conditions under which particular tendencies become evident. For example, the tendencies for individuals to identify with a role and for others around the individual to make such an identification are likely to emerge when[14] (a) allocation of roles is less flexible, (b) roles are highly differentiated, (c) roles are implicated in conflictual relationships, (d) performance of roles is judged as competent, (e) roles are considered difficult, (f) roles are either of high or low rank, (g) power is vested in a role, and so on.[15] These kinds of propositions were very suggestive, but Turner began to feel that they were somewhat ad hoc. Hence, he was led to ask, Are there some underlying processes that can explain the tendencies and the conditions under which they become manifest? This question inspired him, along with various collaborators, to develop what he felt were true explanatory propositions that would stand at the top of a deductive system explaining the tendencies and the conditions under which they are activated.

These explanatory propositions bring Turner's work from the midcentury into the more contemporary theoretical time frame, but for ease of exposition, we will deal with these explanatory "laws" here. In their most recent reworking, Turner and Paul Colomy[16] posit three underlying processes that can explain the other propositions in Turner's developing theory: (1) functionality, (2) tenability, and (3) representation. We will briefly examine each of these.

When activities are organized to meet explicit goals in an efficient and effective manner, then considerations of *functionality* are dominant. Such considerations are most likely when the organization of individuals to achieve goals can potentially involve conflicts of interest among the participants and when these participants must be recruited from diverse pools of individuals who differ in their abilities. Under these conditions, the differentiation and accretion of roles are organized in highly instrumental ways so that goals can be achieved within a minimum of conflict and friction.

When roles form and differentiate in ways that allow individuals to gain personal rewards and gratifications, considerations of *tenability* are evident. Thus, as individuals calculate their costs and rewards, and indeed are encouraged by the organization of roles to do so, tenability dominates functionality.

When the accretion and differentiation of roles involve the embodiment of cultural values, considerations of *representation* are evident. Moreover, the salience of representation of roles increases, when roles are implicated in group conflict and when incumbents in roles are recruited from homogeneous pools of individuals. When representation dominates the organization of roles, tenability will become more important than functionality.

The propositions developed for functionality, tenability, and representation are more complex than this brief discussion, but the general intent is clear. These propositions serve as the higher-order "laws" in deductive systems that subsume the tendency propositions and statements on the conditions under which they hold true. Although this strategy is suggestive, Turner has never fully implemented it by subsuming all the tendency propositions under these three laws in tight deductive systems. Yet, unlike much role theorizing from the midcentury, Turner's approach recognized that generalizations about roles from empirical observations need to be organized in ways facilitating their explanation by more abstract principles.[17] For Turner, the relative amounts of functionality, tenability, and representation would provide the needed explanatory push.

NOTES

1. Jonathan H. Turner, "Role," *Blackwell Encyclopedia of 20th Century Social Thought* (Oxford: Blackwell, 1996). See also the Web site for this book under "role theory." For the most recent review of Ralph H. Turner's role theory, see his: "Role Theory" in J. H. Turner, ed., *Handbook of Sociological Theory* (New York: Plenum, 2002)

2. See, for example, Ralph H. Turner, "Role-Taking: Processes versus Conformity," in *Human Behavior and Social Processes,* ed. A. Rose (Boston: Houghton Mifflin, 1962), pp. 20–40.

3. Ralph H. Turner, "Unanswered Questions in the Convergence between Structuralist and Interactionist Role Theories," in *Perspectives on Sociological Theory,* eds. S. N. Eisenstadt and H. J. Helle (London: Sage, 1985). In particular, this article addresses the argument in Warren Handel's "Normative Expectations and the Emergence of Meaning as Solutions to Problems: Convergence of Structural and Interactionist Views," *American Journal of Sociology* 84 (1979), pp. 855–881.

4. Ralph H. Turner, "Role-Taking: Processes versus Conformity" (cited in note 2).

5. Ibid.; "Social Roles: Sociological Aspects," *International Encyclopedia of the Social Sciences* (New York: Macmillan, 1968).

6. Ralph H. Turner, "The Normative Coherence of Folk Concepts," *Research Studies of the State College of Washington* 25 (1957).

7. Ralph H. Turner, "Role-Taking: Processes versus Conformity" (cited in note 2), p. 23.

8. Ralph H. Turner, "The Role and the Person," *American Journal of Sociology* 84 (1978), pp. 1–23.

9. Ralph H. Turner, "Social Roles: Sociological Aspects" (cited in note 5). Turner has extensively analyzed this process of self-anchorage in roles. See, for example, Ralph H. Turner, "The Real Self: From Institution to Impulse," *American Journal of Sociology* 81 (1970), pp. 989–1016; Ralph H. Turner and Victoria Billings, "Social Context of Self-Feeling," in *The Self-Society Interface: Cognition, Emotion, and Action,* eds. J. Howard and P. Callero (Cambridge: Cambridge University Press, 1990); Ralph H. Turner and Steven Gordon, "The Boundaries of the Self: The Relationship of Authenticity to Inauthenticity in the Self-Conception," in *Self-Concept: Advances in Theory and Research,* eds. M. D. Lynch, A. A. Norem-Hebeisen, and Kenneth Gergen (Cambridge, MA: Ballinger, 1981).

10. Ralph H. Turner, "Rule Learning as Role Learning," *International Journal of Critical Sociology* 1 (1974), pp. 10–28.

11. Ralph H. Turner, "Strategy for Developing an Integrated Role Theory," *Humboldt Journal of Social Relations* 7 (1980), pp. 123–139 and "Role Theory as Theory," unpublished manuscript.

12. Ralph H. Turner, "Strategy" (cited in note 11), pp. 123–124.

13. Ralph H. Turner, "Social Roles: Sociological Aspects" (cited in note 5).

14. Ralph H. Turner, "Role and the Person" (cited in note 8).

15. In his most recent effort, "Strategy for Developing an Integrated Role Theory" (cited in note 11), Turner focused on "role allocation" and "role differentiation" because he views these as the two most critical tendencies. The example of "the person and role" results in the same explanatory principles. Thus, this illustration provides additional examples of Turner's strategy.

16. Ralph H. Turner and Paul Colomy, "Role Differentiation: Orienting Principles," *Advances in Group Processes* 5 (1987), pp. 1–47.

17. For representative examples of the variety of empirical research conducted by Turner, see "The Navy Disbursing Officer as a Bureaucrat," *American Sociological Review* 12 (1947), pp. 342–348; "Moral Judgment: A Study in Roles," *American Sociological Review* 17 (1952), pp. 70–77; "Occupational Patterns of Inequality," *American Journal of Sociology* 50 (1954), pp. 437–447; "Zoot-Suiters and Mexicans: Symbols in Crowd Behavior" (with S. J. Surace), *American Journal of Sociology* 62 (1956), pp. 14–20; "The Changing Ideology of Success: A Study of Aspirations of High School Men in Los Angeles," *Transactions of the Third World Congress of Sociology* 5 (1956), pp. 35–44; "An Experiment in Modification of the Role Conceptions," *Yearbook of the American Philosophical Society* (1959), pp. 329–332; "Some Family Determinants of Ambition," *Sociology and Social Research* 46 (1962), pp. 397–411; *The Social Context of Ambition* (San Francisco: Chandler & Sharp, 1964); and "Ambiguity and Interchangeability in Role Attribution" (with Norma Shosid), *American Sociological Review* 41 (1976); and "The True Self Method for Studying Self-Conception," *Symbolic Interaction* 4 (1981), pp. 1–20.

24

Dramaturgical Theory: Erving Goffman

rving Goffman (1922–1982) was, perhaps, the most creative theorist of interaction processes in the second half of the twentieth century. In one of his last statements before his death, he defined the analysis of face-to-face interaction as the *interaction order*,[1] but unlike many micro-level theorists and researchers, Goffman did not proclaim that the interaction order is all that is real. Rather, he simply argued that this interaction order constitutes a distinctive realm of reality that reveals its own unique dynamics. For, "to speak of the relative autonomous forms of life in the interaction order . . . is not to put forward these forms as somehow prior, fundamental, or constitutive of the shape of macroscopic phenomena."[2] Goffman recognized that, at best, there is a "loose coupling" of the micro and macro realms. Macro phenomena, such as commodities markets, urban land-use values, economic growth, and society-wide stratification, cannot be explained by micro-level analysis.[3] Of course, one can supplement macro-level explanations by recording how individuals interact in various types of settings and encounters, but these analyses will not supplant macro-level explanations. Conversely, what transpires in the interaction order cannot be explained solely by macroprocesses. Rather, macro-level phenomena are always transformed in ways unique to the individuals involved in interaction.

To be sure, macro phenomena constrain and circumscribe interaction and, at times, guide the general form of the interaction, but the inherent dynamics of the interaction itself preclude a one-to-one relation to these structural parameters. Indeed, the form of interaction can often be at odds with macrostructures, operating smoothly in ways that contradict these structures without dramatically changing them. Thus, the crude notion that interaction is constrained by macrostructures in ways that "reproduce" social structure does not recognize the autonomy of the interaction order. For interaction "is not an expression *of* structural arrangements in any simple sense; at best it is an expression advanced *in regard to* these arrangements. Social structures don't 'determine' culturally standard displays (of interaction rituals), they merely help select from the available repertoire of them."[4] Thus, there is a "loose coupling" of "interactional practices and social structures, a collapsing of strata and structures into broader categories, the categories themselves not corresponding one-to-one to anything in the structural world. . . ."[5] There is, then, "a set of transformation rules, or a membrane selecting how various externally relevant social distinctions will be managed within the interaction."[6]

These "transformations" are, however, far from insignificant phenomena. Much of what gives the social world a sense of "being real" arises from the practices of individuals as they deal with one another in various situations. "We owe our unshaking sense of realities,"[7] to the rules of interpersonal contact. Moreover, although a single gathering and episode of interaction might not have great social significance, "through these comings together much of our social life is organized."[8] The interaction order is thus a central topic of sociological theory.

Goffman's approach to this domain is unique.[9] Although we must "keep faith with the spirit of natural science, and lurch along, seriously kidding ourselves that our rut has a forward direction,"[10] we must not become over-enamored with the mature sciences. Social life is "ours to study naturalistically,"[11] but our study should not be rigid.[11] Instead, ad hoc observation, cultivation of anecdotes, creative thinking, illustrations from literature, examination of books of etiquette, personal experiences, and many other sources of unsystematic data should guide inquiry into the micro order. Indeed, "human life is only a small irregular scab on the face of nature, not particularly amenable to deep systematic analysis."[12] Yet, human life can be studied in the spirit of scientific inquiry.

THE DRAMATURGICAL METAPHOR

In both his first and last major works—*The Presentation of Self in Everyday Life* and *Frame Analysis,* respectively—Goffman analogized to the stage and theater. Hence, the designation of his work as "dramaturgical" has become commonplace.[13] This designation is, however, somewhat misleading because it creates the impression that there is a script, a stage, an audience, props, and actors playing roles. Dramaturgy is used to denote Goffman's work in another sense: Individuals are actors who "put on" a performance, often cynical and deceptive, for one another and who manipulate the script, stage, props, and roles for their own purposes. This more cynical view of Goffman's dramaturgy is perhaps closer to the mark,[14] but it too is somewhat misleading. Commentators have often portrayed Goffman as presenting a kind of "con man"[15] view of human social interaction—a metaphor that captures some of the examples and topics of his approach but obscures the more fundamental processes denoted by Goffman's theorizing.

We can use the metaphor of dramaturgy in a less extreme sense. In Goffman's work, there is concern with a cultural script, or normative rules; there is a heavy emphasis on how individuals manage their impressions and play roles; there is a concern with stages and props (physical space and objects); there is an emphasis on stag*ing,* of the manipulation of gestures as well as spacing, props, and other physical aspects of a setting; there is a view of self as situational, determined more by the cultural script, stage, and audience than by enduring and transituational configurations of self-attitudes and self-feelings; and there is a particular emphasis on how performances create a theatrical ambiance—a mood, definition, and sense of reality.

This metaphor provides only an orientation of Goffman's approach. We need to "fill in" this orientation with more details. To do so, we will review Goffman's most important works and try to pull the diverse vocabularies and concepts together into a more unified theoretical perspective—dramaturgical in its general contours but more than just a clever metaphor.[16]

THE PRESENTATION OF SELF

The Presentation of Self in Everyday Life[17] was Goffman's first major work and was largely responsible for the designation of Goffman as a dramaturgical theorist. The basic argument is that individuals deliberately "give" and inadvertently "give off" signs that provide others with information about how to respond. From such mutual use of "sign-vehicles," individuals develop a "definition of the situation," which is a "plan for cooperative activity," but which, at the same time, is "not so much a real agreement as to what exists but rather a real agreement as to whose claims concerning what issues will be temporarily honored."[18] In constructing this overall definition of a situation, individuals engage in performances in which each orchestrates gestures to "present oneself" in a particular manner as a person having identifiable characteristics and deserving of treatment in a certain fashion. These performances revolve around several interrelated dynamics.

First, a performance involves the creation of a *front*. A front includes the physical "setting" and the use of the physical layout, its fixed equipment like furniture and other "stage props" to create a certain impression. A front also involves (a) "items of expressive equipment" (emotions, energy, and other capacities for expression); (b) "appearance," or those signs that tell others of an individual's social position and status as well as the "ritual state" of the individual with respect to social, work, or recreational activity[19]; and (c) "manner," or those signs that inform others about the role that an individual expects to play.[20] As a general rule, people expect consistency in these elements of their fronts—use of setting and its props, mobilization of expressive equipment, social status, expression of ritual readiness for various types of activity, and efforts to assume certain roles.[21] There are relatively few fronts, and people know them all. Moreover, fronts tend to be established, institutionalized, and stereotypical for various kinds of settings, with the result that "when an actor takes an established role, usually he (she) finds that a particular front has already been established for it."[22]

Second, in addition to presenting a front, individuals use gestures in what Goffman termed *dramatic realization,* or the infusion into activity of signs that highlight commitment to a given definition of a situation. The more a situation creates problems in presenting a front, Goffman argued, the greater will be efforts at dramatic realization.[23]

Third, performances also involve *idealizations,* or efforts to present oneself in ways that "incorporate and exemplify the officially accredited values of society."[24] When individuals are mobile, moving into a new setting, efforts at idealization will be most pronounced. Idealization creates a problem for individuals, however: If the idealization is to be effective, individuals must suppress, conceal, and underplay those elements of themselves that might contradict more general values.

Fourth, such efforts at concealment are part of a more general process of *maintaining expressive control.* Because minor cues and signs are read by others and contribute to a definition of a situation, actors must regulate their muscular activity, their signals of involvement, their orchestration of front, and their ability to be fit for interaction. The most picayune discrepancy between behavior and the definition of a situation can unsettle the interaction, because "the impression of reality fostered by a performance is a delicate, fragile thing that can be shattered by very minor mishaps."[25]

Fifth, individuals can also engage in *misrepresentation.* The eagerness of one's audience to read gestures and determine one's front makes that audience vulnerable to manipulation and duping.[26]

Sixth, individuals often attempt to engage in *mystification,* or the maintenance of distance from others as a way to keep them in awe and in conformity to a definition of a situation. Such mystification is, however, limited primarily to those of higher rank and status.

Seventh, individuals seek to make their performances seem *real* and to avoid communicating a sense of contrivance. Thus, individuals must communicate, or at least appear to others, as sincere, natural, and spontaneous.

These procedures for bringing off a successful performance and thereby creating an overall definition of a situation are the core of Goffmanian sociology. They become elaborated and extended in subsequent works, but Goffman never abandoned the idea that fundamental to the interaction order are the efforts of individuals to orchestrate their performances, even in deceptive and manipulative ways, so as to maintain a particular definition of the situation. These ideas are presented propositionally in Table 24.1.

Table 24.1 Goffman's Propositions on Interaction and Performance

I. As individuals make visual and verbal contact, the more likely they are to use gestures to orchestrate a performance, with the success of this performance depending on

  A. Presentation of a coherent front that, in turn, is a positive and additive function of

    1. Control of physical space, props, and equipment in a setting.

    2. Control of expressive equipment in a setting.

    3. Control of signals marking propensity for types of ritual activity.

    4. Control of signals marking status outside and inside the interaction.

    5. Control of signals pertaining to identifiable roles.

  B. Incorporation and exemplification of general cultural values.

  C. Imbuing a situation with a personal mystique.

  D. Signaling sincerity.

II. As individuals in a setting orchestrate their performances and, at the same time, accept one another's performances, they are likely to develop a common definition of the situation.

III. As a common definition of the situation emerges, the ease of the interaction increases.

Although the propositions in Table 24.1 constitute only an opening chapter in *The Presentation of Self,* they are by far the most enduring portions of this first major work. The rest of the book is concerned with performances sustained by more than one individual. Goffman introduced the concept of *team* to denote performances that are presented by individuals who must cooperate to effect a particular definition of the situation. Often two teams must present performances to each other, but more typically, one team constitutes a performer and the other an audience. Team performers generally move between a *front region,* or *frontstage,* where they coordinate their performances before an audience, and a *back region,* or backstage, where team members can relax. Goffman also introduced the notion of *outside,* or the residual region beyond the frontstage and backstage. Frontstage behavior is polite, maintaining a decorum appropriate to a team performance (for example, selling cars, serving food, meeting students, and so on), whereas backstage behavior is more informal and is geared toward maintaining the solidarity and morale of team performers. When outsiders or members of the audience intrude on performers in the backstage, a tension is created because team members are caught in their nonperforming roles.[27]

A basic problem of all team performances is maintaining a particular definition of the situation in front of the audience. This problem is accentuated when there are large rank or status differences among team members,[28] when the team has many members,[29] when the frontstages and backstages are not clearly partitioned, and when the team must hide information contrary to its image of itself. To counteract these kinds of problems, social control among the team's members is essential. When members are backstage, such control is achieved through morale-boosting activities, such as denigrating the audience, kidding one another, shifting to informal address, and engaging in stage talk (talk about performances on frontstage). When they are onstage, control is sustained by realigning actions revolving around subtle communications among team members that, one hopes, the audience will not understand.

Breaches of the performances occur when a team member acts in ways that challenge the definition of the situation created by the team's performances. Attempts to prevent such incidents involve further efforts at social control, especially a backstage emphasis on (a) playing one's part and not emitting unmeant gestures, (b) showing loyalty to the team and not the audience, and (c) exercising foresight and anticipating potential problems with the team or the audience. Team members are assisted in social control by members of the audience who (a) tend to stay away from the backstage, (b) act disinterested when exposed to backstage behavior, and (c) employ elaborate etiquette (exhibiting proper attention and interest, inhibiting their own potential performances, avoiding faux pas) to avoid a "scene" with the team.

What is true of teams and audiences is, Goffman implied, also true of individuals. Interaction involves a performance for others who constitute an audience. One seeks to sustain a performance when moving to the frontstage and relax a front when moving to a backstage region. People try very hard to avoid mistakes and faux pas that could breach the definition of the situation, and they are assisted in this effort by others in their audience who exercise tact and etiquette to avoid a scene. Such are the themes of *The Presentation of Self,* and most of Goffman's work represented a conceptual elaboration of them. The notion of "teams" recedes, but general model elaborating these themes into a theory of interaction among individuals emerges.

FOCUSED INTERACTION

Goffman generally employed the terms *unfocused* and *focused* to denote two basic types of interaction. *Unfocused interaction* "consists of interpersonal communications that result solely by virtue of persons being in one another's presence, as when two strangers across the room from each other check up on each other's clothing, posture, and general manner, while each modifies his (her) own demeanor because he himself is under observation."[30] As will be explored later, such unfocused interaction is, Goffman argued, an important part of the interaction order, for much of what people do is exchange glances and monitor each other in public places. *Focused interaction,* in contrast, "occurs when people effectively agree to sustain for a time a single focus of cognitive and visual attention, as in a conversation, a board game, or a joint task sustained by a close face-to-face circle of contributors."[31]

Encounters

Focused interaction occurs within what Goffman termed *encounters,* which constitute one of the core structural units of the interaction order. Goffman mentioned encounters in his first major work, *The Presentation of Self in Everyday Life,* but their full dimensions are explored in his next book, *Encounters.*[32] There, an encounter is defined as focused interaction revealing the following characteristics[33]:

1. A single visual and cognitive focus of attention
2. A mutual and preferential openness to verbal communication
3. A heightened mutual relevance of acts
2. An eye-to-eye ecological huddle, maximizing mutual perception and monitoring
4. An emergent "we" feeling of solidarity and flow of feeling
5. A ritual and ceremonial punctuation of openings, closings, entrances, and exits
6. A set of procedures for corrective compensation for deviant acts

To sustain itself, an encounter develops a "membrane," or penetrable barrier to the larger social world in which the interaction is located. Goffman typically conceptualized the immediate setting of an encounter as a *gathering,* or the assembling in space of co-present individuals; in turn, gatherings are lodged within a more inclusive unit, the *social occasion,* or the larger undertaking sustained by fixed equipment, distinctive ethos and emotional structure, program or agenda, rules of proper and improper conduct, and preestablished sequencing of activities (beginning, phases, high point, and ending). Thus, encounters emerge from episodes of focused interaction within gatherings that are lodged in social occasions.[34]

The membrane of an encounter, as well as its distinctive characteristics previously listed, are sustained by a set of *rules.* In *Encounters,* Goffman lists several; later, in what is probably his most significant work, *Interaction Ritual,* he lists several more.[35] Let us combine both discussions by listing the rules that guide focused interaction in encounters:

1. *Rules of irrelevance,* which "frame" a situation as excluding certain materials (attributes of participants, psychological states, cultural values and norms, etc.).[36]
2. *Rules of transformation,* which specify how materials moving through the membrane created by rules of irrelevance are to be altered to fit into the interaction.
3. *Rules of "realized resources,"* which provide a general schemata and framework for expression and interpretation for activities among participants.

4. *Rules of talk,* which are the procedures, conventions, and practices guiding the flow of verbalizations with respect to[37]

   a. Maintaining a single focus of attention.
   b. Establishing "clearance cues" for determining when one speaker is done and another can begin.
   c. Determining how long and how frequently any one person can hold the floor.
   d. Regulating interruptions and lulls in the conversation.
   e. Sanctioning participants whose attention wanders to matters outside the conversation.
   f. Ensuring that nearby people do not interfere with the conversation.
   g. Guiding the use of politeness and tact, even in the face of disagreements.

5. *Rules of self-respect,* which encourage participants to honor with tact and etiquette their respective efforts to present themselves in a certain light.

Interaction is thus guided by complex configurations of rules that individuals learn how to use and apply in different types of encounters, logged in varying types of gatherings and social occasions. The "reality" of the world is, to a very great extent, sustained by people's ability to invoke and use these rules,[38] and when these rules are operating effectively, individuals develop a "state of euphoria," or what Randall Collins has termed enhanced "emotional energy." However, encounters are vulnerable to "dysphoria" or tension when these rules do not exclude troublesome external materials or fail to regulate the flow of interaction. Goffman saw such failures as *incidents* or *breaches;* when they can be effectively handled by tact and corrective procedures, they are then viewed as *integrations* because they are blended into the ongoing encounter. The key mechanism for avoiding dysphoria and maintaining the integration of the encounter is the use of ritual.

Ritual

In *Interaction Ritual,*[39] Goffman's great contribution is the recognition that minor, seemingly trivial, and everyday rituals—such as "Hello, how are you?" "Good morning," "Please, after you," and so on—are crucial to the maintenance of social order. In his words, he "reformulated Émile Durkheim's social psychology in a modern dress"[40] by recognizing that, when individuals gather and begin to interact, their behaviors are highly ritualized. That is, actors punctuate each phase of interpersonal contact with stereotypical sequences of behavior that invoke the rules of the encounter and, at the same time, become the medium or vehicle by which the rules are followed. Rituals are thus essential for (a) mobilizing individuals to participate in interaction; (b) making them cognizant of the relevant rules of irrelevance, transformation, resource use, self-respect, and talk; (c) guiding them during the course of the interaction; and (d) helping them correct for breaches and incidents.

Among the most significant are those rituals revolving around deference and demeanor. *Deference* pertains to interpersonal rituals that express individuals' respect for others, their willingness to interact, their affection and other emotions, and their engagement in the encounter. In Goffman's words, deference establishes "marks of devotion" by which an actor "celebrates and confirms his (her) relationship to a recipient."[41] As a result, deference contains a "kind of promise, expressing in truncated form the actor's avowal and pledge to treat the recipient in a particular way in the on-coming activity."[42] Thus, seemingly innocuous gestures—"It's nice to see you again," "How are things?" "What are you doing?" "Good bye," "See you later," and many other stereotypical phrases as well as bodily movements—are rituals that present a demeanor invoking relevant rules and guiding the opening, sequencing, and closing of the interaction.

Deference rituals, Goffman argued, can be of two types: (1) avoidance rituals and (2) presentational rituals. *Avoidance rituals* are those that an individual uses to keep distance from another and to avoid violating the "ideal sphere" that lies around the other. Such rituals are most typical among unequals. *Presentational rituals* "encompass acts through which the individual makes specific attestations to recipients concerning how he regards them and how he will treat them in the on-coming interaction."[43] Goffman saw interaction as constantly involving a dialectic between avoidance and presentational rituals as individuals respect each other and maintain distance while trying to make contact and get things done.[44]

In contrast, *demeanor* is "that element of the individual's ceremonial behavior conveyed through deportment, dress, and bearing which serves to (inform) those in his immediate presence that he is a person of certain desirable or undesirable qualities."[45] Through demeanor rituals, individuals present images of themselves to others and, at the same time, communicate that they are reliable, trustworthy, and tactful.

Thus, through deference and demeanor rituals individuals plug themselves into an encounter by invoking relevant rules and demonstrating their capacity to follow them, while indicating their respect for others and presenting themselves as certain kinds of individuals. The enactment of such deference and demeanor rituals in concrete gatherings, especially encounters but also including unfocused situations, provides a basis for the integration of society. For "throughout . . . ceremonial obligations and expectations, a constant flow of indulgences is spread through society, with others who are present constantly reminding the individual that he must keep himself together as a well demeaned person and affirm the sacred quality of these others."[46]

Roles

In presenting themselves to others, individuals also seek to play particular roles. Thus, as people present a front, invoke relevant rules, and emit rituals, they also try to orchestrate roles for themselves. For Goffman, then, a *role* is "a bundle of activities visibly performed before a set of others and visibly meshed into the activities these others perform."[47] In the terms of Ralph Turner's analysis (see Chapter 23), individuals attempt to "make a role" for themselves; if successful, this effort contributes to the overall definition of the situation.

In trying to establish a role, the individual "must see to it that the impressions of him that are conveyed in the situation are compatible with role-appropriate personal qualities effectively imputed to him,"[48] Thus, individuals in a situation are expected to try to make roles for themselves that are consistent with their demeanor, their self as performed before others, and their front (stage props, expressive equipment, appearance). And, if the inconsistency between the attempted role and these additional aspects of a performance becomes evident, then others in the situation are likely to sanction the individual through subtle cues and gestures. These others are driven to do so because discrepancy between another's role and other performance cues disrupts the definition of the situation and the underlying sense of reality that this definition promotes. Thus, role is contingent on the responses and reactions of others, and, because their sense of reality partially depends on successful and appropriate role assumption, an individual will have difficulty changing a role in a situation once it is established.

Often, however, people perceive a role to be incompatible with their images of themselves in a situation. Under these conditions they will display what Goffman termed *role distance,* whereby a "separation" of the person from a role is communicated. Such distancing, Goffman argued,[49] allows the individual to (a) release the tension associated with a role considered to be "beneath his (her) dignity," (b) present additional aspects of self that extend beyond the role, and (c) remove the burden of "complete compliance to the role," thereby making minor transgressions less dramatic and troublesome for others.

Role distance is but an extreme response to the more general process of *role embracement*. For any role, individuals will reveal varying degrees of attachment and involvement in the role. One extreme is role distance, whereas the other extreme is what Goffman termed *engrossment,* or complete involvement in a role. In general, Goffman argued,[50] those roles in which individuals can direct what is going on are likely to involve high degrees of embracement, whereas those roles in which the individual is subordinate will be played with considerable role distance.

As is evident, then, the assumption of a role is connected to the self-image that actors project in their performance. Although the self that one reveals in a situation depends on the responses of others who can confirm or disconfirm that person's self in a situation, the organization of a performance onstage before others is still greatly circumscribed by self.

Self

Goffman's view of self is highly situational and contingent on the responses of others. Although one of the main activities of actors in a situation is to present themselves in a certain way, Goffman was highly skeptical about a "core" or "trans-situational" self-conception that is part of an individual's "personality." In almost all his works he took care to emphasize that individuals do not have an underlying "personality" or "identity" that is carried from situation to situation. For example, in his last major book, *Frame Analysis*,[51] he argued that people in interaction often presume that the presented self provides a glimpse at a more coherent and core self, but in reality this is simply a folk presumption because there is "no reason to think that all these gleanings about himself that an individual makes available, all these pointings from his current situation to the way he is in his other occasions, have anything very much in common."[52]

Yet, even though there is no transitional or core self, people's efforts to present images of themselves in a particular situation and others' reactions to this presentation are central dynamics in all encounters. Individuals constantly emit demeanor cues that project images of themselves as certain kinds of persons, or, in the vocabulary of *The Presentation of Self,* they engage in "performances." In *Interaction Ritual,* Goffman rephrased this argument somewhat, and, in so doing, he refined his views on self. In encounters, an individual acts out *a line,* which is "a pattern of verbal and nonverbal acts by which he expresses his view of the situation and, through this, his evaluation of the participants, especially himself."[53] In developing a line, an individual presents *a face,* which is "the positive social value a person effectively claims for himself by the line others assume he has during a particular contact."[54] Individuals seek to stay *in face* or to *maintain face* by presenting an image of themselves through their line that is supported by the responses of others and, if possible, sustained by impersonal agencies in a situation. Conversely, a person is *in wrong face* or *out of face* when the line emitted is inappropriate and unaccepted by others. Thus, although a person's social face "can be his most personal possession and the center of his security and pleasure, it is only on loan to him from society; it will be withdrawn unless he conducts himself in a way that is worthy of it. . . . "[55]

As noted earlier, Goffman argued that a key norm in any encounter is "the rule of self respect," which requires individuals to maintain face and, through tact and etiquette, the face of others. Thus, by virtue of tact or the "language of hint . . . , innuendo, ambiguities, well-placed phrases, carefully worked jokes, and so on,"[56] individuals sustain each other's face; in so doing, they confirm the definition of the situation and promote a sense of a common reality. For this reason, a given line and face in an encounter are difficult to change, once established, because to alter face (and the line by which it is presented) would require redefining the situation and recreating a sense of reality. And, because face is "on loan" to a person from the responses of others, the individual must incur high costs—such as embarrassment or a breach of the situation—to alter a line and face.

Face engagements are usually initiated with eye contact, and, once initiated, they involve ritual openings appropriate to the situation (as determined by length of last engagement, amount of time since previous engagement, level of inequality, and so forth). During the course of the face engagement, each individual uses tact to maintain, if possible, each other's face and to sanction, if necessary, each other into his or her appropriate line. In particular, participants seek to avoid "a scene" or breach in the situation; so they use tact and etiquette to save their own faces and that of others. Moreover, as deemed appropriate for the type of encounter (as well as for the larger gathering and more inclusive social occasion), individuals will attempt to maintain what Goffman sometimes termed *the territories of self,* revolving around such matters as physical props, ecological space, personal preserve (territory around one's body), and conversational rights (to talk and be heard), which are necessary for people to execute their line and maintain face.[57] In general, the higher the rank of individuals, the greater are their territories of self in an encounter.[58] To violate such territories disrupts or breaches the situation, forcing remedial action by participants to restore their respective lines, face, definitions of the situation, and sense of reality.

Talk

Throughout his work, but especially in later books such as *Frame Analysis*[59] and in numerous essays (see those collected in *Forms of Talk*[60]), Goffman emphasized the significance of verbalizations for focusing people's attention. When "talk" is viewed interactionally, "it is an example of that arrangement by which individuals come together and sustain matters having a ratified, joint, current, and running claim upon attention, a claim which lodges them together in some sort of intersubjective, mental world."[61] Thus, in Goffman's view, "no resource is more effective as a basis for joint involvement than speaking" because it fetches "speaker and hearer into the same interpretation schema that applies to what is thus attended."[62]

Talk is thus a crucial mechanism for drawing individuals together, focusing their attention, and adjudicating an overall definition of the situation. Because talk is so central to focusing interaction, it is normatively regulated and ritualized. One significant norm is the prohibition against *self-talk* because, when people talk to themselves, it "warns others that they might be wrong in assuming a jointly maintained base of ready mutual intelligibility. . . ."[63] Moreover, other kinds of quasi talk are also regulated and ritualized. For example, *response cues* or "exclamatory interjections which are not full-fledged words"—"Oops," "Wow," "Oh," and "Yikes"—are regulated as to when they can be used and the way they are uttered.[64] Verbal fillers—"ah," "uh," "um," and the like—are also ritualized and are used to facilitate "conversational tracking." In essence, they indicate that "the speaker does not have, as of yet, the proper word but is working on the matter" and that he or she is still engaged in the conversation. Even seemingly emotional cues and tabooed expressions, such as all the "four-letter words," are not so much an expression of emotion as "self-other alignment" and assert that "our inner concerns should be theirs." Such outbursts are normative and ritualized because this "invitation into our interiors tends to be made only when it will be easy to other persons present to see where the voyage takes them."[65]

In creating a definition of the situation, Goffman argued, talk operates in extremely complex ways. When individuals talk, they create what Goffman termed a *footing*, or assumed foundation for the conversation and the interaction. Because verbal symbols are easily manipulated, people can readily change the footing or basic premises underlying the conversation.[66] Such shifts in footing are, however, highly ritualized and usually reveal clear markers. For example, when a person says something like "Let's not talk about that," the footing of the conversation is shifted, but in a ritualized way; similarly, when someone utters a phrase like "That's great, but what about . . . ?" this person is also changing the footing through ritual.

Shifts in footing raise a question that increasingly dominated Goffman's later works: the issue of *embedding*. Goffman came to recognize that conversations are *layered* and, hence, embedded in different footings. There are often multiple footings for talk, as when someone "says one thing but means another" or when a person "hints" or "implies" something else. These "layerings" of conversations, which embed them in different contexts, are possible because speech is capable of generating subtle and complex meanings. For example, irony, sarcasm, puns, wit, double-entendres, inflections, shadings, and other manipulations of speech demonstrate the capacity of individuals to shift footings and contextual embeddings of a conversation (for example, think of a conversation in a work setting involving romantic flirtations; it will involve constant movement in footing and context). Yet, for encounters to proceed smoothly, these alterations in footing are, to some extent, normatively regulated and ritualized, enabling individuals to sustain a sense of common reality.

Talk is thus a critical dimension of focused interaction. Without talk, the gestures and cues that people can emit are limited and lack the subtlety and complexity of language. And, as Goffman began to explore this complexity in later works, earlier notions about "definitions of situations" seemed too crude because people could construct multiple, as well as subtly layered, definitions of any situation—an issue that we will explore near the end of this chapter. For our purposes here, the critical point is that talk focuses attention and pulls actors together, forcing their interaction on a face-to-face basis. But, despite the complexity of how this focusing can be done, talk is still normatively and ritually regulated in ways that produce a sense of shared reality for individuals.[67]

Table 24.2 summarizes Goffman's analysis of focused encounters. Focused encounters occur when social occasions put people in face-to-face contact, and the viability of the encounter depends on rules, rituals, and the capacity of individuals to present acceptable performances. The statements under I and II reveal the basic argument in Goffman's approach.

Disruption and Repair in Focused Interaction

Goffman stressed that disruption in encounters is never a trivial matter:

Social encounters differ a great deal in the importance that participants give to them but, whether crucial or picayune, all encounters represent

Table 24.2 Goffman's General Propositions on Focused Interaction

I. Encounters are created when
   A. Social occasions put individuals in physical proximity.
   B. Gatherings allow face-to-face contact revolving around talk.
II. The viability of an encounter is a positive and multiplicative function of
   A. The availability of relevant normative rules to guide participants with respect to such issues as
      1. Irrelevance, or excluded matters.
      2. Transformation, or how external matters are to be incorporated.
      3. Resource use, or what local resources are to be drawn from.
      4. Talk, or how verbalizations are to be ordered.
      5. Self-respect, or the maintenance of lines and face.
   B. The availability of ritual practices that can be used to
      1. Regulate talk and conversation.
      2. Express appropriate deference and demeanor.
      3. Invoke and punctuate normative rules.
      4. Repair breaches to the interaction.
   C. The capacity of individuals to present acceptable performances with respect to
      1. Lines, or directions of conduct.
      2. Roles, or specific clusters of rights and duties.
      3. Faces, or specific presentations of personal characteristics.
      4. Self, or particular images of oneself.

occasions when the individual can become spontaneously involved in the proceedings and derive from this a firm sense of reality. And this feeling is not a trivial thing, regardless of the package in which it comes. When an incident occurs . . . then the reality is threatened. Unless the disturbance is checked, unless the interactants regain their proper involvement, the illusion of reality will be shattered. . . . [68]

When a person emits gestures that contradict normative roles, presents a contradictory front, fails to enact appropriate rituals, seeks an inappropriate role, attempts a normatively or ritually incorrect line, or presents a wrong face, there is potential for *a scene*. From the person's point of view, there is a possibility of *embarrassment*, to use Goffman's favorite phrase; once embarrassed, an individual's responses can further degenerate in an escalating cycle of ever greater levels of embarrassment. From the perspective of others, a scene disrupts the definition of the situation and threatens the sense of reality necessary for them to feel comfortable. Individuals implicitly assume that people are reliable and trustworthy, that they are what they appear to be, that they are competent, and that they can be relied on; thus, when a scene occurs, these implicit assumptions are challenged and threaten the organization of the encounter (and, potentially, the larger gathering and social occasion).

For this reason an individual will seek to repair a scene caused by the use of inappropriate gestures, and others will use tact to assist the individual in such repair efforts. The sense of order of a situation is thus sustained by a variety of corrective responses by individuals and by the willingness of others to use tact in ignoring minor mistakes and, if this is not possible, to employ tact to facilitate an offending individual's corrective efforts. People "disattend" much potentially discrepant behavior, and, when this is no longer an option, they are prepared to accept apologies, accounts, new information, excuses, and other ritually and normatively appropriate efforts at repair. Of course, this willingness to accept people as they are, to assume their competence, and to overlook minor interpersonal mistakes makes individuals vulnerable to manipulation and deceit.

UNFOCUSED INTERACTION

Goffman was one of the few sociologists to recognize that behavior and interaction in public places, or in unfocused settings, are important features of the interaction order and, by extension, of social organization in general. Such simple acts as walking down the street, standing in line, sitting in a waiting room or on a park bench, standing in an elevator, going to and from a public rest room, and many other activities represent a significant realm of social organization. These unfocused situations in which people are co-present but not involved in prolonged talk and "face encounters" represent a crucial topic of sociological inquiry—a topic that is often seen as trivial but that embraces much of people's time and attention. In two works, *Relations in Public* and *Behavior in Public Places*, Goffman explored the dynamics of unfocused gatherings.[69]

Unfocused gatherings are like focused interactions in their general contours: They are normatively regulated; they call for performances by individuals; they include the presentation of a self; they involve the use of rituals; they have normatively and ritually appropriate procedures for repair; and they depend on a considerable amount of etiquette, tact, and inattention. Let us explore each of these features in somewhat greater detail.

Much like a focused interaction, unfocused gatherings involve normative rules concerning spacing, movement, positioning, listening, talking, and self-presentation. But, unlike focused interaction, norms do not have to sustain a well-defined membrane. There is no closure, intense focus of attention, or face-to-face obligations in unfocused encounters. Rather, rules pertain to how individuals are to comport themselves *without* becoming the focus of attention and involved in a face encounter. Rules are thus about how to move, talk, sit, stand, present self, apologize, and perform other actions necessary to sustain public order without creating a situation requiring the additional interpersonal "work" of focused interaction.

When in public, individuals still engage in performances, but, because the audience is not involved in a face engagement or prolonged tracks of talk, the presentation can be more muted and less animated. Goffman used a variety of terms to describe these presentations, two of the most frequent being *body idiom*[70] and *body gloss*.[71] Both terms denote the overall configuration of gestures, or demeanor, that an individual makes available and gleanable to others. (Conversely, others are constantly *scanning* to determine the content of others' body idiom and body gloss.) Such demeanor denotes a person's direction, speed, resoluteness, purpose, and other aspects of a course of action. In *Relations in Public*, Goffman enumerated three types of body gloss:[72] (1) *orientation gloss*, or gestures giving evidence to others confirming that a person is engaged in a recognizable and appropriate activity in the present time and place; (2) *circumspection gloss*, or gestures indicating to others that a person is not going to encroach on or threaten the activity of others; and (3) *overplay gloss*, or gestures signaling that a person is not constrained or under duress and is, therefore, fully in charge and control of his or her other movements and actions. Thus, the public performance of an individual in unfocused interaction revolves around providing information that one is of "sound character and reasonable competency."[73]

In public and during unfocused interactions, the *territories of self* become an important consideration. Goffman listed various kinds of territorial considerations that can become salient during unfocused interaction, including[74] (a) fixed geographical spaces attached to a particular person, (b) egocentric preserves of non-encroachment that surround individuals as they move in space, (c) personal spaces that others are not to violate under any circumstances, (d) stalls or bounded places that an individual can temporarily claim, (e) use spaces that can be claimed as an individual engages in some instrumental activity, (f) turns or the claimed order of doing or receiving something relative to others in a situation, (g) possessional territory or objects identified with self and arrayed around an individual's body, (h) informational preserve or the body of facts about a person that is controlled and regulated, and (i) conversational preserve or the right to control who can summon and talk to an individual. Depending on the type of unfocused interaction, as well as on the number, age, sex, rank, position, and other characteristics of the participants, the territories of self will vary, but in all societies there are clearly understood norms about which configuration of these territories is relevant, and to what degree it can be invoked.

These territories of self are made visible through what Goffman termed *markers*. Markers are signals and objects that denote the type of territorial claim, its extent and boundary, and its duration. Violation of these markers involves an encroachment on a person's self and invites sanctioning, perhaps creating a breach or scene in the public order. Indeed, seemingly innocent acts—such as inadvertently taking someone's place, butting in line, cutting someone off, and the like—can become a violation or befoulment of another's self and, as a result, invite an extreme reaction. Thus, social organization in general depends on the capacity of individuals to read those markers that establish their territories of self in public situations.

Table 24.3 Goffman's General Propositions on Unfocused Interaction

I. Order in unfocused interaction is a positive and multiplicative function of
   A. The clarity of normative rules regulating behavior in ways that limit face encounters and talk.
   B. The capacity of individuals to provide demeanor cues with respect to
      1. Orientation, or the appropriateness of activities at the present time and place.
      2. Circumspection, or the willingness to avoid encroachment on, and threat to, others.
      3. Overplays, or the capacity to signal that one can control and regulate conduct without duress and constraint.
   C. The capacity of individuals to signal with clear markers those configurations of normatively appropriate territories of self with respect to
      1. Fixed geographical spaces that can be claimed.
      2. Egocentric preserves of nonencroachment that can be claimed during movement in space.
      3. Personal spaces that can be claimed.
      4. Stalls of territory that can be temporarily used.
      5. Use spaces that can be occupied for instrumental purposes.
      6. Turns of performing or receiving goods that can be claimed.
      7. Possessional territory and objects identified with, and arrayed around, self.
      8. Informational preserves that can be used to regulate facts about individuals.
      9. Conversational preserves that can be invoked to control talk.
   D. The availability of configurations of normatively appropriate repair rituals revolving around
      1. Accounts, or explanations for transgressions.
      2. Apologies, or expressions of embarrassment, regret, and penance for mistakes.
      3. Requests, or redemptive inquiries about making a potential transgression.
   E. The availability and clarity of rituals to reinforce norms and to order conduct by restricting face engagements among individuals.
   F. The availability of ritualized procedures for ignoring minor transgressions of norms and territories of self (tact and etiquette).

Violations of norms and territories create breaches and potential scenes, even when individuals are not engaged in focused interaction. These are usually repaired through ritual activity, such as (a) *accounts* explaining why a transgression has occurred (ignorance, unusual circumstances, temporary incompetence, unmindfulness, and so on), (b) *apologies* (some combination of expressed embarrassment or chagrin, clarification that the proper conduct is known and understood, disavowal and rejection of one's behavior, penance, volunteering of restitution, and so forth), and (c) *requests,* or a preemptive asking for license to do something that might otherwise be considered a violation of a norm or a person's self.[75] The use of these ritualized forms of repair sustains the positioning, movement, and smooth flow of activity among people in unfocused situations; without these repair rituals, tempers would flair and other disruptive acts would overwhelm the public order.

The significance of ritualized responses for repair only highlights the importance of ritual in general for unfocused interaction. As individuals move about, stand, sit, and engage in other acts in public, these activities are punctuated with rituals, especially as people come close to contact with each other. Nods, smiles, hand gestures, bodily movements, and, if necessary, brief episodes of talk (especially during repairs) are all highly ritualized, involving stereotyped sequences of behavior that reinforce norms and signal individuals' willingness to get along with and accommodate each other.

In addition to ritual, much unfocused interaction involves tact and inattention. By simply ignoring or quietly tolerating small breaches of norms, self, and ritual practices, people can gather and move about without undue tension and acrimony. In this way, unfocused interactions are made to seem uneventful, enabling individuals to cultivate a sense of obdurate reality in the subtle glances, nods, momentary eye contact, shifting of direction, and other acts of public life.

In Table 24.3, the key propositions implied in Goffman's discussion are enumerated. The relationships among the variables listed in the propositions are multiplicative in that each one accelerates the effects of the other in maintaining order in public situations of unfocused gatherings. This interactive effect allows public order to be sustained without reliance on focused talk and conversation.

FRAMES AND THE ORGANIZATION OF EXPERIENCE

Goffman's last major work, *Frame Analysis: An Essay on the Organization of Experience,*[76] is hardly an "essay" but, rather, an 800-page treatise on phenomenology, or the subjective organization of experience in social situations. It is a dense and rambling work, but it nonetheless returns to a feature of interaction that guided Goffman's work from the very beginning: the construction of "definitions of situations." That is, how is it that people define the reality of situations?

What Is a Frame?

The concept of *frame* appeared in Goffman's first major work, *The Presentation of Self,* and periodically thereafter. Surprisingly, he never offered a precise definition of this term, but the basic idea is that people "interpret" events or "strips of activity" in situations with a "schemata" that cognitively encircles or *frames* what is occurring.[77] The frame is much like a picture frame in that it marks off the boundary of the pictured events, encapsulating and distinguishing them from the surrounding environment. Goffman's early discussion of the "rules of irrelevance" in encounters—that is, considerations, characteristics, aspects, and events in the external world to be excluded during a focused interaction—represented an earlier way of communicating the dynamics of framing. Thus, as people look at the world, they impose a frame that defines what is to be pictured on the inside and what is to be excluded by what Goffman termed the *rim of the frame* on the outside. Human experience is organized by frames, which provide an interpretive "framework" or "frame of reference" for designating events or "strips of activity."

Primary Frames

Goffman argued that, ultimately, interpretations of events are anchored in a *primary framework,* which is a frame that does not depend on some prior interpretation of events.[78] Primary frameworks are thus anchored in the *real world,* at least from the point of view of the individual's organization of experience. People tend to distinguish, Goffman emphasized, between natural and social frameworks.[79] A *natural frame* is anchored in purely physical means for interpreting the world—body, ecology, terrain, objects, natural events, and the like. A *social frame* is lodged in the world created by acts of intelligence and social life. These two kinds of primary frameworks can vary enormously in their organization; some are clearly organized as "entities, postulates, and roles," whereas most others "provide" only a lore of understanding, an approach, a perspective."[80] All social frameworks involve rules about what is to be excluded beyond the rim of the frame, what is to be pictured inside the frame, and what is to be done when acting within the frame. Yet, as humans perceive and act, they are likely to apply several frameworks, giving the organization of experience a complexity that Goffman only alluded to in his earlier works.

Although Goffman stressed that he was not analyzing social structure with the concept of frames, he was clearly developing a neo-Durkheimian argument, recasting Durkheim's social psychology—especially the notion of how the "collective conscience rules people from within"—into more complex and dynamic terms.[81] For, as Goffman argued,[82]

> Taken all together, the primary frameworks of a particular social group constitute a central element of its culture, especially insofar as understandings emerge concerning principal classes of schemata, the relations of these classes to one another, and the sum total of forces and agents that these interpretive designs acknowledge to be loose in the world.

Yet, for the most part, Goffman concentrated on the dynamics of framing within the realms of personal experiences and the interaction order, leaving Durkheim's concerns about macrocultural processes to others. As a result, a problem is consistently evident in Goffman's analysis of frames: He became so intrigued with the interpersonal manipulation of frames for deceitful purposes and with the fluidity and complexity of framing in contingent situations that it is often difficult to discern whether or not the analysis is still sociological. Indeed, it often becomes deeply psychological.

Keys and Keying

What makes framing a complex process, Goffman argued, is that frames can be *transformed*. One basic way to transform a primary frame is to engage in *keying*, which is "a set of conventions by which a given activity, one already meaningful in terms of some primary framework, is transformed into something patterned on this activity but seen by the participants to be something quite else."[83] For example, a theatrical production of a family setting is a keying of "real families"; or a hobby, such as woodworking, is a keying of a more primary set of occupational activities; or a daydream about a love affair is a keying of real love; or a sporting event is a keying of some more primary activity (running, fleeing, fighting, and so on); or practicing and rehearsing are keyings of real performances; or joking about someone's "love life" is a keying of love affairs; and so on. Primary frameworks are seen by people as "real," whereas keyings are seen as "less real"; and the more one rekeys a primary framework—say, performing a keying of a keying of a keying (and so on)—the "less real" is the frame. The *rim* of the frame is still ultimately a primary framework, anchored in some natural or social reality, but humans have the capacity to continually rekey and *layer* or *laminate* their experiences. Thus terms like "definition of the situation" do not adequately capture this layering of experience through keying, nor do such terms adequately denote the multiplicity of frameworks that people can invoke because of their capacities for shifting primary frameworks and rekeying existing ones.

Fabrications

The second type of frame transformation—in addition to keying—is *fabrication*, which is "the intentional effort of one or more individuals to manage activity so that a party of one or more others will be induced to have a false belief about what it is that is going on."[84] Unlike a key, a fabrication is not a copy (or a copy of a copy) of some primary framework but, rather, an effort to make others think that something else is going on. Hoaxes, con games, and strategic manipulations all involve fabrications—getting others to frame a situation in one way while others manipulate them as another, hidden, framework.

The Complexity of Experience

Thus, as people interact, they frame situations as primary frameworks, but they can also key these primary frames and fabricate new ones for purposes of deception and manipulation. From Goffman's viewpoint, an interaction can involve many keyings and rekeyings (that is, layers and laminations of interpretation) as well as fabrications. Once keying or fabrication occurs, further keying and fabrication actually are facilitated because they initiate an escalating movement away from a primary framework. Goffman never stated how much fabrication (and fabrication on fabrications) and keying (or keying on keyings) can occur in interaction, but he did see novels, dramatic theater, and cinema as providing the vehicles for the deepest layering of interaction (because each is an initial keying of some primary frame in the real world, which then opens the almost infinite possibilities for rekeying and fabrication).

Yet, there are procedures in interaction—typically ritualized and normatively regulated—for bringing participants' experiences back to the original primary frame—that is, for wiping away layers of keyings and fabrications. For example, when people have become caught up in benign ridicule and joking about something, a person saying "seriously now . . ." is trying to wipe the slate clean of keyings (and rekeyings) and come back to the primary frame on which the mocking and joking were based. Such rituals (with the normative obligation to "try to be serious for a moment") seek to re-anchor the interaction in "the real world."

In addition to keyings and deliberate fabrications, individuals can *misframe* events—whether from ignorance, ambiguity, error, or initial disputes over framing among participants. Such misframing can persist for a time, but eventually individuals seek to *clear the frame* by getting a correct reading of information so they can reframe the situation correctly. Such efforts to clear the frame become particularly difficult and problematic, however, when fabrication has been at least part of the reason for the misframing.[85]

Thus, framing is a very complex process—one that, Goffman contended, sociologists have not been willing to address seriously. The world that people experience is not unitary, and it is subject to considerable manipulation, whether for benign or deceptive purposes. And, because of humans' capacity for symbol use (especially talk), the processes of reframing, keying, and fabrication can create highly layered and complex experiences. Yet, during interaction, people seek to maintain a common frame (a need that, Goffman was all too willing to assert, makes them vulnerable to manipulation through fabrication). For without a common frame—even one that has been keyed or fabricated—the interaction cannot proceed smoothly. Unfortunately, Goffman concentrated on framing as "organizing experience," per se, rather than on framing as it organizes experience during focused and unfocused interaction. Hence, the analysis of framing is provocative and suggestive, but too often it wanders away from the sociologically relevant topic—"the interaction order."

CONCLUSION

Goffman's works represent a truly seminal breakthrough in the analysis of social interaction. The emphasis on self-presentations, norms, rituals, and frames presented sociological theory at the midcentury with many important conceptual leads that have been adopted by diverse theoretical traditions. There are, however, some questionable points of emphasis that should, in closing, be mentioned. First, Goffman's somewhat cynical and manipulative view of humans and interaction—which have been consistently downplayed in this chapter—often takes analysis in directions that are not as fundamental to human organization as he implied. Second, Goffman's rather extreme situational view of self as only a projected image and perhaps a mirage in each and every situation is probably overdrawn. The denial of a core self or permanent identity certainly runs against the mainstream of interactionist theorizing and, perhaps, reality itself. And, third, Goffman's work tended, at times, to wander into a rather extreme subjectivism and interpersonal nihilism where experience is too layered and fickle and where interaction is too fluid and changeable by the slightest shift in frame and ritual. Yet, even with these points of criticism, Goffman's sociology represents a monumental achievement—certainly equal to that of George Herbert Mead, Alfred Schutz, and Emile Durkheim. Indeed, as the twenty-first century begins, Erving Goffman can be considered the premier micro-level theorist of the last six decades.

NOTES

1. Erving Goffman, "The Interaction Order," *American Sociological Review* (February 1983), pp. 1–17. See also Anne W. Rawls, "The Interaction Order Sui Generis. Goffman's Contribution to Social Theory," *Sociological Theory* 5 (2, 1987), pp. 136–149; and Stephan Fuchs, "The Constitution of Emergent Interaction Orders, A Comment on Rawls," *Sociological Theory* 5 (1, 1988), pp. 122–124.

2. Erving Goffman, "The Interaction Order" (cited in note 1), p. 9.

3. Ibid.

4. Ibid., p. 11. Italics in original.

5. Ibid.

6. Ibid.

7. Erving Goffman, *Encounters: Two Studies in the Sociology of Interaction* (Indianapolis: Bobbs-Merrill, 1961), p. 81.

8. Erving Goffman, *Behavior in Public Places: Notes on the Social Organization of Gatherings* (New York: Free Press, 1963), p. 234.

9. For a useful set of essays on Goffman's analysis, see Paul Drew and Anthony Wootton, eds., *Erving Goffman: Exploring the Interaction Order* (Cambridge, England: Polity, 1988); see also a recent symposium on

Goffman in *Sociological Perspectives* 39 (3, 1996).

10. Erving Goffman, "The Interaction Order" (cited in note 1), p. 2.

11. Ibid., p. 17.

12. Ibid.

13. Erving Goffman, *The Presentation of Self in Everyday Life* (Garden City, NY: Anchor, 1959) and *Frame Analysis: An Essay on the Organization of Experience* (Boston: Northeastern University Press, 1986; originally published in 1974 by Harper & Row).

14. See, for example, Randall Collins, *Theoretical Sociology* (San Diego: Harcourt Brace Jovanovich, 1988), pp. 203–207, 291–298, and *Three Sociological Traditions* (New York: Oxford University Press, 1985).

15. For example, see: R. P. Cuzzort and E. W. King, *Twentieth-Century Social Thought,* 4th ed. (Fort Worth, TX: Holt, Rinehart & Winston, 1989), Chapter 12.

16. See Stephan Fuchs, "Second Thoughts on Emergent Interaction Orders," *Sociological Theory* 7 (1, 1989), pp. 121–123.

17. Erving Goffman, *The Presentation of Self* (cited in note 13).

18. Ibid., pp. 9–10.

19. Note: Randall Collins (see Chapters 9 and 26 in this work) took his idea of situations as either work-practical, ceremonial, or social from this discussion.

20. Note the similarity of this idea to Ralph H. Turner's discussion (see Chapter 23) on "role making."

21. Erving Goffman, *The Presentation of Self* (cited in note 13), pp. 24–25.

22. Ibid., p. 27.

23. Ibid., p. 32.

24. Ibid., p. 35. Note how this idea parallels the notion of "representational" aspect of roles developed by Ralph H. Turner and Paul Colomy (see Chapter 23).

25. Ibid., p. 56.

26. This is a consistent theme in Goffman's work that, perhaps, he overemphasized. See, for example, Erving Goffman, *Strategic Interaction* (Philadelphia: University of Pennsylvania Press, 1969).

27. Erving Goffman, *The Presentation of Self* (cited in note 13), pp. 137–138.

28. Ibid., p. 92.

29. Ibid., p. 141.

30. Erving Goffman, *Encounters*, p. 7 (cited in note 7).

31. Ibid.

32. Ibid.

33. Ibid., p. 18. Note the similarity of this definition to Randall Collins' portrayal of "interaction rituals" (see Chapters 9 and 26).

34. Erving Goffman, *Behavior in Public Places* (cited in note 8), pp. 18–20.

35. Erving Goffman, *Encounters* (cited in note 7), pp. 20–33, and *Interaction Ritual: Essays on Face-to-Face Behavior* (Garden City, NY: Anchor, 1967), p. 33.

36. The concept of frame, which Goffman said that he took from Gregory Bateson, became central in Goffman's later work.

37. These rules come from Goffman, *Interaction Ritual* (cited in note 35), p. 33.

38. Here Goffman anticipates much of ethnomethodology, which is examined in Chapter 25.

39. Erving Goffman, *Interaction Ritual* (cited in note 35).

40. Particularly Durkheim's later work, as it culminated in *Elementary Forms of the Religious Life* (New York: Free Press, 1947; originally published in 1912).

41. Erving Goffman, *Interaction Ritual* (cited in note 35), pp. 56–67.

42. Ibid., p. 60.

43. Ibid.

44. Ibid., pp. 75–76.

45. Ibid., p. 77.

46. Ibid., p. 91.

47. Erving Goffman, *Encounters* (cited in note 7), p. 96.

48. Ibid., p. 87.

49. Ibid., p. 113.

50. Ibid., p. 107.

51. Erving Goffman, *Frame Analysis* (cited in note 13).

52. Ibid., p. 299.

53. Erving Goffman, *Interaction Ritual* (cited in note 35), p. 5.

54. Ibid.

55. Ibid., p. 10.

56. Ibid., p. 30.

57. Erving Goffman, *Relations in Public: Micro Studies of the Public Order* (New York: Harper Colophon, 1972, originally published in 1971 by Basic Books), pp. 38–41.

58. Ibid., pp. 40–41.

59. Erving Goffman, *Frame Analysis* (cited in note 13).

60. Erving Goffman, *Forms of Talk* (Philadelphia: University of Pennsylvania Press, 1981).

61. Ibid., pp. 70–71.

62. Ibid., p. 71.

63. Ibid., p. 85.

64. Ibid., p. 120.

65. Ibid., p. 121.

66. Goffman termed this *reframing* in *Frame Analysis* (cited in note 13) when it involved a shift in frame. However, footing and refooting can occur *within* an existing frame, so a person can change the footing of a conversation without breaking or changing a frame.

67. Again, this emphasis is what gives Goffman's work an ethnomethodological flair. See Chapter 25.

68. Erving Goffman, *Interaction Ritual* (cited in note 35), p. 135.

69. Erving Goffman, *Behavior in Public Places* (cited in note 8) and *Relations in Public* (cited in note 57).

70. Erving Goffman, *Behavior in Public Places* (cited in note 57), p. 35.

71. Erving Goffman, *Relations in Public* (cited in note 8), p. 8.

72. Ibid., pp. 129–138.

73. Ibid., p. 162.

74. Ibid., Chapter 2.

75. Ibid., pp. 109–120.

76. Erving Goffman, *Frame Analysis* (cited in note 13).

77. See Erving Goffman, *Frame Analysis* (cited in note 13), p. 10, for the vagueness of his portrayal.

78. Ibid., p. 21.

79. Ibid., pp. 21–24.

80. Ibid., p. 21.

81. See Émile Durkheim, *Elementary Forms of the Religious Life* (cited in note 40).

82. Erving Goffman, *Frame Analysis* (cited in note 13), p. 27.

83. Ibid., pp. 43–44.

84. Ibid., p. 83.

85. See ibid., p. 449, for a list of the conditions that make individuals inadvertently vulnerable to misframing, and see p. 463 for how misframing can be the result of deception and manipulation.

25

Ethnomethodological Theory

In the 1960s, a new kind of interactionist theorizing emerged. This approach drew more from the phenomenological tradition of Alfred Schutz than from the pragmatist tradition of George Herbert Mead and proposed an alternative approach to analyzing interaction: explore the methods used by people to construct a sense of ongoing reality. This emphasis became known as ethnomethodology. As this label underscores, ethnomethodology is the study of ("ology") the interpersonal "methods" that people ("ethno") use.[1] Like Edmund Husserl and Schutz, ethnomethodologists ask how people create and sustain for each other the *presumption* that the social world has a real character.

THE REFLEXIVE AND INDEXICAL NATURE
OF INTERACTION

Schutz postulated one basic reality—*the paramount*—in which people's conduct of their everyday affairs occurs.[2] Most early ethnomethodologists, however, were less interested in whether or not there is one or multiple "realities," "lifeworlds," or "natural attitudes." Far more important in ethnomethodological analysis was the development of concepts and principles that could help explain how people construct, maintain, and change their lines of conduct as they seek to sustain the presumption that they share the same reality. At the core of ethnomethodological analysis are two basic assumptions about (1) the reflexive and (2) the indexical nature of all interaction.

Reflexive Action and Interaction

Much interaction sustains a particular vision of reality. For example, ritual activity directed toward the gods sustains the belief that gods influence everyday affairs. Such ritual activity is an example of reflexive action; it maintains a certain vision of reality. Even when intense prayer and ritual activity do not bring forth the desired intervention from the gods, the devout, rather than reject beliefs, proclaim that they did not pray hard enough, that their cause was not just, or that the gods in their wisdom have a greater plan. Such behavior is *reflexive:* It upholds or reinforces a belief, even in the face of evidence that the belief might be incorrect.

Much human interaction is reflexive. Humans interpret cues, gestures, words, and other information from one another in a way that sustains a particular vision of reality. Even contradictory evidence is reflexively interpreted to maintain a body of belief and knowledge. The concept of reflexivity thus focuses attention on how people in interaction go about maintaining the presumption that they are guided by a particular reality. Much of ethnomethodological inquiry has addressed this question of how reflexive interaction occurs. That is, what concepts and principles can be developed to explain the conditions under which different reflexive actions among interacting parties are likely to occur?

The Indexicality of Meaning

The gestures, cues, words, and other information sent and received by interacting parties have meaning in a *particular context.* Without some knowledge of the context—the biographies of the interacting parties, their avowed purpose, their past interactive experiences, and so forth—it would be easy to misinterpret the symbolic communication among interacting individuals. To say that an expression is *indexical,* then, is to emphasize that the meaning of that expression is tied to a particular context.

This notion of indexicality drew attention to the problem of how actors in a context construct a vision of reality in that context. They develop expressions that invoke their common vision about what is real in their situation. The concept of indexicality thus directs investigators to actual interactive contexts to see how actors go about creating indexical expressions—words, facial and body gestures, and other cues—to sustain the presumption that a particular reality governs their affairs.

With these two key concepts, reflexivity and indexicality, the interactionists' concern with the process of symbolic communication was retained by ethnomethodology, and much of the phenomenological legacy of Schutz was rejuvenated. Concern was with how actors use gestures to construct a life-world, body of knowledge, or natural attitude about what is real. The emphasis was not on the content of the lifeworld but on the methods or techniques that actors use to create, maintain, or even alter a vision of reality. As Hugh Mehan and Houston Wood noted, "the ethnomethodological theory of reality constructor is about the *procedures* that accomplish reality. It is not about any specific reality."[3]

HAROLD GARFINKEL'S EARLY STUDIES

Harold Garfinkel's *Studies in Ethnomethodology* firmly established ethnomethodology as a distinctive theoretical perspective.[4] Although the book was not a formal theoretical statement, the studies and the commentary in it established the domain of ethnomethodological inquiry. Subsequent ethnomethodological research and theory began with Garfinkel's insights and took them in a variety of directions.

Garfinkel's work saw ethnomethodology as a field of inquiry that sought to understand the methods people employ to make sense of their world. He placed considerable emphasis on language as the vehicle by which this reality construction is done. Indeed, for Garfinkel, interacting individuals' efforts to account for their actions—that is, to represent them verbally to others—are the primary method by which a sense of the world is constructed. In Garfinkel's terms, *to do* interaction is *to tell* interaction, or, in other words, the primary folk technique used by actors is verbal description. In this way, people use their accounts to construct a sense of reality.

Garfinkel placed enormous emphasis on indexicality—that is, members' accounts are tied to particular contexts and situations. An utterance, Garfinkel noted, indexes much more than it actually says; it also evokes connotations that can be understood only in the context of a situation. Garfinkel's work was thus the first to stress the indexical nature of interpersonal cues and to emphasize that individuals seek accounts to create a sense of reality.

In addition to laying much of the groundwork for ethnomethodology, Garfinkel and his associates conducted several interesting empirical studies to validate their assumptions about what is real. One line of empirical inquiry became known as the *breaching experiment*, in which the normal course of interaction was deliberately interrupted. For example, Garfinkel reported a series of conversations in which student experimenters challenged every statement of selected subjects. The end result was a series of conversations revealing the following pattern:

Subject: I had a flat tire.
Experimenter: What do you mean, you had a flat tire?
Subject: (appears momentarily stunned and then replies in a hostile manner): What do you mean, "What do you mean?" A flat tire is a flat tire. That is what I meant. Nothing special. What a crazy question![5]

In this situation, the experimenter was apparently violating an implicit rule for this type of interaction (such as "accepting statements at face value") and thereby aroused not only the hostility of the subject but also a negative sanction, "What a crazy question!" Seemingly, in any interaction there are certain background features that everyone should understand and that should not be questioned so that all parties can "conduct their common conversational affairs without interference."[6] Such implicit methods appear to guide a considerable number of everyday affairs and are critical for the construction of at least the perception among interacting humans that an external social order exists. Through breaching, Garfinkel hoped to discover the implicit ethnomethods being used by forcing actors to engage *actively* in the process of reality reconstruction after the situation had been disrupted.

Other research strategies also yielded insights into the methods parties use in an interaction for constructing a sense of reality. For example, Garfinkel and his associates summarized the "decision rules" jurors employed in reaching a verdict.[7] By examining a group such as a jury, which must by the nature of its task develop an interpretation of what really happened, the ethnomethodologist sought to achieve some insight into the generic properties of the processes of constructing a *sense of social reality.* From the investigators' observations of jurors, it appeared that "a person is 95 percent juror before [coming] near the court," indicating that, through their participation in other social settings and through instructions from the court, they had accepted the "official" rules for reaching a verdict. However, these rules were altered somewhat as participants came together in an actual jury setting and began the "work of assembling the 'corpus' which serves as grounds for inferring the correctness of a verdict."[8] Because the inevitable ambiguities of the cases before them made it difficult for strict conformity to the official rules of jury deliberation, new decision rules were invoked to allow jurors to achieve a "correct" view of "what actually happened." But, in their retrospective reporting to interviewers of how they reached the verdicts, jurors typically invoked the "official line" to justify the correctness of their decisions. When interviewers drew attention to discrepancies between the jurors' ideal accounts and their actual practices, jurors became anxious, indicating that somewhat different rules had been used to construct the corpus of what really happened.

In sum, these two examples of Garfinkel's research strategy illustrate the general intent of much early ethnomethodological inquiry: to penetrate natural social settings or to create social settings in which the investigator could observe humans attempting to assert, create, maintain, or change the rules for constructing the appearance of consensus over the structure of the real world. By focusing on the process or methods for constructing a reality rather than on the substance or content of the reality itself, research from the ethnomethodological point of view could potentially provide a more interesting and relevant answer to the question of "how and why society is possible." Garfinkel's studies stimulated a variety of research and theoretical strategies.

AARON V. CICOUREL'S CRITIQUE

Aaron V. Cicourel has been one of the most persistent critics of sociological research methodologies, particularly the notion that more quantitative methods somehow reduces bias. But he also created a more substantive approach that had much in common with ethnomethodology. Cicourel even questions Garfinkel's assertion that interaction and verbal accounts are the same process.[9] Cicourel notes that humans see, sense, and feel much that they cannot communicate with words. Humans use "multiple modalities" for communicating in situations. Verbal accounts represent crude and incomplete translations of what is actually communicated in interaction. This recognition has led Cicourel to rename his brand of ethnomethodology: *cognitive sociology.*

The details of his analysis are less important than the general intent of his effort to transform sociological research and theory. Basically, he sought to uncover the universal "interpretive procedures" by which humans organize their cognitions and give meaning to situations.[10] Through these interpretive procedures people develop a sense of social structure and can organize their actions. These interpretive procedures are universal and invariant in humans, and their discovery would allow understanding of how humans create a sense of social structure in the world around them.

When analysis is one of the methods that people use to construct a sense of reality, the task of the theorist is to isolate the general types of interpersonal techniques that people employ in interaction. Cicourel, for example, summarized several such techniques or methods isolated by ethnomethodologists: (1) searching for the normal form, (2) doing reciprocity of perspectives, and (3) using the et cetera principle.[11]

1. **Searching for the Normal Form** If interacting parties sense that ambiguity exists about what is real and that their interaction is strained, they will emit gestures to tell each other to return to what is "normal" in their contextual situation. Actors are presumed to hold a vision of a normal form for situations or to be motivated to create one; hence, much of their action is designed to reach this form.

2. **Doing a Reciprocity of Perspectives** Borrowing from Schutz's formulation, ethnomethodologists emphasized that actors operate under the presumption that they would have the same experiences were they to switch places. Furthermore, until they are so informed by specific gestures, actors can ignore differences in perspectives that might arise from their unique biographies. Thus, much interaction will be punctuated by gestures that seek to assure others that a reciprocity of perspectives does indeed exist.

3. **Using the Et Cetera Principle** In examining an actual interaction, much is left unsaid. Actors must constantly "fill in" or "wait for" information necessary to "make sense" of another's words or deeds. When actors do so, they are using the *et cetera principle.* They are agreeing not to disrupt the interaction by asking

for the needed information; they are willing to wait or to fill in. For example, in the conversation reported by Garfinkel about the "flat tire," the experimenter who asked, "what do you mean, you had a flat tire?" was not observing the et cetera principle, and as a result, the subject became angry in an effort to sanction the experimenter to abide by the "folk rules." Or, to take another example, the common phrase "you know," which often appears after an utterance, is typically an assertion by one actor to another invoking the et cetera principle. The other is thus informed not to disrupt the interaction or the sense of reality in the situation with a counter utterance, such as "no, I do not know."

These three general types of folk methods were examples of what ethnomethodologists sought to discover, although most researchers appear reluctant to make these explicit or to theorize beyond their empirical observations of how particularly folk methods are used. For some ethnomethodologists, the ultimate goal of theory is to determine the conditions under which these and other interpersonal techniques would be used to construct, maintain, or change a sense of reality. Yet, few such propositions are to be found in the ethnomethodological literature.

HARVEY SACKS'S ANALYSIS
OF CONVERSATIONAL TURN TAKING

Until his untimely death in 1976, Harvey Sacks exerted considerable influence within ethnomethodology.[12] Although his work was not well known outside ethnomethodological circles, it represented an attempt to extend Garfinkel's concern with verbal accounts, while eliminating some of the problems posed by indexicality.

Sacks was one of the first ethnomethodologists to articulate the phenomenological critique of sociology and to use this critique to build what he thought was an alternative form of theorizing. The basic thrust of Sacks's critique can be stated as follows: Sociologists assume that language is a resource used in generating concepts and theories of the social world. However, sociologists are confusing resource and topic. In using language, sociologists are creating a reality; their words are not a neutral vehicle but *the* topic of inquiry for true sociological analysis—a point of emphasis that is, today, the core topic of ethnomethodological inquiry.

If the pure properties of language can be understood, then it would be possible to have an objective social science without confusing resource with subject matter. Sacks's research tended to concentrate on the formal properties of language-in-use. Typically, Sacks took verbatim transcripts of actors in interaction and sought to understand the formal properties of the conversation while ignoring its substance. Such a tactic resolved the problem of indexicality because Sacks simply ignored the substance and context of conversation and focused on its form. For example, "sequences of talk" among actors might occupy his attention.

In analyzing conversational talk, Sacks and various collaborators would emphasize the fact that conversations involve turn taking. One party in a conversation talks, then another does. The ways in which turns are taken become a key dynamic in the conversation as, for instance, when individuals pause and offer clearance cues that the other can now talk, when they interrupt each other, when they talk over each other, when they pause but keep the conversational floor, and other methods that people use to structure the flow of everyday conversations. For Sacks, the formal properties of turn taking offered a new way to examine action and interaction.

Sacks thus began to take ethnomethodology into formal linguistics, a trend that has continued and now seems to dominate current ethnomethodology in an approach that has been labeled *conversational analysis.* More importantly, Sacks sought to discover universal forms of interaction—that is, abstracted patterns of talk—that might apply to all conversations. In this way, he began to search for the laws of reality construction among interacting individuals.

ZIMMERMAN, POLLNER, AND WIEDER'S SITUATIONAL APPROACH

Sacks and Cicourel focused on the universal properties, respectively, of language use and cognitive perception/representation. This concern with invariance, or universal folk methods, became increasingly prominent in ethnomethodological inquiry. In several essays, for example, Don Zimmerman, D. Lawrence Wieder, and Melvin Pollner developed an approach that sought the universal procedures people employ to construct a sense of reality.[13] Their position was perhaps the most clearly stated of all ethnomethodologies, drawing inspiration from Garfinkel but extending his ideas. To summarize their argument,

1. In all interaction situations, humans attempt to construct the appearance of consensus over relevant features of the interaction setting.

2. These setting features can include attitudes, opinions, beliefs, and other cognitions about the nature of the social setting in which they interact.

3. Humans engage in a variety of explicit and implicit interpersonal practices and methods to construct, maintain, and perhaps alter *the appearance* of consensus over these setting features.

4. Such interpersonal practices and methods result in the assembling and disassembling of what can be termed an *occasional corpus*—that is, the *perception* by interacting humans that the current setting has an orderly and understandable structure.

5. This appearance of consensus is not only the result of agreement on the substance and content of the occasioned corpus but also a reflection of each participant's compliance with the rules and procedures for assemblage and disassemblage of this consensus. In communicating, in however

subtle a manner, that parties accept the implicit rules for constructing an occasioned corpus, they go a long way in establishing consensus about what is in the interaction setting.

6. In each interaction situation, the rules for constructing the occasioned corpus will be unique in some respects and hence not completely generalizable to other settings—thus requiring that humans in each and every interaction situation use interpersonal methods in searching for agreement on the implicit rules for the assembly of an occasioned corpus.

7. Thus, by constructing, reaffirming, or altering the rules for constructing an occasioned corpus, members in a setting can offer one another the appearance of an orderly and connected world, which compels certain perceptions and actions on their part.

From these kinds of assumptions about human interaction, Zimmerman, Pollner, and Wieder's ethnomethodology took its subject matter. Rather than focusing on the actual content and substance of the occasioned corpus and on the ways members believe it to force certain perceptions and actions, attention was drawn primarily to the *methods humans use* to construct, maintain, and change the *appearance* of an orderly and connected social world. These methods are directly observable and constitute a major portion of people's actions in everyday life. In contrast, the actual substance and content of the occasioned corpus are not directly observable and can only be inferred. Furthermore, in concentrating on the *process* of creating, sustaining, and changing the occasioned corpus, we can ask: Is not the process of creating the appearance of a stable social order for one another more critical to understanding how society is possible than the actual substance and content of the occasioned corpus? Is there anything more to society than members' presumptions that society is "out there" forcing them to do and see certain things? Hence, order is not the result of the particular structure of the corpus; rather, order resides in the human capacity *to continually assemble and disassemble the corpus* in each and every interaction situation. This perspective suggested to ethnomethodologists that theoretical attention should therefore be placed on the ongoing process of assembling and disassembling the appearance of social order and on the particular methods people employ in doing so.

EMANUEL SCHEGLOFF'S
CONVERSATIONAL ANALYSIS

Over the last decade and one half, Emanuel Schegloff has been one of the most important figures working within the conversational approach suggested by Garfinkel and firmly established by Sacks. Indeed, some of Sacks's most important early works were coauthored with Schegloff.[14] Like Garfinkel before him, Schegloff has mounted a critique of how sociologists conceptualize action and how actions generate intersubjectivity. Most sociologists visualize action without really looking at what individuals do in face-to-face interaction, while seeing intersubjectivity as achieved by socialization into a common culture. By analyzing the dynamics revolving around conversations as they unfold, it is possible to get a much more fine-grained view of action; equally significant, it is possible to understand the problem of order—of how society is held together—from the elementary and more fundamental processes by which it is constructed: talk and conversation among people in situations.

Conversational analysis is now a highly technical way of analyzing strips of conversations, typically recorded and then converted into a transcript. There is a system of notation for indicating pauses, points of emphasis, overlaps, and other features of conversations. What has typified Schegloff's work is detailed analysis of conversations using this notation system, but for our purposes, the details of how the data are arrayed are less important than the actual methods employed by individuals in conversations. These patterns can contribute to a theory of action at its most fundamental level. Of the various discoveries in Schegloff's ongoing research, several sets of findings can be used to illustrate the potential of conversational analysis.

1. Confirming Allusions[15] In conversations, individuals often allude to something. At times these allusions are explicit; at other times the allusion implies more than the explicit reference. Schegloff notes that in some conversations, another party in the conversation repeats the phrasing of words, indicating an allusion. For example, a phone conversation (made up for illustration) may proceed something like this:

Janice: How are you John?
John: Fine. How are you?
Janice: Doing ok, I guess
John: Oh
Janice: Went drinking
John: Went drinking, eh

The last two turns of the conversation involve Janice making an allusion to drinking (and to the fact that she is only "ok, I guess"), and then John repeats the phrase "went drinking." He could have said "I see," or some other phrase, but rather, he repeats the phrase. This pattern is noticeable in many conversations, and Schegloff asks, Is something special going on here? What are these repeats doing? Schegloff's analysis and answer are complex, but the basic generalization is that when people confirm allusions they indicate that indeed they understand what is being indicated explicitly, but moreover, they understand less explicit allusions accompanying those that are explicit. For instance, if Janice is depressed as a result of drinking, John's repetition of "went drinking" confirms the sense of what drinking does to Janice above and beyond making her tired. Confirmation of allusions thus becomes a mechanism for achieving intersubjectivity, and as such, this particular pattern in conversations can be seen as an ethnomethod used by individuals to create a sense of a shared reality.

2. Repair after Next Turn[16]   In conversations, minor and major misunderstandings occur all the time. When these occur, people's sense of intersubjectivity—that is, of sharing a common sense for what is occurring—breaks down, and if such misunderstandings cannot be "repaired" in the flow of the conversation, the interaction will remain breached. Schegloff initially observed in many conversations that there is what he termed "a third position repair" revealing the following basic structure: Person A makes a statement that he or she feels is adequate (first position); Person B hears this statement and emits a response appropriate to his or her understanding of what person A has said (the second position); but sensing that his or her original statement has not communicated the intended meaning, Person A (in the third position) now seeks to make the repair and communicate the intended meaning; and then, Person B typically begins the response to the repair with the phrase "oh" indicating that the repair has been understood. For example, below is a simplified version of a more detailed and coded conversation reported by Schegloff:

> Annie: Which ones are closed, and which ones are open
> Zebrach: Most of them. This, this, this (pointing)
> Annie: I don't mean the shelters. I mean the roads
> Zebrach: Oh (and after a pause, he tells Annie about roads)

This form of conversation can be found often, and it allows parties to effortlessly make repairs to conversations that are off track. The process can be more complicated in that several more sequences of conversation can occur before the party in the third position of the sequence realizes the misunderstanding, but it is still possible when the third position is taken to make the necessary corrections.

A "fourth position repair" allows the person who has misunderstood to acknowledge the repair effort, and thereafter put the conversation back on an intersubjective footing. For example, (1) Person A makes a statement, (2) Person B responds, (3) Person A makes the repair after sensing that B did not get the intended meaning, and then (4) Person B (now in the fourth position) acknowledges the repair effort, perhaps initially by the phrase, "oh," followed by more talk that moves the conversation further along in the proper direction.

3. Overlaps in Conversations.[17]   People often begin talk at the same time, and this can be problematic because it is in the nature of conversations for people to turn take, with one speaking, then another speaking, and so on. Some overlaps are nonproblematic because they do not deny the speaker holding the floor the right to talk. For example, another person might begin talking just as another is winding down; another speaker might add "conintuers" such as "uh huh" to let the speaker know that his or her talk is understood; another may add a word that the speaker is searching for without grabbing the conversational floor; and others may add speech and other vocalizations in a kind of "chorus" to support the line of talk by a speaker. Moreover, overlaps are generally over very quickly, although at times they can persist.

Schegloff visualizes a number of procedures for dealing with overlaps, and their use constitutes a set of mechanisms or "folk methods" for managing overlaps in ways that allow the parties to sustain the conversation. One set of mechanisms revolves around shifts in the way talk is produced: getting louder, variations of pitch, talking faster, suddenly cutting off talk in progress with special markers (such as bringing teeth and lips together in a dramatic fashion). Another set of mechanisms revolves around the rhythm of the conversation that can be conceptualized as successive "beats" of talk production. Overlaps proceed in such beats, with people often all stopping after the first beat of overlap, or with one person continuing after a beat or two. Yet another is what Schegloff calls "pre-onset" strategies to keep others from starting to talk, such as speeding up the talk, and there are "post-onset" strategies, such as slowing down and deliberating overpronouncing words.

Those working within the broad confines of ethnomethodology have studied these and other aspects of conversations. Such work is highly suggestive, but at present there is virtually no theoretical integration of the many observations of researchers. Thus, there is relatively little theorizing in conversational analysis; most work is highly descriptive, and yet, many scholars like Schegloff clearly have theoretical pretensions.

CONCLUSION

Ethnomethodology has uncovered a series of interpersonal processes that traditional symbolic interactionists, who tend to follow Mead more than Schutz, have failed to recognize. The implicit methods that people use to communicate a sense of social order are a very crucial dimension of social interaction and organization, and the theoretical goal of ethnomethodology is to specify the generic conditions under which various folk methods are used by individuals. But, despite many interesting findings, this goal still seems far away—even after forty years of research.

In the end, ethnomethodology has become a rather isolated theoretical research program. Its practitioners increasingly focused on conversational analysis—a mode of inquiry initiated by Sacks and carried forward by a number of creative scholars. But their work has not had a great impact on mainstream sociological theory, inside or outside the interactionist tradition, although scholars as diverse as Jürgen Habermas (Chapter 13), Pierre Bourdieu (Chapter 29), Anthony Giddens (Chapter 28), and Randall Collins (Chapter 9) have all acknowledged a debt to ethnomethodology. There is, then, something important and fundamental about the assertions of ethnomethodologists.

NOTES

1. For some readable summaries of ethnomethodology, see Hugh Mehan and Houston Wood, *The Reality of Ethnomethodology* (New York: Wiley, 1975); John Heritage, *Garfinkel and Ethnomethodology* (Cambridge, England: Polity, 1984) and "Ethnomethodology," in *Social Theory Today,* eds. Anthony Giddens and Jonathan Turner (Cambridge,

England: Polity Press, 1987); Melvin Pollner, *Mundane Reasoning: Reality in Everyday Sociological Discourse* (Cambridge: Cambridge University Press, 1987); and Wes Sharrock, "Fundamentals of Ethnomethodology," in *Handbook of Social Theory*, eds. George Ritzer and Barry Smart (London, England: Sage, 2001).

2. See, in particular, Alfred Schutz, *Collected Papers I: The Problem of Social Reality*, ed. Maurice Natanson (The Hague: Martinus Nijhoff, 1962); *Collected Papers II: Studies in Social Theory*, ed. Arvid Broderson (The Hague: Martinus Nijhoff, 1964); and *Collected Papers III: Studies in Phenomenological Philosophy* (The Hague: Martinus Nijhoff, 1966). For adaptations of these ideas to interactionism and ethnomethodology, see Alfred Schutz and Thomas Luckmann, *The Structure of the Lifeworld* (Evanston, IL: Northwestern University Press, 1973), as well as Thomas Luckmann, ed., *Phenomenology and Sociology* (New York: Penguin, 1978). See also Robert C. Freeman, "Phenomenological Sociology and Ethnomethodology," in *Introduction to the Sociologies of Everyday Life*, eds. J. Douglas and Patricia Adler (Boston: Allyn & Bacon, 1980).

3. Hugh Mehan and Houston Wood, *The Reality of Ethnomethodology* (cited in note 1), p. 7.

4. Harold Garfinkel, *Studies in Ethnomethodology* (Englewood Cliffs, NJ: Prentice-Hall, 1967).

5. Ibid, p. 42.

6. Ibid.

7. Ibid, pp. 104–115.

8. Ibid., p. 110.

9. Aaron V. Cicourel, *Method and Measurement in Sociology* (New York: Free Press, 1964); "Cross Modal Communication," in *Linguistics and Language Science, Monograph 25*, ed. R. Shuy (Washington, DC: Georgetown University Press, 1973).

10. Aaron V. Cicourel, *Cognitive Sociology* (London: Macmillan, 1973); and

"Basic Normative Rules in the Negotiation of Status and Role," in *Recent Sociology No. 2*, ed. H. P. Dreitzel (New York: Macmillan, 1970).

11. Aaron V. Cicourel, *Cognitive Sociology* (cited in note 10), pp. 85–88. It should be noted that these principles were implicit in Garfinkel's *Studies in Ethnomethodology* (cited in note 4).

12. Harvey Sacks, "Sociological Description," *Berkeley Journal of Sociology* 8 (1963), pp. 1–17; Harvey Sacks, "An Initial Investigation of the Usability of Conversational Data for Doing Sociology," in *Studies in Interaction*, ed. David Sudnow (New York: Free Press, 1972); see also Harvey Sacks, *Lectures on Conversation*, 2 volumes (New York: Blackwell, 1992). Sacks's best-known study, for example, is the coauthored article with Emanuel Schegloff and Gail Jefferson, "A Simplest Systematics for the Analysis of Turn Taking in Conversation," *Language* 50 (1974), pp. 696–697. For a review of the current techniques of conversational analysis, see Alain Coulon, *Ethno-methodology* (London: Sage, 1995); Douglas W. Maynard and Marilyn R. Whalen, "Language, Action, and Social Interaction," in *Sociological Perspectives on Social Psychology*, eds. K. S. Cook, G. A. Fine, and J. S. House (Boston: Allyn & Bacon, 1995).

13. Don H. Zimmerman and Melvin Pollner, "The Everyday World as a Phenomenon, in *Understanding Everyday Life*, ed. J. D. Douglas (Chicago: Aldine, 1970); Lawrence Wieder, *Language and Social Reality* (The Hague: Mouton, 1973).

14. For example, Harvey Sacks, Emanuel Schegloff, and Gail Jefferson, "A Simplest Symatics" (cited in note 12) and Emanuel A. Schegloff, "Opening Up Closings," *Semiotic*, 7 (1973), pp. 280–327.

15. Emanuel A. Schegloff, "Confirming Allusions: Toward an Empirical Account of Action," *American Journal of Sociology* 102 (1996), 161–216.

16. Emanuel A. Schegloff, "Repair After Next Turn: The Last Structurally Provided Defense of Intersubjectivity in Conversation, "*American Journal of Sociology* 97 (1992), pp. 1295–1345.

17. Emanuel A. Schegloff, "Overlapping Talk and The Organization of Turn-Taking for Conversation," *Language in* *Society* 29 (2000), pp. 1–63; see also his "Accounts of Conduct in Interaction: Interruption, Overlap, and Turn-Taking," in *Handbook of Sociological Theory,* ed. J. H. Turner (New York: Kluwer Academic/ Plenum, 2001).

26

Theories of Emotion

In the late 1970s, theories of interaction processes began to shift direction, focusing on how emotions are involved in interpersonal relations and the structuring of social encounters. Not all the theories that emerged during the next two decades were oriented to the legacy of George Herbert Mead. Many were, to be sure, but other traditions were also drawn into theoretical formulations. Thus, in presenting representative samples, or exemplars, of theories on emotions, we cannot easily group them into a few theoretical camps. Instead, a variety of theories will be reviewed to communicate the diversity and eclecticism evident in the study of emotions. This diversity makes the sociology of emotions one of the very exciting areas of interactionist theorizing in sociology; indeed, it could be argued that the cutting edge of interactionism is how emotions shape the flow of interaction processes.

ARLIE HOCHSCHILD'S DRAMATURGICAL
THEORY OF EMOTIONS

Arlie Russell Hochschild[1] was one of the first sociologists to develop a view of emotions as managed performances by individuals within the constraints of situational norms and broader cultural ideas about what emotions can be felt and presented in front of others. For Hochschild, the *emotion culture*[2] consists of a series of ideas about how and what people are supposed to experience in

432

various types of situations, and this culture is filled with *emotional ideologies* about the appropriate attitudes and feelings for specific spheres and activities. *Emotional markers* are events in the biographies of individuals that personify and symbolize more general emotional ideologies.

In any context, Hochschild emphasizes, there are norms of two basic types: (1) *feeling rules* that indicate (a) the amount of appropriate emotion that can be felt in a situation, (b) the direction, whether positive or negative, of the emotion, and (c) the duration of the emotion; and (2) *display rules* that indicate the nature, intensity, and style of expressive behavior to be emitted. Thus, for any interaction, feeling and display rules circumscribe what can be done. These rules reflect ideologies of the broader emotion culture, the goals and purposes of groups in which interactions are lodged, and the distribution of power and other organizational features of the situation.

The existence of cultural ideologies and normative constraints on the selection and emission of emotions forces individuals to manage the feelings that they experience and present to others. At this point, Hochschild's analysis becomes dramaturgic, for much like Goffman before her, she sees actors as having to manage a presentation of self in situations guided by a cultural script of norms and broader ideologies. There are various types of what Hochschild terms *emotion work* or mechanisms for managing emotions and making the appropriate self presentation: (1) *body work* whereby individuals actually seek to change their bodily sensations in an effort to evoke the appropriate emotion (for example, deep breathing to create calm); (2) *surface acting* where individuals alter their external expressive gestures in ways that they hope will make them actually feel the appropriate emotion (for instance, emitting gestures expressing joy and sociality at a party in the attempt to feel happy); (3) *deep acting* where individuals attempt to change their internal feelings, or at least some of these feelings, in the hope that the rest of the appropriate emotions will be activated and fall into place (for example, evoking feelings of sadness in an effort to feel sad at a funeral); and (4) *cognitive work* where the thoughts and ideas associated with particular emotions are evoked in an attempt to activate the corresponding feelings.

As Hochschild stresses, individuals are often put in situations where a considerable amount of emotion work must be performed. For example, in her pioneering study of airline attendants,[3] the requirement that attendants always be friendly, pleasant, and helpful even as passengers were rude and unpleasant placed an enormous emotional burden on the attendants. They had to manage their emotions through emotion work and present themselves in ways consistent with highly restrictive feeling and display rules. Virtually all encounters require emotion work, although some, such as those faced by airline attendants, are particularly taxing and require a considerable amount of emotion management in self-presentations.

Hochschild's work is one of several efforts in the late 1970s to examine emotions sociologically. The emphasis on how culture defines what people are to feel in situations and how these feelings are to be presented became part of all subsequent theories, and her analysis of the mechanisms of "emotion work" added a dramaturgical emphasis to emotional dynamics. At this time, other theories squarely within the symbolic interactionist tradition were also being formulated; these emphasized the centrality of self and identity, thereby providing important conceptual supplements to Hochschild's pioneering work.

SYMBOLIC INTERACTIONIST THEORIES OF EMOTION

David Heise's Affect Control Theory

David Heise[4] and various collaborators,[5] particularly Lynn Smith-Lovin,[6] have developed a theory of emotions that builds on symbolic interactionist theories emphasizing the dynamics of identity. Much of this theory is stated in highly technical terms, involving equations and the language of computer simulations, but fortunately several more discursive summaries are now available.[7] The basic idea in affect control theory is that individuals react affectively or emotionally to every social event and that they do so to the degree of correspondence between *fundamental sentiments* or culturally established affective meanings that transcend particular situations, on the one side, and *transient impressions* or feelings that are specific emotional reactions to the particulars of a situation, on the other. Correspondence between fundamental sentiments and transient impressions will reduce emotional arousal, whereas discordance between fundamental sentiments and situational impressions arouses emotions and motivates individuals to bring their fundamental and situational sentiments into correspondence. Thus, in affect control theory, the basic motivating force in human action and interaction is the reduction of discrepancies, or what is termed *deflection,* between fundamental and transient sentiments and, as deflection is reduced, control of affect or emotion is achieved.

What makes this theory a variation of symbolic interactionism is its emphasis on the dynamics of "defining the situation." Humans are viewed as developing cognitions about every situation, with language being the primary symbolic medium through which cognitions are formed. Thus, people see situations as linguistic designations, and they represent, process, and communicate their cognitions to themselves and others through language. This emphasis on language is typical of symbolic interactionist theories, and it explains why the measurement of the affect associated with cognitions has used the "semantic differential" test in which pairs of words, such as good-bad, big-little, nice-awful, fast-slow, young-old, noisy-quiet, powerful-powerless, sad-happy, strong-weak, and so on—are presented to subjects as they respond to objects, persons, and situations. These linguistic designations for fundamental sentiments were seen in early formulations of the theory to vary along three basic dimensions[8]: (1) *evaluation* or an assessment that determines the degree of goodness or badness; (2) *potency* or the level of power or powerlessness; and (3) *activity* or the extent of animation or passivity. As people define situations, therefore, they invoke fundamental sentiments revolving around evaluations, potency, and activity; then they compare these fundamental sentiments to their more situation-specific impressions or their transient sentiments, which are also constructed in terms of evaluations, potency, and activity. And, as emphasized earlier, individuals are motivated to sustain a correspondence—or alternatively, to avoid deflections—between these two levels of sentiment.

What aspects of a situation are assessed through evaluation, potency, and activity? All definitions of a situation involve cognitions and associated emotions about (1) self or identity, (2) others and their identities, (3) behaviors, and (4) situation or setting. Thus, cognitions invoke affective associations for evaluation, potency, and activity relative to people's identity, their perceptions of others and their identity, their role behaviors, the nature of the situation, and the relevant rituals, scripts, norms, and other situational information. The unit of analysis in affect control theory is thus the *social event,* revolving around an individual (A) performing an act (B) on some object or person (O) in a setting (S), or ABOS. In all situations where social events occur, there are relevant *grammars* that limit the kinds of behaviors toward others that are possible and appropriate, while indicating the form and structure that behaviors are to take. For example, particular grammars indicate how actions toward others occur for situations as various as funerals, graduations, workplaces, or within the family or for each of the fundamental types of situations that constitute social life.

As a brand of symbolic interactionism, the notion of *identity* is central. Identity is composed of the cognitions and associated affect about oneself as an object as well as the person's assessment of the self being presented by others. Just what identities can be presented by self and others in an encounter are, of course, limited by the grammar of the situation. People select identities for presentation that conform to the grammar; in this way, they can minimize deflection. According to Heise, people's cognitions initially sort the range of possible and appropriate behaviors in a situation; then, the emotional reactions to these cognitions are activated along the evaluative, potency, and activity dimensions; and finally, these cognitions and emotions combined influence the kind of identity and role behavior that will be presented.

Thus, people assert identities through their role behaviors in a situation, and they assess the role behaviors of others to impute the identity being asserted by these others. As they do so, individuals present the emotions relevant and appropriate for their identity, and they read the emotions of others to facilitate imputation of the identity of others. The reciprocal reading of associated emotions enables them to achieve intersubjectivity.

More than mutual role-taking and role-making is involved in presenting and imputing identities, however. Identities are presented to avoid deflection or discordance between fundamental sentiments and transient sentiments in a situation. Identity becomes a prime vehicle for asserting and marking fundamental sentiments, as well as for assessing discordance between fundamental and transient sentiments. People see role behaviors as indicators of identities, then they determine if these identities are being played in ways that confirm, or disconfirm, fundamental sentiments. For instance, if a female presents herself in a situation as a mother, a designation that carries a certain evaluation in culturally established sentiments about evaluation, potency, and activity, but then proceeds to hit her child, a deflection has occurred. The fundamental sentiments associated with the identity of mother and the role behavior that mothers should exhibit are being contradicted by the actual role behaviors and transient impressions of what is going on. This deflection motivates people to reduce this discordance. There are three possible options: First, the role behavior can be reconceptualized, leaving the individual's identity intact (for example, the mother is only playfully striking her child). Second, the setting can be reconceptualized (for instance, the child has been very bad and, for its own good, must be disciplined), but there are limits on such reconceptualizations imposed by the grammar of the situation. And third, the imputed identity of the person can be changed (for example, the person is a very bad mother).

This last option is quite common because it is often difficult to ignore or redefine role behaviors, and the grammars of situations limit redefinition of situations. What is left is to impute a new identity to the individual in the face of large deflections and the associated emotional arousal. There are two paths to such change. One is to impute *dispositional traits* to the actors (for instance, the mother was momentarily angry) that modify the identity (a mother with a short fuse, for instance) but leave much of the identity intact. A second and less frequent path is to impute a whole new identity that replaces the older one (this woman was not a mother but rather a mean-spirited caretaker, for example). Because changes in identity are so traumatic, invoking considerable emotion and forcing people to redefine themselves and the situation, individuals can often avoid such reordering of cognition and emotion by emitting and recording emotions that confess to the disconfirming behavior; in essence, an apology offered (for example, the mother expresses how terrible she feels about losing control). When others accept such emotional displays, the person can avoid being shoved into a new identity, and the others in the situation can forgo the cognitive and emotional gymnastics of imputing new identities. Indeed, people will try as long as possible to interpret and reinterpret social events so that deflection can be minimized. Humans seek routines and emotional stability; so they are motivated to keep deflections low by ignoring them—as long as they can.

From the point of view of affect control theory, then, the experience and expression of emotion can be a sign that deflection is occurring. The type of emotion, whether positive or negative, will be related to the nature of the deflection. Positive emotions can arise from deflections where others see a person's identity as better, more potent, or more active than the person himself or herself perceives. Moreover, a negative identity held by a person (as unworthy, impotent, or inactive) will produce negative emotions when others confirm these self-images, even though deflection has not occurred. Thus, emotion and deflection can be related to each other in complicated ways, but affect control theory emphasizes that deflection will arouse people to bring "things back into line" and that emotion is what energizes people to do so.

This emotion mobilizes the individual asserting an identity to do something about the deflection, and the emotion forces others to begin redefining the situation. People will perhaps protest with shining modesty when deflection enhances their identity, or, perhaps if deflection is consistently positive, a new and more highly evaluated, potent, or active identity will emerge. Conversely, people feel "awful" when their role behaviors disconfirm their asserted identity, and they try to bring the two back into line, if they can. Others feel awkward and unsure when such disconfirmation occurs, and they try to redefine situations to bring fundamental and transient sentiments back into correspondence.

Sheldon Stryker's Identity Theory of Emotions

Sheldon Stryker's general theory of identity was summarized in Chapter 22; so, here we only need to focus on the theory as it was later expanded to explain the dynamics of emotion. Stryker initially argued that individuals possess a hierarchy of identities,[9] and those identities high in this salience hierarchy are likely to guide role behaviors. Indeed, role behaviors are orchestrated to reveal an identity to which an individual is committed. The more committed to an identity an individual is, the more the individual's self-esteem rests on others' positive evaluations of the role performances marking this identity. Moreover, identities tend to be presented to conform to broader cultural values, normative expectations of social structures, and definitions of situations.

Emotions are implicated in these processes in several ways.[10] First, those role enactments that generate positive affect and reinforcement from others in a situation strengthen a person's commitment to an identity, moving it higher in the salience hierarchy. As individuals receive this positive feedback, their self-esteem is enhanced, which further increases commitment to the identity, raising it in the salience hierarchy and increasing the chances that this identity will shape subsequent role performance.

Second, when role performances of a person and others are judged inadequate in light of normative expectations, cultural values, definitions of the situation, or identities being asserted, negative emotional reactions mark this inadequacy. Conversely, when role performances are adequate or even more than adequate and exemplary, positive emotions signal this. Thus, emotions are markers of adequacy in role performances, telling individuals that their performances are acceptable or unacceptable. This marking function of emotions works in several ways. The individual reads the gestures of others to see if a role performance has been accepted, and if it has, then the person experiences positive emotions and will become further committed to the identity that was asserted in the role performance. If, on the other hand, the reaction is less than positive, then the individual will experience negative emotions—such as anger at self, shame, and guilt—and mobilize to improve the role performance, or if this is not possible, to lower the commitment to this identity being asserted in the role, moving it lower in the salience hierarchy and selecting a different identity that can be more adequately played out in a role.

Not only do individuals get emotional about their own performances as they role-take with others, but they also inform others about the latter's role performances. Because role performances must be coordinated and meshed together to be effective, inadequacy by others will disrupt one's own role performance, and if this occurs, a person will manifest some form of anger and negatively sanction others. Thus, emotions become ways for individuals to mutually signal and mark the adequacy of their respective role performances in ways that facilitate the coordination and integration of roles.

Finally, emotions are also a sign of which identities are high in a person's salience hierarchy. If emotional reactions are intense when a role performance fails or when it is successful, this intensity indicates that a person is committed to the identity being played in a role and that it is high in the salience hierarchy. Conversely, if the emotional reaction of the individual is of low intensity, then this might signal that the identity is lower in the salience hierarchy and relatively unimportant to the individual.

In identity theory, then, emotions motivate individuals to play roles in which they receive positive reinforcement, and emotions also inform individuals about the adequacy of their performances and their commitments to identities in the salience hierarchy. Emotions thus drive individuals to play roles in ways that are consistent with normative expectations, definitions of the situation, cultural values, and highly salient feelings about self.

STATUS AND POWER THEORIES
OF EMOTION

Randall Collins's Theory of Interaction Rituals

We encountered Randall Collins's theory of interaction rituals earlier in Chapter 9 on Weberian conflict theory.[11] Attention is now drawn to his micro-level theory of emotions. Collins's theory is about the levels of emotional energy that interaction rituals generate rather than about specific types of emotions, although as we will see shortly, he has teamed with Theodore Kemper to address the issue of how power and status produce particular types of emotions (see next section). But the basic theory, as Collins has developed it on his own, borrows from Émile Durkheim's and Erving Goffman's insights about the emotion-generating effects of rituals.

Collins believes that the micro unit of analysis is the *encounter* of at least two people who confront each other and interact. What transpires in such encounters is mediated by the exchange of resources and rituals. Rituals contain the following elements: (1) a physical assembly of co-present individuals; (2) mutual awareness of each other; (3) a common focus of attention; (4) a common emotional mood among co-present individuals; (5) a rhythmic coordination and synchronization of conversation and nonverbal gestures; (6) a symbolic representation of this group focus and mood with objects, persons, gestures, words,

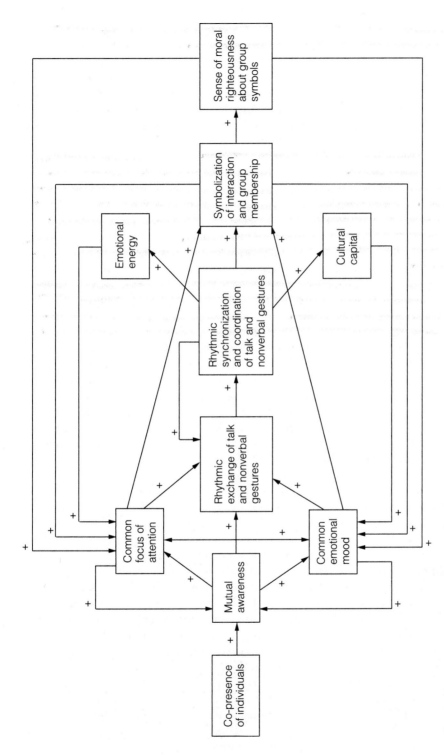

FIGURE 26.1 Collins's Conceptualization of Ritual

and ideas among interacting individuals; and (7) a sense of moral righteousness about these symbols marking group membership. Figure 26.1 portrays the dynamics of such rituals that Collins sees as the "emotional energizer" of interaction because, like Durkheim before him, Collins argues that co-presence, mutual awareness, common focus of attention, rhythmic coordination and synchronization of gestures and talk, common mood, and symbolization arouse emotions that, in turn, feed back and heighten people's sense of co-presence, mood, attention, and symbolization.

Intermingled with these emotion-arousing properties of rituals are exchange processes. Collins visualizes two basic types of resources as crucial to understanding exchanges and rituals: (1) cultural capital and (2) emotional energy. *Cultural capital* consists of such resources as stored memories of previous conversations, vocal styles, special types of knowledge or expertise, the prerogatives to make decisions, and the right to receive honor. The concept of *generalized cultural capital* denotes those impersonal symbols that mark general classes of resources (for example, knowledge, positions, authority, and groupings), whereas the concept of *particularized cultural capital* refers to the memories that individuals have of the particular identities, reputations, and network or organizational positions of specific persons. *Emotional energy* is composed of the level and type of affect, feeling, and sentiment that individuals mobilize in a situation.

Interaction consists of individuals using their cultural capital and emotional energy to talk with one another. Such conversations involve an investment of capital and energy, with each individual attracted to situations that bring the best available payoff in cultural capital and emotional energy. Although individuals also seek a profit in the cultural capital that they spend and receive in interaction, Collins appears to emphasize emotional energy as the real driving force of interaction. Humans find positive emotional energy highly rewarding, and though other rewards are not irrelevant, positive emotional energy is the most valuable. Indeed, individuals seek to maximize their positive emotional energy by participating in those interaction rituals that generate a clear focus of attention, a common mood, emotional arousal, rhythmic synchronization of mood and arousal, and symbolization of these in terms of moral codes.

In Collins's view, there is a kind of market for interaction rituals: Individuals weigh the costs in time, energy, cultural capital, and other resources that they must spend to participate in the various rituals available to them, then they select those rituals that maximize emotional profits. In this sense, Collins proclaimed emotional energy to be the common denominator of rational choice.[12] Thus, rather than representing an irrational force in human interaction, Collins sees the pursuit of emotions as highly rational: People seek out those interaction rituals in a marketplace of rituals that maximize profits (costs less the positive emotional energy produced by the ritual). The search for emotional energy is, therefore, the criterion by which various alternative encounters are assessed for how much emotional profit they can generate.

Humans are, in a sense, "emotional junkies," but they are implicitly rational about it. They must constantly balance those encounters where interaction rituals produce high levels of positive emotional energy (such as love making, family activities, religious participation, and gatherings of friends) with those more practical, work activities that give them the material resources to participate in more emotionally arousing encounters. Indeed, those who opt out of these work-practical activities and seek only high-emotion encounters (such as drop-outs in a drug culture) soon lose the material resources to enjoy emotion-arousing encounters. Moreover, within the context of work-practical activity, individuals typically seek out or create encounters that provide increases in emotional energy. For example, workers might create an informal subculture in which social encounters produce emotional energy that makes work more bearable, or as is often the case with professionals, they seek the rituals involved in acquiring power, authority, and status on the job as highly rewarding and as giving them an emotional charge (such is almost always the case, for instance, with "workaholics" who use the work setting as a place to charge up their levels of emotional energy).

Not only are there material costs as well as expenditures of cultural capital in interaction rituals, but emotional energy is, itself, a cost. People spend their emotional energy in interaction rituals, and they are willing to do so as long as they realize an emotional profit—that is, the emotional energy spent is repaid with even more positive emotions flowing from the common focus of attention, mood, arousal, rhythmic synchronization, and symbolization. When interaction rituals require too much emotional energy without sufficient emotional payoff, then individuals gravitate to other interaction rituals where their profits are higher.

What kinds of rituals provide the most positive emotional energy for the costs involved? For Collins, those encounters where individuals can have power (the capacity to tell others what to do) and status (the capacity to receive deference and honor) are the most likely to generate high emotional payoffs. Hence, those who possess the cultural capital to command respect and obedience are likely to receive the most positive emotional energy from interaction rituals. At this point Collins's theory begins to converge with that developed by Kemper, as we now explore.

Theodore Kemper's Status-Power Model

Kemper was one of the pioneers in the sociology of emotions. Originally, he termed his approach "a social interactional theory of emotions,"[13] and more recently, he has teamed with Collins to develop the theory further.[14] The basic idea of the theory is quite simple: Individuals' relative power and status in social relationships, and changes in their power and status, have important effects on their emotional states. *Power* is the ability to compel others to follow one's wishes and dictates, whereas *status* is the giving and receiving of unforced deference, compliance, respect, and honor. All social relationships reveal power and status dimensions. According to Kemper and Collins, these dimensions are fundamental to understanding interaction and emotions. After reviewing the literature on emotions,[15] Kemper concluded that there are four basic and primary emotions: fear, anger, happiness/satisfaction, and sadness/depression. These primary emotions can, however, be elaborated into more complex combinations and variants, creating such complex and important emotions as guilt, shame, pride, jealousy, love, and other variants and combinations of the four primary emotions. Indeed, Kemper has argued that these primary emotions have a neurophysiological basis, having been selected in humans' evolutionary history because they promoted survival. Kemper thus attempts to explain how power and status generate the four basic emotions and important variants.

Kemper distinguishes among (1) *structural emotions,* which are those affective states aroused by the relative power and status of individuals within social structures; (2) *situational emotions,* which arise by virtue of changes in power and status during the process of interaction; and (3) *anticipatory emotions,* which revolve around individuals' expectations for power and status in social relations. The dynamics of emotion thus inhere in the status and power that individuals actually hold, the status and power that is gained or lost during interaction, and the power and status that was expected in an interaction. The basic propositions of the theory are summarized in Table 26.1. What follows is a more discursive review of the argument.

When people have power and increase their power within social relationships, they experience a sense of satisfaction, security, and confidence. If individuals do not have power and, more importantly, lose power, they will experience anxiety and fear, leading them to lose confidence. Thus, to have power or to gain it gives people the confidence to secure and use more power, whereas to not possess power or to lose it does just the opposite and takes away the confidence so necessary to garnering and sustaining power.

Just what people expect before they interact, and what they actually get, are very important in the production of emotions. When individuals expect or anticipate a gain in power, but do not receive this gain, their anxiety and fear will escalate, and they begin to lose confidence in themselves. Conversely, when individuals have anticipated a loss of power, but do not lose power, they experience satisfaction, and they might begin to gain confidence.

For status, a more extensive set of arguments is presented. Much like power, when people experience a gain in status, they will also experience satisfaction. Moreover, they will come to like those who have given them status and, if the relationship persists, they will form stronger bonds with these supportive others. If individuals experience a loss of status in social relations, they will experience shame and embarrassment, especially if they believe that this loss of status is the result of their own actions and, hence, their own fault. If this loss is sufficiently great, they will experience not only shame but also depression. However, if they perceive that this loss of status is caused by the unfair and inappropriate actions of others, they will experience anger and become aggressive toward these others. As their anger rises, they move into a power mode of interaction—seeking to compel others to acknowledge their status.

The attribution of status loss to oneself or to others is, however, complicated by what people have anticipated before the interaction. If they have anticipated no gain or loss in status, and experience neither, then they feel

Table 26.1 Kemper's Power Theory of Emotions

Power and Emotions

I. The more a person experiences an increase in power in social relations, the greater will be this person's sense of security and confidence; conversely, the more a person experiences a loss of power in social relations, the greater will be this person's sense of anxiety and fear, leading to a loss of confidence.

II. The more a person anticipates a gain in power in social relations but does not receive this gain, the greater will be this person's sense of anxiety and, potentially, sense of fear; conversely, the more a person anticipates a loss of power in social relations but does not receive this loss, the greater will be this person's sense of satisfaction and, potentially, sense of confidence.

III. The more a person experiences an increase in status in social relations, the greater will be this person's sense of satisfaction and well being, and the greater will be this person's sense of liking for those who gave status and the more likely will the givers and receivers of status form bonds of solidarity.

Status and Emotions

IV. The more a person experiences a loss of status in social relations as a result of his or her own actions, the greater will be this person's sense of shame and embarrassment and, if the loss is sufficiently great, sense of depression as well.

V. The more a person experiences a loss of status in social relations as a result of another's actions, the greater will be the person's sense of anger and the more likely will this person be ready to fight, transforming this person's conduct to a power mode of behavior.

VI. A person's reaction to no change in status in social relations will

   A. Lead to satisfaction, if this person anticipated no change.

   B. Lead to shame and perhaps depression, if this person anticipated an increase in status and perceives that the failure to realize this anticipated increase was caused by his or her own actions.

   C. Lead to anger and aggression, if this person anticipated an increase in status and perceives that the failure to realize this anticipated increase was caused by the actions of others.

   D. Lead to satisfaction and well being, if this person receives more status than anticipated.

VII. The more a person gives status, the greater will be the sense of satisfaction, if this status is given freely, and the more the receiver of status will express appreciation and gratitude, which, in turn, increase the sense of satisfaction for the giver of status.

VIII. The more a person withholds status, when the giving of status is due, the greater will be the sense of guilt and shame.

---

satisfied (a mild version of happiness). If they have anticipated an increase in status but did not get it, and if they perceive that this failure to receive status has been the result of their own actions, then they will experience shame and, perhaps, depression. If the failure to receive expected status is seen as the result of others' inappropriate actions, then individuals will mobilize anger and become aggressive. And if individuals get more status than they anticipated, they will become satisfied.

The giving of status to others also generates emotions. When a person freely bestows status on another, the giver of status experiences satisfaction, and the recipient of the status will express appreciation and gratitude, which will feed back and increase the giver's sense of satisfaction. When a person withholds status that another deserves, this individual will feel guilt and shame for not doing what is appropriate, and persons who did not receive what they deserved (and expected) will experience anger if they correctly perceive that the other has wronged them.

In sum, then, for Kemper—and for Collins as well, in their collaborative work—emotion is ultimately tied to the relative power and status of individuals in social relationships, to shifts in status and power, and to both anticipation and attribution of who is responsible for these shifts. In the end, emotion is driven by those conditions (1) that give people the power to tell others what to do, or that take this power away, and (2) that bestow prestige, deference, and voluntary compliance, or that take this status away.

Cecilia Ridgeway's and Joseph Berger's Expectation States Theories of Affect

The central idea in expectation states theories is that members of groups are assigned a status that, in turn, establishes expectations for their competence and for their role behaviors. Such assignment to a status and its corresponding expectations can be based on diffuse characteristics, such as age, ethnicity, gender, wealth, and other traits that individuals bring to the group from the outside, as well as be based on internal organizational forces establishing lines of authority, rank, and division of labor. In more recent years, one of the many creative branches in this general theoretical program has been the analysis of emotions; the work of Cecilia Ridgeway, Joseph Berger, and Cathryn Johnson can be used to illustrate the nature of this program (for a complete review of expectation states theory, see the Web site for this book).

Cecilia Ridgeway's Theory   Like most research and theory within the expectation states tradition, Ridgeway's[16] and Johnson's[17] work focuses mostly on task-oriented groups, where individuals are temporarily assembled to realize a clearly stated goal or purpose. As Ridgeway and Johnson argue, even the most transitory task-oriented group develops an affect structure as members agree and disagree on how to best accomplish the group's goals. Moreover, disagreements can also involve status challenges as lower-status members seek to raise their positions and refuse to defer to the arguments of higher-status members.

In all groups, Ridgeway has argued,[18] the broader societal culture penetrates group structures as a set of norms or *blueprint rules* that indicate how people are supposed to behave in particular types of groups, whether task-oriented work groups or more informal and intimate groups. Following Hochschild's point of emphasis,[19] these blueprint rules include (a) "feeling rules" about what kinds of emotions are to be experienced in a situation and (b) "display rules" about what emotions can be expressed publicly and how they are to be expressed. An affect-arousing event will, therefore, activate these feeling and display rules; yet, status expectation processes are still important in organizing the way affect is mobilized and managed.

Disagreements represent one class of affect-arousing events, and when such disagreements among group members occur, status in the group determines whether individuals will blame themselves or others for the disagreement. If a person holds an equal or higher status compared with the other(s) with whom a disagreement exists, then this person will be likely to attribute the disagreement to other(s), and this person will feel and express annoyance (a mild form of anger). On the other hand, if an individual is of lower status than the person(s) with whom there is a disagreement, then this individual will tend to blame self and experience depression. For this reason, Ridgeway and Johnson note that superiors are far more likely to express anger and annoyance with subordinates than the reverse: The superior is expected to be more competent and, when authority is challenged, anger ensues because expectation states are being violated by inferiors, whereas when subordinates disagree with superordinates, expectation states force them to attribute the blame to themselves (because they are presumed to be less knowledgeable and competent). And, because no reward is to be gained from continuing to blame oneself, individuals tend not to pursue the disagreement. Instead, the lower-status person withdraws, often to the point of experiencing depression.

These disagreement-anger episodes can disrupt the solidarity of the group, however, even as the status order is reconfirmed. Anger and annoyance do not promote positive sentiments of liking and mutual trust. Depression by subordinates leads them to withdraw commitment from the group, thereby eroding solidarity further. In contrast, agreement among people of different status has the opposite effect: It promotes solidarity. If those who agree are of lower status, then the higher-status persons feel satisfaction (a moderate form of happiness) about the fact that subordinates agree with them. If those who agree are of equal or higher status, then individuals are likely to feel a more intense form of happiness, such as gratitude, that comes when superordinates agree with them. When people experience these positive emotions, Ridgeway and Johnson argue, they become motivated to reward those who agree with them; as they do so, all parties develop positive sentiments and become more likely to agree in the future. From this cycle of positive reinforcement comes enhanced group solidarity.

These status processes also help explain why groups typically reveal more positive than negative affect. As noted earlier, disagreements emanating from lower-status persons are sanctioned because they violate the expectations associated with lower- and higher-status group members, and hence, lower-status individuals soon stop punishing themselves and keep quiet. If disagreement can be avoided and agreement can be reached, then the positive emotions of satisfaction, happiness, and gratitude initiate cycles of positive reinforcement that evolve into solidarity that further orients group members to express agreement and to reward each other with positive sentiments.

An interesting dynamic, however, is initiated when a lower-status person is highly assertive and refuses to back down. Expectation states lead others to sanction the lower-status person negatively as being too pushy and self-interested—what is termed the "backlash effect" against those who violate the status order. Thus, lower-status individuals will almost always have difficulty in groups where they seek to raise their status by displaying competence; assertions of such competence will be defined as violating the status order and the expectations associated with this order. One strategy for overcoming this "backlash effect" is to couch assertions of competence in friendly and unthreatening ways, perhaps as suggestions rather than as challenges. In this manner, lower-status group members can, over time, slowly raise their status and change the expectations associated with them.

Another interesting facet of this theory is the argument that the degree of congruence between the status structure and the distribution of affect shapes rates of participation in making decisions. When high-status members are liked more than are low-status members, their power to influence decisions is enhanced. Lower-status members not only see higher-status members as more competent, they also like higher-status members. Because of this congruence in status and sentiment, lower-status individuals are more likely to accept decisions of higher-status members. Congruence of affect and status thus amplifies the influence of status in task groups, and research by Janet R. Johnston demonstrates that such is also the case in more long-term and intimate groups as well.[20] Johnston's findings have, in turn, stimulated Berger's long-standing research program exploring expectation processes in more intimate and longer-term groups.

Joseph Berger's Affect-Expectations Theory   Berger argues that as emotional reactions emerge and are repeated over time within groups, these reactions generate *affect expectation states* that shape and guide the flow of interaction.[21] Such affect expectation states unfold in a series of stages: (a) Affect is aroused during the interaction; (b) an exchange of affect occurs and begins to set up expectation for what will happen in the current interaction; (c) these affect states also begin to generate an emotional orientation toward others in the situation that involves more stable sentiments—whether positive or negative—that will shape the course of subsequent interactions; and eventually, (d) assignment of personality characteristics consistent with the affect that is exchanged and the emotional orientations of individuals will occur, further circumscribing current and future interactions.

Through this approximate sequence, the affect structure of a group stabilizes the interaction, giving it consistency over time. Moreover, people develop situational identities as they exchange affect and impute personalities to each other. Once these identities are formed, they become expectations for what will occur in the situation, thereby further stabilizing the interaction. Individuals thus become driven and constrained to act in certain ways through the exchange of affect and the development of affect expectations. Yet, this kind of affective structure does not completely determine or circumscribe what occurs in the group. For, if expressive exchanges consistently do not confirm the affect expectations that have developed, then the affective orientations of individuals, the imputation of personality traits, and perhaps the situational identities of individuals will all change, and new affect expectations will begin to emerge.

PSYCHOANALYTIC-INTERACTION
THEORIES OF EMOTION

Thomas Scheff's Psychoanalytic Theory of Emotion

Thomas Scheff,[22] at times in collaboration with Suzanne Retzinger,[23] has blended interactionist ideas with psychoanalytic theory. Drawing from Charles Horton Cooley, Scheff emphasizes that people are in a constant state of self-feeling about pride or shame. As individuals read the gestures of others and see themselves in the "looking glass," they experience a sense of pride or, if the self-images are more negative and critical, a sense of shame. Most of the time, individuals experience rather low levels of these emotions and, hence, easily sustain equanimity.

Scheff believes that pride is a positive emotion, promoting mutual attunement of interpersonal responses, mutual respect and deference, mutually agreed on conformity, strong social bonds, and high levels of social solidarity. In turn, these processes feed back and promote further pride among those in interaction. In contrast, shame has the potential to disrupt these solidarity-producing processes. Borrowing from Helen Lewis's psychoanalytic scheme, Scheff argues that when individuals experience a lack of deference from others and, indeed, experience criticism and other negative reactions from others, their self-evaluations also become negative and cause shame. This experience of shame can be fully acknowledged and lead to a healthy reconstruction of bonds of trust, but if the shame is denied and repressed, it activates cycles of unacknowledged shame and outbursts of anger.

From Lewis's analysis, Scheff notes that there are two potential paths by which shame is denied. One is *overt, undifferentiated shame* where the individual has painful self-feelings but hides from the underlying emotion of shame. The shame is, in essence, disguised as feeling "foolish," "stupid," "inadequate," "defective," "embarrassed," "awkward," "insecure," and so on. Under these conditions, individuals reveal disrupted and slowed speech, averted gazes, blushing, and oversoft speech, and though they have painful feelings, the source of these feelings—shame—remains unacknowledged. The second path for denial is termed *bypassed shame,* whereby the individual avoids the full experience of pain before it can be fully experienced. Speech might speed up but take on a repetitive quality that marks the effort to avoid the experience of shame. Later, Scheff termed these two paths of denying shame *under-* and *over-distancing* oneself from the shame. Overt, undifferentiated shame is "underdistanced" because intense feelings are experienced but not fully acknowledged for what they are, and bypassed shame is "overdistanced" because the pain is not perceived as the individual steps outside of self and acts as if the pain is not present.

Once shame is denied, individuals can find themselves locked into shame-anger cycles. Repressed or denied shame generates anger and hostility. Even as this anger is felt or expressed, it causes the individual to experience even more shame (though still denying the shame for what it is), which, in turn, can generate more anger and hostility that lead to more shame. This kind of cycle can last a lifetime, and it can be passed on to subsequent generations. Scheff even argues that shame can be experienced collectively by large groups and even nation-states that, in turn, vent their collective anger in conflict and war-making.

Structural conditions and cultural beliefs can thus inhibit people from acknowledging shame and pride, particularly shame. The more inhibitory these sociocultural forces are, the more likely are individuals to use defense mechanisms and deny their shame, escalating the potential for anger and hostility. In turn, anger and hostility disrupt the attunement of individuals to each other, the development of mutual respect, the maintenance of strong and positive social bonds, and the production of social solidarity. For Scheff, then, the most important emotional substrate of micro-level interaction is the self-evaluations that individuals make relative to pride and shame.

Jonathan Turner's Psychoanalytic Theory

In recent years,[24] Jonathan Turner has sought to integrate a variety of theoretical traditions—primarily, symbolic interactionism, expectation states, and psychoanalytic theory—into a more general theory of emotions. Figure 26.2 outlines the elements of the theory. In all situations, people carry expectations or, if they did not have them on entering the situation, they soon develop them. These expectations come from a variety of sources, such as norms and values, the relative authority or prestige of individuals, needs states that are aroused in situations, past memories of what transpired in past interactions, the density of network ties among individuals, and other forces. The important point is that these expectations become part of individuals' definitions of the situation, especially with respect to what should transpire because of expectations aroused. Emotions are aroused when expectations are met, exceeded, or unmet. As a general rule, when people's expectations are not realized, they experience negative emotions, or various combinations of anger, fear, and sadness. In contrast, when individuals' expectations are realized, they will experience variants of satisfaction and happiness, and if they are exceeded, people generally will feel variants of happiness. The more emotions are aroused, the more interpersonal energy evident in the behaviors of individuals. The most important part of a person's definition of a situation is expectations about self—that is, about how one should be treated by others. Hence, emotions are particularly likely to be aroused when self is confirmed and, most importantly, when others do not confirm expectations for self.

What makes the theory psychoanalytic is the activation of defense mechanisms when people experience negative emotions. The failure to realize expectations, particularly when this failure is the result of negative sanctions from others, is painful; the more core self feelings are salient in an interaction, the more painful is the inability to have this sense of self confirmed. As a result, individuals often activate defense mechanisms and strategies to avoid experiencing this pain.

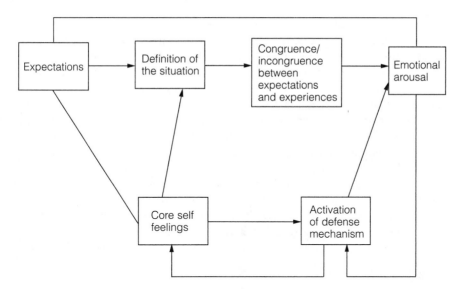

FIGURE 26.2 An Outline of the Elements in Turner's Theory

When incongruities between expectations and responses of others are not severe, individuals can often use defensive strategies, such as selective perception, selective interpretation, or positive memories of past occasions when expectations were met. In this way, individuals can ride out an episode of incongruity between expectations and responses by others. But, if the incongruity cannot be managed in this way, Turner argues that individuals activate more powerful defense mechanisms.

One of these is simple *repression* where the negative emotions associated with incongruity are simply pushed out of consciousness. When habitually used, repression lowers individuals' modal or typical level of emotional energy in all social relations, but at the same time, as repressed emotions build up, they are often released in disproportionate and inappropriate outbursts of fear, anger, or sadness; once these outbursts occur, individuals will be sanctioned by others, forcing them to repress their shame and guilt about their behavior. Individuals can thus get locked into emotional regimes where they repress negative feelings, only to have them erupt in intensity, forcing even more repression, which only ensures that the next outburst will be even more severe.

Another defense mechanism often employed is *attribution,* where blame is imputed to self, others, or social structures for the failure to realize expectations. If individuals blame themselves, they will experience sadness and typically shame as well, and if moral standards are seen to have been violated by the failure to meet expectations, persons will also experience guilt. But individuals often blame others, and under these conditions, they will exhibit anger toward others. If, however, these others have power, repression is likely to occur to hide the anger or, alternatively, the anger is *displaced* onto less power-ful individuals. Oftentimes, people blame the social structures in which they find themselves. Borrowing from Amos Hawley's classification (see Chapter 6), they can blame *corporate units* (or any social structure with division of labor, such a university or business corporation) or *categoric units* (social categories such as ethnicity, gender, and age). If they blame the corporate unit in which the failure to realize expectations occurs, they will express anger toward this unit, and their motivation to stay in the unit will decline or, if they cannot leave, their energy in playing roles will be low. If they blame a social category, they will reveal anger toward members of this category, and they will be likely to develop prejudices toward all members of this category.

Turner's theory is considerably more complex than the brief summary pre-sented here, and he seeks to state the theory as a series of abstract principles, which are too numerous to report here. Nonetheless, this summary offers a sense of the critical sociological dynamics of emotions interpersonal behavior.

CONCLUSION

As is evident, there are many different sociological theories on emotion (see also the Web site for this book for additional theories). Some fall neatly within the symbolic interactionist tradition, others less so, but they all represent the most creative forefront of interactionist theorizing. Mead never developed a theory of emotion, although he offered hints about how one could be devel-oped. Some such as Cooley who saw pride as the basic emotion, and others like Durkheim who saw the connection between emotion and ritual as fun-damental, provided valuable leads, but in the end, not until the middle of the twentieth century did sophisticated sociological theories of emotion begin to surface. And it is really only during the last two decades that these theories have become highly prominent. Today, they mark the leading edge of interac-tionist theorizing, but as is clear from this selective but nonetheless represen-tative review, these theories have not been pulled together into a more integrated theory. Still, the elements for such a synthetic theory are perhaps in place, and perhaps in this new century it will not be long until the emotional dynamics involved in human interaction become an integral part of the evolv-ing interactionist theoretical tradition.

NOTES

1. Arlie R. Hochschild, "Emotion Work, Feeling Rules, and Social Structure," *American Journal of Sociology* 85 (1979), pp. 551–575; *The Managed Heart: The Commercialization of Human Feeling* (Berkeley: University of California Press, 1983).

2. Steven L. Gordon has provided a use-ful analysis of emotion culture, one that has been highly influential in Hochschild's work and by other theo-rists and researchers as well. See "The Sociology of Emotion," in *Social Psychology: Sociological Perspectives,* eds.

M. Rosenberg and R. H. Turner (New York: Basic Books, 1981), pp. 562–592; "Institutional and Impulsive Orientations in Selectively Appropriating Emotions to the Self," in *The Sociology of Emotions: Original Essays and Research Papers,* eds. D. D. Franks and E. D. McCarthy (Greenwich, CT: JAI, 1989), pp. 115–126; and "Social Structural Effects on Emotions," in *Research Agendas in the Sociology of Emotions,* ed. T. D. Kemper (Albany: State University of New York Press, 1990), pp. 145–179.

3. Arlie R. Hochschild, *The Managed Heart* (cited in note 1).

4. See David R. Heise, "Social Action as the Control of Affect," *Behavioral Science* 22 (1977), pp. 163–177; *Understanding Events: Affect and The Construction of Social Action* (New York: Cambridge University Press, 1979); "Effects of Emotion Displays on Social Identification," *Social Psychology Quarterly* 53 (1989), pp. 10–21.

5. David R. Heise and Richard Morgan, "The Structure of Emotions," *Social Psychology Quarterly* 51 (1988), pp. 19–31; Neil J. MacKinnon and David R. Heise, "Affect Control Theory: Delineation and History," in *Theoretical Research Programs: Studies in the Growth of Theory,* eds. J. Berger and M. Zelditch, Jr. (Stanford, CA: Stanford University Press, 1993), pp. 64–103.

6. Lynn Smith-Lovin and David R. Heise, eds., *Analyzing Social Interaction: Advances in Affect Control Theory* (New York: Gordon and Breach, 1988); David R. Heise and Lynn Smith-Lovin, "Impressions of Goodness, Powerfulness, and Liveliness from Discerned Social Events," *Social Psychology Quarterly* 44 (1981), pp. 93–106. For a comparison with expectation states theory, see Cecilia Ridgeway and Lynn Smith-Lovin, "Structure, Culture and Interaction: Comparing Two Theories," *Advances in Group Processes* 11 (1994), pp. 213–239.

7. Lynn Smith-Lovin, "The Sociology of Affect and Emotions," in *Sociological Perspectives on Social Psychology,* eds. K. S. Cook, G. A. Fine, and J. S. House (Boston: Allyn & Bacon, 1995), pp. 118–144. For a detailed but highly readable review of the affect control theory, see Neil J. MacKinnon, *Symbolic Interactionism as Affect Control* (Albany: State University of New York Press, 1994).

8. See David R. Heise and Lynn Smith-Lovin, "Impressions of Goodness, Powerfulness, and Liveliness" (cited in note 6).

9. Sheldon Stryker, *Symbolic Interactionism: A Social Structural Version* (Menlo Park, CA: Benjamin/ Cummings, 1980).

10. Sheldon Stryker, "The Interplay of Affect and Identity: Exploring the Relationship of Social Structure, Social Interaction, Self and Emotions." Paper presented at the American Sociological Association meetings, Chicago, 1987; Sheldon Stryker and Richard Serpe, "Commitment, Identity Salience and Role Behavior: Theory and a Research Example," in *Personality, Roles and Social Behavior,* eds. W. Ickes and E. Knowles (New York: Springer-Verlag, 1982), pp. 199–218.

11. Randall Collins, *Conflict Sociology: Toward an Explanatory Social Science* (New York: Academic, 1975); "Stratification, Emotional Energy and the Transient Emotions," in *Research Agendas in the Sociology of Emotions,* ed. T. D. Kemper (Albany: State University of New York Press, 1990), pp. 27–57; "Interaction Ritual Chains, Power and Property: The Micro-Macro Connection as an Empirically-Based Theoretical Problem," in *The Micro-Macro Problem,* eds. J. C. Alexander, et al. (Berkeley: University of California Press); and *Theoretical Sociology* (New York: Academic, 1988), pp. 187–228; Randall Collins and Robert Hanneman, "Modeling Interaction Ritual Theory of Solidarity," *The Problem of Solidarity: Theories and Models,* eds. P. Doreian and T. J.

Fararo (New York: Gordon and Breach, 1998).

12. Randall Collins, "Emotional Energy as The Common Denominator of Rational Action," *Rationality and Society* 5 (1993), pp. 203–230.

13. Theodore D. Kemper, *A Social Interactional Theory of Emotions* (New York: Wiley, 1979); "Predicting Emotions from Social Relations," *Social Psychology Quarterly* 54 (1991), pp. 330–342.

14. Theodore D. Kemper and Randall Collins, "Dimensions of Microinteractionism," *American Journal of Sociology* 96 (1990), pp. 32–68.

15. Theodore D. Kemper, "How Many Emotions Are There? Wedding the Social and the Autonomic Component," *American Journal of Sociology* 93 (1987), pp. 263–289.

16. Cecilia L. Ridgeway, "Status in Groups: The Importance of Emotion," *American Sociological Review* 47 (1982), pp. 76–88; "Affect," in *Group Processes: Sociological Analysis,* eds. M. Foschi and E. Lawler (Chicago: Nelson-Hall, 1994), pp. 205–220.

17. Cecilia L. Ridgeway and Cathryn Johnson, "What is the Relationship Between Socioemotional Behavior and Status in Task Groups?" *American Journal of Sociology* 95 (1990), pp. 1189–1212.

18. Cecilia L. Ridgeway, "Status in Groups" (cited in note 16).

19. See both works in note 1.

20. Janet R. Johnston, "The Structure of Ex-Spousal Relations: An Exercise in Theoretical Integration and Application," in *Status Generalization: New Theory and Research,* eds. M. Webster, Jr. and M. Foschi (Stanford, CA: Stanford University Press, 1988), pp. 309–326.

21. Joseph Berger, "Directions in Expectation States Research," in *Status Generalization: New Theory and Research,* eds. M. Webster and M. Foschi (Stanford, CA: Stanford University Press, 1988), pp. 450–474.

22. Thomas Scheff, "Shame and Conformity: The Deference-Emotion System," *American Sociological Review* 53 (1988), pp. 395–406; "Socialization of Emotion: Pride and Shame as Causal Agents," in *Research Agendas in the Sociology of Emotion,* ed. T. D. Kemper (Albany: State University of New York Press, 1990), pp. 281–304.

23. Thomas Scheff and Suzanne Retzinger, *Shame, Violence and Social Structure: Theory and Causes* (Lexington, MA: Lexington, 1992).

24. Jonathan H. Turner, *A Theory of Social Interaction* (Stanford, CA: Stanford University Press, 1988); *Face to Face: Towards a Sociological Theory of Interpersonal Behavior* (Stanford, CA: Stanford University Press, 2002); "Toward a General Sociological Theory of Emotions," *Journal for The Theory of Social Behaviour* 29 (1999), pp 133–162; "A Theory of Embedded Encounters," *Advances in Group Processes* 17 (2000), pp. 285–322; "Toward a Sociological Theory of Motivation," *American Sociological Review* 57 (1986), pp. 15–27; "A Behavioral Theory of Social Structure," *Journal for the Theory of Social Behavior* 18 (1988), pp. 354–372; "A Theory of Microdynamics," *Advances in Group Processes* 7 (1989), pp. 1–26; "A General Theory of Motivation and Emotion in Human Interaction," *Österreichische Zeitschrift für Soziologie* 26 (1994), pp. 20–35.

✳

PART VII

Structuralist Theorizing

27

Early Structuralist Theory

The notion of "social structure" or "structure" is central to sociology as an intellectual enterprise. Despite this centrality, the concept of structure is only vaguely theorized; it tends to be used more as a metaphor than as a precisely defined theoretical term. Yet, even with the metaphorical use of the notion of structure, "structuralist" theories can be found in the early masters and, later, in those scholars who served as a bridge to present-day structuralist theorizing.

STRUCTURAL ELEMENTS
IN KARL MARX'S THEORIES

Karl Marx's ideas penetrate just about all macro-level theoretical traditions in sociology; so we would expect to find Marxian concepts in virtually all structural approaches. In particular, two key ideas appear to have been used by those developing a structural or structuralist theory program: (1) system reproduction and (2) system contradiction.[1]

1. Marx was concerned with how patterns of inequality "reproduce" themselves. That is, how is inequality in power and wealth sustained? And how are social relations structured to sustain these inequalities? This metaphor

of social reproduction has been used by many structural theorists who like to view social structures as "reproduced" by the repetitive social encounters among individuals.

From this metaphorical use of Marx's ideas comes a vision of social structure as the distribution of resources among actors who use their respective resources in social encounters and, in the process, reproduce social structure and its attendant distribution of resources. Thus, structure *is* the symbolic, material, and political resources that actors have in their encounters. As actors employ these resources to their advantage, they reproduce the structure of their social relations because they sustain their respective shares of resources. For example, those who can control where others are physically located, who have access to coercion, who control communication channels, and who can manipulate the flow of information can "structure" successive encounters with others who have fewer resources in ways that reproduce inequalities. In so doing, those who have control reproduce structure, but structure is tied to the interactive encounters among individuals using their resources. It is not something "out there" beyond actors and their interactions in concrete situations.

2. Marx was, of course, interested in changing capitalist society, and so he needed to introduce a concept that could break the vicious cycle of system reproduction. His analysis of Georg Wilhelm Friedrich Hegel's dialectics gave him the critical idea of "contradiction." Material social arrangements contain, Marx argued, patterns of social relations that are self-transforming. For example, capitalists must concentrate large pools of labor around machines in urban areas, which allows workers to communicate their grievances and to organize politically to change the very nature of capitalism. Thus, private expropriation of profits by capitalists contradicts the socially organized production process; over time this underlying contradiction will produce conflictual social relations—that is, a revolution by workers—that change and transform the nature of social relations and, hence, social structure.[2]

Again, like so many adaptations of early structural ideas, contemporary theorists have borrowed this notion of contradiction in a metaphorical way. It is used to introduce conflict and change into structural analysis. These theorists posit, in essence, that the distribution of resources that sustains or reproduces social relations is inherently subject to redistribution, under certain conditions. The main condition is inequality. That is, structures reproduced through unequal distribution of symbolic, material, and political resources will exhibit underlying contradictions that will, in turn, generate pressures for interactions that *do not* reproduce the structure but instead transform it in some way through redistribution of resources.

ÉMILE DURKHEIM'S
STRUCTURAL SOCIOLOGY

No one influenced the development of all forms of structural sociology more than Émile Durkheim. Durkheim stood directly in a long line of French thinkers, starting with Charles Montesquieu, proceeding through Jean Condorcet, Jacques Turgot, and Jean Jacques Rousseau, and then moving on to Claude-Henri de Saint-Simon and Auguste Comte. During his career, Durkheim posited four basic types of mechanisms for resolving integrative problems: (1) cultural (collective conscience, collective representations), (2) structural (structural interdependencies and subgroup formation), (3) interpersonal (ritual and the ensuing sense of effervescence and social solidarity), and (4) cognitive (classification, modes of symbolization). In essence, Durkheimian sociology examines how systems of cultural symbols, patterns of group formation and structural interdependence, ritual performances, and systems of cognitive classification integrate variously differentiated social structures. Cultural and structural mechanisms were emphasized in Durkheim's early works, before 1900,[3] whereas interpersonal and cognitive mechanisms became increasingly prominent in his later works in the early years of the twentieth century.[4]

Durkheim viewed structure in much the same way as Comte did—that is, as a form of "statical analysis"—but he used Montesquieu's term "social morphology."[5] For Durkheim, as for Montesquieu, morphological analysis should focus on the "number," the "nature," and the "interrelations" of parts or "elements." This view of structure was emphasized in *The Rules of the Sociological Method*,[6] where Durkheim viewed classification of social facts as involving attention to "the nature and number of the component elements and their mode of combination," whereas explanation "must seek separately the efficient cause (of a social fact) and the function it fulfills." Durkheim's positions on classification of social facts influenced those structuralist approaches that sought to map patterns of relations among the units of social systems. Eventually, this more material approach to structure evolved into network analysis via British anthropology.

Yet, later Durkheim shifted emphasis to the more mental aspects of structure. Indeed, Durkheimian sociology contained an ambiguity about whether structure when broken down to its morphological components is primarily mental, interpersonal, cultural, or material. This ambiguity became more pronounced in the first decade of the century as Durkheim studied how material structures become a part of the mental structure of individuals. For example, Durkheim's early essay on "Incest: The Nature and Origin of the Taboo"[7] along with his and Marcel Mauss's *Primitive Classification*[8] marked a clear movement to the social psychological aspects of structure. This shift became the foundation for much of Claude Lévi-Strauss's structuralism, as we will see in the next chapter, but unlike Lévi-Strauss, who viewed material structures as reflection of mental categories of the mind, Durkheim always insisted that the structures of the mind reflect the material structure of actual social relations. For example, as Durkheim and Mauss noted in *Primitive Classification:*

> Society was not simply a model which classificatory thought followed; it was its own division which served as the division for the system of classification. The first logical categories were social categories; the first classes of things were classes of men, into which these things were integrated. It was because men were grouped, and thought of themselves in the form of groups, that in their ideas they grouped other things, and in the beginning the two modes of grouping were merged to the point of being indistinct. Moieties were the first genera; clans, the first species. . . . And if the totality of things is conceived as a single system, this is because society itself is seen in the same way. It is a whole, or rather it is *the* unique whole to which everything else is related. Thus logical hierarchy is only another aspect of social hierarchy, and the unity of knowledge is nothing else than the very unity of the collectivity, extended to the universe.[9]

Moreover, Durkheim and Mauss provided Lévi-Strauss with yet another lead for his structuralism by emphasizing the importance of mythology, especially as derived from religion, as a reliable source for decoding the "logical hierarchy" and structure of thought. Finally, near the end of this long essay, Durkheim and Mauss introduced another element of structuralist thinking: mental structures are composed of logical connections that reflect how material and cultural "facts" are juxtaposed, merged, distinguished, and, most importantly, opposed. Although they do not pursue this thought, they clearly introduced Lévi-Strauss to what he was to conceptualize later as "binary oppositions." For example, Durkheim and Mauss noted,

> There are sentimental affinities between things as between individuals, and they are classed according to these affinities. . . . All kinds of affective elements combine in the representation made of it. . . . Things are above all sacred or profane, pure or impure, friends or enemies, favourable or unfavourable; i.e., their most fundamental characteristics are only expressions of the way in which they affect social sensibility.[10]

In sum, then, several key elements of structuralism were evident in Durkheim's work at the turn of the century: (1) Mental structures involve the logical ordering and generation of classificatory systems that, although modeled after society, become the basis for individuals' interpretation and action in society. (2) Such structures are designed to show the connectedness of phenomena as part of a coherent, systemic whole. (3) Finally, these structures are created by the logical relations of affinities and oppositions as they are encountered in the cultural and material structure of society.

On this latter point, others in the Durkheimian circle pursued the notion that mental structures are constructed from oppositions. Most notable was

Robert Hertz, who was killed in World War I, like so many of Durkheim's younger colleagues. Hertz's best-known essays were published as *Death and the Right Hand*,[11] in which the notion of binary opposition is developed beyond Durkheim's and Mauss's conceptualization. According to Hertz, mental structures are built up from oppositions: strong-weak, night-day, left-right, natural-social, good-bad, and so on. Yet, although the critical effort in *Death and the Right Hand* is to uncover the underlying principles beneath the surface structure of observed phenomena, an ambiguity exists: Are mental categories—such as "left" and "right"—reflections of social relations, or are they generated from some underlying cognitive capacity? On the surface, Hertz took a straight Durkheimian line—that mental categories reflect social structures—but his work gives consistent hints, supported by his examples, that mental processes per se produce their own structures.

Mauss, by himself, also might have provided Lévi-Strauss with implicit suggestions for reversing Durkheim's position. Although Mauss adhered very closely to Durkheimian principles, seeing himself as "the keeper of the Durkheimian tradition," his book (with Henri Beuchat) titled *Seasonal Variations of the Eskimo: A Study of Social Morphology*[12] emphasized the oppositional nature of thought—in this case the dualistic categories and behaviors created by the facts of winter and summer for the Eskimo. Moreover, in his most famous work, *The Gift*,[13] Mauss emphasized once again the search for underlying principles and practices—in this instance the principle of reciprocity—beneath surface structures and practices such as gift giving. Thus, because Lévi-Strauss read Durkheim, Mauss, and others in the Durkheimian circle, such as Hertz, the basic elements of his structuralism were readily evident. Yet the question remains, What made Lévi-Strauss reverse Durkheim's and Mauss's positions and argue that the material and the cultural structure of society (for example, kinship and mythology respectively) reflect innate capacities of the human mind for generating structures? We will try to answer this question later in the chapter because it is critical not only to sociological structuralism but also to the broad structuralist movement in the humanities and other social sciences.

Structuralist sociology was also influenced by one of the last ideas Durkheim developed in *The Elementary Forms of Religious Life:*[14] the view that conceptions of the sacred as well as the totems that symbolize the sacred and the rituals that are addressed to the sacred are, actually, the worship of society. As individuals feel and sense the power of society beyond them, they have a need to represent this power in the symbols of religion and to arouse the emotion surrounding these symbols through the enactment of rituals. Thus, in enacting religious rituals, individuals in society are not just confirming their faith in the supernatural, they are also legitimating the structure of society. In Durkheim's view, then, religion is the worship of society and of the structures that make up people's daily lives. Thus, social structure, cognitions and beliefs, and ritual practices were seen by Durkheim as intimately interconnected.

GEORG SIMMEL'S
FORMAL STRUCTURALISM

Although Durkheim was the most influential figure in the emergence of struc-turalism, the German sociologist Georg Simmel was almost as influential. Simmel's emphasis on discovering the underlying forms of association among individuals and groups has exerted considerable influence on some modern schools of structural sociology. Simmel believed social structure consists of "permanent interactions," and formal sociology seeks the underlying pattern of these permanent interactions. The content or substantive nature of these inter-actions is far less significant, sociologically, than their basic form. Although interactions can reveal an enormous variety of contents, the underlying form of relations might be the same. As Simmel emphasized,

> Social groups, which are the most diverse imaginable in purpose and general significance, may nevertheless show identical forms of behavior toward one another on the part of individual members. We find superior-ity and subordination, competition, division of labor . . . and innumer-able similar features in the state, in the religious community, in a band of conspirators, in an economic association, in an art school, in the family. However diverse the interests are that give rise to these associations, the *forms* in which the interests are realized may yet be identical.[15]

Social structure must thus be conceptualized as forms or configurations of interaction that undergird and make possible the wide variety of substantive activities of individuals. This point makes Simmel's eclectic approach to soci-ology more understandable, for although he studied widely diverse substantive matters, he was always seeking the underlying form of interaction. In all Simmel's most famous essays, this is the message: Whatever the surface sub-stance and content of social relations, there is an underlying form or structure. For example, as Simmel examined conflict, he could see that conflicts between nation–states, individual people, and small groups all reveal certain basic ele-ments, or forms; or, to illustrate further, as Simmel examined the effects of increasing numbers of people in an encounter, he could argue that the geo-metric increase in the number of possible relations (two people can have two ties, three can have six, four can have twelve, and so on) changes the form or structure of the encounter; or, as Simmel examined the effects of money (a neutral and nonspecific medium of exchange), he could conclude that the form of social relations is fundamentally altered.[16]

Simmel's essay, *The Web of Group Affiliations,*[17] has probably exerted the most influence on more contemporary structural thinking in sociology. Here, Simmel examined the effects of social differentiation on the affiliations of indi-viduals. In less differentiated systems, the individual is absorbed and sur-rounded by one or just a few groups that are lodged inside each other, and as a result, the pattern of group affiliations pulls the individual in one direction. With social differentiation, however, the individual can now have multiple group affiliations, belonging to many different groups and being pulled in many different directions. As a result, no one group can absorb the individual, and the individual only gives a portion of self to any particular group. This process of multiple group affiliations sets the person free and increases individuality because each person can, to a degree, choose and select configurations of group affiliation. At the more macro level, as differentiation encourages multiple group affiliations, it generates many cross-cutting affiliations among individuals who might find themselves in conflict in one sphere and associates in another. As a result, the polarization of society is less likely because group affiliations place individuals in diverse social structures and, thereby, prevent them from being overly mobilized by any one group or small set of groups.

DIVERGING STRANDS
OF STRUCTURALIST THEORY

The ideas of Durkheim, Marx, and Simmel inspired structuralist sociology, although Durkheim was the most influential figure in this trio of early sociologists. As Durkheim's functionalism shifted from a material to more mental view of structure, it shaped two different anthropological traditions, one that is embodied in the French anthropologist, Lévi–Strauss, and the other the British anthropology as carried forward by A. R. Radcliffe-Brown and S. F. Nadel. Partly influenced by this British tradition, an American strain of structural analysis also began to emerge in the middle decades of the century. Later structural theories of the more contemporary era were often either extensions of, or reactions against, these three maturing structuralist traditions. For the present, let us outline in broad strokes how the ideas of early theorists, particularly those of Durkheim, were used to create a distinctly structuralist sociology.

CLAUDE LÉVI-STRAUSS'S
FRENCH STRUCTURAL TRADITION

In *The Elementary Structures of Kinship*,[18] Lévi-Strauss only hinted at the more philosophical view of the world that his analysis of kinship implied,[19] but even at this early stage, Levi-Strauss began to depart from the earlier foundations provided by Durkheim and Mauss.[20] Indeed, Lévi-Strauss was about to "turn Durkheim on his head" in much the same way that Marx had revised Hegel's dialectic. In contrast with Durkheim and Mauss who had argued in *Primitive Classification* that human cognitive categories reflect the structure of society[21], Lévi-Strauss came to the opposite conclusion: The structure of society is but a surface manifestation of fundamental mental processes.

Lévi-Strauss came to this position under the influence of structural linguistics, as initially chartered by Ferdinand de Saussure[22] and Roman Jakobson. De Saussure is typically considered the father both of structural linguistics[23] and of Lévi-Strauss's structuralism as well. Commentators have often viewed Lévi-Strauss's interest in linguistics as decisive in his reversal of the Durkheimian tradition. Yet, the Swiss linguist de Saussure saw himself as a Durkheimian. De Saussure's posthumously published lectures, *Course in General Linguistics,* had a decidedly Durkheimian tone: He argued that the parts of language acquire their meaning only in relation to the structure of the whole; the units of language—whether sounds or morphemes—are only points in an overall structure that transcends the individual; language is "based entirely on the opposition of concrete units"[24]; the underlying structure of language (*langue*) can be known and understood only by reference to surface phenomena, such as speech (*parole*); and the structure of language is "no longer looked upon as an organism that developed independently but as a product of the collective mind of linguistic groups."[25] Thus, in reality, as a contemporary of Durkheim, de Saussure was far more committed to Durkheim's vision of reality than is typically acknowledged, but he made a critical breakthrough in linguistic analysis of the nineteenth century: Speech is but a surface manifestation of more fundamental mental processes. Language is not speech or the written word; rather, it is a particular way of thinking, which, in true Durkheimian fashion, de Saussure viewed as a product of the general patterns of social and cultural organization among people. This distinction of speech as a mere surface manifestation of underlying mental processes was increasingly used as a metaphor for Lévi-Strauss's structuralism. Of course, this metaphor is as old as Plato's view that reality is a mere reflection of universal essences and as recent as Marx's dictum that cultural values and beliefs, as well as institutional arrangements, are reflections of an underlying substructure of economic relations.

Lévi-Strauss also borrowed from the early-twentieth-century linguist Jakobson the notion that the mental thought underlying language occurs as *binary contrasts,* such as good/bad, male/female, yes/no, black/white, and human/nonhuman. Moreover, drawing from Jakobson and others, Lévi-Strauss viewed the underlying mental reality of binary opposites as organized, or mediated, by a series of "innate codes" or rules that could be used to generate many different social forms: language, art, music, social structure, myths, values, beliefs, and so on.[26] In essence, as Lévi-Strauss received these very Durkheimian ideas, he appeared to focus primarily on the distinction between *langue* and *parole* and on the notion of language as constructed from oppositions, while ignoring de Saussure's emphasis on the social structural origins of *langue.*

Why, then, did Lévi-Strauss find linguistic analysis so appealing, and why did he ignore the Durkheimian thrust of de Saussure's work? Lévi-Strauss's own self-reflective answers are not particularly revealing. For example, he claimed that he was probably born a structuralist, recalling that even when he was a two-year-old and still unable to read, he sought to decipher signs with similar groupings of letters. Another childhood influence, he claimed, was geology, in which the task was to discover the underlying geological operations for the tremendous diversity of landscapes.[27] He also constructed many genealogies, and for a time, Lévi-Strauss declared that he was an "anti-Durkheimian" and would embrace Anglo-American methods as an alternative to the Durkheimian approach.[28] Yet, he always kept a foot in the French tradition. For example, he dedicated his essay "French Sociology" to Mauss and emphasized,

> One could say that the entire purpose of the French school lies in an attempt to break up the categories of the layman, and to group the data into a deeper, sounder classification. As was emphasized by Durkheim, the true and only basis of sociology is social morphology, i.e., this part of sociology the task of which is to constitute and to classify social types.[29]

Lévi-Strauss's goal increasingly became one of reworking the French tradition for analyzing morphology or structure. His earlier work seemed to lie squarely in the Durkheimian tradition. In *The Elementary Structures of Kinship* (certainly a very Durkheimian-sounding title), he focused on how kinship rules regulate marriage, which owes a great deal to Mauss's *The Gift*.[30] Lévi-Strauss concluded that exchange is a "common denominator of a large number of apparently heterogeneous social activities," and like Mauss before him, he posited a universal structural "principle of reciprocity." Moreover, drawing from and criticizing Durkheim's early analysis of incest,[31] whereby incest was seen as the product of rules of exogamy, Lévi-Strauss viewed rules regarding incest as ordering principles in their own right. The details here are not as important as the recognition that his work was basically Durkheimian, but there were hints of significant additions. In particular, Lévi-Strauss postulated an unconscious mind involving a blueprint or model for coding operations. For example, "reciprocity" is perhaps a universal unconscious code, lodged in the neuroanatomy of the brain and existing *before* the material and cultural structure of society.

Why, then, did Lévi-Strauss make this change in Durkheimian sociology? The simple answer might be that he wanted to say something new. If he merely borrowed Durkheim's idea of morphology, Mauss's and Hertz's concern with underlying structural principles, Mauss's principle of reciprocity, Durkheim's and Mauss's concern with categories of thought, mythology, and ritual, and de Saussure's as well as Jakobson's basic ideas in linguistics, what would be original about his work? His strategy was simply to turn the Durkheimian school upside down and to view mental morphology as the underlying cause of cultural and material morphology. He decided essentially to convert what Durkheim saw as "real," "a thing," and a "social fact" into an unreality. In doing so, he changed what Durkheim saw as unreal into the ultimate reality. Thus, structuralism was born as the result of Lévi-Strauss's search for something new to say in the long and distinguished French lineage. All elements of the French lineage remain, but they are reversed.

Thus, during the decades of the midcentury, Lévi-Strauss's structuralism became concerned with understanding cultural and social patterns as the universal mental processes that are rooted in the biochemistry of the human brain.[32] In this sense Lévi-Strauss's structuralism is mentalistic and reductionistic. To summarize what became the basic argument:[33]

1. The empirically observable must be viewed as a *system* of relationships among components—whether these components be elements of myths and folk tales or positions in a kinship system.

2. It is appropriate to construct "statistical models" of these observable systems to summarize the empirically observable relationships among components.

3. Such models, however, are only a surface manifestation of more fundamental forms of reality. These forms are the result of using various codes or rules to organize different binary opposites. Such forms can be visualized through the construction of "mechanical models," which articulate the logical results of using various rules to organize different binary oppositions.

4. The tendencies of statistical models will reflect, imperfectly, the properties of the mechanical model. But the latter is "more real."

5. The mechanical model is built from rules and binary oppositions that are innate to humans and rooted in the biochemistry and neurology of the brain.

Steps 1 and 2 are about as far as Lévi-Strauss had gone in the first publication of *The Elementary Structures of Kinship.* Subsequent work on kinship and on myths invoked at least the rhetoric of Steps 3, 4, and 5. What made structuralism distinctive, therefore, was the commitment to the assumptions and strategy implied in these last steps. The major problem with this strategy was that it is untestable. If mechanical models are never perfectly reflected in the empirical world, how is it possible to confirm or disconfirm the application of rules to binary opposites? As Marshall Sahlins sarcastically remarked, "What is apparent is false and what is hidden from perception and contradicts it is true."[34] Yet, despite such criticisms, the imagery communicated by Lévi-Strauss, especially in Steps 1 and 3, has influenced a great deal of structural theorizing. Although not many have adopted the extremes of Lévi-Strauss's approach, the idea of structure as involving "grammars" and "codes" that guide actors in their actions and in the production of social structures has remained appealing.

THE BRITISH STRUCTURAL TRADITION

Radcliffe-Brown's early works, such as his analysis of kinship among Australian tribes[35] and, more significantly, his analysis of ritual in *The Andaman Islanders,*[36] revealed many parallels to the late Durkheim's functional analysis of ritual.[37] Equally important, however, Radcliffe-Brown also developed Durkheim's views on social structure. This latter effort was particularly evident in

Radcliffe-Brown's more theoretical work, especially on kinship. In his classic essay "On the Concept of Function in Social Science," Radcliffe-Brown asserted that "the concept of function . . . involves the notion of a structure consisting of a set of relations amongst unit entities, the continuity of the structure being maintained by a life-process made up of the activities of the constituent units."[38]

In Radcliffe-Brown's thinking, then, structural functionalism was to emphasize structure—that is, relations among entities—over function or the consequence of entities for system integration. Moreover, he emphasized his differences with Lévi-Strauss when he wrote to the latter:

> I use the term "social structure" in a sense so different from yours as to make discussion so different as to be unlikely to be profitable. While for you, social structure has nothing to do with reality but with models that are built up, I regard the social structure as a reality.[39]

In his last major theoretical statement, made in *A Natural Science of Society,*[40] Radcliffe-Brown echoed the sentiments in Durkheim's *The Rules of the Sociological Method*[41] and argued that social systems are an emergent natural system composed of the properties of relations among individuals. Therefore, they must be distinguished from psychological systems, which study relations *within* individuals. In the years between World Wars I and II, however, Radcliffe-Brown and other anthropologists were still welded to functional analysis, allowing notions of the functions of a structure to distort purely structural analysis. Whereas hints of a network approach can be found in a number of anthropological works,[42] Nadel's *The Study of Social Structure*[43] was decisive for many anthropologists in separating "structure" and "function." In so doing, Nadel proposed a mode of analysis compatible with contemporary network analysis. Nadel began his argument with the assertion that conceptions of structure in the social sciences are too vague. Indeed, we should begin with a more precise, yet general, notion of all structure: "Structure indicates an ordered arrangement of parts which can be treated as transposable, being relations invariant, while the parts themselves are variable."[44] Thus, structure must concentrate on the properties of relations rather than actors, especially on those properties of relations that are invariant and always occur.

From this general conception of all structure, Nadel proposed that "we arrive at the structure of a society through abstracting from the concrete population and its behavior the pattern or network (or system) of relationships obtaining between actors in their capacity of playing roles relative to one another."[45] Within structures exist embedded "subgroups" characterized by certain types of relationships that hold people together. Thus, social structure is to be viewed as layers and clusters of networks—from the total network of a society to varying congeries of subnetworks. The key to discerning structure is to avoid what he termed "the distribution of relations on the grounds of their similarity and dissimilarity" and concentrate, instead, on the "interlocking of relationships whereby interactions implicit in one determine those occurring in others." That is, one should examine specific configurations of linkages among actors playing roles rather than the statistical distributions of actors in this or that type of role.

From these general ideas, several anthropologists, most notably J. Clyde Mitchell[46] and John A. Barnes,[47] welded the metaphorical imagery of work like Nadel's to the more specific techniques for conceptualizing the properties of networks. Coupled with path-breaking empirical studies,[48] the anthropological tradition began to merge with work in sociology and social psychology. This merger came about, however, only after network analysis had developed in the United States within social psychology.

THE AMERICAN STRUCTURAL TRADITION
IN SOCIAL PSYCHOLOGY

At about the same time that network analysis was emerging in anthropology in England, a parallel line of development was occurring in the United States, although some figures and ideas in this American program had roots in Europe. Most of this work came from social psychology, a discipline that at the time was unique to America, where the possibilities of experiments in group settings were beginning to create considerable excitement.

Jacob Moreno and Sociometric Techniques

A transplanted European, Jacob Moreno was an eclectic thinker, but perhaps his more enduring contribution to sociology was the development of *sociograms.*[49] Moreno was interested in the processes of attraction and repulsion among individuals in groups; so, he sought a way to conceptualize and measure these processes. What Moreno and subsequent researchers did was to ask group members about their preferences for associating with others in the group. Typically, group members would be asked questions about whom they liked and with whom they would want to spend time or engage in activity. Often subjects were asked to give their first, second, third, and so on, choices on these and related issues. The results could then be arrayed in a matrix (this was not always done) in which each person's rating of others in a group is recorded (see Figure 27.1 for a simplified example). The construction of such matrices became an important part of network analysis, but equally significant was the development of a sociogram in which group members were arrayed in a visual space, with their relative juxtaposition and connective lines representing the pattern of choices (those closest and connected being attracted in the direction of the arrows, and those distant and unconnected being less attracted to each other). Figure 27.2 illustrates the nature of Moreno's sociograms.

This visual representation of choices, as pulled from a matrix, captures the "structure" of preferences or, in Moreno's terms, the patterns of attraction and repulsion among individuals in groups. This visual array can be viewed as a network because the "connections" among individuals are what is most significant. Moreover, in looking at the network, structural features emerge.

Matrix of Friendship Choices in a School Fraternity

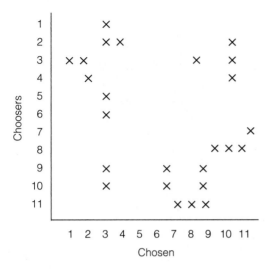

FIGURE 27.1 An Example of an Early Matrix

Source: Constructed from sociogram in J. Moreno, *Who Shall Survive?* rev. ed., New York: Beacon House, 1953, p. 171.

Moreno thus introduced some key conceptual ingredients of contemporary network analysis: the mapping of relations among actors in visual space to represent the structure of these relations. Alongside Moreno's sociograms, however, other research and theoretical traditions were developing and pointing toward the same kind of structural analysis.

Studies of Communications in Groups:
Alex Bavelas and Harold Leavitt

Alex Bavelas[50] was one of the first to study how the structure of a network influences the flow of communication in experimental groups. Others such as Harold Leavitt[51] followed Bavelas's lead and also began to study how communication patterns influence the task performances of people in experimental groups. The network structure in these experiments usually involved artificially partitioning groups in such a way that messages could flow only in certain directions and through particular persons. Emerging from Bavelas's original study was the notion of *centrality,* which was evident when positions lie between other positions in a network. When communications had to flow through this central position, certain styles and levels of task performance prevailed, whereas other patterns of information flow produced different results. Figure 27.3 outlines some chains of communication flow that Bavelas originally isolated and that Leavitt later improved.

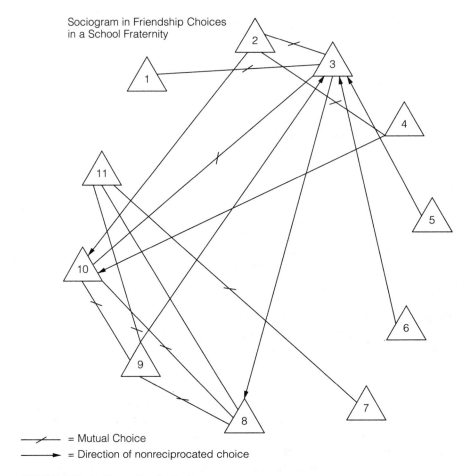

Sociogram in Friendship Choices
in a School Fraternity

```
———✗—— = Mutual Choice
————▶ = Direction of nonreciprocated choice
```

FIGURE 27.2 An Example of a Sociogram

Source: Constructed from sociogram in J. Moreno, *Who Shall Survive?* rev. ed., New York: Beacon House, 1953, p. 171.

The results of these experiments are perhaps less important than the image of structure that is offered, although we should note in passing that occupying central positions, such as C in Figure 27.3, exerted the most influence on the emergence of leadership, task performance, and effective communication. These diagrams in Figure 27.3 resemble the sociograms, but there are some important differences that became critical in modern network analysis. First, the network is conceptualized in the communication studies as consisting of positions rather than of persons, with the result that the pattern of relations among positions was viewed as a basic or generic type of structure. Indeed, different people could occupy the positions and the experimental results would be the same. Thus, there is a real sense that structure constitutes an emergent reality, beyond the individuals involved. Second, the idea that the links among

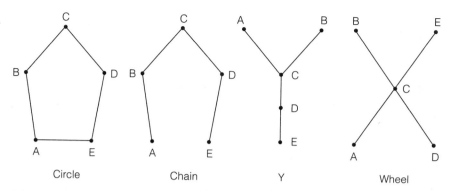

FIGURE 27.3 Types of Communication Structures in Experimental Groups

Source: Harold J. Leavitt, "Some Effects of Certain Communication Patterns on Group
Performance," *Journal of Abnormal and Social Psychology* 56, 1951, p. 40.

positions involve flows of resources—in these studies, information and messages—anticipates the thrust of much network analysis. Of course, we could also see Moreno's sociograms as involving flows of affect and preferences among people, but the idea is less explicit and less embedded in a conception of networks as relations among positions.

Thus, these early experimental studies on communication created a new conceptualization of networks as (1) composed of positions, (2) connected by relations, and (3) involving the flows of resources.

Early Gestalt and Balance Approaches: Heider, Newcomb, Cartwright, and Harary

Fritz Heider,[52] who is often considered the founder of Gestalt psychology, developed some of the initial concepts in various theories of "balance" and "equilibrium" in cognitive perceptions. In Heider's view, individuals seek to balance[53] their cognitive conceptions; in his famous *P,O,X* model, Heider argued that a person (*P*) will attempt to balance cognitions toward an object or entity (*X*) with those of another person (*O*). If a person (*P*) has positive sentiments toward an object (*X*) and another person (*O*), but *O* has negative sentiments toward *X*, then a state of cognitive imbalance exists. A person has two options if the imbalance is to be resolved: (1) to change sentiments toward *X* or (2) to alter sentiments toward *O*. By altering sentiments to *X* toward the negative, cognitive balance is achieved, because *P* and *O* now reveal a negative orientation toward *X*, thereby affirming their positive feelings toward each other. Or, by altering sentiments directed to *O* toward the negative, cognitive balance is achieved because *P* has a positive attitude toward *X* and negative feelings for *O*, who has a negative orientation to *X*.

Although Heider did not explicitly do so, this conception of balance can be expressed in algebraic terms, as is done in Figure 27.4 by multiplying the cognitive links in Figure 27.4(a): (+) x (−) x (+) = (−) or imbalance. This

FIGURE 27.4 The Dynamics of Cognitive Balance

Source: Adopted from Fritz Heider (*The Psychology of Interpersonal Relations* [New York: Wiley, 1958]) with (+) and (–) used instead of Heider's notation.

imbalance can be resolved by changing the sign of the links toward a (–) or a (+), as is done for Figures 27.4(b) and 27.4(c). By multiplying the signs for the lines in Figures 27.4(b) or 27.4(c), a (+) product is achieved, indicating that the relation is now in balance.

Theodore Newcomb[54] extrapolated Heider's logic to the analysis of interpersonal communication. Newcomb argued that this tendency to seek balance applies equally to *inter*personal as well as to the *intra*personal situations represented by the *P,O,X* model, and he constructed an *A,B,X* model to emphasize this conclusion. A person (*A*) and another (*B*) who communicate and develop positive sentiments will, in an effort to maintain balance with each other, develop similar sentiments toward a third entity (*X*), which can be an object, an idea, or a third person. However, if *A*'s orientation to *X* is very strong in either a positive or a negative sense and *B*'s orientation is just the opposite, several options are available: (1) *A* can convince *B* to change its orientation toward *X*, and vice versa, or (2) *A* can change its orientation to *B*, and vice versa. Figure 27.5 represents this interpersonal situation for *A,B,X* in the same manner as Heider's *P,O,X* model in Figure 27.4. Situation 27.5(a) is in interpersonal imbalance, as can be determined by multiplying the signs (+) x (+) x (–) = (–) or imbalance. Figures 27.5(b), (c), and (d) represent three options that restore balance to the relations among *A, B,* and *X*. (In Figure 27.5(a), (b), and (c), the product of multiplying the signs now equals a (+), or balance.)

Heider's and Newcomb's approaches stimulated research that more explicitly employed mathematics as a way to conceptualize the links in interpersonal networks. The key breakthrough had come earlier[55] in the use of the mathematical theory of linear graphs. Somewhat later, in the mid-1950s, Dorin Cartwright and Frank Harary[56] similarly employed the logic of signed-digraph theory to examine balance in larger groups consisting of more than three persons. Figure 27.6 presents a model developed by Cartwright and Harary for a larger set of actors.

The basic idea is much the same as in the *P,O,X* and *A,B,X* models, but now the nature of sentiments is specified by dotted (negative) and solid (positive) lines. By multiplying the signs—(+) = solid line; (–) = dotted line—across all the lines, points of imbalance and balance can be identified. For Cartwright and Harary, one way to assess balance is to multiply the various *cycles* on the graph—for example, *ABCD; ABCDEFGH; HDFG; DFE;* and so on. If multiplying the signs for each connection yields a positive outcome,

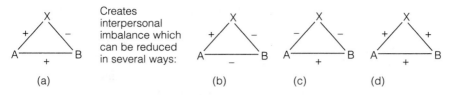

FIGURE 27.5 The Dynamics of Interpersonal Balance

Source: Adopted from Theodore Newcomb ("An Approach to the Study of Communicative Arts," *Psychological Review* 60 [1953], pp. 393–404) with alterations to Newcomb's system of notation.

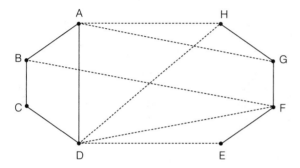

FIGURE 27.6 An S-graph of Eight Points

Source: D. Cartwright and F. Harary, "Structural Balance: A Generalization of Heider's Theory," *Psychological Review* 63 (5), 1956, p. 286.

then this structure is in balance. Another procedure is specified by a theorem: An S-graph is balanced if and only if all paths joining the same pair of points have the same sign.

The significance of introducing graph theory into balance models is that it facilitated the representation of social relations with mathematical conventions—something that Moreno, Heider, and Newcomb had failed to do. But the basic thrust of earlier analysis was retained: Graph theory could represent directions of links between actors (this is done by simply placing arrows on the lines as they intersect with a point); graph theory could represent two different types of relations between points to be specified by double lines and arrows; it could represent different positive or negative states (the sign being denoted by solid or dotted lines); it offered a better procedure for analyzing more complex social structures; and, unlike the matrices behind Moreno's and others' sociograms, graph theory would make them more amenable to mathematical and statistical manipulation. Thus, although the conventions of graph theory have not remained exactly the same, especially as adopted for network use, the logic of the analysis that graph theory facilitated was essential for the development of the network approach beyond crude matrices and sociograms or simple triadic relations to more complex networks involving the flows of multiple resources in varying directions.

CONCLUSION

As structuralist theory matured, it went in many different directions. What is most evident in this divergence is the inability of sociological theorists to agree on their most fundamental idea—social structure. Depending on each theorist's adaptation of earlier traditions—or equally important, their rejection of traditions—very different theories of "structure" are proposed. We will examine only three distinctive approaches among many that have drawn inspiration from the early masters and the French, British, and American variations of structuralist theory. The most general is Anthony Giddens's structuration theory, which is examined in the next chapter. In this approach a wide variety of approaches are synthesized to develop a view of structure as rules and resources that actors strategically use in social relations. Pierre Bourdieu's structuralist approach follows a long French lineage emphasizing culture, but Bourdieu brings in ideas from other approaches as well. Finally, network theory will be examined. Here the British and American structuralist traditions, coupled with ideas from Simmel's formal sociology as well as concepts from American social psychology of the mid-twentieth century, are blended into a view of structure as networks of connections among nodes.

NOTES

1. See Karl Marx, *A Contribution to the Critique of Political Economy* (New York: International, 1970); *The Economic and Philosophic Manuscripts of 1844* (New York: International, 1964); and *Capital: A Critical Analysis of Capitalist Production* (New York: International, 1967).

2. Karl Marx and Friedrich Engels, *The Communist Manifesto* (New York: International, 1971, originally published in 1847).

3. Émile Durkheim, *The Division of Labor in Society* (New York: Free Press, 1947, originally published in 1893) and *The Rules of the Sociological Method* (New York: Free Press, 1938, originally published in 1895).

4. Émile Durkheim, *The Elementary Forms of Religious Life* (New York: Free Press, 1947, originally published in 1912); Émile Durkheim and Marcel Mauss, *Primitive Classification* (London: Cohen and West, 1963, originally published in 1903).

5. Charles Montesquieu, *The Spirit of the Laws* (London: Colonial, 1900, originally published in 1748).

6. Émile Durkheim, *The Rules of the Sociological Method* (cited in note 3), p. 96.

7. Émile Durkheim, "Incest: The Nature and Origin of the Taboo." *Anneé Sociologique* 1 (1898), pp. 1–70.

8. Émile Durkheim and Marcel Mauss, *Primitive Classification* (cited in note 4).

9. Ibid., pp. 82–84.

10. Ibid., pp. 85–86.

11. Robert Hertz, *Death and the Right Hand* (London: Cohen and West, 1960, originally published in 1909).

12. Marcel Mauss and Henri Beuchat, *Seasonal Variations of the Eskimo: A Study of Morphology* (London: Routledge & Kegan Paul, 1979, originally published in 1904–1905).

13. Marcel Mauss, *The Gift: Forms and Functions of Exchange* trans. by I.

Cunnism (New York: Free Press, 1954, originally published in 1925).

14. Émile Durkheim, *The Elementary Forms of Religious Life* (cited in note 4).

15. Georg Simmel, *Fundamental Problems of Sociology* (1918), portions of which are translated in K. W. Wolf, *The Sociology of Georg Simmel* (New York: Free Press, 1950). Quote is from p. 22 of original.

16. For a review of Simmel's work, see Jonathan H. Turner, Leonard Beeghley, and Charles Powers, *The Emergence of Sociological Theory* (Belmont, CA: Wadsworth, 2002).

17. Georg Simmel, "The Intersection of Social Spheres," first published in 1890, best communicates his idea. See *Georg Simmel: Sociologist and European,* trans. Peter Laurence (New York: Barnes and Noble, 1976), but the idea is most available in *Conflict and the Web of Group Affiliations,* trans. Reinhard Bendix (New York: Free Press, 1955).

18. Claude Lévi-Strauss, *The Elementary Structures of Kinship* trans. J. H. Bell, J. R. von Sturmer, & R. Needham (Boston: Beacon, 1969, originally published in French in 1949).

19. Actually, an earlier work, "The Analysis of Structure in Linguistics and in Anthropology," *Word* 1 (1945), pp. 1–21, provided a better clue to the form of Lévi-Strauss's structuralism.

20. Marcel Mauss, *The Gift: Forms and Functions of Exchange* (cited in note 13) is given particular credit. It must be remembered, of course, that Mauss was Durkheim's student and son-in-law.

21. Émile Durkheim and Marcel Mauss, *Primitive Classification* (cited in note 4). Originally published in 1903, this is a rather extreme and unsuccessful effort to show how mental categories directly reflect the spatial and structural organization of a population. It is a horribly flawed work, but it is the most extreme statement of Durkheim's sociologistic position.

22. Ferdinand de Saussure, *Course in General Linguistics* (New York: McGraw-Hill, 1966); originally compiled posthumously by his students from their lecture notes in 1915.

23. Ibid., p. 107.

24. Ibid., p. 108.

25. Actually, Jakobson simply argued that children's phonological development occurs as a system in which contrasts are critical—for example, "papa versus mama" or the contrasts that children learn between vowels and consonants. Lévi-Strauss appears to have added the jargon of information theory and computer technology. See Roman Jakobson, *Selected Writings 1: Phonological Studies* (The Hague: Mouton, 1962) and *Selected Writings 11: Word and Language* (The Hague: Mouton, 1971). For more detail, see A. R. Maryanski and Jonathan H. Turner, "The Offspring of Functionalism: French and British Structuralism," *Sociological Theory* 9 (1991), pp. 106–115.

26. Claude Lévi-Strauss, *Myth and Meaning* (New York: Schocken, 1979).

27. Claude Lévi-Strauss, *A World on the Wane* (London: Hutchinson, 1961).

28. Claude Lévi-Strauss, "French Sociology," in Georges Gurvitch and Wilbert E. Moore, eds., *Twentieth Century Sociology* (New York: Books for Libraries, 1945).

29. Claude Lévi-Strauss, *The Elementary Structures of Kinship* (cited in note 18).

30. Marcel Mauss, *The Gift* (cited in note 13).

31. Émile Durkheim, "Incest: The Nature and Origin of the Taboo." *Anneé Sociologique* 1 (1898), pp. 1–70.

32. See, for example, Claude Lévi-Strauss, "Social Structure," in *Anthropology Today,* ed. A. Kroeber (Chicago: University of Chicago Press, 1953), pp. 524–553; *Structural Anthropology*

(Paris: Plon, 1958; trans. 1963 by Basic Books); and *Mythologiques: le cru et le cuit* (Paris: Plon, 1964).

33. Mirian Glucksmann, *Structuralist Analysis in Contemporary Social Thought* (London: Routledge & Kegan Paul, 1974). A more sympathetic review of Lévi-Strauss, as well as a more general review of structuralist thought, can be found in Tom Bottomore and Robert Nisbet, "Structuralism," in their *A History of Sociological Analysis* (New York: Basic Books, 1978).

34. Marshall D. Sahlins, "On the Delphic Writings of Claude Lévi-Strauss," *Scientific American* 214 (1966), p. 134. For other relevant critiques, see Marvin Harris, *The Rise of Anthropological Theory* (New York: Crowell, 1968), pp. 464–513; and Eugene A. Hammel, "The Myth of Structural Analysis" (Addison-Wesley Module, no. 25, Reading, MA: Addison-Wesley, 1972).

35. A. R. Radcliffe-Brown, "Three Tribes of Western Australia," *Journal of Royal Anthropological Institute of Great Britain and Ireland* 43 (1913), pp. 8–88.

36. A. R. Radcliffe-Brown, *The Andaman Islanders* (Cambridge: Cambridge University Press, 1922, originally published in 1914).

37. Émile Durkheim, *The Elementary Forms of Religious Life* (New York: Free Press, 1947, originally published in 1912).

38. A. R. Radcliffe-Brown, "On the Concept of Function in Social Science." *American Anthropologist* 37 (1935), p. 396.

39. Quote cited in George P. Murdock, "Social Structure" in S. Tax, L. Eiseley, I. Rouse, and C. Voeglia, eds., *An Appraisal of Anthropology Today* (New York: Free Press, 1953).

40. A. R. Radcliffe-Brown, *A Natural Science of Society* (New York: Free Press, 1948).

41. Émile Durkheim, *The Rules of the Sociological Method* (New York: Free Press, 1938, originally published in 1895).

42. For examples, see Raymond Firth, *Elements of Social Organization* (London: Watts, 1952); E. E. Evans-Pritchard, *The Nuer* (London: Oxford University Press, 1940); and Meyer Fortes, *The Web of Kinship among the Tallensi* (London: Oxford University Press, 1949).

43. S. F. Nadel, *The Study of Social Structure* (London: Cohen and West, 1957).

44. Ibid., p. 8.

45. Ibid., p. 21.

46. J. Clyde Mitchell, "The Concept and Use of Social Networks," in Jeremy F. Boissevain and J. Clyde Mitchell, eds., *Network Analysis: Studies in Human Interaction* (The Hague: Mouton, 1973).

47. John A. Barnes, "Social Networks" (Addison-Wesley Module, no. 26, Reading, MA: Addison-Wesley, 1972). See also his "Network and Political Processes" in J. F. Boissevain and J. C. Mitchell, eds., *Network Analysis: Studies in Human Interaction* (The Hague: Mouton, 1973).

48. Perhaps the most significant was Elizabeth Bott, *Family and Social Network: Roles, Norms, and External Relationships in Ordinary Urban Families* (London: Tavistock, 1957, 1971).

49. Jacob L. Moreno, *Who Shall Survive?* (Washington, DC: Nervous and Mental Diseases Publishing, 1934; republished in revised form by Beacon House, New York, 1953).

50. Alex Bavelas, "A Mathematical Model for Group Structures," *Applied Anthropology* 7 (3, 1948), pp. 16–30.

51. Harold J. Leavitt, "Some Effects of Certain Communication Patterns on Group Performance," *Journal of Abnormal and Social Psychology* 56 (1951), pp. 38–50; Harold J. Leavitt and Kenneth E. Knight, "Most 'Efficient' Solution to Communication Networks: Empirical versus Analytical Search," *Sociometry* 26 (1963), pp. 260–267.

52. Fritz Heider, "Attitudes and Cognitive Organization," *Journal of Psychology* 2 (1946), pp. 107–112. For the best review of his thought as it accumulated over four decades, see his *The Psychology of Interpersonal Relations* (New York: Wiley, 1958).

53. The process of "attribution" was, along with the notion of "balance," the cornerstone of Heider's Gestalt approach.

54. Theodore M. Newcomb, "An Approach to the Study of Communicative Acts," *Psychological Review* 60 (1953), pp. 393–404. See his earlier work where these ideas took form: *Personality and Social Change* (New York: Dryden, 1943).

55. For example, D. König, *Theorie der Endlichen und Undlichen Graphen* (Leipzig: Teubner, 1936 but reissued, New York: Chelsea, 1950), is, as best we can tell, the first work on graph theory. It appears that the first important application of this theory to the social sciences came with R. Duncan Luce and A. D. Perry, "A Method of Matrix Analysis of Group Structure," *Psychometrika* 14 (1949), pp. 94–116, followed by R. Duncan Luce, "Connectivity and Generalized Cliques in Sociometric Group Structure," *Psychometrika* 15 (1950), pp. 169–190. Frank Harary's *Graph Theory* (Reading, MA: Addison-Wesley, 1969) later became a standard reference, which had been preceded by Frank Harary and R. Z. Norman, *Graph Theory as a Mathematical Model in Social Science* (Ann Arbor: University of Michigan Institute for Social Research, 1953), and Frank Harary, R. Z. Norman, and Dorin Cartwright, *Structural Models: An Introduction to the Theory of Directed Graphs* (New York: Wiley, 1965).

56. Dorin Cartwright and Frank Harary, "Structural Balance: A Generalization of Heider's Theory," *Psychological Review* 63 (1956), pp. 277–293. See also their "Balance and Clusterability: An Overview," in P. W. Holland and S. Leinhardt, eds., *Perspectives on Social Network Research* (New York: Academic, 1979).

28

Structuration Theory:
Anthony Giddens

D uring the last thirty years, Anthony Giddens has been one of the most prominent critics of the scientific pretensions of sociology. At the same time, he has developed a relatively formal abstract conceptual scheme for analyzing the social world. In the mid-1980s, he synthesized diverse theoretical traditions into what he had earlier titled "structuration theory."[1] This theory represents one of the more creative theoretical efforts of the second half of the twentieth century. Although Giddens has developed theoretical interests in modernity and, indeed, has become an important contributor to the debate about modernity and postmodernity,[2] his theoretical contribution still resides primarily in the more formal statement of structuration theory. Thus, in this chapter we will briefly review Giddens' critique of positivists' natural science view of sociology and, then, devote most of our efforts to summarizing the key ideas in structuration theory.

THE CRITIQUE
OF "SCIENTIFIC" SOCIAL THEORY

Giddens reasoned that there never can be any universal and timeless sociological laws, like those in physics or the biological sciences. Humans have the capacity for agency, and hence, they can change the very nature of social organization—thereby obviating any laws that are proposed to be universal. At best, "the concepts of theory should for many research purposes be regarded as sensitizing devices, nothing more."[3] Giddens buttresses this conclusion with two points.

First, Giddens asserts that social theorizing involves a "double hermeneutic." Stripped of its jargon, this means that the concepts and generalizations used by social scientists to understand social processes can be employed by laypersons as agents who can alter these social processes. We must recognize, Giddens contends, that ordinary actors are also "social theorists who alter their theories in the light of their experience and are receptive to incoming information."[4] Thus, social science theories are not often "news" to individuals; when they are, such theories can be used to transform the very order they describe. Within the capacity of humans to be reflexive—that is, to think about their situation—is the ability to change it.[5]

Second, social theory is by its nature social criticism. Social theory often contradicts "the reasons that people give for doing things" and is, therefore, a critique of these reasons and the social arrangements that people construct in the name of these reasons. Sociology does not, therefore, need to develop a separate body of critical theory, as others have argued; it *is* critical theory by its very nature and by virtue of the effects it can have on social processes.

The implications, Giddens believes, are profound. We need to stop imitating the natural sciences. We must cease evaluating our success as intellectuals by whether or not we have discovered "timeless laws." We must recognize that social theory does not exist "outside" our universe. We should accept that what sociologists and lay actors do is, in a fundamental sense, very much the same. And, we must redirect our efforts to developing "sensitizing concepts" that allow us to understand the active processes of interaction among individuals as they produce and reproduce social structures while being guided by these structures.

THE "THEORY OF STRUCTURATION"

Because Giddens does not believe that abstract laws of social action, interaction, and organization exist, his "theory of structuration" is not a series of propositions. Instead, as Giddens' critique of science would suggest, his "theory" is a cluster of sensitizing concepts, linked together discursively. The key concept is *structuration*, which is intended to communicate the *duality of structure*.[6] That is, social structure is used by active agents; in so using the properties of structure, they transform or reproduce this structure. Thus, the process of structuration requires a conceptualization of the nature of structure, of the agents who use structure, and of the ways that these are mutually implicated in each other to produce varying patterns of human organization.

Reconceptualizing Structure and Social System

Giddens believes structure can be conceptualized as *rules* and *resources* that actors use in "interaction contexts" that extend across "space" and over "time."

In so using these rules and resources, actors sustain or reproduce structures in space and time.

Rules are "generalizable procedures" that actors understand and use in various circumstances. Giddens posits that a rule is a methodology or technique that actors know about, often only implicitly, and that provides a relevant formula for action.[7] From a sociological perspective, the most important rules are those that agents use in the reproduction of social relations over significant lengths of time and across space. These rules reveal certain characteristics: (1) they are frequently used in (a) conversations, (b) interaction rituals, and (c) the daily routines of individuals; (2) they are tacitly grasped and understood and are part of the "stock knowledge" of competent actors; (3) they are informal, remaining unwritten and unarticulated; and (4) they are weakly sanctioned through interpersonal techniques.[8]

The thrust of Giddens's argument is that rules are part of actors' "knowledgeability." Some can be normative in that actors can articulate and explicitly make reference to them, but many other rules are more implicitly understood and used to guide the flow of interaction in ways that are not easily expressed or verbalized. Moreover, actors can transform rules into new combinations as they confront and deal with one another and the contextual particulars of their interaction.

As the other critical property of structure, resources are facilities that actors use to get things done. For, even if there are well-understood methodologies and formulas—that is, rules—to guide action, there must also be the capacity to perform tasks. Such capacity requires resources, or the material equipment and the organizational ability to act in situations. Giddens visualizes resources as what generates power.[9] Power is not a resource, as much social theory argues. Rather, the mobilization of other resources is what gives actors power to get things done. Thus, power is integral to the very existence of structure: As actors interact, they use resources, and, as they use resources, they mobilize power to shape the actions of others.

Giddens visualizes rules and resources as "transformational" and as "mediating."[10] What he means by these terms is that rules and resources can be transformed into many different patterns and profiles. Resources can be mobilized in various ways to perform activities and achieve ends through the exercise of different forms and degrees of power; rules can generate many diverse combinations of methodologies and formulas to guide how people communicate, interact, and adjust to one another. Rules and resources are mediating in that they are what tie social relations together. They are what actors use to create, sustain, or transform relations across time and in space. And, because rules and resources are inherently transformational—that is, generative of diverse combinations—they can lace together many different patterns of social relations in time and space.

Giddens developed a typology of rules and resources that is rather vague and imprecise.[11] He sees the three concepts in this typology—domination, legitimation, and signification—as "theoretical primitives," which is, perhaps, an excuse for defining them imprecisely. The basic idea is that resources are the

FIGURE 28.1 Social Structure, Social System, and the Modalities of Connection

stuff of domination because they involve the mobilization of material and organizational facilities to do things. Some rules are transformed into instruments of legitimation because they make things seem correct and appropriate. Other rules are used to create signification, or meaningful symbolic systems, because they provide people with ways to see and interpret events. Actually, the scheme makes more sense if the concepts of domination, legitimation, and signification are given less emphasis and the elements of his discussion are selectively extracted to create the typology presented in Figure 28.1.

In the left column of Figure 28.1, structure is viewed by Giddens as composed of rules and resources. Rules are transformed into two basic types of mediating processes: (1) normative, or the creation of rights and obligations in a context; and (2) interpretative, or the generation of schemes and stocks of taken-for-granted knowledge in a context. Resources are transformed into two major types of facilities that can mediate social relations: (1) authoritative resources, or the organizational capacity to control and direct the patterns of interactions in a context; and (2) allocative resources, or the use of material features, artifacts, and goods to control and direct patterns of interaction in a context.

Giddens sees these types of rules and resources as mediating interaction via three modalities, as is portrayed in column 2 of Figure 28.1: rights and obligations, facilities, and interpretative schemes. The figure deviates somewhat from Giddens's discussion, but the idea is the same: that rules and resources are attached to interaction (or "social system" in Giddens's terms) via these three modalities. These modalities are then used to (a) generate the power that enables some actors to control others, (b) affirm the norms that, in turn, allow actors to be sanctioned for their conformity or nonconformity, and (c) create and use the interpretative schemes that make it possible for actors to communicate with one another.

Giddens also stresses that rules and resources are interrelated, emphasizing that the modalities and their use in interaction are separated only analytically. In the actual flow of interaction in the real empirical world, they exist simultaneously, thereby making their separation merely an exercise of analytical decomposition. Thus, power, sanctions, and media of communication are interconnected, as are the rules and resources of social structure. In social systems, where people are co-present and interact, power is used to secure a particular set of rights and obligations as well as a system of communication; conversely, power can be exercised only through communication and sanctioning.

Giddens, then, sees social structure as something used by actors, not as some external reality that pushes and shoves actors around. Social structure is defined as the rules and resources that can be transformed as actors use them in concrete settings. But, the question arises: How is structure to be connected to what people actually do in interaction settings, or what Giddens terms "social systems"? The answer is the notion of modalities, whereby rules and resources are transformed into power, sanctions, and communication. Thus, structure is not a mysterious system of codes, as Claude Lévi-Strauss and other structural idealists imply, nor is it a set of determinative parameters and external constraints on actors, as Peter Blau and other macrostructuralists contend. In Giddens's conceptualization, social structure is transformative and flexible, it is "part of" actors in concrete situations, and they use it to create patterns of social relations across space and through time.

Moreover, this typology allows Giddens to emphasize that, as agents interact in social systems, they can reproduce rules and resources (via the modalities) or they can transform them. Thus, social interaction and social structure are reciprocally implicated. Structuration is, therefore, the dual processes in which rules and resources are used to organize interaction across time and in space and, by virtue of this use, to reproduce or transform these rules and resources.

Reconceptualizing Institutions

Giddens believes that institutions are systems of interaction in societies that endure over time and that distribute people in space. Giddens uses phrases like "deeply sedimented across time and in space in societies" to express the idea that, when rules and resources are reproduced over long periods of time and in explicit regions of space, then institutions can be said to exist in a society. Giddens offers a typology of institutions showing the weights and combinations of rules and resources that are implicated in interaction.[12] If signification (interpretative rules) is primary, followed respectively by domination (allocative and authoritative resources) and then legitimation (normative rules), a "symbolic order" exists. If authoritative domination, signification, and legitimation are successively combined, political institutionalization occurs. If allocative dominance, signification, and legitimation are ordered, economic institutionalization prevails. And if legitimation, dominance, and signification are rank ordered, institutionalization of law occurs. Table 28.1 summarizes Giddens's argument.

Table 28.1 The Typology of Institutions

Type of Institution		Rank Order of Emphasis on Rules and Resources
1. Symbolic orders, or modes of discourse, and patterns of communication	are produced and reproduced by	the use of interpretative rules (signification) in conjunction with normative rules (legitimation) and allocative as well as authoritative resources (domination).
2. Political institutions	are produced and reproduced by	the use of authoritative resources (domination) in conjunction with interpretative rules (signification) and normative rules (legitimation).
3. Economic institutions	are produced and reproduced by	the use of allocative resources (domination) in conjunction with interpretative rules (signification) and normative rules (legitimation).
4. Legal institutions	are produced and reproduced by	the use of normative rules (legitimation) in conjunction with authoritative and allocative resources (domination) and interpretative rules (signification).

In this conceptualization of institutions, Giddens seeks to avoid a mechanical view of institutionalization, in several senses. First, systems of interaction in empirical contexts are a mixture of institutional processes. Economic, political, legal, and symbolic orders are not easily separated; there is usually an element of each in any social system context. Second, institutions are tied to the rules and resources that agents employ and thereby reproduce; they are not external to individuals because they are formed by the use of varying rules and resources in actual social relations. Third, the most basic dimensions of all rules and resources—signification, domination, and legitimation—are all involved in institutionalization; it is only their relative salience for actors that gives the stabilization of relations across time and in space its distinctive institutional character.

Structural Principles, Sets, and Properties

The extent and form of institutionalization in societies are related to what Giddens terms *structural principles*.[13] These are the most general principles that guide the organization of societal totalities. These are what "stretch systems across time and space," and they allow for "system integration," or the maintenance of reciprocal relations among units in a society. For Giddens, "structural principles can thus be understood as the principles of organization which allow recognizably consistent forms of time-space distanciation on the basis of definite mechanisms of societal integration."[14] The basic idea seems to be that active agents use rules and resources in accordance with fundamental principles of organization. Such principles guide just how rules and resources are transformed and employed to mediate social relations.

On the basis of their underlying structural principles, three basic types of societies have existed: (1) "tribal societies," which are organized by structural principles that emphasize kinship and tradition as the mediating force behind social relations across time and space; (2) "class-divided societies," which are organized by an urban/rural differentiation, with urban areas revealing distinctive political institutions that can be separated from economic institutions, formal codes of law or legal institutions, and modes of symbolic coordination or ordering through written texts and testaments; and (3) "class societies," which involve structural principles that separate and yet interconnect all four institutional spheres, especially the economic and political.[15]

Structural principles are implicated in the production and reproduction of "structures" or "structural sets." These structural sets are rule and resource bundles, or combinations and configurations of rules and resources, which are used to produce and reproduce certain types and forms of social relations across time and space. Giddens offers the example of how the structural principles of class societies (differentiation and clear separation of economy and polity) guide the use of the following structural set: *private property-money-capital-labor-contract-profit*. The details of his analysis are less important than the general idea that the general structural principles of class societies are transformed into more specific sets of rules and resources that agents use to mediate social relations. This structural set is used in capitalist societies and, as a consequence, is reproduced. In turn, such reproduction of the structural set reaffirms the more abstract structural principles of class societies.

As these and other structural sets are used by agents and as they are thereby reproduced, societies develop "structural properties," which are "institutionalized features of social systems, stretching across time and space."[16] That is, social relations become patterned in certain typical ways. Thus the structural set of private property-money-capital-labor-contract-profit can mediate only certain patterns of relations; that is, if this is the rule and resource bundle with which agents must work, then only certain forms of relations can be produced and reproduced in the economic sphere. Hence the institutionalization of relations in time and space reveals a particular form, or, in Giddens's terms, structural property.

Structural Contradiction

Giddens always emphasizes the inherent "transformative" potential of rules and resources. Structural principles, he argues, "operate in terms of one another but yet also contravene each other."[17] In other words, they reveal contradictions that can be either primary or secondary. A "primary contradiction" is one between structural principles that are formative and constitute a society, whereas a "secondary contradiction" is one that is "brought into being by primary contradictions."[18] For example, there is a contradiction between structural principles that mediate the institutionalization of private profits, on the one hand, and those that mediate socialized production, on the other. If workers pool their labor to produce goods and services, it is contradictory to allow only some to enjoy profits of such socialized labor.

Contradictions are not, Giddens emphasizes, the same as conflicts. Contradiction is a "disjunction of structural principles of system organization," whereas conflict is the actual struggle between actors in "definite social practices."[19] Thus, the contradiction between private profits and socialized labor is not, itself, a conflict. It can create situations of conflict, such as struggles between management and labor in a specific time and place, but such conflicts are not the same as contradiction.

For Giddens, then, the institutional patterns of a society represent the creation and use by agents of very generalized and abstract principles. These principles represent the development of particular rules and the mobilization of certain resources; such principles generate more concrete "bundles" or "sets" of rules and resources that agents actively use to produce and reproduce social relations in concrete settings; and many of these principles and sets contain contradictory elements that can encourage actual conflicts among actors. In this way, structure "constrains" but is not disembodied from agents. Rather, the "properties" of total societies are not external to individuals and collectivities but are persistently reproduced through the use of structural principles and sets by agents who act. Let us now turn to Giddens's discussion of these active agents.

Agents, Agency, and Action

As is evident, Giddens visualizes structure as a duality, as something that is part of the actions of agents. Thus, in Giddens's approach it is essential to understand the dynamics of human agency. He proposes a "stratification model," which is an effort to synthesize psychoanalytic theory, phenomenology, ethnomethodology, and elements of action theory. This model is depicted in the lower portions of Figure 28.2. For Giddens, "agency" denotes the events that an actor perpetrates rather than "intentions," "purposes," "ends," or other states. Agency is what an actor actually does in a situation that has visible consequences (not necessarily intended consequences). To understand the dynamics of agency requires analysis of each element on the model.

As drawn, the model in Figure 28.2 actually combines two overlapping models in Giddens's discussion, but his intent is reasonably clear: humans "reflexively monitor" their own conduct and that of others; in other words, they pay attention to, note, calculate, and assess the consequences of actions.[20] Monitoring is influenced by two levels of consciousness.[21] One is "discursive consciousness," which involves the capacity to give reasons for or rationalize what one does (and presumably to do the same for others' behavior). "Practical consciousness" is the stock of knowledge that one implicitly uses to act in situations and to interpret the actions of others. This knowledgeability is constantly used, but rarely articulated, to interpret events—one's own and those of others. Almost all acts are indexical in that they must be interpreted by their context, and this implicit stock of knowledge provides these contextual interpretations and frameworks.

There are also unconscious dimensions to human agency. Giddens argues that much motivation is unconscious. Moreover, motivation is often much more diffuse than action theories portray, pushing actions to behave in ways

FIGURE 28.2 The Dynamics of Agency

outside their perception. That is, there is no one-to-one relation between *an act and a motive*. Actors might be able to rationalize through their capacity for discursive consciousness in ways that make this one-to-one relationship seem to be what directs action. But much of what propels action lies below consciousness and, at best, provides very general and diffuse pressures to act. Moreover, much action might not be motivated at all; an actor simply monitors and responds to the environment.

In trying to reintroduce the *unconscious* into social theory, Giddens adopts Erik Erikson's psychoanalytic ideas.[22] The basic "force" behind much action is an unconscious set of processes to gain a "sense of trust" in interaction with others. Giddens terms this set of processes the *ontological security system* of an agent. That is, one of the driving but highly diffuse forces behind action is the desire to sustain ontological security or the sense of trust that comes from being able to reduce anxiety in social relations. Actors need to have this sense of trust. How they go about reducing anxiety to secure this sense is often unconscious because the mechanisms involved are developed before linguistic skills emerge in the young and because psychodynamics, such as repression, might also keep these fundamental feelings and their resolution from becoming conscious. In general, Giddens argues that ontological security is maintained through the routinization of encounters with others, through the successful interpretation of acts as practical or stock knowledge, and through the capacity for rationalization that comes with discursive consciousness.

As the top portions of Figure 28.2 emphasize, institutionalized patterns have an effect on, while being a consequence of, the dynamics of agency. As we will see shortly, unconscious motives for ontological security require routinized interactions (predictable, stable over time) that are regionalized (ordered in space). Such regionalization and routinization are the product of past interactions of agents and are sustained or reproduced through the present (and future) actions of agents. To sustain routines and regions, actors must monitor their actions while drawing on their stock knowledge and discursive capacities. In this way, Giddens visualizes institutionalized patterns implicated in the very nature of agency. Institutions and agents cannot exist without each other, for institutions are reproduced practices by agents, whereas the conscious and unconscious dynamics of agency depend on the routines and regions provided by institutionalized patterns.

Routinization and Regionalization of Interaction

Both the ontological security of agents and the institutionalization of structures in time and space depend on routinized and regionalized interaction among actors. Routinization of interaction patterns is what gives them continuity across time, thereby reproducing structure (rules and resources) and institutions. At the same time, routinization gives predictability to actions and, in so doing, provides a sense of ontological security. Thus, routines become critical for the most basic aspects of structure and human agency. Similarly, regionalization orders action in space by positioning actors in places relative to one another and by circumscribing how they are to present themselves and act. As with routines, the regionalization of interaction is essential to the sustenance of broader structural patterns and ontological security of actors because it orders people's interactions in space and time, which in turn reproduces structures and meets an agent's need for ontological security.

Routines Giddens sees routines as the key link between the episodic character of interactions (they start, proceed, and end), on the one hand, and basic trust and security, on the other hand.[23] Moreover, "the routinization of encounters is of major significance in binding the fleeting encounter to social reproduction and thus to the seeming 'fixity' of institutions."[24] In a very interesting discussion in which he borrows heavily from Erving Goffman (but with a phenomenological twist), Giddens proposed several procedures, or mechanisms, that humans use to sustain routines: (1) opening and closing rituals, (2) turn-taking, (3) tact, (4) positioning, and (5) framing.[25]

1. Because interaction is serial—that is, it occurs sequentially—there must be symbolic markers of opening and closing. Such markers are essential

to the maintenance of routines because they indicate when in the flow of time the elements of routine interaction are to begin and end. There are many such interpersonal markers—words, facial gestures, positions of bodies—and there are physical markers, such as rooms, buildings, roads, and equipment, that also signal when certain routinized interactions are to begin and end (note, for example, the interpersonal and physical markers for a lecture, which is a highly routinized interaction that sustains the ontological security of agents and perpetuates institutional patterns).

2. Turn taking in a conversation is another process that sustains a routine. All competent actors contain in their practical consciousness, or implicit stock of knowledge, a sense of how conversations are to proceed sequentially. People rely on "folk methods" to construct sequences of talk; in so doing, they sustain a routine and, hence, their psychological sense of security and the larger institutional context (think, for example, about a conversation that did not proceed smoothly in conversational turn taking; recall how disruptive this was for your sense of order and routine).

3. Tact is, in Giddens's view, "the main mechanism that sustains 'trust' or 'ontological security' over long time-space spans." By tact, Giddens means "a latent conceptual agreement among participants in interaction" about just how each party is to gesture and respond and about what is appropriate and inappropriate. People carry with them implicit stocks of knowledge that signal to them what would be "tactful" and what would be "rude" and "intrusive." And they use this sense of tact to regulate their emission of gestures, their talking, and their relative positioning in situations "to remain tactful," thereby sustaining their sense of trust and the larger social order. (Imagine interactions in which tact is not exercised—how they disrupt our routines, our sense of comfort, and our perceptions of an orderly situation.)

4. Giddens rejects the idea of "role" as very useful and substitutes the notion of "position." People bring to situations a position or "social identity that carries with it a certain range of prerogatives and obligations," and they emit gestures in a process of mutual positioning, such as locating their bodies in certain points, asserting their prerogatives, and signaling their obligations. In this way, interactions can be routinized, and people can sustain their sense of mutual trust as well as the larger social structures in which their interaction occurs. (For example, examine a student/student or professor/student interaction for positioning, and determine how it sustains a sense of trust and the institutional structure.)

5. Much of the coherence of positioning activities is made possible by "frames," which provide formulas for interpreting a context. Interactions tend to be framed in the sense that there are rules that apply to them, but these are not purely normative in the sense of precise instructions for participants. Equally important, frames are more implicitly held, and they operate as markers that assert when certain behaviors and demeanors

should be activated. (For example, compare your sense of how to comport yourself at a funeral, at a cocktail party, in class, and in other contexts that are "framed.")

In sum, social structure is extended across time by these techniques that produce and reproduce routines. In so stretching interaction across time in an orderly and predictable manner, people realize their need for a sense of trust in others. In this way, then, Giddens connects the most basic properties of structure (rules and resources) to the most fundamental features of human agents (unconscious motives).

Regionalization   Structuration theory is concerned with the reproduction of relations not only across time but also in space. With the concept of regionalization of interaction, Giddens addresses the intersection of space and time.[26] For interaction is not just serial, moving in time; it is also located in space. Again borrowing from Goffman and also from time and space geography, Giddens introduces the concept of "locale" to account for the physical space in which interaction occurs as well as the contextual knowledge about what is to occur in this space. In a locale, actors are not only establishing their presence in relation to one another but they are also using their stocks of practical knowledge to interpret the context of the locale. Such interpretations provide them with the relevant frames, the appropriate procedures for tact, and the salient forms for sequencing gestures and talk.

Giddens classifies locales by their "modes." Locales vary in (1) their physical and symbolic boundaries, (2) their duration across time, (3) their span or extension in physical space, and (4) their character, or the ways they connect to other locales and to broader institutional patterns. Locales also vary in the degree to which they force people to sustain high public presence (what Goffman termed *frontstage*) or allow retreats to back regions where public presence is reduced (Goffman's *backstage*).[27] They also vary in how much disclosure of self (feelings, attitudes, and emotions) they require, some allowing "enclosure" or the withholding of self and other locales requiring "disclosure" of at least some aspects of self.

Regionalization of interaction through the creation of locales facilitates the maintenance of routines. In turn, the maintenance of routines across time and space sustains institutional structures. Thus, the reflexive capacities of agents reproduce institutional patterns through routinized and regionalized systems of interaction.

CONCLUSION

Figure 28.3 represents one way to visualize Giddens's conceptual scheme. In a rough sense, as one moves from left to right, the scheme gets increasingly micro. Rules and resources are used to construct structures; these rules and resources are also a part of structural principles that include structural sets;

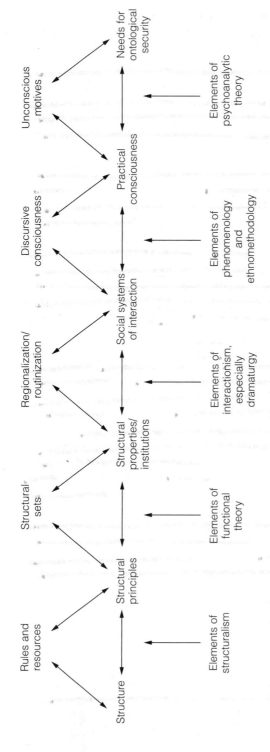

FIGURE 28.3 Key Elements of "Structuration Theory"

these structural properties are involved in institutionalization of systems of interaction; such interaction systems are organized by the processes of regionalization and routinization; and all these processes are influenced by practical and discursive consciousness that, in turn, are driven by unconscious motives, especially needs for ontological security.

Giddens would not consider his "theory" anything more than a conceptual scheme for describing, analyzing, and interpreting empirical events. Moreover, he would not see this scheme as representing timeless social processes, although the reason his works are read and respected is because these do seem like basic and fundamental processes that transcend time, context, and place.

NOTES

1. The basic theory is presented in numerous places, but the two most comprehensive statements are these: Anthony Giddens, *The Constitution of Society: Outline of the Theory of Structuration* (Cambridge, England: Polity, 1984) and *Central Problems in Social Theory* (London: Macmillan, 1979). The University of California Press also has editions of these two books. For an excellent overview, both sociologically and philosophically, of Giddens's theoretical project, see Ira Cohen, *Structuration Theory: Anthony Giddens and the Constitution of Social Life* (London: Macmillan, 1989). For a commentary and debate on Giddens's work, see J. Clark, C. Modgil, and S. Modgil, eds., *Anthony Giddens: Consensus and Controversy* (London: Falmer, 1990). For a selection of readings, see *The Giddens Reader*, ed. Philip Cassell (Stanford, CA: Stanford University Press, 1993).

2. See, for examples, Anthony Giddens, *The Consequences of Modernity* (Stanford, CA: Stanford University Press, 1990); Ulrich Beck, Anthony Giddens, and Scott Lash, *Reflexive Modernization* (Stanford, CA: Stanford University Press, 1994); Anthony Giddens, *Modernity and Self-Identity* (Stanford, CA: Stanford University Press, 1991).

3. Anthony Giddens, *The Constitution of Society* (cited in note 1), p. 326.

4. Ibid., p. 335.

5. See, in particular, Anthony Giddens, *Profiles and Critiques in Social Theory* (London: Macmillan, 1982) and *New Rules of Sociological Method: A Positive Critique of Interpretative Sociologies,* 2nd ed. (Stanford, CA: Stanford University Press, 1993).

6. See Anthony Giddens, *The Constitution of Society* (cited in note 1), pp. 207–213.

7. Ibid., pp. 20–21.

8. Ibid., p. 22.

9. Ibid., pp. 14–16.

10. Here Giddens seems to be taking what is useful from "structuralism" and reworking these ideas into a more sociological approach. Giddens remains, however, extremely critical of structuralism; see his "Structuralism, Post-structuralism and the Production of Culture" in *Social Theory Today,* eds. A. Giddens and J. Turner (Cambridge, England: Polity, 1987).

11. Anthony Giddens, *The Constitution of Society*, p. 29, and *Central Problems in Social Theory,* pp. 97–107 (both cited in note 1).

12. Anthony Giddens, *Central Problems in Social Theory*, p. 107, and *The Constitution of Society,* p. 31 (both cited in note 1).

13. Anthony Giddens, *The Constitution of Society* (cited in note 1), pp. 179–193.

14. Ibid., p. 181.

15. For an extensive discussion of this typology, see Giddens's *A Contemporary Critique of Historical Materialism: Power, Property and the State* (London: Macmillan, 1981).

16. Anthony Giddens, *The Constitution of Society* (cited in note 1), p. 185.

17. Ibid., p. 193.

18. Ibid.

19. Ibid., p. 198.

20. Ibid., pp. 5–7; see also Anthony Giddens, *Central Problems in Social Theory* (cited in note 1), pp. 56–59.

21. His debt to Schutz and phenomenology is evident here, but he has liberated it from its subjectivism. See Chapter 21 on the emergence of interactionism.

22. Anthony Giddens, *The Constitution of Society* (cited in note 1), pp. 45–59.

23. Ibid., pp. 60–109.

24. Ibid., p. 72.

25. This list has been created from what is a much more discursive text.

26. Anthony Giddens, *The Constitution of Society* (cited in note 1), pp. 110–144.

27. See Erving Goffman, *The Presentation of Self in Everyday Life* (Garden City, NY: Anchor, 1959).

29

Cultural
Structuralist Theory:
Pierre Bourdieu

rench structuralism has exerted an enormous influence on modern social
thought—from anthropology and sociology to literary criticism and many
other fields of inquiry in between. These many types of structuralist analyses vary enormously, but they all have a common theme: Most surface phenomena have a deep underlying structure, and this structure can be
conceptualized as a series of generative rules that can create a wide variety of
empirical phenomena. That is, empirically observable phenomena—from a literary text to a social structure—are constructed in conformity to an implicit
logic. Some see this logic as lodged in the biology of the human brain, whereas
others would view this underlying structure as a cultural product.

Purely structuralist analysis has had its greatest impact in linguistics and literary criticism, and for a time it enjoyed considerable popularity in anthropology and sociology.[1] But in recent years, rigid and orthodox structuralist
approaches emphasizing searches for those deep and universal structures that
order all phenomena have declined in sociology; in their place, several more
eclectic perspectives have emerged. These more eclectic theories borrow elements of structuralist analysis and blend them with other conceptual traditions.
There is still an emphasis on symbolic codes. Such codes are causally influenced by material conditions and are subject to interpretation by lay agents.
Thus, just as Claude Lévi-Strauss "turned Durkheim on his head" in seeing
social structure as a reflection of mental structures, many recent efforts have

Note: This chapter was coauthored with Stephan Fuchs.

put Émile Durkheim back on his feet and augmented the emphasis on the structure of symbol systems with Marxian conflict analysis, interactionism and phenomenology, and other traditions in theoretical sociology. The result has been a revival of "cultural sociology" in a less ponderous guise than Parsonian functionalism. In these newer approaches, the structure of cultural codes is causally linked not only to the behavioral and interpersonal activities of individuals but also to the institutional parameters within which such activities are conducted. The most influential of these cultural theorists is Pierre Bourdieu, although the Web site for this book examines others.

PIERRE BOURDIEU'S STRUCTURALISM

Bourdieu[2] has characterized his work as *constructivist structuralism* or *structuralist constructivism;* in so doing, he distances himself somewhat from the Lévi-Straussian tradition:

> By structuralism or structuralist, I mean that there exists, within the social world itself and not only within symbolic systems (language, myth, etc.), objective structures independent of the consciousness and will of agents, which are capable of guiding and constraining their practices or their representations.[3]

Such structures constrain and circumscribe volition, but at the same time people use their capacities for thought, reflection, and action to *construct* social and cultural phenomena. They do so within the parameters of existing structures. These structures are not rigid constraints but, rather, materials for a wide variety of social and cultural constructions. Acknowledging his structuralist roots, Bourdieu analogizes to the relation of grammar and language to make this point: The grammar of a language only loosely constrains the production of actual speech; it can be seen as defining the possibilities for new kinds of speech acts. So it is with social and cultural structures: They exist independently of agents and guide their conduct; yet they also create options, possibilities, and paths for creative actions and for the construction of new and unique cultural and social phenomena. This perspective is best appreciated by highlighting Bourdieu's criticisms of those theoretical approaches from which he selectively borrows ideas.

CRITICISMS OF EXISTING THEORIES

The Critique of Structuralism

Bourdieu's critique of structuralism is similar to symbolic interactionists' attacks on Parsonian functionalism and its emphasis on norms. According to Bourdieu, structuralists ignore the indeterminacy of situations and the practical ingenuity of agents who are not mechanical rule-following and role-playing robots in standard contexts. Rather, agents use their "practical sense" (*sens pratique*) to adapt to situational contingencies within certain "structural limits" that follow from "objective constraints." Social practice is more than the mere execution of an underlying structural "grammar" of action, just as "speech" (*parole*) is more than "language" (*langue*). What is missing, says Bourdieu, are the variable uses and contexts of speech and action.[4] Structuralism dismisses action as mere execution of underlying principles (lodged in the human brain or culture), just as normativism forgets that following rules and playing roles require skillful adjustment and flexible improvisations by creative agents.

Most important, Bourdieu argues that structuralism hypostatizes the "objectifying glance" of the outside academic observer. The "Homo academicus" transfers a particular *relation* to the world, the distant and objectifying gaze of the professional academic, onto the very properties of that world.[5] As a result, the outside observer constructs the world as a mere "spectacle," which is subject to neutral observation. The distant and uninvolved observer's relation to the world is not only systematic but also a passive *cognition*, so that the world itself is viewed as consisting of cognition rather than active practices. According to Bourdieu, structuralism and other approaches that "objectify" the world do not simply research the empirical world "out there"; rather, they construct it *as* an "objective fact" through the distancing perspective of the outside observer.

Bourdieu does not, however, reject completely structuralism and other "objectifying" approaches that seek, in Durkheim's words, to discover external and constraining "social facts." As we will see, Bourdieu views social classes, and factions within such classes, as "social facts" whose structure can be objectively observed and viewed as external to, and constraining on, the thoughts and activities of individuals.[6] Moreover, Bourdieu at least borrows the metaphor, if not the essence, of structuralism in his efforts to discover the "generative principles" that people use to construct social and cultural phenomena—systems of classification, ideologies, forms of legitimating social practices, and other elements of a "constructivist structuralism."[7]

The Critique of Interactionism and Phenomenology

Bourdieu is also critical of interactionism, phenomenology, and other subjective approaches.[8] Bourdieu believes there is more to social life than interaction, and there is more to interaction than the "definitions of situations" in symbolic interactionism or the "accounting practices" in ethnomethodology. The "actor" of symbolic interactionism and the "member" of ethnomethodology are abstractions that fail to realize that members are always incumbents in particular groups and classes. Interactions are always interactions-in–contexts, and the most important of these contexts is class location. Even such an elementary feature of interaction as the possibility that it might even occur among individuals varies with class background. Interaction is thus embedded in structure, and the structure constrains what is possible.

Moreover, in addition to this rather widespread critique of interactionism as "astructural," Bourdieu argues that interactionism is too cognitive in its overemphasis on the accounting and sense-making activities of agents. As a result, interactionists forget that actors have objective class-based interests. And, once again, the biases of "Homo academicus" are evident. By nature, academics define, assess, reflect, ponder, and interpret the social world; as a result of this propensity, a purely academic relation to the world is imposed on real people in social contexts. For interactionists, then, people are merely disinterested lay academics who define, reflect, interpret, and account for actions and situations. But lay interpretations, and academic portrayals of these lay interpretations, cannot accurately describe social reality, for two reasons. First, as noted, these interpretations are constrained by existing structures, especially class and class factions. Second, these interpretations are themselves part of objective class struggles as individuals construct legitimating definitions for their conduct.[9]

Bourdieu then borrows from Karl Marx the notion that people are located in a class position, that this position gives them certain interests, and that their interpretative actions are often ideologies designed to legitimate these interests. People's "definitions of situations" are neither neutral nor innocent, but are often ideological weapons that are very much a part of the objective class structures and the inherent conflicts of interests generated by such structures.[10]

The Critique of Utilitarianism

Rational economic theories also portray, and at the same time betray, Homo academicus' relation to the social world. Like academics in general, utilitarian economic theorists[11] see humans as rational, calculating, and maximizing (*sujets ravauts*), and rational exchange theories thus mistake a *model* of the human actor for real individuals, thereby reifying their theoretical abstractions.

Yet, Bourdieu does not replace the economic model of rational action with an interpretative model of symbolic action. He does not argue that rational action theory is wrong because it is too rationalistic or because it ignores the interpretative side of action. To the contrary, he holds that rational action theory does not realize that even symbolic action is rational and based on class interests. Thus, according to Bourdieu, the error of the economic model is not that it presents all action as rational and interested; rather, the big mistake is to restrict interests and rationality to the immediate material payoffs collected by reflective and profit-seeking individuals.[12]

Bourdieu reasons that all social practices are "interested," even if individual agents are unaware of their interests and even if the stakes of these practices are not material profits. Social practices are attuned to the conditions of particular arenas in which actions might yield profits without deliberate intention. For example, in science the most "disinterested" and "pure" research yields the highest cultural profits—that is, academic recognition and reputation. In social fields other than economic exchange, the structural *denial* of any "interests" often yields the highest gains. It is not that agents cynically deny being interested to increase their gains even more; rather, innocence ensures that honest disinterestedness nevertheless is the most profitable practice.

For example, gift exchange economies, the subject of Bourdieu's early anthropological research,[13] might illustrate this complex idea. Gift exchange economies are typically embedded in larger social relations and solidarities so that exchange is not purely instrumental and material but has a strong moral quality to it. Economic exchanges are expected to follow the social logic of solidarity and group memberships at least as much as they follow the economic logic of material gain. From the narrowly economic perspective of rational action theory, the logic of solidarity would seem like an intrusion of "non-rational" forces, such as tradition or emotion, into an otherwise purely rational system of exchange; but, the logic of solidarity points to those processes by which symbolic and social capital is accumulated—a "social fact" that is missed by the narrow economic determinism of rational action theory. Once the notion of "capital" is extended to include symbolic and social capital, however, apparently "irrational" practices can now be seen to follow their own interested logic, and, contrary to initial impressions, these practices are not irrational at all. The structural denial of narrowly economic interests in gift exchange economies conceals that social and economic capital can be increased as the more the purely instrumental aspects of exchange move into the background. For instance, birthday and Christmas presents are socially more effective when they appear less material and economic; those who brag about the high costs of their presents do not understand the nature of gift exchanges and, as a consequence, are considered rude, thereby losing symbolic and social capital.

Thus, in broadening economic exchange to include social and symbolic resources, as all sociological exchange theories eventually do,[14] Bourdieu introduces a central concept in his approach: *capital*.[15] Those in different classes reveal not only varying levels or amounts of capital but also divergent types and configurations of capital. Bourdieu's view of capital recognizes that the resources individuals possess can be material, symbolic, social, and cultural; moreover, these resources reflect class location and are used to further the interests of those in a particular class position.

BOURDIEU'S CULTURAL CONFLICT THEORY

Although Bourdieu has explored many topics, the conceptual core of his sociology is a vision of social classes and the cultural forms associated with these classes.[16] In essence, Bourdieu combines a Marxian theory of objective class position in relation to the means of production with a Weberian analysis of status groups (lifestyles, tastes, prestige) and politics (organized efforts to have one's class culture dominate). The key to this reconciliation of Karl Marx's and Max Weber's views of stratification is the expanded conceptualization of *capital* as more than economic and material resources, coupled with elements of French structuralism.

Classes and Capital

To understand Bourdieu's view of classes, it is first necessary to recognize a distinction among four types of capital:[17] (1) *economic* capital, or productive property (money and material objects that can be used to produce goods and services); (2) *social* capital, or positions and relations in groupings and social networks; (3) *cultural* capital, or informal interpersonal skills, habits, manners, linguistic styles, educational credentials, tastes, and lifestyles, and (4) *symbolic* capital, or the use of symbols to legitimate the possession of varying levels and configurations of the other three types of capital.

These forms of capital can be converted into one another, but only to a certain extent. The degree of convertibility of capital on various markets is itself at stake in social struggles. The overproduction of academic qualifications, for example, can decrease the convertibility of educational into economic capital ("credential inflation"). As a result, owners of credentials must struggle to get their cultural capital converted into economic gains, such as high-paying jobs. Likewise, the extent to which economic capital can be converted into social capital is at stake in struggles over control of the political apparatus, and the efforts of those with economic capital to "buy" cultural capital can often be limited by their perceived lack of "taste" (a type of cultural capital).

The distribution of these four types of capital determines the objective class structure of a social system. The overall class structure reflects the total amount of capital possessed by various groupings. Hence the *dominant class* will possess the most economic, social, cultural, and symbolic capital; the *middle class* will possess less of these forms of capital; and the *lower classes* will have the least amount of these capital resources. The class structure is not, however, a simple lineal hierarchy. Within each class are *factions* that can be distinguished by (1) the composition or configuration of their capital and (2) the social origin and amount of time that individuals in families have possessed a particular profile or configuration of capital resources.

Table 29.1 represents schematically Bourdieu's portrayal of the factions in three classes. The top faction within a given class controls the greatest proportion of economic or productive capital typical of a class; the bottom faction possesses the greatest amount of cultural and symbolic capital for a class; and the middle faction possesses an intermediate amount of economic, cultural, and symbolic capital. The top faction is the dominant faction within a given class, and the bottom faction is the dominated faction for that class, with the middle faction being both superordinate over the dominated faction and subordinate to the top faction. As factions engage in struggles to control resources and legitimate themselves, they mobilize social capital to form groupings and networks of relations, but their capacity to form such networks is limited by their other forms of capital. Thus, the overall distribution of social capital (groups and organizational memberships, network ties, social relations, and so forth) for classes and their factions will correspond to the overall distribution of other forms of capital. However, the particular forms of groupings, networks, and social ties will reflect the particular configuration of economic, cultural, and symbolic capital typically possessed by a particular faction within a given class.

Bourdieu borrows Marx's distinction between a class "for itself" (organized to pursue its interests) and one "in itself" (unorganized but having common interests and objective location); then he argues that classes are not real groups but only "potentialities." As noted earlier, the objective distribution of

Table 29.1 Representation of Classes and Class Factions in Industrial Societies*

Dominant Class: Richest in all forms of capital

Dominant faction:	Richest in economic capital, which can be used to buy other types of capital. This faction is primarily of those who own the means of production—that is, the classical bourgeoisie.
Intermediate faction:	Some economic capital, coupled with moderate levels of social, cultural, and symbolic capital. This faction is composed of high-credential professionals.
Dominated faction:	Little economic capital but high levels of cultural and symbolic capital. This faction is composed of intellectuals, artists, writers, and others who possess cultural resources valued in a society.

Middle Class: Moderate levels of all forms of capital

Dominant faction:	Highest in this class in economic capital but having considerably less economic capital than the dominant faction of the dominant class. This faction is composed of petite bourgeoisie (small business owners).
Intermediate faction:	Some economic, social, cultural, and symbolic capital but considerably less than the intermediate faction of the dominant class. This faction is composed of skilled clerical workers.
Dominated faction:	Little or no economic and comparatively high social, cultural, and symbolic capital. This class is composed of educational workers, such as school teachers, and other low-income and routinized professions that are involved in cultural production.

Lower Class: Low levels of all forms of capital

Dominant faction:	Comparatively high economic capital for this general class. Composed of skilled manual workers.
Intermediate faction:	Lower amounts of economic and other types of capital. Composed of semi-skilled workers without credentials.
Dominated faction:	Very low amounts of economic capital. Some symbolic capital in form of uneducated ideologues and intellectuals for the poor and working person.

*These portrayals are inferences from Bourdieu's more discursive and rambling text. The table captures the imagery of Bourdieu's analysis; however, because he is highly critical of stratification research in America, he would probably be critical of this "layered" portrayal of his argument.

resources for Bourdieu relates to actual groups as grammar relates to speech: It defines the possibilities for actors but needs actual people and concrete settings to become real. And, it is the transformation of class and class–faction interests into actual groupings that marks the dynamics of a society. Such transformation involves the use of productive material, cultural, and symbolic capital to mobilize social capital (groups and networks); even more important, class conflict tends to revolve around the mobilization of symbols into ideologies that legitimate a particular composition of resources.[18] Much conflict in human societies, therefore, revolves around efforts to manipulate symbols to make a particular pattern of social, cultural, and productive resources seem the most appropriate. For example, when intellectuals and artists decry the "crass commercialism," "acquisitiveness," and "greed" of big business, this activity involves the mobilization of symbols into an ideology that seeks to mitigate their domination by the owners of the means of production.

But class relations involve more than a simple pecking order. There are also homologies among similarly located factions within different classes. For example, the rich capitalists of the dominant class and the small business owners of the middle class are equivalent in their control of productive resources and their dominant position in their respective classes[19]; similarly, intellectuals, artists, and other cultural elites in the dominant class are equivalent to schoolteachers in the middle class because of their reliance on cultural capital and because of their subordinate position in relation to those who control the material resources of their respective classes. These homologies make class conflict complex because those in similar objective positions in different classes—say, intellectuals and schoolteachers—will mobilize symbolic resources into somewhat similar ideologies—in this example, emphasizing learning, knowledge for its own sake, and life of the mind and, at the same time, decrying crass materialism. Such ideologies legitimate their own class position and attack those who dominate them (by emphasizing the importance of those cultural resources that they have more of). At the same time their homologous positions are separated by the different *amounts* of cultural capital owned: The intellectuals despise the strained efforts of schoolteachers to appear more sophisticated than they are, whereas the schoolteachers resent the decadent and irresponsible relativism of snobbish intellectuals. Thus, ideological conflict is complicated by the simultaneous convergence of factions within different classes and by the divergence of these factions by virtue of their position in different social classes.

Moreover, an additional complication stems from people sharing similar types and amounts of resources but having very different origins and social trajectories. Those who have recently moved to a class faction—say, the dominant productive elite or intermediate faction of the middle class—will have somewhat different styles and tastes than those who have been born into these classes, and these differences in social origin and mobility can create yet another source of ideological conflict. For example, the "old rich" will often comment on the "lack of class" and "ostentatiousness" of the "new rich"; or, the "solid middle class" will be somewhat snobbish toward the "poor boy who made good" but who "still has a lot to learn" or who "still is a bit crude."

All those points of convergence and divergence within and between classes and class factions make the dynamics of stratification complex. Although there is always an "objective class location," as determined by the amount and composition of capital and by the social origins of capital holders, the development of organizations and ideologies is not a simple process. Bourdieu often ventures into a more structuralist mode when trying to sort out how various classes, class factions, and splits of individuals with different social origins within class factions generate categories of thought, systems of speech, signs of distinction, forms of mythology, modes of appreciation, tastes, and lifestyle.

The general argument is that objective location—class, faction within class, and social origin—creates interests and structural constraints that, in turn, allow different social constructions.[20] Such constructions might involve the use of "formal rules" (implicitly known by individuals with varying interests) to construct cultural codes that classify and organize "things," "signs," and "people" in the world. This kind of analysis by Bourdieu has not produced a fine-grained structuralist model of how individuals construct particular cultural codes, but it has provided an interesting analysis of "class cultures." Such "class cultures" are always the dependent variable for Bourdieu (with objective class location being the independent variable and rather poorly conceptualized structuralist processes of generative rules and cultural codes being the "intervening variables"). Yet the detailed description of these class cultures is perhaps Bourdieu's most unique contribution to sociology and is captured by his concept of *habitus*.

Class Cultures and Habitus

Those within a given class share certain modes of classification, appreciation, judgment, perception, and behavior. Bourdieu conceptualizes this mediating process between class and individual perceptions, choices, and behavior as *habitus*.[21] In a sense, habitus is the "collective unconscious" of those in similar positions because it provides cognitive and emotional guidelines that enable individuals to represent the world in common ways and to classify, choose, evaluate, and act in a particular manner.

The habitus creates syndromes of taste, speech, dress, manner, and other responses. For example, a preference for particular foods will tend to correspond to tastes in art, ways of dressing, styles of speech, manners of eating, and other cultural actions among those sharing a common class location. There is, then, a correlation between the class hierarchy and the cultural objects, preferences, and behaviors of those located at particular ranks in the hierarchy. For instance, Bourdieu devotes considerable attention to "taste," which is seen as one of the most visible manifestations of the habitus. Bourdieu views "taste" in a holistic and anthropological sense to include appreciation of art, ways of dressing, and preferences for foods.[22] Although taste appears as an innocent, natural, and personal phenomenon, it covaries with objective class location: The upper class is to the working class what an art museum is to television; the old upper class is to the new upper class what polite and distant elegance is to noisy and conspicuous consumption; and the dominant is to the dominated faction of the upper class what opera is to avant-garde theater. Because tastes are organized in a cultural hierarchy that mirrors the social hierarchy of objective class location, conflicts between tastes are class conflicts.

Bourdieu roughly distinguishes between two types of tastes, which correspond to high versus low overall capital, or high versus low objective class position.[23] The "taste of liberty and luxury" is the taste of the upper class; as such, it is removed from direct economic necessity and material need. The taste of liberty is the philosophy of art for its own sake. Following Immanuel Kant, Bourdieu calls this aesthetic the "pure gaze." The pure gaze looks at the sheer form of art and places this form above function and content. The upper-class taste of luxury is not concerned with art illustrating or representing some external reality; art is removed from life, just as upper-class life is removed from harsh material necessity. Consequently, the taste of luxury purifies and sublimates the ordinary and profane into the aesthetic and beautiful. The pure gaze confers aesthetic meaning to ordinary and profane objects because the taste of liberty is at leisure to relieve objects from their pragmatic functions. Thus, as the distance form basic material necessities increases, the pure gaze or the taste of luxury transforms the ordinary into the aesthetic, the material into the symbolic, the functional into the formal. And, because the taste of liberty is that of the dominant class, it is also the dominant and legitimate taste in society.

In contrast, the working class cultivates a "popular" aesthetic. Their taste is the taste of necessity, for working-class life is constrained by harsh economic imperatives. The popular taste wants art to represent reality and despises formal and self-sufficient art as decadent and degenerate. The popular taste favors the simple and honest rather than the complex and sophisticated. It is downgraded by the "legitimate" taste of luxury as naive and complacent, and these conflicts over tastes are class conflicts over cultural and symbolic capital.

Preferences for certain works and styles of art, however, are only part of "tastes" as ordered by habitus. Aesthetic choices are correlated with choices made in other cultural fields. The taste of liberty and luxury, for example, corresponds to the polite, distant, and disciplined style of upper-class conversation. Just as we expect art to be removed from life, so the bodies of interlocutors are expected to be removed from one another and so is the spirit expected to be removed from matter. Distance from economic necessity in the upper-class lifestyle not only corresponds to an aesthetic of pure form, but also entails that all natural and physical desires are to be sublimated and dematerialized. Hence, upper-class eating is highly regulated and disciplined, and foods that are less filling are preferred over fatty dishes. Similarly, items of clothing are chosen for fashion and aesthetic harmony, rather than for functional appropriateness. "Distance from necessity" is the motif underlying the upper-class lifestyle as a whole, not just aesthetic tastes as one area of practice.

Conversely, because they are immersed in physical reality and economic necessity, working-class people interact in more physical ways, touching one another's bodies, laughing heartily, and valuing straightforward outspokenness more than distant and "false" politeness. Similarly, the working-class taste favors foods that are more filling and less "refined" but more physically gratifying. The popular taste chooses clothes and furniture that are functional, and this is so not only because of sheer economic constraints but also because of a true and profound dislike of that which is "formal" and "fancy."

In sum, then, Bourdieu has provided a conceptual model of class conflict that combines elements of Marxian, Weberian, and Durkheimian sociology. The structuralist aspects of Bourdieu's conceptualization of habitus as the mediating process between class position and individual behavior have been underemphasized in this review, but clearly Bourdieu places Durkheim "back on his feet" by emphasizing that class position determines habitus. But the useful elements of structuralism—systems of symbols as generative structures of codes—are retained and incorporated into a theory of class conflict as revolving around the mobilization of symbols into ideologies legitimating a class position and the associated lifestyle and habitus.

CONCLUSION

"Cultural structuralism" oscillates between the extreme positions of objectivism and subjectivism and, therefore, can avoid the conceptual problems of either position. The orthodox structuralism of Lévi-Strauss forgot that underlying generative codes need agents and contexts that transform a system of potentialities into actual historical action. Orthodox structuralism eliminates the "knowledgeable and capable agent" who can do more than simply execute latent schemes of practice. The panstructuralism of Lévi-Strauss opened up "culture" as a systematic area of research about which one can *theorize* but, at the same time, exaggerated the antihumanist notion of "subjectless" structures.

Cultural structuralism also avoids the indeterminate view of culture as a system of symbols that can be defined and negotiated at will by creative and spontaneous agents. Symbolic interactionism in particular exaggerates the capacity of agents to define situations and redefine self-identities in the spontaneous setting of unstructured "situations." Structuralism recovers the materialist notion that definitions of the situation and interpretations of symbols are constrained by external structures that cannot be totally controlled by the will of agents. Cultural practices and symbol use are not self-sufficient systems of unrestrained interpretive creativity; rather, cultural work has its own structures and constraints.

Cultural structuralism, then, does not fall into the traps of subjectless objectivism, and it also avoids the hermeneutic idealism of interpretive approaches to action. It has established the idea that culture has a structure that is itself a reality, *sui generis,* and that it can be analyzed like any other reality.

NOTES

1. For some general works reviewing structuralism, see Anthony Giddens, "Structuralism, Post-structuralism and the Production of Culture," in *Social Theory Today,* eds. A. Giddens and J. H. Turner (Stanford, CA: Stanford University Press, 1987); S. Clarke, *The Foundations of Structuralism* (Sussex, England: Harvester, 1981); J. Sturrock, ed., *Structuralism and Science* (Oxford: Oxford University Press, 1979); W. G. Runciman, "What Is Structuralism?" in *Sociology in Its Place* (Cambridge: Cambridge University Press, 1970); Ino Rossi, *From the Sociology of Symbols to the Sociology of Signs* (New York: Columbia University Press, 1983), and Ino Rossi, ed., *Structural Sociology* (New York: Columbia University Press, 1982); Jacques Ehrmann, *Structuralism* (New York: Doubleday, 1970); Philip Pettit, *The Concept of Structuralism: A Critical Analysis* (Berkeley: University of

California Press, 1977); Charles C. Lemert, "The Uses of French Structuralism in Sociology," and Michelle Lamont and Robert Wuthnow, "Recent Cultural Sociology in Europe and the United States," in *Frontiers of Social Theory*, G. Ritzer, ed. (New York: Columbia University Press, 1990).

2. Indeed, Bourdieu has been enormously prolific, having authored some twenty-five books and hundreds of articles in a variety of fields, including anthropology, education, cultural history, linguistics, philosophy, and sociology. His empirical work covers a wide spectrum of topics—art, academics, unemployment, peasants, classes, religion, sports, kinship, politics, law, and intellectuals. See Loic J. D. Wacquant, "Towards a Reflexive Sociology: A Workshop with Pierre Bourdieu," *Sociological Theory* 7 (1, Spring 1989), pp. 26–63. This article also contains a selected bibliography on Bourdieu's own works as well as secondary analyses and comments on Bourdieu.

3. Pierre Bourdieu, "Social Space and Symbolic Power," *Sociological Theory* 7 (1, Spring, 1989), p. 14.

4. Pierre Bourdieu, *Language and Symbolic Power* (Cambridge, MA: Harvard University Press, 1989).

5. Pierre Bourdieu, *Homo Academicus* (Stanford, CA: Stanford University Press, 1988).

6. Pierre Bourdieu, *Distinction: A Social Critique of the Judgement of Taste* (Cambridge, MA: Harvard University Press, 1984).

7. See Loic J. D. Wacquant, "Towards a Reflexive Sociology" (cited in note 2); Pierre Bourdieu, "Social Space and Symbolic Power" (cited in note 3), pp. 14–25.

8. See Loic J. D. Wacquant, "Towards a Reflexive Sociology" (cited in note 2).

9. Pierre Bourdieu, *Outline of a Theory of Practice* (Cambridge: Cambridge University Press, 1977), pp. 22 *ff.*, and *Distinction* (cited in note 6).

10. Ibid.

11. See Chapter 20 and the Web site for this book.

12. See Loic J. D. Wacquant, "Towards a Reflexive Sociology" (cited in note 2), p. 43.

13. Pierre Bourdieu, *Outline of a Theory of Practice* (cited in note 9).

14. See Chapter 20 and the Web site for this book.

15. Pierre Bourdieu, "The Forms of Capital," in *Handbook of Theory and Research in the Sociology of Education*, ed. J. G. Richardson (New York: Greenwood, 1986). See also Michele Lamont and Annette P. Larreau, "Cultural Capital: Allusions, Gaps, and Glissandos in Recent Theoretical Developments," *Sociological Theory* 6 (2, Fall 1988), pp. 153–168.

16. Pierre Bourdieu, *Distinction* and *Outline of a Theory of Practice* (cited in notes 16 and 9).

17. Pierre Bourdieu, "The Forms of Capital" (cited in note 15).

18. Pierre Bourdieu, "Social Space and the Genesis of Groups," *Theory and Society* 14 (November 1985), pp. 723–744.

19. Bourdieu makes what in network analysis (see Chapter 30) is termed *regular structural equivalence*. That is, those incumbents in positions that stand in an equivalent (similar) relation to other positions will act in a convergent way and evidence common attributes.

20. Bourdieu is not very clear about the issue of how the structural potentialities of a given objective class location become transformed into actual social groups capable of historical action. Like Lévi-Strauss, Bourdieu pursues the formal analogies between deep structures and actual practices, but he lacks a theory about how and when the transformations are going to be made, and made successfully.

21. Pierre Bourdieu, *Distinction* (cited in note 16).

22. Ibid.

23. Ibid. Actually, Bourdieu makes more fine-tuned distinctions, but we focus only on the main oppositions here.

30

Network Theory

During the last thirty years, work within anthropology, social psychology, sociology, communications, psychology, geography, and political science has converged on the conceptualization of "structure" in "social networks." During this period, rather metaphorical and intuitive ideas about networks have been reconceptualized in various types of algebra, graph theory, and probability theory. This convergence has, in some ways, been a mixed blessing. On the one hand, grounding concepts in mathematics can give them greater precision and provide a common language for pulling together a common conceptual core from the overlapping metaphors of different disciplines. On the other hand, the extensive use of mathematics and computer algorithms far exceeds the technical skills of most social scientists. More importantly, the use and application of quantitative techniques, per se, have become a preoccupation among many who seem less and less interested in explaining how the actual social world operates.

Nonetheless, despite these drawbacks, the potential for network analysis as a theoretical approach is great because it captures an important property of social structure—patterns of relations among social units, whether people, collectivities, or positions. As Georg Simmel emphasized, at the core of any conceptualization of social structure is the notion that structure consists of relations and links among entities. Network analysis forces us to conceptualize

---

Note: This chapter is coauthored with Alexandra Maryanski.

carefully the nature of the entities and relations as well as the properties and dynamics that inhere in these relations.[1]

BASIC THEORETICAL CONCEPTS IN NETWORK ANALYSIS

Points and Nodes

The units of a network can be persons, positions, corporate or collective actors, or virtually any entity that can be connected to another entity. In general, these units are conceptualized as *points* or *nodes,* and they are typically symbolized by letters or numbers. In Figure 30.1, a very simple network is drawn with each letter representing a point or node in the network. One goal of network analysis, then, is to array in visual space a pattern of connections among the units that are related to each other. In a mathematical sense, it makes little difference what the points and nodes are, and this has great virtue because it provides a common set of analytical tools for analyzing very diverse phenomena. Another goal of network analysis is to explain the dynamics of various patterns of ties among nodes, although this goal is often subordinated to developing computer algorithms for representing the connections among points and nodes in more complex networks than the one portrayed in Figure 30.1.

Links, Ties, and Connections

The letters in Figure 30.1 represent the nodes or points of a structure. The lines connecting the letters indicate that these points are attached to each other in a particular pattern. The concept of *tie* is the most frequent way to denote this property of a network, and so in Figure 30.1, there are ties between *A-B, A-C, A-D, B-E, C-D,* and *D-E.* We not only need to know that points in a network are connected, but we also must have some idea of what it is that connects these points. That is, what is the nature of the tie? From the point of view of graph theory, it does not make much difference, but when the substantive concerns of sociologists are considered, it is important to know the nature of the ties. As we saw in Chapter 27 on the early sociograms constructed by Jacob Moreno, the ties involved emotional states such as liking and friendship, and the nodes themselves were individual people. But the nature of the tie can be diverse: the flow of information, money, goods, services, influence, emotions, deference, prestige, and virtually any force or resource that binds actors to each other.

Often, as we saw in Chapter 19 on exchange network theory, the ties are conceptualized as resources. When points or nodes are represented by different letters, this denotes that actors are exchanging different resources, such as prestige for advice, money for services, deference for information, and so on. Conversely, if they were exchanging similar resources, the nodes would be represented by the same letter and subscripted numbers, such as A_1, A_2, and A_3.

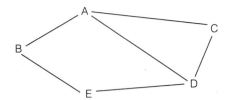

FIGURE 30.1 A Simple Network

But this is only one convention; the nature of the tie can also be represented by different kinds of lines, such as dotted, dashed, or colored lines. In graph theory, the lines can also reveal direction, as indicated by arrows. Moreover, if multiple resources are connecting positions in the graph, multiple lines (and, if necessary, arrows specifying direction) would be used. Thus, the graph represented in Figure 30.1 is obviously very simple, but it communicates the basic goal of network analysis: to represent in visual space the structure of connections among units.

One way to rise above the diversity of resources examined in network analysis is to visualize resource flows in networks for three generic types: materials, symbols, and emotions. That is, what connects persons, positions, and corporate actors in the social world is the flow of (1) symbols (information, ideas, values, norms, messages, etc.), (2) materials (physical things and perhaps symbols, such as money, that give access to physical things), and (3) emotions (approval, respect, liking, pleasure, and so forth). In nonsociological uses of networks the ties or links can be other types of phenomena, but, when the ties are social, they exist along material, symbolic, and emotional dimensions.

The configuration of ties can also be represented as a matrix, and in most network studies, the matrix is created before the actual network diagram. Moreover, when large numbers of nodes are involved, the matrix is often a better way to grasp the complexity of connections than a diagram, which would become too cumbersome to be useful. Figure 30.2 presents the logic of a matrix, using the very simple network represented in Figure 30.1. The mathematics of such matrices can become very complicated, but the general point is clear: to cross-tabulate which nodes are connected to each other (as is done inside the triangular area of the matrix in Figure 30.2). If possible, once the matrix is constructed, it can be used to generate a graph, something like the one in Figure 30.1. With the use of sophisticated computer algorithms in network analysis, the matrix is the essential step for subsequent analysis; an actual diagram might not be drawn because the mathematical manipulations are too complex. Yet, most matrices will eventually be converted in network analysis into some form of visual representation in space— perhaps not a network digraph but some other technique, such as three dimensional bar graphs or clusters of points, will be used to express in visual space the relations among units.

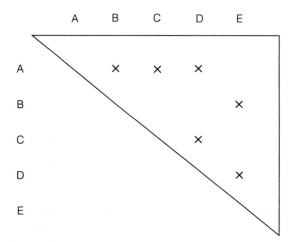

FIGURE 30.2 A Simple Matrix

PATTERNS AND CONFIGURATIONS OF TIES

From a network perspective, social structure is conceptualized as the form of ties among positions or nodes. That is, what is the pattern or configuration among what resources flowing among what sets of nodes or points in a graph? To answer questions like this, network sociology addresses several properties of networks. The most important of these are number of ties, directedness, reciprocity of ties, transitivity of ties, density of ties, strength of ties, bridges, brokerage, centrality, and equivalence.

Number of Ties

An important piece of information in performing network analysis is the total number of ties among all points and nodes. Naturally, the number of potential ties depends on the number of points in a graph and the number of resources involved in connecting the points. Yet, for any given number of points and resources, it is important to calculate both the actual and potential number of ties that are (and can be) generated. This information can then be used to calculate other dimensions of a network structure.

Directedness

It is important to know the direction in which resources flow through a network; so, as indicated earlier, arrows are often placed on the lines of a graph, making it a digraph. As a consequence, a better sense of the structure of the network emerges. For example, if the lines denote information, we would have a better understanding of how the ties in the network are constructed and maintained because we can see the direction and sequence of the information flow.

Reciprocity of Ties

Another significant feature of networks is the reciprocity of ties among positions. That is, is the flow of resources one way, or is it reciprocated for any two positions? If the flow of resources is reciprocated, then it is conventional to have double lines with arrows pointing in the direction of the resource flow. Moreover, if different resources flow back and forth, this too can be represented. Surprisingly, conventions about how to represent this multiplicity of resource flows are not fully developed. One way to denote the flow of different resources is to use varying-colored lines or numbered lines; another is to label the points with the same letter subscripted (that is, A_1, A_2, A_3, and so forth) if similar resources flow and with varying letters (that is, A, B, C, D) if the resources connecting actors are different. But, whatever the notation, the extent and nature of reciprocity in ties become an important property of a social network.

Transitivity of Ties

A critical dimension of networks is the level of transitivity among sets of positions. *Transitivity* refers to the degree to which there is a "transfer" of a relation among subsets of positions. For example, if nodes A_1 and A_2 are connected with positive affect, and positions A_2 and A_3 are similarly connected, we can ask, will positions A_1 and A_3 also be tied together with positive affect? If the answer to this question is "yes," then the relations among A_1, A_2, and A_3 are transitive. Discovering patterns of transitivity in a network can be important because it helps explain other critical properties of a network, such as density and the formation of cliques.

Density of Ties

A significant property of a network is its degree of connectedness, or the extent to which nodes reveal the maximum possible number of ties. The more the actual number of ties among nodes approaches the total possible number among a set of nodes, the greater is the overall *density* of a network.[2] Figure 30.3 compares the same five-node network under conditions of high and low density of ties.

Of even greater interest are subdensities of ties within a larger network structure. Such subdensities, which are sometimes referred to as *cliques,* reveal strong, reciprocated, and transitive ties among a particular subset of positions within the overall network.[3] For example, in Figure 30.4, there are three clusters of dense ties in the network, thus revealing three distinct cliques within the larger network.

Strength of Ties

Yet another crucial aspect of a network is the volume and level of resources that flow among positions. A weak tie is one where few or sporadic amounts of resources flow among positions, whereas a strong tie evidences a high level

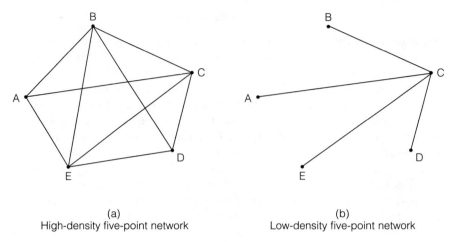

(a)
High-density five-point network

(b)
Low-density five-point network

FIGURE 30.3 High- and Low-Density Networks

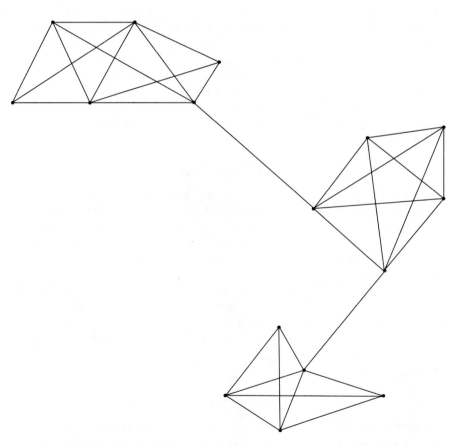

FIGURE 30.4 A Network with Three Distinct Cliques

of resource flow. Clusters and configurations of strong and weak ties significantly influence the overall structure of a network. For example, if the ties in the cliques in Figure 30.4 are strong, the network is composed of cohesive subgroupings that have relatively sparse ties to one another. On the other hand, if the ties in these subdensities are weak, then the subgroupings will involve less intense linkages,[4] with the result that the structure of the whole network will be very different than would be the case if these ties were strong.

Bridges

When networks reveal subdensities, it is always interesting to know which positions connect the subdensities, or cliques, to one another. For example, in Figure 30.4, those ties connecting subdensities are bridges and are crucial in maintaining the overall connectedness of the network. Indeed, if one removed one of these positions or severed the tie, the structure of the network would be very different—it would become three separate networks. These bridging ties are typically weak,[5] because each position in the bridge is more embedded in the flow of resources of a particular subdensity or clique. But, nonetheless, such ties are often crucial to the maintenance of a larger social structure; it is not surprising that the number and nature of bridges within a network structure are highlighted in network analysis.

Brokerage

At times, a particular position is outside subsets of positions but is crucial to the flow of resources to and from these subsets. This position is often in a brokerage situation because its activities determine the nature and level of resources that flow to and from subsets of positions.[6] In Figure 30.5, position A_7 is potentially a broker for the flow of resources from subsets consisting of positions A_1, A_2, A_3, A_4, A_5, and A_6 to B_1, B_2, B_3, B_4, B_5, and B_6. Position A_7 can become a broker if (1) the distinctive resources that pass to, and from, these two subsets are needed or valued by at least one of these subsets, and (2) direct ties, or bridges, between the two subsets do not exist. Indeed, a person or actor in a brokerage position often seeks to prevent the development of bridges (like those in Figure 30.4) and to manipulate the flow of resources such that at least one, and if possible both, subsets are highly dependent on its activities.

Centrality

An extremely important property of a network is *centrality,* as was noted for Alex Bavelas's and Harold Leavitt's studies of communication in experimental groups. There are several ways to calculate centrality:[7] (1) the number of other positions with which a particular position is connected, (2) the number of points between which a position falls, and (3) the closeness of a position to others in a network. Although these three measures might denote somewhat different points as central, the theoretical idea is fairly straightforward: Some positions in a network

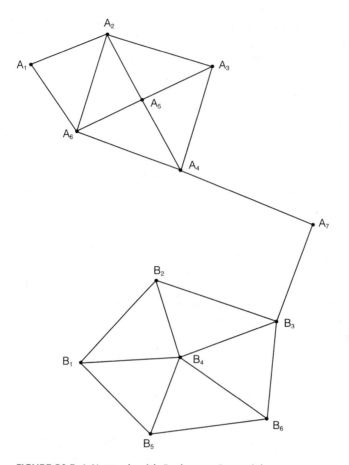

FIGURE 30.5 A Network with Brokerage Potential

mediate the flow of resources by virtue of their patterns of ties to other points. For example, in Figure 30.3(b), point C is central in a network consisting of positions A, B, C, D, and E; or, to take another example, points A_5 and B_4 in Figure 30.5 are more central than other positions because they are directly connected to all, or to the most, positions and because a higher proportion of resources will tend to pass through these positions. A network can also reveal several nodes of centrality, as is evident in Figure 30.6. Moreover, patterns of centrality can shift over time. Thus, many of the dynamics of network structure revolve around the nature and pattern of centrality.

Equivalence

When positions stand in the same relation to another position, they are considered *equivalent*. When this idea was first introduced into network analysis, it was termed *structural equivalence* and restricted to situations in which a set of

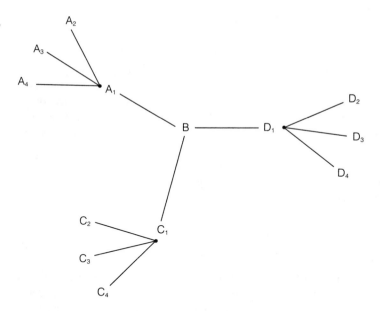

FIGURE 30.6 Equivalence in Social Networks

positions is connected to another position or set of positions in exactly the same way.[8] For example, positions C_2, C_3, and C_4 in Figure 30.6 are structurally equivalent because they reveal the same relation to position C_1. Figure 30.6 provides another illustration of structural equivalence, as well. A_2, A_3, and A_4 are structurally equivalent to A_1; similarly, D_2, D_3, and D_4 are equivalent to D_1; and A_1, C_1, and D_1 are structurally equivalent to B.

This original formulation of equivalence was limited, however, in that positions could be equivalent only when *actually connected to the same position*. We might also want to consider all positions as equivalent when they are connected to different positions but in the same form, pattern, or manner. For instance, in Figure 30.6, A_2, A_3, A_4, D_2, D_3, D_4, C_2, C_3, and C_4 can all be seen as equivalent because they bear the *same type* of relation to another position—that is to A_1, D_1, and C_1, respectively. This way of conceptualizing equivalence is termed *regular equivalence*[9] and, in a sense, subsumes the original notion of *structural equivalence*. That is, structural equivalence, wherein the equivalent *positions must actually be connected to the same position in the same way*, is a particular type of a more general equivalence phenomenon. These terms, "structural" and "regular," are awkward, but they have become conventional in network analysis; so we are stuck with them. The critical idea is that the number and nature of equivalent positions in a network have important influences on the dynamics of the network.[10] The general hypothesis is that actors in structurally equivalent or regularly equivalent positions will behave or act in similar ways.

CONCLUSION

The mathematics of network analysis can become quite complicated, as can the computer algorithms used to analyze data sets of the processes outlined above. This listing of concepts is somewhat metaphorical because it eliminates the formal and quantitative thrust of much network analysis. Indeed, much network analysis bypasses the conversion of matrices into graphs like those in the various figures presented and, instead, performs mathematical and statistical operations on just the matrices themselves. Yet, if network analysis is to realize its full theoretical (as opposed to methodological) potential, it might be wise to use concepts, at least initially, in a more verbal and intuitive sense.

Few would disagree with the notion that social structure is composed of relations among positions. But is this all that social structure is? Can the concepts denoting nodes, ties, and patterns of ties (number, strength, reciprocity, transitivity, bridges, brokerage, centrality, and equivalence) capture all the critical properties of social structure?

The answer to these questions is probably "no." Social structure probably involves other crucial processes that are not captured by these concepts. Yet, a major property of social structure *is* its network characteristics, as Simmel was perhaps the first to really appreciate. For, whatever other dimensions social structure might reveal—cultural, behavioral, ecological, temporal, psychological, and so forth—its backbone is a system of interconnections among actors who occupy positions relative to one another and who exchange resources. And, so, network analysis has great potential for theories of social structure. Has this potential been realized? Probably not, for several reasons.

First, as just noted, network analysis is overly methodological and concerned with generating quantitative techniques for arraying data in matrices and then converting the matrices into descriptions of particular networks (whether as graphs or as equations). As long as this is the case, network sociology will remain primarily a tool for empirical description.

Second, there has been little effort to develop principles of network dynamics, per se. Few[11] seem to ask theoretical questions within the network tradition itself. For example, how does the degree of density, centrality, equivalence, bridging, and brokerage influence the nature of the network and the flow of relations among positions in the network? There are many empirical descriptions of events that touch on this question but few actual theoretical laws or principles.[12]

Third, network sociology has yet to translate traditional theoretical concerns and concepts into network terminology in a way that highlights the superiority, or at least the viability, of using network theoretical constructs for mainstream theory in sociology. For example, power, hierarchy, differentiation, integration, stratification, conflict, and many other concerns of sociological theory have not been adequately reconceptualized in network terms, and hence, it is unlikely that sociological theory will adopt or incorporate a network approach until this translation of traditional questions occurs.

All these points, however, need to be qualified because numerous sociologists have actually sought to develop laws of network processes and to address traditional theoretical concerns with network concepts. Although these efforts are far from constituting a coherent theory of network dynamics, they do illustrate the potential utility of network sociology, as we saw, for example, in our review of network exchange theory in Chapter 19.

NOTES

1. For some readable overviews on network analysis, see Barry Wellman, "Network Analysis: Some Basic Principles," *Sociological Theory* (1983), pp. 155–200; Jeremy F. Boissevain and J. Clyde Mitchell, eds., *Network Analysis* (The Hague: Mouton, 1973) and *Social Networks in Urban Situations* (Manchester: Manchester University Press, 1969); J. A. Barnes, "Social Networks" (Addison-Wesley Module, no. 26, Reading, MA: Addison-Wesley, 1972); Barry S. Wellman and S. D. Berkowitz, *Social Structures: A Network Approach* (Cambridge: Cambridge University Press, 1988). Somewhat more technical summaries of recent network research can be found in Samuel Leinhardt, ed., *Social Networks: A Developing Paradigm* (New York: Academic, 1977); Paul Holland and Samuel Leinhardt, eds., *Perspectives in Social Network Research* (New York: Academic, 1979); Ronald S. Burt, "Models of Network Structure," *Annual Review of Sociology* 6 (1980), pp. 79–141; Peter Marsden and Nan Lin, eds., *Social Structure and Network Analysis* (Newbury Park, CA: Sage, 1982). For advanced research on networks, consult recent issues of the journal *Social Networks*.

2. There are other ways to measure density; this definition is meant to be illustrative of the general idea.

3. The terminology on subdensities varies. "Clique" is still the most prominent term, but "alliances" has been offered as an alternative. Moreover, the old sociological standbys "group" and "subgroup" seem to have made a comeback in network analysis.

4. At one time, "intensity" appears to have been used in preference to "strength." See Mitchell, "The Concept and Use of Social Networks" in *Social Networks in Urban Situations,* edited by J. F. Boisevain and J. C. Mitchel (The Hague: Mouton, 1973). It appears that Granovetter's classic article shifted usage in favor of "strength" and "weakness." See note 5.

5. See Mark Granovetter, "The Strength of Weak Ties," *American Journal of Sociology* 78 (1973), pp. 1360–1380; and "The Strength of Weak Ties: A Network Theory Revisited," *Sociological Theory* (1983), pp. 201–233. The basic network "law" from Granovetter's original study can be expressed as follows: *The degree of integration of a network composed of highly dense subcliques is a positive function of the extensiveness of bridges, involving weak ties, among these subcliques.*

6. Ronald S. Burt has, perhaps, done the most interesting work here. See, for example, his *Toward a Structural Theory of Action* (New York: Academic, 1982) and "A Structural Theory of Interlocking Corporate Directorships," *Social Networks* 1 (1978–1979), pp. 415–435.

7. The definitive works here are Linton C. Freeman, "Centrality in Social Networks: Conceptual Clarification," *Social Networks* 1 (1979), pp. 215–239; and Linton C. Freeman, Douglas Boeder, and Robert R. Mulholland, "Centrality in Social Networks: Experimental Results," *Social Networks* 2 (1979), pp. 119–141. See also Linton C. Freeman, "Centered

Graphs and the Structure of Ego Networks," *Mathematical Social Sciences* 3 (1982), pp. 291–304, and Philip Bonacich, "Power and Centrality: A Family of Measures," *American Journal of Sociology* 92 (1987), pp. 1170–1182.

8. François Lorrain and Harrison C. White, "Structural Equivalence of Individuals in Social Networks," *Journal of Mathematical Sociology* 1 (1971), pp. 49–80; Harrison C. White, Scott A. Boorman, and Ronald L. Breiger, "Social Structure from Multiple Networks: I. Block Models of Roles and Positions," *American Journal of Sociology* 8 (1976), pp. 730–780.

9. Lee Douglas Sailer, "Structural Equivalence," *Social Networks* 1 (1978), pp. 73–90.

10. In many ways Karl Marx's idea that those who stand in a common relationship to the means of production have common interests is an equivalence agreement. Thus, the idea of equivalence is not new to sociology—only the formalism used to express it is new.

11. There are, of course, some notable exceptions to this statement. For an example of what we see as the kinds of laws that need to be formulated, see our formal statement of Granovetter's hypothesis in note 5.

12. Mark Granovetter, "The Theory-Gap in Social Network Analysis" in *Perspectives on Social Network Research,* eds. P. Holland and S. Leinhardt (New York: Academic, 1979).

Name Index

Acker, Joan, 254
Adorno, Theodor, 203
Althusser, Louis, 205
Annett, Joan, 155

Bales, Robert, 45
Baudrillard, Jean, 240
Bauman, Zygmunt, 244
Bavelas, Alex, 467
Berger, Joseph, 444, 446
Bernard, Jessie, 252
Blau, Peter M., 294
Blumberg, Rae Lesser, 183, 254
Blumer, Herbert, 352
Bourdieu, Pierre, 491
Brown, Richard Harvey, 231
Burke, Peter J., 368, 376

Cartwright, Dorin, 469, 470
Chadorow, Nancy, 252
Chafetz, Janet Saltzman, 186
Cicourel, Aaron V., 423
Coleman, James S., 334, 338
Collins, Randall, 151, 438
Comte, Auguste, 23, 76, 457
Condorcet, Jean, 457
Cook, Judith, 258

Cook, Karen S., 308, 315
Cooley, Charles Horton, 344, 447
Coser, Lewis, 131, 142

Dahrendorf, Ralf, 131, 139, 162
Daniels, Arlene, 258
Darwin, Charles, 80
Dawkins, Robert, 100
de Saint-Simon, Claude-Henri, 457
de Saussure, Ferdinand, 462
Denzin, Norman, 242
Dewey, John, 345
Durkheim, Émile, 27, 76, 78, 108, 151, 357, 457

Ekeh, Peter, 321
Emerson, Richard M., 308, 309
Engels, Friedrich, 198

Fonow, Mary, 258
Frazer, Sir James, 271
Freese, Lee, 109, 115

Garfinkel, Harold, 421
Gergen, Kenneth, 242
Giddens, Anthony, 476
Goffman, Erving, 151, 395

Subject Index

Aborigines, 275
Abstraction
  in propositional schemes, 10
  structural, 67
Achievement, 43
Action
  communicative, 221
  dramaturgical, 220
  Habermas's reconceptualization of, 220
  normatively regulated, 220
  Parsons' conception of, 41
  teleological, 220
  theory of, 50
  voluntaristic, 39, 40
Action systems
  generalized symbolic media of
     exchange in, 48
  goal attainment in, 45
  integration of, 44
  interpenetrating, 41
  latency in, 45
  overall, 47
  survival problems of, 45
Adaptation
  in action systems, 45
  in Hawley's ecological theory, 84, 85
Advertising, in postmodern theory, 241

Affect control theory, 434
Affect-expectations theory, 446
Affective neutrality, 42
Affectivity, 42
Affect theory, expectation states in, 444
Analytical functionalism, 24, 38–53
  Parsons' theory of, 38–53
  social system in, 41
Analytical models, 17, 18
Analytical realism, 38
Analytical schemes, 9, 11
Anthropological tradition, functionalism
  and, 29
Anthropology, and exchange theory, 271
Ascription, 43
Axiom, defined, 12
Axiomatic format, 11
Axiomatic propositional schemes, 14
Axiomatic theory, 12

Balance theories, early, 469
Behavior, and macrostructure, 291
Behaviorism
  extreme, 278
  of Mead, 345
Behavioristic exchange theory, of
  Homans, 285–293

519